Registry of Maps

About the Author
Hilke Sue Maunder, author of a number of travel guides published by Hayit, has made her hobby into her profession: having studied English and German and combining her love of travel with her job as a travel director, she now works as a travel journalist. Dedicated to her work, this reporter is extremely knowledgeable of the former German Democratic Republic and a large portion of the former Eastern Bloc.

HAYIT'S BUDGET TRAVEL

Baltic States
(Estonia, Latvia, Lithuania)

by

Hilke Sue Maunder

1993
Hayit Publishing

1st Edition 1993
ISBN 1-874251-07-X

copyright 1993
 Hayit Publishing GB, Ltd, London

copyright 1993 original version: Hayit Verlag GmbH,
 Cologne/Germany

Author: Hilke Sue Maunder
Text on pages 47-48 by Susanne Völler
Translation, Adaption, Revision: Scott Reznik
Print: Scholma Druk, Bedum, NL
Typesetting: Satzwerkstatt Lehne, Grevenbroich, Germany
Cover Photo: Hilke Sue Maunder
Photos: Hilke Sue Maunder
Maps: Ralf Tito

Contents

Contents

Preface

On a Tuesday at the beginning of September 1991.

Somewhere in the Mecklenburg countryside where I have journalistically accompanied the reunification of Germany, I suddenly hear in the radio that the United States plan to recognise the independence of the three Baltic States. On the same day, I request time off.

On Thursday morning, loaded with journalists, the propeller plane from Hamburg lands in Riga. Japanese television is on the scene as I am given one of the first emergency visas to be issued by the young republic of Latvia. A rickety bus takes us to the parliament. A feverish disquiet pervades the atmosphere. Then, after six hours of waiting with President Gorbunovs, journalists clustered around him, the telephone finally rings – it is the President of the United States. The voice of George Bush can be heard throughout the entire city: the United States recognise the independence of Latvia. In Lithuania, the parliamentary president Landsbergis receives the news in Vilnius, surrounded by sand bags and tank barricades. The next morning, accompanied by two fellow journalists, I set out to explore the new countries. 20,000 kilometres of travel over gravel and sand are to follow. The crass contrasts lie side by side – an ecological paradise in a state of emergency, idyllic cities and slum districts. Routine contradictions. What is left are irreplaceable impressions: the calm confidence of the people, their strength in rebuilding their state and state of mind. With the changes in the past two years, difficulties often criticized by spoiled westerners shrink into nothingness. These three countries are basically different for visitors than other tourist destinations; by the same token, this travel guide also differs from others in the "Hayit's Budget Travel" series. The emphasis remains on current and comprehensive information but due to scarcity characterizing the economy, the budget aspect has taken on a subordinate role. One example is the exploding demand for hotels. Because of this, every available bed has been listed – from the most expensive hotel to the most modest hut. Comprehensive is also a description of the culture section: unavoidable when considering that music, literature and art as a basis for the individual's identity have been politically instrumentalized.

Despite the meticulous approach in writing this guide, all information is subject to change to a greater degree than in western nations. I welcome comments, tips and supplemental information from readers.

I would now like to take the opportunity to than those who have contributed to this book in the form of encouragement, suggestions and critique: Mrs. Udze at the Latvian Embassy, Aivars Krons in Riga, Iris and Inkari in Tartu, Albert Caspari at the Information Centre for the Baltic States, the Lithuanian parliamentary representative Algis Klimaitis and my brother Boje Martens, who avoided every pothole with exceptional ease.

Lübeck 1993, Hilke Maunder

Travel Preparations

Addresses / Information

The provisional general representation of the three Baltic States, the "Baltic Information Office," closed during the summer of 1992. These tasks are now fulfilled by the individual embassies.

I. Embassies
Great Britain
– Embassy of the Republic of Estonia
Chargé d'Affaires Eerik Kross
18 Chepstow Villas
London W11 2RB
Tel: (071) 229-6700
– Embassy of the Republic of Latvia
Chargé d'Affaires Marie-Anne Zarine
72 Queensborough Terrace
London W2 3SP
Tel: (071) 727-1698
– Embassy of the Republic of Lithuania
Ambassador Vincas Balickas
17 Essex Villas
London W8 7BP
Tel: (071) 938-2481
United States
– Embassy of the Republic of Estonia
His Excellency Ernst Jaakson
9 Rockefeller Plaza 142
New York, New York 10020
Tel: (212) 247-1450
– Embassy of the Republic of Latvia
Dr. Anatol Dinbergs, Chargé d'Affaires

4325 17th Street N.W.
Washington, D.C. 20011
Tel: (202) 726-8213
– Embassy of the Republic of Lithuania
Dr. Stasys Lozoraitis, Chargé d'Affaires
2622 16th Street N.W.
Washington, D.C. 20009
Tel: (202) 234-5860
Fax: (202) 328-0466

II. Information Centres in the Baltic States
For travel agencies and local tour organisers → *individual entries in the Travel Section.*
Estonia
Estonian Tourist Office, Suur-Karja 23, EE-20001 Tallinn, Tel: 01 42/44 12 39, Fax: 01 42/44 09 63
Latvia
Latvian Tourist Office, Brivibas iela 36, 226170 Riga, Tel: 01 32/22 99 45
Tourist Club of Latvia, Skarnu iela 22, 226050 Riga, Tel: 01 32/22 17 31. Marger Laivins is the director of this travel club.
Lithuania
Since there is no tourist office at present in Lithuania, the Ministry of Economic Relations has temporarily assumed these responsibilities:
Gedimino 30/1, 2695 Vilnius,
Tel: 01 22/62 46 70, 62 21 60,
Fax: 01 22/62 54 32

Eco Centre Alternativa, Kalvariu 130, Vilnius, Fax: 01 22/ 76 67 37. Jonas Jonynas coordinates the Green movement in the Eco-Centre and establishes contacts between environmental and other alternative groups.

VI. Embassies in the Baltic States

Estonia
United States Embassy
Chargé d'Affaires Robert Frasure
c/o Hotel Palace, Room 507
Vabaduse väljak 3
Tallinn
Tel: (358) (49) 303-182; (cellular) (7) (01-42) 444-761
Fax: (358) (49) 306-817; (cellular) (7) (01-42) 444-761

Latvia
United States Embassy
Chargé d'Affaires Ints Silins
c/o Hotel Ridzene
Raina bulv. 7
Riga
Tel: (358) (49) 308-067; (cellular) (7) (01-32) 325-968/185
Fax: (358) (49) 308-326; (cellular) (7) (01-32) 220-502

Lithuania
United States Embassy
Charge d'Affaires Darryl Johnson
Mykolaicio putino 4
Tel: (7) (01-22) 628-049
Fax: (7) (01-22) 627-024

Formalities

Considering the changes to which travels in the Baltic States are subject, even the embassies themselves are not certain of all aspects. The one thing which is certain is the mutual acceptance of the visa throughout all three Baltic States: only one visa is necessary for travel in all three countries. However: the visa is checked regularly and passports are stamped. The Lithuanians are especially exacting in regard to this. On the other hand, the troublesome registration with the police is no longer required – this has been replaced by the registration card at lodgings.

Estonia
Those who plan on travelling to Estonia will need a visa. At present, these are issued at a high fee at the borders – around £13 ($23.50) for one entry and £37.50 ($70.50) for a multiple entry visa. The Estonian Embassy can also issue a visa in a matter of a few days. Necessary documents are as follows: valid passport, a visa application filled out and signed, one passport photo, a self-addressed stamped envelope. Visa fees: single entry (valid 30 days) £9 ($16); multiple entry (valid one year) £27 ($47). These fees are payable in advance by cheque or in person at the embassy. Do not forget to include proof of payment if transferring funds.

Latvia
Necessary Documents: valid passport or children's identification, two copies of the visa application, two passport photos, self-addressed stamped envelope. The visa fee of £15 ($25) is payable in advance to the Republic of Latvia Embassy. Visas are only granted if payment is included. A diplomatic visa, visas for participants in aid programmes and visas for those under 18 years of age

are free of charge. Multiple entry and annual visas are presently only granted to diplomats and businesspersons. Visas are also issued at the borders and international airports.

Lithuania

Necessary Documents: valid passport, one passport photo, two copies of the visa application, self-addressed stamped envelope. Hotel reservations or written invitations are not required but are good to have. Fee: £10 ($17). Rush applications are issued immediately for £20 ($34) for a single entry and £27 ($45) for a multiple entry visa.

Transit

Those who travel through CIS countries to the Baltic States require a transit visa. The Lithuanians require a transit visa for those travelling through Lithuania to Kaliningrad. These visas are usually issued within two weeks from the CIS representation. A tourist visa costs £15 ($25), business visas £18.50 ($32); express visas are issued for a surcharge of £18.50 ($32). The official requirements are one thing, but reality another altogether: in 1991 and 1992, individuals could visit the Kaliningrad/Königsberg region without any formalities at all, no visa, no official invitations and no "financial prompting" of the border officials. Others were turned away at the border.

Money

Even years before independence, there were plans for a Baltic currency.

In 1989, the etchings could be seen in public notices and exhibitions. How many problems that would have to be surmounted on the way to a new currency could have hardly been foreseen by the three Baltic States – through continual Russian ploys and deliveries of energy supplies as a means of political pressure, Russia was repeatedly successful in postponing the Baltic republics from leaving the "Ruble-Zone." However, Estonia was to be the first to accomplish this.

Estonia

On June 20, 1992, the Eesti Kroon was introduced in the entire country, replacing the inflationary Ruble. The exchange rate ranges from 1 to 10 (one Kroon for ten Rubles) to 1 to 50. The Kroon is tied to the German Mark: 1 Mark = 8 Kroon, making one Kroon equal to about 8 US cents or 4 pence. The subdivision of the Kroon is the "Sent," plural "Senti," with coins of 5, 10, 20, and 50 Senti in circulation. Despite the difference in the size, the coins are all rather similar in appearance. The currency is backed by gold and the extensive forests of Estonia. Around £25 million ($47 million) worth of Kroon are in circulation. The full backing of the bank notes through gold as is the case today was only in practice before the First World War during the reign of Czar Nicholas II. However, gold coins were in circulation at that time.

Latvia

The second Baltic State to leave the "Ruble-Zone" was Latvia in the summer of 1992 after the new provisionary currency, the Latvian Ruble, was first introduced as a parallel currency to the Russian Ruble. The small, colourful bank notes which sooner have a similarity to play money have been the only legal tender since September 1992. The Russian Kopeken are, however, still in circulation since coins could not yet be minted due to lacking funds.

Lithuania

The "Vagnorkas," the substitute currency introduced by the former prime minister Gediminas Vagnorkas to reduce the Rubles in circulation is meanwhile no longer in circulation. "Talonas" introduced in the autumn of 1991 as a substitute currency for purchasing food staples like cheese, salt, flour and butter have been the only valid currency since October 1992. Up until the introduction of the freely exchangeable "Litas" – a pressing goal – these coupons are the only means of payment. The banks have been instructed to exchange Rubles in unlimited amounts at the rate of one to one.

Health

No vaccinations are necessary for travelling in any of the Baltic States. However, it is recommended to take out a supplemental health insurance policy. If one should need to visit a physician, one should agree on the charges in advance. In the Baltic capitals, there are emergency medical services with doctors educated in western nations and able to speak a number of languages – their charges must, however, be paid in western currencies. Emergency medical help is available toll-free by dialling the number 03.

Also, one should be sure to bring along medications like pain relievers, medication for digestive problems, ointments for insect bites, bandages, sanitary napkins and any medications taken on a regular basis. All medications are available in the Baltic States, but these are usually produced in Russia and usually have a higher dosage and completely different names. If a pharmacist does not recognise the western name of the medication and therefore does not know its composition, then problems can arise – even when there are comparable products at far more reasonable prices available. There are hardly any health risks connected with travelling in the Baltic States – if one disregards the environmental damage. One should by no means drink water from the tap. In some places the drinking water has had radioactive contamination for years.

Equipment

Since the climate is similar to central and northern European climates, there is no special equipment required for touring the Baltic republics. Good shoes are necessary when considering the cobblestone streets and paths through fields. Rain gear is also necessary due to the sudden showers even during the summer. Other than these two items, normal travel gear and clothing will be sufficient.

Travelling to the Baltic States

... by Air

The entire air network in eastern Europe is presently in a state of radical change. Some of the airplanes from the former state-operated Aeroflot fleet are now used by the new Baltic state-run airlines. Lithuania, for example has had 21 old Aeroflot airplanes and one Boeing 737 since December 1991. The Boeing, the pride of the "Lietuvos Airlines," was eliminated from service by Lufthansa in 1992...

Commercial flights to the Baltic States are offered by: Lufthansa, Hamburg Airlines, SAS, Swissair, Austrian Airlines, Finnair, Baltic International Airlines, Estonian Airlines, Lietuvos Avialinjos and Aeroflot.

Estonia

Frankfurt – Tallinn:
As of March 29, 1992, Lufthansa offers non-stop flights from Frankfurt with 737 Cityjets three times weekly (Wednesday, Saturday and Sunday)
Estonian Airlines: every Saturday
Stockholm – Tallinn:
SAS: Thursday and Saturday departing from Stockholm
Estonian Airlines: Monday, Wednesday and Friday departing from Stockholm
Helsinki – Tallinn:
Finnair: Monday to Friday
Estonian Airlines: Tuesday, Thursday and Sunday

Latvia

Hamburg – Riga:
Hamburg Airlines: commercial flights on Tuesday and Thursday stopping in Berlin; non-stop on Sundays. Charter flights: Thursday and Sunday. Prices: business class: £635 ($1,188), Fly & Save: £380 ($713), Super Fly & Save £254 ($475) and charter flights from £133 ($249).
Frankfurt – Riga:
Lufthansa: commercial flights on Tuesday, Thursday, Friday and Sunday. Prices: first class: £917 ($1,719), business class £634 ($1,188), Fly & Save £380 ($713), Super Fly & Save £254 ($475), weekend fare £196 ($368).
Latvijas Avalinjas: commercial flights Monday, Wednesday and Saturday. Prices similar to Lufthansa.
Hamburg/Frankfurt/Düsseldorf/ Munich – Riga:
SAS: commercial flights via Copenhagen. Tuesday departure, Saturday return. Prices: first class £930 ($1,744), business class £647 ($1,213).
Frankfurt – Riga:
Baltic International Airlines: commercial flights three times weekly (Monday, Wednesday and Saturday).

Lithuania

Frankfurt – Vilnius:
Lufthansa has offered commercial,

non-stop flights since March 29, 1992 in Boeing 737 Cityjets.
The flight lasts two hours. Airfare: Fly & Save: £415 ($779), Super Fly & Save £277 ($519).

Hamburg, Hanover – Berlin/Tempelhof – Vilnius:
Hamburg Airlines with commercial flights with Boeing Dash-8 airplanes on Mondays and Thursdays.

Hamburg – Palanga (Polangen):
Lietuvos Avialinjos: Charter flights from Hamburg once weekly on Sundays, presently only during the summer season.

... by Ship

Those who wish to travel with their own car to the Baltic States should forgo the stress of driving. A ferry is a better option. During the crossing over the Baltic Sea, there is enough time to prepare oneself for the trip and read up on the Baltic States.

Estonia

Helsinki – Tallinn:
– MS Tallink/TALLINK, MS Georg Ots, MS Corbiere/Linda I.
The duration of the trip is 3½ to 4 hours with several departures daily. Visa-free crossings from Helsinki depart on Tuesdays, Fridays and Saturdays. Prices: adults, around £15 ($28); automobile, around £19 ($36); camping vehicle up to 11 metres (36 feet) in length, around £84 ($157); camping vehicle up to 7 metres (23 feet) in length, around £38 ($72).
– MS Kristina Cruises, night cros-

sings every day. Reservations: Korkeavuorenkatu 2, SF-48100 Kota, Finland. Kokeavuorenkatu 45, SF-00130 Helsinki, Finland.
– Hydrofoil Helsinki-Sinilind – Tallinn: the trip lasts only two hours during the summer and is the quickest route to Tallinn; however, the ferries depart only when the Baltic Sea is absolutely calm. Reservations: Sinilind, Lönnerotinkatu 45, SF-00130 Helsinki, Finland; Tel: +35 80/65 10 11.

(Travemünde/Germany) – Stockholm – Tallinn:
– MS North Estonia/ESTLINE
Offers ferry crossings during the entire year at night. The trip lasts 14½ hours; from Stockholm, there are departures at 5:30 pm on Monday, Wednesday and Friday; from Tallinn, at 8 pm on Tuesday, Thursday and Sunday, arriving in Stockholm at 9:30 the next morning. Reservations: Narva maantee 4, Tallinn 200103, Tel: 01 42/44 46 43 or N&T-Estline AB, Box 1215, S-1182 Stockholm, Sweden; Tel: 08/6 13 19 50 or TT-Line Hamburg, Mattentwiete 8, Postfach 11 22 69, D-20457 Hamburg; Tel: +49 40/3 60 12 48, Fax: +49 40/3 60 14 07.

Latvia

Kiel/Travemünde – Riga:
Departing Tuesday and Friday evenings from Kiel, Germany at the eastern side of the harbour. Arrival in Riga at 5 pm two days later (Thursday or Sunday). Travel route: the ferry sets of during the night passing the German islands of Fehmarn and Rü-

gen. On the next morning, Danish Bornholm comes into view on the horizon. The "Mercuri I" reaches the Gulf of Riga on the following morning before continuing at its leisure pace up the river for one hour passing the freight harbour, newer buildings and garden towns to the passenger terminal near the old city. During the 42-hour crossing with the Azerbaidzhani RoRo-ship and its Russian crew, passengers are attended to by a German staff on board. Those who do not plan on bringing their own provisions should book the meal package for £28 ($53) in advance or purchase this on board since dining à la carte is not possible and a single meal like, for example, breakfast is disproportionately expensive at £8.50 ($15.75). "Entertainment" on board is provided by slot machines, a television room and a small duty-free shop.

Prices (one-way): £74 to £295 ($138 to $550) for a cabin; automobile (for up to five passengers), £67 ($125); motorcycle, £34 ($63); bicycle/moped up to 50cc, £8.50 ($16); automobile and camping trailer, £20 ($37.50) per metre; bus prices on request.

Riga – Norrköping:
MS Baltic Clipper: Tuesday, Thursday and Saturday. Reservations: Baltic Tours, Passenger Terminal at Riga Harbour.

Riga – Stockholm:
MS Baltic Clipper: Wednesdays; see above for reservation information.

Lübeck (Hansa Quay) – Riga
Departing once weekly on Wednesday at 8 pm, arriving two days later at 8 am. Returning Sunday at 8 pm, arriving in Lübeck on Tuesday at 7:30 am. This ferry connection has been is offered as of February 1993 during the entire summer. The MS Akademic Serjey Varilev was originally built for Finnish scientists, explaining the relatively high standards on board. Reservations: Baltic Tours, Beim Strohhause 34, D-20097 Hamburg, Tel: +49 40/24 15 80. Prices for one way start at £100 ($200) for a two-bed cabin.

Lithuania
Mukran (Island of Rügen) – Klaipeda/Memel:
In operation during the entire year, the train ferry takes only 12 passengers and a few cars on board. The reason: this is used for the transport of the Red Army back to Russia. German and Lithuanian ships are used for this 20-hour passage.

Reservations for the German ferries can be made by contacting: Deutsche Seereederei Rostock GmbH, Ferry Traffic Neu-Mukran, passenger department, Mrs. Stenzel, D-18546 Saßnitz-Neu Mukran, Tel: +49 38392/4 52 21. For reservations for the Lithuanian ferries, contact: Neu-Mukran, Tel: +49 38392/4 52 27. In Lithuania, the Thieme family accepts reservations for the return trip: Klaipeda, Tel: 5 50 52. After setting an appointment by telephone, written confirmation of the booking is absolutely necessary around two weeks before departure. This ferry route is in very high demand and reservations are accepted around two months in

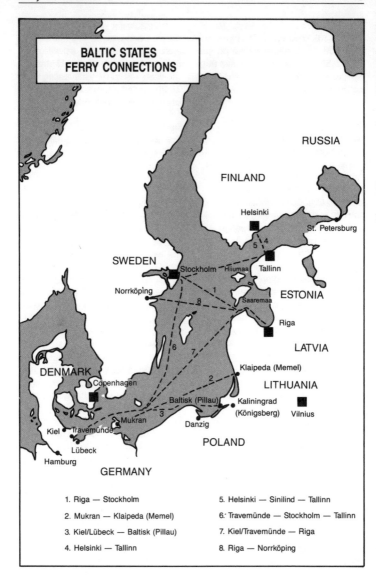

BALTIC STATES FERRY CONNECTIONS

1. Riga — Stockholm
2. Mukran — Klaipeda (Memel)
3. Kiel/Lübeck — Baltisk (Pillau)
4. Helsinki — Tallinn
5. Helsinki — Sinilind — Tallinn
6. Travemünde — Stockholm — Tallinn
7. Kiel/Travemünde — Riga
8. Riga — Norrköping

advance. Prices (one way): adults, £60 ($113); children up to 12 years of age, £30 ($57); insurance per person £2.75 ($5.15); car (for up to five passengers), £67 ($125); vans and camping vehicles, £134 ($250).

Kaliningrad (Königsberg)
Kiel/Lübeck – Baltisk (Pillau):
After more than fifty years, the MS Winston Churchill once again dropped anchor in the harbour of Baltisk/Pillau near Kaliningrad (Königsberg) on October 7, 1992. Up to then, the city and harbour were a restricted military zone off limits to foreign visitors and only accessible to those who could prove that they were born in the city or had special permission. It remains in question whether the newly opened ferry route will endure. The prices per passage begin at £200 ($375) and can be booked by contacting Schnieder Reisen, Harkortstraße 121 in D-22765 Hamburg 50, Tel: +49 40/38 02 06 94, Fax: +49 04/38 02 06 88.

Lübeck – Königsberg:
From April 30 to October 22, a hotel ship sails right past Pillau directly to Königsberg. Sometimes a second ship is put into service from mid-June to mid-August depending on the expected demand. Prices start at £300 ($600) for a return ticket.

... by Train
Travelling to the Baltic States is especially inexpensive and would be quite comfortable if it were not for the borders... During recent years, travellers were either processed slowly or not at all on the Polish border. Distraught travellers report of waits lasting up to 28 hours; others, in contrast, happily recall a speedy procedure.

Berlin – Riga – Berlin:
The express train from Berlin to St. Petersburg with railway cars to Vilnius and Riga departs daily from the Berlin-Zoo railway station. When departing from Berlin, take the train cars D 295. The trip lasts 33 hours, departing from Berlin-Zoo at 10:36 pm, arriving in Vilnius at 9:17 pm the following evening and Riga at 7:03 on the next morning. Return trip: train 621/D 294 departs from Riga at 11:50 pm, arriving at Vilnius at 7:45 the next morning and departing for Berlin at 10:35 am. The train arrives in Berlin the next morning at 6:58. Prices: Riga round trip: £160 ($299); four-bed compartment surcharge £20 ($37.50) each way. Vilnius round trip: £138 ($258), four-bed compartment surcharge £18 ($34) each way. There are daily rail connections from Vilnius and Riga to Estonia.

From May 30 to July 7, a special train called the "Baltic Express" takes passengers from Berlin to Riga. This is the shortest and quickest rail connection on this route, lasting around 25 hours. The train departs from Berlin on Sunday at 8 pm and arrives in Riga on Monday at 9 pm. Prices for return tickets start at DM 390 (£130/ $245) and can be booked through Rail Tours Mochel Reisen, Georg-Vogel-Straße 2, D-77933 Lahr/

Schwarzwald, Tel: +49 78 21/4 30 37 or by contacting Baltisches Reisebüro, A. & W. Wencelides, Bayerstraße 37/l, D-80335 Munich, Tel: +49 89/ 59 63 94.

Riga – Tallinn:
D 652: departing Riga at 11:40 pm, arriving Tallinn 8:12 am (via Tartu). Tallinn – Riga: departing Tallinn at 10:40 pm, arriving at 7:25 am in Riga.

Vilnius – Riga – Tallinn:
Train D 188: departing Vilnius at 10:11 am, arriving Riga at 3:56 pm; departing Riga at 4:14 pm, arriving Tallinn at 11:35 pm.

Berlin – Königsberg – Berlin
Since May 1993, there is a "Königsberg Express" departing for Kaliningrad once weekly from the Main Train Station in Berlin and covering the shortest route (700 kilometres/437 miles)to Königsberg/Kaliningrad. After an interruption of this route lasting 46 years, it was served once again on August 9, 1991 for the first time. This special service will continue up to October 10, 1993. These special trains have only limited seating and can be booked by contacting Rail Tours Mochel Reisen, Georg-Vogel-Straße 2, D-77933 Lahr/Schwarzwald, Tel: +49 78 21/4 30 37. Reservations well in advance are necessary. The train departs from Berlin on Friday around 8 pm and arrives in Kaliningrad Saturday around 9 am. A special offer called "A Visit to Königsberg" is priced from DM 398 (£145/$249), including a bus tour, lunch and the opportunity for a trip to the Baltic coast for DM 25 (£8.50/$15.75).

... by Bus

There is a bus connection from Kiel via Hamburg and Berlin to the Estonian capital of Tallinn, operating on a regular basis since August 24, 1992. The prices each way are 700 Estonia Kroons (around £34/$63) from Berlin and 800 Estonian Kroons (around £37/$69) from Kiel. For information and reservations by fax, contact Autobussikoondis, Kadaka tee 62a, Tallinn, Fax: 53 22 77.

... by Car

Those who chose to drive to the Baltic States will need a good portion of patience – one will need to cover well over 1,000 kilometres in continental Europe alone. Only two variants of the four routes are possible at present. The two transit routes are in relatively good condition with service stations, hotels lining the roadway as well as the cars sold on the black market. Also sold on these routes are smuggled cigarettes and alcohol as the endless caravan of trucks and limousines pass by.

Travel Documents
An international driving licence valid for three years is obligatory when driving to the Baltic States. The insurance card is controlled sporadically at the Polish border. It is *highly* recommended to take out a comprehensive insurance policy for the vehicle for the entire duration of the trip.

Border Crossings
Poland – Lithuania: Ogrodniki – Lazdijai. The only possibility to drive di-

rectly to the Baltic States – meaning without making a detour through Russia or Belorussia. This border crossing is hopelessly overtaxed. Processing by the Poles and Lithuanians at the border takes a very long time and an confusing process of filling out forms with identification numbers for passengers and the car itself causes long waits and an administrative bottleneck. A four hour wait can be considered fast. Those who think they might be able to shorten this procedure by simply passing the mile-long line of cars and forcing their way into the other lane shortly before the border will not only find they will have to pay a high fine to the customs officials who send the delinquent back to the end of the line, it is not uncommon that this could provoke a fistfight.

Poland – Belorussia: Terespol – Brest: a Russian transit visa is required for this route which is 300 kilometres (188 miles) longer than the direct route and has hardly any less traffic.

Poland – Grodno – Vilnius: closed at present.

Poland – Branievo/Bagrationovsk (Eylau) – Sovietsk (Tilsit) – Lithuania: The transit route through the Kaliningrad/Königsberg region is – with the exception of aid shipments – not officially possible. This is not the responsibility of the Russian officials but is due to a law: the Polish officials do not process transit visa because a border agreement for visitors from third countries is not yet in existence.

Practical Information from A to Z

Accommodation → *Camping, Hotels, Private Accommodations*

Aids

Aids is not yet widespread in the Baltic States. What is more common are the classic venereal diseases like gonorrhoea and syphilis. Condoms are inexpensive and available in all pharmacies, most hotels and almost everywhere at public toilets. However, most of the Russian products are not very reliable...

Alcohol

Alcohol separates society: "only the Russians drink" is the proud claim made by the Balts. However, those who travel through these countries will note that one popular pastime – not only after the workday – is drinking. In the morning, it is beer which is followed by vodka during the evening. Even women are not bashful and order vodka by the bottle. Running a close second is the "Shampanskoje," a Russian champagne from the Crimea region. Beer has an unaccustomed 11 to 13 percent alcohol and a sweet flavour. It is only drunk by men – beer-drinking women are considered vulgar. Western brands are highly popular, but cost up to ten times the price of local products.

In Estonia, the "Kommertspood" has been selling alcoholic beverages since 1990 from noon to midnight – albeit at two to three times the normal price. The liqueur "Vana Tallinn" (Old Tallinn) is considered the national drink. It has a high alcohol content and is incredibly sweet.

In Latvia and Lithuania, alcoholic beverages are sold at special counters in grocery stores or at mobile shops on nearly every street corner.

Begging

The Baltic States are very poor countries. It is especially the older people who are helpless in light of the exploding prices. The children reach to entrepreneurial shrewdness by offering services and souvenirs. For having one's windows cleaned at a traffic light or having the car washed at a parking area, dollars or other hard currencies are expected. Others have specialized in selling postcards, "historic" coins or Soviet souvenirs. The frail and ailing can be seen huddled with an outstretched palm on the side of the streets – for the local residents it goes without saying that these people are given a few coins.

Business Hours

Because there are no uniform closing times in the Baltic States, business hours will vary from town to town. Banks usually will open their doors at

8 am and close around 8 pm. Grocery stores are open from around 8 or 9 am to 7 or 8 pm; other shops open at 9 or 10 am and close around 6 or 7 pm. The midday break is relatively late from 2 to 3 pm. Restaurants serving lunch are often closed from 6 to 7 pm. Those who enjoy eating dinner relatively late will have to adapt their eating habits since dinner is often no longer served after 9 pm. The official curfew is 11 pm in the city and 10 pm in villages. The "sanitarine diena" is a socialist relic: a small paper sign in the shop windows announces that the shop will remain closed on that day for cleaning.

Camping

Camping areas are even more affected by the restructuring than hotels. Due to the consolidation of farmland, the return of land to past owners and the lack of sufficient use, many of the once public camping areas have meanwhile had to close. The "current" maps with listings of camping areas are usually not accurate; reliable listings with the capacities and facilities offered at camping areas are not yet available. The camping areas with very modest standards (electricity, water and sanitary hook-ups are either non-existent, faulty or require a high level of patience) are usually located in the popular holiday regions and are only open during the summer season from June to August. In the Baltic States, camping is not only the word for a holiday with a tent, camping vehicle or the like but is also the term used for staying in simply furnished bungalows or huts. Recommended camping areas in *Estonia* are as follows:

– Camping/Motel Peoleo, 12 kilometres south of Tallinn

– Camping Kernu, 40 kilometres south of Tallinn

– Motel Valgerrand in Pärnu

– Camping Malvaste in Malvaste on the island of Hiiumaa

Car Rental

International car rental agencies have meanwhile not only opened up offices in the Baltic capitals but in most mid-sized Baltic cities as well, offering new cars at western rates. The private Baltic agencies have somewhat lower standards when it comes to the vehicles – usually Lada or French models – but these are more often suited to the road conditions. One important recommendation is to take out comprehensive insurance including theft for the duration of rental.

Leading Car Rental Agencies:
Estonia
Tallinn: Finest Auto, Pärnu maantee 22, Tel: 66 67 19; Palace Hotel, Vabaduse väljak 3, Tel: 44 34 61; Refit Limited, 20 Magasini, Tel: 66 10 46, Fax: 44 85 25.
Latvia
Riga: Scorpio Ltd. Trading Company (Volvo 360, 240, 760); book through

Hotel Riga, Tel: 21 60 90; Hotel de Rome, Tel: 21 62 68; Avis/"Auto Ventus" (Volkswagen, Audi): Riga Auto, Eizensteina iela 6, Tel: 53 83 53; 24-hour service in Hotel de Rome, Tel: 21 60 90 from 9 am to 6 pm, all other times Tel: 21 62 68. Service office in the Riga airport, first floor; Hertz: service office in the Riga airport.

Lithuania

Vilnius: Litinterp., Cultural Palace, Sporto 21, Tel: 75 61 72, 35 70 14, Fax: 62 34 15; Rent-a-Car Baltic Optima, Tel: 46 09 98; Eva, Jacioniu 14, Tel: 64 94 28.

Dental Care

Those experiencing problems with their teeth will have to visit one of the local dentists – addresses are listed in the information sections under the individual city entries in this book. In Estonia, the "Baltic Medical Partners" in Tallinn, Tel: 60 22 00, 60 22 01, 60 60 09 will be of help if payment is in hard currency. The state-operated emergency service in Tallinn can be found at Toompuiestee 4; in Tartu, at Raekoja plats 6 and at Otepää Munemäe Street 16-4.

Electricity

In all of the Baltic States, the electrical voltage is 220 volts alternating current. This is appropriate for most normal continental European plugs or adapters.

Emergencies

The emergency numbers are the same throughout all of the Baltic States and are toll-free:
Fire, Tel: 01; Police, Tel: 02; Ambulance, Tel: 03.

Fuel

An unusual procedure: one first pays for the number of litres one plans on buying and then fills one's tank with the prepaid limit of litres. This not only prevents the theft of fuel but also allows for rationing in times of scarcity. Service stations offering diesel, normal and lead-free fuel (A) with octanes of 76, 92 and 93 are quite commonplace, but pumps with premium fuel (super grade) are very rare. A network of service stations with western standards is presently being built by both the Nesté and Standard Oil companies throughout the entire Baltic region. Service stations are listed in the travel section of this guide so that a drive through the country does not become a torturous search for fuel. One should refrain from purchasing fuel directly from tanker trailers. It is uncertain what will come out of the tank-cars – and the motor will most certainly be ruined when instead of fuel, coloured water thickened with flour lands in the fuel tank...

Estonia

Presently, there are enormous supply difficulties for normal fuel and diesel. Lead-free or super grades can only be obtained at service stations supplied by Finland only for hard currencies. Lead-free fuel can be found at the two Union service stations in Tallinn, Pärnu maantee 141 and at the Pirita yacht harbour.

Latvia

At present, fuel is scarce in Latvia as well. One must count on a long wait at the fuel pumps. The sudden appearance of long lines of cars along the main roads means that fuel is being sold directly from tank-cars.

Hard currency service stations: Riga: Pernavas iela 78; Miera iela 3; Nesté Oil Traffic Service Jugla, Brivibas iela 386, Tel: 55 18 06. Saulkrasti: Nesté Oil, Traffic Service, along the road M 12 (Via Baltica), around 40 kilometres north of Riga. 24-hour service, Tel: 95 11 41.

Lithuania

Political tensions are the cause of constant shortages. If Moscow and Vilnius cannot agree on certain disputed topics then the the oil supply is cut off. In October 1992, the energy crisis reached its climax. After the Russian fuel deliveries did not take place for two entire months, the sale of fuel was officially stopped by the government. For the most part, private and public transport came to a standstill. Only ambulances and fire fighting were given fuel from the governmental supply. Prior to this, fuel sold was limited to 20 litres per car and 30 litres per commercial vehicle. Moscow justified the drastic measures with the overdue payments of the Baltic Republic – ten days prior, Lithuania had left the currency union of the Ruble...

The Finnish-Lithuanian joint venture

"Litofinn" is now building a network of service stations with western standards. Only hard currencies will be accepted. Hard currency service stations: Vilnius: Ukmerges 11; Apkasu 13, Tel: 35 86 28; service station accessible to the handicapped: Vilnius, Eisiskiu Motorway, Tel: 26 74 52.

Holidays and Celebrations

Estonia

Official Holidays

New Year's Day: January 1; Estonian Republic Day: February 24; Easter; May Day: May 1; Mother's Day: second Sunday in May; Victory Day: June 23; St. John's Day: June 24; Christmas: December 25 and 26.

Estonian Commemorative Holidays

International Women's Day: March 8; Day of Peace: May 9; Mother's Day: second Sunday in May; Memorial Day for the victims of Stalinism: June 14; Political Revival Day: November 16.

Special Events and Festivals

February: Tartu: ski marathon; May: Tallinn: "Vana Toomas" Rally; Tartu: bicycle races; June: Pärnu: "Fiesta" jazz and blues festival; July: Tallinn-Pirita: sailing regatta; West Virumaa, Lahemaa: "Viru säru" (Palmse) folk art festival; August: Haapsalu: "White Lady" Day; September: Tallinn: flower festival; Tartu: autumn running competitions.

The Estonian Song Festival takes place every five years in Tartu.

Latvia

Official Holidays

New Year's Day: January 1; Ligo Day: June 23; St. John's Day: June 24; Latvian National Holiday: November 18; Christmas: December 25.

Special Events and Festivals

April: Riga: Baltic Spring Theatre Festival; July: Riga: Riga Marathon, Latvian Song Festival, Latvian Dance Festival; Jurmala: Rock Festival.

Lithuania

New Year's Day: January 1; Reestablishment of The Lithuanian State: February 16; Easter; Mother's Day: May 3; Crowning of Mindaugus, State Day: July 6; All Saints' Day: November 1; Christmas: December 25 and 26.

Hotels

The few western oriented hotels are expensive and usually completely booked. Reservations are therefore necessary and should be made well in advance. More simple accommodation, on the other hand, is available in every city. With the least expensive accommodation options, cold running water is the standard, showers with warm water are charged extra. In some places, warm water is only offered during the weekend. In Autumn, the winter chill is already noticeable. Hotels and Restaurants are only heated sparingly and the rooms are only equipped with wool blankets. Beds are narrow and relatively short. Some of the bathrooms require a good deal of patience and to-

lerance. Integrated showers and toilets, poorly mounted basins and tiles falling from the walls are the lesser evils; cockroaches are somewhat harder to tolerate, but the worst aspect are the paper-thin walls. The poor telephone lines become noticeable when shouting can be heard in the neighbouring rooms.

Whether in higher class or simple lodgings: each guest is given a hotel card which must be presented upon request. A widespread relic from the Soviet times is the lady in charge of the floor. She handles the keys, makes sure that quiet and order are upheld on her floor and offers tea and other beverages later in the evening. Many of these ladies have discovered the capitalistic opportunities of their jobs and also offer a wide assortment of services which doesn't stop at selling beer and chocolate.

International News Media

International Newspapers with reports from all of the Baltic States:

"Baltic Independent": P.O. Box 100, Pärnu maantee 67a, EE-0090 Tallinn, Tel: 68 30 74. This paper first appeared as "The Estonian Independent", but meanwhile this weekly paper in English has opened offices in Riga and Vilnius.

"Baltic Observer": Balasta Dambis 3, 226081 Riga, Tel: 46 21 19. This eight-page weekly is printed in Riga and contains the best news summary on the Baltic States.

"Baltic News/Baltijos Naujienos":

P.O. Box 230, Vilnius, Tel: 62 40 90. Weekly newspaper with well founded business information from the entire Baltic region. It appears in English and Lithuanian, focussing on the state of Lithuania.

Estonia

Radio: Eesti Radio has been broadcasting from Tallinn since 1926 in English, Esperanto, Finnish, Swedish and Estonian. Information on the programmes can be found in the "Raadioleht" magazine.

Television: Eesti Television began broadcasting in Tallinn in 1955. The programmes are in Estonian and Russian and are listed in the weekly television magazine "Televiision." In Tallinn, one can receive Estonian broadcasts as well as three ex-Soviet stations (two from Moscow and one from St. Petersburg) as well as four Finnish channels.

CNN broadcasts news on Estonia TV directly from the United States daily from 5 to 6 pm.

Newspapers: Eesti Elu (Estonian Life): founded in 1989, this newspaper contains information on politics, the economy and culture. It is published twice monthly in English and Estonian.

Latvia

Television: Latvia TV broadcasts the CNN News Service daily from 5 to 6 pm directly from the US. Three former Soviet channels (two from Moscow and one from St. Petersburg) can be received in Latvia. Some hotels offer satellite television.

Newspapers: Atmoda (Awakening): this is the most politically radical newspaper of the Baltic. Founded in 1988, this paper is published by the People's Front and advocated independence intensively in Latvian, English and Russian. This, the most widely read newspaper in the country, now accompanies the currents developments very critically.

Lithuania

In Lithuania, radio and television are firmly in the hand of the state. The programmes are controlled by a commission, whose chairman openly advocated censorship during Lithuania's struggle for independence.

Television: "Lietuvos Televizija ir Radijas," Suderves 10, Tel: 45 92 50. Both state programmes Lietuva I and Lietuva II are broadcast from Kaunas. In addition, a Russian channel can be received as well as Polish television in Vilnius and in the regions near the Polish border. Many hotels are equipped with satellite dishes making it possible to receive the British "Sky-TV" among other programmes. Mid-September 1992 marked the first broadcast by a private station. During the test stage, the programme is only broadcast within a 30 kilometre radius of the capital of Vilnius, and this, only on Fridays. It is planned to expand broadcasting time to encompass a daily programme.

Radio: Radio Vilnius offers a 30-minute news summary at 666 kHz. Studija R, Laisves pr. 60, Tel: 42 94 90 at 101.8 mHz was the first private music station able to establish itself on a western FM frequency. At 9 pm, the broadcasts can be heard at 69.5 mHz.

Newspapers: In addition to the English language weekly "Lithuanian Weekly," which can only be purchased for hard currencies, an additional 5 large daily newspapers and 30 regional papers serve as current information sources.

Language Courses

In Lithuania, the University of Vilnius offers summer language courses lasting five weeks from June to August. Lodgings are provided in the student dormitories, in private rooms or in hotels. Lectures on culture and history are taught in English in conjunction with the language as well as a trips to Kaunas and Palanga. Information: Praktines Lietuviu Kalbos Katedra (Faculty of Practical Lithuanian), Vilnius University, Universiteto 3, Tel: 61 09 86.

The fee for the course is US$ 300 (1992).

Maps

There is still only a modest selection of reliable maps for the Baltic States. Most maps are based on old Soviet material – even the so-called "new editions." Those who use maps available in the west will find themselves confronted with inaccurate information. Depicted bridges on the map will often be missing once there, border crossing points are in reality pastures; nature reserves turn out to be restricted areas. An option which is better and less expensive is to purchase the maps after arriving in the Baltic States. The maps available elsewhere are only appropriate for general planning.

Estonia

"Eesti teede-ja Turismi kaart," Moscow 1990. 1:350,000 scale. This is the most precise map on the market.

"Eestu manteed" – Estonian Roads, 1990. 1:200,000 scale. A handy pocket atlas, divided into 75 individual maps. Quite useful, although map formats are often impractical.

"Eesti ved – Estonian Waters," nautical folding map with a scale of 1:400,000. Tallinn/Riga Ltd., 44 Rubles. Produced in cooperation with the University of Tartu.

Latvia

"Latvijas Republika," road map with a scale of 1:750,000 with indications for hotels and service stations. Riga: Jana Seta, 1992. Includes a distance chart.

Lithuania

"Lietuvos Keliai." Lithuanian road map with a scale of 1:400,000. Three maps, Briedis Publishing, Vilnius, 1991.

"Vilniaus Apylinkés," tourist map of the greater Vilnius area with a scale of 1:200,000.

Pets

Those who plan on bringing a pet along on the trip will need an official health certificate for the animal.

Pharmacies

Non-prescription medications are available over the counter in pharmacies, usually open from 8 am to 8 pm. During weekends, at least one pharmacy in each city will be on emergency call; this is also true during the night. Still, it is recommended to bring along any necessary medication. Those who visit the Baltic region during the summer months of July and August should bring along insect repellent.

Photography and Film

Photography shops with quick developing service, a small selection of photographic articles and repair service have established themselves in the Baltic capital cities. The selection and service are financed by charging in hard western currencies. Western brands of film can also be purchased in hotels or at the kiosks along the streets. East German ORWO film and Russian brands are available in every department store.

Postal System

The postal system is better than its reputation. Air mail letters take around a week to be delivered and postcards about two weeks. While the postal charges are escalating, the post office offers an abundance of inexpensive postcards: for a few pennies, the old stockpiles of Soviet postcards are rummaged off at special counters in post offices. Even in the souvenir shops, envelopes and picture postcards are very inexpensive.

In *Estonia,* stamp collectors should not miss a special philatelic opportunity: the first Estonian stamps issued by the young republic had no monetary values printed on them up until the completion of the currency reform in July 1992. The colours alone differentiate the value of the individual stamps. Parallel to this, the old CCCP postage stamps continued to be used with new values rubber-stamped on them. In October 1992, domestic rates for post cards were 10 Estonian cents and sending a post card elsewhere in Europe cost two Kroons.

The "Latvia", the liberty statue in the capital city of Riga, is quite appropriately the motif on the first series of Latvian postage stamps, which *Latvia* issued shortly after its independence. The Soviet CCCP postage stamps have been invalid since then. The postage for a postcard to western Europe was ten Rubles in October 1992.

In *Lithuania,* a postcard must be stamped with five coupons (Talonas) as of October 1992.

Private Accommodation

The lack of sufficient beds in the large cities has led to the first availability of private rooms. These simple apartments, usually located on the outskirts of town are mainly available for weekly or monthly rental. Since there is no central administration for the rental of these private rooms through the tourist office, information on this type of accommodation usually takes on the form of advertisements in informational brochures, notes posted at the airports, ferry docks and train stations or simply word of mouth.

Bed & Breakfast in Estonia

In late 1992, more than one hundred private home owners, landlords, small-scale hoteliers and potential tourism entrepreneurs determined a minimum standard for the accommodation offered. Supported by a consultant from Hamburg, they founded "Eesti Kodu Tourism", the first Baltic bed & breakfast association. A sign based on the Estonian national colours, depicting a black swallow on a blue background in a white circle, now informs travellers where to find clean and adequately furnished rooms along the route. Prices vary from £5 to £10 ($10 to $20).

Shopping

Those who decide to prepare their own meals while travelling in the Baltic States will find a sufficient supply of food staples. The most expensive – and still extremely inexpensive when compared with other European countries – is Estonia followed by Lithuania with the least expensive prices being in Latvia. In all three Baltic states, the prices have shown steep increases with the introduction of new currencies. On the high end of the scale and also relatively popular

are the import goods from western countries. Gradually, these expensive goods with their bright packaging are displacing the locally produced goods on grocers' shelves, even though the quality of these products are just as good or even better. Quite often, prices for cheese, for example, are quoted by the kilogramme. Purchases are totalled using an abacus instead of a cash register. These wooden "calculators" are based on the decimal system, whereby the black beads represent fives and the lighter coloured beads, single digits. Even without any knowledge of the language, the price can be readily recognized. Deposits on glass bottles for milk, juice and beer are present in all of the Baltic States. The deposit per bottle is from three to five Rubles or Kroons. After the official closing time for grocers, there are usually trailers and kiosks which fill demand during the night offering cigarettes, liquor, beer, candy, perfume and condoms.

Souvenirs

In these republics along the Amber Coast, the "gold of the sea" is far and away the most popular souvenir. Not only in the form of jewellery, but even chess figures are produced from amber.

Another popular item are the handicrafts made from leather or wood as well as ceramic articles. Good places to purchase these, in addition to the state-operated handicrafts and souvenir shops (Estonia: Ars, Ukurs; Latvia: Suveniri-Shops; Lithuania: Daile-Shops), are readily found at the outdoor museums at which the artisans sell their wares produced on site. In Riga's Ethnographic Museum at Lake Jugla, one can buy artistic hand-carved wooden spoons and beautiful wrought-iron work. In the Lithuanian town of Rumsiskes, three potters produce clay vessels with traditional decor using conventional potter's wheels. Other nice souvenirs are the colourful woven belts which are worn during celebrations, embroidered with a saying appropriate to the festivity. In Estonia, Haapsalu has been famous for its airy, woollen scarves for centuries – traditionally, it had to be possible to pull these through a wedding ring.

Swimming

Radioactive waste, untreated waste water from paper factories, cities and agricultural operations are often the cause of swimming bans along the coast. This is especially true for the Gulf of Riga. Since there is very little water circulation in this area of the Baltic, the gulf has the murky appearance of cola on some days. The situation in Estonia is hardly any better. Where the Czars once took a dip in the sea, there are now warning signs: swimming is also prohibited in Haapsalu and Narva-Joesuu.

Telephones

Public telephones can be found quite readily in the Baltic States; some-times, up to ten telephone boxes are attached to one building alone. Unfortunately, many of the phones are broken or do not function properly.

Local calls from private telephones or telephones in offices are free of charge. Calls from public phones are charged at two Kopekes per unit of time. An audible signal indicates that the caller must deposit additional coins. The phones accept one, two and ten Kopeke coins. The toll charges are reduced by 50% from 6 pm to 7 am on weekdays as well as on Sundays and holidays. The charges for operator assisted and rush calls are three times the normal rates. Surcharges apply for calls from hotels, telegrams by phone and conference calls. Long-distance calls within the Baltic States and to the former USSR member states can be dialled directly. To do this, one must first dial the access code 8. If a continuous dial tone can be heard, one can proceed with the city code and telephone number. Calls to western European nations and the US require operator assistance or must be placed from selected institutions. A one-minute call to western Europe costs 6 Rubles (October 1992). In Latvia, long-distance calls can be made via satellite in the Riga Business Centre, Elisabethes iela 45/47. As of February 1992, there is also a mobile satellite telephone service in Vilnius. The telephones for this system can be purchased or rented at Comliet, Architektu 146, Tel: 26 98 48 or 26 98 90.

Important Telephone Numbers:
Fire: 01; Police: 02; Ambulance: 03;

Information, telegrams: 06; Information within the city: 09.

Estonia

International dialling code from the United Kingdom: 010 372.

International dialling code from the United States: 011 372.

Country code within the Baltic States: 014.

Haapsalu: 2 47; Kohtla-Järve: 2 33; Narva: 2 35; Pärnu: 2 44; Tallinn: 42; Tartu: 2 34; Viljandi: 2 43.

Latvia

International dialling code from the United Kingdom: 010 371.

International dialling code from the United States: 011 371.

Country code from within the Baltic States: 013.

Bauska: 2 39; Cesis: 2 41; Daugavpils: 2 54; Kuldiga: 2 33; Riga: 32; Valmiera: 2 42; Ventspils: 2 36.

Lithuania

International dialling code from the United Kingdom: 010 370.

International dialling code from the United States: 011 370.

Country code from within the Baltic States: 0 12.

Kaunas: 27; Klaipeda: 2 61; Nida: 2 59; Palanga: 2 36; Panevezys: 2 54; Siauliai: 2 14; Vilnius: 22.

Theft

Status symbols like Mercedes ornaments and Volkswagen logos can disappear from the car in a matter of seconds. Wiper blades are also a favourite booty for thieves as are car radios – therefore, these should be removed when parking the car. A steering wheel and transmission lock is also recommended. One should by no means leave anything that could catch someone's attention in a parked car, whether it is "only" a leather jacket, a walkman or a compact camera.

The "Baltic Mafia" is very active in selling automobiles and other valuables in Eastern Europe and Asia. This criminal ring, dominated by Russians, is also highly involved in organized drug trafficking and prostitution. Youth gangs are presently being intentionally built up. Automobile vandalism is also on the rise, especially directed at foreigners: broken antennas and shattered side mirrors are no longer rare in the larger cities.

In Estonia, burglary in hotels has been reported especially often in the large Tallinn hotels "Viru" and "Olympia" – the burglars seem to have access to the master keys. According to police estimates, eight to ten mostly Russian gangs are active in Tallinn. Their targets are not always foreign visitors but local business and currency exchange offices as well. Latvia's criminal hub – and still only moderate when compared with large Western European cities – is Riga, closely followed by Liepaja, which suffers from an especially poor economy. In Lithuania's capital of Vilnius, the area around the train station and the "picturesque" worker district in the old city can be dangerous and should be avoided at night.

Time of Day

All of the Baltic States and the Kaliningrad (Königsberg) region are on Eastern European Time which is two hours later than Greenwich Mean Time and 7 hours (New York) to 10 hours (Los Angeles) later than in the continental United States. Summer time (daylight savings time) is in effect from the end of March to the end of September.

Tipping

Generous guests will leave a tip of around £1.50 ($3). Just as appreciated are tips in "Marlboro currency." In the eyes of the Balts, leaving no tip is not seen as being tightfisted, but as a sign of bad manners. The gratuity given to a waiter should not be converted to western currencies. Three to five Rubles in a café and ten Rubles in a restaurant is a good and sufficient tip.

Toilets

Clean and more or less hygienic toilets can only be found in the western hotels. Even in the former Intourist hotels, there are often only two squat toilets. With only a few exceptions, the public toilets on the streets are in such a miserable state that a visit to one of this can only be recommended if *absolutely* necessary. The same is true for the cafés and restaurants.

Quite often there is a charge of a few Kopekes or Rubles for the use of the facilities – but at least then, one is given a few sheets of toilet paper.

Youth Hostels

Estonia was the first of the Baltic States join the International Youth Hostel Association. To date, there are eight hostels, some equipped with saunas and conference rooms, are mostly situated near the coast. The prices per night range from £1.25 to £6 ($2.25 to $11.25) per person.

Youth Hostel Addresses:
Tallinn, Narva Street 7; Klooga II: Harjumaa region, around 20 kilometres west of Tallinn; Võsu: Virumaa region, around 70 kilometres east of Tallinn on the Baltic coast; Lahe: near Võsu; Virtsu: Läänemaa region, around 50 kilometres west of Pärnu on the Baltic coast; Varbla: about 30 kilometres west of Pärnu on the Baltic coast; Otepää: Valga region in southern Estonia; Lepaninan: four summer cottages not far from Pärnu on the Baltic coast.

Information and Reservations:
Estonian Youth Hostels, Kentmanni Street 20, 20001 Tallinn, Tel: +7 01 42/44 28 98; Fax: +7 01 42/44 69 71.

Latvia also has plans to build a network of youth hostels. Information: Hans Björkamn, Kolnciema iela 10-12, Riga, Tel: 22 60 46.

In *Lithuania,* concrete plans are not yet in existence.

Travel in the Baltic States

With the exception of Paldiski, Estonia, all cities in the Baltic States are open to visitors from foreign countries; only a few areas are still declared off limits by the last units of the Red Army. For this reason, travelling within the Baltic States presents relatively few problems. However, not all of the inner Baltic border crossing points may be used by foreign visitors. In Estonia, visitors from countries other than the Baltic States may use only four of the fifteen border crossing points – heading toward Latvia, it is only the Ikla (M12) via Luhamaa and Murati which can be used. Foreign visitors may only enter Russia at the Narva border crossing. From Latvia to Lithuania, the border crossing on the road from Jelgava to Siauliai has special status. Since the border is on the transit route to the Russian city of Kaliningrad, a transit document must be filled out and kept for the return trip.

... by Car / Motorcycle

The sparse traffic in the Baltic States compensates for the stress encountered when travelling with one's own car or a rental car from other European countries. The by-ways in Latvia are especially free from traffic; in Estonia, the first stages of increasing traffic are noticeable. In Lithuania, one can already see some of the first traffic jams – and this, not only in the larger cities.

In all of the Baltic States, the **blood alcohol limit** is 0.0 per mill. Those who do not comply with this, risk losing their driving privileges immediately. The speed limits are also very strictly enforced by radar. The following are the **speed limits** in the Baltic States: 50 km/h in cities, in the centre of town it is often 30 km/h, on rural roads 90 km/h and 100 km/h on motorways. Most of the main motorways are in good condition, with turning circles and medians similar to highways in the United States. However, since the motorways often intersect historic paths and divide neighbouring towns and villages, rural residents quite often cross the highways, demanding a high level of caution when driving. Bicycles can also often be seen on the motorways – despite the fact that this is prohibited. An unpaved summer road usually runs parallel to the main paved roads and this is used predominantly by horse-drawn carts. In the rural regions of the Baltic States, there are mostly well packed gravel roads without any larger potholes. This can make for quite a dusty drive, especially in summer. In order to make driving on the loose gravel easier, the roads have been constructed with sloping curves. While the main problems with driving in rural areas are vehicles driven without headlamps, the lack of signposts and wildlife crossing the road especially at dusk, city driving can be quite unnerving due to the unexpectedly poor condition of the roads – especially since local residents do not even slow down for damaged sections of the roadways at railroad crossings, tram tracks or intersections. The fact that a paved roadway can end abruptly and a gravel section begins without any warning can make dangerous driving manoeuvres. This is also true when road construction zones are either not marked or the warning signs come too late. During the evening hours, many of the local residents drive only with parking lights, and in well lit city streets, many drive without turning their headlamps on.

Even the traffic lights are timed differently: a blinking green light signals the change from yellow to red. The approaches to ferries can also be somewhat problematic. The difference in the height of the ramp and ferry deck are often so great that the vehicle can scrape ground – the best way to master this situation is to drive onto the ferry at an angle. The Cyrillic lettering on road signs has, for the most part, been painted over. As a rule now, one will see the Latin names with few exceptions.

The M 12 "Via Baltica" is the main artery between Tallinn and Königsberg through Riga. The through traffic bypasses the Latvian capital on a motorway ring. Of the Latvian motorways, the A 220 from Riga to Jurmala is in the best condition: the two-lane road connects the harbour city of Klaipeda with the capital city of Vilnius. The main police station responsible for traffic is in Tallinn (La-

stekodu Street 31, Tel: 44 54 40), and the officers can be of assistance in English, Finnish, Russian and Estonian.

... by Bus

The fact that the bus network is very extensive and offers good connections makes the bus the main means of transportation. The **bus fares** are very low – even for longer stretches one will end up paying mere pennies. Bus stops are not only in cities, towns and villages but also quite often in the middle of nowhere. Blue signs with a black bus symbol or a large red 'A' indicate bus stops.
Bus tickets can be purchased directly from the driver. For longer distances, ticket can be purchased up to seven days in advance.
Departure times are posted at the bus terminals and bus stops. Printed schedules are not yet available in the shops.

... by Train

The "Eurotrain Explorer Pass" for the Baltic States entitles young people under 26 years of age, students and teachers to unlimited train travel in all of the Baltic States. The price for this pass is around £11 ($21) for 7 days, £16 ($30) for 14 days and £22 ($41) for 21 days. These tickets are, however, less expensive if purchased in the Baltic States. The railway system is not as dense as the bus lines. Train tickets for distances over 50 kilometres can be purchased seven days in advance; tickets for longer distances can be purchased up to 40 days in advance.

In the southern regions of Lithuania near Kybartai, the two sets of parallel tracks have some railway history to tell. This was at one time where Germany ended – and the *Reichsbahn* trains on the normal gauge gave way to railway cars on the Russian wide-gauge tracks.

... by Ship / Ferry

Ship travel within the Baltic States offers a relaxing change in travel. In Estonia, there are ferries to the larger Estonian islands. Ferries depart from the harbour of Rohküla to Vormsi and Heltermaa/Hiiumaa. Virtsu is the departure point for ferries to the island of Muhu with the harbour of Kuivastu and continuing to Saaremaa. From Pärnu, ferries depart on the four hour crossing to the island of Kihnu and excursion ships to the island of Aegna depart from Tallinn.

Departing from Tartu, small ferries chug up the Emajögi to Lake Peipus, continuing past the island of Piirisaar to the Russian city of Pskov. In Latvia, Raketa (hydrofoils) are in operation between Riga and the coastal resort town of Jurmala; in Lithuania, there are ship connections on the Nemunas (Neman) River operating regularly between Klaipeda and Kaunas.

... by Boat

Sailing: The diversity of the Estonian coastline with its coves, bays and islands is the most popular coastal area for sailing. A close second is the area around the Curonian Lagoon and the straits near Klaipeda. The Latvian coastline with its linear sand beaches and coastal cliffs without a single island is less interesting.

The leading source of information for Estonia is the nautical map "Eesti veed"; harbour guides are not yet on the market.

Canoeing: Those who enjoy meandering through waterways will find fantastic rivers where rapids, whirlpools and weirs are rare, placing only limited demands on the ability of canoeists. Popular rivers with paddlers in Estonia are the Emajögi, Pärnu and Kunda; in Latvia, the Salaca and the Gauja are especially popular, surrounded by nature reserve areas. There are not yet any current maps for canoeists on the market.

... by Bicycle

Those who avoid the main routes used for transporting freight and cycle on the gravel or sand **byways** will find themselves in a cyclist's paradise. When cycling through the Baltic States, one will experience beauty, solitude – and dust. The flat landscapes of the rural regions are only sparsely populated, and whenever passing a house or farm, the first to emerge from the doorway is usually the family dog.

Separate bicycle paths are unknown in the Baltic States as is consideration toward cyclists – there are simply too few people who travel by bicycle. Since cycling is uncommon even among children, one should be sure to have sufficient spare tires, a repair kit and proper tools before setting out on a tour – cycle shops are virtually nonexistent in the Baltic States.

... by Air

All inner-Baltic flights are subject to the weather – and the fuel supply. Airplanes, schedules and service are still not up to western standards. Information on Tallinn airport departures is available by contacting Tel: 21 10 92. From Tallinn, there are flights to Tartu, Kärdla/Hiiumaa and Kuressaare/Saaremaa operating sporadically in YAK airplanes seating 40 passengers. Twelve-seater CCCP 29329 airplanes fly from Tallinn to Viljandi and Pärnu and continue to the islands of Kihnu and Ruhnu.

... on Foot

Somewhere in the Baltic States: far from any village a child walks along the roadside with a school pack and a lunch box. Images like these can be seen quite often in the Baltic States by those who choose to explore the country side on foot. While cyclists are quite a novelty, those who make their way through the landscape on foot are a more familiar sight. They will be greeted with far more warmth than those visitors who drive by in a luxury car. Especially beautiful hiking

trails can be found in the national parks of Lahemaa (Estonia), Gauja (Latvia) and Aukstaitijia (Lithuania). The trails are marked and the huts and rest areas have long since been adapted to visiting hikers by the park administration. Those looking for a more challenging climb should visit the Haanja region of Estonia with the highest mountain in the Baltic States, Suur-Munamägi, reaching an elevation of 317 metres (1,037 feet).

... Public Transport

Tickets for municipal lines must be purchased in advance and validated by using the machines to punch the ticket. The municipal buses are not only in poorer condition than the long distance buses, but are also very crowded – even during the weekends. For trips to the outskirts of town and on Sundays and holidays, the fare is double.

... Hitchhiking

On occasion, even the local residents can be seen at bus stops with an outstretched thumb. Hitchhiking as a means of getting home is quite common; however, as a form of travel, it is unknown. Travelling by thumb through the Baltic States can work well on the main freight transport routes, but poorly in rural areas.

The Baltic States:
The Countries and their People

Geography

Estonia

The smallest and northernmost of the Baltic States encompasses a total area of 45,215 square kilometres (17,634 square miles) and has by far the longest and most diverse coastline of the three Baltic States. Along a total length of 3,794 kilometres (2,371 miles), the coastline alternates between idyllic, small bays and seemingly endless sandy beaches. In a matter of only a few kilometres, it changes from lovely islets along the coastline to steep, rugged coastal cliffs and breaks off into the ocean dropping 50 metres at Ontika. The islands themselves are also unique: while Latvia does not have a single island – and for this reason lays territorial claims on Ruhno – Estonia has 1,500 islands, the total area of which is 4,200 square kilometres (1,638 square miles), almost ten percent of the total land area of Estonia. With a surface area of over 2,700 square kilometres, *Saaremaa* (Ösel) makes up over half of the island area. *Hiiumaa* (Dagö), the second largest island is almost half as large. Even more beautiful and diverse in terms of landscape are the smaller islands in the sea – *Muhu* with its eroded stone ridges, Kassari with its wind-swept pine trees and the exotic and secluded islands of *Kihnu* and *Ruhnu*.

Estonia is bordered to the north by the Gulf of Finland, to the east by Russia, to the south by Latvia and lies only a few nautical miles from Sweden to the west. It not only differs from the other Baltic States linguistically, but its landscapes have a marked Scandinavian character. The gently rolling moraine landscape, reaching an average elevation of slightly over 50 (164 feet) metres, ascends to 166 metres (543 feet) near Rakke. The limestone ridge between Rakvere and Paide forms the *central watershed divide* - to the north and west, rivers and streams drain into the sea; to the east, into *Peipsi-järv* (Lake Peipus), and to the south, into *Vortsjärv*. A portion of Lake Peipus – 3,600 square kilometres (1,404 square miles) in surface area, making it the largest lake in Europe – lies in Estonian territory.

Higher elevations can only be found in the southern regions of Estonia. The Haanja region, a diverse landscape of hills and numerous lakes, is also the location of the highest elevation in the Baltic States. Here, the *Suur-Munamägi* reaches an altitude of 317 metres (1,037 feet).

While the extensive plains of central Estonia have been used intensively in agriculture over a period of centuries, moors, swamps and meadows characterize the landscape of western Estonia. The nature reserve of *Matsalu* as well as the extensive forests of Estonia are located in this region. Those who travel throughout the country will quickly notice that Estonia is sparsely populated. The population density is far less than that of other European countries with only 35 people per square kilometre. Over a third of the 1,573,000 residents (1990) live in Tallinn. With over a half a million residents, the capital city is also the country's largest and has been growing through planned resettlement of Russian "guest workers" since 1950. The university city of Tartu has a population of only 114,000. The industrial centre of Narva with 82,300 residents, Estonians account for only three percent of the population; the rest are Russians. A few kilometres farther, a lunar landscape begins with piles of rubble towering to the sky: oil shale is processed industrially between the cities of Rakvere and Narva. Phosphor, glauconite sandstone and diatomite and natural stone building materials like dolomite, gravel and calcium rich sandstone are also quarried and processed. In the country's interior, the approximately 1,000 moors are used in producing peat. On the south Estonian coast, sediments used therapeutically are also industrially produced.

Latvia

Latvia lies between the other two Baltic States, covering an area of 64,600 square kilometres (25,194 square miles), making it the second largest of the Baltic Republics. Latvia is bordered to the north by Estonia, to the east by Russia and White Rus-

sia and to the south by Lithuania. With independence, the ethnic regions have gained new significance. From this point in time, Latvia is once again subdivided into the provinces of Vidzeme (Livonia) north of the Daugava, the coastal plateau of Kurzeme (Curonia), Zemgale (Semgallia) in the south and Latgale (Latgallia) in the east. With a population of 2,868,000, over one third of the total population of Latvia live in the capital city of Riga. Still, Latvians are in the minority among 932,000 residents. Similar proportions are present in other larger cities like Daugavpils, Liepaja, Ventspils and Jelgava.

The 500 kilometres of coastline from Ainazi to Paesciems in the southern portion of the country is bordered by miles of beaches, broad and with fine sand. Coastal cliffs are rare – sand dunes usually make for a smooth transition into the country's interior. The county's largest river and fourth largest river emptying into the Baltic Sea is the highly polluted *Daugava* (Düna), which flows 357 kilometres (223 miles) through Latvian territory. The *Salaca* is less polluted: a biosphereic reserve was established on its banks in 1992. The murky *Gauja* (Livländische Aa) near Sigulda flows sluggishly through the landscape. The 230,000 acre *Gauja National Park*, established in 1972 stretches along its banks. The former landscape of golden-yellow sandstone cliffs, dark green forests and reddish brown fortresses threatens to fall victim to the revolution: investors, builders and planners are pushing for a reduction in the size of the area under protection.

Rising east of the "Switzerland of Latvia" are the *highlands of Vidzeme,* with the highest mountain in Latvia – the *Gaizinkalns* reacing an elevation of 311 metres (1,017 feet).

Hardly developed for tourism but worth exploring are the *eastern regions* of Latvia. The sparsely populated *highlands* on the border to White Russia is characterized by a breathtaking landscape of lakes.

Lithuania

The southernmost of the Baltic States is more than twice as large as Belgium with 65,200 square kilometres (25,428 square miles) of surface area, but only 99 kilometres (62 miles) of coastline. "Lietuva," as it is lovingly called by its 3,761,400 (1990) residents, is bordered to the north by Latvia, to the east and southeast by White Russia and to the south and southwest by Poland. To the west is the Russian enclave of Kaliningrad, formerly Königsberg. The land rises over rolling hills from the *coast* with its unique landscape of sand dunes at the Curonian Lagoon and the miles of sandy beaches near Palanga to the capital of Vilnius. The 15 to 20 kilometre (9 to 12 mile) wide coastal strip of the *Pajuris lowlands* is followed by the rolling hills of *Zemaiciu (Schemaiten),* which are crowned by the *Medviagalis Mountain* reaching an elevation of 234 metres (765 feet). The 60 mile broad, central lowland corridor – a fertile plain at an altitude of 35 to 90 metres (115 to 295 feet) – is bordered to the

south and east by the *Baltic Highlands* with its *Kruopine Mountain* reaching an altitude of 282 metres (922 feet). Farther to the east toward the White Russian border are the *Medininku Highlands* with the highest summit in the country, the *Juozapines,* rising to an altitude of 292 metres (955 feet). The *Aukstaitijos National Park* is situated to the north of the capital city of Vilnius near the Latvian border. This extensive lake area was the first of five national parks to be placed under governmental protection in 1972.

Over 4,000 *lakes* (other sources set the number at 3,000) characterize the landscapes of Lithuania. The largest of them is *Lake Druksiai* in the eastern regions of Lithuania near the Latvian and White Russian borders. The deepest of the lakes is *Lake Tauragnai* dropping to a depth of 60.5 metres (198 feet).

The history of Lithuania is closely tied to its network of rivers: the oldest settlements lie on the riverbanks and fortresses were later built for protection from invaders. Of the 816 rivers (758 in other sources) in Lithuania with a total length of 27,500 kilometres (17,188 miles), the *Nemunas River* measuring 937 kilometres (586 miles) carries special importance: several wars have been fought over this, the economic and transport artery of the country. Today, the Lithuanians stake peaceful claims on the Kaliningrad (Königsberg) region on the opposite banks. A trip on the Nemunas River leads to a remarkable reserve area after 475 kilometres (297 miles). Not far from the *Curo-*

nian Lagoon, the Nemunas branches into the Rusne, Gilia, Skirvite, Atmate and Pakalne. The extensive river delta is a resting place for migratory birds, a breeding ground and sanctuary for endangered aquatic birds under state protection. A small bird station with impressive trapping facilities near Vente has been registering the feathered visitors since 1920. The expansive landscape with its canals, the willows along narrow paths through the fields and the quaint houses beyond the dikes call images of the Dutch marshlands to mind, especially in the springtime when flooding causes the villages to take on the appearance of islands in the sea.

The second longest river in the country is the *Neris* measuring 510 kilometres (319 miles) in length; however, only a length of 235 kilometres (147 miles) flows through Lithuanian territory. While almost half of Estonia and Latvia are covered with forests, a large proportion of Lithuanian land was cleared for agriculture relatively early in its history. Only 22 percent of the area of this country is wooded. Extensive forests, 70 percent of which are composed of pine trees, are therefore under protection as is the case with the Dzukija National Park, located east of Druskininkai. Natural monuments are also protected by law: the gnarled oak of Stelmuze, around 2,000 years old and with an impressive circumference of 13 metres (42½ feet) is said to be the oldest and largest oak in Europe. The tallest Lithuanian pine can be found in Punia with a formidable height of 46 metres (150 feet).

Ethnographically speaking, Lithuania is divided into four *regions*. The western Zemaiciu (Schemaiten) region extends between the Nemunas River and the Latvian border from the coastal region beyond the hills of the Zemaitija National Park and to an imaginary line near Siauliai (Schaulen). Bordering to the east is the largest Lithuanian province. Aukstaitija with its two large cities of Kaunas and Vilnius encompasses more than half of the total land area of Lithuania. Bordered by the Nemunas River and the Polish border in the southwestern regions of the country is the Suvalkija region with the health resort of Birstonas, the forests of Punia and the city of Marijampole. This city had to change its old Christian name during Socialist times to that of the first Lithuanian Communist leader Kapsuka. The fourth region extends from Trakai to the White Russian border and is called Dzukija. This is the smallest province, but contains the largest forests.

Climate

The Baltic States mark a climatic transition: while the interior regions and especially the southeastern area of Lithuania are characterized by the hot summers and cold winters of a continental climate; the currents from the Gulf Stream along the coast and in large portions of Estonia make for a maritime climate with the highest amount of precipitation occurring during the spring and autumn. Although the autumn begins earlier and the summers seem to be shorter and more intense, the weather in the Baltic States is similar to other northern European regions like northern Germany and Denmark. The past winter with average temperatures around the freezing point was quite mild. The last harsh winter with months of snow and ice occurred several years ago. Statistically speaking, however, the ground is covered with 14 centimetres (5½ inches) of snow on 106 days during the year. February is the coldest month with average temperatures of -6°C or 21°F. In contrast, recent summers have been unusually warm. While the meteorologists set the average temperature for the month of July at a constant 16°C (61°F), the Balts enjoyed record-breaking summers during the past two years with weeks of sunshine, dry periods and temperatures exceeding 30°C (86°F) in the shade. In 1991, extensive forest fires made the headlines, fires which required the concerted efforts of the Finns, Swedes, Danes and Balts as well as a number of days of aerial fire fighting to extinguish. A peculiarity to the Baltic States are the "white nights." The endless summer days where even the nights are light in Tallinn and on the northern Estonian coast are an unforgettable experience. On June 21, the longest day of the year, the sun shines up to 19 hours; however, during the winter daylight lasts only a few hours.

Flora

Approximately one third of the total area of the Baltic States is covered by *forests.* The once extensive forests and vegetation, only a few groves remain intact. In Estonia, 43% of the land area is still covered with forests. Deciduous forests composed of oaks, elms, lindens and several bushes including hazelnut, current and the common honeysuckle can still be found scattered around the western and southern regions of Estonia. In central and eastern Estonia are the dense spruce forests with a thick layer of moss covering the ground. Growing in the dry soils from southern to southeastern Estonia and the northeastern beaches as well as the islands are the "alvar forests," sparse pine forests growing in the limerich soil or are characterized by the former sand dunes with heather and cranberry bushes in the underbrush. Pines and spruces are exemplary of the groves, most of which are the result of the cultivation of former deciduous forests. Quite often, the pine forests are interspersed with birch trees. The deciduous broad-leaved forests with the black alder and birch trees can still be found in southwestern and northeastern Estonia. These forests have the marked characteristic of small mounds of soil around the trees' root systems with puddles of water in the hollows.

Rare in other parts of northeastern Europe, *highland moors* with Labrador tea, cranberry bushes and swamp whortelberries still extend over 22% of the land area. Most of the 18,000 moors are located in the northeastern portion of Estonia and in the landscape of Korvemaa. This is the case, for example, with the highland moor of Viru in Lahemaa National Park. Of these swamplands, only few are used for the production of peat. The old *woodland meadows* can only still be found in western Estonia and on the islands. Since it is rare that these are still mown by hand, they are disappearing from the landscape today. "Lood" is the Estonian word for the sparse *pasturelands* which have developed in the lime-rich soil of the deforested alvar forest areas. Extensive marshy meadows are found along the large rivers, for example in the river basins of the Emajögi, Kasari, Pedja and Poltsamaa Rivers.

In Latvia, the nordic vegetation gradually gives way to central European vegetation. 41% of the land area is covered with *forests;* approximately one-third is used in agriculture. Latvia is also called "the grain belt of the Baltic States."

In Lithuania, the "tree of the Baltic States" divides the Lithuanian Republic into halves. Hornbeam forests are limited to the western half of the country. In the country's interior, forest areas are not as extensive as compared to the two Baltic neighbours where approximately 40% of the land area is covered with forests. These are usually mixed forests.

Fauna

The transitional character of the Baltic States are not only reflected in their climate and vegetation, but also in the fauna. In the transitional region between central Europe and Scandi-

navia, a number of arctic species have remained – the golden slover, moorhens and alpine hares find their natural habitat in the highland moors and pine forests. *Moose* and *wild boars* are the best examples for the transitional function of the Baltic States. The originally Scandinavian species of moose are just as at home as are the wild boars, which are otherwise unknown to other regions in northern Europe. The moose population in the "moose forests" of the Curonian Lagoon region, grew from 91 animals in 1948 to around 8,100 in 1984. In addition to this, nineteen thousand wild boars were registered recently in Lithuania alone.

In contrast to this, the *wolf* population has rapidly declined in the Baltic States: although 1,723 animals were counted in Lithuania alone in 1948, the numbers in 1984 had dropped to 300. The relocation of vanished species began under the Soviet rule: in 1947, the Baltic Soviet Republics once again became home to the *beaver* and in 1969, the *European bison.* Today, 20 bisons live in Lithuania and around a dozen individual animals in the two other States. *Red deer, foxes, pine martens* and *badgers* were also threatened with extinction, but now live in the dense forests as do a growing population of *bears.*

To keep the number of western tourists who roam through the hunting areas in check, Latvia and Estonia have already passed very strict hunting regulations. Living in the rivers and lakes – given that the water has not been fully contaminated by un-processed sewage and other chemical contaminants – are *otters*. *Muskrats* make the riverbanks and lake shores their habitat. The freshwater lakes are especially rich in a diversity of *fish*. Around 80 species have been counted. Carp and rainbow trout are bred in ponds. Around 30 species of saltwater fish are processed in the fish processing plants in Estonia, Latvia and Lithuania for the domestic market. The Baltic States are foremost a paradise for *birds:* of the 317 bird species, 225 are migratory and nest in the coastal and lake regions. The numerous bird reserves ensure the survival of the black storks, herons, owls and cranes. In addition to this there is a ban on hunting a number of bird species.

The Baltic People

A legendary amber island in the Northern Sea, the "Baltija," gave the Balticum or the Baltic States their name. As a political entity, the Baltic States are the three nations of Estonia, Latvia and Lithuania. Ethnologically speaking, only the residents of two of the three states are true Balts. Only the Latvians and Lithuanians belong to the indo-Germanic group of people called the Balts – the Estonians, in contrast, belong to the Finno-Ugrians, who moved westward from Asia as early as 3000 BC and settled the land between the Baltic Sea and the Ural Mountains. The differences have become less and less apparent through 4,000 years of common history, almost 700 years of suffering under the Swedish, German, Polish and Russian occupations to the point that even the Estonians proudly refer to themselves as Balts.

Estonians

Today, Estonia is home to a population of 1,573,000; 963,000 Estonians make up 61.5%; Russians account for 30.3% and 1.1% are Finnish. The total fertility rate is rather high at an average of 2.2 children per childbearing woman. The average life expectancy is 71 years of age.

Tacitus was the first to coin the name for Estonia. In the year 98 AD, this Roman historian reported about the "Aestii" in his work "Germania." Six hundred years later, they appear once again in a work by Jordanis (also a historian) this time called "Aestui." Therefore, in the Scandinavian Götar Saga (dating back to the 5th to 6th centuries), Estonia is called "Aistland." At that time the Estonians called themselves "maarahvas" (meaning earth people: maa = earth, rahvas = people). The name is still appropriate to the character of Estonians today. They are very attached to their patch of earth. Their patriotism is understandable. From 1217 to 1990: 700 years of slavery – this is how the Estonians view their history. Assimilation or the preservation of a cultural identity was the central concern for a matter of centuries. Love of country, hatred toward the Germans and Soviets, was a widespread strategy of survival. Estonians resourcefully used the conflicts between Russians and Germany to their advantage (→*History*). The national "awakening" in the Baltic States began with the Estonians. In Tartu, they initiated the first Estonian Song Festival in 1865. With the beginning of the 20th century, Estonians discovered their love of Europe. Today, they are pursuing membership in the European Community. The focal point for Estonians living in exile is Sweden; in Germany, one can find the Centre for the "Estonian Ethnic Community in the Federal Republic of Germany" located in Cologne.

Traditional Costumes

With the growing reflection of Estonians on their own roots, traditional costumes were to experience a renaissance. This is especially true for the islands where they are taken out of the closet, dusted off and worn during holidays and festivals. In some towns, there are even costume and textile museums with some of the oldest Estonian costumes. The traditional dress for women included a dark skirt; – only the Setus (Setukusen) wore light-coloured fabrics. Beads or embroidery were used as decoration, and in the 18th century, colourful stripes came into fashion. On the mainland, they were worn vertically; on the islands, horizontally. A woven belt was wrapped several times around the waist and even worn during the night. This not only helped with posture but also ensured the woman's fertility through its magic power – at least according to folklore. A "soba" made of black fabric,

embellished with braided embroidery served as a coat and, fastened around the hips, it was also worn as a skirt. Especially characteristic of the Estonian dress were the hoods, embroidered differently depending on the region. The traditional and strictly geometric gave way to stylized floral patterns in the 19th century. Earlier, woolen gloves were also worn in summer as protection against all kinds of misfortune. It was only relatively late that stockings were introduced. Before this, cloth pantaloons held to the leg with colourful bands were in fashion. The most popular women's jewellery was the "solg," a curved brooch in the shape of a shield. Bird and plant motifs were used to decorate these silver brooches, measuring up to 3 inches in diameter. Only the Setus wore brooches which almost covered the entire chest. The Setu women enjoyed wearing their wealth: the jewellery of affluent women could weigh up to fourteen pounds.

Latvians

The Latvians call themselves "Latvesi" – which refers to the Latgallians who, together with the Livs and Semigallians, settled the area which is now Latvia.

Today, 53.7 percent of the population are Latvians. Of in total 2,686,000 residents (1990), around 915,000 live in the capital city of Riga. With 41 people per square kilometre, Latvia lies geographically and statistically between the sparsely populated Re-

An Eye for an Eye, a Tooth for a Tooth

The setting is Riga, the capital of Latvia: Russian soldiers kill time on the St. Gertrude Square against shadowy backdrop of their barracks in the distance. They are observed suspiciously by the passing Latvian pedestrians, who do not feel especially comfortable even in their own city. This is because Latvians are in the minority in Riga. Only around a third of the population can speak the native language. Otherwise, one hears mainly Russian phrases. For the visitor, both languages are new, exotic and fascinating; however, for many Latvians, the Russian language sooner has a threatening implication. The presence of the Russian Army brings and uncomfortable feeling with it.

Change of scenery: a department store in Tallinn, a young Russian salesman is addressed by Eastern German visitors in his native language. The salesman prefers to stumble through the conversation in English. The Russian language is not popular in the Estonia city, which is not even far from the Russian border and first formed a continual industrial region with the Russian city of St. Petersburg. Not only the young Russian in the men's wear department knows that the Estonians would prefer his kind gone. Russians go home!

The entry regulations for Russians are becoming more and more strict. Russians can only enter Estonia with a visa, making it difficult and unpleasant when visiting relatives. Still, they can enter the country if they present and invitation. Everything takes longer, is more complicated and requires more time for decisions and processing. It is even more of a problem with, for example, Russians who own a dacha in Estonia and spend the weekends there – an impossibility without a visa. It is a battle of attrition which seems to be effective.

But even the Russians living in the country do not come out untouched. It is increasingly the case that they feel threatened by attacks and draw the consequences which, in Estonia, means: giving up their apartment, work and home and returning to Russia – a land which some have never even seen. A large proportion of the Russian population in Estonia were born there. The gap severs entire families so that even Ellen, a 30-year-old Estonian woman and Alexander, a 33-year-old Russian, who have lived together for ten years are also affected.

Since a few months, he is not even able to consider himself a citizen of the country in which he grew up. He must apply for citizenship although Tallinn is his city of birth. He speaks Estonian fluently and has only been to Russia twice in his life. What seems strange in comparison is that Estonians who have lived in exile for decades and can barely even speak Estonian anymore, are automatically granted Estonian citizenship. Arrogance in regard to Russian residents is often the least severe form of cultural conflict. Now seems to be the time to pay back the humiliations that one once had suffered in the past – even though this also lands at the wrong address.

public of Estonia and the more metropolitan Lithuania. As is true in the two other Baltic States, invasions by foreign powers caused a drastic reduction in the native population in Latvia. In 1941, Stalin had 16,000 Latvians deported and in 1944 and 1945, at least 38,000 Latvians were displaced. In 1946, an additional 60,000 men, women and children were deported to Siberia. Hundreds of thousands were killed in the concentration camps in that country (→ *Travel Section/Salaspils*).

During the Second World War, 15,000 troops served in the Latvian battalion of the German *Wehrmacht*. In 1943, there were also two Latvian SS-Divisions. In the middle of 1944, around 60,000 Latvians fought on the side of the Germans against the Red Army.

Between 1945 and 1948, the partisan movement of the "Waldbrüder" (Brothers of the Forest) reached its height. Those who were not active in the underground resistance either came to terms with the occupying forces or fled the country and lived in exile. The cultural centre for Latvians living in exile is the city of Münster in Germany where there is a high school where lessons are taught in the Latvian language, as well as a cultural centre with dance and theatre groups and a choir, all keeping Latvian heritage alive. The "International Union of Free Latvians" is located at 152 Salzmannstraße in Münster.

Traditional Costumes

The 17th and 18th centuries were a golden age in terms of traditional dress in Latvia. Once overtaken by plain city clothing, traditional costumes came back into fashion during the national awakening in the 19th century, a renaissance which continues at present. Large regional differences in the costumes allow for only generalized descriptions. The "classic" women's costume consists of a skirt, a blouse and a scarf wrapped around the shoulders and pinned together with the "Sakhta," a large brooch. The austra tree, the symbol of the rising sun was the most common motif used earlier in ornamenting the clothing. Men's clothing was sooner practical: a jacket, a shirt and trousers – simple and unembellished.

Lithuanians

In 1990, Lithuania was home to 3.7 million people. Of them, 80% were Lithuanians (around 3 million), 10% Russian and 7% Polish. There are a number of Latvians living in the northern regions of the country who make up 0.1% of the total population. Only 12,000 Jews still live in the southernmost of the three Baltic States. The proportion of Catholics in the population is very high: the church is consistently the largest building in Lithuanian cities.

The wave of emigration to Canada and the United States reached its peak in the 1880's. At the beginning of the 20th century, one-third of all Lithuanians lived in America. Chicago is still considered "the third largest Lithuanian city" due to its high proportion of Lithuanian residents. In the summer of 1954, Catholic intellectuals founded the "Lithuanian Studies Week in Europe." At that time, this was the only opportunity for scientists, historians, literary figures and artists to meet and discuss Lithuanian culture – a meeting of minds and a demand for liberal democratic renewal in the homeland. After the last meeting in Berwang, Tyrol in Austria with over 100 participants, the next "Lithuanian Week" is planned to take place in Germany in 1993.

After the Russians (see below), the Polish residents make up the third largest ethnic group in Lithuania with 7% of the total population. This holds political tension in itself, which could not even be vanquished with the declaration of friendship between these two countries in 1992.

Russians

The systematic Russian settlement of the Baltic States beginning in 1945 has also led to tension in the society: how can the independence of the Baltic States become a reality when Balts are barely in the majority in their own countries? The Russians settled

---

Prostitution – a well-organized service industry

The most popular place and at the same time most discrete meeting point for the "easy" women is the "Jever Pils Bar" on Riga's Kalku iela, where young women throw a shy and unpretentious glance toward the men from the west. Prostitution is long since organized, the market shared by the mafia and pimp gangs. Prostitution is still concentrate in places frequented by westerners – hotel bars and lounges and pubs accepting only hard currencies. Street prostitution can be seen only rarely. Financial necessity forces increasingly younger girls to perform peep-shows in private homes. However, the big winners are – as always – the pimps.

---

predominantly in industrial areas. Narva, in the northeastern region of Estonia, is a Russian city in terms of its residents – only three percent of the city's population are Estonians. Of the three Baltic States, Latvia has the highest proportion of Russian residents at 34% of the total population. In the capital of Riga, the proportion of Russian residents is 70%. In Estonia, 30% of the population is Russian; in Lithuania, only 8.9%. Assimilation and less strict citizenship regulations for Russians is planned in the near future to ease the tensions between the two ethnic groups. Most Russians, however, do not plan on applying for citizenship since they want to maintain the option of returning to Russia. In addition, many Russians think that the citizenship is unnecessary: even without the citizenship, one can live well in the Baltic States – even better than in Russia. Since most live in the industrial or urban areas with high proportions of Russian residents, they feel quite at home anyway. What does cause problems is the high rate of unemployment among Russians. Most of them work in run-down state factories; they are less educated than the Balts and are often trained on the job with no vocational training background and little or no language skills. Animosities surface when the Balts ask themselves why these "lazy drunks" get the same unemployment benefits that a pensioner receives after a lifetime of hard work. Even more of a problem is the situation involving the Russian military. The loss of discipline within the ranks in combination with the uncontrolled sale of equipment breeds massive tensions in the population as well as between the Baltic and Russia governments. The strong military capacity in the Baltic States – which did once belong to Russia, but did not necessarily follow Soviet policy – is a factor which is politically explosive. What is in the first planning stages is to follow in the footsteps of former East Germany.

The Baltic States would "buy" the withdrawal of the troops, for example by providing housing in Russia or by coupling economic aid with the condition that the troops be withdrawn. It is high time for action. The first paramilitary troops have formed in the northeastern regions of Estonia, where an especially large number of Russians live. Lead by former officers in the KGB and the Communist Party, most of these are strict Russian nationalists. Veterans of the Afghanistan war are now training the "Rabodschie Druschini" or "Töölismalevad" in Estonian (meaning worker troops). Threatening signals are coming from Lithuania as well: after the landslide victory for the Democratic Labour Party led by the ex-communist Algirdas Brazauskas, Yeltsin had already halted the withdrawal of Red Army troops during the following week.

Economy
From planned economy to the free market
Estonia, for example

The economic liberation from the Soviet regime began in 1987. During the time when the Communist Party of the Soviet Union passed guidelines for economic reform, two philosophers and two journalists published a "Concept for a Self-sufficient Economy in Estonia." This appeared in the newspaper on September 26, 1987. The political implications of this text were immediately understood by the Balts: the theme was economic sovereignty and the between the lines were political and governmental independence. Two years later, Moscow ultimately had to make concessions: on November 28, 1989, the Supreme Soviet passed the law regarding the economic independence of the Lithuanian, Latvian and Estonian SSR. The transition to the free market economy, integration in the world economic system, the guarantee of unity and a unified economy were the three economic goals. The major problem: dissolving the ties to Russia, which has hindered or blocked all efforts toward these goals even up to the present.

The prolonged economic contact to Finland has proven a major help.

The first reforms made the establishment of small private enterprises possible in 1987. What was not possible within the political theory of socialism was registered under the pseudonym "individual work" and "small co-op." The step-children of the society had one advantage: they were not subject to the governmental production criteria, price regulation, and had up to 20 times less of a tax burden than that of state operated companies. The sluggish reforms were followed by a frenzied development: within one year, 20,000 new businesses were registered; among these were 5,000 private farms. Following the equality in tax status for state and private businesses at the beginning of 1990, a new tax system was implemented based on western models. Sixty percent of the state revenues are now dependent on taxation of income; over 20% come from the value added tax; and an addi-

tional 13% are the result of the turnover-oriented profit taxes on businesses. The separation of state and Soviet budget cause a great deal of turbulence in 1991 in what is now Russia. In 1992, Estonia prepared its first independent budget. The reorganization of the former Soviet Republic brought an avalanche of unsolved problems. The restructuring of the faltering state operated businesses and factories caused a rapid increase in unemployment and the majority of the population in Tallinn was forced to commute to work illegally in the Finnish region of Karelia.

The decontrol of prices at the beginning of 1991, dispensing with decades of governmental price control, paved the way for an explosive rate of inflation. Corruption, the black market and bartering accompanied inflation. Rationing of alcoholic beverages, sugar and cigarettes were to follow. Estonia, well developed agriculturally, experienced a famine which was homespun and unnecessary. Even in the larger cities, one could not even find bread and milk in 1991. The economic crisis ultimately led to the resignation of the prime minister. It was especially the older citizens who were hit hard by the economic crisis – their pensions lay under the sustenance level. For most of the Estonians, a second job had meanwhile become a necessity. The introduction of the Estonian currency, the Eesti Kroon, on June 20, 1992 brought the first small upswing in the economy: the now freely convertible currency allowed the number of joint ventures to develop significantly. While in 1991 there were barely 1,200 private firms, Estonia meanwhile has the most private businesses and new business starts in all of the Baltic States. However, Estonia is still a victim of the Soviet autarkic policy by which the economy looked only to the east. Ninety percent of Estonia's foreign trade was confined to the "Ruble zone" and Russia was the main trading partner for the commodities of metals, oil and other raw materials. The Ukraine supplied sugar, coal and cotton. The CIS nations are the second most important market. Despite economic aid from the United States, the European Community and individual Scandinavian countries, the balance of trade at the end of 1992 shows an enormous deficit: the imports exceed the value of the exports by around 30%.

The largest employer in Estonia is *light industry,* the largest factory in the country is the Kreenholmer carpet manufacturer in Narva. Second place in industrial productivity is the *food processing industry,* followed by *machine production* and the *petrochemical industry.* The largest supplier of energy is the Baltic heat plant, which is supplied with *oil shale* from the region around Kohtla-Järve. The stockpiles of the "brown gold" amont to around 7 billion tons. The first two wagons full were dug up in 1916. Today, around 25 million tons are mined annually and chemical plants process this commodity into over 80 products. The ramification of this industrial exploitation is an ecological

disaster in the northern regions of Estonia. Whether at the Kunda cement factory where a heavy layer of dust darkens the sky or at the phosphate mines in Maardu near Tallinn, the consequences are catastrophic. Even in *agriculture* in which only twelve percent of the population were employed during socialist times, the devastating repercussions of the planned economy are becoming increasingly apparent. While the first Estonian republic exported butter and cheese, the new leaders in Moscow were interested in meat. The plan provided for 800,000 cattle and one million pigs. Today, these animals are sold to western slaughterhouses at dumping prices. They are transported to Poland by road or rail, slaughtered there and reexported to the destitute Baltic States as subsidized aid.

As early as 1988, a large-scale governmental programme for the reprivatization was starting up. Today, the Sovchos silos and stalls stand abandoned along the roads.

Only the most affluent kolkhos' could be transformed into co-ops and agricultural enterprises. Most of those employed in farming chanced a new start with a small farm or moved directly to the city. The exodus into the cities among the young population is enormous.

Similar Problems
in the other two Republics

Problems similar to those of Estonia can be found in the other two Baltic republics as well. The main markets for a number of products was the Soviet Union. To achieve a quick and clean break and establish economic independence is illusionary.

Lithuania can be described as an industrial agricultural country. The number of privatized farms is on the rise here as well. The most important branch of *agriculture* is the production of dairy products, potatoes and grains, pork and beef. Since the land is poor in *mineral resources,* the most important *industries* are in the processing sector: light industry, food processing, petrochemical, machine production and metal processing.

In **Latvia,** there are also very few mineral deposits making similar industries significant: the largest proportion of industry is made up by food and food processing, the chemical industry, machine production and metal processing as well as the manufacture of building materials. *Agriculture* accounts for around 25% of the gross national product; *industry*, for around 45%.

Grains, vegetables and potatoes as well as dairy and meat products are the largest sectors of agriculture here as well. The economic future of agriculture is often seen in connection with the vital *Baltic harbour* in Latvia.

The Bottom Line?

The economic problems in all three Baltic States are obvious: with the dependence on the CIS nations, Baltic products can hardly compete on world markets because of inferior quality. The lack of hard currencies hinders investment in urgently needed machinery and technology... The renewal of the Baltic economy will consume billions – sums of money that no one is willing to invest. The hope lies in the improvement of the present situation through the introduction of Baltic *currencies,* intended to finally put an end to dependence on the Ruble.

History
Estonia

Around 3000 BC, finno-ugrish tribes from Asia moved west and settled the land around the Gulf of Finland. Archaeological finds near Narva and Voru give evidence of these settlements. At that time, the Estonians lived in village communities – the "kihelkondas." Several smaller villages composed a "maakond." Due to their economic significance, some of these groups of villages developed into cities, as was the case with Tartu, Otepää and Tallinn for example. In 1154, Tallinn appeared in the illustrations drawn by the Arab geographer al-Idrisi.

As early as the ninth century AD, the neighbouring nations began to look to the flourishing land in the north with envy. Danes and Swedes repeatedly tried to conquer the Estonian tribes – and failed in their attempts. It was only on the islands in the Baltic Sea that the Swedes were able to gain a foothold.

The Influence of the Teutonic Order
The constant need for defence weakened the Estonia tribes. The Estonians could only counter the German crusaders promoting their teachings of the "correct belief" accompanied by the flame and the sword, with their "heathen" beliefs. In 1217, the Knights of the Teutonic Order were able to conquer the province of Sakala with the fortress of Viljandi. During the ensuing ten years, Bishop Albert I of Riga converted the rest of the nation to *Christianity* with the help of the Danish king Waldemar. In 1227, Saaremaa fell and with it the last Estonian bastion. The victors divided the land among themselves: the north to the Danes and the rest to the Teutonic Order. The victorious Order of Knights were spurred on to further conquests. The Germans conquered the Danish stronghold of Tallinn – only to be forced to return it to the Danes through papal intervention in 1238. Rome was able to uphold peace for almost 100 years. In 1343, the *papal peace* was broken: on the night of St. George, the Estonians freed themselves from Danish dominance. Wherever they met up with Germans, they would kill them and set fire to their possessions. The unequal battle lasted two years before the Teutonic Order came out victorious. Having been scared off by the rebellious Estonians, Denmark gave up its Estonian possessions. In 1346, the German Order also took over the city of Tallinn. Livonia was at the zenith of its influence: nine cities were founded, splendid churches were built all across the country and there was active trade with Russia, Germany and Scandinavia.

The *gradual decline of the Order* began at the end of the 15th century. In 1502, Russia attempted an advance. The German overlord Wolter von Plettenberg was still able to withstand the attack and drive the troops out of Estonia. The last battle of the Order against Ivan the Terrible – with 120 Brothers of the Sword and 500 mercenaries – resulted in a devastating defeat. The leader of the Order fled to Poland; subsequently, he was given the Duchy of Curonia in Latvia. The *end of the Order's rule* meant a *new division of the country:* Tallinn and the surrounding regions came under Swedish, the eastern regions from Narva to Tartu, under Russian influence. During the *first Swedish and Polish war,* the Swedes took hold of southern Estonia, and twenty years later, the Island of Saaremaa.

The Russian General Government
In order to break the Swedish grip on the Baltic Region, Czar Peter the Great and the Polish king Augustus II joined forces with the Danes against King Karl XII of Sweden. The Great Northern War raged on until 1721 ending in the *Treaty of Nystad* which awarded the ruling rights to the Russians. The actual losers were the Estonians: the Swedish reforms (for example education in the local language, the establishment of schools and universities) were suspended, and in 1736, *serfdom* was introduced. It was only in 1817 that the

Estonian peasants were officially freed from bondage by decree of the knighthood.

The German upper class – knights and cities – could maintain their autonomy up until the second half of the 19th century when the Russians began the calculated *combat of German culture*. The Estonians answered this forced *Russification* with their *"National Awakening,"* starting with research into their cultural roots. The *first Estonian song festival in Tartu* followed in 1869. In 1884, the blue, black and white flag of the Estonian student association was elevated to the status of national symbol. In a countermove, the Russian language was introduced as the sole language in education at schools and universities. In 1905 and 1906, *revolutionary uprisings* began in Russia and spread to Estonia. The *Estonian Uprising* was directed both at the Baltic German land owners and the Russian administration. One of the oppositional leaders was Konstantin Päts – eleven years later in 1917, the co-founder of the Tallinn daily newspaper "Teataja" became the first prime minister of the Estonian Republic. However, prior to this, Czar Nicholas II's troops bloodily quashed the uprising. The February Revolution broke out in Russia in 1917 and the Bolsheviks took power under Lenin, concentrating on problems in their own country.

Estonia, no longer occupied, gained hope. While the imperial troops saw their chance to conquer the region for Germany, Konstantin Päts declared the *Republic of Estonia* during the night from the 24th to the 25th of February 1918. The Republic included the Estonian region of Northern Livonia making the republic 47,500 square kilometres in area (18,525 square miles) with a population of 1.2 million. However, the dreams of a new republic were thwarted: the German *Wehrmacht* conquered Tallinn under the command of Baron von Seckendorff. The Estonian government was not recognized and Päts was arrested on June 16. The German interlude would last only a short time: on November 9, 1918, the revolution broke out in Germany as well. The Russians once again attempted an advance. On November 22, 1918, Red Army units begin the *"liberation of Estonia from the yoke of German imperialism"* beginning in Narva. Päts, having meanwhile been released, called the citizens to defence. Supported by Finnish volunteers, the Red Army was driven out in 1919 and the German landlords were dispossessed – Estonia was finally free after 700 year of foreign occupation. In the *Peace Treaty of Dorpat* the independence of Estonia is recognized by the Russians "for all times."

The Free Republic of Estonia
On June 19, 1920, Estonia enacted its democratic constitution. Prime Minister Konstantin Päts was simultaneously voted chief of state. The German minority, now only 1.5 percent of the population, is awarded exemplary *cultural autonomy* in 1925 and representation in the parliament

and on city councils. After a coup in March 1934, the short democratic "interregnums" would come to an end. In fear of the growing strength of the right-wing nationalist "Union of Freedom Fighters," Konstantin Päts declared a state of emergency, cancelled elections and ruled the country under a presidial constitution as a dictator from September 3, 1937. While Estonia struggled to maintain its independence, Germany and Russia had long since decided the fate of the Baltic States. The *Secret Non-aggression Treaty* between Hitler and Stalin, the so-called Molotov-Ribbentrop Pact of September 28, 1939, allowed for the absorption of the Baltic States into the Soviet Union. While Stalin was forcing Estonia to comply with his pact and the first Red Army military units had officially invaded the region, Hitler brought all of the Baltic Germans back to their "homeland," or more exactly, in the occupied Polish regions of West Prussia and the Warthegau area where 100,000 Baltic Germans were settled to "fulfil new assignments." After a demonstration manipulated by Moscow on June 21, 1939, the red communist flag was raised in Tallinn. During the ensuing elections, the Communists received 93% of the vote. The new government, marionettes of Moscow, applied for entry into the USSR on August 6, 1940. The free republic thus became the ESSR, the *Estonian Soviet Socialist Republic.*

The first arrests through the NWKD (Russian Secret Police) were to quickly follow. *Mass deportations* to Siberia began during the night from the 13th to 14th of June 1941: over 10,000 people were deported during this night alone. The liquidation of the Estonian intelligentsia was suddenly interrupted by a *German Wehrmacht attack* on June 22, 1941. The populace misunderstood the intentions of the invaders and greeted them as liberators. The Nazis reached Tallinn on August 28. The perfect and perfidious Nazi brutality continued where the red reign of terror left off – the only difference being that now the victims of mass deportation were mostly Jewish.

As a part of the *Reichskommissariat Ostland,* the general district of Estonia, was granted its own constitution under the leadership of General Karl Litzmann. The battle lost at Stalingrad signalled the end of the Nazi regime and this was true in Estonia as well. Thirty thousands Estonians did voluntarily sign up with the *Wehrmacht* to defend the eastern border on the Narva River rather than submitting to another Soviet occupation; however, after the heavy losses in the battles, the Red Army once again marched into Estonia at the end of July 1944. This time, they would stay.

The Soviet Republic Once More

The reestablishment of the Soviet Republic of Estonia took place within only a few months; the persecution of the former Estonians who collaborated with the Germans was to last over eight years.

While 100,000 Estonians fled into exile, others took to the forests and acted as *partisan guerrillas* - the "Brothers of the Forest" (Waldbrüder) countered the detested Soviets with embittered resistance using guerrilla tactics. The Russian answer to Estonian opposition with *massive Russification and industrialization of former agricultural land*. Around 300,000 Russian "guest workers" arrived in the first few years. During the Eighth Presidium of the Communist Party, all of the Estonian comrades lost their seats as representatives.

With the death of Stalin, Soviet relations generally thawed. Public dissatisfaction first became belligerent when Moscow decided to limit the use of the Estonian language in 1970. Forty leading intellectuals denounced the constant autocracy practised by Moscow in an open letter in 1980. They went on to demand direct participation in all political decisions.

Glasnost and *Perestroika* became Gorbachev's magic words and their magical effects began to unfold beginning in 1987. The *national opposition* was fuelled enormously.

On August 23, 1987, the anniversary of the Hitler-Stalin Pact, over 2,000 people demonstrated in Tallinn against Moscow's political oppression and exploitation.

The Development toward Independence

The year 1988 marked the beginning of a conscious confrontation. On April 2nd, independent popular movements were established "for perestroika and independence." Shortly thereafter, the Presidium of the Estonian Union of Culture declared their vote of no confidence to the government. On June 17, around 170,000 Estonians followed the Popular Front of Estonia's call for a demonstration on the Song Festival Square in Tallinn. The nomination of the Estonian delegates for the Congress of People's Deputies in Moscow was followed up by lifting the ban on the Estonian flag during the next month.

On August 11, over 300,000 people rallied on the Song Festival grounds in Tallinn for a demonstration organized by the Popular Front. The mass demonstration was to go down in history as the *"singing revolution."* During the festival "the Songs of Estonia", one third of the Estonian population sang for freedom. Twelve days later on the anniversary of the Hitler-Stalin Pact, over one million Balts formed a human chain from Tallinn through Riga to Vilnius. On October 2, the Popular Front was officially sanctioned by the government as an oppositional party. *Indrek Toome* was elected chairman of this party with over 100,000 members. The *Estonian Declaration of Independence* was passed by the Supreme Soviet on November 16; this was the first time that national law took priority over Soviet law. The first party to be founded was the ERSP. In January 1989, Estonian replaced Russian as the official language. The Russians, increasingly forced into the defensive, banded together in July to form

"Interfront" and protested against the Estonian voting laws with massive strikes. This law states that only Estonian citizens are allowed to vote. The new year began with a further affront against Moscow. January 1 marked the introduction of extensive *economic autonomy*. On March 30, 1990, the Popular Front won in the elections to the Supreme Soviet of Estonia, securing 43 of the 105 seats. The representative *Edgar Savisaar* became the new president. On May 8, the old *constitution* from 1938 was once again in effect; the supreme Soviet removed the "Soviet Socialist Republic" from the country's name. At least linguistically, Estonia was once again an autonomous republic. Gorbachev reacted with animosity and had a "spontaneous" counter-demonstration organized on Cathedral Hill in Tallinn. During the referendum in March 1991, an overwhelming majority confirmed the political course toward independence. On August 20, 1991, one day after the coup on Gorbachev, the Estonian Parliament declared its *political sovereignty*. The reaction came quickly from Boris Yeltsin: he accepted this step as the Chief of the Russian Republic on August 24. The EC was to follow in recognising Estonia's independence only three days later. It was only on September 6, 1991 that the independence of the Baltic Republic was officially recognized by the USSR. Estonia was admitted into the United Nations on September 17, 1991.

After achieving political independence, the tedious process of disentanglement out of the Soviet Union was to begin. On June 20, Estonia finally left the Ruble zone and introduced the Kroon as the new currency, making it the first of the Baltic States to take this step. One week later, a referendum on the constitution was held. A little over one year after the declaration of independence, 900,000 Estonians – citizens of the Republic of Estonia and their direct descendants – were called to a free election for the first time in 50 years. Despite critique from Moscow, a large portion of the 475,000 Russians living in Estonia were not permitted to vote.

In the presidential election on September 20, 628 representatives ran in the elections for the 101 seats in the "Riigikogu." Entry into parliament is determined by a proportional representation system with a five percent barrier. The voter participation was unexpectedly low at 43%. The winners in the election were the national-conservative Isamaa with 29 seats, followed by Kindel Kodu (Protected Homeland). The former president Arnold Rüütel's party won 17 seats. The Rahvarinne (Popular Front) set their hopes on an Estonian living in exile: Rein Taagepera, Professor of Political Science at the University of Chicago helped the centre party to 15 seats. A moderate 12 seats were won by Moodukad (the moderates). The ERSP (Estonian National Independent Party) led by Lagel Parek followed them with ten seats. The Solumatud Kuningirik (Independent Royalists) and the Eesti Kondanik (Estonian Citizen's Movement) both received eight seats. Represented with only one seat in parliament are Rohelised (Estonian Green Party) and Eesti Etevojate (Entrepreneur's Party). Since all candidates in the direct election of the president failed to receive the required 50 percent of all votes, the 32 year old *Mart Laar* (Isamaa) was elected as prime minister by the parliament. *Trivimi Vellistes* became the foreign minister.

Latvia

While the finno-ugrians migrated from Asia to Estonia around 3000 BC, Indo-European tribes pushed through Lithuania to Latvia. This coiled-pottery culture marked a distinctive change in the social structure: the hunter and gatherer communities gave way to farming and animal husbandry. Gradually, these peoples formed the tribes of the Selonians, the Semigallians, the Latgallians, the Livs and the Cours with regional settlements. Thanks to the heavy amber trade, the Balts were to experience their first age of prosperity from the second to fifth century AD. The "Baltic gold" collected along the beaches and made into jewellery was exported to Rome and Egypt using an advanced trade network. This epoch ended with the appearance of the first Christian ships on the horizon.

The Church and Commerce: The Teutonic Order and the Hanseatic League

The first Hanseatic ships from Visby reached the coast of Latvia in 1186. Also on board these ships from Bremen was Meinhard, the Augustinian from Northern Germany's Bad Segeberg. He not only cared for the spiritual well-being of the seamen on board but more importantly, his religious mission was to spread the Christian faith to the Baltic "heathens." The first Archbishop of Latvia settled near the town of Üxküll and subsequently called himself Meinhard of Üxküll. When the bishop died ten years later having tried to establish the interests of the church in a tolerant manner, humanity was to give way to religious mission by force – first along the coast and the larger rivers. Accompanied by more than 1,000 crusaders, Meinhard's successor Berthold conquered the fortress of Üxküll in 1198 only to fall in battle; however, the prebendary Albert followed him with twenty ships.

On the banks of the Daugava River, Albert reached a stronghold with a harbour: the spiritual and commercial centre of the *Hanseatic League*. On his mission of God, this militant bishop from Bremen was able to force all of the native tribes to convert to Catholicism. The knights, hungry for power through the victorious battles, distance themselves from the Curia in 1202. Under the leadership of Theoderich von Treiden, they established the *Brotherhood of the Sword*, choosing a white coat with a red cross as their coat of arms. Together they built fortresses throughout the country. The conflicts with the Church and the merchants in the

Hanseatic League began as small power struggles only to grow in magnitude resulting in battles and outright wars over dominance in the country. One year after the devastating defeat against the Lithuanians in the battle of Siauliai, the Brothers of the Sword joined forces with the Knights of the Teutonic Order in 1237. From then on answerable directly to the pope, they cleverly withdrew from Bishop Albert's realm of influence. From 1237 to 1561, the Livonian region ruled by the Teutonic Order encompassed the northern regions of Latvia and southern Estonia. Potentially, it could have been even larger had Lithuania not cut off northern Livonia from Prussia in the south. The crusaders tried in vain to unite the two influential regions through war. They were destined to fail: Lithuania, allied with the strong Polish forces was simply too powerful. The battle of Tannenberg signalled the *fall of the Teutonic Order.* On July 15, 1410, the Lithuanian prince Jagiello led the Lithuania-Poland army to victory; in the First Treaty of Thorn, the Knights of the Order were forced to forfeit portions of their possessions.

After the battle of Zarnowitz, the Second Treaty of Thorn dictated the surrender of the possessions in the east. Militarily defeated, the *Reformation* broke the moral back of the weakened Order. In 1522, the first reformed church service was held in Riga.

With Ivan the Terrible, who had made the conquest of Latvia his life's goal, the inevitable would follow. From 1558 on, the Order lost its territories piece by piece to the opponent from the east.

When the Order was officially abolished in 1561, Livonia came under Polish rule while the last leader of the Order, Gottfried Kettler, set sail. He would subsequently be granted Curonia, then a duchy, in gratitude for his efforts.

The downfall of Livonia, as was the case in Estonia, led to a struggle for political power between the nations on the Baltic Sea: Sweden, Denmark, Poland and Russia fought it out over the strategic harbours and commercial centres. During the *Swedish-Polish War* (1600 to 1629), Sweden was able to take power in Riga and large portions of the former Livonian territory. Only eastern Latgallia remained under Polish influence.

Under the Russian Regime

In 1700, King Augustus II of Poland invaded the city of Riga. Simultaneously, Peter the Great marched into Narva – the *Great Northern War* over dominance in the Baltic region had begun. In 1709, Sweden was decisively defeated in the Battle of Poltava. In 1710, Count Scheremetjev conquered Riga for Russia.

In the Treaty of Nystad (1721), Sweden was forced to relinquish Latvia to Russia. With the decay of the Polish-Lithuanian Empire, Latgallia became Russian; in 1792, Peter Biron yielded his independent Duchy of Curonia to the Russian Czaress Anna. Under the *Russian Government,* all of the Swedish reforms were repealed and the established, privileged upper-class of Germans was once again confirmed in their status. The relapse into oppression led to the *development of a Latvian national identity*. Cloaked in a romanticized renaissance of Latvian culture, music and literature, political goals were drafted and also became popular with the proletariat through the budding industrialization.

The *revolutionary uprisings* which shook Russia in 1905 and 1906 spread to Latvia as well. Throughout the country, farmers revolted against the foreign occupation of Germans and Russians. Although the revolts were quashed with undescribable brutality, the uprisings and unrest did not cease during the next few years.

The Free Republic of Latvia

The *First World War* broke out in 1914. The Imperial Army of Wilhelm II pushed into the Baltic regions and occupied Riga. In response to the German threat, Russia formed eight Latvian regiments in which Latvian was the language of command. The "Red Latvian Riflemen" were not able to aid in the defence: in May of 1915, German troops occupied Curonia and conquered Riga during September and October of 1917. While the *October Revolution* shook Russia, the Latvian Riflemen – most of which were Bolshevik sympathizers – founded the "Executive Committee of the Soviet Workers', Soldiers', and Farmers' Deputies of Latvia" in Valka. Their demands were to be adopted into the political programme of the Latvian Social Democratic Party (LSD) founded in 1904. During the elections, the LSD won 73 percent of the vote. Spurred on by the landslide victory of the Bolsheviks, the bourgeois upper-class turned to Wilhelm II for support, demanding annexation into the German Empire. While the local Soviet was once again established in Valka and the Latvian Riflemen conquered Livonia up to the banks of the Daugava River, the *Independent and Democratic Republic of Latvia* was proclaimed for the first time in bourgeois Riga on November 18, 1918 in the National Theatre. The leader of the Farmers' Union, *Karlis Ulmanis* became the chief of state. On January 2, 1919, The Red Latvian Riflemen stood at the gates of Riga.

While uprisings in Curonia and southwestern Estonia continued to strengthen the Bolsheviks, Peter Stucka established his Soviet republic, introduced the eight-hour workday and began with the nationalization of factories. However, even the members of the assembly could not maintain power for long. After months of fighting, the German troops – the so-called "Iron Division" – along with the English Navy and the Latvian militia were ultimately able to overthrow the Soviet Council and establish a *bourgeois government* under the leadership of Karlis Ulmanis once more. On August 11, 1920 in the Peace Treaty of Riga, the Soviets guaranteed "the complete independence and sovereignty of the Latvian State and to voluntarily and for all times forgo any claims on the Latvian people and their territory which were formerly Russian possessions." The Communist Party was outlawed, leaders were executed or imprisoned. A radical *agricultural reform* dispossessed the Baltic-German land owners, who at that time owned over 43 percent of the land. The 1,900 landlords were given 125 acre residual plots; 9.25 million acres were then distributed among the new Latvian farmers.

In 1922, the free state became a member of the League of Nations. However, the exaggerated economic development with the first production of grain and dairy products was brought to an abrupt end with the *World Economic Crisis*. On May 15, 1934, Ulmanis, supported by the "Aiszargi" Militia, attempted to solve the political problems by staging a *coup*. All political parties and labour unions were banned and the parliament was dissolved on May 16. The seventh governmental restructuring under Ulmanis lead to an authoritarian system. It was only in 1938 that this "state of emergency" was lifted.

The Latvian Soviet Socialist Republic

On August 23, 1939, the Supplementary Molotov-Ribbentrop Protocol to the Hitler-Stalin Pact consigned the independent state of Latvia to the Russian realm of influence. While Hitler recalled the Baltic-Germans "home to the *Vaterland*" under the threat of ostracism and to fulfil new duties only to march into Poland seven days later, Moscow demanded that Latvia allow Russian troops to enter the country to set up military bases in an ultimatum on June 16, 1940. According to the time-tested pattern followed frequently by Moscow, the parliament was dissolved and replaced by a "puppet parliament." This event on July 21, 1940 marked the Latvian annexation into the USSR. This annexation was generously ratified by the government. On August 5, 1940, the *Latvian Soviet Socialist Republic* became an official Soviet state in the USSR. The establishment of the Soviet regime was accompanied by terror attacks on the populace: within one year, over 100,000 people were deported or murdered; over 30,000, including 5,000 wealthy Jews from Riga, were exiled to Siberia on the night of June 14, 1941 alone.

The Second World War

In light of the Russian mass murders of Latvians, the Germans were considered liberators when they marched into Riga on July 1, 1941. The hope of reestablishing political autonomy was soon to prove illusory: Latvia was placed under the jurisdiction of the *Reichskommisariat* and the genocide continued without interruption. Over 100,000 people were killed in the pine forest of Salaspils (Kurtenhof) on the outskirts of Riga. The underground opposition lead by the "Central Committee of the National Resistance Movement" began its activities in 1943. Political actions were planned from exile: the leaders were in England and America building up the illegal network to reestablish the free republic. The Latvian Central Committee had hardly declared the Latvian Republic in the autumn of 1944 when Russian tanks began rolling into Riga. In October, the Red Army took occupation of the devastated city. Latvia was once again a *Soviet Republic*. The United States government and most western nations refused to recognize the new Soviet state.

Russian Annexation

Armed farmers, scattered remains of the *Wehrmacht* and discouraged Latvians gathered to form the "Waldbrüder" (Brothers of the Forest). Based in the Latvian forests, those who would not accept the annexation of their country through Stalin staged guerrilla attacks, fighting bitterly for eight years. Stalin answered this with mass executions and deportations. Resulting from the *forced collectivization of agriculture* (in 1949, ninety-three percent of the land was already nationalized) and forced *industrialization of agricultural land* in combination with the planned immigration of 400,000 Russians and 100,000 foreign workers from other nations, the resistance was broken.

The proportion of Latvians fell from 83 to 60 percent from 1945 to 1953. Only after the death of the dictator Stalin would Khrushchev loosen the yoke on Latvia. A number of factories were placed under Latvian management. When, however, the deputy prime minister *Edvards Berklavs* openly demanded the end of the influx of non-Latvian workers, Moscow quickly countered the national Communist sentiment: in July 1959, Berklavs was relieved of duty.

After this, it would take thirty years for glasnost and perestroika to once again make such movements possible. The dissident group "Helsinki 86" was founded in Liepaja, a group which demanded the enforcement of human rights – even Moscow had signed the Final Act of the Helsinki Conference on Security and Cooperation in Europe. June 14, 1987 marked the beginning of the *"Third National Awakening."* In commemoration of the deportations of 1941, over 5,000 people gathered in front of the Freedom Monument in Riga to staged a peaceful demonstration.

The Development toward Independence

Every political demonstration to follow chipped away at the Communist Party's monopoly on political power. Simultaneously, they focussed world attention on the events in the Baltic States and revealed the brutality of the occupying forces. When around 10,000 people took to the streets on the anniversary of the Hitler-Stalin pact, Moscow blamed this on "overseas instigation." During a rally on the anniversary of the first republic, the Soviet Union took more drastic measures: the citizens' movement was brutally broken up. At a memorial ceremony on March 25, 1988 for the victims of the Stalin era, wreaths in the national colours of Latvia were placed on the graves for the first time at Bralu kapi (the Cemetery of Heroes). In June, the red and white banner was raised at demonstrations and in July, the flag itself became the focus of a rally when 30,000 people gathered in the amphitheatre on the outskirts of Riga to protest far more than the planned construction of a subway.

The *National Independence Movement* (LNNK) presented 20 political demands including the stop of Russification, freedom of the press, legalization of independent political parties and the reestablishment of the Republic of Latvia. In September, the Vides aizsardzibas Club (VAK), a club for environmental initiative with around 3,000 members, organized a large-scale demonstration, protesting environmental pollution: 45,000 people linked hands along 36 kilometres (23 miles) of Latvian coastline. With the founding of the *"Latvijas Tautas Fronte"* (LTF) – the Latvian People's Front – on October 8 in the Mezapark in Riga, the first real oppositional party to the Communist Party of the Soviet Union came into being. Dainis Ivans was named leader of the LTF. This journalist set his goals on the independence of Latvia within the socialist confederation. The conservative Communists answered with "Interfront": they demanded the conservation of the old system. On the 18th of November, the anniversary of the founding of the first republic, the red and white Latvian flag was raised once more on the castle in Riga. The election for the *Congress of People's Deputies* resulted in a clear victory for

the People's Front. On August 23, 1989, the extent of the resistance became apparent: over one million people form a human chain measuring 600 kilometres (375 miles) from Tallinn through Riga to Vilnius on the 50th anniversary of the Hitler-Stalin Pact. In October, the People's Front demanded the political and economic independence of Latvia within the USSR. During the elections to parliament on March 18, 1990, the "Tautas Fronte" could still claim the majority; however, the People's Front was subject to ever-increasing pressure from citizens' initiatives and radical groups for national sovereignty outside of the Soviet Union. On May 4, Latvia declared independence. Moscow moved elite military units under the command of the Domestic Ministry to Latvia. While the "black berets" protected the Latvian parliament from the Red Army officers who planned to storm the building on May 15th, the special "OMON troops" carried out Moscow's strict political course in 1991. It came to open acts of violence in January. On January 2, the OMON troops occupied the press building in Riga. During the "week of barricades" from the 13th to the 20th of January, residents were crushed under Soviet tanks and became the target of OMON sharpshooters. Today, large stones stand in memory of those who died here, one of which was a 13-year-old schoolboy.

In the *referendum* of March 3, 73.7 percent of the Latvians answered the question "Should Latvia become in-

Estonia's attractive postcard motifs: here a boathouse near Haapsalu

After having left the suburbs surrounding Tallinn, the city presents itself from its best side as is the case here on City Hall Square or in one
of the numerous restaurants

dependent and democratic?" with a clear "yes." The voter participation was high at 87.6 percent. On August 19, General Kusmin, Commander-in-Chief of the Baltic Red Army, declared a *state of emergency* in the Baltic States. The Latvian parliament answered this declaration on the following day with a vote on the *immediate independence of Latvia*. Four days later, Boris Yeltsin recognized the new state to be followed by the European Community on August 27. On September 1 of the same year, the OMON troops pulled out of Riga. The recognition of Latvia by the United States forced Moscow to action. On September 6, the Soviet Union also recognized the independence of their former member state. With the introduction of a Latvian currency in 1992, Latvia succeeded in leaving the Ruble zone.

On June 5 and 6, 1993, all Latvians – whether living in the country or abroad – will be called to the polls. For the very first time in their lifetime they will ask themselves: which candidates will provide a better future. Who should become a member of the first free parliament? According to "Briva Latvija" (Free Latvia), 25 political parties will participate in the June elections. To clear the hurdle into parliament they must secure at least 4% of the votes. In December 1992, the five most popular parties were: the Latvian Farmer's Block (31.5%), Tautas Fronte (People's Movement) (14.5%), the Latvian Movement for Independence (LNNK) (12.0%), the Latvian Green Party (LZP) (7.1%) and

the Latvian Democratic Labour Party (LDDP) (6.9%). Looking to the upcoming June elections, Latvian television presents the "political top ten" each week with president Gorbunovs being the most popualar and the conservative politician Gadmannis bringing up the rear as the least popular candidate.

Lithuania

In 1009, the Annals of Quedlinburg first reported of a kingdom with the name Lithuania. Around 1230 or 1240, the grand duke Mindaugas united the Lithuanian tribes on the upper Memel (Nemunas) and Düna (Daugava) Rivers. During the *Battle of Siauliai,* Mindaugas was able to defend his land against the crusading knights. Due to political considerations, Mindaugas converted to the Catholic faith. In 1253, the papal court declared him king. On July 13, 1260, the crusaders were once more decisively defeated by the Lithuanian troops near Durbe which is now Latvian territory. In the following year, Mindaugus left the Catholic faith. The external problems were hardly solved when the internal uprisings began: in 1263, Mindaugas was assassinated.

The Grand Duke Gediminas

After a turbulent transition, Vytenis came to power in 1294 and completed the process of political unity by 1316. His brother and successor Gediminas followed a course of expansion: from 1316 to 1341, the grand duke formed a Lithuanian Empire which extended beyond the Dnjepr to the Black Sea by conquering Russian territory.

In 1363, Gediminas' son Algirdas defeated the Tartars in southern Russia, and from that point on, he ruled the empire together with his brother Kestutis. After the death of Algirdas, his son Jogailla ascended to the throne until Kestutis took the empire for himself in 1381. Jogailla avenged this deed with murder – and found a new rival in Vytautas, the son of Kestutis, who did not even shrink back from a pact with the crusaders in order to gain power.

With this, Poland entered Lithuania's political scene. Threatened themselves by the Knights of the Order, Poland offered Jogailla the Lithuanian crown. In 1385, the *personal union* was sealed politically in Kreva. During the following year, Jogailla married Jadwiga in Krakow – the princess and heiress to the throne, although still under age. In 1392, Jogailla and Vytautas buried the hatchet so to speak; the latter was to rule as the grand duke in Lithuania from that time on. The decay of the Ukraine made it possible for the Lithuanian empire to expand to the east. In 1409, Jogailla drove back the German Order from Zemaitija; in 1410, the Polish-Lithuanian army ultimately defeated the crusading knights near Tannenberg in Eastern Prussia. After the death of Jogailla, his son Kasimir was to wear the common crown of Poland and Lithuania; however, the *Union of Lublin* ultimately unified these two countries into the Republic of Rzeczpospolita in 1569. For almost 2,000 years, a common king, a common senate and a common currency could ensure the unity.

With the *three divisions of Poland* (1772, 1793, and 1795), the Lithuanian Territory came under Russian domination.

In the Russian Empire

While the new eastern markets vitalized trade and commerce, the prohibition of the Jesuit Order and the refounding of the University in Vilnius made for an intellectual golden age. However, the situation of the serfs remained unchanged and bitter. It was foremost the oppression through the Russian governor general Count Muravjev which incited an extensive *wave of emigration* beginning in 1860. Farm workers fled from the landlords and czarist exploitation and headed to America and New Zealand.

Under the leadership of Basanaviciaus and Kudirka, the *Lithuanian national consciousness* reawakened at the end of the 19th century. In 1895, the Lithuanian Social Democratic party was founded in Vilnius and even then, demanded that the unity with Russia be only within a federal system.

Independent Lithuania

During the *revolutionary uprisings of 1905* the call for the independence of Lithuania could be heard more and more frequently. Russia, in its only compromise, permitted Lithuanian as the official language. During the *First*

World War, Lithuania was occupied by German troops up to September 1915. While internal political conflicts diverted attention from Lithuania, the Lithuanians made use of the opportunity. In September 1917, the Lithuanian state council (Taryba) was constituted under the leadership of *Antanas Smetona* (1874 to 1944). The provisional government, which professed cooperation with the Germans, proclaimed the *independence* of Lithuania on December 11, 1917. The decision was ratified by the state council on February 16, 1918 and by Emperor Wilhelm II in March of 1918.

On July 9, 1918, Wilhelm von Urach from the House of Württemberg was crowned King Mingas II of Lithuania by the Taryba before Germany consented to a *democratic constitution* on November 2, 1918. Three days later, *Augustinas Voldemaras* (1883 to 1944) was appointed to the office of Prime Minister. With the first party congress of the Lithuanian Communists in December 1918, the undermining of this independence began. A provisional workers' and farmers' government under the leadership of *Vincas Kapsukas* demanded a Lithuanian-Belorussian Soviet Republic. In January 1919, with the help of the Red Army, Kapsukas was successful in occupying portions of Lithuania. Poland laid claim to the Vilnius region. The so-called "Red-West Army" invaded the northern regions of the country in the fall of 1919. The German-Russian Army under the command of Colonel P.M. Bermondt-Avalov could only be stopped with the help of the

entente. On July 12, 1920 in the peace treaty between Lithuania and the Soviet Union, the Vilnius region came under Lithuanian rule. Still, it was annexed by Poland in October 1920 and in spite of the Lithuanian veto, this was recognized at the diplomatic conference on March 15, 1923, awarding ultimate control of this region to Poland. Kaunas became the provisional capital of Lithuania. Territorial problems also awaited in Memelland – but that remained to come.

The constitution of August 1, 1922 replaced the Taryba with the parliament (Seimas). *Aleksandras Seginskis* became the first elected Lithuanian president. The conservative Christian Democrats were in the governmental majority. the *Lithuanian-Soviet Nonaggression Pact* of September 28, 1926 incited internal turbulence. The political destabilization increasingly strengthened the National Party Tautininka. After the coup d'etat of December 1926, the Christian Democrats and the Nationalists sanctioned the first minority government lead by the president *Antanas Smetona* and the prime minister *Augustinas Voldemaras.* The parliament was dissolved and the country was governed by decree from May 1928. The German and Polish pressure on Lithuania increased beginning in 1938. In March 1939, Germany renewed its *claims on the Memelland region.* Under the threat of invasion, Germany demanded the voluntary surrender of Memelland.

Because neither the western powers

The Controversy of Memelland

The territorial controversies were inevitable since the Treaty of Versailles in 1919. Memelland was not conclusively severed from Germany and incorporated into Lithuania, but instead this area was administrated as an allied territory by France. When France marched into the Ruhr region in 1923, Lithuania forced the surrender of the Memelland through a military campaign.

The Memel convention of May 1924 guaranteed territorial autonomy under Lithuanian jurisdiction. At that time the German population predominated with 71,156 citizens compared to a Lithuanian population of 67,259.

an additional 3,600 citizens were imprisoned. In July, the German *Wehrmacht* invaded the country and murdered over 200,000 Lithuanian Jews up to July 1944. Only at the beginning of 1945 could the Red Army drive the *Wehrmacht* back.

The new rulers continued the same policy as before this German interlude; however, oppression, mass deportation, sovietization and forced collectivization could not break the rejection of the Soviet regime, which was most apparent in Lithuania of all three Baltic States. the *National Oppositional Movement,* traditionally supported by the Catholic Church in Lithuania, went underground. It was only under the Gorbachev administration that the oppositional movement would return onto the public scene.

nor the Soviet Union would challenge Germany's lust for power, Lithuania submitted: on March 21, the Lithuanian parliament ratified the cession of the Memelland region.

The Second World War and the Soviet Regime

Prefaced by the *Hitler-Stalin Pact,* of August 23, 1939, Lithuania was the first to be annexed by the Soviet Union in July of 1940. Within the year, the formation of the *Soviet Socialist Republic of Lithuania* was complete. It was then incorporated into the Soviet Union on August 3, 1940. The first mass deportations followed promptly: in July 1941, over 12,000 people were deported to Siberia without a trial and

The Development toward Independence

On the anniversary of the Hitler-Stalin Pact, around 3,000 Lithuanians gathered in Vilnius for the first political demonstration. On June 3, 1988, 500 leading intellectuals founded the Lithuanian reform movement "Sajudis." For the first time on August 23, more than 250,000 individuals commemorated the 49th anniversary of the Molotov-Ribbentrop Pact in Vilnius. From the 16th to the 18th of September, 15,000 people formed a chain around the Ignalina atomic reactor. They demanded the immediate construction stop for this reactor, built according to the Chernobyl proto-type. To ease tension, govenment of-ficials allowed the Lithuanian flag to be flown above the Gediminas for-tress in Vilnius on October 7. Over 100,000 people could be seen sing-ing and dancing in the streets. The Presidium of the Supreme Soviet established Lithuanian as the na-tional language.

Shortly thereafter, Rimgaudas Son-gaila the first Secretary of the Lithua-nian Communist Party was replaced by *Algirdas Brazauskas.* At the same time that the "Sajudis" convened dur-ing the weekend of the 22nd and 23rd of October in the sports palace of Vilnius, 20,000 people gathered on that Sunday for early mass held by Cardinal Sladkevicius on Cathedral Square.

On November 20, the Sajudis an-nounced *"moral independence";* on December 24, for the first time since the end of the Second World War, Christmas Eve was celebrated in public. In January of 1989, Lithuanian was declared the official language. Non-Lithuanians employed in civil service were given a two-year grace period to learn Lithuanian. The Vil-nius Cathedral was consecrated once more on February 5th, an event celebrated by 20,000 people, signi-fying the victory of the Church over communism.

The Soviet control apparatus de-cayed increasingly quickly. On Febru-ary 16, the Sajudis reiterated the de-mand for political independence dur-ing the official celebration of the Lith-uanian Independence Day. In the second ballot for the *Congress of People's Deputies* (March 26 to April 9), the "Sajudis" candidates won 36 of the 42 Lithuanian seats. A reaction to this development was the estab-lishment of the "Yedinstvo" on May 13 and 14, a movement for unity and opposed to Lithuania's independ-ence. Not only the political but the military power of the Soviet Union de-creased rapidly. In answer to a cam-paign by the national youth move-ment on August 3, young Lithuanians gave back their military papers and draft notices for the Red Army. On August 23, the 50th anniversary of the Hitler-Stalin Pact, one million Balts linked hands forming a chain over 600 kilometres (375 miles) in length, extending from Vilnius to Tal-linn in an impressive statement of protest.

The Lithuanian "Baltic Way"

The "Baltic Way" of the Lithuanian cit-izens was flanked by new laws: on September 22, the parliament passed a law on economic autono-my; on November 4, a law regarding Lithuanian citizenship. placed under political pressure, the Supreme So-viet of the USSR ratified a law grant-ing economic sovereignty to the Bal-tic Republics on November 27. Lith-uania expressed its "gratitude" by striking Article 6 from the constitu-tion: on December 7, the dominant role of the Communist Party was re-voked. Two weeks later on Decem-ber 20, the Lithuanian Communist Party declared its independence from the Communist Party of the Soviet

Union. "That is illegal," was the reaction of Mikhail Gorbachev on December 26. By the end of 1989, the Democrats had established themselves as the second party; the Christian Democrats would follow in January as the third political party. When Mikhail Gorbachev visited Vilnius from the 11th to the 13th of January, more than 300,000 people demonstrating for independence provided a turbulent reception of the Soviet chief of state. On February 7, the Supreme Soviet of Lithuania declared the annexation of Lithuania by the Soviet Union as "illegal." In the *first free elections* since 1940, the representatives from the "Sajudis" People's Front won the absolute majority in the second ballot. In response on March 11, the Supreme Soviet declared the *Independence of Lithuania*. The newly elected president, the 59-year-old musician *Vytautas Landsbergis* took office. Moscow reacted on March 16 with an ultimatum. Because the declaration of independence would not be repealed, Moscow initiated a trade blockade for Lithuania. Under the pressure of the economic problems – Lithuania was dependent on Russian oil shipments – the Supreme Soviet struck a compromise on June 30. The declaration of independence would rest for 100 days and the trade sanctions were lifted.

Still, prices climbed without end. Under criticism of the parliament and resulting from rumours of KGB activity, Prime Minister Kazimiera Pruskiene resigned from office on January 7, 1991. Moscow took advantage of this inner-political crisis: on January 11, Soviet paratroopers stormed the press building; two days later, OMON troops attacked the television tower, Black Berets occupied the Ministry of Internal Affairs, killing 13 unarmed civilians in the process. The revenge would follow on February 9: in a nationwide referendum, 79.39% of the Lithuanians voted for independence. Three days later, Iceland was the first and only nation to recognize Lithuania's independence. In a second Soviet referendum, opinions against this step were intentionally promoted. On April 17, between 250,000 and 500,000 people allegedly spoke out for the preservation of the union – this reported by the press. Moscow decided to take a hard course of action. On the border near Krakunai, a Lithuanian border patrolman was shot on May 17. In the following weeks, the Soviet OMON units attacked further Latvian and Lithuanian border patrol stations. On July 31, six border patrolmen were killed by the Black Berets east of Vilnius near Medininkai. These elite Soviet troops stormed the radio, television and telephone buildings on August 19 as well. Although members of the Lithuanian civil defence were still being killed at the parliament building on August 21, the coup against Gorbachev brought the decisive breakthrough for Lithuanian independence. On August 22, the Supreme Soviet of Lithuania banned the Lithuanian Communist Party and confiscated all private assets. The first OMON units which had held the governmental building since January began to withdraw. Four days later on August 26, the Lithuanian government issued the first entry visa for foreign visitors. Sweden was the first country to establish an embassy in Vilnius on August 29. On August 31, the OMON troops withdrew from Lithuania, other troops – like the 80 Black Berets lead by Major Vladislav Makutanovicz – requested political asylum.

The United States recognized the Lithuanian Republic on September 2 and Moscow would follow in this step on September 6, sealing the liberty of the Lithuanian state after 51 years. One week later on September 14, the official state visit by the United States Secretary of State James Baker in Vilnius signalled the restoration of diplomatic relations with the western world.

Negotiations on the withdrawal of the Soviet troops, however, were to first begin on January 30/31, 1992. On March 3, the first 100 units of the Red Army left Lithuania. In a referendum on June 14, 68.74% of all eligible Lithuanians, voted for the immediate withdrawal of the Red Army and for reparations for the injuries and damages dating back to 1940. Russia's answer: the demand for the withdrawal of the troops was a "infraction on the human rights of the Russian military" as stated by Stepaschin, the chairman of the Security and Defence Committee of the Russian Parliament. After the *election victory of the ex-communist* Algirdas Brazauskas in October 1992, Yeltsin immediately stopped the withdrawal of the Red Army from Lithuania. Despite the political tension, Lithuanian athletes marched with the Lithuanian flag in the Winter Olympics in Albertville, France on February 8 and were able to secure a medal for their country. The first western chief of state to visit the independent Republic of Lithuania was the French president François Mitterrand.

Unexpected Ex-Communist Victory in the Elections

After a referendum on the reinstatement of the presidial system failed on May 23, Prime Minister *Gediminas Vagnorius* resigned. On July 21, *Alexandras Abisala* was elected the fourth prime minister of the independent state of Lithuania. On October 25, around 2.5 million Lithuanians were called to the polls to vote for the first time following Lithuania's independence. They were asked not only to ratify a new constitution but also decide on a new parliament to replace the former one elected under Soviet law as the "Supreme Soviet." Seventeen parties – citizens' movements and political parties – had a total of 800 candidates for the 141 seats in parliament. The unexpected victor was the *Democratic Workers' Party of Lithuania* (LDAP) founded by the former communists. President Landsbergis paled as the first election prognoses were reported on television. The LDAP attained 46.57% and 35 seats in the election for the 70 representatives elected by the second ballot. Landsbergis' nationalistic Sajudis movement could only secure

18 seats. Also in the direct election, by which the remaining 71 representatives were elected, the LDAP leader Algirdas Brazauskas enjoyed a landslide victory. The former parliamentary president secured 10 of the former 14 established seats; Sajudis, only one. During the election on Sunday, the LDAP won 45 of the 141 mandates. Sajudis received 27, the Christian Democrats 14, the Polish Voter's Association two seats. In Kaunas, the stronghold of the Sajudis, the frustration of the election defeat was especially apparent on the following Monday: demonstrating students spontaneously burned Soviet flags. On November 8, second ballot elections for the remaining 57 mandates took place in 39 voting districts. Landsbergis used this opportunity to make the Russians the scapegoat, blaming the loss at the polls on the lingering economic and political presence of Russia.

Lithuania's first free presidential elections were held on February 14, 1993. Here, Algirdas Brazauskas won 60.3% of the vote – 1,212,075 Lithuanians voted for the ex-communist. His liberal opponent Stasys Lozoraitis, now Lithuania's ambassador in New York, attained only a meagre 38.28% (772,922 votes).

Culture

Religion

At the times of the hunters and gatherers, the Baltic tribes worshipped deities of nature which could also take on the form of animals. When they later became dependent on wind, water and sunshine as farmers, fertility rituals developed. One example is the celebration of the equinoxes which have endured to present. The attempt at Christianization of the archaic rites and festivals through the Catholic Church was destined to fail in many cases. One example is the St. John's festival on June 23. Nonetheless, the Church plays a more important role in the Baltic States than in other northern European countries. Especially during the Soviet dominance, the church was not only a religious place of worship, but also served as a sanctuary for those with oppositional views. It was also a means of preserving cultural identity and the spark of peaceful opposition. In Lithuania, the majority of the population belongs to the Roman Catholic Church. Most of the residents of Estonia are either Protestant or Reformed Protestant. Latvia is also predominantly Protestant. Only in Latgallia, the eastern region of Latvia, is the populace Roman Catholic; this, due to historical ties to Lithuania.

One Latvian peculiarity especially popular with young people during the National Awakening was the Dievturiba movement. Formed in 1918 as a folklore group, the original members were intensely dedicated to the compilation of Latvian folk culture in the form of music, dance, writings and narrations. Differing from the other folklorists who set out in search of a national Latvian identity at that time, the leader of this group Ernests Brastins attempted to politically revitalize the mythological origins of the songs. The resonance from the populace remained limited at first. Brastins' neo-Latvian paradigm met with much more interest in the writer Janus Veselis, whose work was greatly influenced by his literary colleague. After the Red Army's occupation of Latvia, the Dievturiba movement was persecuted; Brastins was arrested and deported in 1940. However, Brastins' brother was able to flee to the United States. In the safety of exile, he continued to propagate his brother's life's work by continuing to publish articles in the "Labietis" magazine. This publication by and for Latvians in exile was banned in Latvia under Soviet rule but is now readily available.

From 1989, the movement viewed itself as the official religion. The triad belief system goes back to the roots of an ancient Latvian faith. In it, the heavens are ruled by Dievs (the fatherly and creative supreme god), Mara (mother earth) and Laima (lucky fairy). The evil counterpole of the gods is Veins, a "devil" which is sooner a divine blunderer and quite popular with the Latvians. The creators of the universe were banned from "paradise" by Dievs' "human" mistakes and insufficiencies...

Film

The "Nordic Film Festival," which takes place every year in November in Lübeck Germany presents a broad spectrum of Scandinavian-Baltic film productions, increasing the exposure of films from Latvia, Lithuania and Estonia. In the Baltic States, the cinema is firmly rooted in Baltic culture.

In 1896, the age of cinema began in Tallinn, the capital of **Estonia.** Twelve years after the first cinema presentation, the first permanent cinema in Estonia was opened here in 1908.

Counting among the Estonian film pioneers was Johannes Pääsuke, whose first film "Bear Hunt in Pärnumaa" was completed in 1914.

The establishment of the film company "Estonia" (1919) by the brothers Peeter and Georg Johannes Parikas as well as Konstantin and Theodor Märska brought a breakthrough for motion pictures. "Estonia" produced films up until 1932.

The documentary film "With the Camera through Estonia" was released in 1924. "Gold Spider" by Konstantin Märska marked the release of the first Estonian feature film in 1930. Small clubs and studios like "Regina Film" and "Taara-Film" sprang up. From 1931 to 1940, "Eesti Kultuurfilm" produced weekly newsreels and documentaries. After the takeover by the new Soviet rulers in 1940, its name was changed to "Kinokroonika Eesti Studio" making propaganda films like "The Will of the People" (1940) their main realm of activity. With the film "When the Evening Begins" (1955) "Tallinn Film" began its production of feature films. Documentary films were produced by "Eesti Telfilm" where directors like Mati Poldre, Toomas Lepp, Märs Müür and Hagi Sein worked.

Especially popular are the animated and puppet films by Reiho Unter or Hardy Vomer. The most famous animator in Estonia is Priit Pärn. With Estonia's independence from Moscow, smaller studios like "Estofilm" and "Eesti aeg" began working parallel to "Tallinn-Film."

The effects of glasnost and perestroika on the Baltic cinema were apparent earliest in **Latvia.** For the first time in 1988, an international film festival in Riga presented 200 films from 25 countries. While the Soviets increasingly suppressed the call for independence, films from Argentina, England, France, China and the United States were shown during the nine-day "Arsenals" festival – a novum for the Baltic States. Meanwhile, the "Arsenals" festival has become an institution.

The first silent documentary films by the US-Lithuanian Antanas Raciunas marked the beginning of cinema in **Lithuania.** Filmed from 1909 to 1913, these films showed only scenes in the exile centres for Lithuanians in the United States. However, from 1921, newsreels were shown in Lithuanian cinemas. In 1926, the film production company "Akis" was founded in Kaunas. Under the direction of Jurgis Linarta, "Akis" produced the first Lithuanian feature films "Doctor against his Will" (1927) "The Soldier" (1928) and "Onyte and Jonelis" (1931). In 1932, "Akis" found competition: Jonas Vaickus founded the film studio "Musu Lietuva." from its headquarters in Kaunas, it mainly produced news features and docu-

mentaries. In 1938, the first Lithuanian puppet film was released: "The Fat Man's Dream" with figures by Stasys Usinskas. The Soviet feature and documentary film studio founded in 1940 in Kaunas produced over 40 films up to June of 1941. In 1944, production began once more. From 1946 – after having changed the name to "Lithuanian Film Studio" – pro-Soviet "documentaries" were produced here. "Popular" directors in the 1950's and 1960's who documented the struggle to build up a Soviet society were Voktoras Staosas, Liudgardas Maculevicius and Loeonas Tautrimas. In the 1970's, films were produced with a strong emotional impetus. Such was the case with "Outside at the Door" (1966), a co-production by Algirdas Dausa, Almantas Grikevicius, Henrikas Sablevicius and Rimtautas Silinis. In 1953, Alexandr Faintsimmer produced the first feature film of the Soviet period: "Dawn Over the Nemuna." "The Bridge" (1956) by Boris Shreiber was the result of the cooperation with film studios in Moscow and St. Petersburg. The children's film "The Blue Horizon" by Vytautas Mikalauskas followed in 1957. Two years after the Association of Cinematographers was founded in the Lithuanian SSR, Lithuanian motion pictures became more widely known internationally.

In 1960, the film "Living Legends" directed by the quartet Marijonas Giedrys, Balys Bratkauskas, Arunas Zebriunas and Vytautaus Zalakevicius, won an award at the Karlsbad Film Festival. "The Last Days of Vacation" filmed in 1964 by Arunas Zebriunas premiered in 1965 at the Locarno Film Festival and in 1966 in Cannes. At the end of 1981, the impressive archives of the Lithuanian Film Studio included 533 documentaries, 300 television films (produced by the "Telefilmas" studio founded in 1968) and 77 feature films. As of 1972, the current activities of the Lithuanian cinema and film industry are reported in the monthly publication "Kinas" and the weekly magazine "Savaites ekranas" (The Weekly Stage).

Literature
Estonia
The history of the printed book, "raamat" in Estonian, began in 1525. At that time, the convention in Lübeck confiscated a barrel filled with Lutheran books and missals in the Livonian, Latvian and Estonian languages so that these writings would not "contaminate the peoples, who were still naiive to the Christian faith." These texts were publicly burned on the marketplace. In 1631, the first Estonian printing house began production in Tartu; however, it was 1739 before the first complete Estonian translation of the bible appeared in Tallinn. The "Kalev" marked the beginning of the actual history of Estonian literature. The main figure in the epic poem "Kalevipoeg" written by Friedrich Reinhold Kreutzwald from 1857 to 1861 combines folkloric sagas, fairy tales and old songs. The work simultaneously united and severed the nation. Although the heroic

cycle was a national treasure, at the beginning of the 20th century it became an unpleasant historical burden. During the Soviet rule, it was a means of maintaining distance to the Russians – a symbol of Estonian identity. The renaissance of Estonian literature introduced Jaan Kross in 1958. The works of this, the most popular contemporary Baltic author (born in 1919 in Tallinn) helped the Estonians in finding a national identity. His works have meanwhile been translated into twenty languages and include poems, essays and novellas as well as a historical novel. Also highly respected are the authors of children's books. Even adults enjoy reading books by Ellen Niit, the most renowned children's author. Born in 1928, she is also a gifted poet. Short stories and novels made Mihkel Mutt famous and excellent poetry can be found in the works of Paul-Erik Rummo. Ain Kaleep enjoys a special status among Estonian authors: this writer is able to realize his literary vision through his office as parliamentary representative. Now that governmental oppression and censorship are no longer problems, paper shortages and insufficient print capacity increasingly hinder literary productivity. Still, around 2,000 books are published annually in Estonia.

Latvia
Spiritual literature translated by pastors and disseminated among the people was the only reading material in Latvia for centuries. It was only during the 19th century that a nation-

al Latvian literature could develop in its own right. During the era of national awakening, "young Latvianism" furthered the tradition of folkloric poetry and the epic folk poetry of Kris Baronis would later culminate in the romantic lyric of Alunans (1832-1864) and Auseklis (1850-1879). Andrejs Pumpur, born in 1841, published the Latvian epic poem "Lacplesis" in 1888, the year of his death. Written in the same style as the German "Nibelungen" epic, the "bear hunter" tells the story of oppression and liberation: in the battle with the German knights (the Brothers of the Sword) Lacplesis is defeated and falls into the Daugava River. According to the saga, Latvia would suffer from oppression until Lacplesis returns – no wonder that the Latvian dissident has become a political symbol in this country. Pumpur's has also proven political vision in other areas as well. His play "The Witches of Riga" warned against Russian aggression long before the Soviet occupation during the Second World War. With the novel "Mernieku laiki" (The Time of the Surveyor), Reinis and Matiss Kaudzite introduced realism to Latvian literature. These two brothers worked for twenty years on the first great Latvian novel, published in 1879. The new literary movement was predominantly continued by Rudolfs Blaumanis, a novelist and dramatist. He unites two extremes in his work: while he earned his livelihood with texts for the humour pages of the newspapers, his tragedies form the basis of his literary fame. The most widely known classic Latvian

author is Janis Plieksans (1856-1926) better known under his pen name Rainis. His works "Fire and Night," "Blow Breeze," "Ave Sol" and "The Golden Horse" reflect the Latvian yearning for freedom and national strength. His wife Elza Rosenberg, also called "Aspazija" (1868-1943) was a dramatist, feminist and poet, renowned for her temperament: not only are her poems riddled with churning emotion. Born in the countryside, Anna Brigadere (1861-1933) began her writing career after she was well beyond the age of thirty. In her works, she described what she knew best: lovingly and vividly, she paints the literary picture of life on the Latvian farms. Just how dynamic and diverse Latvian literature was at the beginning of the 20th century can be seen from the production of a Latvian literary almanac which appeared in 1916 in Moscow thanks to the initiative of Maxim Gorki. Twenty-two Latvian authors are introduced through their texts translated into the Russian language. Karlis Skalbe (1879-1945) dedicated his work solely to the genre of fairy tales and is described by his people as "their own Latvian Hans Christian Andersen." The youngest of ten children, his father a blacksmith, he was forced to live in exile due to his anti-czarist activities. In sharp contrast to his fairy tales, Skalbe was very political. This militant writer was not only one of the first intellectuals to discuss the complete autonomy of Latvia but also stood in the front lines, so to speak, in founding the first Latvian republic. Two decades later with the Russian invasion, Skalbe fled to Sweden in a boat where he died shortly thereafter. The first free Republic of Latvia brought completely new aspects to the nation's literature. With Alexandrs Caks, for example, it is Riga. Using rhythm instead of rhyme this tailor's son pays homage to the old city and its atmosphere. The authors of Latvia were also subject to the mass deportations in connection with the Soviet occupation. Many died – among others, the author A. Grins (1895-1945). After 1944, the development in Latvian literature polarized: in Sweden, Germany and the United States, the poets V. Strelerte, V. Snikere, the storyteller Anslav Eglitis (born 1906; in Californian exile), the dramatist Martins Ziverts (born 1903; in Swedish exile) and J. Klidzejs created the basis for a significant Latvian exile literature. On the other hand, in the Latvian SSR, the only goal of literature was to praise Stalinism. Older socialist authors like V. Lacis (1904-1966), Andrejs Upitis (1877-1970) or J. Sudrabkalns (1894-1975) were honoured as "poets of the people." Only after the death of Stalin in 1953 did authors have more freedom in their work. Some Latvian authors were rehabilitated; literary classicists like Fricis Barca or Janis Rainis were misused for party propaganda beginning in 1957. Counting among the most widely known contemporary poets is Imants Ziedonis born in 1933. Regina Ezera, deported to Germany in 1944, returned to Latvia in 1945. Her popular novel "Aka" (The Well) was filmed in Riga under the title "Sonata from the Sea." Alberts Bels, born in 1938,

is the most often translated Latvian author. His most renowned work, a historical novel, was entitled "Codename Harrison." Lisvaldis Lams took a literary approach to his heritage. Born into a dockworker's family, this author wrote prose for books and newspapers about the worker milieu.

Lithuania

"Metai" is the name of the first significant Lithuanian literary work: "The Seasons" written in hexameter by Kristijonas Donelaitis (1714-1780) was published posthumous. One of Donelaitis' contemporaries was more popular at first. Many poems by Antanas Strazdas (1760-1833) are now folk songs. Antanas Baranauskas (1853-1902) whose prose is virtually riddled with didactic value, was the most famous poet during the middle of the 19th century. Works by Simonas Daukantas (1793-1864) are pertinent and vivid with romantic and patriotic elements.

After the Russian government's ban on publishing Lithuanian literature in Latin script in 1864, literary productivity stagnated. From 1883 to 1886, the "Ausra" (Dawn) newspaper rang in Lithuanian identity from exile in Tilsit. The advocates of the national renaissance were foremost Maironis (= Jonas Maciulis) with his collection of poetry entitled "Pavasario balsai" (Voices of Spring); A. Drambrauskas (= A. Jakstas) and Pranas Vaicaitis. The national Romantic Period was followed by Realism, personified by Zemaite (= Julija Zymantiene, 1845-1921), Satrijos Ragana (= Marija Pekkauskaite, 1877-1930), Jonas Biliunas (1879-1907) and Vincas Kurdirka (1858-1899) the father of the satirical short story. In 1904, the ban on printing was finally lifted.

In 1913 and 1914, the first literary journal was published in Vilnius entitled "Vaivorykste" (Rainbow). During the period of political autonomy, the Lithuanian literature developed under the influence of foreign trends. Among the most significant storytellers were Vincas Kreve-Mickevicius (1882-1954), Juozas Tumas-Vaizgantas (81869-1933), Petras Cvirka (1909-1947), Vincas Mykolaitis-Putinas (1893-1960) and Juozas Grusas (born in 1901). Salomeja Neris (= Bacinskaite-Buciene, 1904-1945) was a literary leader in the genre of poetry. The dramatists Balys Sruogo (1896-1947) and Petras Vaiciunas (1890-1959) established international renown.

After the occupation by the USSR, the constraints of "Soviet Realism" dictated the literary works in Lithuania from 1944 to at least 1956. Successful Soviet-Lithuanian writers include Jonas Avyzius (born in 1922), Mykolas Sluckis (born in 1928), Romualdas Lankauskas (born in 1932) and J. Kondrotas (born in 1918). Works by the dramatists Jonas Marcinkevicius (born in 1930) and Kazys Saja (born in 1932) were presented on stage. The poets E. Miezelaitis (born in 1919) and J. Vaiciunaite (born in 1937) were honoured by the gov-ernment; however, the highest readership concentrated on underground and exile literature.

Visual Arts
Estonia

In the area of painting, Estonia has also experienced a development closely related to the national awakening. If the graphic arts were previously something reserved for upper-class German descendants, then the founding of a drawing school in 1803 at the University of Tartu brought them closer to Estonian nationals. The German graphic artist Karl August Senff was appointed to the office of president of the first Estonian Academy of the Arts. Due to the close artistic ties to Germany, many painters studied in Düsseldorf and later also in St. Petersburg. The first truly Estonian painter was Johann Köler (1826-1899), who never renounced his origin from a farming family. After his education at the St. Petersburg Art Academy, Köler departed for Italy, stayed four years and perfected his late classicistic-romantic painting style. Ultimately, he was appointed professor at the St. Petersburg Art Academy in 1867 because of his flattering portraits of members of the upper social class. Köler not only mixed colours but also diligently mixed in politics: he was the leader of the radical wing of the national movement in Estonia.

Oscar Hoffmann (1851-1911) is considered the "Rembrandt of Estonia." Educated at the Düsseldorf Academy, his travels through Belgium and Holland influenced his portrayals of scenes from the Estonian countryside. His contemporary Tonis Granzstein (1863-1916) rose to fame through his altar paintings in the southern Estonian city of Noo.

Sculpture developed later than painting. The work of August Weizenberg (1837-1921), influenced by the Danish sculptor Thorvaldsen signalled a breakthrough. Weizenberg became famous for his plastic interpretation of stories and characters from the national epic poem "Kalevipoeg." The sculpture "Linda" portraying the mother of the national hero is one example which can be viewed in Tallinn. The "Russalka" at the Kadriorg Park in Tallinn is among the most widely renowned monumental plastics by Amandus Adamson (1885-1891). During his Parisian period from 1886-1891, this sculptor, whose work is predominantly concerned with the war of independence, won a prize for his three wooden figures. A dazzling personality in painting during the turn of the century was Ants Laikmaa (1866-1942). This art-inspired young man hiked from Riga to Düsseldorf to visit the Art Academy there. When Laikmaa returned to Tallinn in 1900, he opened the first school for the graphic arts, took part in the first national art exhibition in 1906 and founded the Estonian Artists' Association shortly thereafter. This dedication, however, brought him little satisfaction: in 1907, Laikmaa had to flee to Finland. From there, he then emigrated to Italy folowed by Tunisia.

It was only in 1913 that Laikmaa returned to Estonia to teach at the art school in Tallinn.

The Raud brothers brought outstanding, although contrasting influence to the art scene in Estonia. Progressive revitalization best describes the influence of Kristjan Raud (1865-1943) who settled in Tartu in 1904 after having studied in Munich, Düsseldorf and St. Petersburg. His energetic activities in collecting Estonian folk art led to a programme for national art. Conservative, classic portraits of members of the upper social class made his twin brother Paul (1865-1930) famous. The aftermath of the Russian revolution of 1905 drove many artists into exile. It was formost the members of the literary "Association of Young Estonia" who fled the country. The sculptor Jan Koort (1883-1935) for example, educated in St. Petersburg, was forced to flee through Finland and Norway because of his anti-czarist statements. His flight led him to Paris where he taught up to 1908 and found a new artistic home in the avant-garde artist colony of "La Ruche." This sculptor, who chiefly used black granite, basalt and other hard types of stone, was forced to leave once more in 1934: Koort fled from the Nazis to the Soviet Union. A companion of his during his stay in Paris was Nikolai Triik, born in 1884 in Tallinn. In the confrontation with the modern western European movement, Triik developed his own style of painting portraits which was the concentration of his activity up until his death in 1940.

Amidst the economic and political confusion of the first republic, the year 1919 marked the founding of the "Pallas" Academy for the Graphic Arts in Tartu; thus, the opening of Estonian Art to all social classes and artistic styles. Shortly thereafter, the establishment of artists' groups and associations followed. In the 1920's, close relations to Germany influenced Estonian art. Ado Vabbe met his artistic colleagues Kandinsky in Munich and the sculptor Anton Starrkopf and examined the German expressionistic style during his time as a prisoner of war. In Paris, A. Akberg, M. Laarmann and other Estonian painters formed the artists' group "Ryhm." The internationalization of Estonian art abruptly ended with the annexation into the Soviet empire. Cut off from the rest of the world, artistic life was left to its own devices, politically instrumentalized or suppressed. The artists reacted in three different ways: withdrawal into the private sphere, emigration or coming to terms with the new rulers by joining the artists' association. In 1945, the first attempts by the Soviets to Russify Estonian art began. The artistic ideal of "Socialistic Realism" was propagated in campaigns against "Formalism" and "Cosmopolitanism." After the liquidation of the art school in Tartu through a merger with the conservative school in Tallinn, only "official art" remained under Stalin's rule.

In the 1960's the political grip started to loosen considerably, which was also noticeable in art. Works by artists from the neighbouring socialist countries like Poland, Czechoslovakia and East Germany could suddenly be seen at exhibitions and more modern directions in art were tolerated. Today, Estonian art is experiencing a dramatic renaissance: galleries showing works by young Estonian artists are springing up in all of the cities. Also, waiting lists for entry to the art academy and numerous applications for foreign scholarships are evidence of the artistic potential in Estonia which was suppressed for so long.

Latvia

The second half of the 19th century is often referred to as the "golden age" of Latvian painting. Almost all of the prominent artists went on a "grand tour" of the western European art metropolises after completing their education in St. Petersburg before the national awakening movement gave art realism the typical Latvian brush stroke. The portrait painter Janis S. Roze (1823-1927), for instance, first worked in Paris and Munich before returning to Riga. Karlis Hune (1830-1877) showed his works at various art exhibitions in Paris along with Cezanne, Monet and Renoir. Latvian art during the turn of the century was decisively influenced by three contemporaries who could not be more different from one another: Janis Rozentalis (1866-1916), Janis Valters (1872-1945) and Vilhelms Purvitis (1869-1932).

Janis Rozentalis is considered the founder of Latvian national painting.

The outstanding portrait painter brought the rural lifestyle to the canvas as no other. Vilhelms Purvitis is considered *the* Latvian landscape painter. The works of this impressionist whose favourite motive was landscapes in spring were recognized with a bronze medal at the 1900 World Fair in Paris and with the gold medal in Munich in 1901. Janis Valters, known as Johannes Walter Kurau during his time in Dresden, painted mainly "plein-air," meaning in nature. In 1919, Valdemar Tone (1892-1958), Konrads Ubans (1893-1981), Jekab Kazaks (1895-1920), Niklavs Strunke (1894-1966), Romans Suta (1896-1944) Uga (1895-1963) and Oto Skulme (1889-1967) founded the "Riga Group," which occupied itself intensively with expressionistic trends. An extensive collection of works by the Riga Group can be seen in the National Art Museum in Riga. The art academy in Riga, founded in 1919 by Purvitis, became the centre for Latvian painting; today, it remains a centre of education for young artists. The Sovietization of the country ended artistic freedom. While the most prominent artists fled into exile, "Socialistic Realism" was declared the official artistic style. All creativity was forced into governmental limits. Art during the early post-war period was influenced by Janis Pauluks, Eduards Kalnins, Valdis Kalnroze and Arijis Skride. Maija Tabaka counts among the most widely known contemporary artists. Works by the painter and graphic artist Gunar Krolis could be seen at the 1980 Latvian Graphic Exhibition in West Berlin. Also represented there was the work of the director of the Latvian Art Academy Indulis Zarins. The 1990 "Unexpected Encounters" exhibition in the National Art Gallery of Berlin was dedicated to the Latvian avant garde. This exhibition of Latvian artists from 1910 to 1930 was followed by an exhibition in Riga of Art from Berlin from the 1960's to the 1980's.

Information on the current events in the art scene in Latvia can be found at the "Art Days," taking place annually at the end of April as well as in the magazines "Maksla" (Art), "Literatura un Maksla" (Literature and Art), "Liesma" (Flame), "Avots" (Spring).

Lithuania

Neolithic Ceramics, pieces of art made from bone and amber as well as wooden figures of humans and animals excavated by archaeologists during the past decades are the oldest evidence of the Lithuanian culture; book illustrations and decorations for weapons from the Middle Ages offer evidence of western and Byzantine influence.

During the early 1500's, Italian, German and Flemish masters propagated the art of the Renaissance. A separate school of painting developed under the influence of the humanistic paradigm which was dedicated solely to painting portraits. The leading proponent of this trend was Steponas Olandas. Baroque painting was especially influenced by Poland and Italy. Religious portrayals and portraits of respected contemporaries determined the choice of artistic motifs. The establishment of departments for the graphic arts at the University of Vilnius – painting and drawing (1797), sculpting (1803), graphic arts (1805) – brought enormous progress to the graphic arts. Up until 1832, graphic artists were professionally educated and "modern" painting styles promoted in Vilnius. Works could be seen from 1810 in Vilnius at frequent art exhibitions. Genre and history paintings, including psychologically interpreted portraits of families, friends and professional superiors determined the paintings of the Romantic period, influenced mainly by the painters Jonas Rustemas, Valentinas Vankavicius and Karolis Ripinskis. Landscape paintings characterized by national ardour made Vincentas Dmnochovskis and Konstantas Kukevicius renowned.

The establishment of the Lithuanian Art Society in 1907 as well as the first national art exhibition from 1907 to 1914 supported by the art society had a very stimulating effect on the artistic productivity around the turn of the century. Among the numerous artists who displayed their work, one stood out especially: Mikalojus Konstantinas Ciurlionis (1875-1911). In his paintings and graphic works, the composer and painter from the southern regions of Lithuania masterfully combines the tradition of Lithuanian folklore with characteristics of Art Nouveau and Romanticism. The proximity to the people in the symbolism of his paintings elevated this artists status almost to the point of becoming a national saint. Ciurlio-

nis became especially famous through his attempt to present music on the canvas. To this end, he used the mathematical principles of music in his paintings enhanced by the dimension of time and created such unique spatial cycles; holistic works of art in a new metaphysical dimension. The establishment of the art school in Kaunas (1922), the Lithuanian Sculptors' Society (1920-1929) and the opening of the M. K. Ciurlionis Art Gallery in Kaunas (1925) offered Lithuanian art – subdivided into its highly diverse ideological and artistic trends – a broad basis for creativity.

The art of the 20th century, based mainly on the tradition of Realism, was especially influenced by the painters Justinas Vienozinskis (1880-1960), Petras Kalpokas (1880-1945), Jonas Sileika (1883-1960) and Adomas Varnas (1879-1979). Among the sculptors, Petras Rimsa stood out especially. The establishment of the Society of Independent Artists (1930) was followed by the formation of the "Ars" group two years later. This group meshed elements of Lithuanian folk art with characteristics of Cubism and Expressionism in an unconventional manner, yielding a unique style in painting. While some painters like Antanas Gurdaitis (born in 1904) and Viktoras Vizgirda (born in 1904) accentuated the rhythm of the painting and used bold colour contrasts, others like Justinas Vienozinskis emphasized the subtle harmony of soft tones. Sculpture was dominated by monumental plastics.

Juozas Mikenas (1901-1964) sculpted (among other works) "The First Swallow," a work which stands high above the banks of the Neris River next to the "Lietuva" Hotel. In the beach resort of Palanga, the "Egle Sculpture" dedicated to the queen of the nocturnal snakes is a work of fantasy by Robertas Antinis (1898-1981).

Music
Estonia

The earliest musical works in Estonian folklore were runic songs. Cliff drawings on the east shores of the Änis-järv are evidence that these verses were sung in unison to diatonic melodies and were varied when repeated. These melodies, handed down over generations, are around 1,000 years old. They were even kept alive in some regions of Estonia into the 20th century.

As in other northern European countries, the collection of folk songs and texts began during the era of the national awakening. The return to one's own national origin led to the first national *Folk Song Festival* in Tartu in 1869. Initiated through the commemoration of the abolition of indentured servitude fifty years prior, 845 participants in men's choirs sang songs that year filled with national romanticism in support of an Estonian national identity. One song by Lydia Koidula "Mu isamm on minu arm" (My Country, My Love) has since become the unofficial anthem of the Estonians and is sung at every *Song Festival*. Up until the sixth Song Festival in 1896, held for the first time in Tallinn instead of Tartu, only men's choirs took part. In 1910, children's choirs were also allowed to perform. At the first Song Festival in the independent Republic of Estonia in 1923, only Estonian songs were sung.

The twelfth festival, held in 1947 in Tallinn with 25,760 singers was spurred by Soviet pressure: more a demonstration staged by the new rulers, hymns praising Stalin displaced the old Estonian folk songs. During the following festival in 1950 in Tallinn, 31,907 participants were to sing in praise of Stalin as well. At the fourteenth festival, the fading ability of the Estonians to sing was bolstered by Russian choirs made up of soldiers and miners. The present-day stage was dedicated at the fifteenth festival in Tallinn. The song festival in 1990 (with 28,000 active participants) drew an audience of around 500,000 to the stadium. The first festival since the independence of Estonia from the Soviet Union will take place in 1995...

As was the case in the 14 national dance festivals from 1934 to 1990 in which 9,000 dancers participated, the political significance of the song festival took precedence over the musical content in support of unity and independence.

Thirty-one years after the beginning of the folk music tradition, *classical music* was to also find its audience in Estonia. The year 1900 marked the founding of the first Estonian symphony orchestra followed by the opening of the first opera in 1906. In the year following the independence of 1918, music academies were founded in Tallinn and Tartu. As early as 1940, during the first year of Soviet rule, they were degraded to second class educational facilities and later combined into one music academy in Tallinn. For this reason, Estonian composers studied mainly in St. Petersburg, some also in Dresden, Germany. Counting among the founders of Estonian music was Rudolf Tobias (1873-1918). A student of Rimsky-Korssakov, he composed his main work in Leipzig, Germany. The oratorio "The Mission of Jonah" combines the early folk tradition of the Kalevala epic with modern tonal composition. Contemporary music was also performed by the Estonian National Symphony Orchestra (ESSO) under the direction of Peeter Lilje.

In 1926 when the Radio Chamber Ensemble was founded, the musicians joined the theatre orchestra of the "Estonia" in Tallinn during large performances – on March 26, 1927 for the first time commemorating the 100-year anniversary of the death of Beethoven. In 1928, Estonian music students founded "Fidentia." This association had around 140 members up until 1941, then over half of them were forced to flee from the Soviets into exile.

The most famous Estonian modernist was Maart Saar (1882-1963), who in addition to atonal works like the solo "Black Bird" (1908), and the piano piece "Sketch," also composed traditional choir music. Religiously motivated works were composed by Peeter Süda (1883-1920; Artur Kapp (1878-1970) composed sonatas, Heino Eller (1887-1970) composed "Four Pieces for String Quartet" among other works. Almost all of the Estonian composers today are students or descendants of Heino Eller, who taught at the music academy in Tallinn up to 1970. Eduard Tubin (1905-1982) gained international renown through his opera "Barbara von Tiesenhusen" (→ Travel Section/Kavilda) which was premiered in 1968. Also worth hearing are also the suites on Estonian dance music for solo violin and orchestra.

Among the contemporary composers, the most famous is Edgar Arro born in 1911 in Tallinn. After visiting organ courses at the conservatory in Tallinn, Arro worked from 1936 to 1940 as an organist for radio broadcasts. From 1948 to 1953, he led the seminar for young composers in the Estonian Composers Association and wrote cantatas, piano pieces and "Kümmel Pala," ten pieces for the organ based on Estonian folk melodies.

Around 50 composers are presently active in Estonia. Arvo Pärt, born in 1935 in Paide visited the conservatory in Tallinn up until 1963. In 1980, Pärt fled into exile, first to Vienna, then to Berlin where he has lived since 1982. In 1964, his orchestral symphony "Perpertuum Mobile" premiered at the festival in Venice. In 1980, "Annum per Annum" was completed, a work composed for the radio station in Baden-Baden, Germany in commemoration of the 900th anniversary of the Cathedral in Speyer. Mati Kuulberg (1947) composed ballets and chamber concerts; in 1976, he completed his sonatas for two pianos. Veljo Tormis (1930) created modern pieces from traditional folk songs. In the ballet cantata "Estonian Ballads" (1980) Tormis used old folkloric elements from extinct tribes like the Ishoric and Votic. Erkki-Sven Tüür, born in 1959 on the island of Hiiumaa studied the flute from 1976-1980 at the conservatory in Tallinn. After his first successful attempts, he continued studying the composition of music from 1980 to 1984. A member of the chamber-rock band "In Spe" from 1979 to 1983, Tüür loves the combination of rock and Renaissance. Tüür couples electronic and acoustic instruments – apparently with success: the 33-year-old has been honoured three times with the annual Estonian music prize. In 1989, his second symphony was among the top ten at the UNESCO music tournament in Paris. Quite unconventional for the established music industry, Tüür's works have short, unusual titles: "24 Marginalias for Two Pianos" is the title of one work; "Mythos for String Quartet and Audio Tape" is his "live electronic" piece.

Raimo Kangro, born in 1949, composed the "Maiden from the North," the first rock opera which debuted in 1980. In 1989, he completed his piano concert "Klimper."

The Estonian *Choirs* are renowned in Estonia as well as abroad. The Estonian Philharmonic Chamber Choir – a professional choir since 1981 – holds around 50 concerts annually. In 1991, the mixed choir won three gold medals at the Takarazuka Chamber Choir Competition in Japan. The Tallinn Boy's Choir with 300 members at present was founded in 1971 by its present conductor Professor Venno Laul. The boys begin musical training at the age of six and the top candidates can then become members of the concert choir at the age of ten. Rehearsals take place two times a week; in addition to this each boy must also learn an instrument.

The National Men's Choir of Estonia (RAM) founded in November of 1944 by the composer and director Gustav Ernesaks, rehearses three hours daily. The sixty vocal musicians sing all works in the original (meaning 23 languages) and hold around 100 concerts annually. The "Linnamusikud" Ensemble is now in its third year. This youth group from Tallinn under the direction of Taivo Niitvägi musically presents the historical liturgy of the church year. In addition to the Estonia folk instruments like the zither, shepherd's flute and an instrument similar to the bagpipes, European and Oriental musical instruments are also used.

Walter Ojakäär and Uno Naissoo were considered the most prominent advocated of the forbidden jazz during the Soviet rule. Tiit Paulus, whose career began in 1964 at the Tallinn Jazz Festival, is considered the best jazz guitarist in Estonia.

Also very successful as a jazz-blues and pop vocalist is the 37-year-old Sergej Manukyan. Hard rock with a tendency to heavy metal is the repertoire of the rock band "Gold Digger." Among the groups who have gained fame all across the country are "Friday's Deal," "Compromise Blue," "Ultima Thule," "Merry Christmas Mr. Lawrence" and "Kevin Coyne and the Paradise Band."

Latvia

"Riga dimd" (Riga sounds) is the title of an old folk song, the melody of which can be heard at noontime from the tower of St. Peter's Church. To be certain, anyone who strolls through the alleyways of this Hanseatic city will be confronted by music every step of the way: jazz here, classical there, heavy metal and folk songs come from the windows and street musicians hold spontaneous concerts. It was especially *folk music* which experienced an unexpected renaissance in recent years. "Skandinieki" is considered the most successful folk ensemble. They perform songs on historical instruments: the zither-like "Kokle," the wooden bells "Koku zvani," the "Kalbatas," a type of xylophone and the "Stabules" a type of recorder. The group performs solely "Dainas." These Latvian folk songs – comprising mostly four lines and combined to form longer songs – reflect the daily life of the Latvians. The process of collecting folk song culture was initiated by Johann Gottlieb Herder, who published a selection of Dainas in 1807 in Tübingen, Germany. After his death an additional 78 Dainas were found. In 1869, Janis Cimze began collecting Dainas,

some of which were over a thousand years old. It was Krisjanis Barons (1835-1923), however who is acclaimed as the "father of the folk song" by the Latvians. In 1894, Barons began to publish his collection of folk songs in stages: six volumes in twenty-one years. The national poet Janis Rainis wrote enthusiastically after the publication of the final volume: "Our tongues can be silenced, but the songs you collected will ring in our ears and echo in our hearts" – which can be read in the Rainis Museum in Riga.

While Barons collected song texts, Emilis Melngailis began his search for melodies. This composer listened to the songs of the rural population, recorded the melodies on paper for posterity and consequently created over 5,000 folk songs.

With that, Barons and Melngailis laid the foundation for the establishment of the Latvian *Song Festival,* a festival whose tradition began on June 26, 1873 with 1,003 singers and 16 orchestras in what was formerly the Keizardarzs (Czar's Gardens). Since 1955, the Song Festival takes place every five years in Riga's Mezapark on a monumental stage which can accommodate 10,000 musicians and an audience of 30,000. Among the most widely known choirs taking part in this event is "Ave Sol." Under the direction of Imants Kokars, the director of the Jazeps-Vitols Conservatory, this choir was celebrated enthusiastically during a concert tour through the United States in 1987 – and not only by the Latvians living there in exile.

One of the greatest Latvian composers of more artistic music is Jazep Vitols (1863-1948), often better known as Joseph Withol. After completing his education at the St. Petersburg Conservatory, Vitols founded the Music Conservatory in Riga in 1919. Later, he fled from the Soviets and died shortly thereafter in Lübeck, Germany. Alfred Kalnins (1879-1951), also active as a vocalist and organist, wrote the first "Latvian" opera. "Banuta" premiered in 1920 and is based on an old Latvian legend. As early as 1919, the music critic Pavuls Jurjans (1866-1948) had established the national opera. Famous musicians of that time also included the three Medins brothers. The eldest, Jazeps Medins (1890-1966), was active in forming the first opera ensemble, for which he composed the lyric opera "Vaidelote." In contrast, Jekab, a music teacher, was occupied with composing piano pieces. Janis, the youngest, not only composed film music but also the opera "Fire and Night" based on a libretto by the national poet Janis Rainis. With the arrival of Elvis Presley, the Beatles and the Rolling Stones, *rock and pop music* took over the Latvian music scene, much to the chagrin of the Soviet regime. Young bands attempted to measure up to international stars and performed the "imperialistic ghetto music" in cellars and courtyards. In order to be tolerated, the rock music had to have a sufficient amount of pro-Soviet content, which was verified on a regular basis at concerts. Underground rock developed in parallel to the official pop music. The Latvian bands became, much like the folk music choirs, symbols of Latvian identity – and for this reason they remain just as popular as foreign musicians today. The *Summer Rock Festivals* in Jurmala, Rezekne and Daugavpils also contribute to the popularity of Latvian bands. One of the most popular bands in the country is "Elpa." The band of five from Daugavpils was founded ten years ago by Valdis Rundzans and combines folk elements with hard rock. Janis Logins, vocals and keyboard in the band "Elpa," has meanwhile started a successful solo career. Most rock groups can be found in the greater Riga area. Among the widely known "official" bands even during Soviet rule are "Remix," "Livi," "Zodiaks" and "Turaidas Roze." Those who refer to themselves as "independent" bands include "Linga," "Arhivs," "Dzeltenie Pastnieki" and "Melna Kafija."

Lithuania

What the Dainas are to the Latvians are the Dainos to the Lithuanians: old songs, reflecting the spirit of the people. The *song Festival tradition* began later than in the neighbouring Baltic States. It was only in 1924 that Lithuania celebrated its first Song Festival in Kaunas; additional song gatherings followed in 1928 and 1930. Regional folk song festivals took place in other cities like Klaipeda in 1927, 1933 and 1938 for example.

Popular instruments used in folk music were the Kankles (zither), Birbyne (fife), Skuduciai (panpipe), Daudytne and Lamzdelis (pipes of varying sizes) and Ragas (horn). The collection of Lithuanian folk melodies was especially practised by Liudvikas Reza (1776-1840), Friedrich Kurschat (1806-1884), Antanas Juska (1819-1880) and Christian Bartsch (1832-1890). They compiled their notes starting in 1935 in the *Lithuanian Folklore Archives* which scientifically researches the old folk song tradition and provides the numerous folklore ensembles with songs and dances. Upholding this folk tradition, the leading groups of this type today were all founded at the end of 1970: the ethnographic ensembles of Ziurai and Luoke, the dance ensembles of the University and Teaching College of Vilnius and the Folk Music Group of the National Outdoor Museum of Rumsiskes.

The first golden age for more classical music began in Lithuania during the Russian Revolution. In 1905, "Adam and Eve," the first Lithuanian operetta, was performed in St. Petersburg; in the following year (1906), the first national opera "Birute" by the same composer Mikas Petrauskas debuted on the stage. The centre for the bourgeois music scene was the provisional capital of Kaunas from 1919 to 1940. While Juozas Grudis, Antanas Raciunas or Juozas Zilevicius composed, music journals discussed the new self-perception: in 1924 and 1925, "Musikos menas" (The Art of Music) appeared on the market followed in 1926 by "Muzikos

aidai (Echo of Music). During the Second World War when Germany occupied Lithuania, Moscow documented its claim to power with a ten-day festival of Lithuanian Literature; Stasys Simkus composed his opera "Kaimas pri davro" especially for this spectacle. His contemporaries like Feliksas Bajoras, Osvaldas Balakauskas, Vytautas Jurgutis and Bronius Kutavicius avoided such lucid political statements.

During Soviet rule, music was firmly bound within political structures. Still, some ensembles were able to gain international reputations, and thus, maintain contact to the international music scene. Counting among the musical "bridges" of that time were foremost the Lithuanian String Quartet founded in 1946 and acclaimed in Budapest in 1959 and Liège in 1964; the Vilnius Quartet and the Ciurlionis String Quartet, a group which debuted in 1976 at the West Berlin Festival. Founded in 1974, the Humana Ensemble has dedicated itself to the preservation of the old musical tradition. The Trimitas Brass Band, in contrast, has been playing top-notch jazz since 1959.

Photography

Photography has much more significance in cultural life in the Baltic States than in many other countries. Art and information simultaneously – the number of visitors to a photography exhibition even in remote towns is surprisingly large and the names of the photographers are almost as widely known as the international pop stars.

Estonia

Counting among the elite Estonian photographers are Peeter Langovits, Harald Leppikson, Malex Toom, Henn Soodla, Kalju Suur, Tiit Vermäe, Vambola Salupuu and Artur Rätsep all of whom are members of the "Estonian Photographic Art Association." In May 1992, these photographers all presented their work during the "European Culture Exhibition" in Karlsruhe, Germany. Peeter Linnap's photographs of abandoned Red Army military bases drew particular attention.

Latvia

Controversial and critical is the motto of members of the photographic group "A" in Riga. As a freelance photographer, Valts Klein, born in 1960, compiled a photograph series on the ostracized in the Soviet society – the ill, alcoholics and the dying – in the idyllic town of Ogre. Valts loves series: his gravestone portraits of Soviet officers during the January barricades in 1991 attracted numerous visitors to the exhibition hall.

Aivars Liepins, born in 1953, also dedicated his work to fringe groups of the society like prisoners or orphans.

Broad public resonance was also the result of the political photographic features shot during the turbulent events in 1991. Wilhelms Michailowski photographed the military activities of the Black Berets (the attack troops of the Soviet Ministry of the Interior) disguised as a "KGB officer"; Uldis Briedis documented these events as a photo journalist.

Lithuania

As late as 1986, an exhibition of Lithuanian photographers – Stanionis, Macijauskas, Pozerskis, Sonta – was closed. Aleksandras Macijauskas, born in 1938, captured Lithuanian country life in his photographs with a touch of surrealism. Romualdas Pozerskis, born in 1951, works as a freelance photographer in Kaunas. Juozas Kazlauskas, born into a farming family in 1941 in Zvirbliskiai, has been a photographer since 1965. After studying the motion picture arts in Moscow (1972), the main theme of "Man and his Environment" has determined the content of his photographic series since 1975. With the political changes acting as a catalyst, Kazlauskas' uses photography to work through the past. His photographic series on the victims of Stalinism makes a poignant statement: looking back frees the path forward. Algimantas Kuncius displayed his black and white works at the "Zango" and Kampl" photo-galleries in Munich. Born in 1939 in Pakruojis, Kuncius first worked for the weekly journal "Literature and Art" before he took on the position of photographic editor for the monthly journal "Milestones in Art." Together with Macijauskas, Rakauskas and Sutkus, Kuncius founded the "Lithuanian Association for the Photographic Arts" in 1968, which quickly became a motivating factor for Lithuanian photography.

Kuncius' speciality is presenting the everyday in a special light. It is especially his black and white photography which exudes a special attraction, like in the series "Sunday in the Country" (1975-1985) or "Reminiscences" (1975-1986).

Antanas Sutkus was born in 1939 in Kluoniskiai and honoured during the Soviet regime as the "deserved cultural artist of the Lithuanian Soviet Republic." The only child in a working class family, Sutkus is now president of the "Lithuanian Society for Photography." Growing out of his first autodidactic origins in 1954 was his series "People in Lithuania," in 1962 and his sole exhibition in Munich in 1984.

Cuisine

One statement straight away: no one starves in the Baltic States. Even though the selection is more limited than one would encounter at home, the foods are tasty and prepared with care – and still incredibly inexpensive. Those who chose not to prepare their own meals, will find a broad spectrum of culinary selections.

Kohvik/Kafejnica/Kavine: These "cafés" offer not only cake and pastries but smaller meals, sandwiches and salads as well.

Söökla/Ednica/Valgykla: the inexpensive cafeterias with self-service are usually associated with the central department store. The selection of warm and cold dishes offered is similar to that of an institutional cafeteria.

Restorans/Restoranas: Whether expensive or dirt cheap – a doorman stands at the door of many restaurants. For this reason, an advance reservation, especially in the larger cities, is recommended. Admission is charged at the door for the music which is often performed live by a band at dinner. It is also common that an additional charge for the service is added to the bill – this, from five to ten percent of the total sum. In the more exclusive restaurants, a luxury tax is added. During the autumn and winter, the restaurants are usually not heated and can be quite chilly.

The largest problems are caused by the menus. These are written in the country's language and Russian. One will however gradually become acquainted with recurring dishes: "Snitzel" or "Bifteek" are easy to guess even without the help of a language dictionary. What is quite unusual are the references to the amount of food served: prices are orientated on the weight of the meal – even slices of cake are weighed in advance to determine the price.

The seasons dictate the dishes served. In winter, hearty meat and potato dishes dominate the menu, often fatty and heavy; the contrast of spring is announced with the addition of cucumber salad for breakfast. Tasty rolls, jam or marmalade early in the morning are a rarity in the Baltic States. Breakfast is a more heavy and less continental occasion: cheese, eggs, cottage cheese, smoked fish, grey or white bread. Often a warm dish is served. Sausages,

Theatre: Tallinn, Tartu and Touring Troupes

The premier of the play "The Cousin from Saaremaa" by Lydia Koidula in the Community House of Vanemuine laid the foundation for the development of the *Estonian National Theatre* in 1870. During the national awakening, theatre as well as music and art served to "protect national rights." At the beginning of the 20th century, the first professional theatres were founded: In 1906, the "Vanemuine" in Tartu and the "Estonia" in Tallinn; in 1911, the "Endla" in Pärnu. Not only classics ranging from Shakespeare to Schiller were performed, but also works by Anton Hansen Tammassare, Estonia's national dramatist which enthused the audiences.

At the end of the 1920's, the *Musical Theatre* developed into an independent branch of vocal drama. At first small operas by European composers were on the calender of performances. The premier of "The Vikings" by Evalöd Aav in the "Estonia" made this national opera an integral part of musical drama in Estonia. In 1922, *ballet* developed into a separate division in the "Estonia." In 1935, the "Vanemuine" in Tartu established its own ballet troupe. During the first republic, experimental theatre provided contrast to the predominantly classical programmes in the larger theatres. The "Morning Theatre" with its expressionistic repertoire from 1921 to 1924 caused a number of dramatic uproars. Today, the theatres – large and small alike – are in a battle for survival.

The small stages in Rakvere, Viljandi or Pärnu go on tour through the country with their productions, while the theatres in Tartu and Tallinn vie for sponsors to fill the deficits in the coffers.

The state subsidies are hardly sufficient for heating.

---

scrambled eggs and porridge can ward off hunger for the entire day.

Popular dishes for lunch in Estonia is "green soup," a vegetable broth with bacon and onions and served with a dollop of sour cream. Another popular dish is "blinys" or blintzes, small pancakes garnished with sour cream. Due to the high prices, meat dishes are relatively rare. One speciality of the country is, however, moose. Due to the increasing radioactive contamination of wild game resulting from the Chernobyl accident, one should forgo ordering this.

The most popular *beverage* is black tea, with strong, sweet black coffee running a close second. The fruit juices are especially tasty and can be purchased in half litre or five litre bottles in the stores: sour, red northern cranberry juice (Punasesotra Mahl), the somewhat sweeter pomegranate juice and the interesting mixed fruit juices. Beer has an unusually high alcohol content. The deep yellow

Saaremaa Ölu in the brown half-litre bottles packs a punch with 16% alcohol. For those who are not beer drinkers, there are also Russian sparkling wines from the Crimea region.

In *Latvia,* grey Riga bread is served with every meal. This is a dark bread with a slight caraway flavour. In addition to this are the fresh-smoked Riga sprats – herring which is even served for breakfast. The warm lunches are less hearty: milk soup with potato dumplings or mushroom soup with barley can be considered typically Latvian. This is also true for the green peas with bacon or the Vidzeme cabbage. Creamy desserts will satisfy the sweet tooth or one can also try the black bread cake or sour cream dessert "gotina" (little cow). Men conclude the meal with Allazu kimelis (Allasch caraway) or Rigas Balzams (Riga balsam), the popular bitter herbal liqueur in the ceramic jug. Women usually sip on "Melna Aronija" a blackberry wine served with coffee.

Lithuania's national dish has the melodious name "cepelinai." These oblong dumplings made from raw potatoes and filled with minced meat are served in a light bacon gravy.

A Brief Language Guide

Estonian

Estonian is a member of the finno-ugrish language family. Because of its mellow sound, it is often considered the "Italian of the Baltic Region." Now subdivided into three dialects and numerous accents, north and south Estonian were earlier separate written languages. The Estonian grammar differs fundamentally from the indo-European languages. For example, Estonian has 14 declinations. A word can also have up to three different meanings: by differentiating between three pronunciation levels with consonants and almost all vowels – short, middle and long emphasis – the meaning of the word is varied.

Pronunciation: double vowels are always pronounced long; double consonants, harder. The emphasis in a word is always placed on the first syllable.

Estonian for Beginners

Hello	Tere
Good morning	Tere hommikust
Good day	Tere päevast
Good evening	Tere ohtust
Good night	Head ööd
Good-bye	Head aega
Please	palun
Thank you	tänan
Yes	Jah
No	Eih
Excuse me	vabadungst

Eating and Drinking

menu	menüü
bill	arve
beer	õlu
(white) bread	Sai
butter	voi
ice cream	jäätis
fish	kala
meat	liha
vegetables	aedvili/köögiviljad
beverage	joogid
potatoes	kartul
cheese	puust
coffee	kohv
cake	kook
milk	piim
mineral water	Mineralveesi
dessert	magusroad
fruit	puuviljad
juice	mahl/jook
cream	vahukoor
salad	salat
salt	sool
soup	supp
tea	tee
wine	vein
sugar	suhkur
breakfast	eine
lunch	louna
dinner	ohtusööl
café	kohvik
cafeteria	söökla
restaurant	restoran

Shopping

I would like	ma tahaksin
Could you please show me...	palun näidake mulle...
How much does it cost?	kui palju maksab?
expensive	kallis
cheap	odav
open	avatud/lahti
closed	suledtud/kinni
store	kauplus
shop	pood
kiosk	kiosk
antique book shop	Antikvaariat
art supplies	kunstitooted
bakery	pagariäri/leiva-pood
bank	pank
barber shop/salon	juuksur
book shop	raamatukauplus/raamatud
butcher	lihääri
department store	kaubamaja
envelope	ümbrik
flower shop	lille kauplus/lilled
fruit and vegetable store	aia ja puuviljüääri
grocery store	toiduainete kauplus/toidupood
market	turg
newsstand	ajalehekiosk
pastry shop	kondiitrikkauplus
post office	postkontor/post-maja
postage stamp	marka
records	helipaadid
shoe store	jalatsikauplus/jalatsid
souvenir shop	suveniirid
wholesale store	komisjonikauplus

Colours

black	must
blue	sinine
brown	pruun
green	roheline
pink	roosa
white	valge
yellow	kollane

Travelling Around

Where?	kus?
To where?	kuhu?
From where?	kust?
How far?	Kui kaugel?
here	siin
there	sekak
right	paremal
left	vasakul
large	suur
small	väike
city	linnas
suburb	eeslinn
street	tänav (tn.)
rural road	tee (t.)
main street	puiestee (pst.)
motorway	maantee (mnt.)
square	väljak
bridge	sild
hotel	hotelli
church	Kirik
museum	Muuseum
post office	postkantor
theatre	teater
exit	ährasoit
arrival	saabamuine
trolleybus	trolley
streetcar	trammi
autobus	autobuss
bus station	autobussijaam
railway station	raudteejaam
train	rong
ship	laev
harbour	sadam
airport	lennujaam
aeroplane	lennuk

ticket	pilet	**Numbers**	
travel agency	reisibüroo	1	üks
		2	kaks
Feeling under the Weather		3	kolm
ill?	haige?	4	neli
pharmacy	apteek	5	viis
physician/doctor	arst	6	kuus
dentist	hambarst	7	seitse
emergency ward	esmaabi	8	kaheksa
hospital	haigla	9	üheksa
ambulance	kiirabi	10	kümme
		11	üksteist
The Calendar		12	kaksteist
When?	millal?	13	kolmteist
day	päev	14	neliteist
week	nädal	15	viisteist
month	kuu	16	kuusteist
year	aasta	17	seitseteist
yesterday	eile	18	kaheksateist
today	täna	19	üheksateist
tomorrow	homme	20	kakskümmend
later	hiljem	25	viiskakskümmend
earlier	varem	30	kolmkümmend
evening	ohtu	40	nelikümmend
night	öö	50	viiskümmend
Monday	esmaspäev	60	kuuskümmend
Tuesday	teisipäev	70	seitsekümmend
Wednesday	kolmapäev	80	kaheksaküm-
Thursday	neljapäev		mend
Friday	reede	90	üheksakümmend
Saturday	laupäev	100	sada
Sunday	pühapäev	1000	tuhat

Latvian

Latvian is grouped within the Baltic language family which was once spoken by the tribes of Prussia, Lithuania, Latgallia, Semigallia, Curonia and Selonia. While the Selonian language developed into the Lithuanian language, Latvian arose from the fu-sion of Latgallian, Semigallian and Curonian. Old Prussian was complete-ly lost through the eastern settlement of the Germans; Latgallian is still pre-sent today in the form of a dialect. The Latvian language reflects the hi-story of foreign occupation: in addition to Swedish and Russian traces in the vocabulary, German influences have remained not only in borrowed words but also in the grammar itself. Latvian, which does have 12 vowels but only two genders (masculine and feminine), always has the emphasis on the first syllable of a word.

Latvian Basics

Hello	Sveiki
Good morning	Labrit
Good day	Labdien
Good evening	Labvakar
Good night	Ar labu nakti
Good-bye	Ata
Please	Ludzu
Thank you	Paldies
yes	Ja
no	Ne
Excuse me	Atvainojiet, ludzu
I'm sorry	Atvainojos
My name is	Mani sauc
Do you speak English	Vai jus runjiet angliski?
I don't speak Latvian	Es nerunaju latvieski
Please speak slowly	Ludzu runajet lenak
I don't understand	Nesaprot

At the Restaurant

I would like to order...	Veletos
Some more, please	ludzu ver
That is enough, thank you	pietiek, paldies
I would like to pay, please	ludzu rekinu
bill	rekins
breakfast	brokastis
lunch	pusdienas
dinner	vakarinjas
menu	edienkarte
beer	alus

bread	maize
butter	sviets
cake	kuka
cream	krejums
fish	zivis
fruit	augli
ice cream	saldejums
juice	sula
milk	piens
mineral water	mineraludens
salt	sals
soup	zupa
sugar	cukurs
tea	teja
vegetables	saknes
wine (red/white)	vins (sarkans/ balts)

At the Hotel

hotel	viesnica
restaurant	restorans
café	Kafejnica
cafeteria	Ednica
room	istaba
bed	gulta
bath	vanna
floor attendant	dezurante
suitcase	koferis/cemodans
room key	atslega
small	maza
large	liel

Shopping

store	veikals
bakery	maizes veikals
book store	gramatu veikals
barber/salon	frizetava

Rising proudly into the sky are the towers of St. Catherine's Church in Pärnu named after the Russian czaress

Estonia draws visitors through its cultivated landscapes, the coastal regions near Muhu or merely the chance to experience nature and meet
local residents like on the Emajögi River

department store	universalveikals
grocery store	partikas preces/ veikals
optician	brillu veikals
post office	pasts
business hours	darba laiks
cleaning day	sanitaria diena
open	atverts
closed	slegts

Travelling Around

trolleybus	trolejbuss
autobus	autobuss
streetcar	tramvajs
railway	dzelzcels
train station	stacija (central)
train	vilciens
bus stop	peturas vieta
board	iekapt
debark	izkapt
transfer	parseties
When/where must I transfer?	kad/kur man ja- parsezas?
ticket	bilete
return trip	turp un atpakal
When does the train depart?	Kad atiet vilciens?
When does the train arrive?	Kad pienak vil- ciems?
hydrofoil	Rakete
harbour	osta
airport	lidosta
aeroplane	lidmasina
commercial flight	reiss
taxi	taksometra
to the left/right	pa labi/pa kreisi
straight ahead	taisni
forwards	uz prieksu
near	tuvu
far	talu
city	pilseta
suburb	priekpilseta
village	ciems

in the country	uz laukiem
beach	jurmala
sea	jura
mountain	kalns
lake	ezers
river	upe
bridge	tilts
street	iela
square	laukums
boulevard	bulvaris
path	cels
fortress/castle	pils
church	baznica
cemetery	kapi *or* kapseta
park	parks
exhibition	izstade
museum	muzejs

Feeling under the Weather

emergency ward	ambulance
hospital	slimnica
ambulance	atro palidzibu
pharmacy	aptieka
medication	zales
physician/doctor	arsts
dentist	zobu arsts
Could you give me something ...	dodiet ludzu kaut ko ...
... for a headache	pret galvas sapem
... for diarrhoea	pret caureju
... for constipation	pret vedera aiz- cietejumu
I have a fever	man ir karstums
I have a headache	man sap galva

Weights and Measures

centimetre	centimetrs
metre	metrs
kilometre	kilometrs
gram	grams
pound	marcina
kilogramme	kilograms
litre	litrs

The Calendar

Monday	pirmdiena
Tuesday	otrdiena
Wednesday	tresdiena
Thursday	ceturtdiena
Friday	piektdiena
Saturday	svestdiena
Sunday	svetdiena
day	diena
week	nedela
month	menesis
year	gads
yesterday	Yakar
today	Sodien
tomorrow	Ritdien

The Time

minute	minute
half an hour	pisstunda
in the morning	no rita
before noon	priekspusdiena
afternoon	pec pusdienam
evening	vakara

Numbers

1	viens
2	divi
3	tris
4	cetri
5	pieci
6	sesi
7	septini
8	astoni
9	devini
10	desmit
11	vienpadsmit
12	divpadsmit
13	tirspadsmit
14	cetrpadsmit
15	ciepadsmit
16	sespadsmit
17	septinpadsmit
18	astonpadsmit
19	devinpadsmit
20	divdesmit
25	divdesmitpieci
30	trisdesmit
40	cetrdesmit
50	piecdesmit
60	sesdesmit
70	septindesmit
80	astondesmit
90	devindesmit
100	simts
1000	tukstots

Lithuanian

The Lithuanian language also belongs to the Baltic group of languages within the Indo-European linguistic family of languages. Considering all of the lines, hooks and dots on the letters, the pronunciation of Lithuanian is most easily accomplished by listening closely to the language being spoken – listing all of the rules for emphasis would go far beyond the limits of this small guide. As a brief summary: a point means the vowel is pronounced short and hard; a bar over the vowel indicates that it is pronounced long and soft. An "inverted roof" over a consonant indicates a sh, ch or zh sound.

Lithuanian from Square One

Hello	Sveikas
Good morning	Laba rytas
Good day	Laba diena
Good evening	Laba vakaras
Good night	Labanaki
Good-bye	Viso gero
Please	prasom
Thank you	aciu
yes	Taip
no	Ne
Excuse me	atsiprasau
I'm sorry	apgailestauju

At the Restaurant

bill	saskaita
menu	valgiaraistis
beer	alus
beverages	gerimai
bread	duona
butter	sviestas
cheese	suris
coffee	kava
dessert	desertas
fish	zuvis
fruit	vaisiai
ice cream	ledai
juice	sultys
mineral water	mineralvanduo
rice	rugiai
salt	druska
soup	sriuba
sugar	cukrus
tea	arbata
vegetables	darzoves
wine	vynas

Shopping

store	parduotuve
bakery	duonos parduotuve
book store	knygynas
barber/salon	kirpykla
department store	universaline parduotuve
grocery store	maizes preces
market	turgus
optician	optika
post office	pastas
cheap	pigus
expensive	brangus
How much does this cost?	kiek kainuoja?
I would like ...	as noreciau ...

Travelling Around

city	mieste
suburb	priemiestis
street	gatve (g.)
rural road	kelias
main street	prospektas (pr.)
motorway	plentas (pl.) autostrada
square	aikste
bridge	tiltis
river	upe
lake	ezeras
field	lauka
museum	muzeijs
post office	pasta
autobus	autobuso
trolleybus	troleybus
train station	gelezinkelio stoti
airport	aerouosta
streetcar	tramvajaus
service station	degaline
taxi	taksi
near	arti
far	toli
forwards	pirmyn
straight ahead	tiesiai
to the left/right	i desine/i kaire

Feeling under the Weather

pharmacy	vaistine
emergency ward	greitoji pagalba
hospital	ligonine
physician/doctor	gydytojas
dentist	dantu gydytojas
head	galva
hand	ranka
leg	koja
eye	akis
ear	ausis
nose	nosis
mouth	burna
tooth	dantis
heart	sirdis

The Calendar

day	diena
night	naktis
morning	rytas
winter	ziema
spring	pavasaris
summer	vasaris
autumn	ruduo
Monday	primadienis
Tuesday	antradienis
Wednesday	treciadienis
Thursday	ketvirtadienis
Friday	penktadienis
Saturday	sestadienis
Sunday	sekmadienis

Colours

black	juodas
blue	melynas
brown	rudas
green	zalias
red	raudonas
white	baltas
yellow	geltonas

Numbers

1	vienas
2	du
3	trys
4	keturi
5	penki
6	sesi
7	septyni
8	astuoni
9	devyni
10	desimt
11	vienuolika
12	dvylika
13	trylika
14	keturiolika
15	penkiolika
16	sesiolika
17	septyniolika
18	astuoniolika
19	devyniolika
20	dvdesimt
25	dvidesimt penki
30	triesdesimt
40	keturiasdesimt
50	penkiasdesimt
60	sesiasdesimt
70	septynaisdesimt
80	astuoniasdesimt
90	devynioasdesimt
100	simtas
1000	tukstantis

Travel Section

The travel sections for each of the Baltic States are structured similarly. In the extensive portion covering the *capital city,* tips for *excursions* in the surrounding regions are followed by the *Estonian Islands* and 15 *districts.* In the sections on Latvia and Lithuania, the capital cities are followed by *ethnographic provinces* including their respective sights. If *national parks* extend over the district or provincial boundaries, then they are covered individually. The Russian enclave of Kaliningrad was intentionally omitted since there are meanwhile comprehensive and current travel guides covering the former Königsberg region.

The "Top Ten" on Travel Itineraries

I. Cities & Castles

Tallinn: Estonia's capital city attracts visitors with its medieval and maritime flair.

Tartu: For centuries, Estonia's university city has been characterized by "Tartu vaim," an open-minded and vivacious lifestyle.

Haapsalu: The former spa, renowned for its mud-baths, is impressive for its Bishop's Castle and the surrounding old buildings.

Riga: The Middle Ages in the old city contrast with the Art Nouveau architecture of the newer districts and the folklore on the banks of Lake Jugla – the capital of Latvia successfully combines the Hanseatic with the present.

Kuldiga: Picturesque small town in Curonia on the famous Rumbla Waterfall.

Rundale: This location could hardly be more bombastic: the castle of Birons shines anew after complete restoration.

Vilnius: Baroque and concrete offer a fascinating contrast in the capital of Lithuania. A southern lifestyle determines the rhythm of this metropolis.

Kaunas: Churches and commerce characterize the lifestyle in the second largest city of Lithuania. Even Satan is honoured here: a visit to the Devil Museum is definitely worthwhile.

Trakai: The most beautiful water castle in the Baltic States stands at Lake Galvas. The Karaïtes, Jewish religious refugees from Crimea, once settled on this peninsula.

Klaipeda: The old city of Memel is being meticulously restored to its former grandeur. The entire old city has been classified as a historic monument since 1969.

II. Sand and Sunshine

Estonia

Narva-Joesuu: Where the Russian Czars went swimming up until the war are now warning signs for the polluted water. The beach and chain of sand dunes, however, have remained as beautiful as ever.

Pärnu: Even the long tradition of this beach resort with its long sandy beach could not spare it from the effects of water pollution and the proximity of the harbour. The combination of spa facilities, cultural life, and breathtaking mansions along the coast make it easier to forgo swimming in the sea.

Latvia

Ainazi: Long, secluded beaches on the Estonian border are inviting for a day in the sun.

Jurmala: Twelve beach resorts carry the simple name "beach," but unfortunately also suffer from the ban on swimming.

Kemeri: The old spa town in the middle of a wooded park is situated near the light sandy beach on the Bay of Riga.

Kolka/Mazirbe: Secluded and untouched beaches in the Sliteres nature reserve are surrounded by "pristine" forests and small lakes.

Liepaja: The clean beach before the gates of the city offers miles of swimming and recreation.

Lithuania

Palanga: A beach measuring 25 kilometres (16 miles) – who could ask for anything more?

Curonian Spit: The wonderful world of dunes to the lagoon and the long beaches on the sea side of the island – this barrier island is a sheer paradise.

Nature –
as far as the eye can see

Lahemaa National Park/Estonia: Wild romanticism in the forest and meadow landscape in the northern regions with pretentious manor houses and idyllic farm cottages.

Matsalu Bird Sanctuary/Estonia: Flocks of birds in the marshlands.

Gauja National Park/Latvia: The river determines the landscape: sometimes languid, then churning as the river flows by the sandstone cliffs and through dense forests; secluded farmyards, steadfast fortresses and quaint towns.

Sliteres Nature Reserve/Latvia: Cleared by the Soviets, now untouched coastal hinterland surrounding Kolka point.

Salaca Biosphere Reserve/Latvia: The largest colony of white storks with 120 birds nesting in this area – an area under protection since 1991.

Curonian Lagoon National Park/Lithuania: Pine trees, sand and oaks combined with the old fishing boats make the moderately modern resort with an invigorating climate attractive to visit.

Aukstaitija National Park/Lithuania: Extensive lake basins northeast of Vilnius near the Ignalina atomic power plant.

Dzukija National Park/Lithuania: forests as far as the eye can see – solitude in the eastern regions, located near the White Russian border.

Estonia

Estonia at a Glance

Country Name: "Eesti vabarik" (Republic of Estonia)

Capital City: Tallinn (population: 500,000)

Larger Cities: Tartu (population: 114,000), Narva (population: 82,300)

Area: 45,215 square kilometres (17,634 square miles)

Length of Coastline: 3,749 kilometres (2,343 miles)

Population: 1,573,000

Population Density: 35 per square kilometre (13.5 per square mile)

Ethnic Groups: Estonians (61.5%), Russians (30.3%), Ukrainians (3.1%), White Russians (1.8%), Finns (1.1%).

Language: Estonian (Finnish-ugrish origin) and Russian.

Economic Structure: Industry and construction (42%), commerce and transport (24%), agriculture and forestry (13%).

Declaration of Independence: Recognition by the Soviet Union on September 6, 1991.

Tallinn (Reval)

One third of all Estonians live in the capital city of Tallinn: with a population of around 500,000. Tallinn, located on a peninsula extending into the Gulf of Finland, is the political, cultural and economic centre of Estonia. A ring of monotonous prefabricated settlements, in which predominantly Russians live, surrounds the new city from the period of promotorism. A massive ring of walls encloses the medieval Hanseatic centre of Tallinn with the Toompea (Cathedral Hill) and the Vanalinn (the lower city). Due to the proximity to Finland only two hours away, Tallinn makes the most western impression of all Baltic cities: construction is taking place everywhere, western products can be seen on the shelves in stores and the city is marketed and sold according to western principles.

History

The history of Tallinn is as diverse as the city's historical names: Lindesnäs was the Swedish name for the city around 800 AD. In 1154 in Palermo, the Arab geographer al-Idrisi drew the fortified settlement on the Toompea onto his world map and called it "Qualeveni." When, on June 15, 1219, the *Danes* under King Waldemar conquered the fortress, they founded "Revle" which was later called "Reval" by the Germans. The Estonians, however, were more consistent in what they called their city, the settlement was called "Taani linn" – Danish City, which developed into "Tallinn" over the centuries.

In 1227, the *Brothers of the Sword* reached Tallinn from Riga on a conquest which had more to do with murdering than missioning and conquered the fortress. After the crusaders, the merchants arrived. In 1230, the order called 200 Lübeck merchants to Tallinn from Visby/Gotland, awarded exempted them from taxation, and thus, laid the cornerstone for the metropolitan settlement (the lower city today).

The St. Nicholas Church became the cultural centre of German commerce. After the defeat of the Brothers of the Sword in the battle of Saule, Tallinn and northern Estonia fell under Danish rule once more as specified by the *Treaty of Stenby* in 1236. This time the Danish rulers held power up to 1346. In 1248, King Erik Plogpennig awarded the aspiring harbour and commercial centre the *Lübeck City Status* and in 1284, Tallinn became a member of the *Hanseatic League.* In 1265, the guilds had the say in the city: the organizations of craftsmen and merchants had meanwhile become so powerful that they freed themselves from obligation to the king. In the same year construction on the city wall began.

Having little or no benefit from the economic well-being of the city, the Estonians staged an uprising in 1343. The revolt of the 10,000 enraged Estonians against foreign domination went into the annals of history as the *St. George Uprising.* Weary and discouraged from battles and wars, Denmark withdrew. Estonia was then sold for 500 kilograms of silver to the German Order. The crusaders settled on the Cathedral Hill; the merchants and guilds se-

cured power in the lower city. As the tensions between the Church and the merchants grew, a wall was built. The two gates, the only passageways from the lower to the upper city, remained closed at night. The Church and the guilds posted several guards to protect their respective territories. It was only in 1889 that the division of the city came to an end. The ring of walls caused space to become scarce in the lower city: in 1370, Tallinn had a population of 4,500. The houses were built increasingly close together making the streets and alleyways more and more narrow. The wealth of the merchants increased as well. Around 1400, Tallinn, along with Novgorod, had the most influence in the Hanseatic League. When almost the entire city and the buildings on the Cathedral Hill were destroyed in a fire in 1433, the combined homes and warehouses were built – buildings which have been preserved to date.

The year 1524 marked the beginning of the *Reformation:* the convention of Livonian tribes decided to introduce the teachings of Luther. During the raids on religious buildings in the city, only the St. Nicholas Church was spared. The 16th century still held other terror in store. In 1553, an extensive fire broke out on Cathedral Hill. In 1558, Ivan the Terrible marched into Estonia and occupied Tallinn. Three years later, the city revoked its oath to the Order and subjected itself to the rule of the Swedish *King Erik XIV,* who confirmed the privileged status of this city. The in-

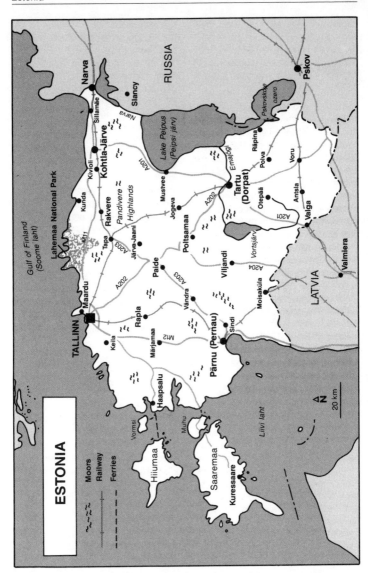

crease in Sweden's power drew envy: the Danes were on the lookout for seven months in 1570; in 1570 and 1571, the Russians occupied the city for ten weeks and once again in 1577.

In 1603, the *plague* raged in Tallinn, claiming one-third of the population by 1657. Thus weakened, Tallinn could hardly counter the Russian occupation of the city during the *Great Northern War*. In 1710, the city finally surrendered to *Czar Peter I*. The Swedish privileges were immediately revoked and members of the German upper class where given back their former rights. Commerce boomed thanks to the new eastern markets and the city quickly recovered from the aftermath of the war. Beginning in 1772, the city had its own news medium: "The Reval Weekly News." Neither the nautical battle between Russia and Sweden in the harbour of Reval (1790) nor the blockades by the English fleet (1801, 1809, 1855) could break the Russian regime.

In 1816, Tallinn had a population of 11,983, of which 5,000 were Germans, 4,000 were Estonians and 2,000 were Russians. The *policy of Russification* in the city was accompanied by the expansion of the infrastructure into the new hinterlands. Tallinn became Russia's gateway to the west, the harbour was expanded and became the main harbour in the Russian Empire. The year 1837 marked the establishment of ship lines between St. Petersburg and Tallinn; in 1870, trains began to chug

regularly from Baltic stations to St. Petersburg. In 1871, Tallinn's population comprised 10,020 Germans, 15,097 Estonians and 3,300 Russians, ten years later (1881) the city's population had grown to 45,880 with 26,324 Estonians, 12,737 Germans (27.8%) and 10,318 Russians. In 1887, the Russian language was introduced to all schools. The growing *industrialization* of the city increasingly fostered social tension. In 1901, the first illegal labour movement was founded. Using flyers and word of mouth, they propagated the ideas of Marx and Lenin. To nip the growing restlessness in the bud, the city administration was transferred to the Estonians in 1904. While the first revolution broke out in St. Petersburg in 1905 and 1906, *labour demonstrations* were bloodily quashed in Tallinn by the Czar's brigade. Simultaneously, the "German Society of Estonia" was founded, the secret goal of which was to secure German influence. With the laying of the cornerstone of the *war harbour* in 1912, the expansion of nautical influence began. The *October Revolution* of 1917 brought the short victory of communism: on October 26, the Bolsheviks proclaimed Soviet rule. At the beginning of 1918, the German *Wehrmacht* marched into Estonia. On February 24, 1918, the Committee of Estonian Chivalry resolved to proclaim independence. In 1938, the capital city of this now *Free Republic of Estonia* had a population of 145,191. Under pressure from the *Hitler-Stalin Pact,* Estonia signed a protocol with the German Empire concerning the relocation of the German populace on October 30, 1939. In the summer of 1940, when the Communist Party of Estonia had just 133 members, the bourgeois government of Estonia was toppled after the invasion of the Red Army on June 21. On August 6, Moscow had already annexed the *Estonian Soviet Republic* into the USSR. One year later, on June 14, 1941, Stalin had almost 11,000 Estonians deported to Siberia, two-thirds of which were women and children.

The *Second World War* only temporarily drove the Red Army out of Estonia. The *Wehrmacht* did conquer Tallinn on August 28, 1941; however, three years later on September 22, 1944, the red banners returned to Tallinn. In October, the Russian SSR was given five percent of Estonia: 2,350 square kilometres (917 square miles) of Estonian territory in the Trans-Narva region as well as a large portion of the Petschur (Petseri) district. The rest would follow within only a few weeks: the Estonian SSR was once again annexed into the USSR. The *Collectivization of Agriculture* (1948-1951) met with strong resistance in the rural population. On March 25 and 26, 1949, tens of thousands of Estonians were once again deported to Siberia as "enemies of the people." Ninety-two percent of those deported were women, children and elderly people. While the population of Tallinn was still around 280,000 in 1960, Moscow's Russification policy brought the city's population to almost half a million within the following 30 years. The Esto-

nians became a minority within their own country. On the anniversary of the Hitler-Stalin Pact in 1987, the open resistance began with a large-scale demonstration of 2,000 citizens in Tallinn. Since the 6th of September 1991, Tallinn is once more the capital of the free Estonian Republic. The return into the realm of western nations is supported by Tallinn's partner cities: Kotka (Finland), Kiel (Germany), Venice (Italy), Gent (Belgium) and Malmö (Sweden).

Walking Tours of the City
The Old City / Toompea
(Upper City)

The *Toompea,* or Cathedral Hill, dominates the old city of Tallinn. The cultural and political centre is situated on a 48-metre-high, and 15 acre large rock plateau. It belongs to the "Glint," a geological fault system which extends from St. Petersburg to the Swedish island of Gotland. The strategic location of the Cathedral Hill above the Bay of Tallinn was recognized quickly by the Estonians. In the 11th century they erected an agricultural fortress. In 1219, the walled fortress was conquered and destroyed by the Danish fleet under King Waldemar II. In 1227, an attack by the Brothers of the Sword brought the division of the Toompea: the southeastern portion (the small fortress) was cut off from the rest of the fortress (the so-called great fortress) by trenches. The small fortress and the great fortress occupy the southern quarter of Cathedral Hill. *The Small Fortress*, a type of forerunner for the subsequent fortresses, was built as a fortified castle by the Teutonic Order in 1222 and expanded by the Danes in 1238. After being extensively remodelled, there followed a change in function which combined the fortress function with that of a monastery. The cloisters surrounding an inner courtyard connected the living quarters of the monks. On the southeastern corner, the *Pikk Hermann* (Tall Herman) was constructed during the second half of the 14th century. At first, the tower was only 35 metres (115 feet) tall, but construction was then continued bringing the tower to a height of 50.2 metres (164 feet). The "Tall Herman" is easily recognized among the other structures in the wall complex: the Estonian flag has flown atop this tower since February 24, 1989. Earlier, the Stürden Kerl Tower (Strong Man's Tower) supplemented the southeastern fortifications, but this small octagonal tower was dismantled during the 18th century. The northwestern corner was secured by the *Pilsticker Tower* (Arrow-Sharpener Tower). A steep stairway leads down to the lower city from here. In 1502, the round tower *Landskrona* was built in the northeastern corner of the fortification. At the end of the 16th century, the tedious remodelling of the fortifications into a stately castle began. The "Imperial Hall" building was built in the Renaissance style along the western wall in the southern outer courtyard from 1585-1590; during the 17th century, the farm buildings

followed. In consequence to the damage caused during the Great Northern War, Catherine II ordered the "renovation" of the fortified castle in 1766 in order to prepare this as the seat of the Russian governor general: the imperial hall and the Stürden Kerl Tower were dismantled; a new *castle* built in the style of early classicism was erected in 1773. This pink and white structure with its "white hall" takes up the broad flank of *Lossi plats* (Castle Square). While the Minister's Council resided here during the Soviet times, the government and parliament assemble here today. Only the eastern, western and northern walls with their three towers remain of the original fortifications. Also with the *Great Fortress* constructed during the first half of the 14th century, the fortification structures have been dismantled for the most part or the building materials were used for civil purposes. What has remained, however, is the axial street system of the Great Fortress: all streets begin at the Cathedral Square and radiate to the surrounding walls of the fortress complex. A small governmental district has established itself around Lossi Plats. Lossi plats 1a is the address of the Foreign Ministry; number 7 houses the Ministry of Health. The Technical Inspection Administration has reserved house number 4. The golden yellow, bulbous spires of the *Alexander Nevski Orthodox Cathedral*, erected on Cathedral Hill from 1894 to 1900, almost seem out of place – it was exactly for this reason that the nationalists demanded that this church

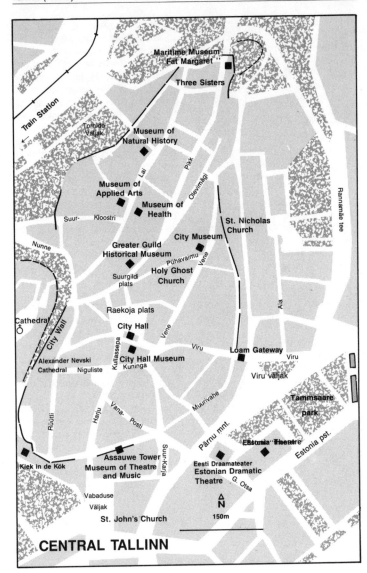

Maritime Museum
"Fat Margaret"

Three Sisters

Train Station

Tornide
Väljak

Museum of
Natural History

Pikk

Lai

Museum of
Applied Arts

Olevimägi

Museum of
Health

Suur- Kloostri

St. Nicholas
Church

Nunne

City Museum

Vene

Greater Guild
Historical Museum

Pühavaimu

Suurgildi
plats

Holy Ghost
Church

Raekoja plats

Cathedral

City Wall

City Hall

Vene

Viru

Alexander Nevski
Cathedral Niguliste

Kullassepa

Aia

City Hall Museum
Kuninga

Loam Gateway

Viru

Rüütli

Harju

Vana-

Posti

Muurivahe

Viru väljak

Rannamäe tee

Tammsaare
park

Kiek in de Kök

Assauwe Tower
Museum of Theatre
and Music

Suur-Karja

Pärnu mnt.

Eesti Draamateater
Estonian Dramatic
Theatre

Estonia Teater

Estonia pst.

G. Otsa

Vabaduse
Väljak

△
N
150m

St. John's Church

CENTRAL TALLINN

be torn down during the period between the two World Wars. Even today, these demands are becoming increasingly explicit. However, this symbol of the Czar's power still remains standing on the sturdy foundation of Finnish granite and the 4.7 ton bell continues to call the pious to prayer. The Toomkooli (Cathedral School Street) connects the castle with the cathedral, secular and spiritual power so to speak. The house at Toomkooli 4 dates back to 1691 but was remodelled in the classicistic architectural style during the 19th century. Passing the Technical Archives, a side-street before house number 13 leads off to the right and to the "Toomkooli" Restaurant. The neighbouring villa is home not only to the Canadian Embassy, but also the International School of Tallinn. The small terrace in the courtyard offers a good view of the old walls, the harbour and the newer district of Mustamäe. Passing the palace from the 17th century, the Toomkooli street leads directly to the *Toomkirik*, St. Mary's Cathedral. In 1219, a provisional wooden church was the forerunner of this, the oldest church on the Estonian mainland before construction began on a stone church in 1229. First mention of a consecrated St. Mary's Church was in 1233; in 1319, the Cathedral School was founded. The cathedral in the heart of the Great Fortress was continuously remodelled and rebuilt: in the last quarter of the 13th century, the church was expanded considerably; around 1560, the nave church was transformed into a basilica; during

the following years, a chapel was added. In 1684, a fire destroyed the church and no services were held for two years. It was only at the at the end of the 17th century that the restorations of the church could be completed. There was, however, still no tower – the western tower was first built in 1778 and 1779 with a baroque crown. As was common up until the baroque period, the church was used as a burial site over the course of many centuries. Even today, numerous limestone and dolomite grave slabs are evidence of the former pantheon of nobility. The oldest grave slabs date back to the 13th and 14th centuries. In 1595 Arent Passer, the famous architect and mason from Tallinn, finished the sarcophagus for general Pontus de la Gardie and his wife; the sarcophagus for Ferdinand von Tiesenhausen dates back to 1599. Among the 107 preserved epitaphs are the top plates for the sarcophagi of Otto von Üxküll and for the Swedish general Carl Horn and his wife. The marble memorial for Admiral Samuel Greigh (1788) is more monumental. In 1848, a monument was erected for the Estonia navigator Adam Johann von Krusenstern (1770-1845), who circumnavigated the world. Also worth seeing are the pulpit from 1686 and the altar, carved from 1694 to 1696 by Tallinn's master craftsman Christian Ackermann. The altar picture was painted in 1881 by the German artist Eduard Franz Karl von Gebhardt. The chandeliers date back to the 17th century; the organ was built in 1878 in Berlin.

Stately mansions are evidence that the Toompea was the residential area preferred by nobility. While the upper class enjoyed the fresh air, the "lower" class was cramped into the lower city in narrow, stifling alleyways. The Toompea retained its independence from the City Council of Tallinn up until 1889. The largest proportion of the older buildings on Cathedral Hill were destroyed in the fire of 1684. The *oldest house* is directly behind the Toomkirik on the edge of the plateau.

The former mansions of the aristocracy now predominantly house administration offices and ministries. Only 375 residents are registered as living on Cathedral Hill. The residential houses on Kiriku Plats (Church Square) date back to the 18th century. The *Rüütelkonna Hoone* (House of Knights) across from the Cathedral was built during the 19th century and is now home to the National Library. Interesting buildings can also be found in *Kohtu Street*. The *Count's House* (house number 8) built as a house for the noble class from 1809 to 1814) is considered the perfect example of classicistic architecture in Tallinn.

Located at the edge of Cathedral Hill, a splendid portal composed of six Ionian columns forms a gateway to the old city below. Today, this is the address of the Financial Ministry.

Scenic Terraces:
– Patkuli Stairway: via Rahukohtu.

– Kohtu Street, behind house number ten to the right: The small square offers the best view of Tallinn: the entire old city from the Olai Church to the Niguliste Church.

– Estars Platform: via Toom-Rüütli, head right to the passageway, take the small alleyway to the left, the portal at the yellow house leads to a tourist terrace next to a souvenir shop and Café "Estars" which offers a view of the bay and harbour as well as the Olai Church.

The Old City / Vanalinn (Lower City)

The old city has been blocked off to private traffic since the summer of 1992. The entry fee is five Kroon which must be paid at the control booths. Those who park illegally on the ring street around the old city risk being towed immediately.

I. Around City Hall Square

The Viru Väljak cannot be missed: it has the heaviest traffic in the city on the traffic circle where the former Intourist Hotel Viru rises 22 stories into the sky. The hotel was completed in 1972 and has 362 rooms. Diagonally across from the hotel is the main post office. The walking tour begins at *Viru Värav* (loam gateway). The two slender, round towers were built in 1454. To the right, a plaque of old Tallinn provides information on the streets in the old city. Large retail stores selling fashions, shoes and porcelain line the broad shopping street Viru (loam street). In the corner house to the right, "Gallery Molena" sells handicrafts as well as some tacky items. On the small square, kiosks sell flowers and beer, shoes and silk stockings. The Viru leads to *Vana Turg* (old marketplace). Out of town merchants could once store their wares in the former municipal warehouse (No. 1), built during the 15th to 17th century. A beautiful gable ornament with a grapevine motif adorns the medieval residential house (No. 6); on house number 7, a commemorative relief honours Juhan Smuul. This Estonian poet lived in this house from 1955 up to his death in 1971.

From the Kuninga, turn left on to the Kullassepa. On this gold smith's street amid the currency exchange offices and restaurants, gold smiths still keep the old tradition alive. The Kullassepa leads into the *Raekoja Plats*. Formerly the main marketplace and now the City Hall Square, a small tour train departs from this point, rattling tourists through the old city and up to Cathedral Hill. This train has only been in operation since the summer of 1992. Since only recently, the tourist information office is the corner house on Kinga Street next to the "Vana Toomas" restaurant. The tourist information office is open weekdays from 9 am to 5 pm and weekends from 10 am to 4 pm during the summer and will be able to help in planning one's stay in Tallinn. Information is available by phoning 66 69 50.

The plain grey *City Hall* with its incomparably slender tower dominates this area of Tallinn. The oldest secular building and simultaneously the last remaining Gothic city hall in the former USSR can be toured daily from 10 am to 5 pm (advance notice: Tel: 44 08 19). Pointed out during the tour through the city hall building are the key to the city and the old bench from 1374, the highlight being the old main assembly hall; the lunette paintings by Johan Aken are explained and the wax figure cabinet of citizens of Tallinn over the centuries is presented as the main attraction. In 1322, the city hall of Tallinn was first mentioned in historical documents.

The present-day structure, however, presumably dates back to 1351. Extensive remodelling followed during the period from 1402 to 1404 as well as in the 17th century. The building, measuring 37 metres (121 feet) in length and 14.5 metres (48 feet) in width is crowned by a saddleback roof, which is typical for Tallinn's medieval structures. The slender city hall tower, built after a sketch by the Oriental researcher Olearius after a minaret, was later added to the building. When the wooden city hall was replaced with a stone building in 1436, a weather vane was added to the tower. The citizens of Tallinn call this formidable figure with the impressive sword and moustache "Vana Toomas" (Old Thomas). When a new baroque tower was subsequently built, Old Thomas kept his accustomed place. Today, a replica of the traditional city patron crowns the tower. The original from 1530 now stands in the City Museum. The row of arcades which lead to the square (once simultaneously serving as the pillory and marketplace) was inspired by the Italian social buildings on the Palazzi dei Signori from the 14th century. Also notable is the irregularity in the placement of the windows on the first floor – the city hall is composed of two buildings fused together. For this reason, the floors are at different levels in the eastern and western portions of the ground and first floors.

On the first floor are the representational rooms: the assembly hall, council hall (which also served as the court of law), the rathskeller and city treasury. The wood carvings on the banks in the council hall depict the love stories of Tristan and Isolde and Samson and Delilah as well as the battle between David and Goliath.

The ground floor houses the warehouse and torture chamber, somewhat further and more hidden is the treasure chamber. The *municipal prison* from the 14th century located behind the city hall was converted to a residential building during the 19th century. Founded in 1422, the *Ratsapotheke* is one of the oldest pharmacies in Europe. For over 300 years from 1585 to 1911, the pharmacy was owned by the Burchard von Belavar family from Hungary. When the plague broke out in 1571 in this house, it had devastating consequences for the entire city. The present-day baroque façade covers three medieval buildings. diagonally across from the pharmacy, the *Operetta House* (Raekoja plats) attracts visitors with its turn-of-the-century architecture. On the corner of Aptee-

gi (Pharmacy Street) is the oldest and smallest *Craftsman's House* in Tallinn. Two wonderful handicrafts shops have set up business in the garden levels on Apteegi street, both with reasonable prices. In house number 2, scarves from Haapsalu, straw decorations for saunas and cane work can be found; across the street on the basement level of house number 3, wool blankets, wood and leather goods are offered for sale. On the corner of Vene (Russian Street) is the impressive, four-storey *Postal Building* built in 1918. A short jaunt on the Vene is worth the while for the "Aragats" Gallery at number 12. A few steps further is the inner courtyard of a Catholic church, a plain classicistic plastered building painted yellow. The Pühavaimu (Holy Ghost Street) leads up to the *Pühavaimu Kirik* (Holy Ghost Church). This church to the rear of the old pharmacy was first mentioned in 1316 and remodelled from 1375 to 1380; it first served as a chapel for the city hall and the church for the neighbouring infirmary. The plain whitewashed building houses an opulent interior. The two-panelled altar shrine was created by Bernd Notke in 1483. This master craftsman from Lübeck Germany also carved the rows of reliefs depicting the saints on the pulpit. Also worth noting among the abundant art treasures are the 57 paintings on the gallery railings. In the open belfry of the octagonal steeple is the lighter-sounding counterpart to the dark ring of the City Hall tower. The church bell, having rung since 1433 is meanwhile the oldest bell in

Estonia. It inscription: "Boys and girls, ladies and gentlemen I always ring the correct time and no one can turn this into an accusation" refers to the oldest clock in the city, the face of which dates back to 1684 and can be seen on the exterior wall facing the Pikktänav Street. Next to the church, the "Saiakaik" (white bread) Alley is reminiscent of the delicious white bread which was once baked here.

On Suurgilde Plats, "Café Maiasmokk" has been an inviting address for coffee and cake since the 1930's. A pastry shop has stood here as early as 1860, which was taken over by Georg Stude in 1864, who transformed it into a mecca for pastrylovers. The Pikk (Long Street) connects the Great Sea Gate with the Pikk Jalg, the gateway to Cathedral Hill. Magnificent bourgeois buildings line what was formerly the main street of Tallinn during the Middle Ages. The Suurgilde (Greater Guild) resided behind the magnificent Gothic façade of *Pikk 17* from 1410 to 1920. This association of affluent merchants accepted only major merchants and ship owners into their organization. Only members of the Greater Guild were allowed to be on the city council. Beginning in 1623, the cellar of the Guild was used as a wine tavern. Ebullient balls were held in the ballroom, modelled after the citizen's hall in the city hall. A popular festival was the selection of the "Count of May": a young man was crowned Count of May in the rose garden and could then chose his "bride" the Countess of May from eight

maidens. The couple would then ride in a festively decorated carriage on a parade through the city. However, real weddings were also held in the Guild House. The young couple would then retire to the "bride's chamber" for the evening. At Pikk 18, the Dragondi Gallery has been selling Estonian and international art since 1980, including every type of art from classic to modern. The Brotherhood of the "Black Heads" had its domicile at Pikk 26, the *Mustpeade Vennaskond* (Black Head House). The patron saint of this brotherhood for unmarried merchants (in existence up to 1940) is St. Maurice. The black skin tone of this saint, whose profile can be seen on the coat of arms, gave this guild its name. The magnificent portal in green, red and gold from 1640 is also embellished with a portrait of the patron. The coat of arms of the Hanseatic cities of Bruges, Novgorod, London and Bergen hang above the ground floor. Between the windows on the first floor, proverbs augment two reliefs. Written in large letters is: "Helf Gott alle Zeidt" (Help God at all times) and following under the stone relief are the allegories Pax (peace) and Justitia (justice), with a depiction of Jesus throned above.

The portraits and furnishings of the "Black Heads" can now be seen in the City Museum; the silver treasures, in the Art Museum. Directly adjacent is the *Olevi Gild Hoone* the Olai Guild House at number 27. Tallinn's oldest guild was founded in 1341 as a spiritual brotherhood for citizens and then developed into a organization of social standing for Estonian crafts-men. The members of this, Tallinn's lowest ranking guild were forbidden to wear expensive clothing made of velvet, silk, leather or taffeta; nor were they allowed to wear gold jewel-lery. The German craftsmen were combined in the Kanuti (St. Kanutus) Guild. In 1698, the two guilds were united. The guild house, remodelled from 1419 to 1422, is composed of two buildings; the larger of the two houses the guild hall, probably the most impressive secular room from the Middle Ages in Tallinn. After the guild was closed, the building first served as a warehouse. In 1806, the "Black Heads" purchased the house; today the building is used for social receptions. At house number 30/39, the street branches. On the triangular square under the tall linden trees, a snack bar sells burgers and beer.

Bear left, through the narrow Vaimu Street to Lai (Broad Street). Here, magnificent *bourgeois manors* also line the wide street. House number 29 is a residential house from the Middle Ages. The residential store-house from the 15th century (No. 23), now houses the Noorsooteater (Youth Theatre founded in 1965); at No. 1 is the Nunkuteater (Puppet Theatre). Founded in 1952, the Esto-nian Puppet Theatre performs pro-ductions for children and adults alike. Those who would like to continue their tour with a walk to Cathedral Hill can reach the upper city through the Pikk Jalg (Long Cathedral Hill; "long leg" in English). The narrow Voone-mehe alleyway leads back to City Hall Square.

II. Fortified Walks

Twenty-five of the original 35 fortifi-cation towers have been preserved in the 2 kilometre (1¼ mile) long fortifi-cations around the old city. These characterize the profile of Tallinn. Planned construction on the *City Wall* presumably began during the third quarter of the 13th century. Although construction continued into the 14th century, the wall still did not com-pletely encircle the city. A new con-struction phase began in 1410 when the Dane Jens Kande was brought to the city to coordinate the construc-tion of Tallinn's fortifications. When the ring of fortification walls finally stood in 1346, the trenches surround-ing it were filled with water. The in-creased spread of firearms in the 14th and 15th centuries made it ne-cessary to remodel the fortifications. In 1475, the "Kiek in de Kök," the first artillery tower was built. During the second half of the 15th century, new bastion towers would follow – this complex, once the strongest of its kind in the country, came into being. Its walls were even twice the height of the fortifications in Nürnberg Ger-many which were considered the largest and most secure during the Middle Ages.

On Vabaduse Väljak (Liberty Square), formerly Voidu väljak (Victo-ry Square), is *Joani Kirik* (St. John's Church). During Tallinn's golden age in the 17th century, this church with an abundance of terra cotta sculpt-ings was considered the most signifi-cant brick building of that time along with the Cathedral in Tartu. The church, already heavily damaged during the 18th century, was burned to the ground in 1944 during the battles to conquer the city. Both the interior and exterior of this three-naved Gothic church built before 1330 were embellished with statues. The interior ornamentations were once again exposed by the fire of 1944 which destroyed the plaster.

Due to the construction of the "Tallinn Business Center" turn left at the Harju Mägi and then continue up the stairway on the left leading up to the park and out onto the fortification walls past the *Assauwe Tower* housing the Museum for Music and Theatre (Müürivahe 12) and continuing up to *Kiek in de Kök* (Museum open daily 10:30 am to 5:30 pm; Sundays and holidays from 11 am to 4:30 pm). The walls of this 49.4 metre (162 foot) artillery tower built in 1475 are four metres (13 feet) thick. The name is a result of the fact that from the upper floors of this tower, one could easily peek (Kiek) into all of the kitchens (Kök) of the city. During the seven-day occupation of the city in 1577, a cannonball tore a large hole in the fourth floor of the tower. In commemoration of this event, six cannonballs (three stone and three iron) have been embedded into the tower. To the left is the Alexander Nevski Cathedral (→ *Upper City / Toompea Walking Tour*). A tunnel through the wall leads to a small scenic terrace, dominated by the *Neitsitorn* (Maidens' Tower). First referred to as the Maidens' Tower in 1373, this tower was three storeys high in 1378 according

to historical sources. Supplemental construction from 1455 to 1458 brought the tower to its present-day height. The roof was constructed by the town stone-cutter Hans Kotke. During the 18th and 19th centuries, the tower decayed; the interior was occasionally used as living quarters even into the 20th century. After extensive restorations during the 1980's, a pub was opened in the dungeon cells, serving hot spiced wine instead of bread and water. In the second and third storeys of the former prison for "easy girls," a café offers a beautiful view of the old city. From the square, the Lühike Jalg (short leg), an 80 metre (220 foot) staircase leads down to the *Sweden Gate*, which separates the upper from the lower city. Those who wish to do so can turn off onto Rüütli Tänav (Knight Street). In the shadows of the city wall, the city's executioner lived in the inconspicuous house at number 42. The executioner had the following engraved on his sword: "The grace of God dawns each morning, when I raise my sword to help the pitiful sinners to eternal life." Today, the executioner's sword is kept in the City Museum.

Then, turning left onto Rataskaevu (Wheel Well Street), one will see a well which has stood at the Dunkri Street crossing which gave the street its name. The *Niguliste Kirik* (St. Nicholas Church; No. 11/13), first mentioned in 1010, is one of the oldest churches in Tallinn. Dedicated to St. Nicholas, the patron saint of seafarers, the original wooden church was replaced with a lower stone building as early as the 13th century. Only the early Gothic portal to the north has been preserved. A steeple and several chapels would first follow in the 14th century before the first structural modifications were made in the 15th century. This three-naved church not only fulfilled a religious function; the church roof also sheltered a storeroom for especially valuable wares. In 1944, the church was destroyed in the war. Reconstruction began in 1956 and the metal tower roof followed from 1970 to 1972. Remaining from the once majestic interior are only a few art treasures like the carved two-panelled altar by the craftsman Hermann Rode (1481) from Lübeck, Germany and the famous "dans macabre" fragment by Bernd Notke (also of Lübeck) which dates back to the 16th century. The chandelier with seven arms also originates from Lübeck and was a gift from this Hanseatic city. "Kelch's Sarcophagus" stands in the southern apse. According to the legend, this is the final resting place of Christian Kelch, catechist of the Niguliste Church who fell victim to the plague in 1710. "Kelch's Linden," presumably the oldest tree in the city, stands before the southern portal, growing on the actual grave of the chronicler Christian Kelch. In his Livonian Chronicle of 1695, Kelch wrote: "Estonia is heaven for estate owners, a paradise for the parson, a goldmine for foreigners and hell for farmers."

The restored Niguliste Church serves as a museum for medieval art. Organ concerts take place here on Wednesdays, Saturdays and Sundays.

Passing the former *Infirmary* (No. 15) and the *City Hall*, the alleyway leads to *Rataskaevu Square*. The "von Krahl Theatre" (No. 10) opened its doors here on this small triangular square with a fountain in October 1992.

The tower gate *Pikk Jalg Torn* (Long Cathedral Hill; literally: long leg), built in 1380 was formerly locked up at nine in the evening. If there was any indication of danger, then the tower gate was further secured with iron chains and sturdy grates made of oak. The Pikk Jalg beyond this, a small and narrow cobblestone alleyway between high limestone walls, connects the lower city with Cathedral Hill. While this alleyway is only open to pedestrians today, the English woman Elizabeth Rigby reports in her travel memoirs that the coachmen used to shout in warning before beginning their descent down this road. Continuing via Nunne and Väike Kloostri, now a huge construction area for a new hotel, one will come to the Gustav Adolf Gymnasium (secondary school) at Gümnasiumi 2/corner of Suur Kloostri 16, which houses the *Pedagogic Museum* (side entrance; open 10 am to 6 pm, Tel: 44 30 84). The public pathway leads directly across the schoolyard to a narrow alleyway which runs along the shadows of a longer continuous section of wall. First, one will see the *Saunatorn,* a tower which originally did not reach the earth but was built on the outer side of the retaining wall, followed by the *Kuldjala Torn* (Golden Foot Tower) from the early 14th century.

Continue along the Kooli (School Street) past the *Nunndetagune Torn*, standing off by itself, to the *Loewenschede Torn*. The Laboratooriumi (Laboratory Street) leads to the *Koismäe Torn* from the 14th century. The *Platetorn*, named after the former Commander Herbord Plate, once controlled the entrance to the city from the Suurtüki Street. Continuing straight ahead, one will see three more towers: *Eppingi Torn* (Epping Tower), *Grusbeke-Tagune-Torn* (Grusbeke Tower), and *Wulfardi-Tagune-Torn*. To the left is the round *Horse Mill* from 1379. If the water level was insufficient, the mill was run by horse power. Up to the fire of 1757, the mill served as a military storage depot. Despite reconstruction, nothing remains of its original equipment and furnishings. Take the Lai (Broad Street) to the right and down to *Oleviste Kirik* (Olai Church; No. 50). Its tower, measuring 124 metres (406 feet) in height and even taller (159 metres/520 feet) earlier, characterizes the profile of the city.

As reported in the city chronicle, an Italian tightrope artist fixed his rope to the tower and performed his act...

One can certainly also enjoy the view all the way to the coast of Finland during clear weather with more sturdy footing. The church with the highest nave – 31 metres (101 feet) at the central nave – was built before 1297, burned down to its foundations in 1625 and 1820 and was given its present day form during re-

construction lasting from 1829 to 1840. Inside, the altar painting was created by the German Balt Wilhelm von Kügelgen in 1830. Continue past the church on the left and turning onto the Pikk (Long Street). Standing at house number 71 are the most famous houses in the Baltic States, the *Kolm Ode* (Three Sisters). These are Tallinn's answer to Rigas "Three Brothers" and date back to the 15th century. The most magnificent is the corner house, the other two houses are smaller and more plain in comparison. Continue the walking tour by heading to the right and down to the *Suure Rannavrava Eelvaräv* (the Great Sea Gate), one of the original six gates in the city wall. Its reconstruction in 1518 marked the beginning of the last major phase of construction on the city's fortifications.

The coat of arms from 1539 depicts two winged lions with the heads of eagles. One of the city's youngest towers is the *Paks Margareeta* (Fat Margaret). Built as a defence tower from 1510 to 1529, the impressive, squat round tower with walls five metres (16 feet) thick served as an arms depot, barracks and as a prison up to 1917, before the *Maritime Museum* moved in. Outside the fortification wall, a footpath leads through a small greenbelt to the *Stollingi Torn* (Stolting Tower). Passing the *Hattorpe-Tagune-Torn* (Hattorpe Tower) continue to Uus Street and Olevimägi before the *Bremeni Torn* (Bremen Tower) on Brookus plats, named after Commander Hinze van Bremen, marks the beginning of a new section of the wall. From the *Munkadetagune Torn* (Monks' Tower), the Müürivahe (Wall Street) closely parallels the city wall. Past the *Hellemani Torn* (Hellemann Tower) and a short section of wooden embattlements, the alleyway leads to Viru Varäv (→ *Walking Tour I: Around City Hall Square*) and farther to Karjavärava Plats. Where once another gate stood is now dominated by the neo-classicistic monumental Soprus Cinema building, its façade consisting of six tall, plain columns. The *Museum of Music and Theatre* in the *Assauwe Tower* is worth a visit. Ending the walking tour is the former *Harju Gate,* where the landlord Johann Üxküll was publicly beaten in 1533 for mishandling his serfs.

III. Modern Tallinn:
From the Turn of the Century to Socialism

At the end of 1911, the Tallinn city council called on the internationally renowned Finnish architect Eliel Saarinen to consult them in the planning the city. In the spring of 1912, Saarinen won the architectural competition for the spatial planning of the city. His model for the new centre created an attractive contrast to the neighbouring old city: monumental squares and broad boulevards contrasted with picturesque squares, quaint inner courtyards and charming alleyways. Saarinen's magnificent general plan was to fail in the light of reality: the First World War dashed all hopes of realization of these plans. The only building constructed by the famous Finnish architect which has

remained preserved to date is the Credit Bank, erected in 1911/1912.

The best point of departure for a walking tour of Tallinn of the 19th and 20th century is the *Viru Väljak.* Two pools separate the busy traffic circle of the capital from the square-shaped *Tammsaare Park,* in the middle of which there is a memorial for the Estonian author of the first republic, A. H. Tammsaare. On Estonia Puiestee is the monumental "Estonia" Building. Built from 1909 to 1913, the grand opening of this, the only ballet theatre and opera house in Tallinn in 1914 was an event of national significance. Not far from here, on Pärnu Maantee, the *Eesti Draamateater* (Estonian Dramatic Theatre) has presented plays by Estonian and foreign dramatists since 1916. The Pärnu Maantee is the main business street in the city. Those who find the Kaubamaja department store across from the "Viru Hotel" a bit too hectic should take a stroll through the "Laste Maailu" department store (No. 6). Since only recently, a number of galleries have opened up shop on the side-streets. Worth visiting are Vaal Galerii at Väike 14 (open noon to 6 pm) and the Luum Gallery at Harju 13. Located on the corner of Harju and Müürivahe is the site of the Estonian-US Joint Venture TBC Ltd., the "Tallinn Business Center." Construction on this complex began in the summer of 1992. The grand opening of this post-modern monumental structure with over 5,800 square metres (56,900 square feet) of office space is scheduled for 1993. Although the Pärnu Maantee was transformed into a prototypical socialistic example of city planning and renamed Lenin Boulevard, only the 12-storey high-rise for the Central Committee of the Communist Party has left a noticeable scar on the inner city's profile. The really unsightly socialist structures surround the city. Mustamäe, located on the western arm of the bay is Tallinn's oldest suburb. It can be emphatically warned against going swimming on the public beach due to water contamination. In the 1970's and 1980's, the socialist "sleeping centre" (as the Tallinn residents call their urban settlement) Lasnamäe housing around 100,000 residents was built above the Kadriorg Park.

Pirita

The Moscow Olympic games brought international renowned to Pirita: in 1980, the Olympic sailing competitions were held here. On the two-lane motorway to Pirita running parallel to the bay, now seems somewhat out of place as does the cement basin for the Olympic flame. The other Olympic buildings also make quite a deserted impression today. Where once the athletes stayed in the Sports Hotel now offers beds to the general public. Barbed wire still separates the stair-shaped hotel complex from the coastal promenade, blocking direct access to the former yacht harbour. Pizza and petrol are available at the former foreign currency service station across the street. The better part of Pirita begins beyond

the bridge over the Pirita Jõgi. To the left is a swimming pool and the "Regatt Bar." One should definitely forgo swimming in the Baltic at Pirita, however – the organic contamination of the seawater is ten times higher than the maximum allowable limits set in the Helsinki Convention. To the right-hand side are first a department store and cinema and shortly beyond that is the actual attraction of the Pirita area: the *ruins of the Bridgettine Monastery*. The monastery which gave this small settlement the name "Pirita" was first built by the Bridgettine Order in 1436, first using wood and then stone. Three wealthy Tallinn merchants – Heinrich Schwalberg, Heinrich Huxer and Gerlach Kruse – along with ten other citizens donated their fortunes to this monastery. The legends surrounding the establishment of this monastery was recounted by the Estonian author Eduard Bornhöhe in a novel. At that time the Bridgettine monastery was together with the Dominican monastery and open to both sexes: the separate convents of monks and nuns stood under the same administration of an abbess. The peaceful cloistered life ended abruptly with the Livonian War. In 1577, Ivan the Terrible had some of the occupants of the monastery killed and others imprisoned. During the summer months, concerts take place against this picturesque backdrop. In 1992, the theme was "Pirita Blues." Continuing up the Kloostrimetsa Avenue, one will come upon the *Botanical Gardens* (No. 44). Beyond is a shady wooded park with several rare specimens of

The Park of the Czars – Kadriorg (Katharinental)

The most beautiful and largest park in Tallinn lies between the extensive bay and the steep Lasnamägi. In 1714, Peter the Great bought a small plot of land at the base of the hill and built a summer cottage there. Still present today, the original house consisted of three rooms and a kitchen with an open hearth. In 1718, Peter the Great also purchased the land between the summer cottage and the nearby city, planted a chestnut boulevard and began construction on the Czar's Palace and Park during the same year. The plans for this were designed by the Italian architect Niccolo Michetti, the name "Jekatarinetal" was provided by Czaress Catherine II. Open to the general public in 1721, the Germans called the park "Katharinental" and the Estonians shortened it to "Kadriorg." In the oldest section of the park on the swan pond, a memorial commemorates Friedrich Reinhold Kreutzwald, the founding father of Estonian national literature. The sundial with astrological signs and markings for the hours is made from Estonian marble. The splendid summer residence Kadriorg Castle (Weizenbergi 37) was built by a trio of leading architects – Niccolo Michetti, Gaetoano Chiaveri and Michael Grijojewitsch Semzov. The cornerstone of the main building was laid on March 21, 1720. However, after the death of Peter the Great on February 8, 1725, construction proceeded only sluggishly. The present-day structure – one main wing and two side wings – is in accordance with the original plans for the most part. The large hall on the first floor is two storeys high. The initials of Peter and Catherine point to the planned use of this room as a throne room. It was only in the 1930's that the banquet hall was completed. The first baroque castle in Estonia is now home to the National Art Museum. Behind the museum, one can still see the old summer cottage of the czar, the so-called "Peter's Cottage" (memorial) as well as a governmental building erected in 1938 by the Estonian architect Kotli. The expansive Kadriorg Park extends all the way to the coastal promenade. The "Russalka" has stood at this point since 1902. This sculpture by Adam Adamson is a popular backdrop for a photograph with friends and not only among Estonians. The monumental memorial with the mermaid sculpture measures 16 metres (53 feet) in height and stands in remembrance of the Russian cruiser which sank in the Gulf of Finland in 1893.

The granite pedestal depicts a ship run aground on a reef; on the post office is a merciful bronze angel. The names of the victims of this disaster are engraved on the marble tablets. Not far from the Russalka is a small amusement park on the promenade with a carousel and ferris wheel.

trees on a high pine-covered hill called *Metsakalmistu* (Forest Cemetery; No 36).

Where culture was the root of opposition against 700 years of foreign dominance, the cemetery of heroes is similar to a pantheon of the fine arts: poets like Anton Hansen Tammsaare, Juhan Smuul and Lydia Koidula and composers like Evald Aav and Konstantin Türnpu have found their final resting places here, neatly ordered according to genre. Another famous person buried here is Jonannes Vares-Barbarus, the first president of the Estonian Soviet Socialist Republic.

Rocca al Mare

The suburb on the Kopli Bay was given its Italian name meaning "rock at the seaside" in 1863 by the mayor and merchant Girard de Soucatoun, who built his summer residence here. In the same way, another town on the bay is called "Sala y Gomez," named after a rocky island in the ocean in a novel by Adalbert von Chamisso. Just as wonderful as the melodic name is the *Ethnological Open-Air Museum* (Vabaohumuuseum tee 12, open daily from 10 am to 8 pm; bus number 21 and 45), which has kept the rural Estonian folk culture alive since 1957 on its 70 hectares (175 acres) of land. Farmhouses, barns, stalls and windmills from all over the country have been collected and rebuilt in this extensive wooded park. Folk dance groups provide animation in the scenery; during the summer, craftsmen demonstrate old techniques and when farmers use these pastures, the sheep and goats can be seen grazing. Tasteful handicrafts are for sale at a stand at the entrance. Instead of a sterile cafeteria, picnic areas provide an inviting backdrop for a break. For the kids are old playground contraptions like an wooden swing. This park is constantly growing through the addition of new structures.

Nomme

The garden city, the name of which is based on the Estonian word "nomm" meaning heather, is built on sand in the literal sense. The magnificent villas stand on the dunes surrounded by pine forests. The attraction of the Glehn Park is the monumental *sculpture of the Kalevipoeg*. The idyllic Nomme suburb is accessible by buses 14 and 18.

Museums

– *Ajaloomuuseum* (Museum of History): 17 Pikk, Tel: 44 34 46, 60 21 63; open Thursday to Tuesday from 11 am to 6 pm. Housed in the Great Guild Building from 1410, The Museum of History founded in 1864 exhibits specimens from the Estonian Provincial Museums. Branches: *Maarijamäe Loss* (Maarijamäe Castle), Pirita puiestee 56, open Wednesday to Sunday from 11 am to 5 pm. Bus lines 1, 5, 8, 34 and 38. In the former summer residence of Adjutanten A. Orlov-Davydov, this permanent exhibition shows the history of Estonia up to present. The neo-Gothic limestone building high above the sea was built in 1874.

– *Kunstimuuseum* (Art Museum): 37 Weizenbergi, Tel: 42 63 50; open Wednesday to Monday from 11 am to 6 pm. Streetcar 1, 3; bus lines 1, 5, 8, 44 and 56. This gallery was opened in the baroque castle of Kadriorg and dedicated to modern Estonian paintings. Today, the permanent collection includes Estonian paintings from the 19th century to 1940. Located behind the building is the sculpture garden.

– *Linnamuuseum* (Tallinn City Museum): 17 Vene, Tel: 44 58 56, 44 18 29; open Wednesday to Monday from 10:30 am to 6 pm. Opened in 1937 and housed in a medieval merchant's house in the heart of the old city, the exhibits illustrates the history of the city from the 14th to the 18th century. The permanent collection comprises porcelain and handicrafts from the period of the first Estonian republic.

– *Loodusmuuseum* (Museum of Natural History): 29 Lai, Tel: 44 42 23; open Wednesday to Monday from 10 am to 5:30 pm. Founded in 1941, this permanent exhibition shows the flora and fauna of Estonia.

– *Meeremuuseum* (Maritime Museum): 70 Pikk, Tel: 60 18 03; open Wednesday to Sunday from 10 am to 6 pm. The impressive cannon tower Paks Margareeta has been home to the collection on the development of ship travel and fishing in Estonia since 1935.

– *Rae Muuseum* (City Hall Museum): 4/6 Raekoja, Tel: 44 87 67; open Thursday to Tuesday from 10:30 am to 5:30 pm. The Raekelder (Rathskeller) is an informative stroll through the history of Tallinn from the 10th century to the end of the Swedish domination in 1710.

– *Teatri-ja Muusikamuuseum* (Museum of Theatre and Music): Müürivahe 12, Tel: 44 28 84; open Wednesday to Monday from 10 am to 6 pm. The entryway in the old city wall leads to this museum filled with documentation of the history of music, including books and manuscripts. Founded in 1924, this museum also has a collection of old musical instruments.

– *Tarbekunstimuuseum* (Museum of Applied Arts): 17 Lai. Tel: 44 59 89; open Wednesday to Sunday from 11 am to 6 pm. A store from the 17th century houses this collection of Estonian handicrafts from the 20th century.

– *Tervishoiumuuseum* (Museum of Health): 28/30 Lai, Tel: 60 16 02, 60 17 08; open Tuesday to Saturday from 11 am to 5 pm. Electronic models and videos augment the exhibition on the human anatomy, physiology and sexuality under the motto "the human, health and family."

– *Tulettörjemuuseum* (Museum of Fire-Fighting): 14 Vana-Viru, Tel: 44 42 51; open Tuesday to Saturday from noon to 6 pm. The old fire department building exhibits historical fire fighting equipment.

A. H. Tammsaare Memoriaalmuuseum: 12 A. Koidula, Tel: 42 72 08, 42 63 00; open Wednesday to Monday from 11 am to 6 pm; streetcars 1 and 3. The wooden mansion from the 19th century, the last residence of

this poet, is now a memorial on the Tammsaare and is also considered a forum for the "Estonian Youth Movement" which celebrates Estonian tradition within the framework of Europe.
– *Eduard Vilde Memoriaalmuuseum:* Roheline aas 3, in the Kadriorg castle park.
– *Peter Esimese Majamuuseum* (Museum on Peter the Great): Maekalda 2.
– *K. Raua Majamuuseum:* K. Raua 8, memorial in the home of K. Raua.
– *F. Tuglas Majamuuseum:* Vaikese Illimari 12.
– *Tallinn Zoo:* 145 Paldisk maantee, Tel: 55 99 44; open daily from 9 am to 3 pm.

Exhibitions and Galleries
– *Eesti Näitused,* Pirita tee 28. Exhibition grounds.
– *Lillepaviljon,* Pirita tee 26. Flower pavilion.
– *Tallinna Kunstihoone* (House of Art): 8 Vabaduse väljak, open Monday from noon to 6 pm, Tuesday to Sunday from noon to 7 pm.
– *Eestinäitused:* 28 Pirita tee, open Monday to Sunday from 11 am to 7 pm.
– *Vaal Galerii:* 12 Väike-Karja, open Tuesday to Friday from 2 to 7 pm, Saturday from noon to 4 pm.
– *Kunstihoone Galerii:* 6 Vabaduse väljak, open Monday from noon to 6 pm, Wednesday to Sunday from noon to 7 pm.
– *Draakoni Galerii:* 18 Pikk, open Tuesday to Friday from 11 am to 6 pm, Saturday from 11 am to 4 pm.

– *Galerii G:* 2 Narva maantee, open Tuesday to Friday from noon to 6 pm.
– *Galerii Molen:* 19 Viru, open Tuesday to Friday from 11 am to 6 pm, Saturday and Sunday from 11 am to 4 pm. Graphic arts and handicrafts.
– *Hansa Ait:* 10 Sauna, open Monday to Friday from 11 am to 6 pm, Saturday from noon to 4 pm.
– *Kalamaja Galerii:* Käsperti 28, open Wednesday to Sunday from 10:30 am to 5:30 pm.
– *Tornigalerii:* 56 Pirita tee, open Wednesday to Sunday from 11 am to 6 pm.
– *Kiek in de Kök:* 1 Komandandi tee, open Tuesday, Wednesday and Friday from 10:30 am to 5:30 pm, Saturday and Sunday from 11 am to 4 pm.
– *Laste Loomingu Maja* (House of Children's Art): 6 Kuninga, open daily from noon to 6 pm, closed Tuesdays.
– *Munkadetagune Galerii:* 58 Müürivahe, open daily from 9 am to 6 pm, Saturday from 11 am to 5 pm.
– *Gallery Deco:* 3 Vabaduse väljak, exhibition and sales in the Palace Hotel, Tel: 44 34 61.
– *Õpetaja Maja Pildigalerii:* 14 Raekoja plats, open weekdays from noon to 6 pm.
– *Gallery "Aragats":* 12-7 Vene, open Tuesday to Saturday from 10 am to 6 pm; Aragat Kalatsjan exhibits and sells his pictures here.

Sports and Recreation
Body Building
Club "Fortius," 4 Toompuiestee, Tel: 66 65 53; aerobics, freestyle dance

studio, body-building weight room, solarium.

Cycling
Velodroom, Rummu tee 3.

Figure and Speed Skating
Linnahaal Indoor Arena, 20 Mere-puiestee, Tel: 42 51 58.

Football (Soccer)
"Kadriorg" Stadium, 124 Roheline aas, Tel: 42 51 58.
"Kalev" Stadium, 3 Staadioni, Tel: 66 16 65.

Gymnasiums
Harjuoru voimla, Toompea 3.
"Kalevi" spordihall, Juhkentali 12.
"Kalevi" spordibaas, Herne 28.

Horseback Riding
Hippodrom, Paldiski maantee 50.

Ice Hockey
"Talleksi" hokiväljak, Pirni 1.

Ice Skating
Jäähall, L. Koidula 21.

Sailing
Tallinn Yachting Centre, 1 Regati puiestee; 1 Pirita.
Tallinn Sailing Service; Tel: 23 76 55, Telex: 17 32 77.

Sports Stadiums
"Dvigateli" stadioon, Leningradi maantee 16.
Kadrioru stadioon, Roheline aas 24.
Lastestaadion, Suur-Amerika 14.
"Kalevi" keskstadioon, Staadioni 3.
"Kalevi" spordiväljak, Narva maantee 65.
"Norma" spordiväljak, Kose tee 4.
"Töörjoureservide" spordiväljak, Toompark.

Ski Jumping
Mustamäe suusahüppebaas, Vana-Mustamäe 16.

Swimming
Outdoor pool: Pirita.
Indoor pool: Kalevi siseujula, 18 Aia St., Tel: 44 05 45.
Indoor pool: "Dünamo," 3 Aia St., Tel: 44 66 17.

Tennis
Tennisebaas "Kaarli," Kaarli puiestee 2.
Dünamo tennisehall, L. Koidula 38.
"Kalev" Courts, 28 Herne St./Vabaduse väljak, Tel: 44 21 69.
Hotel tennis courts: Palace Hotel, Vabaduse väljak, Tel: 44 34 61.

Theatres and Concert Halls
– Ooperi-ja Balletiteater "Estonia" (Estonia Opera and Ballet): 4 Estonia puiestee; for tickets, contact Tel: 44 90 40, Monday and Wednesday to Saturday from 1 to 7 pm, Sunday from 11 to 7 pm.
– Eesti Draamateater (Estonian Dramatic Theatre): 5 Pärnu maantee, Tel: 44 33 78; tickets can be purchased daily from 1 to 7 pm, closed Monday.
– Eesti Noorsooteater (Estonian Youth Theatre): 23 Lai tee, Tel: 44 85 79; tickets available weekdays from 1 to 4 pm.
– Vanalinnastuudio (Old City Theatre): 14 Raekoja plats, Tel: 44 84 08. Ticket sales: 2 Kullasepa St., daily except Sundays from 1 to 7 pm. Sakala 3. Comedies.
– Eesti Nukuteater (Estonian Puppet Theatre): 1 Lai St., Tel: 44 12 52. Ticket sales: Thursday to Monday from 2 to 6 pm.
– Vene Draamateater (Russian Dramatic Theatre): 5 Vabaduse väljak,

Tel: 44 37 16; ticket sales: daily except Mondays from 11 am to 7 pm.

Concerts

– Estonia Kontserdisaal (Estonia Concert Hall): 4 Estonia tee, Tel: 44 31 98, Fax: 44 53 17; daily from 1 to 7 pm.

– Niguliste Kirik (Museum Concert Hall): 13 Niguliste, Tel: 44 99 91.

– Olvi Saal: 26 Pikk.

– Väravatron: 9 Lühike Jalg.

– Mustapeade Maja Valge Saal: 26 Pikk.

– Matkamaja: 18 Raekoja plats.

Dining Out

Advance reservations are recommended, especially during the evenings. Quite often, meals are accompanied by live music – a tip is expected for the entertainment.

Cafés

– Maiasmokk: 16 Pikk, 1 Pühavaimu, Tel: 60 13 96. The oldest marzipan and chocolate manufacturer in Estonia, founded in 1864, this café is especially attractive because of its interior decor, the baking pans full of irresistible cakes and calorie-packed pastries and the good coffee and tea. Seats 58, open daily from 11 am to 10 pm.

– Matkamaja: Raekoja plats 16. A small, cozy café in a medieval cellar.

– Neitsitorn: 1a Komandandi tee, Tel: 44 08 96, 44 05 14. Open daily from 11 am to 10 pm. Today, coffee and cake are served in the old dungeon cells; in the cellar, even cognac and hot spiced wine. This café has a balcony with a view of the city and is on four levels in the old city gate. Seats 80.

– Harju: 4 Suur-Karja, Tel: 44 66 66, open daily from 9 am to 9 pm. A quaint café that seats 60.

– Kadriorg: 90 Narva maantee, Tel: 42 74 72; open daily from noon to 5 pm and 6 pm to midnight.

– Moskva: 10 Vabaduse väljak, Tel: 66 67 90; open daily from 8 am to 9 pm. A meeting place for young intellectuals; live music is performed during the evenings.

– Narva: 10 Narva maantee, Tel: 42 44 59; open daily from 8 am to 10 pm, located near the Viru Hotel. Seats 64.

– Pärl: 1 Pikk, Tel: 44 07 10; open daily from 9 am to 9 pm.

– Schwerin: 124 Vilde tee, Tel: 53 28 47; open daily from 11 am to 11 pm. Located in the district of Mustamäe, this café is named after Tallinn's German sister city. The café can seat 76 and another 46 at the bar.

– Tallinn: 6 Harju, Tel: 44 49 25; open daily from 8 am to 8 pm.

– Vigri: 19 Narva maantee, Tel: 42 15 13; open daily from 11 am to 8 pm. A children's café with an extra ice cream menu, located in the middle of the city and seats 65.

Top Restaurants

– Astoria: 5 Vabaduse väljak, Tel: 44 84 62, for reservations call Tel: 66 60 48; open daily from 1 to 7 pm and 9 pm to 2 am. Has been re-opened after renovations, seats 100 and an additional 25 at the bar. A dance band performs during the evening.

– Carina: 26 Pirita tee, Tel: 23 74 75; open daily from noon to 5 pm and 6 pm to midnight. The red, black and white decor is in post-modern style.

From the terrace in the garden there is a view of the Bay of Pirita and the Tallinn Harbour. Piano music on occasion during the evening, if so admission is charged. Two dining rooms seating 86 and 24 respectively as well as a bar.

– Eeslitall: 4 Dunkri, Tel: 44 80 33. An old, renovated restaurant in the old city. Live music on occasion, usually folk and solo vocalists.

– Galaxy: in the television tower; 58a Kloostrimetsa tee, Tel: 23 82 50; open daily from 2 to 6:30 pm and 8:30 pm to 2 am. Fantastic view of Tallinn and the surrounding regions. Video programmes during the evening – if the breathtaking view does not suffice. Seats 60. Advance reservations are a must – otherwise one is not even allowed into the elevator.

– Gloria: Müürivahe 2, Tel: 44 69 50, open noon to 4 pm and 8 pm to midnight, Fridays and Saturdays from noon to 6 pm and 8 pm to 2 am. Large and good with a variety show from Tuesday to Saturday, dance band. Seats 145.

– Palace: 3 Vabaduse väljak. Hotel restaurant serving renowned cuisine. Tel: 44 34 61; payment is only accepted by credit card or in hard currencies.

– Sub Monte: 4 Rüütli, Tel: 66 68 71; open daily from noon to 6 pm and from 7 pm to midnight. Located in a medieval cellar in the old city; payment accepted only by credit card or in hard currencies. Serves Estonian specialities; seats 50

Restaurants in the Middle Category
– Gnoom: 2 Viru, Tel: 44 24 88; open daily from noon to 6 pm and 7 pm to midnight; restaurant, bar and grill in a combination of locales on several floors with decors ranging from medieval to Biedermeier.

– Kullassepa Kelder: 7/9/11 Kullassepa, Tel: 44 22 40; open daily from noon to 7 pm and from 8 pm to midnight. Chicken is the main dish served in this small restaurant located in a cellar; seats 48.

– Kännu Kukk: 71 Vilde tee, in the district of Mustamäe, Tel: 52 32 43; open daily from noon to 5 pm and from 7 pm to midnight. This restaurant is especially popular with Finnish tourists. Seats 176 and has a banquet hall which can seat up to 90 guests, a café which seats 35 and a pancake bar seating 36.

– Kevad: Lomonossovi 2, open daily except Sundays from noon to 4 pm and from 7:30 pm to midnight. Located in the Tallinn department store; seats 130.

– Kolde: Ehte 2, Tel: 49 21 60. Seats 100 with two banquet halls and a dance band; open daily from noon to 5 pm and from 7 pm to midnight.

– Nord: 3/5 Rataskaevu, Tel: 44 46 95, 44 85 91; five dining rooms over a number of levels; hunting room, fish restaurant, fondue room, bar and grill, and the "Foxhole" bar in the cellar.

– Pirita: 5 Merivälje tee, Tel: 23 81 02; open daily from noon to 5 pm and from 7 pm to midnight. Beach restaurant near the sea with a beautiful view of the Bay of Tallinn. Seats 200; 40 at the bar, dance band. Slow service, cool to cold food in autumn and winter. Tip: check the bill carefully...

– Rae: 1 Roosikrantsi, Tel: 66 60 78; open weekdays from 7 pm to midnight; Saturdays and Sundays from 1 to 5 pm and from 7 pm to midnight.

– Raekook: 5 Dunkri, Tel: 44 35 40; open daily from noon to 5 pm and from 6 pm to midnight.

– Rataskaevu: 7 Rataskaevu, Tel: 44 10 89; open daily from 6 to 11 pm. Cozy inn-style restaurant in the old city. Seats 64.

– Reeder: 33 Vene, Tel: 44 65 18; open daily from noon to midnight. Even more popular after the completion of renovations. Seats 36 and 30 at the bar.

– Vana Saku: 555 Pärnu maantee, Tel: 55 65 66; open daily from 5 pm to midnight; located at the "Peoleo" Motel.

– Vana Toomas: 8 Raekoja plats, Tel: 44 58 18; open daily from noon to 5 pm and from 7 pm to midnight; Fridays and Saturdays from 7 pm to 1 am. A restaurant on the city hall square located in the cellar service Estonian cuisine; dance band during the weekend. Seats 100.

Speciality Restaurants

– Kalinka: 69 Kopli puiestee, Tel: 47 81 66; open daily from noon to 6 pm and from 7 pm to midnight. Russian cuisine; can only be recommended for lunch, evenings can become dangerous. Dance band; seats 120.

– Maharaja: 13 Raekoja plats, Tel: 43 76 03; open Monday to Thursday from noon to 4 pm and from 5 pm to midnight, Friday to Sunday from noon to 5 pm and from 6 pm to midnight. First opened in 1990, excellent Indian cuisine in the historical cellar. Payment is accepted only in hard currencies; seats 50.

– Szolnok: 101 Vilde tee, in the city district of Mustamäe, Tel: 53 22 53; open daily from noon to 5 pm and 7 pm to midnight. This restaurant was named after Tallinn's partner city in Hungary and serves Hungarian cuisine.

Night Life

Bars

– Arabella: Dunkri 3. For the younger crowd, open from 8 am to 8 pm, serving only non-alcoholic beverages.

– Karolina: Komandandi tee 3, open 11 am to 6 pm and 7 pm to midnight. Spiced wine for the connoisseur.

– Karikabaar: 3 Kuninga, Tel: 44 17 80; open daily from 11 am to 6 pm and 7 pm to midnight. Located in a medieval cellar in the middle of the old city.

– Kliff: a beer hall on board the "Salme" near the Kadriorg Park.

– Kuller: Piiskopi 1, on the Cathedral Hill. Fresh draught beer served on the small terrace or in the crowded pub.

– Kuningaaiabaar: between Neitsitorn and Lühike Jalg.

– Mündibaar: 3 Mündi, Tel: 44 67 41; open daily from noon to 7 pm and from 8 pm to midnight. The first bar in Tallinn which has really earned the right to be called a bar, and fittingly popular.

– Regatt: Pirita, 1 Merivälja tee, Tel: 23 83 59; open daily from 7 pm to midnight. Young people, live music and dancing.

– Sinine Bar: Pirita tee 28, open daily

from 11:45 am to 11:30 pm. A quiet bar with videos.

– Sky-Bar and Casino: located in the Palace Hotel, 3 Vabaduse väljak, Tel: 44 34 61; open daily from 9 pm to 3 am.

Cabaret

– Gloria: 2 Müürivahe, Tel: 44 69 50.

– Night-Club, in the cellar of Hotel Viru. Admission: 20 Kroons. Live show lasts until midnight, dancing until 4 am.

Discotheques

– Lucky Luke's: 20 Merepuiestee (on the sea side of the Linnahall); open daily from 1 pm to 3 am; country, disco and occasionally live music.

– Partarei: 20 Merepuiestee (small hall in the Linnahall); open Friday to Sunday from 11 pm to 4 am.

– Laplaya: 5 Merivälja tee (beach hall Pirita), open Friday to Sunday from 9 pm to 2 am.

– Mängude Maja: 124 Vilde tee, in the district of Mustamäe, open Wednesdays and Sundays from 8 pm.

– Raudteelasta Klubi: 60 Telliskivi, open Wednesdays and Friday to Sunday from 8 pm. Predominantly Russian clientele.

– Ehitajate Klubi: 8 Endla, Friday to Sunday from 7 pm; Russian clientele.

– Restoran "Gloria": 2 Müürivahe; dance evenings once a month.

Accommodation

Hotels

– Palace: 3 Vabaduse väljak, Tel: 44 34 61. International four-star hotel on the main square of Tallinn, 45 single rooms, 41 double rooms and 5 suites. Car rental, tennis courts.

– Viru: 4 Viru väljak, Tel: 65 20 93. 22 storey, modern hotel.

– Olümpia: 33 Liivalaia, Tel: 60 24 38. 26 storeys high, fantastic view of the old city.

– Rataskaevu: Rataskaevu 7, Tel: 44 19 39. Renovated quaint hotel in the old city with a large number of VIP and governmental guests

– Kelluka: Kelluka tee 11, Tel: 23 88 11. Small, well-managed hotel in a residential district; bar and restaurant.

– Sport: 1 Regati, Tel: 23 85 98. Three-storey building in the Olympic yachting centre of Pirita. Those who can get past the bright green reception area which is sooner like a counter at the airport, will find the least expensive rooms in Tallinn – single rooms are priced at 405 Kroons and double rooms cost 560 Kroons including a breakfast buffet. One should only consider seeking other accommodation if it is raining: rain can drip through the gaps in the concrete slabs. Patrolled parking area; a Neste service station is located behind the hotel.

– Tallinn: 27 Toompuiestee, Tel: 60 43 32. Four storeys.

– Kungla: 23 Kreuzwaldi, Tel: 42 14 60. The seven-storey tourist hotel in the centre of the city is still strictly under Soviet management and should therefore only be used as a last resort.

Smaller Hotels and Guest Houses

– Kullervo: 27/29 Tedre, Tel: 55 64 18; Fax: 49 50 62. Eleven rooms with 24 beds.

– Silva: 14 Laulu, Tel: 51 49 90. Eight

rooms, two luxury rooms, sauna, swimming pool, fireplace and car rental.

– EMI Hotel: J. Sütiste tee 21.
– Kajakas: Pärnu maantee 123.
– Kopli: Kopli 2c.
– Mihkli: Endla 23, Tel: 45 37 04.
– Narva: Soo 46.
– Neptun: Asunduse 15.
– Ookean: Paljassaare tee 39.
– Ranna: P. Tsaikovsky 11.

Motels

– Kernu: 40 kilometres (25 miles) south of the city on the motorway to Pärnu; built in 1991. Tel: 77 16 30, Fax: 21 49 41.

– Peoleo: 55 Pärnu maantee, Tel: 55 65 66. Brand new motel with two restaurants, a souvenir shop and a hair salon.

Transport

Automobile Repair
"Autoteenindus": 232 Pärnu maantee.
VAZ-Centre: 72a Kadaka puiestee.
No spare parts are available for foreign models!

Car Rental
Finest Auto: 22 Pärnu maantee, Tel: 66 67 19.
Hertz Rent-a-Car: Tel: 42 10 03. Volvo 240.
Ideal: Tallinn Airport, International Terminal, open daily from 9 am to 5 pm, Tel: 21 92 22, Fax: 21 27 35. Volvo, Toyota, Samara.
Mercedes-Benz AG: Tel: 60 62 05. Mercedes, Volvo, Wolga and RAF.
Palace Hotel: 3 Vabaduse väljak, Tel: 44 34 61. Mercedes, Peugeot, Chevrolet, Tschaika and Wolga.

Refit Ltd.: 20 Magasini, Tel: 66 10 64; Fax: 44 85 25. Least expensive car rental in the city (Toyota Corolla).

Patrolled Parking Areas (day and night)
Mere pst. 20; Liivalaia 38a; Regati pst. 1; Sole 29; Narva maantee 130; Oismäe tee 112; M. Harma 6; A. H. Tammsaare tee 93a and 133; Linnu tee 64; Pärnu maantee 100; E. Vilde tee 75; Tartu maantee 105.

Parking Areas (open during the day; subject to a fee)
Viru tn.; Nunne tn.; Viru väljak; Vabaduse väljak.

Fuel
Union Service Stations (credit cards or hard currencies):
Pärnu maantee 141, Tel: 52 92 00, 24-hour service: 95E (lead-free), 99 octane, diesel, lead-free, car wash.
Pirita Yacht Harbour: Regati puiestee, Tel: 23 84 04, open daily from 10 am to 6 pm, 99 octane, boat diesel, 76 octane.
Pääsküla: 552 Pärnu maantee, Tel: 51 90 67, 24-hour service: A-99.
Auto Pesula: service station with a car wash: Rocca al Mare on the road to Paldiski, open 6 am to 11 pm.

Traffic Police
Tallinna Liikluspolitsei, Lastekodu 31, Tel: 44 54 50.

Train
Baltic Train Station (Balti jaam): Toompuiestee 39. A sober new building has replaced the old Tudor train station which was destroyed in the war. One unique characteristic has remained: every morning a steam locomotive has been put into service to provide the train station laundry with

steam – and this, forty years running.

Boats

Passenger trips (Reisisadam): Sadama 25.

Buses

Cross-country bus terminal (Maalinide autobussijaam): Lastekodu 46.

Airport (Lennujaam)

Tallinn's airport lies in the southeastern regions of the city, fifteen minutes from the centre of the city by car. There is no special airport bus line; only Bus 22 goes to the airport via the train station, the Tallinn Hotel, Vabaduse väljak, the Estonia Theatre and the Kaubamaja department store. Tickets should be purchased in advance at the ticket sales counters and then validated when in the bus. Those who ride the bus without a valid ticket are subject to a fine of ten Rubles. The airport was built in 1980 for the Olympics and first equipped with an international terminal in 1989 when service began between Tallinn and Stockholm.

Airline Information Offices:

SAS, Tel: 21 25 53.

Estonian Airlines, Vabaduse väljak, Tel: 44 63 82.

Finnair, Tel: 42 35 38.

Travel Agencies

"Raeturist," Matkamaja, Raekoja plats 18, Tel: 44 43 33.

Estonian Tours, Roosikrantsi 4b, Tel: 44 20 34.

Tallinn Excursions Office (tours of the city), Adamsoni 2, Tel: 44 28 12.

Baltic Tours, Laikma 45, Tel: 43 06 63.

Estonian Holidays, Viru 4, Tel: 42 14 45.

Esktravel, Pikk 37, Tel: 44 48 86.

Sputnik Travel Bureau, Mundi 2, third floor, Tel: 44 05 00.

Tallinn Travel Bureau, A. Adamsoni 2, Tel: 44 46 24.

Municipal Transport

Tram

1 Kopli	– Kadriorg
2 Kopli	– Ülemiste
3 Tondi	– Kadriorg
4 Tondi	– Ülemiste

Trolleybus

1 Mustamäe	– Kaubamaja
2 Mustamäe	– Estonia
3 Mustamäe	– Kaubamaja
4 Keskuse	– Balti jaam
5 Mustamäe	– Balti jaam
6 Väike-Oismäe	– Kaubamaja
7 Väike-Oismäe	– Balti jaam
8 Väike-Oismäe	– Vabaduse väljak
9 Keskuse	– Kopli

Bus

Municipal Bus Station (Linnalähilinide autobussijaam): Balti jaam

1 "Baltika"	– Merivälja
2 Väike-Oismäe	– Nomme
3 "Baltika	– Pelgurand
4 Balti jaam	– Mähe tee
5 Männiku	– Kose
6 Kallavere	– Kunstiülikool
7 Seli	– "Polümeer"
8 Balti jaam	– Mähe aedlinn
9 Express Bus:	
Kadaka	– Teenindusmaja
10 Väike-Oismäe	– Vana Pässküla
11 Express Bus:	
J. Sütiste tee	– Kaubamaja
12 Express Bus:	
Viru väljak	– Mähe tee

13 Kallavere	– Tallinna Uusa-dam		49 P. Pinna	– Pirita
			50 Seli	– Pae
14 Express Bus:			51 Priisle	– Teenindusmaja
Viru väljak	– J. V. Jannseni		52	– not in service
15 "Baltika	– Sojamäe		53 Express Bus:	
16 Väike-Oismäe	– Tallinn-Väike		Priisle	– Teenindusmaja
17 J. Sütiste tee	– "Polümeer"		54 Express Bus:	
17A J. Sütiste tee	– Autobussijaam		Kallavere	– Kunstülikool
18 Viru väljak	– Laagri		55 P. Pinna	– Pae
19 P. Pinna	– Kauplus "Tallinn"		56 Express Bus:	
20	– not in service		Seli	– Kauplus "Tallinn"
21 Balti jaam	– Kakumäe tee		57 Viru väljak	– Raudalu
22 Balti jaam	– Lennujaam		58 Priisle	– Pae
23 Kadaka	– Juhkental		59 Balti jaam	– Paljassaare
24 Balti jaam	– Oomi		60 Priisle	– Maneezi
25 Express Bus:			61 Väike-Oismäe	– Harku-Kadaka
Viru väljak	– Muuga aedlinn		62 P. Pinna	– Lennujaam
26 Väike-Oismäe	– Paljassaare		63 Priisle	– Maneezi
27 Laagri alevik	– Harkujarve		64 Väike-Oismäe	– Pääsküla
28 "Baltika	– Haabersti			
29 Viru väljak	– Iru Internaat-kodu-Kärmu		Taxi Buses	
			1 Viru väljak	– Merivalja
30 Teenindusmaja–	Lauluväljak		2 Viru väljak	– Tahertorni
31 Express Bus:			3 Viru väljak	– Pääsküla
P. Pinna	– Teenindusmaja		4 Viru väljak	– Pääsküla
32 Männiku	– Kopli		5 Viru väljak	– Mustamäe
33 Männiku	– Kopli		6 Viru väljak	– Kopli
34 Viru väljak	– Muuga aedlinn		7 Viru väljak	– Nomme
35 Seli	– Kauplus "Tallinn"		8 Viru väljak	– Laagri
36 Kadaka	– Viru		9 Viru väljak	– Kose
37 Kallavere	– Maardu		10 Viru väljak	– Väike-Oiesmäe
38 Viru väljak	– Muuga		11 Viru väljak	– Manniku
39 "Baltika	– Lasnamägi		12 Viru väljak	– Seli
40 Viru väljak	– Pelgurand			
41	– not in service			
42 Kallavere	– Petrooleumi		Taxis	
43	– not in service			
44 P. Pinna	– Teenindusmaja			
45 Viru väljak	– Kakumäe			
46 Väike-Oismäe	– Vabaduse väljak			
47 Väike-Oismäe	– "Polümeer"			
48 Express Bus:				
Viru väljak	– Pelgurand			

Taxis

Tallinna Taksopark, Tel: 60 30 44; Kooperativa "Esra," Tel: 43 03 30. Official taxis are required to have the appropriate sign on the roof of the car as well as taxometers inside. As a safety precaution, one should not use the other, probable less expensive taxis. There are taxi stands in the centre of the city on Vabaduse and Viru väljak. Outside the city limits, taxis charge twice the normal fare

Information

Emergency

Emergency Hospital: 19 Sütiste tee. Accident centre: 10 Sütiste tee and 18 Ravi.

Pharmacies

Raeapteek: 47 Pikk. One of the oldest pharmacies in Europe, established in 1422. Open Monday 11 am to 6 pm, Tuesday to Friday 9 am to 8 pm, Saturday and Sunday 9 am to 3 pm.

Apteek No. 1: 5 Tönismägi. Open Monday to Friday from 8 am to 9 pm, night service, closed during the weekend.

Apteek No. 2: 10 Pärnu maantee. Open Monday to Friday from 8 am to 8 pm, Saturday from 9 am to 5 pm. No night service.

Vanaturu Apteek: 1 Vene. Open Monday to Friday from 9 am to 7 pm, Saturday from 9 am to 4 pm, no night service.

Apteek No. 205: 7 Rävala puiestee, Monday to Frideay from 8 am to 8 pm, Saturday from 9 am to 4 pm.

Post Office

Main Post Office: 1 Narva maantee, first floor. Open Monday to Saturday from 8 am to 8 pm. Postal Information Service, Tel: 44 19 09. General Delivery letters and parcel can be picked up from 9 am to 8 pm at this address.

Telex/Telefax/International Calls

Main Post Office, counters 43 and 44, open Monday to Saturday from 8 am to 8 pm, Tel: 44 23 47 and 44 18 03. International calls within Europe as well as overseas can be placed directly at the "Palace Hotel"; otherwise these can be ordered in advance by calling Tel: 0 07. Urgent calls are placed as "Kirikone" (express calls) within the hour; these are charged at twice the normal rate.

Telephone Information Tallinn: Public Facilities and Offices: Tel: 09; private numbers: Tel: 0 65.

Toilets

Usable facilities, but only in the utmost emergencies are (N = Women, M = Men): Valli Street: 50 Senti fee, but does have a diaper changing table behind a curtain. 5 Dunkri; 1 Maneezi; Kaubamaja department store, building B, first floor; Kadriorg Park near Russalka. Another option is to head for the nearest first-class hotel.

Tourist Information

Information Office on Raekoja plats, Tel: 66 69 50, open weekdays from 9 am to 5 pm and also during the weekends in summer from 10 am to 4 pm.

Estonian Tourist Information Office, Suurkaja 23, 200001 Tallinn, Tel: 44 12 39; Fax: 44 09 63.

Intourist Tallinn, 4 Viru väljak, 200001 Tallinn, Tel: 65 07 70; Fax: 44 04 16.

Estonia's Island Country

According to an advertising brochure (information varies), Estonia has 1,500 islands which can be subdivided into three groups: the *Gulf of Finland islands* (from the eastern border to Osmusaar in the west), the *the islands in the Gulf of Riga and Bay of Livonia* (between Pärnu and Kuremaa), and the large *Väinmere island group,* also called the Moonsundi Archipelago, in the strait between the mainland and the large islands. The diverse world of the western Estonian islands was place under governmental protection immediately after independence was declared. The biospheric reserve "West Estonian Islands" comprises 1,560,000 hectares (3.9 million acres). Linguistically, the islands are also exactingly subdivided. "Saar" is the term for the larger, inhabited islands; in contrast, "Laid," "Kari" or "Rahu" are small, unwooded islands.

Abruka (Abro)

A ferry chugs over to Abruka from Kuressaare harbour of Roomassaare on the island of Saaremaa. The island is covered with a deciduous forest more typical of central Europe than of Estonia. This dendrological peculiarity prompted *Theodor Lippmaa* (1892-1943) to begin research on this phenomenon. The secluded, frugal life of the island's residents was documented by the author *Jüri Tuulik* who was born on this island, in his narratives.

Aegna (Wulf)

The popular excursion destination for Tallinn residents has a very beautiful landscape and lies off the point of the Viimsi Peninsula near Tallinn. Ferries depart from the fishing village of Viimsi to this island, which is now planned to be touristically developed.

Hiiumaa (Dagö)

With 1,023 square kilometres (399 square miles) of land area and a population of 11,540, Hiiumaa is only one-third the size of Saaremaa, but is still the second largest island of Estonia. The predominantly flat island is mostly covered by forests in the northern regions and to the south, fields and swamps provide some diversity in the landscape. "Insula deserta" – deserted island – is how old writings referred to Hiiumaa during the 18th century. Today, people still settle predominantly in the coastal regions. The island's interior with its swamps and forests is almost completely uninhabited. The main town on the island is **Kärdla** and is located on the northern coast; **Käina** in the south. The Väinameri Strait separates the island from the mainland.

Travelling to Hiiumaa: There is a ferry from Heltermaa to Rohuküla; the trip lasts 90 minutes.

The flight from Tallinn to Hiiumaa lasts half an hour. Earlier the crossing took an entire day. Thus, the Swedes called this island "Day Island."

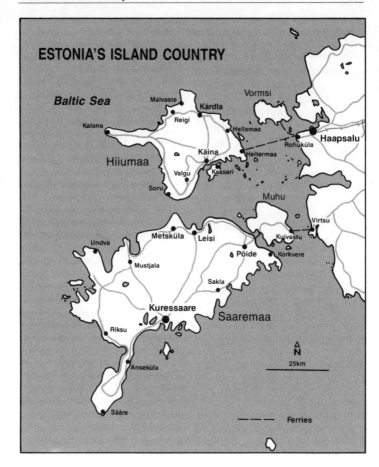

Heltermaa / Suuremoisa

Passports are checked in the ferry harbour of Hiiumaa: at the gate, Russians and other "undesirables" are sent back by the police outpost. Directly beyond this, a bronze statue of a woman with windswept hair sitting on a rock welcomes the visitors. Six kilometres (4 miles) farther to the west is *Suuremoisa Castle*. A beautiful walk lined with black alders leads up to the late baroque landowner's

Pre-Christian Symbol of Atonement or Hiding Place for Gold?

North of the Chapel of Suuremoisa is a mysterious pile of stones on a square plot of land. This is most likely a *stone grave* which is around three metres (10 feet) high, composed of stacked granite blocks with a diameter of 16 metres (52 feet). However, the legends interpret this pile of stones as a pre-Christian symbol of atonement, an Estonian pyramid, the grave pile of a king or even a hiding place for golden treasures...

castle, built in 1772. Today children romp in the 64 rooms all laid out symmetrically. One peculiarity has remained to date: the double ceiling. The area between the two ceilings can be reached through a secret door in the closet and often served as a hiding place for the landowners. The estate's domestic buildings, most of which are dilapidated, are presently being rebuilt from the foundation up. The extensive castle gardens has meanwhile become very "close to nature." The old tree-lined walk, now bisected by a road, connected the estate with the nearby *church* in earlier times. The church from the 13th century has a stone pulpit from the 17th century. Buried in the adjacent *chapel,* is Ebba Margarethe Stenbock, once the sole ruler on Hiiumaa. *Information:* Hiiumaa Harbour, Tel: 9 42 12.

Käina (Keinis)

The main southern town on Hiiumaa is Käina, renowned as the birthplace of the Estonian composer Rudolf Tobias. In his home (Tel: 9 26 20) is a small *memorial museum* in honour of the man who composed the first national oratorio "The Mission of Jonah." From 1912 to 1918, Tobias taught at the Music Academy in Berlin. Through coupling old traditions with modern movements, he had a significant influence on the Nordic art nouveau in music – an aspect which is also documented in the museum. The *church,* built around 1500 at the beginning of town, was once the bishopric of Ösel-Wiek and now stands in ruins because of a bomb dropped during the Second World War. The organ, built by Rudolf Tobias was also destroyed at that time.

Surroundings

Kassari: Two earthen dikes lead off to the east and to the west from Käina over to Kassari – a trip that one should by no means forgo (→ *Islands/Kassari*). Between these two islands surrounded by extensive reeded marshes is the bird sanctuary of Käina Laht, the Bay of Käina.

Kärdla

With a population of 4,200, the only city on the island – awarded this status in 1938 – has more the profile of a garden town: the Nuutri River and its tributaries flow directly through Kärdla. The Artesian wells are another "natural" attraction of this city on the northern coast, a settlement that was first mentioned in 1564 as a Swedish village. The establishment of a textile mill by the Ungern-Sternberg brothers brought industry to the idyllic rural town in 1829. In 1845, the textile magnates, who were reputed all the way to St. Petersburg and Moscow, employed over 500 workers. A harbour was constructed so that the fabrics could be exported to various countries. In 1941, the factory was destroyed in the war. The former location is still a vacant lot today and the remaining fishermen work at the harbour.

The most lively area in Kärdla is around the *Keskväljak*. This oblong square is dominated by the *church* built from 1861 to 1863 with an organ from 1904. In the centre of the square, an impressive wooden signpost provides information on the distance to the sights in the city and on the island. All located on this square with are the bus stop, fire department, a furniture store and "Voorastemaja," a simple inn. The department store with an adjacent restaurant is only a few steps away. The *Cultural Park* begins next to the *church*. The concert hall has been used for song festivals, theatre performances and concerts since 1926. Also worth seeing is the *Paul Tamm Residence and Museum* (Tiigi 40, Tel: 9 14 41). The *beach* is more or less modest and begins to the west of the harbour: more gravel than sand, the numerous rock fragments in the shallow water make swimming a less enjoyable experience.

Surroundings

A short trip to the south is worthwhile to see the *meteorite crater* with a diameter of four metres (13 feet), which dates back 400 million years when a meteorite plummeted into the sea. Now people began drilling for mineral water in the centre of the crater – since then, "Kärdla Water" has been produced here.

Not far from the main road to Heltermaa, one-half kilometre (one-third mile) north of Palade is the *Soera Talumuuseum*. The farmhouse museum can only be toured officially during the summer but is worth a visit at any time during the year. The oblong wooden cabin squats under the thick thatched roof which covers the living area and stalls. The fence composed of diagonal branches is just as typical for old Hiiumaa as the moss-covered erratic blocks in the grass.

Information

Accommodation: Kärdla Hotel, Vabaduse 13, Tel: 9 14 81.
Airport: Tel: 9 12 17.
Automobile Repair/Service Stations: Korgessaare maantee 47, Tel: 9 13 59.
Café-Bar: Kärdla-Baar, Kalevipoja Street, Tel: 9 15 50; Rannapargu, Lubjaahju Street, Tel: 9 12 87.
Cultural Centre: Voidu 22.
Hospital: Rahu 2, Tel: 9 14 49.
Post Office: Posti 7.
Restaurant: Kärdla Restoran, Vabriku väljak, Tel: 9 15 62.
Travel Agency: Dagö, Vabriku väljak 1, Tel: 9 12 41.

Kopu

The peninsula in Hiiumaa's western regions protrudes 21 kilometres (13 miles) into the sea. For the most part uninhabited, the peninsula is almost completely wooded with the exception of the 10 square kilometre (4 square mile) sand dune belt of the Korbi Mountains in the southwestern region. The highest elevations are the Andrusmägi (54 metres/177 feet) and the Tornimägi (Tower Mountain) (68 metres/222 feet) with its famous *Kopu Lighthouse (Tuletorn)*. The lighthouse here has been in operation atop this mountain since 1480 warning seafarers of the Hiiumadal (Nackmensgrund), a sandbank which suddenly rises out of the Baltic Sea. The first lighthouse, a stone structure from the 16th century was just 20 metres (65 feet) tall. Earlier, the wood burned for the beacon was hoisted up to the top of the tower by pulley. When the structure was built up to its present day height of 37 metres (121 feet), a staircase with 130 steps was built in the lighthouse. Over 100 metres above sea level together with the height of the mountain on which it stands, the beacon can be seen at a radius of 48 kilometres (30 miles) or 26 nautical miles, well before the treacherous sand bank.

A gravel road leads out to the tip of the peninsula. A pier, a lighthouse, a house, a merchant and some pine trees – in Kalana one feels sequestered from the world.

Korgessaare (Hohenholm)

The craggy coastline near Korgessaare with its underwater reefs and shoals was the doom of many a ship. The reason for this was the "false lighthouse" of the feared Count Ludwig von Ungern-Sternberg.

Surroundings

A beautiful natural beach with fine sand extends along the *Luidja Laht* in the southwestern regions of Korgessaare. This beach, in parts quite heavily overgrown, is now concealed by a relatively flat belt of sand dunes. It is only a few yards to the beach from the parking area on the main road near the merchant's.

Reigi

Now the smallest village on the western coast, first mentioned in historical documents in 1470, Reigi was once the cultural centre of Hiiumaa. The ruins of a tavern are reminiscent of the days when the village was bordered by the Baltic Sea: the fishermen could sail directly up to the bar. Richly embellished wooden gates open to the *church* and the adjacent cemetery. The whitewashed church with a weather vane from 1801 displays Count von Ungern-Sternberg's coat of arms on its tower portal. Within the wrought-iron fence are graves of some members of this legendary family: Eduard (1782-1861), James Archibald (1811-1842) and Otto-Dietrich, who died in 1799.

Takhuna (Tachkona)

The peninsula in the northern regions of Hiiumaa was the object of several battles. The remaining ruins of fortifications were built before the First World War. A lighthouse marks the outermost point of the peninsula: manufactured from cast iron in Paris, the 43-metre (140-foot) tall tower was erected here in 1875. Its beacon has a radius of 18 nautical miles. At the beginning of the peninsula is the *Mihkli Farm.* The oldest buildings date back to the 18th century. When the Swedes were resettled in the Ukraine, the Estonians moved to this farm – in this way, the farm united the farming traditions of both peoples. The Mihkli farm museum also possesses one of the last smoke saunas of Hiiumaa.

Near **Malvaste,** a small village composed of a cluster of wooden houses, is the only *camping area* on the island of Hiiumaa.

The False Lighthouse

Count von Ungern-Sternberg was the demise of numerous seafarers who ran aground having fallen victim to the Count's false lighthouse. In the evening the despot placed a beacon in a rock near Korgessaare on Hiiumaa which shone through the forest glade to the open sea – signalling the way to disaster. According to old law, the wreckage and cargo of the ships that were stranded or ran aground on the reef became the property of the landowner. No one was ever able to prove that these beacons were the work of the count. Still, justice was finally served: after many "successful" years, the count was banned to Siberia for murdering a captain whose ship had run aground.

Kassari

Those who are a little disappointed with Hiiumaa will be enthusiastic about Kassari: on only 19 square kilometres (7½ square miles), this island offers a unparalleled diversity of landscapes and culture. Two land bridges surrounded by reeded swamp areas lead over to the island of Kassari. Simultaneously, these form the borders of the *Käina Laht,* the bird sanctuary in the bay. Extending out from the western of the two land bridges is the *Orjaku Säär,* a promontory and the beginning of a chain of hills which extends over the entire island. Juniper hedges line the streets on the island, apple plantations, potato and rape-seed fields are interspersed with meadows, forests and solitary pine trees on gravel banks. The island's small yacht harbour with its wharf lies in the western regions near **Orjaku.**

Worth seeing in the village of **Kassari** is the Museum of Local History *Kassari Koduloomuuseum,* housed under the red roof of a whitewashed residential house (Tel: 9 71 21, open from 11 am to 5 pm). Nearby, a gravel road leads off from the main road to the

Aino Kallas Suvemaja. This was the summer cottage of the Estonian-Finnish author Aino Kallas, who spent the summers here from 1924 to 1938. It is concealed within trees and shrubs in a wonderful landscape of junipers. Two kilometres (1¼ miles) farther, the *Kassari Kabel* will give visitors an impression of how the people lived on this island in earlier days: the farmhouse with its thatched roof built of stacked stone slabs found locally, was plastered yellowish-gold around the entryway. Also in the village of Kassari, a two-kilometre (1¼ mile) long side-street leads past the ruins of a post windmill to *Sääre Tirp.* This natural monument was formerly blocked off to visitors and portions of it are more similar to a park. Extending against the background of the bay and the scattered islands is a landscape which holds an attraction all its own: green solitary pine trees on grey gravel.

Keri

The island Keri Saar is a mere 0.05 square kilometres (0.02 square miles) in area and is located north of Prangli on the periphery of the main shipping route. For this reason, a lighthouse was built on the island of Keri as early as 1719 and the beacon was fuelled with natural gas from under the surface of the island up to the beginning of the 20th century.

Kihnu

Pine forests and fields are the main characteristics of this, the largest island in the Gulf of Riga. Kihnu is accessible by ferry from Pärnu in four hours; by air, the flight lasts half an hour. Due to the limited contact with the outside world, old customs and traditions are better preserved on this island which has been inhabited since the Middle Ages. It is more common to find the traditional costumes here than on the mainland. A famous local celebrity was "Kihnu Jonn." This sea captain sailed all of the seven seas with his ship. The only *restaurant* on the island now bears the name of his last ship: "Rock City." While *Juhan Smuul* recorded the adventures of Enn Uuetoa (Jonn's real name) in the form of a novel, *Mark Soosar* captured the present-day men of Kihnu on film: this Estonian documentary producer filmed "Kihnu mees – The Men of Kihnu" here in 1968. The *Kihnu Muuseum* provides information on the history of this seven-kilometre (4¼ mile) long island whose four villages once belonged to the Bishop of Saare-Lääne.

Manilaid

A mere 30 people live on the island of Manilaid where electricity was only installed a few years ago. There is a boat connection to Manilaid from the harbour near the village of Liu south of Pärnu.

Muhu (Moon)

Wild romanticism distinguishes the island of Muhu, the third largest Estonian island with an area of 198 square kilometres (77 square miles). The rocky island, the landscape of which is characterized by juniper forests and dwarf pines, is accessible by two automobile ferries departing from Virtsu. The trip lasts around 30 minutes. Ferry tickets are not available on board, they must be purchased in advance in the ferry building. Passports are checked upon arrival in Muhu's harbour Kuivastu: it is rumoured that Russians are sent back. Muhu's population is almost completely Estonian.

An asphalt road leads via Hellamaa to the 3 kilometre (2 mile) land bridge which has connected Muhu with Saaremaa since the 19th century. All other roads on the island are wide gravel roads. The highest hill on the island is near Paelda: the Sepa "mountain" reaches an elevation of 25 metres (82 feet). The Ekumägi Mountain near Igaküla, bordered by a coastal wall made from erratic blocks, reaches the lofty altitude of 21 metres (69 feet). The island, formerly subdivided into six estates, had a population of 6,000 at that time, including a large number of free farmers. Their traditional costume was so widely known that it was commonly considered the national costume of all of Estonia. The most beautiful of these articles of clothing are displayed in the annex of the *Koguva Village Museum*.

Island Tours

I. Northern Route

An asphalt roadway leads from **Kuivastu** (Kuiwast) to Hellamaa. From there, turn right onto the gravel road to **Oetmetsa**. Continue via **Raugi** to **Kalaste.** At the signpost for "Üügu Pank," turn right onto the sand road and continue to the parking area and rest stop after one kilometre (½ mile).

The sea has washed out two caves – "Kitsekamber" and "Sokutuba" – in the recessed coastal cliffs. The marshy headlands with countless small streams is a veritable cornucopia for botanists; orchids and rare plants bloom here in abundance. The narrow beach is a combination of sand and gravel; small boulders in the water line the coast.

Continuing via **Nommküla** to **Riutsi,** and several hundred yards further is a turn-off to **Päelda** - located near **Sepa Mountain,** Muhu's highest hill (25 metres/82 feet). Continue farther toward **Viiri** on the main route heading to Saaremaa via **Igaküla** to **Koguva.** Keeping traditional Estonia alive, the picturesque village with the typical stone walls, its humble fishing huts and the blossoming gardens was first mentioned in historical documents in 1532. All 105 buildings in this village are classified as historical monuments "in tribute to the free farmers." The *Family House of the National Author Juhan Smuul* has been a memorial site since 1973; the *Tooma Farm* is now a farming museum. Smuul, born here in 1921, lived in Koguva until 1940 and in Tallinn up to his death in 1972. His stark work room with a bed and a small wooden desk in which Smuul authored the famous work "Kihnu Jonn" (The Wild Captain) among others, has remained unchanged. The residential house from the 19th century with a chimney from 1895 houses an interesting exhibition on the island's history. In the adjoining building are costumes and textiles from Muhu. In addition, the well and the bakehouse on the grounds are also worth seeing. The post windmill on the edge of the village near the parking area is built on a boulder as its base. The wooden mill housing and typical mill sails have remained completely intact.

Koguva Village Museum. open daily from 10 am to 6 pm, Tel: 9 86 18. There is a large parking area next to the bus stop.

Koguva was also where the free farmer Hanske's farm was located since the 16th century. From there, travellers and the mail were safely transported over the small channel (Väike Väin) to Saaremaa. It was only in the 19th century that ships departed for Orissaare from Linnuse. Subsequently a land bridge was constructed providing a firm connection with the large neighbouring island. The top portions of the Muhu fortress fell victim to the pickax during the construction of this land bridge. 400 cubic spans of stone were used in the construction of this land bridge. The land bridge is currently being widened. At the beginning of the land bridge is a post windmill with a souvenir stand and a comical sign for a bar. Small islands of reeds protrude from the calm tides to the right and left of the land bridge – numerous aquatic birds can be observed here especially during twilight.

II. Southern Route

Beyond **Kuivastu** turn left onto a gravel road to **Pädaste** (Pädast). In Pädaste is the former *Castle* of the Buxhoeveden family. The castle grounds include some rare trees. Returning to the main route via Mähla, continue to **Liiva,** located at the centre of the island which is the location of the *Church of Muhu.* Built in the 13th century as a one-naved church, it was reconstructed a number of times during the subsequent centuries. Several of the murals depict ships. *Carl Wilhelm Freundlich* was also active here from 1825 to 1872 as a sexton.

Naissar (Nargen)

This island with an area of 17.9 square kilometres (7 square miles) was mentioned in historical documents as "terra feminarum" (meaning woman's land) as early as the 11th century. Naissar is the largest island in the Gulf of Finland and only a few nautical miles from the capital of Tallinn. Civilians have no access to this island because it is still in the possession of the Soviet military. When the troops have withdrawn, it is planned to develop this island with a lighthouse dating back to 1489 into a recreational area for Tallinn's residents. *Bernhard Schmidt* invented a new telescope system here, where in addition to the soldiers, only a few fishermen and farmers are allowed to live today.

Osmussar

This island was named after an animal: a type of marten called "Osmu" (meaning wolverine). Earlier, the coastal Swedes settled on this small island located ten kilometres (6¼ miles) from the Poosasepa Peninsula in the western portion of the Gulf of Finland. Today, it is inhabited only by a handful of fishermen.

The northern coastline comprises a small sea cliff, on the southern coast a lime-sandstone surface gradually falls off into the sea. Numerous erratic blocks can be found scattered around the island's interior.

Prangli (Wrangelsholm)

This sandy and stony island, measuring 6.2 square kilometres (2½ square miles) in area, is still a military zone. Around 200 residents live in the three fishing villages all with a school, a church and a cultural centre. The beach is just as flat and stony as the island itself. Two lighthouses stand at the northern and southern tips of this island with its small archipelagos of ten smaller islands surrounding it.

Ruhnu (Runö)

This small island with an area of 15 square kilometres (6 square miles) is located in the middle of the Gulf of Riga. It was home to only Swedish fishermen from 1341 to the end of the Second World War. Outsiders hardly ventured a journey to this island because of the numerous shoals and sandbars which made docking ships difficult at best. Due to the secluded location which inspired *Theodor Luts* to produce the documentary film "Ruhnu Saar" in 1931, the island was spared the numerous wars and battles in the Baltic region. Today, a more peaceful type of battle is underway: while Latvia now claims territorial rights to the island – and with Ruhnu, they would get their first and only island – Estonia refuses to give up control of the island. Estonia's most exotic island is accessible by air from Pärnu on an irregular basis.

In the island's only village located directly at the centre of the island is the oldest *wooden church* in Europe. When the first parson came to Ruhnu in 1644, he had the Magdalene Church built for the congregation. The lead glass paintings originate from the 17th century. A painting in the church's interior depicts Duke Wilhelm of Curonia. It was only in 1912 that a new stone church was built. The *Haubjerre Moor,* more similar to a lake after heavy rains, provides the island's residents with drinking water. With the exception of this area, the island is barren: the sand dunes on the beach reach a height of up to 20 metres (66 feet). In the island's interior, the dunes are mostly covered with pine forests.

Saaremaa (Oesel)

Together with the neighbouring island of Muhu and 500 additional islands, Saaremaa (Estonia's largest island) makes up an Estonian province with a land area of 2,911 square kilometres (1,135 square miles) and a population of 40,490.

The provincial capital of Kuressaare is located in the southern regions of this island with an area of 2,671 square kilometres (1,042 square miles). The highly articulated coastline offers 854 kilometres (534 miles) of sandy beaches, coastal cliffs, reeds and swamps. On the western coast near Kihelkonna is Estonia's oldest nature reserve: in Vilsandi, the extraordinary diversity of birds is under protection.

On Saaremaa which has been inhabited since the Stone Age, the main economic factor is agriculture. Large fields with one solitary tree characterize the interior of the island. Large industrial areas can be found only in Kuressaare near the harbour. Dolomite is quarried industrially for use in construction. Juniper heath and windmills are characteristic of the Sorve Peninsula. The "Saaremaa vats" (Saaremaa waltzes) by *Georg Ots* brought renowned to the island in a musical way. *Mark Soosar* filmed his documentary "Miss Saaremaa" here in 1988.

Kuressaare (Arensburg)

Kuressaare, the provincial capital of Saaremaa has a population of 17,000. It is located on the southern coast, in the coastal depression of Tori Bay. A ring of monotone and stereotypical concrete tourist bunkers and an extensive industrial area (for the production of cement, construction materials and chemicals) surround the city; they hardly are an indication of the fact that the first mud-baths brought a boom to this city as a spa and health resort. The main attraction of this town is the impressive fort of the Teutonic Order.

History

The history of this city begins with the "Eagle Fortress": first mentioned in historical documentation in 1384, a settlement developed around the bishop's fortress, the see of his bishopric Saare-Lääne/Oesel Wiek, which quickly grew in significance. Even before the entire diocese fell to Denmark as a result of the Livonian War, the last bishop, Johann von Münchhausen, sold his land to the Danish king. Friedrich II gave this land to his brother, Duke Magnus von Holstein in 1560 in feudal tenure who then awarded Hanseatic city status to Arensburg in 1563. The island came under Swedish rule from 1645 to 1710. In 1648, Queen Christine gave Arensburg to Count de la Gardie in feudal tenure. While the plague raged in Kuressaare, the Russians conquered the island in 1710 during the Great Northern War and burned the city to the ground. It is said that only eleven residents survived this attack. In 1840, a German physician opened the first therapeutic mud-baths and more were to follow in 1876 and 1883. The health resort of Kuressaare quickly gained renown and popularity – in 1858 a steamship route to Riga was opened, operating on a regular basis. The increase in tourism also brought new residents: the population grew from 1,379 in 1782 to 3,378 in 1863 and 4,483 in 1897. The city's most famous son was *Eugen Dücker,* born on January 29, 1841 in Arensburg. This landscape painter died on St. Nicholas Day in 1916 in Düsseldorf. On old maps, Kuressaare is still called Kingiseppa after a communist revolutionary.

Sights

Beyond the tall trees of the fortification wall is the stalwart *bishop's fortress* which has hardly been changed over the centuries. The square fortress was built with the locally quarried Kaarma dolomite with walls over 20 metres (65 feet) high and battlements. The construction of the convent building, completed in 1380, was begun around 1338. From 1648, the Swedes used the fort's chapel as a storehouse for grain. The Russians, who acquired the fort without resistance in 1710, continued the tradition: they also used the chapel for storing grain over a period of 100 years. Finally in 1836, the oldest fortress in Estonia was ultimately stricken from the czar's imperial list of fortresses. At 29 metres (95 feet) the five-storey "Tall Hermann" is the highest of the two defence towers. Where once prisoners were locked in the dungeon, the *Saaremaa Museum* (open Wednesday to Sunday from 11 am to 5:30 pm) now provides information on the multi-faceted history of the city and the island. Song festivals are held in the fortress' inner courtyard. A solitary cannon has stood in front of the fortress gate since 1971:

formerly 67 cannons provided for the defence of the episcopal see. The spa park extends between the fortress and Pargi Street. A place with grave markers and a commemorative plaque indicates that during the construction of the park human bones were unearthed – the remains were then laid to rest under the monument.

The old spa building from the turn of the century was rebuilt according to the original plans in 1988 after having been destroyed by fire. Today, the building houses a café and restaurant. Across the way is the concert "shell." Magnificent wooden villas from the turn of the century featuring "Victorian eclecticism and artistically forged Art Nouveau gates characterize Pargi Street. Set somewhat back from the street is the *Linnakodanik Muuseum* (City Museum) with an adjacent *Art Gallery* (Pargi 5a, open Wednesday to Sunday from 11 am to 5:30 pm). The old city centre is at Kesk väljak. While Lossi Street leads from here past the orthodox St. Nicholas Church and old houses directly up to the fortress, a number of side-streets lead off to the Turg (marketplace) at Tallinna maantee 5. Sold daily both outdoors and in historical vaults are flowers, fruits and vegetables, meat and eggs. In contrast, the shelves in the *market hall* on Turu Street, now classified as a historical monument, are completely empty – a use for this historic building has not yet been determined. The *city hall* from 1670 with the city's coat of arms above the portal, the *Cultural Centre* (No. 6) and *St. Laurentius*

Church are also on Tallinna maantee. Jean Baptiste Holzmayer found his last resting place somewhat outside of town near Kudjape in 1807. This director of the Kuressaare Academy studied the old customs of Saaremaa. The old cemetery is also the burial site of *Johann Wilhelm Ludwig von Luce*. This physician and ardent collector of plants founded the Estonian Literary Society in Kuressaare in 1817.

Surroundings

Beaches and Swimming: The best beach for swimming is located on Sutu Bay east of Kuressaare near the village of Kailuka on the Väta Peninsula. To the west, sand dunes line the beach on Loode Point to the Sorve Peninsula. The oak forest of Loode with trees over 300 years old is especially impressive because of its diversity of birds. Next to the yacht harbour of Nasva, the fish processing plant dumps untreated sewage directly into the sea.

Kaarma (Karmel): A trip to Kaarma, located 15 kilometres (9 miles) to the north is worthwhile to visit the church here. Built in 1270, a hiding place for the persecuted after the bloody uprisings of 1298 was built above the sacristy. During the 14th century the church was enlarged to accommodated pilgrims and 100 years later, the church tower was added. The dolomite quarries begin beyond the graveyard where generations of local land owners are buried. The grey stone from Kaarma was used in building the fortress of Kuressaare and for the stately palaces in Tallinn, Riga and Moscow.

Information

Accommodation

Hotel Tarsa, Kauba 10, Tel: 5 72 93. Six rooms in a villa from the 19th century.

Lossi-Hotel, Lossi 27, Tel: 5 71 42. A brown villa from the turn of the century situated in the park near the bishops' fortress. Hotel guests may ignore the "no entry" sign and park in front of the building. Simple accommodation, toilet/shower in the hall. £7 ($12.50) per person per night in a double room (hard currency required).

Hotel Panga, Tallinna 27, Tel: 5 79 89. Built in 1986, this hotel is equipped with showers on each floor.

Hotel Mardi, Vallimaa 5a, Tel: 5 74 36. Single rooms £5 ($9.50), double rooms £7 ($12.50).

Outside of the city: Hotel Männikäbi, Mändjala, Tel: 7 51 06. Eleven kilometres west of town near the coast on the road to Salme. Built in 1992, 34 beds, sauna.

Cottage Village Tagranna, 40 kilometres north of town. Built in 1991, 5 cottages each for two persons. Shower/toilet in a separate building, sauna. Tel: 5 48 75.

Airport Roomassaare: Tel: 5 57 56. Airline tickets: Tel: 5 42 61. Flights to Tallinn and Pärnu depart from this small airfield which is also used militarily.

Automobile Repair: Kalevi 2, Tel: 5 74 78.

Banks: Houidsbank, Tallinna 11; Kuressaare Bank, Tallinna 27.

Bus Station: Pihtla 25, information Tel: 5 73 80.

Café-Bars

Kuursaal, in the spa park, Kingiseppa 2.

Kuressepa, Kastani 2, Tel: 5 94 66.

Kodulinn, Tallinna 11.

Levikaabel, Niidu 11.

Cinema: Oktoober, Tallinna 6.

Fuel: Roomassare 89, Tel: 5 55 75.

Harbour Roomassaare: Tel: 5 55 74.

Pharmacy: Saaremaa Apteek, Lossihoovi corner of Raekoja plats.

Post Office: Torni 1.

Restaurants

Café/Bistros: Pinguin, Turu 1.

Grill-bar: Raekoja plats. A rustic, smoky pub offering chicken dishes.

Kuursaal: in the park, Kingiseppa 2. The interior is far more impressive than the food: this restaurant and café is housed in the central spa's leisure building which, after a fire, was restored to its original, turn-of-the-century resort architecture. Its clarity and simplicity in style with charming luxury instead of heary lustre evokes the care-free feelings of summer.

Restorans Kuressaare: Raekoja 1, on the third floor in the building next to the department store (Kaubamaja), Tel: 5 51 39, open from noon to 5 pm and 6 to 11 pm, closed Sundays.

Taxi: Tel: 5 49 39, 5 55 77.

Tourist Information: Tallinna 4, open 9 am to 5 pm, currency exchange and souvenir shop open 10 am to 3:30 pm.

Train Tickets: Sales: Tallinna 50, Tel: 5 74 70.

Travel Agencies: Lossihoovi 4, Tel: 5 62 63; Thule, Pargi 1, Tel: 5 74 70; Saaremaa Reisebüroo, Pärna 2, Tel: 5 79 70; Viisam, Uus 22, Tel: 5 57 00.

Kärla

Kärla is somewhat to the north, halfway from Kuressaare to Kihelkonna. In 1843, the present-day classicistic *church* replaced its medieval predecessor. All that remains of the former church are a carved wooden relief on the eastern wall from 1637 and the epitaph for the feudal lord von Buxhoeveden dating back to 1598. Not far from town, the Kärla River has washed out a valley in the sand dunes up to 6 metres (20 feet) deep. Lake Karujärv to the north is also called "Pühajarv," meaning "holy lake."

Kihelkonna (Kielkond)

The "centre" on the western coast reveals itself as a widely scattered parsonage with a military base and a fishing harbour. More economically significant are the Jaagurahu quarries where pure, crystalline limestone is extracted. The whitewashed *church* with its pointed tower on Kiriku Street dates back to 1270; its sacristy was added in 1899. The small, angular bell tower is offset from the church.

Surroundings

Farm Museum Viki Village: Open daily except Mondays from 10 am to 6 pm, Tel: 7 66 13; bus stop, parking. Directly on the main road to Kuressaare is the Mihkli family estate. The family had already begun transforming it into a museum in the 1930's. In family ownership for over six generations, the estate provides an impression of rural life from 1840 to present. Eight

buildings have been preserved –
among them a sauna, a storehouse
and stalls and a 130-year old windmill.

Lümanda: Eight kilometres (5 miles)
to the south is the parish with the
highest church tower on the island.
East of town is the *Viidumäe Nature
Reserve.* This highland moor has the
widest variety of species in Estonia.
(Information: Viidumäe Looduskaitseala, Lümanda, Tel: 7 63 21).

Vilsandi Nature Reserve: Several glint
islands with a large bird population
surrounding the main island of Vilsandi were consolidated into a nature
reserve in 1907, making this Estonia's oldest reserve. Since over
10,000 nesting pairs of birds are registered here, Vilsandi is only accessible to those with a special permit.

Tagamoisa Peninsula: North of Kihelkonna, an extraordinary landscape
attracts visitors with more than 50
small lakes near the beach and an
area of coastal cliffs near Undva near
the northeastern point. On the western point, a narrow strip of land leads
out to the former island of Harilaid
with its lighthouse.

Leisi (Laisberg)

The centre of northern Saaremaa has
the only harbour in the region near
Triigi to the northeast. South of town,
one can see the last *post windmills*
on Saaremaa on an elevation near
Angla: only five of the former nine
windmills remain. Somewhat farther
to the south is the *church of Karja* on
the road to Kuressaare. Its richly em-

bellished arcades and columns decorated with statues make this
church an architectural jewel.

Orissaare

The first town on Saaremaa when
coming from Muhu is Orissaare. In
the old harbour from which ferries
used to depart to Koguva before the
land bridge was built, scuba divers
recently discovered a sunken ship
from the 16th century. The shipwreck is now to be salvaged, restored and exhibited to the public.

Pöide (Peude)

Even at a distance, the Kahutsi fortress can bee seen from a hill near
Pöide. In the centre of town is the
largest *fortified church* on Saaremaa.
Walled up windows, high walls and a
monumental, stocky tower lend this
church, completed after the uprising
of 1343, the appearance of a fortress. The staunch exterior stands in
contrast to the artistic interior. It is
especially the masonry which is
worth closer inspection – masterly
floral   ornamentation   augment
sculpted busts. A console is embellished with the busts of two
Estonian farmers.

Sorve Peninsula (Sworbe)

The peninsula in the southwestern
regions of Saaremaa projects 32 kilometres (20 miles) into the Baltic Sea.
Only an alluvial land bridge connects

Sorve with the mainland. This is also the location of the sand beaches which are even a rarity on Sorve.

There is a beautiful swimming area surrounded by sand dunes and pine trees near Järverand. The western coastline is wild and rugged, whereby the interior regions are covered with forests. The highest hill reaches an elevation of almost 37 metres (120 feet). In 1863, Pastor Martin Körber organized the first song festival on Sorve. The *War Memorial of Tehumardi* leaves a more sombre impression: on October 8, 1944, the nightly hand-to-hand combat between Russians, Germans and Estonians claimed thousands of lives.

Along the road to Samle, ruins testify to the embittered battle for the island; only overgrown gardens remain of former villages and farms. Even the lighthouse on the peninsula's point built in 1646 and renovated in 1770 was destroyed during the Second World War. Surrounding the new lighthouse from 1949, the remnants of fortifications are reminiscent of the Hitler-Stalin Pact of August 1939, which enabled the Soviets to construct a military base here. During clear weather, the view from this point extends far past the sound to the Curonian coast of Latvia. Also located in a beautiful landscape is the lighthouse of Loo near the coastal cliffs of Kaugatuma. In addition, there is a forest area near Viiersti with a number of rare plants.

Valjala (Wolde)

Halfway from Orissaare to Kuressaare, Valjala extends along the Maadevahe River. Only one impressive limestone *fortification wall* with a thickness of 5 to 8 metres (16 to 26 feet) remains from the once mighty fortress of the island. Construction on the neighbouring *church* began before 1261 but was only completed in 1270. This is considered the oldest church in Estonia. With the reconstruction of the church as a fortified church at the end of the 15th century, the windows were walled up. Inside, fragments of frescoes have remained preserved over the years.

Surroundings

Lake Kaali (Saal): Located three kilometres (2 miles) from Valhaja, amid fields and forests is a small circular lake 110 metres (360 feet) in diameter. The steep shores climb up to 7 metres (23 feet). According to the legend, it was here that Phaeton (Estonian: Päikesepoeg) fell to earth. When the geologist Reinwald began research into these mythological origins, he found a number of meteorite splinters. In the area surrounding Lake Kaali are seven additional craters, also around 2,700 years old. A small *Geological Museum* on the shores of Lake Kaali provides further information on the impact of the meteor shower.

Vohma

Only a few kilometres north of Vohma are the magnificently beautiful coastal cliffs of Saaremaa. A sand trail leads up to the highest point of the *Panga Pank,* which rises to a height of up to 21 metres (70 feet). From here, the view down to the sea past the weathered glint layers is dizzying. A narrow mule track leads along the coast. There is also a picnic area here which makes a nice place to stop for a break.

Vormsi (Worms)

Over 30 small islands surround Vormsi, Estonia's fourth largest island with an area of 93 square kilometres (36 square miles). Around 500 people live on this flat island, actually a gravel ridge. The numerous summer villas show how popular Vormsi has meanwhile become as a second residence. On Vormsi, which belonged to Sweden in the 13th century, historical buildings from before the Second World War have remained preserved through the Soviet offensive in the autumn of 1944. The island, an almost unknown idyll ten years ago, now has a good touristic infrastructure – especially for cyclists and hikers. Hullo, a village with a church from the 14th century, is the location of the junction of the island's roads. Several interesting erratic blocks make short side trips worthwhile: in Borbby, the 22.5 metre (74 foot) thick "Smen" rises several metres high; near Diiby is the 5.8 metre (19 foot) "Kirikukivi" (Church Stone); and in Kärssläti, the "Vargstain." In Saxby, a 24 metre (79 foot) lighthouse has sent its beacon out to a radius of up to 15 nautical miles since 1864; a ki-

lometre-long spit of land begins near Ramp Säär (Rumpos). Also worth seeing is the 2.5 metre (8 foot) coral reef "Valgemägi" in Hoitburg.

Along the Baltic Coast

Ida-Virumaa (Ostwierland)

This northeastern Estonian province comprises the region between Lake Peipus and the Gulf of Finland, bordered by the Narva River to the east, also forming the border to the Russian Republic. A population of 222,030, most of Russian descent, lives in this region. The provincial capital is Kohtla-Järve; however, the largest city is Narva with a population of 82,300 – only three percent of which are Estonians. The forced industrialization during the past decade has transformed large areas of the formerly beautiful landscape into a surreal lunar landscape. Just one example: the mining of oil shale has left piles of debris; the underground corridors in the mines have in part collapsed. The two heating plants near Narva, which supply around 80% of Estonia's energy demand and even supply energy to Latvia and Russia are the largest polluters in Europe: the burning of oil shale in the two 1,600 megawatt plants contaminates the soil with 50 kilograms of ash per square metre annually. Barren areas blanketed in ash extend for miles. 124,000 tonnes of nitrogen oxide and soot are discharged into the air each year; 300 cubic metres of water used in the extraction of the fuel is pumped out of the ground. Sillamäe is no isolated instance in this ecologically distressed area. The waste products from the uranium stored here are dumped at the disposal site for household waste near the sea...

Narva

The former Hanseatic city on the border to Russia was completely destroyed during the Second World War. Estonia's third largest city, also the administration centre for the province of Ida-Virumaa, is home to a population of 82,300, most of which are of Russian descent. In protest of against the turn in political tides – now the young Estonian Republic is chipping away at the rights of Russian foreign workers – the last remaining statue of Lenin in the Baltic States still stands on the city's central square.

History

The history of the city began downstream from the powerful rapids on the Narva River which connects Lake Peipus with the Gulf of Finland. After the area around Narva fell to the Danes in 1171, Dietrich von Kyvel secured the city from Russian attacks by building a fortress which was continually reinforced and expanded during the decades to follow. The small settlement which developed in the safety of the fortress was awarded the status of a city by the King Menved of Denmark at the beginning of the 14th century. In 1346, the Danes sold the city and the land to the Teutonic Order which enclosed the area in a fortification wall in 1380. The Grand Duke Ivan III built the mighty fortress of Ivangorod on the eastern banks of the river across from the Teutonic Order's fortress (Hermann's Fortress), situated on the western banks of the Narva. During the Livonian War, the Russians were able to gain possession of the city on the western bank. Their victory was, however, short lived. Iin 1581, under the command of Pontus de la Gardie, the Swedes stormed the fortress and subsequently awarded Narva the status of a Swedish city. In 1704, King Karl XII of Sweden was first able to drive out the Russian Czar Peter I, but would consequently accept defeat when the Treaty of Nystad ultimately placed Narva under Russian control in 1721. During the Second World War, the city and the Narva River were once again the focus of embittered battles and the entire city was destroyed with the exception of the fortress complex.

Sights

The contrasts could not be sharper: the Estonian wade in the shallow waters of the Narva River below the staunch Hermann's fortress on the western banks across from the impressive Ivangorod Fortress. On the Russian side, there is not a soul in sight. The reason is that the border area is off limits to the Russian populace.

The *Hermann's Fortress* was first mentioned in historical documents as a Danish border fortress in 1256. The castellated ring wall with the low bastions was first built by the Teutonic Order who resided here up to 1558.

The fortress was named after its tallest tower "Tall Hermann." The view from the wooden embattlements which lead along the outer walls at a dizzying height, extends over the city and far into Russian territory. Hermann's Fortress as well as the Ivangorod Fortress (called Jaanilinn by the Estonians) were both destroyed in 1944 and subsequently rebuilt. Today, the old Teutonic fortress houses the _Narva Linnamuuseum_ (Narva City Museum; St. Peterburi 2, Tel: 3 32 01, open Saturday to Tuesday from 10 am to 6 pm). A _Pimead_ or "dark garden" was laid out along the steep embankments next to the fortress in 1853. A monument has stood in the park in memory of the Russian soldiers who fell in the battle for Narva during the Great Northern War since 1704. In the inner city, only a few buildings remain from the period before the Second World War. The baroque _city hall_ dates back to the 17th century. In 1648, construction began on _St. John's Church,_ also called the "Swedish cathedral." After the Russian invasion, the three-naved church was dedicated to the Russian Saint Alexander Nevski in 1704. In 1733, Czaress Anna relinquished the church to the German congregation which dedicated it after thorough renovations on St. Michael's Day in 1734 with a festive service. The slender tower with an unusual crown was built in 1789 and contrasts with a sooner weighty, plain interior: a simple cross-vaulted ceiling rests on massive stone columns; subdued light falls into the church through the Gothic windows.

Somewhat outside the city on an island in the Narva River, the _Kreenholmi Textile Mill_ has produced cotton thread, flannel and silk for export to over 20 countries since 1857. With around 12,000 employees, the textile mill is still the largest industrial plant in Estonia. The spirit of socialism remains intact in the _Kreenholmi Muuseum_ (Lenini 10, Tel: 2 41 18, open Tuesday to Sunday from 10 am to 6 pm). In 1872, Kreenholmi employees staged the first worker's rebellions in Estonia.

Surroundings

Narva-Joesuu: → _individual entry_
Narva Veehoidla: To the south is the "Narva Sea," a 240 square kilometre (94 square mile) municipal reservoir. The construction of this reservoir caused the Narva River to lose its rapids.

Information

Accommodation
Hotels: Narva, Puskini 6, Tel: 3 15 52. A dilapidated, dingy building.
Vanalinna, L. Koidula 6, Tel: 2 24 86, single room £10.75 ($20), double room £16 ($30)
Airline Tickets: Puskini 14, Tel: 4 98 57.
Automobile Repairs: Kirovi 1a, Tel: 4 92 49.
Border Crossing: Next to Hermann's Fortress from the Peetri plats head-

ing toward the river, rarely traffic jams. CIS visa is required.

Bus Station: Vaksali 2, Tel: 3 15 95.

Café-Bars: Bistroo, Puskini 10; Café Kevade, Keskallee 6; Narva, Puskini 6; Oksana, Tallinna 19; Café Randel, St. Peterburi 2; Café Tempo, Tallinna 56; Vikerkaar, Voidu 1.

Cinema: Punane Täht, Kommunaaride 1.

Fuel: Tallinna 64, Tel: 4 98 53. Tallinna 55a, Tel: 4 24 00.

Hospital: Komsomoli 3, Tel: 2 24 43.

Post Office: Kingiseppa 10, Tuleviku 3.

Restaurants: Baltica-Restorans, Puskini 10, Tel: 2 22 53; Joala, Kreenholmi 6, Tel: 3 35 63; Regatt, Anveldi 34a, Tel: 4 09 40; Tempo, Tallinna 52, Tel: 4 14 68.

Swimming: an extensive and pristine bathing area at the foot of the Hermann's Fortress on the Narva River with slopes, grassy and sandy beaches, on the Russian side there isn't a solitary swimmer.

Taxi: Tel: 3 15 95.

Theatre: Stuudioteater Ilmarine, Lenini 8, Tel: 9 52 42.

Train Station: Vaksali 2, Tel: 3 14 54.

Narva-Joesuu (Hungerburg)

Ten kilometres (6¼ miles) north of Narva where the River flows into the Baltic Sea, Narva-Joesuu stretches several miles along the coast. A belt of sand dunes wooded with pine tress separates the former summer resort preferred by the Russian elite from the seven kilometre (4½ mile) beach with fine sand. One should, however, forgo a dip in the sea: the untreated waste from the Narva River and the highly polluted industrial waste make the tides murky. Still, the population of this town of 3,000 increases by a number of times during the summer months and the guest houses and spa facilities are booked to capacity with families and those seeking relaxation. A ferry departs to the Russian side from the small harbour near the mouth of the river. During the summer, there are tour ships to Narva. On Linda Street, the *Vladimir wooden church* (no. 15) is worth seeing.

Information

Café-Bar: Ankur, Koidula 19; Grillbaar, Vabaduse 44.

Camping: Narva-Joesuu Kämping, Koidu 6, Tel: 2 24 86.

Restaurant: Majakas, Pargi 8, Tel: 7 29 31.

Sillamäe

The first larger city on the motorway from Tallinn to St. Petersburg was one of the most mysterious cities in Estonia up until 1990: the Estonians were not allowed to set foot in the youngest city in Estonia. All 20,000 residents were resettled here from the Soviet Union. The monotone brick and concrete wasteland suffers from massive ecological problems – not only resulting from the nearby oil shale processing industry but also from the uranium plant in this town. The contaminated waste still lands at the disposal site for household waste even today. Radioactive contaminants can seep unhindered into the Baltic Sea. Over 1,200 tonnes of uranium and 800 tonnes of thorium are registered near the coast according to the Estonian Environmental Minister Tonis Kaasik. The exact impact of this ticking time bomb is to be revealed by 30 investigations to be undertaken by the three Baltic States in cooperation with Sweden, Finland and Norway.

Surroundings

Sinimäed (Blue Mountains): Seafarers gave the "Blue Mountains" their name: due to the mist off the coast, the wooded hills appeared to be blue from a distance. The highest elevations in this range are the Tornimägi to the west (69.9 metres/226 feet), the Porguhauamägi at the centre (83.3 metres/272 feet) and the Pargimägi to the east at 84.6 metres (277 feet). From the spring to the autumn of 1944, the front between the Russian Red Army and the German *Wehrmacht* ran along the ridge of the Blue Mountains.

Information

Automobile Repair: Tallinna maantee 19.

Café-Bar: Skazka, Tel: 7 43 80.

Fuel: Tallinna maantee 40.

Toila

Twenty kilometres (12½ miles) of steep coastline extend from Saka to Toila. Near Ontika, where the glint reaches its highest elevation of 55.6 metres (182 feet), the beach below lies in perpetual shade. The Voka coastal cliffs "only" reach a height of

43 metres (141 feet). Toila, located at the mouth of the Pühajögi (sacred river) was once brought fame by a Russian merchant: Jelissejev had the Oru castle built here from radiant white stone. The former summer residence of the president of the first Estonian Republic was destroyed during the Second World War. Only the tree-lined walkways, terraces and a few secondary buildings remain. Toila was once known as a holiday resort even before the First World War. It was mainly the Russian elite who built their stately villas here concealed in the pine forest above the coastal cliffs; the Soviet working class had to be satisfied with the multistoried brick holiday apartment buildings.

Kohtla-Järve

Fifty kilometres (31¼ miles) west of Narva is the industrial centre for the extraction of oil shale, surrounding the Kohtla Järve lake. This industrial city with a population of 76,800 came into existence in 1946 through the consolidation of the five small villages Kohtla, Kukruse, Johvi, Athme and Sompa. The old mass housing for workers surrounding the mines and quarries became districts of the city. The wooden barracks were replaced with concrete buildings. The high proportion of Russians in the population is typical for Estonian industrial areas. In **Kohtla,** two museums are worth visiting: the *Kohtla-Järve Art Museum* (Pargi 40, Tel: 2 23 00) exhibits works by local artists. Interesting insights into the extraction and processing of the "flammable stone" is provided by the *Polevkivimuuseum* (Oil Shale Museum; Narva 9, Tel: 4 57 54). In 1991, **Johvi** celebrated its 750th anniversary. Worth seeing here is the *fortified church* from the 16th century. An old mound of rubble with an *observation platform* in **Kukruse** located between Kohtla and Johvi commemorates the fact that the mines began production here in 1916. The cupel grounds near the estate of Kukruse are still in operation. This is also the location of the grave sites of the aristocratic von Toll family. One member of this family, *Eduard von Toll*, died in the North Sea in 1902 during a polar expedition. The year 1916 also marked the beginning of surface mining in **Järve.** Oil shale was transported to Kohtla by horse-drawn wagon and from there, by train to St. Petersburg. With the consolidation of the Kukruse and Järve mines, the "collective oil shale industry" was established in 1918. North of the road to Narva is the *Järve estate building and park,* similar to a fortress. In **Edise,** the old estate stalls have been converted to a restaurant.

Surroundings

Purtse: The restored *fortress of the Teutonic Order* in Purtse from the 13th century is now the venue for cultural events and is also the most significant historical site in the proximity of the Kohtla-Järve. A feudal lord's limestone palace from the 16th century has been recently renovated. The nearby *Taaramägi Hill* is actually a fortified farm from the first century AD.

Kivioli: Kivioli is located 25 kilometres west of Kohtla-Järve not far from the Ojamaa River. In 1922, the first quarries began producing oil shale.

Information

Accommodation: Guest House, Vahtra 2, Tel: 5 89 21.

Café-Bar: Vigri, Metsa 5, Tel: 5 70 67.

Fuel: Lepa tee 86, Tel: 5 74 17.

Restaurants: Kevade, Keskpuiestee 33, Tel: 5 73 39; Porter, Keskpuiestee 1, Tel: 5 80 98.

Lüganuse (Luggenhusen)

Eight kilometres (5 miles) west of the Kohtla Järve is a larger village, situated on the picturesque Purtse stream which was already historically documented in Danish chronicles in the 13th century. The village *church,* surrounded by the Purtse on three sides has a tower which is quite unusual for Estonia – it is round at the top. Also worth seeing are the old round crosses in the graveyard. A pleasant walk leads out to the mouth of the Purtse where it flows into the Baltic Sea. Adjacent to the sand beach are more than 40 kilometres (25 miles) of coastal cliffs to the east. Upriver is the old marketplace of **Püssi** (Isenhof). The dried-up Purtse riverbed with its interesting chalk formations is under nature conservation.

Information

Accommodation (Guest Houses): Narva maantee 30, Tel: 4 92 06; Kitzberg 10, Tel: 2 22 68; Tsaikovski 11, Tel: 2 26 01.

Automobile Repair: Kohtla-Järve,

Kaevuri 1, Tel: 4 01 44; Kohtla-Järve, Narva maantee 44, Tel: 4 57 88.
Café-Bars: Kohtla-Järve: Maias-mokk, Rakvere 12, Tel: 2 27 72; Mi-kro, Tsaikovski 11, Tel: 2 12 01; Tuu-leke, Tel: 4 57 33; Johvi: Kajakas, Tel: 2 18 40.
Fuel: Kohtla-Järve, Narva maantee 5, Tel: 4 54 91; Johvi-Athme, Tel: 3 33 71; Athme 49, Tel: 3 33 66; Ehi-tajate 27, Tel: 4 40 00.
Restaurants: Kohtla-Järve: Turist, Kesk-Allee 12, Tel: 4 41 53; Trilobiit, St. Peterburi 10, Tel: 4 41 01; Athme, L. Tolstoi 19, Tel: 3 41 37; Fööniks, Rakvere 12, Tel: 2 27 70. Johvi: Valge Hobu Trahter, Tel: 2 27 42.
Theatre: Noorte Vaatajate teater, Voi-du väljak 5, Tel: 2 20 75.
Travel Agency: Kohtla-Järve Reise-büroo, Varese 6, Tel: 4 71 63.

Iisaku

Iisaku is located on the A 201, 45 kilometres (28 miles) south of the Kohtla-Järve and around 20 kilome-tres (12½ miles) north of Lake Pei-pus. Worth seeing here is the *Mu-seum of Local History*. The nearby *Täriveremägi* with its 94 metre (307 foot) summit is the highest elevation in northern Estonia.

Illuka

On the secondary road from Kohtla-Järve to the eastern shores of lake Peipus is the small village of Illuka, set back somewhat off the roadway. The village's main attraction is 8 kilo-metres (5 miles) long and 3 kilome-tres (2 miles) wide: scattered among the 30 square kilometres (12 square miles) of pastoral, heather-covered hills are the *forty lakes of Kurtna*. A few miles to the south is **Kuremäe** with the only operating convent in Estonia. Time seems to have come to a standstill in the *Pühtitsa Convent*. Founded in 1892, during the govern-mental policy of forced Russification, the nuns still tend their own fields, sowing, weeding and harvesting the gardens just as they had done in years long past. The quiet, contem-plative cloistered life within the con-vent's walls is only interrupted during the weekends when the pious pilgrim to the religious services held here.
The nearby *Kuremägi* is a hallowed site for the Estonians. A sacred spring, a 1,000 year old oak tree and a beautiful view of the moor of Aluta-guse make the climb up the 22 metre (72 foot) "summit" worthwhile.

Surroundings
Northeast toward Sillamäe is the *Mu-raka Highland Moor* with its peculiar swamp islands. This area is a natural sanctuary for a number of endan-gered species: flying squirrels and over 100 bears make this their habi-tat. Rare birds of prey can raise their broods here undisturbed.

Lake Peipus

The border between Russia and Estonia runs directly through the fifth largest lake in Europe: the eastern shores are already the Republic of

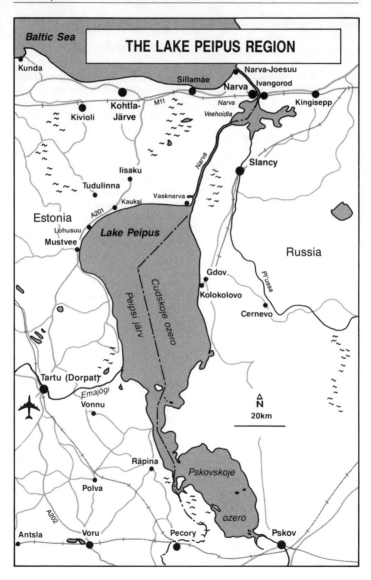

Baltic Sea

THE LAKE PEIPUS REGION

Kunda

Narva-Joesuu

Sillamäe

Narva

Ivangorod

Kohtla-Järve

M11

Narva

Veehoidla

Kingisepp

Kivioli

Slancy

Narva

Iisaku

Tudulinna

Vasknarva

Kauksi

A201

Estonia

Lohusuu

Lake Peipus

Mustvee

Russia

Gdov

Kolokolovo

Cudskoje ozero

Pl'ussa

Peipsi järv

Cernevo

Tartu (Dorpat)

Emajõgi

Vonnu

△
N

20km

Räpina

Pskovskoje

Polva

A202

ozero

Antsla

Voru

Pecory

Pskov

Russia. With a total surface area of 3,555 square kilometres (1,386 square miles), large portions of this lake are grown with reeds; only at a few places do sand dunes and pine forests line the shores.

Vasknarva (Neuschloß)

The largest town on the northern shores of Lake Peipus evolved at the source of the Narva River. From 1346, the small harbour village was protected by a fortress. The castle now stands in ruins; only the walls with a thickness of 3.6 metres (12 feet) remain. The beach of Vasknarva is quite popular for swimming.

Kauksi

This holiday resort on the northern shores of Lake Peipus is the only Estonian "Tourismibaas" on the lake. This beautiful section of beach lies three kilometres to the south, where the Rannapungerja River empties into the lake.

Lohusuu

The village of Lohusuu comprises two parts: the Russian Vene-Lohusuu on the shores of Lake Peipus and Eesti-Lohusuu, the Estonian portion on the Avijögi River. Both ethnic groups make their living from fishing. Located up the Avijögi River is **Avinurme,** known for its manufacture of wooden vessels.

Lääne-Virumaa (Westwierland)

The region between the Gulf of Finland and the Pandivere range is the Lääne-Virumaa province with an area of 3,464 square kilometres (1,351 square miles). The provincial capital is Rakvere (Wesenberg). In 1987, the citizens were barely successful in hindering an ecological catastrophe: since the province is rich in phosphate deposits, the Soviets had planned to begin the industrial extraction of this raw material with the help of foreign workers for the use in the production of artificial fertilizers. The deterioration of the region and the threat of widespread pollution provoked a landslide of protest – the people took to the streets all over Estonia to protest this industrial giganticism.

Rakvere (Wesenberg)

Even from quite a distance, one can already see the ruins of the Teutonic fortress of Rakvere. Rakvere itself is a small provincial capital 90 kilometres (57 miles) east of Tallinn. Seen from the southern perspective, high wooden fences and watchtowers evoke other associations: what has the appearance of a "concentration camp" reveals itself as an abandoned pig stall from the nearby slaughterhouse after a peek over the fence.

History

The Danes built a castle and city atop the Estonian fortress hill of Tarvanpepa in 1252. Only fifty years later, the town at the base of the fortress – a commercial centre situated on the trade route from Tallinn to Novgorod – was awarded the rights of a city in 1302. In 1343, the administrative governors of the Teutonic Order moved into the fortress. In 1558, the fortress and city were taken by the Russians during the Livonian War and subsequently pillaged. In 1581, the Swedes had their turn and conquered the city under the leadership of commander Pontus de la Gardie. The Polish-Swedish War from 1602 to 1605 brought Rakvere under Polish rule. With a population of only 375, Rakvere became the provincial capital in 1783 – and with this, began to grow: in 1881, 3,228 people lived in this city; in 1897, the number of residents had already reached 5,860. In 1989, the population had grown to 19,900. The most famous resident of the city is *Johann Hornung.* In 1693, this religious philosopher published a book on Estonian grammar. The lithographer *August von Pezold* (1794-1859) who brought Estonian folk life to paper, was born here as well.

Sights

The main attraction of this otherwise rather modern city is the *Teutonic Fortress* (open 11 am to 5 pm, charging admission) on the Vallimägi, belonging to the Pandivere (Pontifer) range. The impressive ruins from 1252, the stones of which were used in the construction of the city during the 18th century, are presently being restored. The defence tower crowned by the Estonian flag offers a panorama of the city and the Pandi-

vere landscape of rolling hills. Housed in the Kohtuasutuse Hoone, designed and built by John Moor from 1785 to 1790, the *Rakvere Muuseum* (Tallinna 3, Tel: 4 43 69; open Tuesday to Saturday from 11 am to 5 pm) is worth seeing. The historical architecture of the city is best preserved on Pikk (Long Street). From Tallinna Street up to the church, the street is characterized by stately bourgeois buildings mostly constructed of stone. Beyond the church are predominantly one-storey wooden houses from the 18th and 19th centuries, painted in dark opaque tones. The whitewashed *church* built in 1427 by the Tallinn master craftsman *Andreas* is embellished with a lavishly decorated blue and grey portal with Gothic elements. Those who go inside should take a closer look at the four evangelists created by *Elert Diel,* one of the most significant sculptors of Tallinn during the 17th century. The altarpiece was created from 1710 to 1730 by *Johann Valentin Rabe* from Lübeck, Germany; the pulpit (1690) by *Christian Ackermann.* On Kastani, a boulevard with two rows of chestnut trees on the median is a *memorial* in memory of the Estonians who fell in the Second World War (1941-1944). What was once the central market is now a modern city centre with a department store and bus terminal.

Surroundings

Haljala: the fortified church (15th century) on the marketplace near the junction of the rural road from Tallinn to Narva not only served its spiritual purpose but was also subject to secular uses – it has also served as an outpost and signal tower for the fortress of Rakvere. In 1730, the master craftsman *Rabe* created the altar and pulpit.

The Pandivere Range: The Pandivere (Pontifer) range begins to the south of Rakvere. While neither a lake nor a stream is to be found on this plateau with heavy chalk deposits and an area of 2,000 square kilometres (780 square miles), the sources of a number of rivers can be found in the periferal areas.

The railway junction of **Tapa** (Taps) lies on the northwestern edge of this region. The solitary railway building in the birch forest dates back to 1876. Situated in the heart of the Pandivere range, 23 kilometres (14½ miles) south of Rakvere is the train station of **Tamsalu.** The town stands in sharp contrast to the idyllic landscape: surrounding Terko, a completely dilapidated industrial complex, are neglected houses and vegetable gardens. Located to the southeast, the marketplace of **Simuna** is the site of an interesting *church* with a carved wooden altar created by the master craftsman *Ackermann* in 1684. Not far from here, **Rahkla** offers a beautiful view of the *Kellavere – Mägi* from a height of 155 metres (507 feet).

Information

Accommodation: Oktoober, Tallinna 25, Tel: 4 34 20.

Automobile Repair: Ruut, Tel: 3 85 07; Siil, Tel: 4 17 75.

Bus Station: Laada 38.

Fuel: Rägavere tee 46, Tel: 4 31 21. On the outskirts of town heading toward Narva, left beyond the traffic circle.

Restaurants: Kolhida, Tallinna 68, Tel: 4 44 64; Koidula 1-3, Tel: 4 27 43.

Theatre: Kreutzwaldi 2a, Tel: 4 56 61 and 4 28 97.

Kunda

The city lives and suffers under a cloud of cement dust, a result of the huge cement factory on the banks of the Kunda River. Even at a distance of ten kilometres (6 miles), one will notice the fine dust and the grey cloud hanging over the city. Estonia's second cement factory was built 30 kilometres (19 miles) to the east in Aseri (Assern) in 1899.

Surroundings

Toolse (Tolsburg): Located in a picturesque setting on the tip of a spit of land in the Baltic Sea, Toolse is probably the most widely known Teutonic fortress in Estonia. Built in 1471 for protection from pirate attacks, the Russians conquered this fortress in 1558, followed by the Swedes in 1581. Although ships still docked in the Toolse harbour which later silted up as late as the 19th century, the fortress has been left to decay since the 18th century. Beyond the *Kronskallas,* a small waterfall in the Toolse Stream, is the beginning of a diverse coastline with sand dunes, retaining walls and isolated coastal cliffs. Rising up from Ulgu Point is the massive seven metre (23 foot) *Ehakivi* erratic block. Near **Karepa** the *witch's house* is worth seeing. This summer cottage belonging to the artist *V.*

Earlier, the Bishop's Castle of Kuressaare served as a fortress, today it houses a museum within its walls which presents the diverse history of the city

While the beach on the Estonian side of the Jaanalinn in Narva is heavily frequented, there is not a soul in sight on the Russian riverbanks

Important impulses in the struggle for independence originated from the University of Tartu

Lember-Bogatkina is built solely from root wood is "decorated" with countless wooden and stone figures.

Lahemaa National Park

With an area of 64,910 square kilometres (25,315 square miles), Lahemaa National Park is located 40 kilometres east of Tallinn. The park was founded on June 1, 1971 and roughly encompasses the area north of the E 40 between the villages of Kuutsalu and Viitna, extending to the coastline on the Gulf of Finland. It lies within the two provinces of Lääne-Virumaa and Harjumaa.

Landscapes in the National Park
The Lavamaa limestone plateau extends between the two heavily wooded areas of Korvemaa to the south and the Baltic Sea coastal depression to the north, an area predominantly used for agriculture. This plateau is scattered with large stones and erratic blocks. The highest mount in the national park reaches 115 metres (376 feet). The coastline is very rugged; the limestone plateau also shows chalk formations. Fourteen lakes are the spawning grounds for salmon and lake trout; eight rivers – the Loo, Pudisoo, Valgejõgi, Loobu, Võsu, Altija, Musotoja and Vainupea – transverse the area from west to

LAHEMAA NATIONAL PARK

east. 67% of the national park's area is covered with forests and 5% is swampland. The park administration subdivides Lahemaa into natural landscapes (70%), cultivated landscapes (22%) and reserve areas under absolute protection (8%). Among the latter areas are the Suurekorve, Laukaso, Udriku, Koljaku-Oandu and Vainupea Reserves. The *Viru Highland Moor* has a special status, with an area of 150 hectares (375 acres) it is the smallest highland moor with lakes, located in the middle of Lahemaa.

The massive layer of peat, now six metres (20 feet) thick and increasing at a rate of 1.5 centimetres (½ inch) per year is the basis for a unusual landscape: scattered among the gnarled pine tress from one to two hundred years old are shellberries, sundew and Labrador tea. The essential oils give the moorland its characteristic fragrance. In the autumn, red cranberries cover the ground. The early of the 20th century marked the beginning of the draining of the northern portions for peat production. Meanwhile, peat production has been discontinued. Instead a network of hydrological observatory stations cover the moor, to research the influence of the old peat milling areas on the water balance as well as the atmospheric supply of moor water. While eagles and cranes brood here, endangered species have found their refuge in the dense forests: brown bears, lynxes and minks make this their habitat. Trumpeter swans, black storks, loons and other rare bird spe-

cies nest in this area. In total there are 37 types of mammals, 213 types of birds and 24 types of fish in Lahemaa.

Lady's slipper and beach peas grow here in abundance. The tourist route through the national park leads from Tallinn past the left shores of Lake Kohala to Kotka, Vatku, Vohma, Ilumäe, Palmse and Vosupere to Viitna and farther to Narva. An *educational hiking trail with observation points* leads through the Viru Highland Moor.

Information on the National Park: 202 128 Viitna, Tel: 4 57 59 and 4 92 53. *Park Information:* Tel: 4 56 39. *Tours:* Lahemaa Tourist Camp, Tel: 9 33 51.

Towns in the National Park

Altija

The idyllic fishing village of Altija on the road to Vergi lies directly on the coast. In addition to the thatched roofed Uustalu farm, now an *open-air museum,* the well and dark moire huts offer an impression of old Estonia. Offering diversion is a bus stop with a rest area including a playground with wooden equipment for the children. The *Koljaku-Oandu Reserve* begins near this town.

Kolga (Kolk)

The classicistic ensemble of estates owned by the Swedish noble Stenbock family was built in 1765, rebuilt in 1820 and is now being restored. North of Kolga is the *Suurekorve Reserve*.

Konnu

The *Udirku Reserve* begins south of the town of Konnu.

Loksa

A ship wharf dominates the small city of Loksa on the Valgejögi (White River). The wharf workers make for a high proportion of Russians in the population.
Café/Restaurant: Pohjarannik, Tallinna maantee, Tel: 77 51 75.

Muuksi (Mukenkul)

Muuksi has been historically documented since 1290. The city with its limestone houses, stone fences and walls will take visitors back to a world of long ago. North of town, the glint cliffs along the coast tower up to 47 metres (154 feet) and a waterfall at Turjeberg plunges four metres (13 feet). South of Muuksi is the picturesque lake Kahala-Järv. An *educational hiking trail* leads to Sillikorve.

Palmse (Palms)

The most magnificent northern Estonian estate became a village during the 13th century, which the King of Denmark gave to the Cestercian monastery in Tallinn along with other villages. The village of Palmse (Palkemas) was already mentioned in the old annals as a possession of the monastery. The location was ideal at the edge of the Estonian coastal depression and the limestone plateau.

The fresh springs enabled the construction of fish ponds. Later the water was used by the breweries and distilleries and in animal husbandry. The appearance of the medieval state complex, presumably composed of wooden buildings – is unknown today. From 1674 to 1923, the estate belonged to the Baltic-German von Pahlen line of aristocracy, who began construction on the stately manorhouse in the 17th century. From 1697 to 1698, the first building (the manorhouse) was constructed and then remodelled in the baroque style by the governor general's architect J. G. Mohr. Livery stables, grain storehouses, stalls, a caretaker's house, the carpenter and gardener's house, a sauna, a beer and brandy kitchen, a malt kiln, a lime kiln, a mill and the miller's house were to follow during the 18th and 19th centuries. The stately park is among the largest of its kind in Estonia. The old monastery park was transformed during the construction of the manorhouse. The stately baroque park was augmented by a free-flowing, landscape park with architectural elements created on the estate grounds. The total length of all the tree-lined walkways and paths leading through the park was 36 verst (equal to 38.4 kilometres or 24 miles) at that time. Filigree wooden bridges spanned the small stream, an artificial lake provided the opportunity for gondola rides and aquatic games. The 32 buildings in Palmse are being restored by the National Park Administration and new uses are being made possible: the former nobleman's house now serves as a book and souvenir shop; the kiln, now provides lodgings and refreshments in a small cafeteria. It is planned to transform the entire estate into a "cultural centre." *Summer concerts* and *folklore festivals* like the annual "Viru Säru" in June already provide revitalising impulses within the old walls with folk dancers and musicians.

Surroundings

Hiking Trail to the Monastery: The stone blocks are reminiscent of the fact that the devil himself is said to have bothered the nuns – and he was turned to stone in punishment.

Ilumäe Chapel: Located on the roadway heading toward Loksa, members of the von Pahlen family are buried in this chapel's graveyard. This family owned the Palmse estate for a number of centuries. The chapel is embellished with the coats of arms of these free farmers. Located to the west of Palmse is the *Laukasoo Nature Reserve.*

Sagadi (Saggad)

Less widely known, but no less worth seeing is the group of estates (Sagadi Mois) on the road from Vosu to Haljala. Surrounded by rebuilt domestic buildings and a white wooden fence, the gatehouse from 1785 opens to an oblong inner courtyard with lawn areas and the manorhouse. The manorhouse is a classicistic building from the 18th century. Behind the antique rose façade with applied white columns are the forestry school and the *Metsamuuseum* (Forestry Museum; open from May 1 to September 15). A majestic staircase with a veranda enclosed in class leads down to the estate's gardens with a small pond.

Transport: There is a bus stop directly in front of the estate.

Vainupea

Stones in the water are a substitute for boat docks at the harbour mole. The church here is over 100 years old and is now used for religious services and concerts. The *Vainupea Nature Reserve* extends along the coast.

Vergi

The centre in this extensive settlement of wooden houses in the coastal pine forests includes a merchant, residential blocks and numerous single-family homes. Vergi has a secluded location on the old army base. Travelling through the former military zone west of town is now possible. Beyond the gatepost is a broad road with a number of curves leading by Lahti, a collection of wooden houses in the middle of nowhere, to Vosu.

Vihula (Viol)

A tree-lined avenue leads to the Vihula estate, presently under renovation. The main building from the 18th century seems out of place with its gable which was later added in the 19th century. The park is the most beautiful part of this estate. Beyond the mill, the stream was dammed up near the manor house. White wooden bridges span the tributaries and the lake is line with landings and bathing huts. The rear areas of the park were designed more close to nature: the small, steep riverbanks lined with pine trees and ferns may make one forget that this is actually a planned park. The trail leading through the landscape park leads up to the estate wall made from glint slabs. The end of the trail is marked by a small octagonal pavilion in white.

Viitna

The village of Viitna on the old trade route from Tallinn was already historically documented in the 13th century. Where the reception centre for guests now stands were once forty taverns. The *Viitna Tavern* belongs to Palmse and is among the oldest and most historically significant of its kind which has remained preserved in Estonia. The exact date of construction is unknown. What is certain, however, is that as early as 1802, this was the site of some heavy drinking. The left part of the tavern was the "gentlemen's hall" with the stables for the guests' horses; the right-hand portion was reserved for the less noble farmers, their horses and the kitchen. The barn, which burned down in 1989, is presently being rebuilt.

Information

Accommodation: Motel Viitna, located directly on the M11, on the right-hand side of the road when coming from Narva, shortly before Viitna, Tel: 4 94 19. Situated on Lake Väikejärv (small lake), the waterlilies bloom on the lake during the summer. An educational hiking trail begins at the motel and leads to Suurjärv (large lake) and farther to Lake Nabudi.

Fuel: At the intersection in Viitna, Tel: 9 36 58.

Vohma

Archaeological excavations were underway from 1969 to 1972 on the Tandemägi, a small hill near the village of Vohma. On the northwestern periphery of the hill, archaeologists found the remains of three *stone coffin graves;* on the southeastern edge, the found an early *tarand grave.* Decorative pieces and fragments of pottery are evidence that these grave sites date back to the time of Christ. The complex surrounding the tarand grave has meanwhile been reconstructed.

Vosu

This village of Vosu along a street is framed with wooden villas, hotels and the concrete buildings of the youth hostel. During the summer this is an active little town; in the winter, a miserable hamlet. Several footpaths lead through the flat sand dune belt to the beach with its fine sand, extending along the bay of Käsmu.

Accommodation: Youth Hostel, Tel: 9 91 89, open from June 1 to September 15.

Harjumaa (Harrien)

The region measuring 4,147 square kilometres (1,618 square miles) in area surrounding the city of Tallinn not only encompasses Estonia's largest province but, with a total population of 128,500, it is also the most densely populated.

Aegviidu (Charlottenhof)

Southeast of the barren, lunar landscape of Korvemaa is the holiday resort of Aegviidu with around 1,200 residents. A very nice camping area is located around 2 kilometres (1¼ miles) from town in **Nelijärve** (Four Lakes). The name of this place is misleading: actually, there are seven lakes which surround this town; however, only four can be seen from the 106 metre (347 foot) summit of the Valdehobusemägi, now equipped with an observation tower.

The holiday resort has high season during the entire year. In summer, sports enthusiasts come to the orienteering competition and during the winter to the ski marathon. In the nearby pine forests, signs in Russian warn against the use of firearms: the Red Army's troop training area extends over an area of 360 square kilometres (140 square miles). The unusually well-maintain roadway leading through the middle of nothing quickly reveals itself as the runway for the Soviet reserve airport. The train station of Aegviidu was built in Russian architecture when the railway route from St. Petersburg to Tallinn was originally opened.
Accommodation: Youth Hostel.

Harku

The Great Northern War drew to an end here in 1710. The Russian domination began in the Swedish garrison barracks with the signing of the treaty of surrender.

Joelähtme (Jegelecht)

Seventeen kilometres (10½ miles) east of Tallinn where the rural road crosses the river on a bridge from the 19th century, *2,800- year-old graves* were discovered – the oldest evidence of human settlement in northern Europe. To the left of the road are old houses in the village of **Rebala** which once gave the province of Rävala and the city of Tallinn (= Reval) their respective names. When the village was scheduled to come under the pickax for extraction of phosphorite for the nearby Maardu plant, objections voiced by the scientists in 1985 saved the village. The whitewashed *church* with walls measuring 1.65 metres (5½ feet) in thickness had only firing slits instead of windows since it was a fortification church.

Surroundings

Chalk Range: Between Joelähtme and Kostivere are the largest caves in the Estonian chalk formation area.

The river from Joelähtme suddenly disappears beyond a meadow only to reappear as a spring near the church before flowing into the larger Jägala River with its rapids. The *stone grave* is a mushroom shaped, eroded sandstone block, one chalk spring in Tuhula is called the *witch's spring* by the local residents.

Jägala Waterfall: Next to the eight-metre (26 foot) waterfall on the Jägala River, a number of other small waterfalls line the glint coast. The *Linnamägi,* the fortress hill on the mouth of the Jägala River is considered one of the largest farm fortresses in Estonia. One should forgo swimming in the river as well as in the Bay of Ihasalu Laht: up the Jägala River, a paper and wood-pulp combine was set up near Kehdra and this dumps its untreated sewage into the river.

Keila (Kegel)

Fourteen thousand residents live in the suburb of Keila on the banks of the Keila River. The old settlement southwest of Tallinn was founded in the early 13th century and later belonged to the estate of the Teutonic Order. It experienced a short period of prosperity because of the rail route from Tallinn to Paldiski. The wooden Danish *church* built in 1220 on the Keila River was replaced with a two-naved stone church in the early 14th century. The *Harjumaa-Muuseum* (Linnuse 9, Tel: 74 61 36) provides interesting insight into the local history of the area.

Surroundings

Keila-Joa: Residential blocks and heavy industry surrounding the small church prompt the question: why is this filthy area highlighted on numerous maps? It could be the fact that this town is located near the six-metre (20 foot) waterfall on the Keila River or because it is near the *Tudor Castle* which belonged to the family von Benckendorff completed in 1830 – either way there are nicer places in Estonia.

Fuel: At the entrance to town to the right when coming from Tallinn.

Klooga (Lodensee): The idyllic appearance is deceptive: in 1943 and 1944 around 2,000 people were killed in the Klooga concentration camp. Not far from here, the stream falls over cascades into the sea. This spectacle of nature is most beautiful after the thaw in spring. In summer, the stream is often dry.

Laulasmaa: "the singing land" (Laulma = singing, Maa = land) is the name of this village, which gained repute as the "African beach of Europe" during the past century.

Keila/Information

Automobile Repair: Tel: 74 43 30.
Restaurant: Paldiski maantee 4, Tel: 74 53 41.

Kernu (Kirna)

The tallest juniper bushes reaching a height of up to four metres (13 feet) have brought renown to the small town of Kernu on the M 12 toward Pärnu. At kilometre marker 35-1 is the "Swedish King's Staff": this is classified as a *natural monument* and consists of a 300-year-old tree trunk

twisted seven times and almost 1.5 metres (5 feet) in circumference. The manor house in this town was built in the classicistic architectural style at the beginning of the 19th century.
Accommodation: Kernu Motel, Tel: 21 56 96.

Kose (Kosch)

The southeastern centre of the province is located on the A 202 toward Paide on the Pirita River. A *park* with old walkways lined with linden trees borders the meandering river in the centre of the city; white waterlilies bloom on the pond. The *church* from the 15th century also includes a graveyard where *Otto von Kotzebue.* This was the son of the German author August von Kotzebue who circumnavigated the globe.

Padise

The ruins of the old *Monastery Fortress* on the road to Haapsalu are the oldest historical monument in Harjumaa. In the 13th century, Cistercian monks began construction. When Estonian farmers killed 28 of the monks in the Jüriöö uprising in 1343, construction was stopped. The building was first completed in the 16th century.

The fortified monastery, surrounded by the river on all sides, suffered during the Livonian War. In 1766, fire destroyed large sections of the structure. Now, plans exist to rebuild the monastery with secular aid. Located near the ruins of the monastery is the old Estonian *Vana Linnamägi Fortress.*

Paldiski (Baltischport)

The Red Army's naval base 60 kilometres (37½ miles) west of Tallinn on the A 205 is still a military zone. The expansion into a military harbour and naval base began during the time of Peter the Great. While the harbour stood uncompleted at first, the fortress whose walls are still preserved today, was used as a type of prison. Near the fortress and harbour, a settlement developed during the 18th century, which was awarded the tights of a city in 1783 under the name "Baltic Port" (Baltisk Port). In 1796, it became the provincial capital of the province with the same name. Paldiski attempted in vein to break the Tallinn's hegemony – despite the ice-free harbour and a railway connection, Paldiski remained a quaint beach and health resort and centre for the local fishing industry up until the turn of the century. In 1782, the city had 211 residents; in 1913, 1,300; and today ??? – these statistics are just as taboo as are the things that happened in this area during the Soviet regime. It was only after Estonia's independence that the press suddenly informed the public that the Soviet army had operated two atomic reactors on their marine base without the knowledge of the Estonian government. What remains unclear to date is whether the sea has been radioactively contaminated as a result. The most famous resident of this city was the sculptor *Adam Adamson,* who still praised the city as a "pearl in the landscape."

Surroundings

Pakri Peninsula (Roger Wiek): A picturesque lighthouse stands along the steep coast on Glint Point, still a prohibited Soviet military zone.

Saku

The small settlement of Saku quickly grew around a brewery founded here in 1876. The classicistic manor house dates back to 1830. The nearby surroundings consist of an extensive landscape of heather, which is especially beautiful when it blooms in the autumn.

Tabasalu

Fourteen kilometres (9 miles) west of Tallinn, beyond a 9% grade on the coastal road, the town of Tabasalu comprises three brick apartment towers with adjacent maintenance facilities and a camping area in the pine forest. In the nearby town of **Rannamoisa** (Strandhof) is the beginning of a section of coastal cliffs. Beyond the extensive pine forests from **Väna Joesuu,** which then merges into a deciduous forest near **Naage** is a beautiful sand beach. The parking area to the right of the road offers a nice view of the bay, otherwise the trees block the view to the sea. One should be careful when going on a walk through the forest: the glint ridge suddenly drops off in the middle of the forest, concealed by the under-

brush in many places. Hikers could unexpectedly suffer a fall of 6 metres (20 feet).

Refreshments: Café Merepiiga (Café Mermaid), Tabasalu, Tel: 47 03 33.

Vaida

The oldest Estonian sewer system can be found in Vaida. Today, this is classified as a historical monument. The pipes originate from England and have been in use since 1852.

Läänemaa (Wiek)

Extending from the Gulf of Finland in the north to the Gulf of Riga in the south is the province of Läänemaa with an area of over 2,417 square kilometres (943 square miles) and a population of 33,839. The landscape is characterized by a very rugged coastline, which – similar to the Swedish cliffs – offer a number of larger and smaller island and boulders off of the coast. Fields, meadows and junipers are typical for the flat interior regions, which rise to a height of 51 metres (167 feet) at Pikajala Hill (Longfoot Hill) near Palivere. The land, which was pillaged during the course of numerous wars, was even shaken by nature itself: 1877 was the date of the last earthquake here. The touristic and economic centre of Läänemaa is the provincial capital of Haapsalu with a population of 15,200.

Haapsalu (Hapsal)

The former summer resort with old wooden houses and narrow alleyways was once highly praised by *Pjotr (Peter) Tchaikovsky* and other Russian artists from the 19th century. Today, huge and dilapidated residential high-rises and industrial areas are characteristic of this city. The railway borders the town to the north and east; to the south and west, the lake forms the natural city limits. The motorway leads through the unsightly portion of town in a broad arc – one would hardly expect such a beautiful city centre.

History

The year 1220 marked a turn in the historical development of the old fishing village. With the establishment of the diocese of Saare-Lääne, construction of the castle began around 1228 followed by the founding of a cathedral in 1279. Haapsalu was awarded the "ius regense," the rights of Riga. The bishop established the city limits in 1323 on horseback. Up to the middle of the 14th century, Haapsalu remained the bishop's seat; then the men of Saare-Lääne moved to Arensburg on the island of Saaremaa. Only the cathedral chapter remained in Haapsalu. Under Swedish rule the city experienced a short period of prosperity at the end of the 17th century before the Russians destroyed the fortress and conquered the city in 1710. Peter I visited Haapsalu in 1715; however, he found the town ill-suited as a naval base. The provincial capital since 1784, the first economic boom as a beach and health resort began with the opening of the first therapeutic mud-baths by the local physician Dr. Karl Abraham Hunnius in 1825. The so-called Bergfeldt Sanatorium was in existence up until 1940. In 1845, Hunnius founded the second mud-baths, which endured up to 1953. During the 19th century, Haapsalu gained renown as a fashionable resort preferred by nobility and aristocracy. Members of the czar's family visited Haapsalu and possibly paged through the weekly newspaper "Hapsalsche Wochenblatt" which has been published since 1895 or the "Hapsalsche Stadtblatt" from 1886. In 1869, Tchaikovsky composed the "Souvenir of Hapsal" – the notes for these three piano pieces can be seen in the local museum. Just as airy and light as the music are the white woollen shawls, a traditional souvenir from Haapsalu.

Sights

The 100-hectare (250-acre) old city is a closed ensemble of history and is classified as a historical monument in its entirety. The most impressive structure is the "Bishop's Fortress." The central portion, the "small fortress" was built in 1291. From 1391 to the beginning of the 15th century, the stone anterior fortress to the west followed. At the beginning of the 16th century, the eastern anterior fortress was completed. The entire ring of walls, which reaches a height of up to 10 metres (33 feet), has a total length of around 800 metres (½ mile) today. The rectangular fortress building with an inner courtyard was transformed into a castle from 1641 to 1647 by Jakob de la Gardie. Church services have been held on a regular basis since Christmas of 1990 in the *fortress church.* This church was restored from 1886 to 1889 and given a neo-Gothic portal with a rounded archway. The baptistery on the south side of the church dates back to the 13th century.

Czar Peter I stopped at the municipal governor's house at Wiedemanni 2 during his visit to Haapsalu in 1715. Housed in the former town hall from 1775, the *Museum of Local History* (Lossi plats) provides information on the history of the resort and the surrounding regions with extensive exhibits. Those who would like even more information should visit the *Läänemaa-Muuseum* (Kooli 2, Tel: 4 46 48). Not far from the Protestant *Jaani Church,* Count de la Gardie had a small park with a pond called the *Count's Garden,* laid out on the harbour area which had since silted up. On the *beach promenade,* one might notice the white park bench made from Saaremaa marble with musical notes chiselled on the backrest. This was set up in honour of the Russian composer *Peter Tchaikovsky,* who composed the work "Souvenir of Hapsal." Not far from this point, stone steps lead to the Baltic Sea, now overgrown and stinking with algae. Passing the *Spa Building* built in 1905 by the architect *R. Knüpfer,* the tour leads along a belt of reeds in Tagalaht Bay to the *therapeutic mud-*

Waiting for the White Lady

The Bishop's Fortress conceals a mystery. It is said that during the "white nights" in August, a woman's silhouette could be seen from the wall on the centre window of the baptistery – the famous "White Lady of Haapsalu," who was entombed in the walls of this fortress. The Prebendary's former lover had dared to cross the threshold of the Order's fortress out of love for this priest. At that time entrance to the fortress was strictly forbidden for women. Every year in August, the Estonians celebrate the "White Lady" festival. After the performance of the "White Lady" play on the square in front of the fortress, all stand in anticipation waiting for the apparition.

baths. A monument stands here in honour of the physician *Abraham Hunnius* who discovered the therapeutic effects of Haapsalu mud. Somewhat outside of the old city is the train station which was built in 1905 for the route from Keila to Haapsalu. Dedicated in 1906, the building has a length of 216 metres (706 feet) which makes it the longest railway structure in Estonia.

Information

Accommodation

Camping: Roosta Camping, Ehitajate tee 3, Tel: 9 37 32, Noarootsi vald, 40 kilometres (25 miles) to the east on the coast.

Hotels: Haapsalu, Posti 43, Tel: 4 48 47. Five single rooms, 26 double rooms, two suites with western standards. This hotel is an Estonian-Swedish joint venture.

Pippi Boarding House, Posti/corner of Nurme, WC/shower in the hallway, 20 beds, sauna.

Automobile Repair: Tallinna 73, Tel: 5 58 84; Stop, Tel: 4 47 76.

Café-Bars: Café Greitz, Lossi plats (right next to the fortress); Meirist, Tallinna maantee 1; Venta, Jalaka 1a, Tel: 5 57 66.

Fuel: Lihula maantee 11, Tel: 5 51 02; Tallinna maantee, Tel: 4 47 76.

Harbour: Rohuküla merevaksal, Tel: 9 11 38 (ferries to Hiiumaa).

Hospital: Suur-Liiva 15, Tel: 4 45 02.

Marketplace: Jüriöö (next to the Alexander Nevski Cathedral).

Post Office: Tamme 21.

Restaurants: Maritima, Tallinna 1, Tel: 4 44 45, open 11 am to 5 pm and 7 pm to midnight; Paralepa, Tel: 4 40 54.

Travel Agency: Westra, Posti 67, Tel: 4 56 49, Fax: 4 51 91.

Kirbla (Kirrefer)

The *smallest medieval church in Estonia* stands on the beach of Kirbla. However, it is the landscape surrounding the town which is more widely known than this church with its late baroque altar. Reed and marshlands border the Kasari River over a distance of 15 kilometres (9½ miles) all the way to Matsalu Bay. The nicest view of this pastoral landscape of Estonia is from the bridge over the Kasari, built in 1904 and measuring 300 metres (980 feet) in length (→ *Matsalu*).

Koluvere

On the A 207 from Lihula to Risti is the village of Koluvere. The *Teutonic fortress* from the 13th century is surrounded by a deep moat fed by the Liivi River. This was also the site where Catherine II once had the princess of Württemberg Augusta Carolina imprisoned. This domicile of the Brothers of the Sword was transformed from a castle to a convent around 1400 and was the subject of embittered battles: the Swedes conquered the fortress in 1564, to be followed by the Danes and later the Russians. After the end of the Great Northern War, the fortress temporarily served as a prison. In 1905, revolutionaries burned the fortress to the ground; it has meanwhile been reconstructed and completely restored. Also worth seeing is the old *watermill* on the Liivi River with the interior preserved in its original state.

Lihula (Leal)

The small rural city of Lihula on the road from Virtsu to Tallinn was the site where the history of Estonia was decided in 1220. In the battle over the Lihula fortress, Denmark was able to gain control over western Estonia. Up to 1265, Lihula was the bishop of Saare-Lääne's seat before the archbishop went to Haapsalu. All that remains today of the old fortress on the hill are ruins.

Accommodation: Lihula Camping.

Matsalu Nature Reserve

The huge reeded areas at the Kasari delta in which individual reeds can grow up to 4 metres (13 feet) has been under protection since 1958. The official recognition of this area first followed in 1970. The nature reserve has an area of 400 square kilometres (156 square miles) – the largest area in the Baltic States – and the adjacent Bay of Matsalu with its islands off the coast. One hundred years before the recognition, in 1870, observation of the birds began. Even today, 120,000 birds are spotted, banded and registered each year in Penijoe. in the *Haeska Manorhouse,* a classicistic structure from the 19th century on the northern shore of Matsalu Bay houses a research centre with a bird museum, video show and an observation tower (Matsalu Riiklik Looduskaitseala: Penijoe, Tel: 7 84 13).

The focal point of this nature reserve is the *Penijoe River;* trips into the marshlands and the bay are possible from the harbour. The *observation towers* on the low sand dunes offer a view of the nesting areas of 68 species of birds during the summer. Over 100 different species of birds are registered on the islands in Matsalu Bay. Hundreds of thousands of swans on their migration to the north and northeast stop in the reserve beginning in mid April. The mounds on the southern edge of Matsalu originate from prehistoric coral reefs and erratic blocks. The large stones are called "Näärikivid" (New Year's stones) by the local residents: according to the legend, they are said to have been deposited here during the ice age on New Year's Eve.

Information: Nature Reserve Administration, Avro Millmets (Director), 203 190 Lihula, Tel: 7 84 13.

Noarootsi (Nuckö)

A small strip of land usually submerged in water connects the 100 square kilometre (39 square mile) Noarootsi Peninsula with the mainland. Those who have a soft spot for barren juniper heath scattered with stone blocks should definitely make the crossing. The history of the island is closely tied to the Swedes living here. As early as 1294, the privileges of the coastal Swedes who lived here up to 1944 were mentioned in historical documents. **Pürski,** the main "city" of Noarootsi, is said to have been named after the Estonian birch ("Björk" = Birch). Others claim that the origin of the name of this town is related to the Swedish city of Birka. The *church of Noarootsi* built around 1390 is near **Hosby,** which was restored with financial aid from the Swedes. The region near **Österby** offers a beautiful view across the sea to Haapsalu, around 3 kilometres (2 miles) away.

Palivere

The highest hill of Läänemaa, the Pikajalamägi, rises 51 metres (167 feet) near the A 207 to Tallinn. The *church* of Lääne-Nigula from the 13th century is considered a jewel of architectural history. Somewhat surprisingly, however, since only the choir has retained its medieval appearance... The *Teutonic fortress* of Palivere is also called "Vallipealne."

Puhtulaid

The wooded Puhtulaid Peninsula, which protrudes from the water like an island during high tide, is a very famous site. In 1813, the world's first monument for the leading German poet Friedrich Schiller was erected here – *Wilhelmine von Helvig* so admired the German poet that she honoured him with a monument in the estate park. A *600 year old oak tree* with a trunk 1.4 metres (4½ feet) in diameter in the Park of Puhtu is reminiscent of the former deciduous forest here. The 137 types of birds in the deciduous forests often perch in the oak's branches which reach a height of up to 23 metres (75 feet). The last owner of the Puhtu estate was the famous philosopher and natural scientist *Hermann von Keyserling.*

Puise

In the autumn of 1944, the beach on the peninsula of Matsalu Bay was flooded with refugees: countless Estonians tried to flee from the Red Army by sea from the Puise Peninsula, first to Sweden and then farther to the United States, Canada and Australia.

Ridala (Röthel)

Ridala is situated south of Haapsalu on the rural road to Lihula. The town attracts archaeologists, who hope to find the grave of the Swedish king. King Ingvar of Sweden landed here with his men around 600 AD and devastated the country. During the Estonian counterattack, the king was killed in the ensuing battle and buried near the coast. The search for the grave site has remained unsuccessful. A sign on the street points the way to the whitewashed *fortified church* from the 13th century. The pulpit and altar were created by *Elert Thiele* in 1655. The weathered round crosses made of stone in the graveyard date back to the 13th and 14th centuries. Up on the old fortress hill *Ridala Tubrilinn,* one can still see the remnants of the old fortification wall.

Taebla

A painter made the town of Taebla famous. Located on the A 206 before the gates of the city of Haapsalu, Taebla was the home and workplace of the artist *Ants Laikmaa* (1866-1942). The landscape painter had his home and atelier built in the nearby hamlet of Kadapirku in the style of old Estonian country cottages. The house with its triangular windows, a thatched roof and a room with a bay window is surrounded by an extensive park. Today it houses the *Ants Laikmaa Museum* (Tel: 9 66 88). The *Clock Spring of the Polish King* can be found near the school of Taebla: when the Polish king was caught in the act of stealing the church clock, the ruler is said to have thrown it into this spring during his flight.

Virtsu

Today, this former island is connected to the mainland by a narrow isthmus. Ferries to Muhu and continuing to Saaremaa depart from Virtsu (Information: Virtsu Harbour, Tel: 7 55 20). The former Üxküll family castle was almost completely destroyed with the exception of a few sections of walls. The Üxküll family once had sole rule over the island.

The Grindstone of Kalevipoeg

The *erratic block* halfway between Rapla and the train station 3 kilometres (2 miles) away is called the "grindstone of Kalevipoeg" by the local residents. According to the legend, Kalevipoeg had thrown the boulder at a wolf which had attacked a young lamb. However: with a circumference of 20 metres (65 feet), the stone killed both the wolf and the lamb...

Raplamaa (Rappel)

The least known Estonian province of Raplamaa was established 40 years ago from the peripheries of the four adjacent provinces. The provincial capital of Raplamaa is Rapla with a total area 2,980 square kilometres/ 1,162 square miles and is home to 6,390 of the province's total population of 40,000. The city of Rapla is devoid of any significant touristic highlights, but does offer attractive landscapes in the surrounding regions.

Rapla (Rappel)

Rapla was first documented historically in 1241 when the Danish king added this village to his list of possessions. The construction of the Mary Magdalene Church elevated this village to the status of parish; however, the fate of Rapla was determined by the Alu Estate located three kilometres (2 miles) away. In 1945, the small city became the provincial capital. The *parsonage* on the riverbanks is the oldest building in Rapla. The *oak of peace* in front of the parsonage was planted in commemoration of the abolition of serfdom. Rapla's *church* is the only rural church in Estonia with two towers. The alter from 1737 was a gift from the municipal judge Hans Ludwig Fock, according to the inscription. The pulpit was donated by *Christian Ackermann* around 1700 and depicts the coats of arms of Matthias von Stauern and those of his two wives.

Surroundings

Hagudi: Nine kilometres (5½ miles) to the north near the railway route lies the *Krusenstern Estate*. The history of this estate spans centuries and began with a romance: in 1637, Philipp Crusiks, born in Thuringia Germany, planned a journey to Persia. Because of a shipwreck in the Baltic Sea, he came to Estonia. There, he met the daughter of the estate owner in Kunda. He fell in love and married her. Twelve years later, having been elevated in status to nobility, the Swedish king gave Crusiks the Hagudi Estate. A monument at the entrance to the estate commemorates one of the estate's famous offspring: *Adam Johann Krusenstern* was born on the estate in 1770; later he was to circumnavigate the globe.

Horeda: Surrounding he manorhouse – presently left to decay – an Estonian-Finnish company now plans to lay out the first golf course in Estonia.

Keava: This small village 5 kilometres (3¼ miles) east of Rapla was already historically documented in the chronicle of Novgorod: Prince Izposlav Jaroslavovits was able to push through to the fortified farm of Keava on his military campaign through Estonia – then this Russian commander was devastatingly defeated. The expansive moorlands of Keava extend all the way to the base of the 82 metre (268 foot) Fortress Hill.

Kehna (Kechtel): A horse thief made this town located 12 kilometres (7½ miles) from Rapla on the rural road to Viljandi famous: Juri Rumm always emerged untouched from his thieving escapades to return to the Kehna estate. The adjacent park is widely known for its 30 metre (98 foot) larch tree and the former sovkhoz, for its advances in animal husbandry research – it was here that the first successful artificial insemination of pigs took place.

Information

Automobile Repair: Tallinna 19, Tel: 7 33 77.

Café-Bar: Hariduse 3, Tel: 5 78 37.

Fuel: Tallinna 1, Tel: 5 53 35.

Restaurant: Rapla, Kooli 1, Tel: 5 60 96.

Järlepa

This small village north of Rapla on the periphery of a swampland area made theatre history: while August von Kotzebue was alive, actresses from the neighbourhood formed a small ensemble under Kotzebue's direction. When Kotzebue discovered that his wife was continuously disloyal, the author moved to Varbala and began a new career as a potato farmer – and the court theatre was disbanded only three years later. After this theatrical intermezzo, the turkeys arrived: today, this estate is now known for its poultry breeding. North of the village is a the small Järlepa-järv (Lake Järlepa).

Surroundings

Angerja: In the spruce forest near Angerja, northwest of Järlepa near the road to Kohila is the *King of Stones*, an erratic block which has been split exactly in the middle by the elements. The golden watch belonging to the estate owner of Pahkla is said to have once fallen into this crevasse...

Juuru (Jörden Church)

The town's name "Juuru," Estonian for root, refers to the sacred grove on which a *church* was built in 1238. Less "sacred" was the "War of Mahtra," and there is a *museum* in Juuru covering this historical period. On June 14, 1858, 700 to 800 farmers began a nation-wide uprising in the forests beyond the Mahtra estate directed against the German land owners. While the land owners fled to St. Petersburg, Czar Alexander II sent troops to combat the revolutionaries. His 2,000 soldiers surrounded the farmers and drove them out. The two leaders were sentenced to 1,000 lashes and 20 years of forced labour. The gauntlet and exile in Siberia awaited thirty-three other farmers. Three years after the uprising, the banishment of serfdom began in Russia, which was later adopted in all of Estonia in 1871.

Lohu

The Lohu Estate is located on the rural road to Kohila near the Keila River. The Estonian sculptor *Anton Starrkopf* was born here in 1889. In the manorhouse, significant black and white tempera paintings from the 18th century were discovered when the tapestry depicting scenes from "Don Quixote" was removed from the walls. Having been restored in Moscow, the tapestry now hangs in the Historical Museum in Tallinn.

Märjamaa

This town on the M 12 between Tallinn and Pärnu has presumably been in existence since the 13th century. The town's Gothic *church* from the middle of the 14th century is dedicated to the Virgin Mary. The Rangu Heath begins five kilometres (3 miles) to the northwest of Märjamaa.

Raikküla

Only a few kilometres south of Rapla is the *Estate of Raikküla* which belonged to the Count von Keyserling family. The nobleman shocked the public with his taste for the avantgarde during his renovations: not only did Alexander set up Estonia's first alpinarium, but also caused a good deal of fear in the farmers by building chimneys. Since the farmers feared that the warmth escaped through the flue, they would stop it up with straw and the disaster was inevidable: fire.

Arnold von Keyserling also tried his had at something new: since the summer of 1990, this son of the natural scientist *Hermann von Keyserling* has run a philosophical summer school every year. The classicistic manorhouse on the estate was built in 1820.

Velise

The small city of Velise on the banks of the Velise River southwest of Märjamaa is known for its "heavyweights": Georg Lurich, an athlete by trade, wandered with his camels from one fair to the next. His most famous trick was to have two horses pulling in opposite directions try to separate his clasped hands – never were the horses successful. Tonis Ervin, a wrestler who performed at the Tallinn circus, is said to have single-handedly beaten up fifty masons. In 1905, the men of Velise also demonstrated their strength: during the time when the estates were being "nationalized" they declared the "free city-state of Velise" within the district borders – a stone in front of the church commemorates this event.

Surroundings

Only one kilometre (½ mile) from Velise, the *Village Museum of Silloatsa* exhibits agricultural equipment, most of which were built by hand by the farmers themselves.

Vigala

The scattered settlement south of Märjamaa comprises the districts of Vana-Vigala (Old Vigala), Kivi-Vigala and Kesk-Vigala. The loamy soil up to 20 metres (65 feet) thick brought relative prosperity to the farmers in this region. The church of Kivi-Vigala dates back to the 14th century. Only a few trees remain from the avenue lined with larch trees which once led to Vana-Vigala. Vana-Vigala is also the largest village in Estonia with residents numbering 1,000. The rather dilapidated *manorhouse* in Vana-Vigala which now houses the agricultural school belongs to the oldest Baltic-German line of nobility, the Üx-küll family. There are graves scattered throughout the narrow and elon-gated *estate park* which includes a pond. What has also been preserved is the so-called *wall of hunger* from the Middle Ages. Music seminars take place in Vana-Vigala each summer.

Surroundings

The painter *Ants Laikmaa* was born in **Avaste** in 1866. The *Avaste Hill* offers a nice view of the Velise River and the distant *Fortress of Soontagana* in the Järve Moor.

Pärnumaa

This seaside resort region of Estonia has much more to offer than merely the beach: from the beach on the Bay of Pärnu, this province stretches over 4,771 square kilometres (1,861 square miles). With 54,000 people living in the capital of Pärnu, the countryside is less densely populated with 41,000 residents.

Pärnu (Pernau)

Annually, around 300,000 visit Pärnu, Estonia's oldest health resort on the Gulf of Riga with its beach measuring 100 metres in width, its shady parks and Art Nouveau villas. Pärnu, the port city and provincial capital is located 135 kilometres (85 miles) south of Tallinn and is home to a population of 54,000, making it the fifth largest city in Estonia.

History

Originally, two cities were named Pärnu: The first, Vana-Pärnu (Old Pernau) lay on the right banks of the

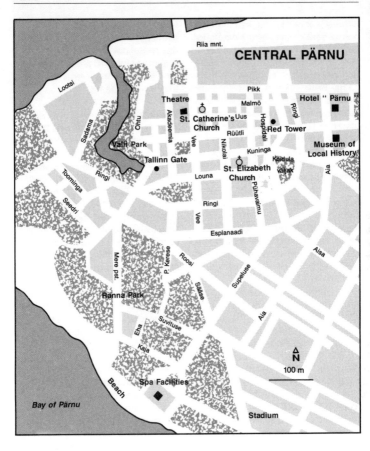

Pärnu River and was founded by the Bishop of Saare-Lääne. When the Lithuanians burned down the fortress in 1236, the bishop moved to Haapsalu. In 1575 and 1577, Old Pärnu was burned to the ground twice more. On the left banks of the Pärnu River was Uus-Pärnu (New Pernau), originally called "Embecke." The city's membership in the Hanseatic League caused the city to flourish. With the end of the Teutonic Order's rule, Pärnu first went to Poland and then came under Swedish rule in 1699, resulting from the Swedish-Polish War, and then even became a university town: Pärnu was the temporary seat of the Tartu alma mater until 1710, when the Russians conquered the city. In 1782, Pärnu had a population of 1,954. When the mudbaths were opened in 1838, this marked the beginning of a turbulent development into a health and beach resort. In 1890, therapeutic silt baths were to follow.

In 1857, the first daily newspaper in Estonia, the "Perno Postines" (Pernau Post) appeared in Pärnu. In 1897 with a population of 12,842, Pärnu had grown to the fourth largest city in Estonia.

Paper pulp dictates Pärnu's economic well-being: over 3,000 employees worked in Russia's largest paper factory. The factory owned by the Waldhof company from Mannheim, Germany was blown up by the Russians during the First World War. The year 1938 marks the official founding of the resort town of Pärnu: the first therapeutic baths replaced the old therapeutic silt baths. The drawback to this resort is the untreated sewage from the fish combine as well as from the city which result in the poor quality of drinking water and polluted seawater. Adding to this is the noise from the nearby Soviet airport.

Sights

The Pärnu River bisects the city: beyond the old city "island" between the river and the Baltic Sea is the residential district of Ülejoe (meaning "above the river") with the *Lydia Koidula Museum* (J. V. Jannseni 37, Tel: 4 16 63)

which was first opened in 1953. The memorial museum is open Wednesday to Sunday from 10 am to 5 pm, Saturdays form 10 am to 4 pm. Also on this side of the river is the industrial area of Rääma.

Walking Tour

The city's network of streets through the centre of Pärnu are at right angles almost without exception. The main shopping and business street is the Rüütli (Knight's Street) which is closed off with flowerpots beginning at house number 43, making it a pedestrian zone. Lining the old shopping street are two-storey stone houses from the 18th century, either plastered or left in the natural red brick. At the lower end of the street not far from Hotel Pärnu is the *Pärnu Koduloomuuseum* (Museum of Local History; Rüütli 53, Tel: 4 34 64; open Wednesday to Friday from 11 am to 6 pm, Saturday and Sunday from 11 am to 5 pm). In 1996, the museum will celebrate its 100th anniversary: one year after the establishment of the Pärnu Society for Historical Studies, a small museum was founded, an idea initiated by the amateur archaeologist Dr. Paul Schneider. From 1898 to 1938, the society published a twelve-volume chronicle of the city in the German language. In 1901, the number of articles on display had already increased to 884 with 2,000 coins and 1,569 books. Nine years later, the society and museum moved into an old house at Elevandi Street 7, where they stayed up until the fire on September 23, 1944. In 1953, the museum moved to its present location; in 1963, the number of articles on exhibition at the municipal museum numbered 20,466 with 16,585 visitors in that year. Today, this collection has grown to 60,000 articles. The museum hosts around 80,000 visitors annually. The ground floor shows the flora and fauna of the Pärnu Province as well as having special exhibitions. On the upper floor, a collection of traditional costumes augments the presentation of the city's history.

The skyline of Pärnu is determined by two churches. The new apostolic orthodox *Jekaterinen Church* (Catherine Church; Vee 16) was built from 1765 to 1768, funded by Czaress Catherine II. *Elizabeth Church* (Nicholai 22) was given its name by Jelisatev, the daughter of Peter I, who gave the congregation funds to finance the construction of their church. The builder from Riga finished this church in 1747.

The classicistic *city hall* from 1788 with its white, columned façade has an impressive ornamented door. The last remnants of the former city wall are the *Punane Torn* (Red Tower; Hommiku 11) and the *Tallinna Värav* (Tallinn Gate; Kuninga). The name Red Tower refers to the red bricks used to build this round tower in the 15th century. The defence tower, restored in the 19th century, served as a prison around 1500 and as the city archives from 1895 to 1907. The Tallinn Gate was built in the baroque architectural style.

The old wall complex was turned into a *park* in 1862. This extensive green-belt around the old city merges with the beach park. The city's streets are also green: the old tree-lined boulevards are over 40 kilometres (25 miles) long. They have a harmonious appearance because only one type of tree was planted. All of the Lindens now have the same circumference and height.

The pride of Pärnu is the 40 kilometre (25 mile) long sand beach which is up to 100 yards wide in some places. The beach was the basis for the establishment of the sanatorium and convalescence homes. Today, Pärnu is Estonia's largest health resort. Up to 25,000 people are treated here for cardio-vascular, circulatory and joint ailments annually. The central street of the resort district is Rannapuiestee (Beach Boulevard) along the *Rannapark* (Beach Park), which was laid out in 1891. The old resort building was constructed in 1890.

The Beach Hotel and Beach Café with the mushroom-shaped observation tower were built in 1940. With a length of two kilometres (1½ miles), the mole, built from boulders to shelter the mouth of the river, offers a beautiful view of the beach and the skyline of the city.

Surroundings

Pärnu-Jaagupi: Pärnu-Jaagupi is situated on the northern edge of an extensive moor, an area which was once called "Korbe." It was first in the 16th century that the name of the church's patron saint (Jaagup) was used to denote this city. To the north of town is a type of forest rare to Estonia, the *Oak Forest of Enge.*

Sindi (Zintendorf): 14 kilometres (9 miles) northeast of Pärnu is a worker's district which grew up around a textile mill 160 years ago. The textile mill remains the largest employer and focal point of the city. The Sindi-Lodja Bridge offers a beautiful view of the Reiu-Jögi and the lower Pärnu-Jögi.

Information

Accommodation

Camping/Motel: Valgerand, Seedri 4, Tel: 4 23 38.

Camping Kavaru: 5 kilometres (3 miles) outside of town in the forest by a beach.

Hotels: Pärnu, Rüütli 44, Tel: 4 21 45; double rooms for 100 Rubles.

Victoria, Kuninga 25, Tel: 4 34 12, Fax: 4 34 15; foreign-currency hotel with western standards; opened in 1991 by the Best Western hotel chain. 12 single rooms, 9 double rooms and two junior suites.

Emmi, Laine 2, Tel: 2 20 43; Kajakas, Seedri 2, Tel: 4 21 81 and 4 30 98; Kalur, Rüütli 2, Tel: 4 01 92; APBN Pensionaat.

Youth Hostel: Tostamaas Puhkebaas: Tel: Tallinn 44 72 74. On the coastal road from Pärnu to Virtsu is a youth hostel located near the beach and equipped with a sauna. Varbla, 30 kilometres (19 miles) to the west; open from May 1 to October 1, accessible via the small coastal road via Tostamaa.

Automobile Repair: Erki, Karja 6, Tel: 4 27 67; ; Tallinna maantee 89a, Tel: 4 22 43; Pappsaare, Tel: 4 15 91.

Bank: Kommertspank, Rüütli 51.

Beaches and Swimming: The pride of Pärnu is its beach: around 100 yards wide and a seemingly endless stretch of fine white sand bordered by low dunes and framed in the deep blue of the Baltic Sea. A nudist beach for women is the Naiste beach to the right of the spa building.

Bus Station: Ringi 1, Tel: 4 15 54.

Cafés: Atlantika, Tallinna maantee 2; Baar Bristol, Rüütli 45; Bristol Kohvipood, Rüütli 43; Baar Crown Mary, Pühavaimu 8; Ekspressbaar, Tallinna maantee 14; Florett, Voidu 26; Humal, Auli 1a; Männi, Riia maantee 28; Perona Baar, Rüütli 45; Vahtrabaar, Kerese 4; Victoria, Kuninga 25, Tel: 4 30 41 (located in the Victoria Hotel); Vikerbaar, Vee 2, Tel: 4 15 64.

Cinemas: Kiir, Vee 10, Tel: 4 03 30; Mai, Papniidu 10; Ranna, Mere puiestee 22, Tel: 4 06 37.

Fuel: Hommiku 2, Tel: 4 05 37; Riia maantee 24, Tel: 2 19 06; Nesté Service Station (at the entrance to town on the opposite side of the road when heading for Riga), Niidu 1, Tel: 4 28 77.

Hospital: Polyclinic, Suur-Sepa 16, Tel: 4 25 45 and 4 19 67.

Marketplace: Suur-Sepa 18.

Museum: Aia/corner of Rüütli, open 11 am to 6 pm.

Pharmacies: Rüütli 39, Tel: 4 11 47; Riia maantee 15, Tel: 4 28 43.

Post Office: Rüütli 5/corner of Akadeemia 7; late evening service.

Restaurants: Hermes, Riia maantee 74, Tel: 4 26 81; Neptun, Ranna puiestee 3, Tel: 4 34 85; Pärnu, Rüütli 44, Tel: 4 11 05; Postipoiss, Vee 12, Tel: 4 02 04; Raanahoone, Ranna puiestee 3, Tel: 4 02 22; Roosikelder,

Kuninga 18; Tallinn, Akadeemia 5, Tel: 4 04 68; Victoia, Kuninga 25 (in the Victoria Hotel).
Spa Facilities: Sanatoria: "Estonia," Ranna puiestee, Tel: 4 24 90; "Rahu," Sääse 7 Tel: 4 26 36; "Soprus," Eha 2a, Tel: 2 21 03; "Tervis," Seedri 6, Tel: 4 32 69.
Special Events
June: "Fiesta": Jazz, Blues and Gospel Festival, every year lasting one week. The eighth festival in 1993 once more included international participation.
Sports and Recreation: Kalev Stadium, Ranna puiestee 2, Tel: 4 30 08; Kalev Yacht Club, Lootsi 6, Tel: 4 19 48.
Taxi: Central switchboard, Tel: 4 12 40.
Theatre: Eesti Draamateater: Pärnu maantee 5, Tel: 44 20 65. Large theatre seats 548; small hall seats 128.
Endla-Theatre, Käskväljak 12, Tel: 4 22 53.
Train Station: Tammiste, Tel: 4 07 73.
Travel Agencies: Travel Agency Riese, Uus 2, Tel: 4 07 51, Fax: 4 06 90; ATP Tourist, Ringi 3, Tel: 2 31 25, Fax: 2 23 86; Pärnu Reisebüroo, Kuninga 32, Tel: 4 27 50.

Audru (Audern)

Situated on the mouth of the Audru River is a clean beach with white sand – even the name "Valgerand" meaning white sand is an indication of this. The *Audru Estate* was founded in 1449. The *church* was newly constructed in 1636 for an Estonian Lutheran congregation.

Information
Restaurant: Kuldlovi (Golden Lion), in the old tavern, Tel: 4 06 03.

Häädemeeste (Gutmannsbach)

Thirty-five kilometres (22 miles) south of Pärnu is the largest town on the coast toward Latvia. While mineral water is produced today in Häädemeeste, ship-building brought renowned to this town by the sand dunes even beyond the borders of Estonia. The 20 kilometre (12½ mile) Timm Canal was built in order to better transport the wood from the nearby forests to this village (historically documented since 1560). East of town is the *Rannametsa* chain of sand dunes, the highest in Estonia. While wind-swept pine trees cover the 40 metre (131 foot) Tootuse Hill, Torni Hill is completely barren. South of Häädemeeste toward Tali is a *highland moor* near **Nigula** with 370 moorland pools, lakes and islands. This area has been classified as a nature reserve. The cranberry fields in the nearby peat regions yield a copious harvest in autumn: two tonnes per hectare are picked here for processing into cranberry juice.
Information
Accommodation: Numerous camping areas like "Rannametsa Kämping" are nestled in the pine forests on the sand dunes.
Fuel: Tel: 9 82 12.

Ikla

The border crossing point is open to pedestrians in this last village before the Latvian. Drivers must turn back to the dirt road M 12 and cross the border there. Not far from the border is a mineral spring – the Ravimuda.

Kabli

The protracted fishing village along the secondary route from Pärnu to Ikla consists of only a few houses. The waiting area for the bus stop is built from a ship's bow and is reminiscent of the fact that this village was once widely known for the construction of sailing ships.

Accommodation
Camping: Looderanna Kämping, Tel: 9 84 58; Camping in the coastal pine forests near Majaka.

Kilingi-Nomme (Nömme)

The extensive, green settlement of Kilingi-Nomme situated in the forest is the southern centre of the province. Located on the Sakala chain, the wooded sand dunes extend up to the edge of town. The elongated small city, whose double name can be traced back to the Kilingi Estate and the Nomme Inn was classified a city in 1938. The birch-lined avenue in the centre of town connects the estate with the church. The marketplace with its massive pine tress in the centre of town is the location of a café and the church. The *Tihetmetsa* lies on the eastern edge of town with a

park and manorhouse – golden lions guard the classicistic entrance to both sides.

Information
Accommodation: Kilingi-Nomme, Pärnu maantee 53, Tel: 9 22 94.
Café: Kilingi-Nomme, Pärnu maantee 42, Tel: 9 21 89. Across from the department store in the centre of town.
Fuel: Pärnu maantee.
Police: Pärnu maantee 27, Tel: 9 25 02.

Lavassaare

Surrounded by extensive swampland areas north of Pärnu is the centre for peat production. The Lavassaare mount (31 metres/102 feet) offers a sweeping view of the expansive peat area and the small lake Lavassaare at the centre.

Taali (Staelendorf)

Surrounding the village of Taali on the banks of the Pärnu River is the most fertile soil in the province. Therefore, it is no wonder that archaeological finds from this area are evidence of human settlements having existed here over thousands of years. Worth seeing is the river with its red sandstone boulder. In the middle of the river is an erratic block. According to the legend, Kalevipoeg the national hero, is said to have once tried to destroy Vonnu (Cesis) by hurling this 4.2 metre (14 foot) stone called *Vonnukivi* at the Latvian city.

Tahkurand (Tackerort)

Twenty kilometres (12½ miles) south of the road from Pärnu in the birthplace of *Konstantin Päts*, a memorial has once more stood here in honour of the authoritarian president of Estonia during the first independent republic. A memorial is housed in a sheep stall. The orthodox church originates from 1874.

Tori (Torgel)

Powerful horses make Tori famous. Located upriver on the Pärnu, Tori is the town where horses have been bred since 1865. The "Tori Race" is used as a work and draught-horse. The *Eesti Pollumajandusmuuseumi Tori filiaal* (Agricultural Museum; Tel: 6 69 97) provides information on the history of the estate and the adjacent stud-farm.

On the gently sloping banks of the Pärnu-Jögi is the partially collapsed *Cave of Tori* reaching a depth of almost 10 metres (33 feet). The sandstone caves on the 150 metre (490 foot) wide Pärnu River resulted from the erosion of springs.

Tostamaa

Thirty kilometres (19 miles) west of Pärnu, a chain of sand dunes lines the coast near Tostamaa. The highest elevation in this series of dunes is the "Leevarotimägi" (Rat Bread Mountain) reaching a height of 20 metres (65 feet). Within town is the only service station on the way to Haapsalu. On the coastal road is a youth hostel equipped with a sauna.

Vändra (Fennern)

In the northeastern regions of the province, 54 kilometres (34 miles) from Pärnu is the birthplace of *Lydia Koidula,* situated on the A 203 toward Paide. This is not the only famous citizen of this town. The founder of Estonian journalism *Johann Voldemar Jannsen* was born here as well. Vändra's third "VIP" lies in the cemetery: *Lilli Suburg* founded the local girls' school. The *Vändra Kolhoosi Koduloomuuseum* (School and Local History Museum) in Vändra-Alikonnu keeps the history of this town alive. Vändra also had a school for the deaf for many years, which was founded in 1866.

In the nearby town of **Kurgija,** the *Carl Robert Jakobson House Museum* commemorates this citizen of Vändra by choice, who revolutionized the agriculture. The museum is a prototype farmyard. *Jakobson,* editor of the radical "Sakala" newspaper, developed a new feed combination for cows and achieved impressive increases in the harvest yields through adoption of the Finnish crop rotation system. Jakobson died in 1882 and today, memorial hikes along the 12 kilometre (7½ mile) "Sakala tee" take place in his honour on his birthday and the day of his death.

There are still brown bears living in the forests of Vändra located near the border of Old Estonia and Livonia.

Information
Accommodation: Vändra, Tiigi 2, Tel: 9 56 89.
Automobile Repair: Tel: 9 36 75.
Café-Bar: Karu Baar, Tuuru 2, Tel: 9 56 63.
Restaurant: Vändra, Tel: 9 57 42.

Järvamaa (Jerwen)

This province in central Estonia measures 2,620 square kilometres (1,022 square miles) in area and is characterized by agriculture. The administration centre of the province with a population of 43,800 is the city of Paide on the A 203.

Paide (Weißenstein)

The materials used in its construction gave the city its name: Paide was built from the light Paekivi limestone. The Germans called the city Weißenstein or Wittenstein (white stone) because of the light coloured houses.

History

One of the most historically significant Teutonic fortresses in Estonia built in 1265, furthered and protected the development of Paide which was awarded the status of city in 1291. However, the fortress also attracted wars: in 1558, Ivan the Terrible burned the settlement to the ground; in 1560, Paide once again stood in flames before the Poles, Swedes and Russians successively took control of the city and fortress. In 1783, Paide became the provincial capital with only 440 residents. In the middle of

the 19th century, the grandfather of the German author Hermann Hesse worked in Paide as a local doctor.

Sights

The town still has the profile of a small classicistic city. On the central Kesk väljak (Church Square) the spiritual centre and political centre stand vis-à-vis: to the left, the city hall; to the right, the church. Another sharp contrast is provided by the *cultural centre,* built from long stone blocks: post modern style in its purest form, but with colourful rose window windows over the entry way. Old Paide, predominantly composed of one-storey wooden houses with patinas, has been preserved in the streets Pärnu, Pikk, Tallinna and all around the Kesk väljak. The Teutonic fortress is now mostly in ruins. The castle, built from 1265, was stricken from the list of fortresses in 1636. Restorations took place from 1895 to 1897, which were then continued in 1985. The octagonal fortress tower Vallitorn-Rampart (Tall Hermann), was destroyed by the Russians in 1941, but has meanwhile been reconstructed. In addition to this tower are also the ruins of Püssirohutorn (Gun Powder Tower), the embattlements at the western gate, the convent building, the Orthodox Uspenski Church as well as a stage for the song festival on the fortress hill. The committee for historical monuments meets in the caller of the fortress. In the park on Vallmägi is a memorial for the Estonians who died in the battle against the Germans on the night of St. George in 1343. The *Koduloo-*

muuseum (Museum of Local History; Lembitu 5, Tel: 2 12 76) provides information on the history of the city.

Information

Accommodation

Paide Voorastemaja: Telliskivi 8, Tel: 2 12 27.

Hotel: Neili Kuningat (Four Kings), is presently under the management of the Swedish-Estonian joint venture "Estkompexim" built to western standards. The planned opening of this hotel is in 1993.

Motel: Mäo-Manor, a motel with a business and tourist centre is being built on the intersection on Mäo Street.

Automobile Repair: Telliskivi 17, Tel: 4 18 69.

Beer Hall: Kaval-Ants, Väike-Aia 20.

Fuel: Tallinna maantee 59, Tel: 2 11 05; Prääma tee 12, Tel: 4 13 72.

Police: Tallinna maantee 12.

Post Office: Pikk 2/4, corner of Kesk väljak.

Restaurant: Paide, Kesk väljak, Tel: 4 13 30; Varo, Tallinna maantee 3.

Türi (Türgel)

Thirteen kilometres (8 miles) south of Paide on the A 206 is the small city of Türi, located on the railway route from Tallinn to Viljandi. The sluggish Pärnu River meanders directly through the centre of this town with a population of 6,800. The river is very narrow, silted up and overgrown in many places. It was only in the 20th century that this former parish began to develop into a city – a fact reflected by the generous spatial planning

in Türi. Broad boulevards and extensive parks make up the profile of this "green city," which is famous for its annual *flower market*. In addition to the gardening tradition, the large yellow cranes of the Türi Metsa Combine (wood processing plant) determine the city's appearance. The Kirna-Kolchos is located at the exit from town when heading toward Paide. The Viljandi maantee runs directly through the centre of town. The old rural road to Viljandi is lined with small, pruned linden trees on both sides. The *church* from the beginning of the 14th century has a remarkable portal to the south. Also worthwhile is a visit to the *Flower Museum*. The small lake near town is quite clean.

Information

Accommodation: Türi Voorastemaja (guest house), Jaama 7, Tel: 7 82 62.

Automobile Repair: Tel: 7 85 07.

Bus Station: Viljandi maantee, on the southeastern edge of town.

Fuel: Tallinna maantee 64, Tel: 7 84 26; open 8 am to 8 pm on weekdays.

Pharmacy: Paide maantee 7.

Restaurants: Pärna Kohvik (café) and Restaurant II Korrussel in the Toidukaubad (department store), Viljandi maantee.

Ambla (Ampel)

The small village of Ambla on the edge of the Pandivere range to the northeastern plain is located 37 kilometres (23 miles) north of Paide on the A 203 toward Rakvere. Its unadorned *church* built from limeston in 1280 is dedicated to the Virgin Mary. The altar was carved by the Dutch master *Berent Geistman* from 1620 to 1628, the column capitals are adorned with stylized sculptures. In the churchyard is a memorial in honour of those who fell in the war of independence. Not far from town is the Ambla River, the source of which can be found near Lake Vanaveski.

Surroundings

Albu: Six kilometres (4 miles) southwest of Ambla, the *home of Anton Hansen Tammsaare* (Vargamäe, Tel: 3 77 56) is a memorial to the Estonian national poet who was born on a moor island near Albu on January 30, 1878.

Imavere

On the fork of the A 202 and A 204 around 20 kilometres (12½ miles) southeast of Paide, the *Piimandus-muuseum* (Milk Museum; Tel: 9 75 53) provides information on the history of the first Estonian dairy cooperative, founded by farmers here in 1907. *Hermynia von zur Mühlen* (1883-1951) grew up on the Eistvere farm. Later she would become famous in Austria as an author.

Jäneda (Jendel)

South of the railway route from Tapa to Tallinn is the old Jäneda estate, located on the edge of the Pandivere range and the moor plain of Korvemaa. The village's existence was first documented in 1353. The former *estate* of Hans von Benckendorff now houses the Jäneda agricultural school. One of its most widely known students was *Arnold Rüütel,* the first president of the free Estonian Republic in 1991. The ponds in the park are in part man-made.

Surroundings

Lehtse (Leetse): This workers settlement west of Tapa is situated along the railway to Tallinn. The *Pakase Lake* north of the town is one of the most beautiful moorland lakes in Estonia.

Koeru

The town of Koeru lies in the eastern regions of the province on the verge of the Pandivere range. The *Mary Magdalene Church* originates from the 13th century; famous Estonians are also buried in the churchyard. The old village *tavern,* built from 1825 to 1833, still serves its original function. Earlier, postal carriages also stopped here on their routes. The *Endla Moor* begins south of Koeru. Portions of the nature reserve are under absolute protection and not accessible to visitors. Educational trails lead to the deepest spring in Estonia, reaching a depth of 5 metres (16 feet), as well as to a number of small rivers which transverse the region. Permits for a visit to the reserve are available at the forester's office.

Tartumaa

The province of Tartumaa extends to both sides of the Emajögi. This very fertile plain is bordered by the provinces of Vorumaa to the north and the Otepää chain of hills to the south. The university city of Tartu lies in the centre of this province with an area of 3,150 square kilometres (1,229 square miles) and a rural population of 41,400.

Tartu (Dorpat)

The university city on the Emajõgi (Embach) in southern Estonia is considered the intellectual centre of the country. The Toommägi (Cathedral Hill) offers a beautiful view of this city with a population of 115,500.

History

In addition to Riga and Tallinn, Tartu was one of the largest cities in Livonia. The earliest settlements on the Toommägi hill above the Emajõgi River date back to the 5th and 6th century. Around 1030, *Prince Jaroslav* from Kiev built his fortress Jurjev here. At the beginning of the 13th century, "Tarbatu" was one of border cities which was the object of rigourous battles between the Estonians and the Teutonic Order. In 1211 and 1212, the Germans burned down the fortress of Tartu. In 1224, the city fell to the Teutonic Order despite the bitter resistance of the Russian *Prince Vladceslav* and his 200 men – here too, a bishop's fortress of the Teutonic Order was built on the ruins of the fortified Estonian farm around 1234. While construction began on the nearby cathedral, the settlement at the base of the fortress developed quickly into a significant centre for southern Estonia. As soon as the

middle of the 13th century, Tartu had a municipal constitution according to Rigan law and shortly thereafter became a member of the Hanseatic League. The collapse of Livonia lead to Russian rule from 1558 to 1582 – they abducted the last bishop of Tartu to Russia. In 1582, the city came under Polish rule; in 1625, Tartu was occupied by the Swedes and remained under their rule until 1704.

In 1630, Sweden established a court of law in Tartu, opened a printing house and founded an academy which was then converted to the "Academia Gusaviana" by *Gustav Adolph of Sweden* on June 30 1632 – the University of Tartu was born. With the renewed threat of war, the University was temporarily moved to Pärnu in 1699.

In 1704, during the Great Northern War, the Russians occupied the city, which was forced to surrender to the greater Russian forces. Four years later, the demolition of the old fortifications began – up to that time Tartu was surrounded by a city wall with 18 towers. After an extensive fire swept through the city in 1775, the city centre was rebuilt in the manner which can be seen today: the inner city was rebuilt in the unified style of Russian classicism. The reopening of the university on April 21, 1802 under *Czar Alexander I* brought a revitalization of the city's cultural life. A observatory was built and a number of academic societies were founded. The much alluded to "Tallinn vaim," the free spirit of Tartu was especially apparent during the 19th century: the university city was the origin of the "National

Awakening Movement. In 1865, the "Vanemuine" song and dance society was founded and four years later in 1869, Tartu celebrated its first song festival. From 1876 on, the railway connected Tartu with Tallinn and St. Petersburg. In 1889, a railway to Riga and Pskov via Valga was to follow.

Walking Tours of the City
I. Cathedral Hill

The first encounter with Tartu should begin with a stroll around the *Toome* (Cathedral Hill). This is considered the "green lung" and sightseeing mile of the city. The *Holy Grove* of old Tartu was degraded to a rubble pile for refuse, sand and gravel. Livestock grazed on the slopes. This deplorable state of affairs displeased *Emperor Paul I*. At the end of the 18th century, he decreed that the land would be divided into parcels and sold to the faculty members of the University. The plan to pave the green heart of the city with homes sparked protest in the populace. A stormy conflict arose with Rector Parrot; he, in turn, wanted to convert this area into a park. Parrot was finally able to achieve his goal: watchmen enforced the ban on grazing cattle here and landscapers began work, transforming Cathedral Hill into an English landscape park. The park was presented to the public upon the reopening of the university. In the oak forests of Taara on Cathedral Hill is an old *sacrificial stone* considered sacred by the Estonians. Newlyweds

go to this site after the wedding and place flowers on the stone; students burn their notes after having passed their exams... Surrounded by tall trees, the *cathedral ruins* with a length of 76 metres (249 feet) and walls with a height of 23 metres (75 feet) count among the most monumental structures built in Estonia during the 13th century. Founded in 1231 as the cathedral of the bishopric by *Bishop Hermann I of Buxhoeveden*, construction took an unusually long time – the building was often destroyed overnight and the plans were constantly changed. The present-day structure with the two towers originates from the 15th century. In 1624, a fire almost completely destroyed the church. Later secularized, the church served as a storehouse and grain silo and was increasingly left to decay. In 1806, the choir became the university's library; the cathedral church now houses the *Museum of History for the University of Tartu* with a concert hall. The old man peering down from the nearby pedestal was erected in memory of the embryologist *Karl Ernst von Baer* (1792-1876) who taught at the University of Tartu. A second memorial depicts a young man with a walking stick and long hair: *Kristjan Jaak Peterson* (1801-1822) walked from his home city of Riga to Tartu to attend the university. The inscription on the pedestal quotes a few lines from the poetry of this farmer's son.

Not far from the church, the *Bridge of Sighs* leads to *Musumägi* (Kissing Mountain), a small hill with a bank.

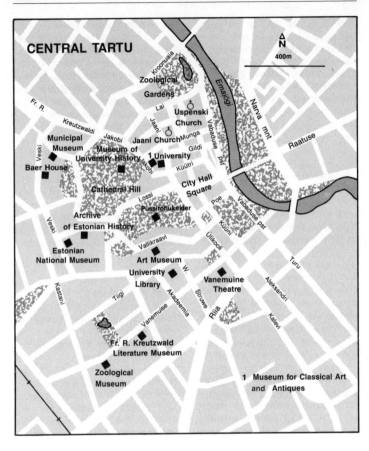

CENTRAL TARTU

N
400m

Emajõgi

Fr. R.

Kreutzwaldi

Kroonuaia

Zoological Gardens

Lai

Uspenski Church

Jaani

Jakobi

Jaani Church

Munga

Vabaduse pst

Gildi

Narva mnt

Raatuse

Municipal Museum

Museum of University History

Jakobi

1 University

Küütri

Baer House

Veski

Cathedral Hill

City Hall Square

Lossi

Pussirohukelder

Poe

Küüni

Vabaduse pst

Archive of Estonian History

Veski

Vallikraavi

Ülikooli

Turu

Estonian National Museum

Kastani

Art Museum

University Library

W.

Vanemuine Theatre

Aleksandri

Kalevi

Tiigi

Akadeemia

Struve

Riia

Vanemuise

Fr. R. Kreutzwald Literature Museum

Zoological Museum

1 Museum for Classical Art and Antiques

This is likely the base of the former fortress tower where Russian merchants were imprisoned in the dungeon during the era of the Hanseatic League. It is now a point where lovers meet. At the base of the hill is a small artificial grotto, where it is said that couples have often committed suicide together in protest of the injustice in the world. The *limestone obelisk* on the slope of Cathedral Hill at the corner of Lai Street was erected in honour of *Professor J. K. S. Morgenstern.* Earlier, a high fence blocked off the view of the sports field for male students: this was intended to hinder women passing by from being offended by the sight of sweating men... Both slopes of Cathedral Hill are connected by bridges. The *Inglisild* (Angel's Bridge) leads toward the centre of town. The name of this bridge is actually derived from "ingli" meaning English, not from the heavenly beings. Those coming uphill from the city will see the inscription "Otium reficit vires" (rest renews vitality). At the opposite end of this bridge built in the classicistic style from 1836 to 1838 shows a relief of the dean *Georg Friedrich Parrot* with the inscription "Promo Rectori Universitatis Dorpatensis" (the first rector of the University of Dorpat). The counterpart at the other end of Lossi Street is the *Kuradisild* (Devil's Bridge).

This, the third bridge to be built on this site, was erected in commemoration of the 300th anniversary of the Romanovs in 1913 in honour of Czar Alexander I who had reopened the university in 1802. Since the past century, a choir competition on the bridges has become a city tradition: the women sing on the Angel's Bridge and the men, on the Devil's Bridge. On the Toome slope below the church is the *Püssirohukelder* (Gun Powder Cellar), now a café and restaurant with a variety show. The cellar, commissioned by Czaress Catherine II, was first under ownership of the brewer Shramm for 70 years before the physics Professor Lewitzky's experimental pendulum station moved in. The professor claimed that the cellar was especially well suited

for research into earthquakes because of its constant temperature and walls resistant to vibrations. The former *barracks* on the edge of Cathedral Hill were converted to a gynaecological clinic according to the plans of *Johann Gabriel Kranhals*. On the opposite side of Cathedral Hill where the fortified farm and later the bishop's castle stood is now the old *observatory* of Tartu. Built at the beginning of the 19th century, this planetarium with an nine-inch Frauenhofer telescope offered the world's best view into the cosmos at that time. The memorial in front of the then world famous observatory is in memory of its director *Georg W. Struve* (1793-1864).

II. City Hall Square

The medieval central market is now *Raekoja plats* (City Hall Square) and remains the centre of the city. The open square between Cathedral Hill and the Emajögi River is bordered to the west by the City Hall, whereby toward the river it once lead to the old stone bridge. This, the oldest landmark of Tartu, was destroyed in 1941 during the Second World War. It has been replaced with the plain, arched *Raatuse Bridge*. This is unfortunate. Construction on the old bridge began in 1775 after the extensive fire in the city and it took six years to collect the materials and all of the stones – the majestic stone bridge, completed in 1784, was built from 300 handchiselled granite blocks. A Latin inscription once commemorated the fact that the bridge in Tartu was the

A bird's eye view of Riga and the cathedral from St. Peter's Church

Kemeri, especially renowned for its therapeutic springs, also offers impressive architecture: whether one of the wooden villas or the façade of the old sanatorium

first bridge built of stone in all of Livonia. Toward Cathedral Hill, the *city hall* dominates the oblong square. This pink and white building constructed from 1782 to 1789 according to the plans of *Johann Heinrich Bartolomäus Wolter,* rests on a framework of aspen wood. In the middle of the black, slate-shingle hip-roof is a small tower with a carillon. At city hall square No. 6 is the so-called *Old University:* built in 1789 by *Baron Ungern-Sternberg,* it was later sold to the university. City Hall Square No. 16 belonged earlier to the "Great Guild." Number 18 is widely known as the *crooked house:* the building leans considerably to the right due to the settlement of the subsoil. As the house was once owned by the wife of the army commander *Barclay de Tolly,* it is also often called "Barclay House." On the ground floor is the old Bridge Pharmacy; on the upper floor, the *Kivisilla Gallery* (side entrance).

On Ülikooli (University Street) the *Jaani-Kirik* (St. John's Church; No. 25) is presently being restored. The church was built by architects from Lübeck in 1310 and destroyed in 1944; it was famous for its terra cotta plastics. Surrounding the church are several school buildings. The *Princess' Building* was used as a sanatorium for noble Livonian girls after the death of *Hedwig Czerkassova,* the princess of Curonia. The *Treffner Secondary School,* called "Secondary School No. 1" under the Soviets, was founded by *Hugo Treffner* as a private school for the sons of socially deprived families – according to his motto: "An Estonian boy must study like crazy." Across from the church is the *Hospital for Inebriates.* This was a university building under Swedish rule; the Soviets occasionally used it as a prison. In 1941, the Soviet Secret Police murdered 192 people here. On Lai tänav (Broad Street) is the *oldest wooden house* in the city (No. 24), now a branch of the *City Museum.* It is worthwhile to make a detour from Lai Street to Magasini 7, the orthodox *Uspensky Church,* built in the early classicistic style from 1776-1782.

To the left-hand side of City Hall Square, modern facades determine the street's profile. Next to the concrete block housing a shopping centre, the Vanemuise Street leads slightly uphill to the right. The Peace Treaty of Tartu was signed in *House Number 35* in 1920. In this treaty, Russia renounces all territorial claims on the independent Republic of Estonia for all times... The famous *Vanemuine Theatre* holds performances at two locations: the Suur Maja (Large House; No. 6) was built according to the Finnish architect *Armas Lindgren's* plans in 1906. At that time it was considered one of the most beautiful theatres in the Baltic States. The old Vanamuine was replaced with new building in 1967, which united the opera, ballet and theatre under one roof. The Väike Maja (Small House; No. 45a), formerly "German Theatre" was reopened in 1990 after a fire.

III. The University District

The Ülikooli leads directly to the oblong main building of the _university_. The history of the Tartu alma mater began with the Swedes: founded in 1630 by _Johann Skytte,_ the governor general of Livonia, Ingermanland and Karelia it first served as an academic secondary school. However, demand was so great that Skytte requested that _Gustav Adolf II_ make the school into a university only one year later. The Swedish king signed the documents to found the university in the army camp at Nuremberg during the Thirty Years' War. Because of this, the university was officially founded on October 15, 1632.

Having been paralyzed by war and constant changes in power, the university was founded again in 1802.

The First World War interrupted the operation of the educational institution once more. Plans to move the university Woronesch had been made, but these preliminary plans were never realized. However, a large portion of the educational materials were transported their to ensure their safekeeping – the return of these materials has not taken place to date, although this was stipulated in 1920 in the Treaty of Tartu... Around 5,500 students attend the nine faculties of the University of Tartu. During the construction of the main building from 1804 to 1809 according to plans drawn up by _Johann Wilhelm Krause,_ enormous difficulties emerged. The first medieval remnants of St. Mary's Church had to be razed, then five thousand wooden beams were driven into the marshy ground to support the foundation. The broad façade has six columns supporting the tympanum, which projects somewhat from the façade. The two-storey lecture hall on the first floor is widely known for its excellent acoustics. Twenty-eight lathed cedar columns support the gallery around the lecture hall. Also belonging to the university is the anatomy theatre, built in 1805 according to the plans of the architect von Krause as well as a botanical garden (Lai 40, Tel: 3 53 53; open daily from 8 am to noon and 1 to 5 pm). Exhibitions also take place in the two greenhouses on the grounds.

The university of Tartu was also the only university in Russia where student associations, fraternities and duelling brotherhoods were allowed. The first student association (EÜS) was founded here in 1870. The colours of the EÜS – blue, white and black – were elevated to the Estonian national colours during the time of the national awakening. The Estonian fraternities had adopted many of the traditions present in German fraternities. The eve of May 1st was the traditional climax of the year: for over 100 years, students have paraded with torches through the city to Cathedral Hill where, at the Karl Ernst von Baer memorial, they first wash the statue's hair with shampoo and then rinse it with champagne. The EÜS fraternity house combines Art Nouveau with Estonian folk elements. (Information: Eesti Üliopilaste Selts, EÜS = Estonian Student Association, Tonissoni Street 1). The *Eesti Pollumajanduse Akadeemia* (Agricultural Academy, EPA for short) is located on *Riia Hill*. Atop this hill is a *memorial for deported citizens,* who were exiled to Siberia during the Soviet era as well as those who lost their lives under the communist regime. Not far from there is the *Hall Maja* (Grey House). What was once the local KGB headquarters is now the administration centre for the province of Tartumaa.

Museums, Galleries and Exhibitions

Antiik-Muuseum (Antiques Museum): Ülikooli 18, Tel: 3 53 84; open Tuesday to Friday from 11 am to 4:30 pm, Saturday from 10 am to 1:30 pm.

Archive of Estonian History: J. Liivi 4, Tel: 3 42 02.

Baer House: Veski 4, Tel: 3 35 14; open Monday to Friday from 9 am to 5 pm. This was the home and workplace of Karl Ernst von Baer, the medical doctor and scientist.

Eesti Rahva Muuseum (Estonian National Museum): Veski 32, Tel: 3 42 79; open Wednesday to Sunday from 11 am to 6 pm, exhibiting Estonian folk art.

Kivisilla Gallery: Side entrance of the "crooked house," Raekoja plats 18; open Tuesday to Sunday from 11 am to 6 pm, exhibiting Estonian paintings from the early 18th century to present as well as a permanent exhibition "Tartu maal." This is also the exhibition hall of the Artist's Association of Tartu.

Art Museum: Vallikraavi 14, Tel: 3 25 21; open Tuesday to Sunday from 11 am to 6 pm. Special exhibitions from Estonia and abroad as well as paintings from the era of the "Pallas" art academy, but also works of socialist realism, harvest paintings and the private art collection of Matti Milius.

Agricultural Museum: Torvand (4 kilometres/2½ miles outside of Tartu; accessible by the bus to the airport); exhibits on the rural farm life in Estonia.

Fr. R. Kreutzwald Museum of Literature: Vanemuise 42, Tel: 3 00 53; open Monday to Friday from 8 am to 5 pm; exhibiting the collection of the Estonian on folk culture and linguistics compiled by Jakob Hurt (1839-1907).

Ülikooli ajaloo Muuseum (Museum for the History of the University of Tartu): Toomemägi, in the ruins of the cathedral; open Wednesday to Sunday from 11 am to 5 pm; covering the history of the university, teaching materials and laboratories.

Oskar Luts Memorial: Riia 38, Tel: 3 37 05; open Wednesday to Monday from 11 am to 6 pm, Sundays noon to 6 pm.

Sports Museum: Riia 27a (in a wing of St. Paul's Church), Tel: 3 46 02; open Wednesday to Sunday from 11 am to 6 pm; covering the history of sports from the early 19th century to present.

Linnamuuseum (City Museum): Oru 2, Tel: 3 20 33; open daily except Tuesdays from 11 am to 6 pm; exhibiting articles of daily use and furniture from the 18th and 19th centuries. There is a affiliate museum at Lai St.

24 in the oldest wooden house in Tartu.

Starkopf Atelier Museum: E. Vilde 2; open Wednesday to Monday from 11 am to 6 pm; exhibiting works by the sculptor Anton Starkopf (1889 - 1966).

University Library: W. Struve 1, Tel: 3 24 67; open Monday to Friday from 9 am to 10 pm, Saturdays from 10 am to 8 pm and Sundays from 10 am to 6 pm.

Zoological Museum: Vanemuise 46, Tel: 3 06 33; open Wednesday to Sunday from 11 am to 4:30 pm.

Surroundings

Several kilometres northwest of Tartu toward Jogeva are the *Caves of Aruküla,* situated near the old Vasula estate. The underground corridors in the white sandstone have ceilings 1 to 1½ metres high supported by bizarre columns. A large proportion of the corridors, which extend over a network covering 10 hectares (25 acres), have meanwhile collapsed. Fish fossils were found in this underground world in 1834. The caves also once served as a hideout for the Estonians. The nearby Lake Vasula is a popular recreation area with the residents of Tartu. Near *Muuge,* the walls of an old monastery can be seen on the banks of the Emajögi River.

On the southern outskirts of Tartu, accessibly by the A 202, a stop in **Ülenurme-Kuuste** and a visit to the *Agricultural Museum* (open Tuesday to Sunday from 10 am to 8 pm) is worthwhile. The first institute for agri-

cultural sciences was on the site of the Vana Kuuste estate from 1834 to 1839. This institute, a branch of the University of Tartu, was founded by *Johann Friedrich Leberecht Schmalz.* Now a museum, the estate includes a caretaker's building, livery stables, a carpentry workshop, stalls and a carriage house. Newlyweds often visit this estate; they are welcomed here according to old tradition.

Information

Accommodation

Hotels: Rändur, Vasara 25, Tel: 7 17 13, 7 56 91; Pro, Tuglase 13, Tel: 6 18 53; PS-Hotel, Tuglase 13, P.O. Box 133, Tel: 6 13 86; Taru Hotell, Rebase 9, Tel: 7 37 00, Fax: 7 40 95, opened in 1989, 2 kilometres up the river from the centre of the city. This hotel belongs to the Tallinn "Finest Hotel Group"; Park Hotell, Vallikraavi 23, Tel: 3 36 63. Quiet and located centrally near the cathedral park.

Guest Houses operated by the University of Tartu: Information on this type of accommodation is available at the university.

Airport: Voru/Torvandi, Tel: 3 49 85.

Automobile Repair: Septa 21, Tel: 7 48 16; Ringtee 56, Tel: 2 87 75.

Banks: Kommertspank, Munga 18, Tel: 3 31 97; Dunkri 9, Tel: 44 69 77.

Bars: Taverna, Raekoja plats 20, those wearing jeans are refused admission; a meeting place for the western guests in Tartu.

Kuulikelder, Lossi, open until 8 pm, a tiny cellar in the corner house.

Bus Station: Riia/Turu 2; Information for cross-country buses: Tel: 7 61 19 and 3 24 06; municipal buses, Tel: 7 73 53.

Cafés: Rukkilill: Tuglase 2; Säde, Küüni 2; Tempo, Küütri 6; Vana Ülikooli Kohook: on Ülikooli Street to the right of the main university building, student café on the first floor of a villa; self-service in the university cafeteria: lower floor of the main university building, Ülikooli 18.

Cinemas: Athena, Küütri 10, Tel: 3 46 22; Ekraan, Riia 14, Tel: 7 54 94; Illusioon, Raatuse 97, Tel: 3 44 79; Varia, Noukogude v. 16, Tel: 3 49 34.

Fuel: Külitse, Tel: 9 73 44; Voru/Aardla, Tel: 3 17 13; Kaunas puiestee 21, Tel: 3 72 62.

Hospital: Puusepa 8.

Marketplace: Vabaduse puiestee 1 (market hall).

Pharmacy: Raekoja plats 18.

Post Office: Lai 29.

Restaurants:

Fox: Rebase 9, Tel: 7 39 54; Kaseke, Tähe 19, Tel: 7 06 08; Kaunas, Narva maantee 2, Tel: 3 48 47, dancing on Wednesdays, Fridays and during the weekend; Püssirohukelder, Lossi 28, Tel: 3 42 31, a café and restaurant in the historical gun powder cellar, variety programme on Wednesdays, Fridays and Saturdays beginning at 8 pm (admission is charged); Restorans Volga, Küütri 10, Tel: 3 39 60; Restorans Tarvas, Riia 2, Tel: 3 22 53, open daily from 1 to 6 pm and 8 pm to 1 am, small and cozy; Taverna Raekoja plats 20, restaurant in the cellar, entrance on the side-street diagonally across from the "crooked house," exclusive and small – the management is the Swiss-Estonian firm "Estkompexim."

Service Stations: Voru/Aardla, Tel: 7 39 13; Kaunase pst. 21, Tel: 3 72 62; Ringtee 52, Tel: 2 88 64.

Ship Travel: Ships depart for Pirisaar (an island in Lake Peipus) and continuing to Pskov/Russia from June to September from the harbour, Soola 5, Tel: 3 45 53 (docks are near the bus terminal).

Theatre: Vanemuine Theatre, Vanimuise 6, Tel: 7 28 49, Fax: 3 22 35. Tickets can be ordered in advance by phoning Tel: 3 03 01, 3 40 59 or 3 07 85.

Train Station: Raud tee/Vaksali 6. Information: Tel: 3 09 67 and 3 99 50.

Travel Agencies: Asteele, travel and tour agency, Lai 35, Tel: 3 15 17; Pro Studiorum, Tuglase 13, Tel: 6 18 53.

University of Tartu: Main Building, Ülikooli 18.

Alatskivi

On the southern periphery of the Alatskivi prehistoric river valley, 30 kilometres (19 miles) north of Tartu toward Lake Peipus is the small village of Alatskivi. In the centre of the village, the birthplace of the Estonian author *Juhan Liiv,* is now a memorial. Liiv is buried in the village cemetery. An avenue lined with linden trees leads through a gateway arch to the *Castle of Alatskivi*. This whitewashed building in the Tudor style was designed in 1870 by the estate owner himself *Ernst von Nolcken*. A portion of the landscape park which surrounds the manorhouse is also called "deer park." The mill or castle lake lies at its centre.

Surroundings

Peatskivi: Situated one and a half kilometres (1 mile) from Alatskivi is one of the most famous resting places of Kalevipoeg. On the crest of the hill, the Estonian later erected a fortified farm.

Elva

6,500 people live in this small city, 20 kilometres (12½ miles) southwest of Tartu on the railway route. The diverse landscape of rolling hills on Lake Verevi surrounded by dense spruce forests makes Elva a popular destination. Later, artists discovered the attraction of Elva and built wooden villas here.

In the centre of town is Arbi Lake with its swampy shores. Those who choose to forgo a swim in the lake, renting a boat or walking along the shores, should visit two exhibitions: the *Leopold Hansen House Museum* (Vilde 2a, Tel: 5 62 89) and the *Tartumaa Museum of Local History* (Pikk tänav 2, Tel: 5 61 41).

Surroundings

Eight kilometres (5 miles) To the northwest of town toward Noo is the small town of **Toravere** with the *Estonian Astrophysical Institute.* A star chart decorates the observatory's façade; this is the work of *Lagle Israel* made from 20,000 stones from the sea. Wonderful walks lead along the meandering *Elva-jögi,* which has cut

Elva – "Eleven" or "Lightning"?

Two legends exist in explanation of the origin of Elva's name, a city which gained the status of city in 1938.

The first version: a Swedish estate owner built eleven villas here and called the settlement Elva, which simply meant eleven in his language. The second version: the builder of the railroad to Elva, a man from the Georgian Republic is said to have had a terrible fear of thunderstorms. When he heard the thunder, he is said to have looked skywards and shouted "Elva, Elva" which meant "lightning" in his language. What is more likely than either of these two explanations is that the town was named after the Elva River which flows along the eastern edge of town.

deep into the valley, or up to *Vapramägi,* offering a panorama of the nearby range of hills and the river.

Information

Accommodation: Elva Voorastemaja (guest house): Heidemanni 31, Tel: 5 61 71; Vehendi Motell, Tel: 7 37 00.

Automobile Repair: Järve 5a, Tel: 5 63 07.

Restaurant: Elva Restoran, Pikk tänav 1, Tel: 5 61 30.

Swimming/Boat Rental: At Lake Verevi along the road to Tartu.

Kallaste

The fishing city of Kallaste with a predominantly Russian population is around 40 kilometres (25 miles) southeast of Tartu on the western shores of Lake Peipus. The town's name originates from the Estonian word Kallas, meaning beach. Because of its location on the 8 metre (26 foot) high shoreline of red sandstone, the Russians also call this city "Krasnaja Gora" (Red Mountain). As is the case with most of the settlements on the shores of Lake Peipus, Kallaste also originates from the 19th century, when the religiously persecuted fled from Novgorod and settled here. Their old fishing cottages line the steep shores up to the harbour, which is a restricted zone off limits to visitors. A small sand beach lies 5 kilometres (3 miles) to the north near the town of **Ranna.**

Mehikoorma (Ismene)

The fishing village of Mehikoorma is located on the Lämmijärv, the narrow strip between Lake Peipus and the Pihkva Järv, situated around 50 kilometres (31 miles) southeast of Tartu. The lake reaches its deepest point in this area at 17.6 metres (58 feet). The small park with the wooden *mermaid sculpture* offers a nice view of the lake. A commemorative plaque was placed on the *lighthouse* from 1938 in memory of the Estonia fighters of 1944. In the hinterlands is **Järvselja.** The Christmas trees for Tartu are harvested each year in the extensive forests in this area. An iron wolf

guards the *Järvselja Nature Reserve,* which is only accessible to those with a special permit. A stroll through the *botanical gardens* leads by silver spruces to witch hazel trees several metres tall. These trees bloom in the winter. On the edge of town are the experimental grounds of the Agricultural University of Tartu.

Noo (Nüggen)

Twenty kilometres (12½ miles) southwest of Tartu in the middle of an expansive landscape of fields and meadows is the small town of Noo on the A 201. A school brought renown to this settlement: it was here that Soviet pilots had their theoretical training. The *fortified church* from 1330 stands out with its richly embellished façades. The altarpiece is the work of *Tonis Grenzstein* (1895). The statues of the apostles were created by *Juan Koort* in 1909 and 1910. In the nearby town of **Lemmatsi** is a *memorial* to those who fell in the Second World War.

Piirisaar (Porka Island)

The only larger island in Lake Peipus was repeatedly the subject of conflict between Russia and Livonia/Estonia. From the Middle Ages up to the Treaty of Tartu in 1920, Piirisaar was divided – and was also called "border island." What was once a sanctuary for young men who wanted to avoid military service in the czar's army is now a popular destination for excursions. During the summer, the ship from Tartu stops here on the way to Pskov. The island is also accessible by air from Tartu if demand is sufficiently high. A ferry departs regularly from Piirisaar to **Mehikoorma**

Praaga

The only village on the alluvial land at the mouth of the Emajõgi is accessible only by boat or on foot. There is no road to this village – the extensive moor and swamplands make it impossible to reach this settlement built on piles by bus or car. However, this makes it possible to enjoy this unique moor landscape almost completely undisturbed – and not only in the autumn. This is when the city residents flock to this area with baskets in hand to pick the sour red cranberries.

Ranna (Rangen)

This town near the eastern shores of the Vortsjärv was first mentioned in 1347. Ranna's *church* from the 14th century has a carved pulpit from the early 16th century. The most impressive aspect of this town is the landscape surrounding it: the swampy alluvial eastern shores of the Vortsjärv are almost uninhabited. The 8 metre (26 foot) steep *shores of Tamme* north of Ranna are especially beautiful. During the summer months, Ranna is the destination of steamboats offering tours on the Vortsjärv. (Information and tickets are available at the travel agency in Tartu, Lai 35). Around 3 kilometres (2 miles) off the shore near Rannaküla is the legenda-

ry *Tondisaar* (Devil's Island) in the middle of Vortsjärv.

Rongu

Thirty-three kilometres (21 miles) south of Tartu on the A 201 is Rongu with the only *one-naved church* in southern Estonia. Inside, the church has stained glass windows worth seeing as well as 16 valuable altar paintings. The nearby *Hill of Souls* was once a holy grove and burial site; today, festivals are celebrated there.
Information
Restaurant: Koverkorts (Crooked Tavern).

Ulila-Puhja

Thirty kilometres (19 miles) west of Tartu toward Vortsjärv is an extensive peat production area near Ulila-Puhja. The prehistoric river valley of *Kavilda* separates the two towns – for the local residents, this is the most beautiful area in their province. The sight most worth seeing is the three-naved Gothic *church* from 1499.

Vonnu (Wendan)

In the southeastern regions of the province is Vonnu, the birthplace of the poet *Gustav Suits*. The *church* commissioned by *Bishop Hermann of Tartu* was built from 1232 to 1235 and changed a number of times over the centuries. Across from the church, the *Pudrokool* (Porridge School) was founded in 1876 as one of the first home economic schools in the Baltic States. After completion of primary school, girls would learn how to run an orderly household here... The *park* was first laid out by a pastor. With the symbolic planting of an oak, *Eduard Körber* welcomed the end of serfdom.

Sakalamaa (Viljandimaa)

The province of Sakalamaa surrounding the provincial capital of Viljandi is 3,589 square kilometres (1400 square miles) in area and its landscape is characterized by the Sakala range. These hills extend in the southern regions well into Latvia. The *prehistoric valley of Viljandi* divides the ridge of hills. On the edge of the valley are extensive forests and swamplands. It is especially the moors in the northwestern regions which are hardly inhabited and have, therefore, remained "true to nature." Sakalamaa is also the land of the "Mulgid," the farmers who were first able to buy their farms free from the German estate owners. The Mulgids are considered the "Scots" of Estonia: they are viewed as being affluent, but extremely frugal – sometimes even stingy.

Viljandi (Fellin)

The location is idyllic: in the heart of the Sakala range on the northwestern shores of *Lake Viljandi* is the city of Viljandi, the provincial capital. The sixth largest city in Estonia with a population of 24,000 bustles as the lively hub of a very productive agricultural region.

History

Even before the Brothers of the Sword conquered the settlement at the base of the old Estonian fortress, Viljandi had already appeared on the earliest world maps: in 1154, the town was first mentioned by the Arabian geographer Al-Idrisi. Well within the hands of the Christians from 1224, Viljandi was awarded city status in 1283 and, as an important commercial centre, became a member of the Hanseatic League in the middle of the 14th century. Around 3,000 people lived in the medieval city which was also the site of a Franciscan monastery in addition to six parish churches. In 1560, Viljandi fell to the Russians who burned the city and fortress to the ground. In 1582, the city became the seat of the Polish starosta (administration centre for the Polish district council). One hundred years later the city chronicles note: Viljandi has only 43 houses left, inhabited by 55 families. The ultimate decay of the Teutonic fortress caused the Great Northern War. In 1744, the population sank to 100. The appointment of this city as provincial capital in 1783 marked the beginning of a dramatic development. In 1897, the city's population climbed back up to 7,701.

An annual footrace around the lake is held every year, covering a distance of 12 kilometres (7½ miles). The record set in 1960 still stands today.

Sights

The main attraction of this town is *Castle Hill* with the ruins of the Teutonic fortress. Lossi tänav (Castle Street) leads from the centre of the city to the red and white *suspension bridge* with the original bridge gateways. This bridge spans the deep ravine and leads to the *castle park* at the summit of Castle Hill, offering a wonderful vies of the prehistoric ravine and lake. This was once the location of one of the most mighty fortresses in the country. The tower ruins on the southwestern corner of the fortress, the *Villu Kelder*, was named after *Villu*, the leader of an Estonian revolt in the 14th century.

At that time, the rebels hid themselves in grain sacks in order to gain access to the fortress. They were discovered and the sacks were pierced with spears – and Villu died in the dungeon which was named after him. The *Jaani-Kirik* (St. John's Church) originates from the 15th century and is located on Vabaduse väljak. The former Franciscan monastery, also used as a fortified church, is presently being restored. Diagonally across is the neo-Gothic brick tower of *St. Paul's Church*. Tallinna, the main business street in the city begins at Vabaduse väljak and leads directly into the centre of the old city with classicistic wood and stone villas from the 18th and 19th centuries. The *city hall* on City Hall Square dates back to the 18th century. The *City Museum* (Laidoneri Plats 12, Tel: 5 26 63) is housed in a classicistic building. The *Museum of Local History* (Tombi 12, Tel: 5 33 16; open Thursday to Monday from 10 am to 5 pm) expounds on the history of the region. The *Uga-*

la Theatre near the castle park on the opposite banks of the river is considered the most modern theatre building in Estonia. The huge brick structure conceals the stage for the "Viljandi draama teater Ugala."

Wrought iron gates and columns of marble and granite enclose the *cemetery*, which extends beyond the theatre. In 1911, the *water tower* was completed making Viljandi one of the first Estonian cities to be equipped with waterworks. Although long since inoperative, the tower remains the landmark of Viljandi.

Surroundings

Sanatorium of Jämelja: Konstantin Päts, the authoritarian president of the first Estonian Republic was sent here to convalesce after having been held prisoner in a KGB prisoner camp in 1954.

A tourist centre is presently being built on *Lake Viljandi*.

Southwest of Viljandi on the Raudna River is the small village of **Heimtali.** The *Heimtali estate manorhouse* was built in the classicistic style at the beginning of the 19th century.

Information

Accommodation

Camping: Viiratsi Kämping: 10 kilometres (6, miles) outside of town, Tel: 5 23 71; in Holstre-Nõmme, Tel: 2 97 77 or 5 23 71.

Hotels: "Viljandi," Tartu tänav 11, Tel: 5 38 52; Viljandi filiaal, Väike turu 4, Tel: 5 32 54.

Airport: Päri, Tel: 5 33 49. Airline tickets: Tartu 14, Tel: 5 39 85.

Automobile Repair: Tallinna 97a, Tel: 5 36 56.

Bank: Tallinna 3.

Bus Station: In the centre of town, Ilmarise 1/Tallinna/Uus, Tel: 5 39 80.

Café-Bars: Draakon, Tartu 34; Iva, Tasuja 2; Marleen, Jakobsoni 11; Mulgi Keller, Tartu 5; Posti Trahter, Posti 18; SM, Väike 12; Viljandi Café, Lossi 31, Tel: 5 34 24.

Cinemas: Rubiin, Lossi 21; Täht, Posti 18.

Fuel: Tallinna 99a, Tel: 5 50 50 at the entrance to town.

Hospital: Jakobsoni.

Marketplace: Turu plats.

Pharmacy: Riia maantee 2.

Post Office: Tallinna maantee 11.

Restaurants: Vikerkaar, Roo 3/5, Tel: 5 29 09; Viljandi, Tartu 11, Tel: 5 47 59.

Sports and Recreation: Ski-jump, tennis courts, stadium, facilities of the sport club "Kalev," swimming pool, boat harbour.

Taxi: Taxis can be ordered in advance by phoning Tel: 5 34 43 or 5 34 44.

Theatre: Ugala, Vaksali 7, Tel: 5 36 17.

Train Station: Located on the outskirts of town, Metalli 1, Tel: 5 38 25.

Travel Agency: Tallinna 6, Tel: 5 23 71.

Karksi (Karkus)

Only a few kilometres from the Latvian border is the double town of Karksi-Nuia. The steep *prehistoric river valley of Halliste,* which is 300 metres wide (980 feet) wide and 32 metres (105 feet) deep near Nuia separates the two portions of the city. In the side valleys are eroded cliffs with free standing Devon sandstone rock formations with such striking names as "Vana Porguhaud" (Old Inferno) and "Uus Porguhaud" (New Inferno). Rising to the valley side of Nuia are the *ruins of the Kantrimägi fortress,* a fortress which was first historically documented in 1248 and ultimately destroyed in 1620 after having had a number of different owners. The *church* of Karksi was built on the foundation the old fortress church in 1778. Just as famous as the fortress' strength in battle with two heavy stone catapults, eight cannons and 75 crossbows were the private beer brewers in this town. Under the Soviets, hops and malts maintained their status, making this one of the few places where Estonia private breweries have endured.

Surroundings

Kärstna (Kerstenshof): 5 kilometres (3 miles) to the east is the Kabelmägi (Chapel Hill) rising above the old village estate. The view from the summit extends beyond the small Veisjärv to the large Vortsjärv. In the small *chapel* the Russian lieutenant-general *Reinhold Anrep,* lays buried under a gravestone crowned with an iron lion. Anrep fell in the battle against Napoleon in 1807.

Information

Fuel: Nuia, Tel: 3 16 50.

Restaurants: Kauka-Baar, Nuia, Tel: 3 16 60.

Karkski, in the department store in Nuia, Tel: 3 12 90.

Note: The Lilli border crossing on the A 204, a gate on a sand road is only open to citizens of the Baltic States.

Foreign visitors must use the boarder crossings in Ikla or Valga.

Kolga-Jaani
(St. John's Church)

The small market town on the junction of the Poltsamaa – Viljandi road was earlier a group of islands inhabited by fishermen; however, the water level of the Vortsjärv sank, and farmers built their wooden houses around the *church* from the 14th century. In 1917, the militant pastor *Villem Reimann,* author of the "Estonian Cultural History," call the Estonians to arms in the struggle for national independence from the pulpit. A commemorative church service is held every year in honour of the militant man of the cloth now buried in the graveyard.

Meleski

Two kilometres (1¼ miles) north of Vaibla on the northern shores of Vortsjärv is a museum commemorating the largest Estonian industrial enterprise of the past century. In 1792, a glass factory was established in Meleski, which soon employed 538 workers. While the factory now produces masses of bottles, a *Glass Museum* provides information on the former glass and mirror manufacturer.

Moisaküla

The small Estonian city of Moisaküla on the Latvian border is home to a population of 1,400. The industrial

area in the country was gained the status of a city in 1938. A railway route runs via Kilingi-Nomme to Pärnu. East of Moisaküla is **Abija,** the old "Mulgid" centre. Flax farming brought relative affluence to these first free Estonian farmers. The *Moisaküla Muuseum* provides information on the history of the region.

Suure-Jaani

One of the smallest cities in Estonia came into being at the end of the 19th century and was raised in status to a city in 1938. Suure-Jaani is located around 20 kilometres (12½ miles) north of Viljandi. In front of the *church* built as a fortified church at the beginning of the 14th century, is a memorial commemorating the battle of 1217, in which *Lembitu* (a famous Estonia general) was devastatingly defeated by the Teutonic Order. A number of famous Estonians are buried in the graveyard: the composers *Artur Kapplh* and *Mart Saar* as well as the painter *Johann Köler.* The *Kapp Muuseum* keeps the memory of the musician Artur Kapp and his father *Joosep* alive.

Surroundings

Hüpassare: The birthplace of the composer Mart Saar is now a *memorial museum.* In the nearby *Kanoss Moor* is the famous "Vest Pocket Stone" of Kalevipoeg with a circumference of 24 metres (79 feet) and a height of only four metres (13 feet).

Lohavere: Three kilometres (2 miles) away is the former fortress hill of Lembitu, the most famous Estonian general in the early Middle Ages. No traces remain of the old fortified farm.

The 130 metre (425 foot) *Surgavere-Mägi* rises to the south of Suure-Jaani on the road to Viljandi.

Information

Fuel: Oja tee 2, Tel: 7 11 86.

Vohma (Wörma)

A train station, fallow land, a run-down industrial area, monotone apartment blocks and right in the middle an idyll: deep yellow houses almost hidden by the thick layer of leaves – this is Vohma, the small city in the Navesti Valley. The bridge there already connected northern with southern Estonia in the 13th century.

Surroundings

Kabala Estates: Two kilometres (1¼ miles) to the north and one kilometre (½ mile) to the right on the A 204 is a classicistic manorhouse concealed in a rather overgrown park by the tall trees. A rather monotonous concrete apartment building makes for a rather sharp contrast to the rust-brown manorhouse, which could only be saved from complete decay by timely renovations.

Pilistvere: On the Navesti River toward Poltsamaa is the small village of Pilistvere, first mentioned in historical documents in 1454. It Gothic *church* from 1300 with a tower 66 metres (216 feet) tall is considered one of the largest rural churches in Estonia.

Information

Bus Station: Tallinna 27.

Pharmacy: Tallinna 17.

Restaurant: Kaleva, Tallinna 26, Tel: 2 33 95; in the department store.

Vortsjärv (Wirzsee)

The Vortsjärv lies in the provinces of Valgamaa and Tartumaa. the north-eastern lakeshore to both sides of the Emajögi River which finds its source here, is very marshy. During the winter, access to the lake is often only possible on sled; during the spring, high water hinders traffic. A special show of nature takes place during the spring when large ice floes drift from Vortsjärv to Lake Peipus. The *nicest beach for swimming* on this lake with a high fish population can be found in **Vaibla** on the northern lakeshores where the water only gradually becomes deeper, making it an ideal area for children.

Valgamaa

The southernmost province of Estonia – 2,044 square kilometres (797 square miles) in area with a population of 41,380 – extends around the provincial capital of Valga. The border town is a divided city: the Latvian portion of the city is called Valka (→ *Travel Section/Latvia*). The most attractive landscape is the hilly region of the *Korgendik range* near **Otepää.** The highest elevation in this, the "Switzerland of Estonia" is the 217 metre (710 foot) *Kuuste,* followed by the *Meegatse* (214 metres/700 feet) and the *Harimägi* (212 metres/693 feet).

Valga

The Latvian border runs directly through the city: in the Estonian Valga, the southernmost city in the country are 17,500; in Latvian Valka, around 8,000.

History

Located at the intersection of the rural roads from Tartu to Riga and Riga to Pskov, Valga was first mentioned in historical documents in 1286. Different from other Estonian border towns, this settlement was never secured with a fortress. The small commercial centre remained quite significant up to the Livonian War: the Livonian provincial government convened here – and they decided that the parsons and farmers need to be taught religious basics. In 1577, Ivan the Terrible came and devastated the land to such a degree that even his own soldiers deserted because of hunger. After the region became Polish in 1582, Valga was awarded the status of city despite its low population in 1584 by King Stefan Batory as well as receiving additional privileges: three annual markets and regular weekly markets were permitted to take place on Fridays. The plague and the Thirty Years' War, brought this economic recovery to a halt. The chronicles note for the year 1627: the "city" of Valga has only three residents; among them, the pastor and a widow. The reform of the province raised Valga's status to an administrative centre in 1783. The city and national border have been a point of conflict since having been determined: as soon as 1224, the Konnaoja River was confirmed as the national border between the Teutonic Order the Bishop of Tartu by a special papal envoy. The border river was the subject of conflict between Poland and Russia in the 16th century and in 1920 the conflict flared between Estonia and latvia during the first Estonian Republic and almost led to a war on the Konnaoja – had this not been settled by an international border conflict commission lead by the British Colonel Tallent, which confirmed the river as the national border.

Sights

The sleepy provincial city offers ample sightseeing with a good deal of atmosphere. Construction work on the *Janni-Kirik* (St. John's Church) on Septa tänav was begun in 1787; however, it was first completed in 1816 due to lacking funds. The plans for the early classicistic church were drawn up by *Christoph Haberlandt;* the organ was built by master organ builders from Leipzig. The *city hall* across from the church was built in 1865. Earlier, the old Swedish smiths' workshops stood here, which gave the street its name. In the *city park* on Kungla Street, a *soldier's memorial* stands in honour of *Jakob Palvadre.* This commander of the Red Army was executed in 1936 as ordered by Stalin. Earlier, the Raja was the residential area preferred by the local dignitaries. The former *court of law,* built in 1783, had a number of different uses over the years: the editorial office of a communist newspaper, city administration, seat of the military, a prison and a storehouse for one of the cooperatives. Even the former *beer brewery* experienced unexpected changes: where over

70,000 kegs of beer were brewed at the turn of the century, a distillery was in operation during the first Republic before the Soviets were to bottle brandy here up to 1985. After having been closed for a number of years, this brewery supplied the Hummel kolkhoz before Estonia became independent and the factory faced economic problems once more.

During the Second World War, Valga became infamous as the location of the military prison Stalag 351: horse stalls were used as a prison camp. Over 30,000 lost their live in the 300 metre (826 foot) trench of Priimetsa. The *Valga Koduloomuuseum* (Museum of Local History; Pärnu puiestee 11, Tel: 4 14 92) in the former Säde Company building provides detailed information on both gloomy and light aspects of this border region.

Information

Accommodation: Säde Hotel, Jaama puiestee 1, Tel: 4 16 50.

Automobile Repair: Valli 47, Tel: 4 19 40; Metsa 21, Tel: 4 17 60.

Café-Bar: Koidu kohvik, Vabaduse 2/4, Tel: 4 10 14.

Fuel: Pikk 1, Tel: 4 15 84.

Restaurants: Hämarik, Vabaduse 37, Tel: 4 06 07; Säde, Jaama puiestee 1, Tel: 4 26 48.

Jogeveste (Beckhof)

Four kilometres southeast of Torva in a forest area near the Väike-Emajögi is the mausoleum of the field marshal *Barclay de Tolly,* which has stood here since 1812. In 1823, a small classicistic chapel was built next to

the grave in which Madame de Tolly is also buried. Inside, a monument by the Russian sculptor *Demut-Malinovski* depicts the Scottish aristocrat on horseback, who emigrated to Livonia. The relief on the base is a reminder of the glorious days of the commander: after his victory over Napoleon in the battle of Borodino, Prince Michael Bogdanovich Barclay de Tolly marched into Paris with his troops on March 31, 1814.

Karula (Karolenkirche)

Fifteen kilometres (10 miles) east of Valga is a landscape of wooded hills scattered with a number of lakes. This is the backdrop of the town of Karula. The nearby *Pikk-Järv* (Long Lake) is rightfully named, with a width of 170 metres (468 feet) and a length of around 3 kilometres (2 miles). The *church* in Karula and the *Rebasemägi* in **Lüllemäe** to the east offer nice views of the in part very marshy landscape. South of Karula is **Koikküla,** with the *Kantijärv,* ranking among the most beautiful lakes in southern Estonia. Those who take a stroll along the border river of Koiva should not forget to bring along their passport.

Koorküla

Around 13 kilometres (8 miles) south of Torva, Koorküla lies on the Ohnejögi River. The river has carved a deep valley – the *stone walls* rise up to 30 metres (98 feet). Natural springs have washed out small caves in the soft sandstone. Surrounding the town are a number of lakes. The largest among them, the Valgjärv, was the site where 70 beams were found during scientific diving expeditions. These indicate – as do the pottery fragments in the mud – that this was the site of a lake settlement, presumed to have lined the shores between the 5th and 10th centuries.

Otepää (Odenpäh)

The tourist centre of the province halfway between Valga and Tartu is equally popular as a summer and winter resort. Otepää, the "gateway to Estonia's Switzerland," a landscape of rolling hills with numerous lakes, has a population of around 2,600.

Otepää, first documented in 1116, came into existence in its present-day form during the second half of the 19th century. Information on the city, awarded this status in 1936, is provided by the *Keskooli Koduloomuuseum* (City and School Museum; Hariduse 9). The *church* has the largest organ in Estonia.

The actual attraction of Otepää is located outside of town. The *Pühajärv* (Holy Lake) is considered a "pearl of nature" located to the south of Otepää. According to the legend, it originated from the tears shed by a mother who had lost her five sons in war. The lake is around 16 kilometres (10 miles) long, 3½ kilometres (2¼ miles) wide and almost 9 metres (30 feet) deep. It also has a number of smaller islands which, according to

the legend, are said to be the gravestones of the five sons. On the road from Otepää to Puka is an *oak tree* with a diameter of 6.5 metres (21 feet) classified as a natural monument.

From the 214 metre (700 foot) *Meegaste Mountain* also on the road from Otepää to Puka, the view extends all the way to Vortsjärv, the city of Tartu and the Suur-Munmägi, Estonia's highest mountain during clear weather. South of Otepää in **Kääriku**, a town on the lake with the same name, is the University of Tartu sports centre. Not far from *Nüpli Järv* on the southern edge of town, a visit to the *Talumuuseum* (Farm Museum) of *G. Wulff-Oie* is worth the trip.

Information

Accommodation

Guest Houses: Esta, Kolga tee 22a; Kikkas, Tamme 9; Suuaspordi pansionnat, Tehvandi 1a, Tel: 5 54 71.

Youth Hostel: On the outskirts of town, Tel: 5 59 34, open all year, sauna.

Café-Bars: Nuustaku baar, Visulombi 2, Tel: 5 52 22; Oti baar, Tel: 5 59 52.

Restaurants: Otepää, Tennisväljak 1, Tel: 5 58 98; Pühajärve, Tel: 5 52 27.

Travel Agency: IMO, Lipuväljak 13, Tel: 5 53 82. Telephone information Monday to Friday from 9 am to noon: Tel: 5 40 31.

Sangaste (Sagnitz)

Halfway between Valga and Otepää is the village of Sangaste east of the A 201, amid a pastoral landscape of rolling hills. The estate belonging to the Bishop of Tartu and constructed in 1287 was considered one of the most beautiful in all of the diocese.

The last Count of Sangaste was *Friedrich Georg Magnus von Berg,* who took over the estate in 1873. Up to his death in 1938, Count von Berg worked for sixty years on developing the rye hybrid "Sangaste" after which the estate was named. A tradition in commemoration of this is that a handful of grain is scattered on his grave every year. The grave site is now marked with a stone set up by the Grain Research Centre in Jogeva.

The castle which belonged to this "grain prince" is similar to the British Palace: architect *Otto Hippicus* built this copy of the Windsor Castle in 1874 and 1875. The bricks for this Tudor castle were provided by the local kiln; the granite for the foundation originates from Finland. Several of the 149 rooms gained special renown: the 300 metre (980 foot) long ballroom, the 200 metre (655 foot) long dining room and the vaulted cellar with an echo that the prince liked to demonstrate for his guests. Today, there are only a few trees left from the former oak lined avenue which lead from the town to the castle. The extensive *park* comprising a forest and the castle gardens offers a number of beautiful walking paths. On an elevation above the Väike-Emajögi is the *church,* built during the 14th century using local building materials. Destroyed to the foundations during the numerous wars, the present structure dates back to 1742. The organ is the work of the *Kriisa* brothers

– *Tanniel, Inhan* and *Jakob.* A somewhat steeper climb leads up to the *Härimägi.* From the highest elevation in the province, there is a beautiful view of the town and the surrounding regions as well as the Väike-Emajögi.

Taagepera (Wagenküll)

Ten kilometres (6¼ miles) west of Torva is a softly rippling landscape with the small estate village of Taagepera. Today, a sanatorium is housed in the former *estate* belonging to the von Stakkelberg family and surrounded by a *landscape park.*
Surroundings
Near the Latvian border is **Holdre** which has an Art Nouveau estate house built in 1910. The village, located 8 kilometres (5 miles) southwest of Torva is only accessible via an unpaved road.

Torva (Törwa)

Old peat kilns gave this town its name. Torva is located around 20 kilometres (12½ miles) to the north on the road from Valga to Karksi. The Ohnejögi flows through the middle of this town over a length of 3.5 kilometres (2 miles). On the southern edge of town, the sandstone walls of the *Tikste Valley* climb to a height of up to 30 metres (98 feet); to the southeast are *Riiksa-Järv* and *Vanamoisa-Järv* – both popular lakes for swimming. The history of this young town is quickly recounted: a small settlement developed around the Patküla estate beginning in 1875 which then became a market town in 1921. Finally, in 1927, it became a city. Since there is hardly any industry in Torva, it remains a quiet garden city with a lot of green. The *Liimmägi fortress* is considerably older than the town and is located around ½ kilometre to the south on a hill with the Ohnejögi at its base. The fortress complex with walls of 3.5 metres (11½ feet) and an outwork was presumably completed during the 12th century.

Surroundings

Helme (Helmet): The Helme estate only a few kilometres west of Torva was the site of the first assembly of the "Estonian Literary Society" (Eesti Kirjameeste Selts). Among others, the national poet *Lydia Koldula* was also in attendance. The baroque manorhouse from the second half of the 18th century now houses an agricultural school. The *Teutonic fortress* of Helme was probably built during the early 14th century. A fortress wall, now in ruins, encircled the complex. In the northern slopes below the fortress are the *Helme caves:* the two sandstone grottoes – the "Devils' Belly" and the "Moses Church" – each have two entrances. The spring in the valley was once attributed with miraculous powers. It is said that a young girl sacrificed here pearls to the healing water in order retain her youthful beauty.

Information

Accommodation: Torva Voorastemaja, Veski 2, Tel: 3 35 52.
Automobile Repair: Kangro 7, Tel: 3 38 97.
Fuel: Valga maantee 59, Tel: 3 35 82.

Restaurant: Torvik, Valga 55, Tel: 3 34 90.

Vorumaa

With an area of only 2,305 square kilometres (899 square miles), Vorumaa is one of the smallest provinces. Still it offers one of the most diverse landscapes: it is here that one will find the highest mountains and deepest lakes. In the core of Vorumaa, the Haanja range rises to 318 metres (1,040 feet) at *Suur-Munamägi,* the highest mountain in the Baltic States. The southwestern regions of the province are flat and sandy, covered with extensive wooded areas. The administrative centre of the province is Voru.

Voru (Wesso)

This city in the centre of the province with a population of 17,800, lies in a deep valley basin on the 231 hectare (578 acre) *Lake Tamula.*

Voru, whose coat of arms depicts a green pine tree, has remained a quiet, quaint provincial city, despite the construction of a railway route which connected Voru with Valga and Petseri in 1918. First founded in 1784, the population was recorded in the civil registry in the following year. Among the 67 citizens were 23 Balts, 17 Germans, 20 Russians, 1 Swede and six other foreigners. The main employers are the "Kodu" knitting factory of with branches in Rouge and Antsla; the "Voru Aparaat" machine factory, a furniture factory and a dairy farm. During the era of the first Estonian Republic, *Paul Ebber's* cocktail champagne made Voru internationally known. While Voru was expanded to include a new modern district, as was the case with Nöörimaa in 1974, the perpendicular streets and alleyways of the inner city have been completely preserved. The old centre extends between Kreutzwaldi (Riga Street), Jüri (George Street), Tartu (Dorpat Street) and Voidu väljak (Marketplace). The few sights in town are in close proximity to one another. The *Apostolic Church* was built in 1793 according to the plans of the Livonian architect *M. Schons* and construction was supervised by *Johann Karl Ott*. The orthodox yellow and white *Jekaterinenkirik* (Catherine's Church) dates back to 1806 and was built according to the plans of *Christoph Haberlandt* as a one-naved, baroque church. The interior includes some valuable icons. The organ was built by the famous *Kriisa Brothers* in 1913. The former *manorhouse* built during the second half of the 18th century as municipal offices now houses a secondary school. The one-storey baroque building has been a schoolhouse since 1804 – from 1921 to 1930, this school was for future teachers. Voru keeps the memory of *Dr. Friedrich Reinhold Kreutzwald* alive with a *memorial museum* (Kreutzwaldi 31, Tel: 2 17 98). The co-founder of the autonomous Estonia culture, whose "Kalevipoeg" advanced to the become the popular national epic poem, worked in Voru from 1833 to 1877 as a medical doc-

tor. The building from 1793, in which Kreutzwald lived beginning in 1839, remains unchanged from the times when the poet lived here: furnishings, books, documents – everything has been completely preserved for posterity. The Kreutzwald Memorial Museum was opened on June 28, 1941 and is also used for readings, exhibitions and concerts today. In the *Kreutzwald Park* on the Tamulajärv, a bronze monument to the poet made by *Adam Adamson* in Italy was unveiled on August 29, 1926, and was set on a pedestal in 1988. Located since 1983 on the former site of the private boy's school of Heinrich Krümmer is the plain building which houses the *Koduloomuuseum* (Museum of Local History; Kreutzwaldi 16, Tel: 4 14 79, open Tuesday to Sunday from 11 am to 1:30 pm and 2 to 6 pm). Visitors have "glided" through the extensive exhibitions illustrating regional and local history in felt slippers since 1985. In the north of the city on the banks of the Vohandu River is the *Bishop's Fortress of Kirumpää*. This tower fortress from 1322 was transformed into a military camp during the second half of the 15th century and destroyed from 1656 to 1658 during the Russian-Swedish War. In 1701, the field troops were based here. Later, the ruins were used as a type of "quarry" to provide the city with construction materials.

Surroundings

Three small watercourses connect Lake Tamula with Vagula-Järv to the west. This, a popular area with hikers is the green district of Kubija, equipped with a tourist centre and camping area.

Information

Accommodation: Voru Voorastema-ja, Tel: 2 12 26; Voru Kubija Tourist Station, Männiku 43, Tel: 4 12 16.

Automobile Repair: Antsla maantee 23, Tel: 2 23 54.

Cinema: "Noorus," Jüri.

Fuel: Räpina maantee 10, Tel: 2 12 23; Antsla maantee 34, Tel: 3 15 23.

Post Office: Jüri.

Restaurants: Voru, Koidula 16a, Tel: 2 17 72; Guest House Vohandu, Koidula 16a, Tel: 2 19 32.

Travel Agency: Männiku 43, Tel: 4 12 16 and 7 15 79.

Antsla (Anzen)

On the rural road halfway between Voru and Valga is the old estate village of Antsla with a population of 2,300. The old *estate,* now an agricultural school, belong to the aristocratic family Üxküll from 1405. The landscape park of Vana-Antsla is one of the most beautiful in southern Estonia. The first fish breeding ponds that were fed with fresh spring water in the Baltic States were constructed in Antsla during the past century. The main employer in town is the "Marat" textile mill, which produces hosiery and knitted goods. South of town is the Karula landscape of rolling hills with a wealth of lakes, which can best be explored from the village of **Kaika** (→ also *Valgamaa*)

Haanja (Hahnhof)

The Haanja is with 19 "summits" not only the most hilly (and rainy...) region of Estonia but also the poorhouse of the country: according to the legend, the devil is said to have dug through the region looking for peanuts in vain.

While earlier, carving wooden pipes enabled the farmers to supplement their meagre income during the winter months, today the Estonians use their "natural capital": the touristic potential of the over 30 lakes surrounding the highest mountain in the Baltic States is being increasingly discovered.

The main attraction is the 318 metre (1,040 foot) *Suur Munamägi,* the name of which means "big egg mountain" and refers to the form of its dome. Built in 1939, the 29 metre (95 foot) observation tower (Tel: 7 88 57, closed from November 1 to April 30) offers a view of the towns of Voru, Polva, Räpina, Lake Peipus and the distant towers of Pskov and Petseri. An exhibition in the tower provides information on the "protection of natural and cultural monuments in Estonia." Below the observation tower, a memorial stands in honour of *Juhan Kunder,* who composed the well-known song: "Kui siit pilvepiirilt" (If from this border of clouds...). Since Estonia's independence, the Estonian national flag is flown once again on the highest summit in the Baltic States. At the base of the mountain, surrounded by flower beds in the Estonian national colours, a monument in honour of the

Estonians who fell in the war of independence was erected on August 7, 1988. From the parking area with the bus stop on the main road, a steep footpath leads up the mountain – one should forgo attempting the drive up the sand road. East of the Munamägi is the *Vaskna-Järv*. There are a number of small islands in this lake, the largest in the Haanjas region. At 297.5 metres (973 feet), the *Vällamägi* is the second highest mountain of Haanjas. At the foot of the *Tsalbamägi* near the village of **Plaksi** is the highest lake in Estonia, the *Tuuljärv* (Wind Lake) at an elevation of 257 metres (840 feet) above sea level. The picturesque *Kavadi-Järv* near **Uee-Saaluse,** is a popular motif for numerous artists. It is a man-made lake from the second half of the 19th century – the estate owner dammed up three lakes directly next to one another and created one large body of water. The most beautiful view is from the 274.3 metre (899 foot) *Hällimägi* on the southern shores of the lake. **Kasaritsa** (Kasseritz), located on the northern edge of the Haanja range, is also surrounded by birch forests and lakes. Not far from **Plaani,** a small settlement on the ridge of the road to Suur Munamägi with a field-stone church from 1873, is a small secondary road to **Kokemäe.** In the *Kuremäe Tree Nursery* located there, over 400 trees and bushes grow on terraces, making this the largest dendrological collection in the country. The phylogenetic trees can be traced back over nine generations.

Rouge (Range)

Fourteen kilometres (9 miles) southwest of Voru is the small town of Rouge. The lake plateau in this area counts among the most beautiful regions in the Haanja range. The *church,* a small, simple building on the slope of the Rouge valley was built in 1730. The organ with 31 registers was constructed by the *Kriisa Brothers* in 1930. A monument by *V. Melnik* in honour of the citizens of Rouge who died from 1914 to 1920 has stood across from the church since 1926. From *Rouge Linnamägi,* on which an Estonian fortified farm stood from the 8th to 11th century, one can see the seven lakes of Rouge connected by the Rouge River like a shimmering string of pearls. At 38 metres (124 feet), the *Suurjärv,* also called "Kalevipoeg's Well" is the deepest lake in Estonia. At the end of the prehistoric river valley of Rouge meas uring 10 kilometres (6¼ miles) in length and 52 metres (170 feet) in depth is the oblong *Kahrila-Järv.* Dense deciduous forests and all kinds of chirping birds give the *Ööbikuorg* (Nightingale Valley) a pleasant note, while the deep *Tindi Valley,* the slopes of which have a number of springs, makes a much more rugged impression with its free standing dolomite formations.

A good opportunity to get a closer impression of the beauty of this landscape is to hike along the 8.5 kilometre (5¼ mile) *Rouge Haanja Trail.* During the winter, marked cross-country skiing trails transverse the area beginning at the central intersection in Rouge. Seventeen kilometres (10½ miles) to the west is **Sänna** (Sennen). After the ruthless exploitation in the interest of the Czar, hardly any pearls can still be found in the river mussels in the Pärlijogi.

Krabi (Schönangern)

Isolated on the Latvian border, 15 kilometres (9¼ miles) south of Rouge is the small village of Krabi. "Pagamaa," Devil's Land, is what the local residents call the secluded area on the border river Kolga. They interpret the deep depressions all around this area as the devil's footprints and thus give them foreboding names like "Horguhaud" (Hell's Grave). Marked hiking trails lead there. In the schoolhouse of Krabi, a small *museum* provides information on the less satanic history of the settlement. In the middle of the Pagamaa Nature Reserve is the Piiriorg (Border Valley) of the Kolga with its four lovely valley lakes. The largest of them, the *Kikkajärv*, has one island; the *Liivjärv*, a 20 metre (65 foot) observation tower and a nice swimming area. The reserve includes two educational trails with lengths of 6 and 10 kilometres (3½ and 6¼ miles).

Misso (Illingen)

In this southeastern town of Estonia, the borders of Estonia, Latvia and Belorussia meet, forming the border regions of three countries. Where

traffic now buzzes along the A 212, it can hardly be imagined that this was the site of the first cobblestone road from Riga to Pskov. Two kilometres to the west is another memorial for the fallen soldiers in the first mounted regiment during the war of independence which was unveiled on August 27, 1988. North of the thoroughfare is the *Pullijärv;* three kilometres (2 miles) to the south, the *Hino-Järv* with its eight islands, one of which came into being only 130 years ago through the sinking of the water level. Northwest of Misso, a visit to the *manorhouse* in **Ruusmäe** (Rogosi) is worth the detour. This complex consisting of manor and servants house bordering the inner courtyard on all sides, still has old construction elements from the 16th century.

The gateway tower houses a *School Museum* worth seeing.

Moniste (Menzen)

Between Varstu and Saru in the southwestern regions of the province is the small village of Moniste in the broad Muustjögi Valley. This village has had a *Village Museum* since 1948 (Kuutsi küla, Tel: 9 36 22, open Tuesday to Sunday from 9 am to 1 pm and 2 to 5 pm), which was founded by *Alfred Lepa* as a lay museum. With a smokehouse (a house without a fireplace), a smoke sauna, a barn, a well and summer kitchen, it illustrates rural life during the past century.

Urvaste (Urbs)

Eight kilometres (5 miles) north of Antsla, around 33 kilometres (53 miles) west of Voru is the small parish of Urvaste. Its *church* on the edge of the valley was built during the 13th century, rebuilt a number of times and first equipped with a tower in 1899. It is the only basilica among the rural churches in Estonia. Growing next to the school, the *Tamme-Lauri Oak* is considered a sacred tree. The tree has a height of 18.5 metres (60.5 feet) with a circumference of 8 metres (26 feet) and is now classified as a natural monument. The *Uhtjärv* extends to the south of Urvaste. This is an elongated valley lake with a depth of up to 40 metres (131 feet). The *Loolajärv* has a small island. One trip worth making is to the *Luukuse-Mägi* with a height of 161 metres (527 feet).

Vastseliina (Neuhausen)

The old Russian border point during the reign of the Teutonic Order has an idyllic location 20 kilometres (12½ miles) southeast of Voru. Six kilometres (4 miles) east of the town, the ruins of the old fortified *Bishop's Castle* is perched atop a steep slope. The location on the confluence of the Meeksi Stream in the Piusa River was well chosen: the tower fortification, built in 1342, enjoyed the natural protection of the waterways on three sides.

A chronicle from 1379 mentions Vastseliina as the strongest fortress in Livonia. To better protect it against firearms, the fortress was fortified and huge artillery towers were added during the 15th century. After having been destroyed during the Great Northern War, the fortress lost its significance. This was not the case for the old *Border Tavern:* already included on an old map from 1695, this is still a site of merriment today.

Surroundings

The entire *Piusa Valley* is classified as a nature reserve.

From Vastseliina, a hiking trail leads to the north along the river until it flows into the Vohandu. Near **Möldri** (3 kilometres/2 miles) are the "Müürimäed," the Wall Mountains. These yellowish-red sandstone cliffs on the Piusa River originated around 400 million years ago; today, they reach a height of up to 19 metres (62 feet). A few kilometres farther past the 15 metres high *Tamme-Müürmägi,* the old *Tamme Mill* stands on the confluence of the Puise and Vohandu. In the Lindora Forests toward Tabina are Slavic *grave mounds.* Northeast of Vastseliina, the 212 metre (693 foot) *Kuksina-Mägi* and the 204 metre (667 foot) *Meremäe-Mägi* offer a good view of the Piusa Valley to the west and the nearby city of Petseri with the Pihkva Järv (Lake Pskov) to the northeast.

Jogevamaa

Long ranges of hills transverse the Province of Jogevamaa from the west to the southeast. The province itself covers an area of 2,604 square kilometres (1,016 square miles) and is home to a population of 42,650. The provincial city of this typically moraine landscape with its drumlins is Jogeva with a population of 7,300.

Jogeva (Laisholm)

Jogeva is quite a young city. Although the polish revisional report mentioned the state's possessions of Jogeva in 1599, it was only after the construction of a railway route to Tartu in 1876 that a settlement would first develop around the railway station with an inn, stores and a postal station. When the estate owner *Count E. von Manteuffel* began in 1903 to lease his land along the rural road to Tallinn and around the train station, the village grew by bounds. The rural road became the main road to the new town. In 1919, the town with 95 houses and 817 residents was declared a market town and the status of city would follow in 1938. During the Second World War, 60% of Jogeva was destroyed; today, it is a centre for gardening. Among the most important institutions is the state breeding station. Sculptures by the famous Estonian sculptor *Anton Starkopf* can be seen in the decorative garden of Rudolf Tamme.

Surroundings

In the town of **Kurista** five kilometres (3 miles) from Jogeva, roses are grown in the middle of the spruce forest. On a glade, one *rose garden* exhibits 500 different types of roses. **Siimusti,** west of Jogeva is renowned for the production of colourful flowerpots and functional garden ceramics. South of Jogeva among several lakes is the widely known *Experimental Forestry Station of Kaarepere* with the adjacent *Metsamuuseum* (Forest Museum). To the southwest of Jogeva not far from *Kuremaa-Järv* is the church village of **Palamuse.** The history of this town began in 1234 with the construction of the slender, three-naved *St Bartholomew's Church,* around which a settlement quickly developed. The church, remodelled during the 15th century, contains a remarkable pulpit: reliefs depicting six apostles decorate the balustrade, the crown shows an angel on Jacob's ladder.

The village became known beyond its borders through the work of the author *Oskar Luts.* His rascal's novel "Kevade" (School Days), with memories of his school days made Luts one of the most popular authors in Estonia. His home, now a *museum* (Tel: 3 30 32) documents his life and works.

Around 12 kilometres (7½ miles) northeast of Jogeva is **Laiuse** (Lai's Church) on the verge of the range of hills 10 kilometres (6¼ miles) long and 2 kilometres (1¼ miles) wide. The 144 metre (471 foot) summit offers a very nice view. The former *Teutonic fortress* east of Laiuse Mountain was presumably built at the end of the 14th century as the first castle fortress in Estonia in the form of a irregular rectangle. The *church* on the eastern slope was the site of the registration of gypsies in 1841 by order of the Russian governor general in order to force them to settle permanently. The *linden tree* in the

northeastern corner of the churchyard was planted on May 29, 1701
by Charles XII.

Information

Accommodation: Jogeva Voorastemaja (guest house), Jaama 4, Tel:
2 14 54.
Automobile Repair: Tel: 2 12 78.
Fuel: Tel: 2 17 65.
Restaurant: Jogeva, Gagarini 33, Tel:
2 29 82.

Kärde

Twenty kilometres (12½ miles) north
of Jogeva on the road to Rakvere is
the *Stone of Peter the Great* – the
Russian czar is said to have once
rested and eaten lunch here, according to the local residents. The *Maiden's Stone* is reminiscent of less
pleasant events: out of unrequited
love for a boy not suited in social
class, the noble maiden Stackelberg
from the Kärde estate drowned her-
self. The *Peace Cottage* in the nearby
park was where the peace treaty between Russia and Sweden was
signed on June 21, 1661. The *Peace
Trench* above Peter's Stone was dug
during the peace negotiations to
busy the soldiers.
The moorlands have been re-
searched for over 100 years in the
Experimental Institute of Tooma on
the edge of the Endla Nature Reserve.
Taking sample specimens is quite
a tricky endeavour: narrow board-
walks aid in traversing the swampy
area.

Mustvee (Tschorna)

Two thousand people live in the largest "city" on the western shores of
Lake Peipus, situated around 60 kilometres (38 miles) north of Tartu on
the A 201. As early as the 16th century, the Estonians inhabited a small
fishing village at the mouth of the
Mustvee River at Lake Peipus. The
dark water of the lake which shim-
mers black at the mouth of the river
gave the town its name (Mustvee =
black water). At the beginning of the
19th century, religiously persecuted
Russians came to this area, built up a
new existence as fishermen and began farming "local" vegetables like
cucumbers, onions and carrots.

Surroundings

Ten kilometres (6¼ miles) west of
Mustvee is **Torma.** Before the railroad was built, this old postal station
linked western Europe with St. Petersburg: Catherine II, Paul I, Alexander I, Nikolai I, Joseph II all stopped
here during their travels. After this
the sleepy village was to make headlines only once more – the local pastor *Johann Eisen von Schwarzen-
berg* published a standard reference
work for preserving vegetables.

Information

Accommodation: Mustvee Voorastemaja (guest house), Tartu maantee
58, Tel: 2 42 76; Mavi Motel.
Fuel: Tel: 2 44 26.
Restaurant: Ankur, Tartu 5, Tel:
2 44 40.

Poltsamaa (Oberpahlen)

Sixty kilometres (38 miles) northwest of Tartu on the main route to Tallinn (A 202) is the garden city of Poltsamaa on the banks of the Poltsamaa River and with a population of 5,300. This former residence of *Duke Magnus* (1558), was destroyed during the Great Northern War and then experienced a new era of prosperity during the 18th century. Mayor *Woldemar Lauw* opened a glass factory, a coppersmith's, a mirror factory and a porcelain plant. *Peter Wilde* founded the last of the six printing houses in Russia here in 1766. The others are in Moscow, St. Petersburg, Kiev, Riga and Tallinn. Still during the same year, a pharmaceutical journal was published; from 1766 to 1780, Wilde printed 16 works in Estonian, Latvian and German. Poltsamaa became a city in 1926.

Sights

Nestled in the *Linnapark,* the expansive city park on both banks of the sluggish Poltsamaa River is the old heart of the city. The *church* including *ruins of a monastery* (Tallinna maantee) is surrounded by a moat. The walls of almost 7 metres (23 feet) built from field-stones and bricks date back to the 16th century. The three-storey *castle,* built in 1771 by Woldemar Lauw on the ruins of the old fortress has an interesting rococo interior: artificial marble in yellow, pink and light blue, the work of the Berlin master craftsman *Michael Graff* embellishes the walls of the rooms.

Surroundings

Timotheus von Bock was born in 1787 on the former *Voisiku estate* southwest of Poltsamaa. This man became famous through the novel "Keisri Hull" (The Czar's Lunatic) by *Jaan Kross.* Bock had criticized the czar to prompt him to change the Russian constitution, demanding the prohibition of serfdom in a letter in 1816. Bock had hardly sent the letter to the czar when the aristocrat was imprisoned, only to be freed twenty years later as a broken man.

Estonia's only saint was born in **Umbusi** in 1883 under the name of *Karl Tennisson.* Tennisson, who preached the Buddhist belief from 1915 and called himself "Brother Vahhindra," sought after immortality. Because he wandered through the country without shoes, the bald monk became known among the local residents as "barefoot Tennisson." A pilgrimage to Tibet was followed by a period in Burma during the Second World War, where Tennisson led a congregation of monks. After his death, when his corpse lay in the sun for three days and did not decay, this Buddhist by choice was canonized in 1962.

Information

Accommodation: Poltsamaa Voorastemaja, Joe 1, Tel: 5 14 60.
Bus Station: Tartu maantee/Kesk väljak.
Café-Bar: Poltsamaa bar, Pajusi 2, Tel: 5 13 36; Urvebaar, Lossi 1, Tel: 5 12 55; Kinobaar, J. Kuperjanovi 2.
Fuel: Pajusi 18, Tel: 5 16 06; Paustvere, Tel: 5 23 95; on the A202 at the

Poltsamaa exit, three kilometres (2 miles) east of town.
Hospital: Polyclinic, Viljandi maantee 3.
Restaurants: Konvent, on the riverbanks in the park behind the church; Ranna, Veski 1, Tel: 5 14 92.

Puurmani

Thirty-nine kilometres (24 miles) northwest of Tartu and 22 kilometres (14 miles) south of Poltsamaa is the old settlement of Puurmani on the A 202. Despite the fact that the medieval fortress of the Kurse Order steward has long since been destroyed, the 112 year old estate castle is definitely worth a stop. The *Count of Manteuffel's manorhouse* began with a total of 42 rooms when it was built in 1880 in its stately park. The countess added a 43rd room – the "snoring room" for the count – shortly thereafter.

Polvamaa

The Polvamaa province in the southeastern regions of Estonia surrounding the provincial capital of Polva covers an area of 2,165 square kilometres (845 square miles) and is hardly industrialized. The population is dominated by Estonians at a proportion of 90%. Most of the Russians living in this province have settled along the banks of lake Peipus and in Räpina. One interesting aspect among the 36,150 inhabitants of Polvamaa are the Setukese people in the eastern areas, whose region has also been

called "Setumaa" since 1920 (→*Setumaa).*

Polva (Pölwe)

The small provincial capital of Polva with a population of 7,270 in the Ort Valley is a relatively young city. The towns name comes from the word "polv" meaning knee: in order to appease the devil, who repeatedly let the church collapse during its construction, a kneeling girl was entombed in the walls of the church as a sacrifice. Just as unusual as the legend surrounding the name of the city is tower of this plain church from the 15th century: the centre of town cannot be missed because of this slender, bright red steeple. Somewhat outside Polva is the *Song Festival Field* on the Intsikurmägi. The small Johann Käis House Museum is worth the trip to **Rosma.** *Jakob Hurt,* founder of the Estonian Folk Museum, was born in the schoolhouse of **Himmaste** in 1833.
Information
Accommodation: Polva Voorastemaja (guest house), Voru 12, Tel: 9 53 74.
Automobile Repair: Pat, Piiri 16-11.
Bus Station: Tel: 9 51 39.
Café-Bar: Hämariku Bar, Kesk 10, Tel: 9 69 90.
Fuel: Jaama 70, Tel: 9 60 06, three kilometres (2 miles) outside of town heading for Räpina.
Hospital: Polyclinic, Uus 2/4.
Restaurant: Polva, Kesk 10, Tel: 9 57 25 and 9 50 55, a restaurant,

cafeteria and canteen in the "Tervis" department store.

Train Station: two kilometres (1¼ miles) outside of town, Tel: 9 57 56.

Räpina (Rappin)

On the banks of the Vohandu River which has been dammed up, making it into a reservoir in the town, is the eastern centre of the Polvamaa province. The small metropolitan town of Räpina came into being in the 18th century surrounding the church, the paper factory and the estate. The *Moisanhoone* (manorhouse) on Pargi Street, built after the classicistic castle of Sillapea, now houses Estonia's largest school of gardening. The park surrounding the manorhouse was created at the beginning of the 20th century by the landscape architect *Walter von Engelhardt.* Beyond the bridge spanning the small stream, a man sheds his shackles – this is a *memorial* to the abolition of serfdom. The *church of Räpina* was built in 1785 in the classicistic style. The moats date back to the Great Northern War (1700-1721).

Information

Automobile Repair: → *Fuel*

Fuel: Räpina maantee 18, Tel: 2 12 23.

Police: Joe 2.

Restaurant: Vohandu, Voopsu 29, Tel: 3 12 96 and 9 12 96.

Leevi

Twenty-three kilometres (14 miles) southeast of Polva, mid-river on the Vohandu are sandstone cliffs which tower to both sides of the valley up to 20 metres (65 feet). The local residents call the colourful cliffs "walls." Some of these cliffs like the "Podramuur" (Moose Wall) are under nature protection.

Petseri (Petschory/Pecory)

The former small Estonian city now lies in Russian territory. In October 1991, two-thirds of the populace voted to stay under Russian administration during a referendum. Declared a city in 1782, Petseri is known for its *caves,* which were first dug into the soft sandstone by monks and used as living quarters during the 15th and 16th centuries. Another attraction in Petseri is the *monastery complex* in the deep valley. Surrounding the *Uspen skaja* (Church of the Ascension) built in 1473, a metropolitan settlement quickly developed. To protect the town, a ring of walls with six towers and three gates was constructed from 1558 to 1565. Beyond the fortified monastery today are eight churches, among which is the *Michail Church,* built in the classicistic style in 1827 as well as a *bell tower* and a *sacred spring.*

Piusa

On the northern banks of the Piusa River only a few kilometres from the Russian border near Petseri is an underground labyrinth of artificial *caves.* The cave system is kilometres in length and extends between the

Setumaa

The southeastern portion of the Polvamaa province is inhabited by the Setukese people; their region extends in the Vorumaa province from Vastseliina to Petseri on the Piusa River. The interesting melting pot, called Setumaa since 1920 begins near Voopsu. At first glance, the fortress-like villages look quite different – in **Tona** the yards are closed off to the street and open to the lake; in **Voporzova,** the individual farmhouses form a protective ring around a central courtyard.

What is less commonly seen is the traditional dark women's consume with white lace and a light bonnet. The Setu women wear their wealth: the ornate jewellery, usually made of silver, can weigh up to seven kilograms (14 pounds).

Every year during the summer, the Setukese celebrate a large *song festival* in Värska. The most widely known vocalist to perform was *Anne Vaberna* - this woman is said to have known over 100,000 verses of folk songs by heart...

village and the railway route. The "Sammaskoo bas" is over 400 metres (1,308 feet) in length with ceilings up to six metres (20 feet). As with all of the other grottoes, the caves are the result of the industrial extraction of quartz from 1922 to 1966.

Taevaskoda (Himmelreich)

The small train station of Taevaskoda is located six kilometres (4 miles) north of Polva. The picturesque setting on the Ahja River, which is lined with bizarre eroded sandstone formations make the name Himmelreich (heaven) more than appropriate. Below the 150 metre (490 foot) long walls of sandstone in various colours, is the *Suur-Taevaskoja,* a monumental rock with a height of 24 metres (79 feet). This huge erratic block on the edge of the rapids is called "witch's stone" by the local residents. They also refer to the summer villas with exotic gardens in the resort of Valgemetsa "witch cottages." The nearby *Schoolhouse Museum* with a classroom from the past century is also worth visiting. A dense network of hiking trails leads through the forest. The marked trails lead to **Kiidjärve** among other destinations. Farther upstream is the *Väike-Taevaskoja Rock,* with a length of 190 metres (621 feet) and a height of 13 metres (43 feet). In it is the *Neitsi koobas* (Girl's Cave). According to the legend, it is said that one can hear the sound of girls sitting at the loom weaving cloth. They only appear on St. John's Day (June 23) – given that one finds a fern blossom to be used as a "magic wand." The hiking trail on the meandering river leads farther up to the hydraulic power plant where there is an *ecological exhibition* in the turbine room. Another trail leads from Kiidjärve north to the *Akste Reserve,* where over 1,200 anthills are under protection on the 200 hectares (500 acres) of land. The densely populated colony – over 800 million "inhabitants" per square kilometre – offers yet other superlatives of nature: the highest anthill is 1.6 metres (over 5 feet); the oldest anthill is sixty years old. Access to the reserve is not permitted. A befitting end of a day of hiking is **Ahja** (Aya), the birthplace of the author *Friedebert Tuglas.* It was especially the children's book "Little Illimar" which put this estate village on the lakeshores on the map.

Saatse

The small settlement of Saatse is close to the Russian border. The *Setu Museum* provides information on the history and customs of the Estonian-Russian population. The Russian Orthodox *Paraskeva-Pjatnitsa Church* has an icon from the 18th century.

Värska

Between the pointed arm of the Pihkva-Järv and Lake Orsava in the south is the small settlement of Värska. The harbour and therapeutic mud are determining factors in this town's economy; mineral water is also bottled and sold from the *Värska Springs.* a holiday hotel for teachers provides for a limited amount of tourists and some diversion. South of Värska, the landscape is "wind swept." In the *Setumaa Sahara* a sand area extending to Lutepää, botanists find a wealth of steppe flora. The highest elevation is the *Pikkmägi.*
Information
Accommodation: Värska Kämping.
Sanatorium: Tel: 9 46 30.

Latvia

Latvia at a Glance

Country Name: Republic of Latvia
Capital City: Riga (population: 915,000)
Larger Cities: Daugavpils (population: 130,000), Liepaja (population: 114,000)
Area: 64,600 square kilometres (25,195 square miles)
Population: 2,868,000
Longest River: Daugava (357 kilometres/223 miles)
Ethnic Groups: Latvians (52%), Russians (34%), Belorussians (4.5%), Ukrainians (3.5%), Poles (2.3%), Lithuanians (1.3%).
Language: Latvian (indo-European language) as official language; Russian is also spoken.
Economic Structure: Industry and construction (40%), commerce and transport (25%), service industry (20%), agriculture and forestry (15%).
Declaration of Independence: Recognition by the Soviet Union on August 21, 1991.

Today, Latvia is subdivided into 469 administrative districts, forming 26 provinces with 56 cities. Historically, the central Baltic State comprises four ethnographic regions – Kurzeme (Curonia) to the west, Zemgale (Semigallia) to the south, Latgale (Latgallia) to the east and Vidzeme (Livonia) to the north with Riga at its centre.

Vidzeme

The province of Vidzeme extends north of the Daugava River to the Baltic Sea. It has a magnificently beautiful sedimentary coastline with fine, broad sandy beaches which are not at all crowded...yet. Toward the interior of the province, the landscape becomes more hilly. With the 900 square kilometre (350 square mile) Gauja National Park, Vidzeme has an incomparable nature reserve. In the highlands of Vidzeme, east of the "Switzerland of Latvia (or Livonia)" is the highest mountain in Latvia: the Gaizinkalns with an elevation of 311 metres (1,017 feet).

Riga

Riga is today what it always was: the western gateway to the Baltic States. A bishop from Bremen once founded the city on the Daugava – and today the city of Bremen is helping Riga as its sister city on the way from the planned to a market economy. What was once the commercial centre of the Hanseatic League is now a pulsating international harbour and Riga is a vital big city that makes a very western impression.

Almost one million people live in the Latvian capital – 55% Russians, 40% Latvians and 5% are minorities from the Ukraine and Belorussia. The city has many faces: Hanseatic houses like in Lübeck, art nouveau like in Berlin, wooden structures as in Moscow and stately palaces as in Paris. These contrasts concentrated on only a few square kilometres in the heart of the city reduce the scars of Socialism to a minimum. Desolate streets, over-crowded busses, pushing and waiting in line are soon forgotten when the golden stars of the "Latvija" sparkle in the sunshine. At the base of the freedom monument where women lay down flowers in memory of the victims of the uprisings. The entire city begins its new era in a calm matter-of-factness. Nowhere else in the Baltic States are the people so full of life despite the daily drudgery and no where else do the people complain so little about the empty shops and inflationary prices.

History

Bishop Albert von Bremen founded the "Locus rige" in the middle of the uninhabited swamplands where the Riga River flows into the Daugava and later into the Baltic Sea. He granted the fortified settlement city status in 1201. At that time, the germination point of the city is said to have been exactly on the site of the present-day Alberta laukums (Albert Square). Already in 1226, the har-

bour city had a council with its own voting rights. While the harbour, church and administration was firmly under German control, foreign merchants founded guilds and merchant associations. In the middle of the 13th century, a general guild for local and foreign merchants came into existence. In 1304, the merchant's guild developed into the so-called "Greater Guild." The "Lesser Guild" was made the society for the craftsmen. It was first in 1785 that a reform made these guilds accessible to non-Germans.

From then on, membership was dependent only on financial standing and not on nationality. In 1282, Riga joined the Union of Northern German Cities which later became the Hanseatic League. During conflicts similar to a civil war between the citizens and the clerics, the first Rigan fortress including a church was destroyed in 1297. Around 1300, the city wall measured around 9 metres (30 feet) in height and was 2 metres (6½ feet) thick. During the 14th century, 18 towers and 14 gates were added to the cities defences. Two hundred years later, the construction of embattlements, several entrenchments and an artificial canal followed. The oldest preserved illustration of Riga appeared in 1547 in *Sebastian Müller's* "Cosmography." The old wood engraving printed in Basel shows the cathedral, St. Peter's, St. Jacob's, the city hall, the castle and St. John's. In 1581, Riga was annexed by Poland and during the following year, the Polish king festively marched into the city. During the following years, Riga was not destined

The Gauja River meanders through the lush green of pristine forests — what catches one's eye are the bizarre sandstone formations which have come into being over the course of centuries

Street scenes in Tukums and Cesis: the long years of communism have left their mark on the buildings

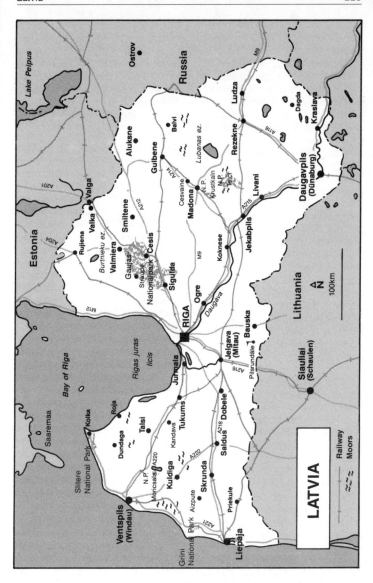

to come to rest: from 1584 to 1587, the "Calendar Uprisings," religiously motivated conflicts in protest of the replacement of the Julian calendar by the Gregorian, swept through the city. In 1600, the Swedish-Polish War of Succession broke out. In 1622, *Gustav Adolf* conquered Riga. In 1656, Russian troops occupied the city for weeks on end during the Swedish-Polish-Russian War and bombarded Riga with around 2,000 cannonballs, weighing up to 160 pounds each. This was, however, in vain – in 1660, Riga was declared the second capital of Sweden in the pact of Oliva. This fragile peace lasted for fifty years. In 1710, the czar's troops were successful in taking the city during the Great Northern War. In the Treaty of Nystad, the Swedes were forced to relinquish their predominance in the Baltic region and Riga became Russian. In 1802, Riga was home to a population of 28,882 – 45.9% of them were of German descent (13,216).

In 1812, a state of emergency was declared because of the advancing French army and the grain supplies were brought to St. John's Church. Although Napoleon's troops passed by Riga, over 800 buildings in the outer city were burned down as a precautionary measure. During Russian rule lasting almost 200 years, Riga developed into the most important commercial centre in the western regions of the Russian empire. The expansion of the harbour, the railway (1861) and the abolishment of the requirement of guild membership

(which opened access to all occupations for Latvians) fostered an enormous boom. Within only a few decades, the population of Riga climbed to a quarter of a million. In 1905, the worker's uprisings of St. Petersburg also reached Riga. In October, the czar's troops brutally shot down the demonstrators.

During the First World War, the German troops were able to break through a line of Latvian riflemen and march into the city. When the October Revolution reached Riga, the German upper class turned to *Emperor Wilhelm II* for help. The desire to be incorporated into the German Empire was thwarted when the monarch fell victim to the November Revolution. In 1918, two governments grappled over control of the city: The bourgeois conservatives under the leadership of *Karlis Ulmanis* and the socialist Soviet government under *Peter Stucka*. Ulmanis was the victor. In the peace treaty of August 11, 1920, the Soviet Union guaranteed national sovereignty: Karlis Ulmanis became the president of the first Republic of Latvia. In 1939, the fragile dream of democracy was shattered. In the supplementary protocol of the Hitler-Stalin Pact, Latvia was delegated to the Soviet realm of influence. The resettlement of the German Balts began, affecting around ten percent of Riga's population of 385,000 at that time.

Stalin continued the "cleansing process" of the city: thousands of citizens were deported to Siberia. When Hitler's henchmen marched into Riga in 1941, the genocide of the Jewish population began *(→ Salaspils)*. In October of 1944, the German *Wehrmacht* had to surrender the city to the Red Army. However, acts of terror directed against the civilian population continued: Stalin had undesirable citizens deported, "liquidated," or had them simply disappear in several waves up to 1952. With massive economic aid from the Soviet Union, the devastated city was rapidly rebuilt.

Today, the change from planed to market economy is especially supported by German and Scandinavian firms who enter into joint ventures with Latvian companies. The economic backbone, in addition to the harbour and commerce, is industry. The Riga Automobile Factory (RAF), manufactures automobiles, vans and special vehicles; radios and turntables come off of the assembly lines of VEF-Telecommunications; beyond the impressive gates on Brivibas iela is the "Valst Electro-Technology" plant.

Acute problems are caused by the sewage which is hardly treated and the high level of air pollution. The planned construction of a subway sparked protest in the populace. The desired but completely oversized dam project on the Daugava River also resulted in large-scale demonstrations.

Riga is subdivided into five administrative units: on the right banks of the river are the districts of central Riga, Ziemelu and Vidzeme; on the left banks, Urzeme and Zemgale. The residents prefer the names of their city districts: Bierini (Lindenruh), Bolderaja (Bolderaa), Ciekurkalns (Schreyenbusch), Daugavriva (Dünamünde), Nordeki (Nordeckshof), Purvciems (Moordorf), Vecmilgravis (Alt-Mühlgraben) and Ziepnickkalns (Seifenberg).

Walking Tours
Vec Riga (Old Riga)
Of the 590 buildings in the old city, 79 are classified as historical monuments. Where the alleyways are especially narrow, cannon barrels were driven halfway into the ground earlier to block them off to transport vehicles.

I. Old City Tour
The tour through the city begins in the geographical centre: the *Latvija* at the southern end of Brivibas iela towers 41 metres (134 feet) into the sky. This Latvian liberty monument, designed from 1931 to 1934, by the sculptor *K. Zale* and the architect *E. Stalbergs,* is connected with the Latvian self-esteem and aspiration for independence like no other structure in the country. Erected on the fifteenth anniversary of the declaration of the republic on November 18, 1935, the monument has since been a continual thorn in the side of the Soviet Union. What is considered politically provocative is not only the golden inscription on the base formulated in Latvian: "Tevzemei un Brivibas" (For Freedom and Fatherland). The figures on the corners are sculpted from Finnish granite and depict nation-

al Latvian virtues – the work of the people, defence of the homeland, the fruits of the arts and the advances of science. In the central structure, the warrior _Lacplesis_ and the prophet _Vaidelots_ are reminiscent of bold Latvian folk epics. The nine metre (30 foot) female figure of mother earth with a shield and sword symbolizes the yearning for a homeland. Her three golden stars represent the three historical provinces of Kurzeme, Vidzeme and Latgale. While, during the late 1950's, there were turbulent discussions on tearing down the national memorial, the topic of debate at the base of the _Latvija_ is now the continuation of freedom. Conservative, pro-Russian demonstrators unroll their banners of protests here. A few steps away, a street musician hopes for a few coins and farther along, religious groups recruit sinners by offering spiritual salvation. One's attention is repeatedly drawn to the bas relief on black travertine where flowers in the national colours lay in memory of those who died in the January uprisings of 1991.

A narrow sand walkway leads off to the right to the _fortification walls_ toward the old city. Flat erratic blocks decorated with flowers are in memory of those who died in the _week of barricades_ in 1991. One victim: _Edjis Rieks,_ a schoolboy who was killed on January 20, 1991 by OMON riflemen (→ _History_).

Before reaching the bridge over the brook running through the park, a bust stands in memory of the scien-

tist _M. Keltys_. The man-made _Pilseta_ (city stream) resulted from the fact that the moats were made narrower and flooded. Passing the _Kalnins Memorial,_ erected for the 100th birthday of this composer (1979), the walking tour leads to the _National Opera._ Built from 1860 to 1863 by _Ludwig Bohnstedt_ in the German classicistic style, the building burned to the ground in 1882 and was first reconstructed five years later. At first a dramatic theatre, the first Latvian opera brought music to this stage in 1913. The impressive building with a classicistic columned portico on the exterior and bombastic neo-baroque interior is presently being restored. Performances are, however, still held – a performance by the internationally renowned ballet troupe is highly recommended. On the other side of the Aspazijas Boulevard (formerly Theatre Boulevard) is the "Hotel Riga," the old "Hotel de Rome." The new "Hotel de Rome," opened in 1991, is around 100 yards up the street.

At the beginning of Teatras iela, three Atlas statues crown the roof of the corner house (No. 9). The three men burdened by the weight of the globe are illuminated from inside at night. Passing the Finnish Embassy to Kaleju iela and diagonally off to the _Jana Seta,_ are the last remnants of a medieval monastery. It is presumed that lepers were cared for here by Dominican monks. The lepers gained access to the monastery through a small doorway in the wall.

Traces of the old _city wall_ from the 13th to 15th century and rebuilt in

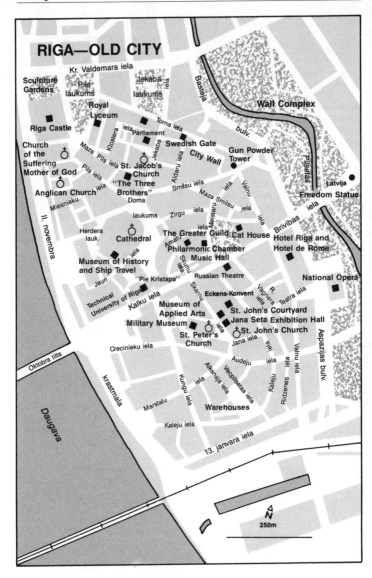

RIGA—OLD CITY

Sculpture Gardens

Kr. Valdemara iela

Pils laukums

Jekaba iela

Jekaba laukums

Basteja

Wall Complex

Riga Castle

Royal Lyceum

Torna iela

Klostera iela

Maza Pils iela

Parliament

Swedish Gate

City Wall

bulv.

Gun Powder Tower

Pilsetas

Church of the Suffering Mother of God

Pils iela

St. Jacob's Church

Jekaba iela

Aldaru iela

Latvija

Freedom Statue

Anglican Church

iela

"The Three Brothers"

Smilsu iela

Doma

Maza Smilsu

Valnu

iela

iela

iela

Miesnieku

laukums

Zirgu iela

iela

Meistaru

Cat House

Brivibas

Herdera lauk.

Cathedral

The Greater Guild

Amatu

Hotel Riga and Hotel de Rome

iela

Philarmonic Chamber Music Hall

Skarnu

iela

II. novembra

Museum of History and Ship Travel

Jaun

iela

"Pie Kristapa"

Russian Theatre

National Opera

Skarnu

Vagnera iela

R.

Teatra iela

Technical University of Riga

Kalku iela

Eckens-Konvent

Museum of Applied Arts

iela

St. John's Courtyard

Military Museum

Jana Seta Exhibition Hall

Crecinieku iela

St. Peter's Church

St. John's Church

Jana iela

iela

iela

Audeju

Valnu iela

iela

Oktobra tilts

Krastmala

Kungu iela

iela

Alksnaja iela

Vecpilsetas iela

Kaleju iela

Ridzenes iela

Aspazijas bulv.

Marstalu

Warehouses

Kaleju iela

13. janvara iela

Daugava

N

250m

1960 can still be seen in the inner courtyard. The *Jana Seta Exhibition Hall* (Jana Seta 1, Tel: 21 01 72 and 21 01 39; open daily from 11 am to 7 pm and 10 am to 6 pm in winter) exhibits Latvian art on the ground floor.

On the second and third floors are special exhibitions of works by international artists. The passageway leads through to Skarnu iela. The *Juras Kirik* (St. George's Church; No. 10/16), built at the beginning of the 13th century, belonged to the fortress complex as its chapel. After the destruction of the fortress, the church had a number of different owners and uses: for a while, it served as a convent (an orphanage and home for the poor); in 1488, it became a domicile for the Tertiary monks; and from the middle of the 16th century – fully secularized, it was used as a storehouse. To the rear of the building, it can still be seen how three storehouses were made out of the rear portions of the church.

The longitudinal nave was transformed into the storehouse "white dove," the rest of the altar choir formed the "leaden grey dove," and the former anterior hall became the "brown dove." The freshly renovated façade now houses the *Museum of Applied Arts*. The *Eka-/Ecken's Convent* (No. 22) a plain two-storey building was transformed into an inn for foreign visitors in around 1453. Initiated by Mayor Ecke, the end of the 16th century saw its transformation into a home for needy widows. Directly next door is the *Janis Kirik* (St. John's Church; No.24). The former

monastic church from the 14th century was first documented in 1297. At that time it served as a chapel for the Dominican Monastery, which stood on the grounds of the fist Bishop's Fortress as early as 1234. In 1330, the first expansion of the church took place; in the 15th and 16th centuries, three Renaissance ancillary naves were added to the church. Thus, the church can be seen today as being composed of two portions: the high Gothic portion from the 13th to 15th century and the lower, more modest additions. Worth seeing inside are the baroque altar and the lectory (cupboards between the choir and storehouse) from 1768/1769. The 73 metre (239 foot) tower was first added to the church in 1835. In the small park across the street are the *Bremen Town-Musicians,* a sculpture by *Christa Baumgärtel*, based on a famous German fairy-tale. This was a gift from the city of Bremen for its Latvian partner city. Beyond this is the mighty old *St. Peter's Church* First built in 1209 as a congregational church, it then served less Christian purposes in 1297: from atop the tower, enraged citizens shot flaming arrows during the conflict between the city and clerics, setting fire to the nearby St. Juras. The 123 metre (403 foot) tower of St. Peter's, built of wood in the 14th century and officially serving as "Luginsland" (watchtower) for the municipal garde from 1353 also enraged the religious world. Since the congregational church was much higher than the cathedral, the cathedral was ultimately built up two more storeys. However, this did not prevent that Riga's first clock was installed on St. Peter's church in 1352. In 1666, the old wooden tower collapsed after 170 years of being in dire need of repair. The master builder from Strasbourg *Rubbert Bindenschuh* built a new crown for the tower in 1690. Said to be the highest church spire in the world at that time, it was struck by lightning and destroyed in 1721. *Peter the I* who experienced the catastrophe first-hand, ordered immediate reconstruction according to the original plans – however, this was to be financed from municipal coffers. When *Johann Heinrich Wülbern* set the new crown on the roof of the tower in 1746, he impertinently threw a glass down from the tower saying: "May the tower stand as many years as glass shatters." The glass fell on a nearby haystack. Despite this story which always leads to a chuckle during any tour of the church, the tower stood undamaged for almost two hundred years. On June 29, 1941, German bombs caused the church to go up in flames, the organ made by the Walker company from Ludwigsburg in 1886 was destroyed along with the tower and almost all of the furnishings. In 1954, the main nave could once again be roofed. The new tower crown was to follow on August 20, 1970 and every three hours, the melody of the Latvian folk song "Riga dimd" can be heard from the St. Peter's clock tower since 1976. Today, an elevator inside the tower takes visitors up to the observation platform at a height of 72 metres (236 feet). Taking the elevator up the tower is

only possible in groups, i.e. when the elevator is full. Tickets are sold at the kiosk in the anterior hall and include a tour of the church. To the right of the church are several apartment houses and a playground with wooden equipment.

Standing in sharp contrast to the bourgeois is the nearby *Latviesu Sarkano Strelniku Laukums* (Square of the Latvian Red Riflemen). Hardly any traces remain of the old City Hall Square which was barely one-sixth as large. The House of the Black Head Guild from the 15th century with the famous Renaissance is the seat of the "Honourable Company of the Black Heads," the city hall across the way from 1765 and the Roland's Column, now in the interior of St. Peter's Church are missing from the picture. The dismal cement block beyond the construction area, unveiled in 1970 in the middle of square as a memorial to the Latvian Red Army houses a branch of the *Latvian (Revolutionary) Military Museum*. G. Lusi-Grinbergs and D. Driba are responsible for the "architecture" of this building in the form of a cube raised out of the earth. In front of the museum with slabs of oxidized copper, a daring trio has stood since 1971 – at least it is still standing to date: the dismantling of this is a controversial topic of debate. Meanwhile the new Penguin ice cream parlour has long since won the hearts of visitors... Beyond the streetcar tracks on the right-hand side of the square is the oblong *Riga Technical University (RTU)* built in 1968 as a polytechnical university. An archway under the laboratory building leads to Kramu iela. A glance to the right will reveal that all the buildings on the street are being renovated. To the left-hand side on Jauniela, carved figures embellish the yellow Lithuanian Art Nouveau façade of the cellar restaurant "Pie Kristapa," whose "Bear Hunter Beer" is served in earthenware mugs. Despite a hearty base of moose-meat dishes – whether dumplings or stew – this beer will make visitors hang on to the table...

On Jauniela corner of Palasta iela is the house where Peter I lived during his stay in Riga in 1745. His treasurer had already purchased the house in 1711 from a wealthy merchant and had it remodelled by the court architect. Passing Gallery A & E (Jauniela 17), the alleyway leads to the *Doma Laukums* (Cathedral Square), called "Square of June 17th" under Soviet rule. Here, a high metal sculpture with the seven coats of arms of Riga's seven partner cities. The nearby *cathedral* is considered the largest sacred structure in the Baltic States. The cathedral in Ratzeburg, Germany is said to have served as a prototype for this building. Whatever the case may be: with a length of 87 metres (285 feet), a width of 43 metres (141 feet) and a height of 26 metres (85 feet) at the central nave and 16 metres (53 feet) at the side naves, the "Domus Dei" (House of God) has impressed visitors for centuries. Only the tower, almost 90 metres (295 feet) tall is not a part of this holy grandezza. The corner stone had already been lain in 1211. Bishop Albert,

however, would not live to see the completion of the cathedral. It was only twenty years after the death of this founding father of Riga that the papal legate *Wilhelm von Modena* could dedicate the St. Mary's Church in 1226. The completion of the cathedral was financed through funds from the pious: forty years of forgiveness was sold for a few coins for the construction. All that remains of the old church is the northern portal which originates from the end of the 13th century because 100 years after completion, the cathedral was thoroughly remodelled. Due to other architectural changes, the cathedral has elements of Romanic, Gothic, Renaissance and Baroque architecture. The old furnishings fell victim to the pillagings of the reformation in 1524. The paintings of the saints were then replaced by grave slabs: for a price, merchants, aristocrats and tradesmen could purchase a grave in the church. The closer to God (the altar), the more expensive the grave sites were. Graves remaining preserved to date are those of Archbishop Albert and the last resting place of Meinhardt, the first bishop of Livonia, whose remains were transported here from Iksile (Üxküll). In the centre of the church is the pulpit, built in 1641 in the Renaissance style and "Gothicized" during the beginning of the 19th century. The wooden statues of the apostles, evangelists and angels as well as the allegorical depictions of Christian virtues were presumably carved by *Tobias Heincs* from Jelgava. The Renaissance front of the organ was the work of the *Ja-*

kob Rabe, built from 1594 to 1601. Later the organ front was added. The organ itself, one of the largest and most famous in the world, is renowned for its extraordinary sound. The Walker Company from Ludwigsburg also responsible for the organ in St. Peter's Church, built this impressive instrument from 1883 to 1884. The organ comprises 6,768 wooden and metal pipes grouped in 127 different registers. With this, it has a tonal spectrum of 9½ octaves. The largest pipe measures ten metres (33 feet) and the smallest is only 13 millimetres (½ inch). Those who master the four keyboards for the hands and two pedal keyboards can bring out the sound of rushing wind or the soft purring of a cat. The monumental masterpiece was restored by Dutch organ craftsmen from 1981 to 1984.

Organ concerts once again draw a large audience several times a week. After the Soviets degraded the cathedral to a museum and concert hall, the church once again served its original religious purpose on October 9, 1988. The first church service in the cathedral simultaneously marked the founding of the Popular Front.

Construction of the cathedral monastery began during the 13th century on the southwestern side of the cathedral. Surrounding an open rectangle at the eastern wing were the parlatorium for receiving guests, the keeper's lodge and assembly hall; the monk's cells were on the upper floor. The refectory, the monk's dining hall as well as the kitchen and storage rooms were in the southern wing. The west wing housed a religious seminary. Today, the southern and western buildings are used as a Museum for City History and Navigation.

Across from the cathedral is the Latvija Radio/Radio Riga building in the sand-coloured palace. During the January uprisings, long cement barriers blocked off the entrance to the OMON tanks. The elegant stock exchange building was designed by *Harald Julius Bosse.* Four years after the cornerstone was laid on June 3, 1852, the building was completed in the Italian neo-Renaissance architectural style. A short detour leads to *Herdera Laukums* (Herder Square). A memorial for *Johann Gottfried Herder* has stood in the shadows of the cathedral since 1864. Herder lived in Riga from 1764 to 1769 and taught history, geography and German at the cathedral school. This small square dedicated to Herder was first came into being in the 1860's, when the earthen walls were removed. From Cathedral Square, Pils´ iela (Castle Street) leads past a small bistro (No. 13/15; open 10 am to 10 pm) and farther past decorative house doors to Anglikanu iela. The *Anglican Church* here was built from 1857 to 1859. On the corner of Pils iela and Pils laukums is a grey, angular Roman Catholic *Church of the Suffering Mother of God,* a classicistic church from the 18th century. The Pils laukums (Castle Square) was called "Pionieru laukums" up until Latvia's independence. The memorial for *Peter Stucka,* leader of the conciliatory government of the first republic has meanwhile been removed as is the case with the monument for the literary couple *Janis Rainis and Elza Rosenberg.* Making a stop in the Pils and Café garden accessible via a small side street (the way is marked) on can enjoy a rest on the terrace surrounded by chestnut trees and look down to the motorway along the river. Renamed by the Soviets at that time as "Komjaunatas krastmala," nothing more is reminiscent of the quays, the harbour or the city market for fish, meat, fruit and vegetables which was first closed in the 1920's with the construction of a central market. The restructuring of the waterfront is not yet complete. The *Pils* (Riga Castle), built as a second fortress for the Livonian Order between 1330 and 1353, who lived here up until the 16th century later served as the residence of Polish, Swedish and Russian rulers. In 1919, the Social Democratic Party held their fifth congress here. Then they voted for the Bourgeois Latvian Government chose the castle as its governmental seat during the first independent republic. From 1944 to 1990, this was the palace of Young Pioneers and now a bronze plaque praises the building as the "Castle of Schoolchildren." The 2.5 metre (8 foot) thick walls now enclose three museums: the *Museum for Latvian History* (3rd floor and Holy Spirit Tower) is presently under construction; the *Janis Rainis Museum for the History of Literature and Art* on the second floor;

and the *Museum of Foreign Art* on the ground and first floors. The small *Skulpturu darzs* (Sculpture Garden) at the western end of the building was laid out in 1967.

The Maza Pils iela (Small Castle Street) was originally in a suburb and was first incorporated into the city during the 13th century. The narrow alleyway, once a broad boulevard leads past an *Antique Shop* (No. 13) with furniture, icons and books to the landmark of Riga *Tris Brali* (The Three Brothers; Maza Pils iela 17, 19 and 21). Their counterpart "The Three Sisters" stand in Tallinn. House number 17 was built during the 15th century and is the *oldest preserved residential house* in Riga. This craftsman's house with the step-gable has been used as a bakery since 1687.

House number 19 was built by a merchant in 1646: the living quarters on the ground floor and storerooms in the upper storey. *House number 21* is an architectural illusion: the historical façade from the 18th century conceals a modern building from 1966.

At the beginning of Klostera iela is the Royal Lyzeum; following on the same side of the street is the *St. Jekab Church* (St. Jacob's Church). First mentioned and consecrated at the same time as the cathedral (1226), this three-naved basilica was then situated outside of the city walls. This church with its late Romanic choir has a the only Gothic church tower in the city. This church is now the seat of the Catholic archbishop and changed confessions a number of times throughout its history. The first Protestant church service in Latvia was held here after the reformation in 1522. After that, the Jesuits directed this church and then it went back to Protestant control from 1621 to 1922, before ultimately becoming Catholic. Across the way is the *Augstaka Padome* (House of Latvian Chivalry). Where the supreme council of the Latvian SSR, the highest organ of the state convened during the Soviet regime, is now the seat of the Latvian parliament. The Florentine palace was designed by two students who later became the most famous Latvian architects: *R. Pflug* and *J. Blaumanis* drew up the plans for this building in fulfilment of their graduation requirements in 1867. The barricades surrounding the governmental district strictly guarded by the Latvian civil defence beginning in 1991 were first removed in July of 1992.

The Maza Troksnu iela and Aldaru (Brewer) iela lead to the *Zviedru Varti* (Swedish Gate) built into the city wall during the Swedish occupation (1698). A lion's head above the archway with the date marks the first time that an opening was added to the city wall. This is the last preserved city gate in Riga and is flanked by cannons – they were taken from the Swedes during the Great Northern War. The *George Tower,* once a fortification tower next to the Swedish Gate, now forms an architectural unit with Tornu iela 11, the *House of Architects.* Next door, Tornu iela 9 was once the home of the executioner.

The Tornu iela leads up to the left to the *Arsenal,* built by *I. Lukini, A. Nelingers* and *J. Spacirs* from 1828 to 1832, partially using materials from the old city walls. One tract of the former arsenal houses an exhibition hall for modern Latvian art.

Down to the right, a portion of the old city walls from the 13th to 15th centuries were unearth and restored in an exemplary manner. Built from stones, erratic blocks, bricks and limestone, each guild was responsible for "their" portion of the wall. The 10 metre (33 foot) high and 2 metre (6½ foot) thick ring of walls surrounding the city is steep and smooth on the exterior. Inside, the supports form small niches. During peace times, these were used as small sales stands; during wars, they were filled with sand and stones. Leading along the entire length of the wall is a roofed gallery for the guardsmen, equipped with gun slits. During reconstruction of the fortifications in 1987, only a few historic sections of the walls could be incorporated. It is especially the angular tower with a weather vane which has a somewhat unreal appearance. A few steps farther is a convincing defence fortification – the *Gun Powder Tower.* First historically documented in 1330, this was one of the largest fortification towers in the city: 25.5 metres (83 feet) high, 14.3 metres (47 feet) in diameter and walls almost 3 metres (10 feet) thick. The five metre (16 foot) thick underground portion of the tower rests on a grating made from oak trunks. The steps chiselled into the wall lead up to the gun slits out of which cannons protruded into the 19th century... Nine cannonballs were later embedded in the façade, reminiscent of the Russian occupations of 1657 and 1710. The Gun Powder Tower, converted to the *Rubonia Fraternity House* during the 19th century, now houses a small gallery. The military legacy is held for posterity in the adjacent *Military Museum.* In front of the tower is a small *granite sculpture:* a horseman covers his face with his hands. The Meisteru iela leads to the Amatu iela on which the *Guild Houses* are located. The *Liela-Gilde* (Greater Guild; No. 6) also called "Münster Room" was first historically documented in 1330. Its present-day appearance in the English neo-Gothic style was added to this palatial building in 1856. The former merchants' guild with the old Ministeres istabā (Münster Room) from the 14th century now serves as a philharmonic concert hall. During the 16th and 17th century weddings were celebrated in the rooms of the Great Guild: the newlyweds spent their wedding night in the bridal suite from 1521. Th adjacent *Maza Gilde* (Lesser Guild; No. 5) was the craftsmen's guild and adapted to the neo-Gothic architectural style during its remodelling from 1864 to 1866. The "Cat House" diagonally across the way of the two majestic guild houses is the work of an irate merchant. "You can kiss my ..." he thought when his membership in the Greater Guild was denied and subsequently had a black cat added to the tower of house. The cat prominently displays its backside to the guild. The small courtyard near the "Cat House" is one of the most popular oases during the summer. Souvenir painters sell their "originals"; art students produce minute portraits. Ice cream and beer stands offer summer refreshments. Across from the guilds is the *Philharmonic Chamber Music Hall;* on the corner of Kalku iela is the *Russian Theatre.*

Down to the right, the Kalku iela leads to the *Jever Bistro,* the first western pub in Riga opened in the spring of 1991 by a restaurateur from Hamburg. The meeting point for men, girls and the wanna-be prominence is unthinkably expensive for the local residents: steaks are only sold for hard currencies is the motto – and envious Latvians observe this with curiosity as sums equal to their monthly earnings are paid for a beef filet, their rent goes down western gullets in nothing flat – and how the rightly reserved Latvian women sell more than their souls for hard currencies. Similarly decadent: the casino with its "Forum Café." For a mere Latvian's daily wage, the westerners flock to their own kind; Balts remain outside. Quite stately, in contrast is the "Hotel de Rome." The first new hotel building in Riga opened in 1991 is run by the former manager of the top-class Hotel Atlantik in Hamburg. The "Café Otto Schwarz" on the uppermost floor offers a beautiful view of the wall complexes and the city.

However, beforehand, one should take a quick peek into "Riga Modes." In the *Riga Fashion Centre's* exhibition halls three to four shows annually present the newest trends in textiles, jewellery and ceramics – admission is charged. Contemporary art by Latvian painters has been exhibited in *Rigas galerija* (Aspazija bulv. 20, Tel: 21 63 87; open 11 am to 8 pm except Sunday and Monday) on two floors since August 1992.

Beginning on the other side of the street is the greenbelt with the wall complex. A sand walkway leads back to the Latvija. Those who want to experience more of this city should continue through the new section of the city.

II. The New City

The epithet of "garden city" is well deserved by Riga with its 15 large parks, 7 forests and 150 smaller parks. Although the old city has next to no green areas, the new portion of the city came into being during the second half of the 19th century on the site where the earthen walls and embattlements once stood: The new city – green, spacious and with Art Nouveau houses and extensive parks. The walking tour begins on *Bastejkalns* (Bastion Hill). A park with a pavilion (which has long since been torn down) and a greenhouse was

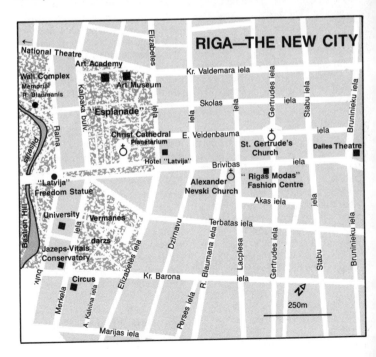

laid out on the site of the old wall complex in 1887. In 1898, the city had a stream built with a series of small cascades. At the base of the man-made hill, a small *Alpinum* (Alpine Park) was to follow. The sculpture called *"The Foal"* was created by the Rigan sculptor *Gaida Grundberg*. A bridge spanning the Pilseta (city stream; one can feed the swans...) leads to the *memorial for Rudolf Blaumanis* (1863-1908), the classic author of Latvian literature. The inscription on the base quotes his work "The Trumpeter": "Mans zelts ir mana tau. Ta mans gots ir vin as gods" – "my gold is my folk. Their honour is my honour." The memorial, created in 1929 by *Teodors Zalkans* (1876-1973), was the first memorial to be erected in a Rigan park – it was only at the end of the 1960's that others would follow. The nearby *Trio "Dance of Peace"* is the work of *Parsla Zalkalne.*

Large erratic blocks lining the way with flowers on them are in memory of the victims of the January blockades when the Soviet Tanks with OMON troops crossed the greenbelt towards the old city and the people tried to stop them by standing in their paths. Among those who died on January 20th of this fateful year was a 13-year old schoolboy in addition to the film projectionist *Gvido Zvaigzne*. Crossing the Kr. Valdemara iela (formerly Gorki iela) continue past the *city hall* built from 1869 to 1913, down to the left to the neo-baroque *National Theatre* on the corner of Kronvalda bulv. 3. Where the Rus-

sian National Theatre performed up until the First World War became a place where politics were practiced on November 18, 1918: on the stage which symbolized the world, Latvia declared its independence. While political independence was shattered, freedom in art remained: since then, the theatre was known for its modern and provocative productions but also for classical performances of Latvian and international dramatists. The six theatrical busts on the façade – Schiller, Puschkin, Molière, Gogol, Goethe and Shakespeare – are a pure understatement of the multifaceted repertoire of this theatre. This can be experienced first-hand by an audience of 1,000 in the large auditorium and 100 in the small chamber theatre. On the opposite side of the street, the Kr. Valdemara iela leads up to the right to the *Art Academy*. The neo-Gothic building erected from 1902 to 1904 first housed the commercial stock exchange school. The *Art Museum* (Kr. Valdemara iela 10a), built from 1903 to 1905 by *V. Neumanis* has a breathtaking interior: stately flamboyance with an impressive staircase at the portal, the rich wall coverings and the heavy chandeliers.

On the first floor, murals depict views of Riga and Latvian landscapes. The house, opened in 1905 as a municipal museum, was converted into a national museum. During the German occupation of Riga, the Nazis pillaged the museum – meanwhile, the majority of the over 500 stolen paintings have been returned. Only a small proportion of the total collection of

14,000 works are on display in the permanent exhibition. Still, the works in the two main exhibition halls, Russian and Latvian paintings from the 18th to 20th centuries, hang very close together – for western museum-goers, an unusual visual experience... (→ *Museums*). The adjacent *park* the name of which was only recently changed back to "Esplanade" was formerly called "Park of the Communards" during the Soviet occupation from 1955 – this after the 27 Latvian "communards" who fell in 1919 and were buried next to the cathedral. An "Avenue of Heroes" leads past ten busts of famous Bolsheviks and deserving workers of the Soviet Union. Around 200 years ago, sand dunes stretched over this area. When Napoleon's troops were marching toward Riga, these "Kubes" were removed – the enemy would have otherwise had a good view of Riga from this vantage point. Thus, the city officials had the sand dumped at the defence areas (French: "Esplanade") and made into a park. During folk festivals, carousels offered amusement for the younger visitors, travelling performers entertained adults. The fun and worldly entertainment brought chagrin to the religious world – the construction of the Russian-Orthodox *Cathedral* put an end to the merriment.

While the *Christ's Church* was secularized and made into a planetarium and used as a House of Science after the war, culture returned to the park in 1948: it was here that the first song festival was celebrated after the war.

Every year on September 11th, the birthday of the national poet *Janis Rainis,* the preliminary events of the *Literature Festival* take place in the park. The *Christ's Cathedral,* on the other hand, is hidden behind a wooden fence. The priceless icon wall inside and the five domes once covered with gold leaf are presently being restored.

Hotel "Latvija" rises 22 storeys across the way on Brivibas iela (formerly Lenina iela). This former Intourist hotel, officially closed in September of 1991 for renovations and removal of monitoring devices, serves one of the best cups of coffee in Riga in its rather sterile cafeteria. On the opposite side of the street, the former Ministers Council of the Latvian SSR building, erected from 1936 to 1938 according to plans by *S. Skuljins* now houses the *Ministry of the Interior*. At Brivibas iela 38, a visit to the third floor is worthwhile. The apartment of *Andrejs Upits* was converted into a memorial museum for this Latvian author (open Tuesday to Sunday from 11 am to 6 pm).

On the other side of Brivibas iela, a sign with exaggerated lettering points the way to *Rigas Modas* (No. 49/53). Viewings and shows in the fashion centre of Riga are held on weekdays from 11 am to 7 pm. Passing "Radiotehnika," once the largest factory for entertainment electronics in the Soviet Union the tour leads to Lacplesa iela, and passing the Swedish Embassy (No 15) to the right, onto Baznicas iela (Church Street). The old *St. Gertrude's*

Church, a neo-Gothic brick structure from 1865 is surrounded by more or less renovated residential buildings from the turn of the century. Amid the peaceful atmosphere, the "Senite" marks the beginning of a new era: this restaurant with a cellar and terrace recruits guests with a bright banner, loud music and a doorman.

At Brunienku iela 24a is a masterpiece of Latvian Art Nouveau: *Reinholfs Smelings* designed this building, a schoolhouse, from 1913. The *Dailes Teatras* at the end of the street on the corner of Brivibas iela 75 was founded in 1920. International stars performed here under the direction of *E. Smilgis* who worked here for 50 years. Housed in this modern building since 1976, this permanent ensemble has two stages: the large theatre seats an audience of 1,000; the small theatre, around 400. In the small park grounds surrounding the theatre, Latvian artists exhibit their *sculptures.* On the opposite side of Brivibas iela, continue past the small shops, cafés, street merchants and women selling flowers back to the city. The yellow building similar to a villa is now the Russian-Orthodox *Alexander Nevski Church,* dedicated to the most popular Russian saint.

Five to six-storey residential buildings in Art Nouveau architecture line Blaumanis iela. On Terbatas iela, one will notice the last *remnants of the barricades:* they stand here to protect the newly founded Ministry of Economic Reform. Those tired of walking can turn back to the "Latvija" from here. The more extensive tour continues through the *Vermanas darzs (→Parks)* to the exit on Kris Barona iela at the corner of Merkela iela. The broad, bustling street is one of the main traffic arteries of Riga. It was named after the Latvian author and philosopher *Garlibs Merkelis* (1769-1850). Across from the flower market on the intersection of Brivibas iela, the "Sakala" department store offers an interesting impression of the Latvian shopping routine. Those who purchase their clothing here must be in the upper income brackets. At the *Staburadze house* (Merkela iela 13), the entrance is especially interesting: the bronze door is embellished with reliefs of St. Peter's Church and Gun Powder Tower. The former *Salamonskij Circus* (no. 4) built in 1889 now shows only "parttime" artists and other attractions; during the summer, the beat of the music drones through the building as young Rigans dance the night away in the disco. The *Jazeps-Vitols Conservatory* (Merkela/Kris Barona iela) built from 1873 to 1874 by Janis Blaumanis, has housed the conservatory of music since 1920. It was named after its first director, the composer *Jazeps Vitols* (1863-1948). In addition to the professional training of vocalists, choir directors, composers and conductors is the "Folk Conservatory" which offers education to more amateur musicians. Especially gifted and talented children are encouraged and fostered in the adjacent music school and secondary music school. Next to the conservatory is the *University.* The front portion of this block of buildings constructed in 1869 for the Riga Polytechnical School, is decorated with medallions depicting the sciences which were first taught here: architecture, chemistry, physics, economics, agriculture, technics and geology. In 1919, the subjects were expanded to include medicine, biology, geography and pharmacology. Also, the coat of arms of the former provinces Kurzeme and Vidzeme as well as the island of Saaremaa reveal who financed the transformation into a university which took place in 1896. The university has maintained close contacts to its partner university in Rostock/Germany since 1971. The Raina Boulevard leads back to the "Latvija."

III. Art Nouveau Tour

In the former "German quarter," the area between Hanzas iela and Tallinna iela is around ten times as large as the old city and over entire streets lined in Art Nouveau architecture. The boom of this "new style" began in 1896: at that time the German architect *Edmund von Trompowsky* erected the first six-storey residential house on Lacplesis iela. In 1904, the construction of wooden houses in this area was prohibited. Additional residential buildings quickly followed: in 1913 alone, 210 six-storey residential houses were built in this area. The rich ornamentation on the façades mostly originates from the workshop of the German sculptor *August Volz* in Riga. In 1910, *Henry van der Velde* (1863-1957) received

an invitation to take part in an architectural contest to design the parsonage in Riga. Although bombs destroyed his building completed in 1912 on Valnu iela (Wall Street), the memory remains: in "Story of My Life" the then 90 year old man reports of repeated trips to Riga. Local architects also created outstanding buildings in Art Nouveau – more than 250 buildings were designed by *K. Peksens; Janis Alkins* created over 130 houses. The list of masters of Rigan Art Nouveau can be continued almost indefinitely: *A. Aschenkampff, B. Bielenstein, W. Bockslaff, M. Eisenstein, E. Laube, A. Malvess, P. Mandelstamm, H. Scheel* and *A. Vanags* are only the prominent elite of the sweeping movement who aspired to new "natural" architectural forms.

Literature Tip
Janis Krastins, "Jugendstils Rigas archtektura," Riga, 1980: 664 examples of Rigas Art Nouveau by 128 architects.
Pamphlet "Jugendstils Riga – Art Nouveau in Riga," available in the larger hotels and book shops in Riga.

IV. From the Train Station to the Banana

The walk through the "city's stomach," the largest marketplace in Europe, begins near the train station. The approximately 20,000 visitors who arrive in Riga every day are confronted with contrasts upon leaving the station building. On the walls of the buildings near the bus terminal is a panorama of old Riga next to garish

Riga's Art Nouveau – the Highlights

The following is a suggested walking tour to discover an architectural "sampler"...

Alberta iela (Albert Street; under the Soviets Fricis Gailis iela):

No. 2a: At the entrance, a symphony of blue and white with a harmonic combination of Art Nouveau and classicistic elements, created in 1906 by *Michail Eisenstein*. Also the work of Eisenstein are the house numbers 4, 6 (both 1904) and 8 (1903).

House number 12 with the grand staircase was built by the Latvian *Konstantins Peksens*. A short jaunt up to the *Rozentals-Blaumanis Museum* is worth the detour: in the home where the artist met with his friend the author is a small collection representing their creative encounters.

Elisabethes iela (Elizabeth Street, under the Soviets Kirova iela; originally named after the Russian Czaress Elizabeth):

No. 10b: Deep blue Art Nouveau in the upper portions, the lower part is sand coloured classicism united by Michael Eisenstein in 1903.

At number 33, the Russian combined Art Nouveau elements with forms from the Renaissance, baroque and classicistic architectural styles.

Hanzas iela (Hansa Street):

No. 5: The fire department now houses the *Museum of Fire Fighting* and was created by *Reinholfs Smelings* in 1909.

Stabu iela:

No. 19: It was here that decorative ornaments from Latvian folk art appeared on the façade, complementing the Art Nouveau.

Terbatas iela:

No. 15/17: The A Kenina School, built by *Konstantins Peksens* and *E. Laube* in 1905, makes the impression of an anthroposophic building by Rudolf Steiner: no right angles, no straight halls, subdued lighting – terse and heavy with folk art elements.

Valdemara iela:

No. 23 was built in 1901 by the German architect *Heinrich Scheel* and the German-Balt *Friedrich Scheffel* in cooperation with the Berlin architect *Albert Gieseke*.

billboards advertising western products. Flower merchants offer inexpensive lilies of the valley. Slender and angular, a rectangular cement column with a steel pattern on the broad face displays the digital time. The underpass leading to the inner city is a bustling centre for street merchants and kiosks: books, flowers and western consumer goods are sold here. A few steps further, women with drawn faces sell young puppies, a pair of worn shoes, their last piece of silver cutlery... On the huge open area of the *Centralais Tirgus* (Central Market), accessible via the Gogola iela, the wooden stands sag under the weight of the fresh produce offered for sale by private farmers: cucumbers, apples and potatoes are stacked metres high and bananas lay temptingly on the scales. Tropical fruits and silk stockings await their buyers. Only one thing is surprising: little is actually purchased here – the prices at the private market are beyond the means of the local residents. It is also hardly any less expensive in the *Zeppelin Halls.* Once hangers for the German Zeppelin, built from 1924 to 1930, meat and fish, bread and butter are sold on an area of around 80,000 square metres (856,000 square feet). From the self-service fish hall, accessible over a stairway at the western end of the market hall, is a bird's eye view of the bustling marketplace.

Beyond the official market grounds, the black market extends to Krasta iela along the river, where everything is sold that has any value at all: gears and shoes, but also cars and liquor. Women hold up what they have for sale, men usually lay their wares out on their car or a blanket. Caution: those who stroll through this area in their western clothing must be prepared for pickpockets and latent aggression against "rich" western visitors.

The high-rise building of the *Academy of Science* (Odesas iela) in the typically Stalinistic style is the address of 13 research institutes and stood amid the bustling market life up to the end of the Second World War. At that time, the so-called "Louse Market" for knick-knacks and second-hand goods was held on the

lawn in front of the building at that time. Farther up the Odesas iela, one will come to a small circular plaza with the largest round building in the country: the *Jesus Baznica.* This classicistic church built on a cross shaped floor plan is the fourth building to stand on this site. The first church, consecrated in 1638, was destroyed 18 years later during the Russian occupation. The second church burned to the ground in 1710 during the Great Northern War through the conquest of Riga by *Peter I.* The subsequent wooden church also went up in flames in 1812. In the Jesus Church, the centre of the German Lutheran congregation of Riga, German language services are held every second Sunday.

V. Kipsala (Kiepenholm) and Agenskalns (Hagensberg)

The island of Kipsala in the Daugava River was once inhabited by fishermen and mariners. The maritime legacy is upheld by the street names: Matrozu iela – Sailor's Street, Locu iela – Navigator's Street, Zvernieku iela – Fishermen's Street. While the island was earlier only accessible by ferry, the Vantsu tilts Bridge has provided access to the island for pedestrians and vehicles since the summer of 1991. The bridge itself is an experience: one 109 metre (357 foot) reinforced concrete pillar bears the supporting steel cables of the 312 metre (1,020 foot) long bridge without any other supports. Those who visit Kipsala should do so as Herder did – this philosopher, teacher, pastor and librarian enjoyed his evening walks here. From Balasta Dambis, an old residential cobblestone street lined with villas from the turn of the century offers a breathtaking view of the old city. Not far from the magnificent *villa* (No. 38/40) a dream in turquoise, the *Kipsala Keramika* farther up the street (No. 32; open Monday to Friday from 11 am to 4 pm), is the workshop and showroom for 16 ceramic artists in the Latvian Art Union who have worked here in eight studios on the ground floor with their works displayed in the showroom on the upper floor.

The tour continues over the bridge to Pardaugava on the opposite banks of the river. Those tired of walking can take the streetcar, a trip leading past the *memorial of the fortieth anniversary of the victory of the Red Army,* to *Agenskalns tirgus* (Hagensberg Market). Beyond the monumental central market, the weekly market in this residential area provides more typical impressions. Surrounded by shops for the more modest population, factories and dusty wooden houses, it sooner provides insight into daily life in Riga. On the Agenskalns tirgus, L. Laicena iela 84/ corner of Uzvaras bulv., a brick building with a steel and glass frame was built in 1911 by Riga's star architect *Reinholfs Smelings.* Behind the protective wall is the open marketplace in the inner courtyard beyond the market hall. Those who feel a bit hungry will find a small cooperative "Viesmilies" (cellar; Laicena iela 58) a cozy, clean restaurant with a limited but moderately priced selection. The trip back by streetcar leads over the Saltu Bridge via two other islands in the Daugava. The first island is *Lucavsala* (Lutzausholm) on the right-hand side. A *monument for the Great Northern War* has stood here in memory of the fallen Russian soldiers since 1891. On *Zakusala* (Rabbit Island) a television broadcasting antennae rises to the right with the new architecturally interesting station all in black. The *Friendship Park* planned for this site is being designed together with seven partner cities: Ruse/Bulgaria, Bremen and Rostock/Germany, Sczcecin/Poland, Calais/France, Kobe/Japan and Pori/Finland.

VI. Bolderaja (Bolderaa)

The suburb at the confluence of the Lielupe, Curonian Aa and Daugava Rivers was a formidable competitor with Riga 780 years ago. The harbour, also fortified, was thrown out of the race by decree: Riga alone was awarded depot rights. When the harbour increasingly silted up during the 18th century, however, Rigan merchants were forced to make concessions: the ships were partially unloaded in Bolderaja, Beginning in 1895, the goods were transported to Riga by rail.

Today, two churches, numerous wooden houses, fruit and vegetable gardens all show that this competitor has remained a small city – and once again must come to the rescue of Riga: help with the sewage problems is now the topic of discussion. The Daugava, fourth largest river flowing

Ceramics Show

Not hobbyists but internationally recognized artists can be observed at the workshop and showroom of the Latvian Art Union: *Skaidrite Cihovska* with her teapot creations, *Violeta Jatniece, Mirdza Dreimane, Izabella Krolle* and *Dzintra Indrikone. Latvite Medniece* produces ethnographic figures: fable characters with two heads, imaginative horses, mythological figures from the Latvian legendary world. *Peteris Martinsons* won the bronze medal at the international ceramics competition in Mino, Japan in 1992.

Educated as an architect and a ceramic artist since 1963, he teaches ceramics and design at the Riga Art Academy. He works predominantly with porcelain. His ceramic collages are fascinating through their differing surface textures resulting from experimental firing techniques.

Also belonging to this creative circle of ceramic artists are Aija Zile, Mara Linkaite, Silvija Smidkena, Daina Gailite, Dainis Krastins, Ilga Anaga, Valdis de Burs, Kornelija Ozolina and Arniss Pelss.

---

into the Baltic Sea and the drinking water supply for the capital, transports huge levels of pollutants daily into the sea. Swimming is prohibited in the entire Bay of Riga. Up until only recently, Riga did not even equipped with a water treatment plant. Today, the current situation has long since made the plant in Bolderaja obsolete. The water treatment plant, built to handle 70,000 cubic metres of water can only treat 70% of the sewage. The explosive mixture of pollutants is already causing problems: the microorganisms in the biological treatment stage cannot hand the uncontrolled levels of heavy metals, chlorine compounds and other pollutants. Finances are insufficient for supplemental treatment stages for phosphates or nitrogen reduction. Also remaining to be determined is the disposal of the highly contaminated silt and mud.

Museums

For those who do not want to embark on a marathon through the almost twenty museums of the city, the following provides a tempting selection of the best museums in Riga:

– *Museum of Latvian History:* Pils laukums 3, Tel: 22 74 29. Tram 7, 9; trolleybus 7, 21. Displaying finds from the Middle Ages, the grave marker of a Livonian Knight of the Order, wooden sculptures from rural churches, a show on Riga's production of porcelain, native costumes and amber jewellery.

– *Museum of City History and Ship Travel:* Palasta iela 4, Tel: 21 13 58. Tram 7, 9. The displays in this museum revolve around the rare collection of the Rigan doctor *N. Himzels,* who left his collection to the city after his death. All of the pieces were first displayed in 1773. Today 17 exhibition halls and the special hall for "Navigation on the Baltic Sea" can only accommodate a portion of the extensive collection on the development of the city of Riga and navigation. Among the pieces displayed is the *Great Kristaps* (Christopher), the colourful sculpture of the patron saint of ship travel on the Daugava River – even the poem dedicated to St. Christopher by *Joachim Ringelnatz* is not missing from the exhibition. A branch of the museum is located at the Riga Cathedral. *Cathedral Museum:* Palaste iela 2, Tel: 21 34 98.

– *National Art Museum:* Kr. Valdemara iela 10a, Tel: 32 32 04 and 32 44 61. Open Tuesday to Friday from 11 am to 5 pm, Saturday and Sunday from 11 am to 6 pm. Tram 3, 5, 7, 10 and 21; bus 11 and 13. Latvian paintings on the upper floor: Janis Feders, Janis Rozentals, Janis Valters, Vilhelms Purvitis, Eduard Kalnins, Valdemar Tone – the masterpieces of Latvian art are hung unusually close together here. Latvian sculpture is exemplified by the works of T. Zalkalns, G. Skiters, Karlis Zendega. Russian art is displayed on the ground floor to the right: V. Borovikovskij, F. Rokotov, V. Perov, I. Kramskoj, V. Polenov, Ilja Repin, W. Kusotodiev, Levitan, K. Korovin. A special exhibition hall is dedicated to the works of Nikolai Rerichs – one simply must see his luminous blue paintings of mountain landscapes.

– *Museum for Foreign Art:* Pils laukums 3, Tel: 22 64 67, 22 06 47 and 22 52 09. Open Tuesday to Sunday from 11 am to 5 pm. Egypt, Greece and Rome. German masters from the 16th to 18th centuries; Dutch artists from the 17th century. German art is represented by works of Carl Spitzweg, Ludwig Richter, Wilhelm von Lenbach. Also includes a collection of porcelain as well as East Asian art.

– *Janis Rainis Museum for Literature and Art History:* Pils laukums, second floor. Manuscripts, texts and documents by and about this Estonian national poet. Since Rainis had active contact to other artists like the Rigan architect Blaumanis, this collection also offers a dynamic cross-section of cultural life in Riga from 1860 to 1930.

– *J. Rozentals and R. Blaumanis Memorial:* Alberta iela 12, Apartment 9, Tel: 33 16 41.

– *Kris Barona Memorial:* K. Barona iela 3, Apartment 5, Tel: 28 42 65.

– *Ugunsdzesibas Muzejs* (Fire Fighting Museum): Hanzas iela 5 (Fire Department), Tel: 33 13 34. Tours offered Tuesday to Saturday from 10 am to 5 pm and by appointment. Fire fighting vehicles manufactured by the former Riga car factory "Russobalt" from the period before the First World War.

– *Museum of Applied Arts:* Skarnu iela 10/20, Tel: 22 22 35 and 22 78 33. Handicrafts enjoy wide popularity in Latvia.

– *Stradins Museum of Medical History:* L. Paegles iela 1, Tel: 22 43 96 and 22 26 56. Tram 1, 10 and 24; bus 2 and 24. Over 70,000 pieces are displayed in the 44 halls covering medical history from the Orient and the Occident, from ancient Greece and Rome to present. Among these are:

the coat of arms of the barber's guild from 1494, a guild which also performed surgery at that time; a Rigan pharmacy from the 19th century; the history of the Riga Medical Institute.

– *Pharmaceutical Museum:* Vagnera iela 13/15.

– *Theatre Museum:* E. Smilga iela 37/39, Tel: 61 18 93 and 61 77 08. Tram 2; bus 4, 7, 8, 25, 38, 42. Housed in the former home of E. Smilgis, this museum was opened in 1976. It especially provides information on the history of the Rainis Daile Art Theatre, of which Smilgis was the director for 50 years. His office has been preserved in its original state. A special exhibition hall is dedicated to the Latvian vocalist *Malvine Vignere-Grinberga (1873-1949).*

– *Latvian War Museum:* Smilsu iela 20, Tel: 22 81 47. Tram 5, 7 and 9. Covers the First World War, the 1917 Revolution and the Second World War.

– *Museum of the Latvian (Red) Riflemen:* Latviesu (sarkano) strelnieku laukums, Tel: 21 10 30.

– *Lenin Memorial:* closed at present. Lenin House: Cesu iela 17, Tel: 37 14 41. Lenin's residence: Elisabethes iela 18, Tel: 28 78 63.

– *Andrejs Upits Memorial:* Brivibas iela 38. The former flat of this writer is now open to the public.

– *Latvian Museum of Natural History:* Kris Barona iela 4, Tel: 21 32 91. Open Wednesday to Sunday 11 am to 5 pm, Thursdays noon to 7 pm. Tram 4, 6 and 11; trolleybus 3, 5 and 17, bus 11, 14, 16 and 32. Petrified shellfish from Lode (Lohde); in 1970,

the 350 million ancient animals were found near Cesis.

– *Arsenal Exhibition Hall:* Tel: 22 95 70. Open Tuesday to Sunday from noon to 6 pm. Modern Latvian art.

– *Latvia Exhibition Hall:* Brivibas iela 31, Tel: 22 24 61; trolleybus 4, 14 and 17; bus 1, 21, 32, 34 and 47.

– *Exhibition Hall on the island of Kipsala:* Balasta dambis 34; trolleybus 7 and 21; bus 13, 22, 30 and 53. Exhibition of ceramics, numerous modern pieces.

– *Photoclub "Riga":* Blaumana iela 21; tram 4, 6 and 11; trolleybus 11, 18, 22 and 23. Works by Latvian photographers.

Museums outside the City

– *Automobile Museum Mezciems:* Eizensteina iela 6, Tel: 53 79 25. Bus 21. Open Tuesday to Sunday from 10 am to 6 pm. Behind the glass façade which looks like a cooler grille from a Rolls-Royce, the automobile museum has displayed 50 old-timers, 30 motorcycles and numerous historical bicycles. The first floor is reserved for the vehicles of famous people – Maxim Gorky's 1933 Lincoln, Molotov's 1939 Rolls-Royce and Stalin's limousine from 1949 to 1951 for example. The Soviet copy of a Packard with a red flag on the radiator grille is presented especially well: Stalin is getting out of the car – portrayed by a wax figure. A number of Daimler models are also displayed on the ground floor: a horse drawn model from 1885 and a motor carriage from 1886. The yellow German automobile club vehicle from 1924 is on loan from the Berlin Transport Museum.

After admiring the 1912 Russobalt fire engine and the bright blue 1938 Opel convertible, the collection of model automobiles along the wall is also worth seeing. Displayed on the upper floor are sportscars, bicycles and compact cars. Directly at the entrance is the fastest diesel in the world. The metallic grey Volkswagen "Pfeil" set a world record in 1980 at 362.07 kmph (227.72 mph). A few yards farther: an East German Trabant P 50... Through the broad glass façade of the building, one will see the *Bikernieku Racetrack,* which was opened on July 30, 1966. Automobile, motorcycle and go-cart races take place here during the entire year. On June 20, 1992, the "veterans" were at the starting line for an old-timer rally.

– *Museum of Applied and Decorative Art:* Skarnu iela 10/20, Tel: 22 78 33. Well worth a visit, especially for the textiles.

– *Ethnographic Open-Air Museum* (Brivdabas Muzejs): Brivibas iela 440, Tel: 99 45 10. Bus 1, 823 and 825. Open daily from 10 am to 5 pm. A visit to this open-air museum on the shores of Lake Jugla is an absolute must. Founded in 1924, this exhibition of farm houses from all over the country was opened in the summer of 1932 with the first six structures. Today, more than 80 buildings on 100 hectares (250 acres) display over 30,000 individual pieces from the four historical and cultural provinces of Latvia: Kurzeme, Vidzeme, Latgale and Zemgale. Structures include farmyards, workshops, churches, schools and tar factories. Also represented in this exhibition are Livonian farmers, who have long lived in the northern regions of Kurzeme as well as Russian farmers, who moved into Latgallia in the 18th century. Folklore performances, demonstrations of old handicraft techniques and wood carving bring the old tradition to life. Historical handicrafts are also sold at the marketplaces or during presentations. In the summer, services take place on a regular basis in the church; and exhibitions and lectures are held in the cultural house. Our tip when visiting the museum: be sure to stop by "Priedes Krogs" (open 11 am to 5 pm, closed Mondays and Tuesdays), a cozy, rustic tavern housed in a building from 1841 from the Bauske region.

Despite the proximity of a paper factory which dumps its untreated waste directly into *Lake Jugla,* this is still a popular destination for excursions. Lake Jugla is connected to Lake Kis by a canal. The bridge over the canal marks the city limits of Riga.

Galleries

A & E, Skarnu iela 17; open daily from noon to 6 pm.

Kolonna, Skarnu iela 16/corner of Doma laukums, Tel: 22 60 70; open Tuesday to Friday from 10 am to 6 pm, Saturdays from 10 am to 3 pm.

Ars Longa, R Vagnera iela 4; open Tuesday to Sunday from 11 am to 5 pm.

Bastejs, Basteja bulvaris 12; open Tuesday to Saturday from noon to 5 pm.

Pulvertonis, Smilsu iela 20, Hall 13;

open Tuesday and Wednesday from 11 am to 6 pm, Thursday from noon to 7 pm and Friday to Sunday from 11 am to 6 pm. In the Gun Powder Tower.

Rigas Galerijas, Aspazija bulvaris 20, Tel: 21 63 87; open Tuesday to Saturday from 11 am to 7 pm. This gallery was opened in August 1992 and exhibits Latvian art on two floors.

Vecpilseta, corner of Kalku and Meistaru iela; open Monday to Wednesday from 8 am to 2 pm, Thursday and Friday from 3 to 6 pm and Saturday from 9 am to 3 pm.

Shopping
Marketplaces

Central Market: Negu iela 7, Tel: 22 99 81. The largest market in Europe takes place at the man train station. It is easily recognised by the Zeppelin Halls from the period before the First World War. Surrounding the halls are sales stands and open market stands. The black market section extends to the banks of the Daugava River along Krasta iela.

Agenskalna Market: L. Laicena iela 64, Tel: 61 15 64.

Vidzemes Market: Brivibas iela 90, Tel: 27 22 63.

Handicrafts and Souvenirs

Sakta, Brivibas iela 32.

Gallery for Folk Art, Brivibas iela 48

Department Stores

Universalveikals, Audeju iela 16.

Perfume

The Latvian perfume company "Dzintars" sells its products in their own outlet store: Kr. Barona iela 3.

Chocolate

Sporta iela 2, selling Uzvara products.

Parks and Gardens

Arkadijas Park: O. Vaciesa/corner of F. Brivzemnieka iela. This park on the opposite side of the river was preceded by a private garden laid out in 1850. In 1911, when the park was completed, this park was named after Arcadia, the mythological landscape in ancient Greece. It must have been just as idyllic for those who lived in the former wooden houses (which have now given way to modern apartment complexes) surrounding this park with cascades, ponds, bridges, an amphitheatre and playground. However, the most beautiful aspect of this park is the view of the Marupite River and the Tower of Riga.

Basteikalns: → *Walking Tour II.*

Botanical Gardens: Kandavas iela 2, on the opposite banks of the Daugava River. Covering 15 hectares (37½ acres) the botanical gardens include of 8,000 individual plants representing 900 species from decorative flowers to pharmaceutical plants and an Arboretum (a grove comprising various types of trees for scientific and educational purposes) with rare trees and shrubs.

Dziesmu svetku parks (Song Festival Park): Sverdlova iela/corner of Hanzas iela. The oldest municipal park in Riga, covering 7.6 hectares (19 acres), was laid out in 1721 by order of Peter I as the "Czar's Garden." In 1920, this park with its 15 indigenous and 57 imported species of trees was renamed "Viestura darzs." Since the

100th anniversary of the Song Festival tradition which was celebrated with a enormous choir concert, this park has been called Song Festival Park. During the celebration, a monument was unveiled, commemorating seven Latvian composers, *Peteris Barisons* (1904-1947), *Janis Cimze* (1814-1881), *Emilis Darzins* (1875-1910), *Andrejs Jurjans* (1856-1922), *Alfred Kalnins* (1879-1951), *Emilis Melngailis* (1874-1954) and *Jazeps Vitols* (1863-1948). The original Dutch architecture of the garden was destroyed by fire and flood. Only one pond and one elm which was planted by the czar himself have endured. The "Alexander Gateway" at the main entrance on Hanzas iela was built as a triumphal arch to commemorate the victory over Napoleon. It originally stood on the edge of the city and was then moved to its present location in 1935.

Esplanade: → *Walking Tour II.*
Mezaparks: Koknes prospekt/corner of Meza prospekt, tram 11 to Zoologiskais darzs. There is also a steamer-ferry connection. The forest park, formerly the Czar's Forest, begins adjacent to the zoo. The concentration camp "Kaiserwald" was located here in 1943. 19,000 Jews from Riga housed here for six months in the cramped barracks. Ultimately, they were transported elsewhere and killed. Today, the meadows and forests along the Kisezers (Stintsee) make up the "Kulturas un atputas parks" (the cultural and recreational park). The centre of the park features the permanent economic exhibition, the showcase for Latvian factories. Adjacent to this is the monumental amphitheatre built for the Song Festivals, in which numerous choirs from Latvia and abroad sing Latvian "Dainas" along with the populace every five years – also in 1993. A new development is that automobiles are sold on the grounds during the weekends – and these "shows" draw almost as many spectators as the Song Festivals themselves.
→ *see also Cemeteries*

Vermanes darzs (during the Soviet regime: Kirowa darzs): bordered by Elisabethes iela, Terbatas iela, Merkela iela and Kr. Barona iela. Formerly, the suburban houses were cramped into this small area 150 years ago. In 1812, they were burned to the ground – out of fear of Napoleon's troops who were advancing on Riga on their Russia campaign. The expansion of the defence buffer was intended to prevent that the enemy could invade Riga unnoticed. Still, the desolate, swampy square only 8,450 square metres (90,922 square feet) at that time, is just one-sixth of its area today. The over 2,000 trees planted at that time are no longer in existence: they fell victim to the dampness. The health sanatorium with an artificial mineral spring has also disappeared. The festive dedication of the park took place on July 8, 1817 – shielded by a high, wooden fence. The party was intended to remain a private affair – the park was at first only accessible for the aristocracy of Riga. From 1850 to 1870, the park grew to its present dimensions.

An estrade was built, a drainage system installed and a bronze fountain was ordered for the park in Berlin. Equipped with an ice skating rink, a sundial and the first rose garden in the city, this park was an idyllic retreat. This was also noticed by the citizens of Riga – and they demanded entry. However, it was only in 1930 that the fence finally toppled. The park was given its socialist name when a bust of *S. M. Kirow,* one of Lenin's compatriots, was unveiled in the park in 1954. In 1991, the park reverted to the name honouring the woman who once donated the land for this beautiful park to the city.

Zoological Gardens: Located in a beautiful landscape near the Kisezers (Stintsee) not far from the Forest Park is the Riga Zoo. It has been at this location since 1912. The collection of 2,500 animals includes 350 species.

Cemeteries

Cemeteries, not normally a place frequented by tourists. In Latvia, however, one should definitely pay a visit to them because they are a symbol of national pride. All of the three main cemeteries in Riga are located in the Mezaparks district: Rainis, Bralu and Meza cemeteries. The Bralu kapi (Brother's Cemetery) is especially helpful in providing insight into the Latvian mentality.

Bralu kapi (Brother's Cemetery)
Also called the Cemetery of Heroes, this memorial cemetery is the final resting place for soldiers who fell during the two world wars. It was de-

signed by the trio *A. Birznieks* (architect), *A. Zeidaks* (gardening engineer) and *K. Zale* (sculptor). After twelve years of construction, they were to see their plans come to fruition in 1936. Through the gateway arch embellished with two groups of statues, the long central avenue (ceremonial avenue) leads to the main terrace. Linden trees line the walkway. The Latvian symbols for love and femininity stand here for sisters, mothers, lovers and brides who pay their last tributes to the soldiers buried here. The rose bushes at the base of the lindens symbolise the thorny path that the soldiers had to tread. A broad, flat staircase leads up to the main altar terrace flanked by 100 oak tress – a symbol of the soldiers' perseverance. On the altar terrace, an eternal flame has burned since 1958 when the last Latvian soldier was laid to rest here. The cemetery itself lies below. The plots are laid out in regimented rows; plain grey stones provide names, rank and date of birth. On 300 gravestones is only one word "nezinams" – "unknown." In the struggle for independence, the cemetery became a place for political demonstrations: on June 14, the demonstrators commemorated the beginning of the deportations by Stalin; every year on November 18, the Latvian independence is celebrated.

Meza kapi (Forest Cemetery)
The Forest Cemetery is well suited for a contemplative walk. Each of the old graves has its own story to tell. Under the gravestone with the stylized Baltic waves lies *Vilis Lacas,* the

Latvian writer and minister. The graves with crosses in the form of a propeller are in memory of young pilots who died while testing sport aircrafts during the 1920's and 1930's in Riga.

Rainis kapi (Rainis Cemetery)

The municipal cemetery extends over site of an older graveyard: it came into being in 1929 on the former location of a small cemetery dating back to the 19th century. This old cemetery was used for those who died without their final confession and therefore no longer had the right to a gravestone or cross. After *Rainis'* death, donations enabled the construction of the entry archway and the restructuring of the cemetery. The focal point became a monumental Rainis memorial, sculpted from a 60 ton block of Finnish granite by Professor *Karlis Zemdaga* in 1935. In accordance with the inscription "a strong man, I greet the sun," the sculpture depicts a young man awakening to the sun, a symbol for happiness and freedom. Rainis' wife *Elza Rosenberg* was buried next to him with less pomp and pathos. Even high-ranking Soviet officials, artists and scientists and former "heroes of the Soviet Union" like *Imants Sudmalis* and *Otomar Oskalns* have found their final resting place in this cemetery.

Sports and Recreation

Daugava Stadium, Augsiela iela 1, Tel: 27 48 15.

Dynamo *Stadium,* E. Melngaila iela 1a, Tel: 33 12 11.

Mezaparks *Sports Complex,* Tel: 51 85 68.

Riga *Sports Manège,* Maskavas iela 160, Tel: 24 17 70.

Riga *Sports Palace,* Kris Barona iela 75, Tel: 27 71 33.

Daugava *Tennis Club,* Kronvalda bulvaris 2a, Tel: 32 29 20.

Riga Technical University *indoor swimming pool,* Kipsalas iela 5, Tel: 61 69 89.

Central *Yacht Club,* Sturmana iela 1, Tel: 43 33 44.

Seaman *Yachting Club,* Laca iela 1a, Tel: 32 32 61.

Yachting Club, Liela iela 6, Tel: 43 32 50.

Saunas: Lubanas iela 1/3, Tel: 2 42 59; Tallinnas iela 37, Tel: 27 33 67; Dagmaras iela 7, Tel: 45 86 16; Martina iela 12, Tel: 61 79 89.

Information on Sporting Events as well as the outcome of matches are listed in the newspaper "Sports" which is published four times weekly.

Theatres and Concert Halls

National Theatre (Nacionalis teatris): Kronvalda bulvaris 2, Tel: 32 28 28 and 32 27 59. Ticket sales daily from 10 am to 2 pm and from 4 to 7 pm.

Dailes teatris: Brivibas iela 75, Tel: 27 04 24 and 27 10 36. Ticket sales daily from 10 am to 2 pm and from 4 to 7 pm.

Russian Theatre (Krievu Drama teatris): Kalku iela 16, Tel: 22 76 46 and 22 54 23. Ticket sales daily from 11 am to 1 pm and from 2 to 4 pm.

Youth Theatre (Jaunatnes teatris): Lacplesa iela 25 (Latvian ensemble), Lacplesa iela 37 (Russian ensemble). Tel: 28 75 58 and 22 30 52. Founded in 1940 and directed by Adolfs Sapiro, this theatre troop was present at the Bertolt Brecht Festival in 1988 in Berlin.

Puppet Theatre (Lellu teatris): Kris Barona iela 16/18, Tel: 28 51 45 and 28 54 18. Ticket sales daily except Mondays from 11 am to 6 pm. Founded in 1943, this theatre has both a Latvian and Russian ensemble. They are often on tour and even perform overseas.

Operetta Theatre (Operetes teatris): Brivibas iela 96, Tel: 27 12 64 and 27 37 88. Ticket sales Monday to Friday from 10 am to 2 pm and from 3 to 7 pm; Saturday and Sunday, only until 6 pm. Founded in 1945, Latvian and Russian ensembles perform both classical and modern operettas.

Independent Studio Theatre "Kabata": Kramu 4, Tel: 22 53 34. An experimental theatre troupe; performances take place on an irregular basis.

Riga Chamber Theatre: Caka 30.

Riga Circus (Rigas cirks): Merkela iela 4 (near the train station), Tel: 21 34 79. Circus fantasies come to life at the building from 1889. Still: in addition to regular performances of this, the only stationary circus in the Baltic States (only during the winter), disco evenings are held here during the summer.

National Opera: Aspazijas iela 3, Tel: 22 84 02.

Philharmonic Concert Hall: Kalku iela 11a, Tel: 21 34 97.

Richard Wagner Hall: Vagnera iela 4, Tel: 21 08 17.

"Ave Sol" Concert Hall: Citadeles iela 7.

Cinemas

Since 1988, the "Arsenals" International Film Forum presents more than two hundred films from Latvia and abroad each year during nine days at the end of September. These include both old and new productions. Information on the current films is posted on public bulletin boards and is also listed in the "Rigas Balss" newspaper.

Aina: Valnu iela 19, Tel: 21 69 29.

Daile: Kris Barona iela 31, Tel: 28 38 54; trolleybus 2, 4, 6 and 11.

Etna: Gertrudes iela 72; trolleybus 1, 11 and 23, bus 6 and 17.

Gaisma: Tallinnas iela 54; trolleybus 5, 18 and 23.

Lacplesis: Lacplesa iela 52/54, Tel: 28 58 84; trolleybus 11, 18, 22 and 23, bus 6.

Palladium: Maijas iela 21, Tel: 28 63 80; trolleybus 11, 18, 22 and 23.

Pionieris: Skodas iela; trolleybus 3, 5, 10, and 21, bus 11 and 33.

Riga: Elisabethes iela 61, Tel: 28 63 80; trolleybus 1, 4, 14 and 17, bus 1, 14, 21 and 32.

Spartaks: Elisabethes iela 61, Tel: 28 63 80; trolleybus 1, 4, 14 and 17, bus 1, 14, 21 and 32.

Cafés

Architekt, Amatu iela 4, Tel: 22 51 72.

Balta Roze (White Rose): Laipu iela 1, upper floor. Small but nice: a co-op café serving tea and pastries.

13 Kresli (13 Chairs), Cathedral Square, one of the most famous cafés in Riga. Small and crowded.

Imeretia, Kijevas iela 32, Tel: 22 75 64.

Leningrad, Raia iela 25, Tel: 22 65 16.

Magdalene, Smilsu iela 2/4, Tel: 22 43 78.

Melpomena & Tersiphora, Akmenu 13, Tel: 61 45 83.

Mozums, Skunu iela 19/Doma laukums.

Nota Bene, Jurmalas gatve 14, Tel: 40 36 11.

Palette, Gleznotaju 12/14, Tel: 21 60 37; new wave in white.

Pils (Castle) Café, self-service on the terrace under chestnut trees with a view of the Daugava River; a popular meeting place for young people – unfortunately, only during the summer.

Petergailis, Skarnu iela 26 (near St. Peter's Church).

Put Veni, Jauniela 18/22, Tel: 22 88 41.

Rigonda, Jerjomenko iela 2, Tel: 59 63 61.

Rostok, Terbatas iela 13, Tel: 28 15 34.

Senite, Veidenbauma iela 33, Tel: 37 33 80.

Vecriga, Valnu iela 18, Tel: 21 68 50.

Vigante, Stabu iela 49a, Tel: 27 55 40.

Restaurants
Foreign Currency Restaurants

Jever Bistro: Kalku iela 6, Tel: 22 70 78; open daily from 11 am to 3 am. The destination for hungry western tourists and prestigious Latvians, among other reasons for the "easy women" who frequent this pub. The restaurant is a virtual gold mine for the proprietor from Hamburg.

Lido: Lacplesa iela 53, Tel: 28 79 27.

Otto: in the Hotel de Rome.

Other Restaurants

Astorija, Audeju iela 16, Tel: 21 14 75.

Baltija, Melnsila 22, Tel: 45 19 59.

Daugava, Kugu iela 24, Tel: 61 36 00.

Metropol, Aspazijas iela 36/38, Tel: 21 60 21; hotel restaurant.

Pie Kristapa, Jauniela 25/29, Tel: 22 63 54 and 22 75 90; a beer bar in the cellar; restaurant on the ground floor with a very friendly doorman. Serving tasty "Bear Killer Beer" which lives up to its name... hearty cuisine.

Priedeskrog, a pub located in the open-air museum at Lake Julga.

Put Vejini, Jauniela 28; "Blow Wind" is the name of this restaurant, which many consider the best in Riga.

Rusa, Lokomotives iela 68, Tel: 26 35 25.

Schtsin, Maskavas iela 264, Tel: 25 73 47.

Sonata, Lidonu iela 27, Tel: 46 76 11.

Turist, Slokas iela 1, Tel: 61 00 38 and 61 56 82; hotel restaurant.

Vec Riga, Aspazija iela 22, Tel: 21 66 69 and 21 60 01.

Night life
Night life ends early in Riga, namely around 11 pm. This is when most of the cafés and restaurants close. Those who would rather not spend their last dollars in the foreign currency bars in the larger hotels and want to observe the managers and powerful flirting with the girls will find only a few sparse alternatives:

Bars and Cafés

Café Forum, Kalku iela (near the casino).

Café Luna, Brivibas iela/Basteja bulvaris; rough but sincere, heavily frequented by Russians.

Discotheques and Dancing

Galaktika, Brivibas iela 24, with the adjacent Café Allegro.

Szczecin, Maskavas iela 264, in the Kengarags district, Tel: 25 73 47.

Disco Ships (only in summer): MS Liepaja, MS Maskava, at the Krastmala iela docks on the outskirts of the old city.

Casino Latvija, Kalku iela 24, Tel: 21 23 22.

Accommodation

Four-Star Hotels

Hotel de Rome: Kalku iela 28, Tel: 21 62 68; centrally located with double rooms priced at £95 ($178).

Hotel Ridzene: Raina bulvaris 7, Tel: 32 44 33; built in 1984, centrally located.

Three Star Hotels

Hotel Latvia: Elisabethes iela 55/ corner of Brivibas iela, Tel: 21 26 45; on the 14th through 16th floors of the Danish-Latvian joint venture "Fremadrejser" modernised to western standards. Prices for suites £94 to £117 ($175 to $220); double rooms, £70 to £95 ($132 to $178); single rooms, £47 to £59 ($88 to $110).

Hotel Riga: Aspazijas bulvaris 22, Tel: 21 61 04. In the same building:

Eurolink: the second floor of Hotel Riga, modernised to western standards by a Swedish corporation. Tel: 21 63 17, Mobile Tel: 00 46 10-68 28 32. Single rooms cost £42 ($78); double rooms, £50 ($94). All of the food is brought over from Sweden,

only soup vegetables and flowers originate from Latvia.

Simple Hotels, not always the cleanest and often loud

Atlantija, Tel: 34 01 78.

Aurora, Marijas iela 5, Tel: 22 44 79.

Baka, Elisabethes iela 3, Tel: 32 15 08.

Baltija, Raina bulvaris 33, Tel: 22 74 61.

Daugava, Kugu iela 24, Tel: 24 79 97.

Family Hostel, Elisabethes iela 22-4a, Tel: 28 48 68; three price categories with an average of £5.35 ($10).

Jurnieks, Tel: 39 27 32.

Karavelle, Katrinas Dambis 25, Tel: 32 98 76, on the sea harbour.

Metropole, corner of Padomju bulvaris/Janvara iela 13, Tel: 21 61 84.

Plavnieki, Salnas iela 26, Tel: 13 70 40; bus 47 and 52.

Saulite, Merkela iela 12, Tel: 22 45 46.

Sports, Gogola iela 5, Tel: 22 67 80.

Sportistu, Tel: 52 23 47.

Turists, Slokas iela 1, Tel: 61 54 55.

Viktorija, A. Caka iela 55, Tel: 27 23 05.

Zemgale, Valdeku iela 66, Tel: 62 27 14; bus 40.

Tip: YMCA-YWCA Interpoint Programme, Kalnciema iela 10/12, Tel: 33 21 31 and 61 38 48, Fax: 22 50 39. Open from July 1 to August 15 daily from 8 am to 11 pm. Assistance, activities and inexpensive accommodation. Also includes a café and is managed by a Danish staff.

Houses and Apartments in Riga and the surrounding regions are rented out by the "House and Flat Rental

Service," Tel: 26 63 39 and 37 48 74. A room on Slepotabu iela costs around £32 ($60) including meals; half of a bungalow in Jurmala Dzintari costs around £22 ($40). Prices quoted are as of 1992.

Transport

Airport: Lidosta "Riga." Eight kilometres (5 miles) to the southwest. Bus 22 departs from the airport to the city and the main train station. Lufthansa office at the airport, open Monday to Saturday from 9 am to 4 pm, Tel: 20 71 83; Latvijas Aviokompanija, Airport Counter, Tel: 22 37 75; SAS Airport Counter, open Monday to Saturday from 9 am to 4 pm, Tel: 20 70 55; Hamburg Airlines, City Office, Marstalu iela 12, a/k 541, Tel: 22 76 38, Fax: 22 76 52.

Airport Spilve: Near the centre of town on the southern banks of the river. From here, the "Baltic Helicopter Service" (Tel: 45 86 68) offers helicopter flights to every destination in the Baltic States.

Bus Station: Autoosta, Pragas iela 1.

Ferries: Passenger Terminal, Eksporto iela 1.

Ship Travel: Trips on the Daugava River, Balasta dambi 1a. Raketa (hydrofoils) up the river past the harbour to Jurmala. The trip on the hydrofoil lasts around one hour. There are also connections to Engure (70km/44 miles). Shorter distances are also offered on the hydrofoil to the interior of the country on the Daugava and Lielupe Rivers. The hydrofoil docks are at Komjanautas krastmala between the October and Gorki Bridges.

Train Station: Centrala dzelzcela stacija, Stacija laukums.

Travel Agencies: Baltaa Tour, Elisabethes iela 63, Tel: 28 53 90; Baltic Tours, Eksporta iela 1, Tel: 32 95 19; BLIK, Brivibas iela 219, Tel: 55 13 43; Ergo, 13 Janvara 3, Room 401, Tel: 22 97 60; Fremad Riga, Vagnera iela 3, Tel: 21 07 73; Jurmala Tours, Basteja bulvaris 16, Tel: 22 29 19; K & G, Basteja bulvaris 14, Tel: 22 96 19; Lattour, Brunienku iela 29/31, Tel: 27 49 52; Latvia Tours, Grecinieku iela 22/24, Tel: 21 36 52, Fax: 21 36 66; Pavadonis, Elisabethes iela 45/47, Tel: 33 42 02; Saulite, A. Caka 79/6-34, Tel: 27 41 13; Tour Service, Elisabethes iela 207, Tel: 32 34 47.

Municipal Transport:

Tram S

2 Ropauzu iela	– Tapesu iela
4 Imanta	– Cierkalns
5 Ilguciems	– Milgravis
6 Ausekla iela	– Lake Jugla
7 Ausekla iela	– Sarkanais kvadrats
9 Aldaris	– Sarkanais kvadrats
10 Centralais tirgus (central market)	– Biumuiza
11 Stacija laukums (train station square)	– Kulturas un atputas parks

Trolleybus

1 Petersalas iela	– Valmieras iela
2 Sarkandaugava	– Saules darzs
3 Centralais tirgus (central market)	– Sarkandaugava
4 Centralais tirgus (central market)	– Smerlis

The economic situation in Latvia is anything but rosy, many people must make ends meet by selling their belongings on the street; however, the shelves in stores are slowly filling

Cultural diversity in Lithuania: the statues before the Dramatic Theatre in Vilnius draw spectators — bands perform on the streets of Klaipeda

5 Centrala stacija
(main train sta-
tion) – Daugavas
Stadium

6 Republikas slim-
nica – Riga Technical
University (RTU)

7 Kafejnica "Prie-
des" – Keguma iela

8 RTU – Abolu iela

9 RTU – Ilguciems

10 Ausekla iela – Daugavas
Stadium

11 Stacija laukums
(train station
square) – Ieriku iela

12 RTU – Livciema iela

13 Centralais tirgus
(central market) – Vaidavas iela

14 Brivibas
bulvaris – Mezciems

15 Inzenieru iela – Pavlova iela

16 Katlakalna iela – Smerlis

17 Merkela iela – Purvciems

18 Stacija laukums
(train station
square) – Mezciems

19 Inzenieru iela – Livciema iela

20 Inzenieru iela – Zakusala

21 Lacplesa iela – Ilguciems

22 Centrala stacija
(main train sta-
tion) – Katlakalna

23 Stacija laukums
(train station
square) – Purvciems

24 Inzenieru iela – Malu iela

Buses

1 Bus Terminal – Bergi

2 Centrala stacija
(main train sta-
tion) – Vecmilgravis

3 Bolderaja – Centrala stacija
(main train station)

4 Stacija laukums
(train station
square) – Beberbeku iela

4Z Stacija lau-
kums (train sta-
tion square) – Zolitudes iela

5 Abrenes iela – Tiraine

6 Stacijas laukums
(train station
square) – Rigas 2. precu
stacija

7 Abrenes iela – Upesgrivas iela

8 Abrenes iela – Zolitude

9 Abrenes iela – Saules darzs

10 Abrenes iela – Bruklenu iela

11 Bus Terminal – Suzi

12 Abrenes iela – Katlakalna

13 Centrala stacija
(main train sta-
tion) – Eksperimentala
baze

14 Stacija laukums
(train station
square) – Zversaimnieciba

15 Jugla – Veikals "Starts"

16 Centrala stacija
(main train sta-
tion) – Jugla Paper Fac-
tory

17 Bus Terminal – Jugla Paper Factory

18 Visku iela – Brivibas gatve

19 Juglas tilts (Jug-
las bridge) – Jaunciems

20 Express bus 13.
janvara iela – Birzes iela

21 Planetarijs (Pla-
netarium) – Mezciems

22 Architektu iela – Lidosta "Riga"
(Airport)

23	Abrenes iela	– Balozi		

23 Abrenes iela – Balozi
24 Express bus
   Centrala stacija
   (main train sta-
   tion) – Mangalsala
25 Abrenes iela – Marupe
26 Abrenes iela – Katlakalns
27 Skirotava – TEC
28 Juglas tilts (Jug-
   las bridge) – Upesciems
29 Veikals "Starts" – 4. celu buves ra-
   jons
30 Rumbula – Kipsala
31 not in service
32 Centrala stacija
   (main train sta-
   tion) – Jugla
33 Bus Terminal – Kundzinsala
34 Express bus
   Jugla – Kleistu iela
35 not in service
36 Imanta – Vakabulli
37 Express bus
   Planetarijs
   (Planetarium) – Imanta
38 Stacija laukums
   (train station
   square) – Imanta
39 not in service
40 Abrenes iela – Ziepniekkalns
41 Express bus
   Planetarijs
   (Planetarium) – Imanta
42 Stacija laukums
   (train station
   square) – Imanta
43 not in service
44 not in service
45 Imanta – Plavnieki
46 not in service
47 Planetarijs (Pla-
   netarium) – Plavnieki
48 not in service

49 Sarkandaugava – Visku iela
50 Centrala stacija
   (main train sta-
   tion) – Skirotava
51 Mezciems – Jaunceltnes
52 Stacija laukums
   (train station
   square) – Ulbrokas kapi
53 Planetarijs (Pla-
   netarium) – Zolitude

Route Taxis
T-1 Centrala stacija – Imanta
T-2 Centrala stacija – Kengaras
                     – Darzini
T-3 Centrala stacija – Jugla
                     – bernu slimnica
T-4 Centrala stacija – Purvciems
                     – Akademijas iela
T-5 Centrala stacija – Spilve
T-6 Centrala stacija – Vecmilgravis
T-7 Centrala stacija – Lidosta "Riga"
                       (Airport)
T-8 Centrala stacija – Ziepniekkalns
T-9 Centrala stacija – Bolderaja
T-10 Centrala staci-
     ja – Mezciems
T-13 Centrala staci-
     ja – Zolitude

State Taxis
Yellow vehicles with a black and white chequered sign on the roof are state taxis. Licence plates begin with a number combination before the letters.

Information
Banks: Baltija, Aspazijas bulvaris 34, Tel: 21 34 44; LR Banka, Kr. Valdemara iela 2a, Tel: 32 34 73; Orints, Berzinas iela 13L, Tel: 37 00 93; Rigas Banka, Katlakalna iela 2, Tel:

24 97 19; Rigas komercbanka, Smil-su iela 6, Tel: 32 39 67.

Dental Care: Emergency Service, Stabu iela 9, Tel: 27 45 46.

Film Developing: Kodak Photo Shop, Brivibas iela 40, Tel: 28 86 62; open daily from 10 am to 6 pm. Film supplies and developing services, payment accepted only in hard currencies.

Hospital: Hospital P. Stradina Republikaniska slimnica, Pilsonu iela 13, Tel: 61 14 12. Emergency clinic: Traumatologiskais instituts, Duntes iela 16/22, Tel: 39 30 08.

Lost and Found Office: For the public transport system; Tel: 21 96 35. For articles lost at the train station, Tel: 23 21 78.

Pharmacies: Audeju iela 20, Tel: 21 33 40; Brivibas iela 38, Tel: 28 97 61; Kalku iela 18, Tel: 22 49 08; Alnu iela 26, Tel: 22 34 34; "Amfa," Elisabethes iela 21, Tel: 33 31 96 (accepts only hard currencies).

Post Office: Main Post Office, Brivibas iela 21, Tel: 22 31 63. 24-hour service; express letters can be posted at the train station from Monday to Friday from 8 am to noon. Immediate long distance calls can be placed directly at the "Riga Business Centre," Elisabethes iela 45/47, Tel: 22 51 89.

Travel Agency: The first international travel agency in Riga: Fremadrejser, a Danish-Latvian joint venture, Richarda Vagnera iela 3, Tel: 21 07 73, with a branch office in Hotel Latvija, Suite 1612.

Surrounding Regions of Riga

Salaspils (Kurtenhof) Memorial
Eighteen kilometres (11¼ miles) east of Riga on the left-hand side of the motorway is a sign for the 2 kilometre (1¼ mile) side road leading to a parking area in the Rumbul Forest where over 100,000 people were murdered from 1941 to 1944 during the Nazi reign of terror. The Kurtenhof concentration camp (as Salaspils was called then) is accessible by taking the suburban train to Darzini and from there it is a 1 kilometre (½ mile) walk. The memorial on the former concentration camp grounds was established in 1967. The builders – G. Asaris, O. Sakamenny, O. Ostenbergs, I. Strautmanis and the sculptors L. Bukovskis, J. Zarins and O. Skarainis – were awarded the Lenin Prize in 1970 for their accomplishments. The entrance to the memorial is "blocked" by a 13 metre (43 foot) high and 100 metre (327 foot) long cement beam. "Aiz Inem Vartiem Vaid Zeme" – "The earth moans beyond this gate" is the inscription on the "guillotine." The gateway between life and death presents a small exhibition of black and white photos of the concentration camp. In the flat, black marble block on the right edge of the lawn is the "admonishing heart" of the complex. The dull ticking of a metronome symbolizes the beating of the hearts of the victims who died here. In this "work and rehabilitation camp" in the middle of the forest, the solitary sound breaks the silence, creating a stifling atmosphere. Gravel covers the "path of suffering" which leads

Nazi Terror in Salaspils/Latvia

The setting: 46 prisons, 23 concentration camps, 18 ghettos. The victims: 313,789 civilians, 330,032 prisoners of war, 39,835 children. As the Red Army approached Salaspils in 1944, the mass braves were opened and the corpses burned – the survivors were transported to other camps... The wooden barracks were quickly set on fire by SS troops. The camp burned to the ground. However: not only in western Europe, in Latvia, radical right movements are also forming at present. The Latvian civilians police "Aizsargi," which once hunted Jews and communists is once again permitted by the government. This is the military backbone of the radical right-wing opposition.

Those who are emotionally shaken by a visit to the memorial should make a stop at the *Botanical Gardens of the Academy of Sciences.* During a stroll through the colours of the rose plantation one has the opportunity to collect one's thoughts.

around the central open area with meadow flowers and herbs growing on it. Six monumental sculptures tower at the centre – three victims and three "victors." The "unbending" tries to raise himself from the ground. The "humiliated" covers her face and breast with her hands. Next to a small birch the "mother" protects here children with her body. The trio on the outer edge symbolize the resistance: "oath," "red front" and "solidarity" are the names of the individual figures. White slabs mark the former sites of the barracks; dark black slabs mark the sites for laying wreaths. A narrow path leads to the execution site in the pine forest. The Nazi bullets have riddled the cement wall where the victims stood blindfolded. A lower cement wall overgrown with rose bushes marks the site of the former children's barracks.

Vidzeme – Western Baltic Coast

Jurmala (= Beach)

Train, taxi, bus or hydrofoil provide transport to the holiday and beach resort of the Rigans – it is with good reason that the area was earlier called "Riga Beach." Jurmala first came into existence in 1959 through the conglomeration of eleven holiday destinations which line the broad bay over 40 kilometres (25 miles): *Priedaine* (Kiefernhalt), *Lielupe* (Bullen), *Bulduri* (Bilderlingshof), *Dzintari* (Edingburg), *Maiori* (Majorenhof), *Dubulti* (Dubbeln), *Jaundubulti* (Neudubbeln), *Pumpuri* (Karlsbad), *Melluzi* (Karlsbad II), *Asari* (Assern I) and *Vaivari* (Assern II). The melodic name of the "city" divulges what Jurmala actually is – a "seashore": all of the towns lay on a 90 square kilometre

(35 square mile) peninsula between the Lielupe River and the Baltic Sea. This area was formerly only built up with villas of the wealthy Rigan bourgeois and scattered fishing cottages. In 1879, the railway made this idyllic landscape of sand dunes accessible to everyone: Jurmala's boom as a beach resort began. In 1965, the German author *Heinrich Böll* spent a few weeks in Jurmala. Even today, despite the ban on swimming in the entire bay – due to the untreated sewage from the city of Riga, agriculture and the nearby paper factory – the sun-hungry crowd the beach and the more courageous or reckless actually do go into the filthy brew, which stinks terribly on some days. 300,000 day guests, 100,000 holiday guests and 60,000 residents – the peninsula is very crowded during the summer. The threatening breakdown of traffic is hindered by gates to the peninsula: only the residents and hotel guests area allowed to drive past the control station. Others may not drive beyond this point without a special permit – at least theoretically.

At the beginning of the peninsula is **Priedaine;** situated in the middle of a pine forest are the brick buildings of the Uzvara Kolkhoz.

Lielupe was named after the Lielupe River on which this village, now a resort town, developed. At the end of Vikungua iela is the "Raketa" dock Stirnurags. Those who enjoy sailing, paddle boats or rowing will find ample opportunity for aquatic sports on the river. The clubhouse of the "Daugava Yacht Club" is also situated on the riverbanks. The small core of this town is dominated by the impressive "Pensionats Lielupe" complex, a retirement home for the more well-to-do seniors.

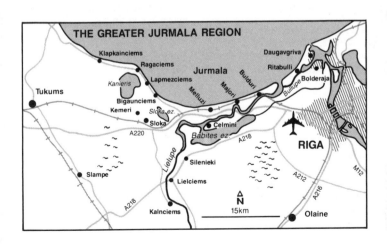

Information

Accommodation: A branch of the Jurmala Hotel (Maiori) is located in Lielupe, Vilnu iela 3, Tel: 5 11 57.

Bars: Bura, Vikingu 3; Olimspiskais, Pardomju prospekt 18

Restaurants: Restaurant Ednica at the "Science House", Zinatnes nams, Vikungua iela 5/7; Bura, Vikingu 3, open 1 pm to midnight; Laivas, Tiklu 1, open noon to 11 pm.

Without any distinctive border or region separating the two towns, Lielupe continues into **Bulduri.**

Information

Cafés: Bulduri, Meza prospekt 27; Pie veva Edgara, in the sand dunes; Kafejnica Turist, Bulduri prospekt 3.

Cinema: Vienibas prospekt 5, next to a small park in the centre of town.

Marketplace: Vienibas prospekt 13 (near the train tracks).

Pharmacy: Bulduri prospekt 17.

Post Office: Bulduri prospekt 29, Tel: 5 30 27.

Restaurants: Juras Perle (directly on the beach), Vienibas prospekt 2; Kulinaria, Vienibas prospekt 3, in the centre of town.

Dzintari (Edingburg) was named after the "Baltic gold"; "dzintars" is the Latvian word for amber, which can still be found on the high-tide line along the Baltic coast, especially after autumn storms. The church (Lienes iela 14), once secularized and now used as a Museum of Art and History, has meanwhile been converted back to its original function.

The light and dark brown church was built as a classicistic temple with a turret. On the border to Maiori is the concert hall (Turaidas iela) built in 1936. From May to September, up to 1,000 spectators enjoy summer concerts during the "Riga Summer Festival" performed by orchestras from around the world. In a small park next to the concert hall, a stream of water shoots out of the roofed drinking fountain from a mineral spring. The cool water was discovered in 1959 during construction work on the "Baltija" sanatorium from a depth of 400 metres (1,308 feet). The nearby exhibition hall (Turaidas iela 11, Tel: 6 44 63) displays various special exhibits during the summer, open daily (except Tuesdays) from noon to 7 pm.

Information

Bars: Balzams, Dzintaru prospekt 58, open noon to 11 pm; Boulings, Dzintaru prospekt 32, open noon to midnight and serving cocktails; Soul Bar, Turaidas iela 13; Club Gamma, Dzintaru prospekt 66; Casino Bar and Restaurant.

Restaurant: Pie Patvara (at Samovar), Dzintaru prospekt 32, open noon to 11 pm.

In **Maiori,** the tourist centre of Jurmala, nothing remains that is reminiscent of the former fishing village which once stood here. The busy artery of this seaside resort is the Jomas iela. The pedestrian zone runs from the edge of town to Dzintari over about 1.5 kilometres (1 mile) parallel to the coastline to the train station with a bus stop and taxi stand. Only occasionally is the row of shops in the wooden villas from the turn of the century interrupted by modern architectural eyesores – for example, the "Universalis" department store with its showcase façade or the central hotel building.

One of the most quiet streets in town is the Juras iela (Sea Street) in the shade of a low belt of sand dunes. Those who stroll through this area will find no shops or cafés but only holiday apartments and guest houses from the turn of the century next to old chestnuts, lindens and pine trees. Near the "Janis Fabricius" sanatorium, a wooden datcha houses the *Rainis Memorial Museum* (Plieksana iela 7). In the summer cottage of this folk poet in which Rainis lived with his wife *Elza Rosenberg* (the poet "Aspazija") during the last years of their lives. In 1949, this was converted into a small museum and the adjacent building was integrated into the memorial museum in 1965.

Information

Accommodation

Hotel: Julia, Dzintaru prospekt 50, Tel: 5 21 11; Jurmala, Jomas iela 47/49, Tel: 6 13 40; DM 70, $40 and less expensive in Latvian currency. Warm showers, clean and simple rooms. Patrolled parking area in front of the hotel.

Bar: Sencis, Jomas iela 33.

Cafés: Omega, Jomas iela 42; Aero/Anita Café, Jomas iela 35 including an arcade; Joma, Jomas iela 54; Kafejnica Exkurs at the beach entrance

near the polyclinic above the beach playground; Septinas Masinas, Jomas iela 37.

Currency Exchange: Jomas iela 79/81 and 53.

Gallery: Doria, Jomas iela 43, open 11 am to 6 pm.

Pharmacy: Jomas iela 41

Post Office: Lienas iela (main coastal road) 6/8, Tel: 6 20 12.

Restaurants: Jura, Turaidas iela 3, open noon to midnight; Jurmala, Jomas iela 47/49, open 1 pm to midnight (hotel restaurant in the pedestrian zone); Lido, Turaidas iela 8, open 1 pm to 1 am; Miezitis, Konkordijas iela 86 (restaurant complex including a Kafejnica and bar).

Train Station: There are rail connections from Maiori to Riga and Tukums.

Dubulti has a very impressive railway station: a sweeping, daring cement structure full of Socialist metropolitan ambience stands in crass but interesting contrast with the summer villas with patinas in town.

Also odd is the Protestant *church* on Baznica iela. The church has characteristics of Latvian Art Nouveau: half timber and exposed stone, strict geometrical ornaments at the windows. The church building is surrounded by old linden trees and *wooden villas* from the 18th and 19th centuries.

Information

Café: "Dubulti," Muzeja iela 8/10, open noon to midnight; Ednica, Baznica iela 10. The neighbouring "Rubin" Bar belongs to this café as well.

Those who overlook the small sign for **Jaundubulti** will notice which district they have meanwhile entered when they see the tennis courts and the radiant light blue *Church of the Orthodox* on Strelnieku prospektas. The transition to **Pumpuri** is just as fluent.

Information

Accommodation: Hotel Pumpuri, Upes 2, Tel: 6 75 54. Only open during the summer season.
Bar: Kabura, Piejuras 1, open 5 pm to 1 am.

After **Melluzi,** a holiday resort with a cinema and tennis courts follows **Asari:** the huge children's playground with a small amusement park on Vapu iela/corner of the main street is a paradise for the smaller guests. **Vaivari** hardly has the character of a beach resort with its numerous allotment gardens. Only the monumental "Vaivari" holiday complex, a mountain range of brick – each building being a peak – is reminiscent of the days of mass tourism. On the western edge of town is the beginning of an extensive forest area between the coastline and coastal road. In the autumn, this is a paradise for mushroom pickers.

Information

Accommodation: Hotel Atbalss, Tel: 3 63 92. Open only during the summer season.

Kemeri (Kemmern)

The coastal road to Tukums leads farther to Kemeri. The old health resort lies around 5 kilometres (3 miles) from the coast in a huge forest park with an area of 60 hectares (150 acres). The Versupite (Oxen) River winds its way through the entire spa park, spanned by numerous bridges. Especially picturesque: the Muskalny (Musical Bridge) with its wrought iron landings. The history of this spa began over 150 years ago. In the late 18th century, the ranger of Kemeri offered "therapeutic baths" in his house – without medical supervision. In 1839, the first official therapeutic baths were opened with 32 pools. The rail connection on the route from Riga to Tukums brought guests to Kemeri from St. Petersburg and Moscow – around 8,000 spa patients visited Kemeri annually up to the First World War. Today around 30,000 visitors come to the spa every year in hopes of alleviating their ailments in the mud and sulphur baths.

Sights

During the construction of sanatorium number one, the architect *E. Laube* was only given one stipulation: the spa building for 300 patients had to be able to compete with stately European sanatoria like that in Baden-Baden/Germany. It was a success: the *neo-classicistic spa building* in radiant white is just as impressive today. The western façade opens to an extensive flower garden with an arbour vitae; the eastern façade faces the forest. International chess tournaments with the Soviet master

S. *Flor* brought the hoped for PR to the sanatorium in 1937 and 1939. The spa has ample bookings even today.

The *Rotunda* on the *Island of Love* in the middle of a man-made lake was designed by the architect *E. Stalberg* in 1930. The old wooden bridge was replaced at that time with the stone "Bridge of Women's Whims." On the "Avenue of Sighs" satisfied patients erected a *monument* for their doctors in 1861 modelled after the medical Aesculapius rod, with a snake winding around an oak trunk. The wooden church on the banks of the Versupite, the seat of the Russian-Orthodox *Church* was built in 1893 without using a single nail. The bizarre carvings were created by Latvian artists. Those who died in the two World Wars are buried in the two "cemeteries of heroes" next to the church. The extensive spa area, now a pedestrian zone, was designed by the Rigan landscape architect *M. Wagner.* A straight avenue leads from the sanatorium to the *oak meadow,* where a memorial has stood in memory of the two authors *Maxim Gorky* and *Janis Rainis* since 1953. The area surrounding Kemeri is rich in sulphur springs. On spring number six, the "Spring of Youth and Beauty" discovered in 1889 near the Versupite, a drinking fountain with a stone base on the stream is an inviting place to stop for a quickening sip. The 13 °C (55.4°F) warm "Kemeri" water, bottled and available in shops and pharmacies, is used to treat digestive ailments.

Information

Accommodation

Camping: Ventspils iela, Tel: 3 68 85, in the Jaunkemeri district on the road from Jurmala to Kolka.

Hotel: Ventspils iela 6, Tel: 3 65 75, in the Jaunkemeri district on the road from Jurmala to Kolka.

Marketplace: Tukuma iela.

Post Office: Kathedrales iela/corner of Tukuma iela 30, Tel: 6 55 60.

Restaurants: Kemeri, Tukuma iela 21, open 11 am to midnight; Café Toritu iela 8/14; Neptun in the Jaunkemeri district.

Spa Facilities: Sanatoria for adults: "Latvia," "Kemeri," "Tschaika," "Dzimtene," "Jaunkemeri," "Jantarny bereg," as well as two sanatoria for children. These treat skeletal and muscular disorders, disorders of the central nervous system, skin diseases and digestive problems.

Vidzeme – Northern Baltic Coast and Hinterlands

Adazi (Neuermühlen)

The former model project of the Soviets lies several kilometres northwest of Riga. The prototype kolkhoz was lead by Gorbachev's former agricultural advisor *Albert Kauls.*

Only the *church* is old: burned to the ground by the Russians in 1656 and destroyed once more in 1666, the present-day church was consecrated in 1775.

Surroundings

A nice excursion is to the **Baltezers** (Weißensee) to the *small or large white lakes* with five islands. The weekend settlement of **Garkalne** to the southeast developed near the former combine for reinforced concrete construction, which began production in 1959. Located two kilometres (1¼ miles) away, a workers' settlement in the forest shows more clearly how ruthlessly man and nature were sacrificed to industrial giganticism.

Ainazi (Hainasch)

A linden boulevard traverses the northeastern town on the Latvian Baltic Coast. Earlier, it led to the Estonian town of Ikla – today, it is a border crossing point open only to Balts. Foreign visitors must take the M 12 to enter Estonia.

The *Buhweta Church* near the centre of town was built of brick in 1894 and 1895. The *Ungusdzesibas Muzejs* (Main Street 69; open Wednesday, Thursday and Saturday from 10 am to 4 pm) quickly reveals itself as a fire fighting museum. In the former school of navigation (Kr. Valdemara iela 21b) is a branch of the *Riga Museum* for *City History and Navigation*. From 1864 to 1915, over 1,000 captains and helmsmen were trained for their professions in the Latvian and Estonian languages.

Café: Kafe Ainazi, Main Street 32, next to the central bus terminal.

Salacriva

The old fishing village of Salcriva extends on both sides of the mouth of the Salaca River on the Baltic coast. The southern banks make up the harbour now off limits to visitors and large portions of the northern banks are military zones. For this reason, the actual town is rather disappointing – however, not the small pub at the bus stop. "Pie Bocmana (Boatman) is the name of this rustic inn, all in wood serving good and hearty food – open to 10 pm.

Vecsalaca lies four kilometres (2½ miles) upriver. The town's name awakens false hopes: the sand path leads only to a few private homes in the middle of nowhere...

Saulkrasti (Neubad)

The first larger town to the north of Riga along the coast was founded at the beginning of the 19th century and is more similar to a small city than a resort; this, despite the beach and sanatorium. Most of the 10,000 residents commute to work in Riga. The nearby **Vecaki** (Wezahken) is less crowded than Jurmala.

Vidzeme – The Interior

Burtnieki (Burtneck)

The small city of Burtnieki lies 20 kilometres (12½ miles) northwest of Valmiera on the southern shores of Lake Burtnieku is the small city of Burtnieki. Along the steep coastline, the castle rises amid a small park. It was built as a bishop's fortress in the middle of the 14th century. From 1582, it belonged to the Catholic diocese of Cesis. Later *King Gustav Adolf of Sweden* handed the castle over to his chancellor *Axel Oxenstierna*. Made almost devoid of function due to the spread of firearms, the fortress made way for a manorhouse – however, portions of the old walls were incorporated into the new structure.

The *church,* first documented as a three-naved basilica in 1283, not only lost its original ancillary naves over the centuries, but its old interior furnishings as well: all that remains are two carved wooden figures, one of the Virgin Mary and one of St. John the evangelist. Both were once a part of the pulpit or choir. But the church did already possess a musical instrument that other Livonian churches could only dream of at that time: its own organ.

Cesis (Wenden)

Eighty-five kilometres northeast of Riga, the small city of Cesis is well worth a visit. The provincial city is situated above the Gauja in the middle of a national park.

History

Because of the favourable location on the trade route between Riga to Tartu, Cesis was already mentioned in historical documents as early as 1206. in 1383, this fortified city gained the status of a city and became a member of the Hanseatic League in the same year. During the 14th century, the city became the seat of a lesser guild. In 1577, *Ivan the Terrible* attacked this prospering Hanseatic

Cesis – "Birthplace" of the Latvian Flag

Cesis is also considered the birthplace of the Latvian national flag. According to the legend, a Latvian King laid down on a white flag signalling surrender to the enemy. While the old king died, his blood stained the flag soaking it in deep red. Under the body of the king, the flag remained white. In 1270, the red and white striped banner was first declared the official flag of Latvia.

city. According to an old legend, the residents of the fortress are said to have preferred to fill the cellars with gun powder and go up with the fortress than to submit to the Russian aggressor. Cesis was almost completely destroyed in a massive fire in this city in 1671. During the War of National Independence (1918-1920) Cesis was the site of a decisive battle: from June 19 to 23, a Latvian-Estonian regiment defeated the German troops. The planned development of this city as a tourist centre for the Gauja region began in 1930. Famous personalities were born in and around Cesis: A monument in the nearby town of Kalaci stands in honour of the poet *Eduards Veidenbaums;* a museum in Vecpiebalga is dedicated to *Karlis Skalbe,* referred to by Latvians as "their own H. C. Andersen."

Sights

Poles mark off the inner city around the shopping street Rigas iela as a pedestrian zone. Some of the numerous old houses have been classified as historical monuments. One of these is the former _Municipal School,_ which served as a district school from 1886 and has been used by the labour union since 1920. An impressive outdoor staircase made of limestone leads up to the _Müller School,_ the former residence of the poet and physician _Alexis Adolphi_ (1815 - 1874). The _city castle of Cesis,_ which served as the seat of _Count Sievers_ during the 18th century, now houses the _Museum of Local History_ (historical museum on the ground floor, special exhibitions on the upper floor; open Tuesday to Sunday from 10 am to 5 pm). In the foyer of the palace, a doorway leads to the main attraction of this building, the mighty _Wenden Fortress._ The Order's fortress on Castle Hill, built in 1209 and 1210 by the Brothers of the Sword, was expanded inn 1495 by the Livonian Order Master _Wolter von Plattenberg._ It later became the headquarters of the Teutonic Order in Livonia.

The Poles gained control over the fortress in 1562; in 1577, Ivan the Terrible – the feudal lord and citizens chose to blow themselves up rather than surrendering. In 1777, Count Sievers bought the ruins and began laying out a _castle park._ The count laid special emphasis on the design of the pond: fed with water from the Duckern Springs through a pipeline, the pond was intended as a reflecting pool for the fortress. The best preserved portion of the fortress is the western tower. The former living quarters of the Order Master with walls 4 metres (13 feet) thick was renovated in 1914 and a conic roof was added. The _St John's Church_ with the 65 metre (213 foot) tower was built from 1283 to 1287, expanded repeatedly and ultimately destroyed by fire in 1748 – and rebuilt. Several Livonian Order Masters are buried in this Romanic-Gothic church, among others _Wolter von Plettenberg_ (died in 1535), _Johann Freytag von Loringhoven_ (died in 1494), _Hermann von Brüggeney_ (died in 1549). The coats of arms of the Livonian nobility embellishes the altar room. The altar piece showing Christ on the cross was created by the famous Estonian painter _Johann Köler._

Surroundings

Araizu ezers (Lake Arrasch): Seven kilometres (4¼ miles) south of Cesis on the road to Riga is the largest lake in Gauja National Park with an area of 393.6 hectares (984 acres). On the small, wooded island in the middle of the lake was the site where a Livonian settlement from the 9th and 10th centuries was recently discovered during _archaeological excavations._ The _church_ directly on the shores of the lake was built in 1225. On the western shores are the last remnants of the Old Wendan Fortress from 1577.

Ungurmuiza Castle: Northwest of Cesis on Lake Ungura is the estate of Lord von Ungur. The wooden structure has wonderful wall decorations.

A tea house, barn and chapel augment the estate ensemble.

Hiking in Gauja National Park: One popular hike leads along the Gauja to **Ligatne** (Ligat). From there, one can return by bus.

Information

Accommodation: Hotel Tervete, Vienibas laukums 1, Tel: 2 23 92.

Automobile Repair: Lapsu iela 36, Tel: 2 29 00; Priekulu iela 7, Tel: 2 36 21.

Bus Station: Raunas iela 1, Tel: 2 36 13.

Cafés/Bars: Cesis, Rigas iela 10, open 7 am to 3 pm and 4 to 9 pm. Kafejnica, Raunas iela 13 (across from the Culture Centre). Kafejnica, Raunas iela 10; Kafejnica Terrasse, Plavas iela 5 (self-service). Cirulisi, Cirulisu iela 28, open 9 am to 3 pm and 4 to 9 pm. Cocktail Bar, Rigas iela 25; Lauma, Rigas iela 53, open 10 am to 3 pm and 4 to 11 pm; Pie Raunas Vartiem, Rigas iela 1/3; Pie Kurmisa, Valdemara iela 13.

Culture Centre: Kulturas Nams, Raunas iela 12.

Hospital: Beverinas iela 11, Tel: 2 23 71.

Marketplace (Tirgus): Plavas iela 9.

Pharmacy: Rigas iela 7; Rigas iela 19.

Post Office: Raunas iela 14.

Toilets: new: Plavas iela 13; old: Rigas iela (on the central square, corner of Katrinas).

Train Station: Raunas iela 1 (at the end of the street).

Dining in a Mushroom

Restaurant Senite (Little Mushroom): near Incukalns on the M 12, hidden by the motorway rest stop among the trees. Open daily from 1 to 11 pm, reservations can be made by calling Tel: 99 15 83. Appropriate dress is expected – jeans, shorts or beach attire are not acceptable. The building with a spherical roof at the fork in the main road is indeed similar to a mushroom architecturally speaking. "Senite" is considered one of the best restaurants in the country. While Latvian specialities are served in the light and friendly dining room, domestic beer is tapped from the keg in the cellar.

Incukalns (Hinzenburg)

Twenty-nine kilometres (18 miles) northeast of Riga near the A 21 is the traditional summer resort for the citizens of Riga. Artists also came to Incukalns: over a number of years, the writer *Janis Sudrabkalns* lived and worked here as did the author of children's books *Doku Atos*. The famous Latvian sculptor *K. Zale* died here. Nearby is the *Gauja Fur Farm,* on which silver foxes and minks have been bred since 1945.

Limbazi (Lemsal)

The train station on the Svetupe, 20 kilometres (12½ miles) from the Baltic coast of Vidzeme was heavily damaged during the Second World War. As soon as 1747, the town was burned down with the exception of four houses. Thus, the *Bishop's Fortress* formerly the main fortress of the archbishop of Riga on the "Livonian side" is reminiscent of the former importance of the small city. As soon as 1368, Limbazi, surrounded by several monasteries, had been awarded the rights of a city. The walls at the eastern end of the fortress, built in 1223, have been preserved to date as have the gun slits along the embattlements and portions of the northern front and the main gate with its portcullis.

The impressive whitewashed building of the Lutheran *church* with high, runged windows overgrown in green was built in 1860. The *war memorial* in the churchyard is in memory of the soldiers who fell during the war of independence from 1914 to 1920. Also on this square are the hospital and the *Russian-Orthodox Church* with its greenish blue domes.

Information

Bar/Restaurant: Lielezers, Rigas iela 8; restaurant open from 1 to 11 pm; Ednica, from 6 am to 4 pm. Kafejnica, Rigas iela 14.

Hospital: Klostera iela 13.

Ligatne

Halfway between Cesis and Sigulda on the southern edge of Gauja National Park, the small village of Litgatne extends in the Litgatne River valley. The town, which developed around a paper mill in 1896, comprises the centre of the "educational and recreational zone" in Gauja National Park. It was established in 1975 with the goal of expounding on animal and plant life as well as geological aspects.

Along the various *hiking trails* traversing the park, *stands* and *observation areas* have been set up from which one can observe – given some patience – moose, wild boars or even bears in their natural habitat. The *educational nature trail of Ligatne* is lined with several cages with endemic birds and other animals.

Those who would rather explore the area on horseback can rent horses at reasonable prices by the hour or by the day at the *Ligatne Stables*. Also offered are guided horseback tours along the river. One should, however, voluntarily forgo the automobile tours through the national park – the wild, romantic and pristine landscape is better experienced on foot anyway. One *recommended hike* leads to the sandstone formations of Launaga iezis, Katrinas iezis, Kuku iezis and Springu iezis in and on the banks of the river. The *Zvartas iezis* rock formation rises to an impressive height of 46 metres (150 feet). The only opportunity to cross the river between Sigulda and Cesis is with a single wooden ferry.

Information

Gauja National Park Information Office: "Pauguri," Tel: 5 33 23 and 5 33 24; open during the season from 8 am to 8 pm.

Hospital: Komjaunatnes iela 7, Tel: 5 31 74.

Post Office: Komjaunatnes iela.

Train Station: a few kilometres outside of town.

Mazsalaca

The small city of Mazsalaca midstream on the Salaca River, 20 kilometres (12½ miles) south of the Latvian-Estonian border and around 60 kilometres (38 miles) from the coast in the hinterlands offers no special highlights. Surrounded by flat, often swampy land, the attractions extend along the riverbed: in the centre of town, a *church* above a steep slope; outside of town up the river are wonders of nature like the *Vilkacu priede* (werewolf pines), the *Sapnu kapnes* (Stairway of Dreams), the *Velna ala* (Devil's Cave), the 62 metre (203 foot) *Skanakalns* (Mountain of Dreams) and *Echo Point*. Around 10 kilometres (6¼ miles) to the southeast in a picturesque setting is *Lake Burtnieku* (→ *Burtnieki).*

Information

Accommodation: Hotel at Rigas iela 17, Tel: 5 12 35.
Café: Aura, Rujienas iela 31, open on weekdays from 11 am to 7 pm.
Fuel: Baznicas iela 24, Tel: 5 17 67.
Medical Care: Brivibas bulvaris 4, Tel: 5 13 13.

Gauja National Park

Extensive forests line the banks of the Gauja; caves, cliffs and sandstone formations accompany the third largest river in Latvia which flows lazily along in some places and churns, falling over rapids in others.

The uniqueness of this diverse central region of the Gauja River and its countless tributaries was recognized as early as the 1930's when flora and fauna were placed under governmental protection for the first time. In 1974, the 920 square kilometre (359 square mile) region was officially declared a national park. The 100 kilometre (63 mile) long and 10 kilometre (6¼ mile) wide nature reserve is subdivided into seven zones. Only three of these are open to visitors: *Sigulda, Ligatne* and Araisu. The area of the national park also comprises the cities of **Cesis, Ligatne, Sigulda** (including Krimulda and Turaida), the towns of **Straupe, Araisu** and **Ungura** as well as five larger and 33 smaller lakes.

The largest lakes are *Lake Ungura* (393.6 hectares/984 acres), *Lake Vaidavas* (87.2 hectares/218 acres) and *Lake Raiskuma* (78.3 hectares/196 acres). The diverse region between Cesis and Sigulda carries the epitaph "Switzerland of Livonia." In the winter, this is a popular destination for winter sports enthusiasts offering cross-country ski trails and bobsled tracks.

Sigulda (Segewold)

This spread-out, very green small city (population: 10,000) in the heart of the *Vidzemes Svice* (Livonian Switzerland) is the number one tourist centre in Gauja National Park. It is renowned as a summer resort and winter sport destination alike. Belonging to this city, first founded in 1889, are the districts of Paragauja, Turaida and Krimulda.

History

The banks of the Gauja near Sigulda were already inhabited during prehistoric times. In the 2nd and 3rd centuries, it was the finno-ugrish tribes who secured their livelihood here through hunting and fishing. Thanks to the favourable location on a trade route which connected the lower Daugava with Cesis, Trikata and Tartu, a bustling commercial centre developed near Sigulda. Up to the beginning of the 13th century, Turaida, Metsepole and Idume were areas inhabited by the Livs, protected by wooden forts atop hills. At the end of the 12th century, knights of the Teutonic Order pushed into the region, conquered it and destroyed the Livonian fortresses. By order of the pope, the Gauja-Livonian region was partitioned off in 1207: the right bank of the Gauja went to the bishop of Riga, the left bank was placed under the control of the Teutonic Order. In Sigulda, Turaida and Krimulda, mighty fortresses were built. A settlement quickly developed in the shadows of the fortress in Sigulda, which was mentioned as a city as early as the 15th century. This old settlement of Sigulda presumably lay between the church and the new castle. In the middle of the 17th century, the estate of Sigulda came into existence there and remained until around 1890. The development as a spa town brought the opening of a railway connection on the route Riga – Pskov – St. Petersburg. *Prince Kropotkin,* the estate owner of Sigulda , began selling off parcels of land for the construction of guest houses and summer cottages. Sigulda became a preferred summer resort for nobility and aristocrats from Moscow, St. Petersburg and Warsaw. The city had a population of around 1,000 at the beginning of the year 1900 which rapidly tripled during the summer months – Sigulda was "in." Awarded the rights of a city on February 28, 1928, Sigulda was the district capital from 1950 to 1962. The incorporation of Turaida and Krimulda on the opposite banks of the Gauja followed in 1953.

Sights

Even from a distance one can see the pride of Sigulda: the *"Sarajevo" bobsled track.* Designed by the architects *A. Purgailis* and *M. Jostins,* a Yugoslavian firm built the track above the Gauja. Two runs lead through steep curves down into the valley. Run S1, 1,200 kilometres (three-quarters of a mile) long allows for top speeds of 120 kmph (75 mph); on the S2 run 988 metres (1,077 yards) in length) speeds of 105 kmph (66 mph) can be attained. Those who have no fear of heights should take a closer look at the track. A narrow path leads along the cement bobsled track to the starting house, in which a small exhibition is displayed in the sportsmen gallery. However, the breathtaking view of the extensive forests and the river valley in the Gauja National Park from this vantage point alone is worth the climb.

The walk to the centre of Sigulda first leads past the *train station.* The present-day structure replaced its splendid predecessor in 1951. Tuff slabs from Allazi adorned the façade of the old train station, a building constructed by Professor *Peteris Feders* in 1925 as the most impressive railway building in Latvia. The Janis-Rainis iela leads to the whitewashed *Siguldas baznica* (Municipal Parish Church), located on the edge of town toward Turaida. Built in 1225, the church was altered in 1671, 1701 and most recently in 1930 by the famous Rigan Art Nouveau architect *Konstantins Peksens*. The small *chapel* in the graveyard originates from 1856. Diagonally across from the church is the cableway terminal, next to Café "Tourist" and the *ferris wheel*. The gondolas take passengers over the

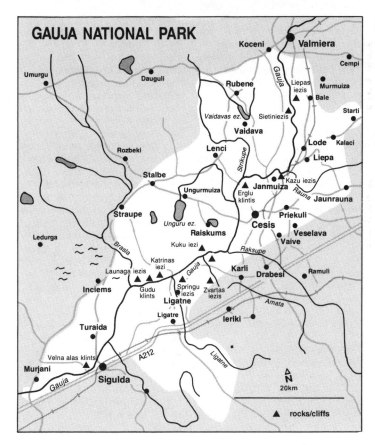

Gauja at a height of 40 metres (130 feet) to Krimulda, the "Bishop's" side of the river. At the parking area behind the church and the National Park Administration building, the tour leads to the *Jaunapils* (New Castle). Built from 1878 to 1881 by the architect *H. Birkhana* as a medieval castle, the Tudor structure has housed the sanatorium for cardiology and climatology since 1953. In front of the sanatorium, a monument stands in memory of the linguist and journalist *Atis Kronvaldis* (1837-1875). The name "New Castle" can be attributed to the fact that the two anterior fortresses of the old Order's fortress once stood at this site, extending over two hills. From 1973 to 1977, the last remnants of the *Pilsdrupas* (fortress ruins) were secured. This saved the ruins at the last minute: only the main building and two towers remain of this fortress built from 1207 to 1226 by the Brothers of the Sword and destroyed in the Great Northern War. The underground corridors used to access the buildings during attacks have mostly collapsed or have been filled in. Today, the fortress is used for cultural events: theatre performances are held on the outdoor stage against the romantic backdrop during the summer, in addition to concerts and evenings of singing.

The *Krisjanis Barons Memorial* on the Kris Barona iela, corner of Livkalna Street near the entrance to the bird park was erected in commemoration of the 150th anniversary of the compilation of Latvian folk songs. From the *People's Park,* numerous trails lead down to the river. With a length of 153 metres (500 feet) and a width of almost 17 metres (56 feet), the Gauja Bridge has connected Sigulda with Turaida since 1936. The bridge provides a nice view of the Gauja River, its light coloured sand bars, the valley walls the radiant red fortress of Turaida.

Surroundings

Gelznotaju kalns (Artists' Mountain): At an elevation of 93 metres (304 feet) above sea level, this vantage point offers a breathtaking view of the Gauja River extending over 12 kilometres (7½ miles) – no wonder that this mountain became popular with landscape painters. Latvian painters like *Janis Feders, Janis Rozentals* and *Vilhelms Purvins* set off for this destination with easel and canvas in hand. The *Keizeras Kresls* (Czar's Chair) is also a popular overlook. On the *Satezeles Fortress Hill* are the last remnants of an old Livonian settlement from 1212. Passing the Krauklu Ravine, a hiking trail leads to *Petera ala* (Peter's Cave), a cavern around six metres (20 feet) deep and with ceilings of five metres (16 feet) on the steep banks of the Vejupite.

Information

Accommodation: Hotel Sigulda, Pils iela 6, Tel: 7 22 63; Tourist Base Sigulda, toward Turaida 5 kilometres/3 miles from town, bus station. The four-storey yellow building offers simple accommodation for hikers with youth hostel standards. The hotel was built in 1955.
Art Gallery: L. Paegles iela 4; open

Monday to Friday from 10 am to 5 pm, Saturday from 10 am to 3 pm.
Bus Station: Raina iela 3, Tel: 21 06.
Cableway (Troses cels): Baumana iela.
Cafés: Café Turist, at the cableway station; Café Pie raiba suna, Vidzemes soseja; Café Sigulda tirgus, Gales iela 27; Café Bucefalns, Instituta iela 1.
Fuel: Vidzemes sosteja 69, on the main road from Riga to Pskov.
Gauja National Park Administration: Raina iela 15.
Hospital: Lakstigalals iela 3, Tel: 7 20 03.
Pharmacy: Pils iela 3.
Post Office: Pils iela 2.
Restaurants: Salons Aparjods, in the Culture Centre (Kulturas Nams), Tel: 7 31 43; opened in May of 1992, decor in white, romantic and modern, very clean and serving delicious cuisine; prompt polite service, 5 tables plus booths. Under the same management: Bar Aparjods, Ventas 1a, Tel: 7 10 88; Restaurant Gauja, L. Paegles iela 3.
Sports and Recreation: A miniature golf course and tennis courts are located on Raina iela. Winter sports: 13 cross-country skiing trails.
Train Station: On the railway route Riga – Pskov – St. Petersburg.

Sigulda-Krimulda (Cremon)

On this, the "Bishop's side" of the river is the district of Krimulda, accessible via the bridge over the Gauja or by cableway. The old fortress of the Vikmestians, seat of the cathedral chapter of Riga from 1255 to 1273, was destroyed in the 17th century. In the *sanatorium* (Mednieku iela 3), built as the municipal castle in the classicistic style in 1854, has housed a renowned pulmonary sanatorium since 1922 – the ill, mostly children, recuperate during the summer in the fresh air. Lying on cots in a semicircle covered with light cloths to protect against the sun, the sight is reminiscent of Thomas Mann's "The Magic Mountain."

Surroundings

Tauretaju kalns (Trumpeter's Hill): Guardsmen once warned of the approach of strangers and enemies by trumpet from this hill.

Sigulda-Turaida (Treyden)

The road to Turaida leads up over an 11% grade. The city district on the opposite banks of the Gauja has belonged to Sigulda since 1953. On the intersection with the road to Saulkrasti in the centre of town is an ugly, monotone supply centre with a bakery, Kafejnica and restaurant beyond a huge parking area. More idyllic is the portion of town surrounding the village pond with the post office and farmhouses. The actual attraction of this town lies across from the parking area: the *National Cultural Centre* "Turaidas Muzejsreservats" laid out in 1988. The *park* extending over four hills has a point of interest on each of the hills: *Baznica Kalns* (Church Hill): the small wooden church from 1750 with baroque towers is considered the oldest wooden historical building in the Vidzeme region. The old altarpiece inside is relatively well preserved. The church, a branch of the *Sigulda Museum of National History* is open daily from 9:30 am to 6 pm. Behind the church is the last remaining grave of the former graveyard, the *Grave of the Maija*.

Pils Kalns (Castle Hill) with the *Bishop's Fortress:* The first castle on this hill was built by the Livonian King Kaupo in the 12th century in the form of a wooden fortress. The fortress was destroyed by the German Crusaders in 1206 or 1212. The structure subsequently built on this site by the Rigan Bishop in 1214 was of red brick on a foundation made from erratic blocks. The bishop lived here from 1776 and the fortress was renovated and restored in 1953. The main tower as well as the northern and western towers and the majority of the outer walls have meanwhile been rebuilt. The fortress' former domestics building now houses an exhibition of the *Sigulda Museum of National History*. The 14 metre (46 foot) tower offers a beautiful view of the Gauja region. A trail with explanatory markers leads around the fortress – unfortunately, the text is only in Latvian and Russian.

Dainu Kalns: The former site of an old Livonian settlement was renamed in 1985: since then Daina Way leads over the "Song Mountain," so named in commemoration of the 150th birthday of the folk song collector *Kris Barons*. The fifteen large sculptures in the *Sculpture Garden* under the blossoming apple trees or surrounded by autumn leaves are the work of *Indulis Ranka*.

On the fourth hill, the *Janu Kalns*, a small orchard produces delicious apples in the late summer months. The service facilities of the outdoor museum are directly at the entrance: the Café "Turaida" in the old grain storehouse, the small grocery store and the outdoor sanitary facilities with brick dividers.

Surroundings

A beautiful hiking trail leads to the *steep Pikere Riverbanks with the Devil's Caves.* The Liele Velnala (Big Devil's Cave) is eleven metres (36 feet) deep, 5½ metres (18 feet) wide and 2½ metres (8 feet) high. The Maza Velnala (Little Devil's Cave) is one metre shorter. Mothers used to wash their babies in the waters of the nearby *Gudribas avotins* (Wisdom Spring) – they strongly believed that the water possessed supernatural powers and made the children smart and happy...

Beyond the bridge to Turaida on the left-hand side is the largest cave in Latvia, the *Gutmana ala* (Goodman's Cave). It is 10 metres (33 feet) high, 12 metres (39 feet) wide and 19 metres (62 feet) deep. The walls of this cave are covered with the inscriptions of visitors. A spring bubbles to the surface within the cave, which has a constant temperature of 5°C (41°F) in the summer as in the winter. Its water is said to have healing properties. The name of the cave refers to the "good man," who is said to have given water from this spring to pilgrims and strangers. Only a few minutes away one will find two more grottoes: the *Revolutici ala* (Revolution Cave) and the *Viktora ala* (Victor's Cave), Viktors – according to the legend – is said to have dug this cave for Maija his lover so that she could watch him from the cave at work as the Sigulda castle gardens...

Smiltene (Smilten)

The small city of Smiltene to the west on the A 212, 150 kilometres (94 miles) northeast of Riga is nestled in the northern edge of the *Hills of Vidzeme*. The Abuls River flows through the city, which later flows into the Gauja near the town of Valmiera. Protected by the Archbishop of Riga's fortress, a tiny village came into existence in the 14th century. The importance of this "spiritual" settlement was soon discovered: in 1601, the city chronicles state that all ten houses were taverns... In 1650, the Russians destroyed the town and did so once more in 1702 during the Great Northern War. The present-day city came into being at the end of the 19th century, when the lord of the Smiltene Castle, *Prince Lieven,* sold off parcels of land for the construction of houses. Smiltene, granted the status of city in 1920, was not left untouched by the Second World War: the town was once again heavily damaged. All that is left of old Smiltene are the ruins of the fortress and the parsonage built in 1790. The neighbouring *church* is also interesting. The tonal quality of its organ was described as "shrill" in 1784 – for this reason, the reformed congrega-

The Grave of Maija

A stairway leads up to a slate slab decorated with flowers below the tall trees. This is the grave of a young girl, the "Rose of Treyden" (1601-1620) according to the legend: she is said to have died because she was courted by two men – the Polish officer Jakubovsky, who desired her for her beauty and the simple gardener Viktors, who truly loved Maija. One evening, Jakubovsky killed her with his sword... and Viktors buried his beloved at this site before he disappeared forever.

tion of Riga donated a better sounding organ in 1874. The new organ was built in the workshops of the Valmiera organ craftsmen *Contius* and *Stein* in 1783.

Straupe (Lielstraupe-Roop)

Along the road from Sigulda to Valmiera through Gauja National Park is the village of Straupe. Earlier, one of the oldest fortresses in the Baltic States stood here. Today, the beautiful park comprising a *castle, pond and church* has been classified as a historical monument. The Lielstraupe castle, first mentioned in 1206, belonged to a convent director. *Otto von Rosen* awarded was awarded the land in feudal tenure by the Archbishop of Riga. In the 14th century, the Roop region was subdivided in

Large Roop, Small Roop and Hochrosen. Construction on the castle presumably began around 1500 since historical documents only refer to "hoff to Roope" (estate of Roop) before then, but call it "dat slothe Roope" (the castle Roop) after 1512. Up to 1529, Lielstraupe belonged to a family without interruption until the sale on a member of the Hochrosen clan began a series of change in ownership. In 1797, Czar *Paul I* bought the castle and placed the estate under the his imperial control. In 1856, purchased by *Johann Gustav Baron von Rosen* brought the 8,000 hectare (20,000 acre) wooded estate grounds back under the control of the Rosen family. In 1905, during the revolutionary uprisings, the castle was set aflame but rebuilt by *Hans Baron Rosen* and his architect *Wilhelm Bockslaff*. The last owner of the Roop castle lived on the 50 hectares (125 acres) that remained of the estate after the land reformation of 1919 – until Hitler called the German Balts "home" in 1939. The entire castle complex is presently being restored and being equipped with informational signs in Latvian.

Rising from the wooded park are the onion crowns of the majestic four-storey castle tower. Also preserved to date are the western wing with a gable originating from 1750, the short southern wing and the northern wing with the main entrance. The whitewashed castle church with the light blue window frames and red tile roof was restored in 1971 and was originally built as a three-naved structure with a vaulted choir. Remains of

the old fortress can be recognized in the steeple. Old gravestones rest against the church wall built from erratic blocks.

Valmiera (Wolmar)

Valmiera lies 120 kilometres (75 miles) northeast of Riga outside the national park on the Gauja River. This small city on the old trade route Riga – Pskov – St. Petersburg was for the most part destroyed during the Second World War. In the centre of town, the construction of new administration and residential buildings continues even today. The economic backbone of this city are the glass, furniture and food industries.

Three kilometres (2 miles) outside of town was once the famous Baltic *Kokenhof Brewery*.

History

The banks of the Gauja, within the city limits today, were inhabited since the 11th century. Although the city was only first mentioned in 1323, the settlement is presumed to be much older. While the competing city of Riga became a member of the Hanseatic League, Valmeira changed hands ten times between 1560 and 1622: Poland, Russia and Sweden conquered and consequently lost the city. In 1625, the majority of the population succumbed to the plague. The Russians marched into Valmiera in 1702 during the Great Northern War. They razed the fortress and killed or banished the residents. Seventy years later, fire destroyed what had remained standing in spite of the war: within two years, the city burned to the ground twice. In 1869, a railway connection to Riga was to follow. During the first Latvian Republic, Valmiera was considered the most Latvian of all cities: the proportion of Latvians in the population was said to have reached 95%. The intentional industrialization of the city by the Soviets turned the tides: with the settlement of Russian industrial labourers for the glass fibre and furniture factories, Russians now make up the majority of the 20,000 residents.

Sights

The *Sveta Simana baznica* (St. Simion Church), a brick structure with white windows and door frames, is perched high above the Gauja River. The church was built as a basilica by the Teutonic Order from 1280 to 1283 and repeatedly modified architecturally up to 1908 when it was most recently renovated, as divulge by a stone over the side entrance. Inside, the altar was donated by *Michael Kayser* in 1748. The pulpit bears the coat of arms of Count Oxenstierna. Behind the church is a wall built from erratic blocks which reaches a height of up to 5 metres (16 feet).

The "ruins" of the old Teutonic fortress in the small park are classified as a historic architectural monument. The last remnants hardly indicate how fortified the fortress once was. It is presumed to have been built from 1212 to 1214 by the bishop's official *Woldemar*. To left side of the wall, a narrow path leads off to the *Museum for Art and History* (Brunnieku iela 3, Tel: 3 27 33; open Tuesday to Friday from noon to 6 pm, Saturday and Sunday from 11 am to 6 pm). This collection covering the history of the city is worth seeing and extends over two floors of the building. The artists of Valmiera make up a special focal point. A small exhibit displays portraits by *Theodor Uders* (1868-1915) and the works of *Rudolf Petersohn* (1905-1992) are exhibited in a special room. This Russian who settled here captured the city and surroundings in hushed scenes on canvas. Also worth seeing in more detail is the extensive collection of postcards and black and white photos of Valmiera at the turn of the century, donated to the museum by *Jana Matula* (1912-1989). Amber jewellery, souvenirs and guides for the local regions are sold at the reception. The *Museum of Local History* (Varonu laukums 3, open Monday to Friday from noon to 6 pm, Saturday and Sunday from 11 am to 6 pm) is also worth a visit.

The Rigas iela runs through the middle of town. Those who stroll by the shops on this street will come to the *Teacher's Academy,* built from 1900 to 1903 by the architect *Kieselbasch* and now used as a school. Continuing along this street, one will also pass the *Russian Orthodox Church.* An inviting place to stop for a break is the park surrounding the mill pond.

Surroundings

Burtnieku ezers (lake): → *Burtnieki* and *Mazsalaca.*

Gauja River Valley between Valmiera and Strenci: The *Erglu klints* (Eagle Cliff) lies on this especially picturesque section of the river with boulders, rapids and sand bars.

Information

Accommodation: Hotel Gauja, Terba-

tas iela 2, Tel: 2 21 65 and 24 11 25.
Bus Station: Central terminal, Cesu
iela, Tel: 2 26 56.
Café: Kafejnica Saule, Rigas iela 12.
Cinema: Rigas iela 19.
Fuel: Koceni, Abelites, Tel: 5 55 98 (8
km/5 miles outside of town on the
road to Incukalns).
Hospital: Jumaras iela 195, Tel:
2 61 20.
Marketplace: Terbatas iela 8a; Tues-
days, Thursdays and Saturdays from
7 am to 3 pm.
Pharmacy: Rigas iela 16.
Post Office: Diakonata iela 6.
Restaurant: Ednica, Rigas iela 34,
simple restaurant; hotel restaurant
Gauja, Terbatas iela 2, Tel: 24 11 25.

Kurzeme (Curonia)

The province of Kurzeme comprises
the area between the Baltic Sea and
the Daugava River, and since 1795,
Zemgale as well. The flat region characterized by agriculture is interrupted
by two ranges of hills: the 153 metre
(500 foot) Smiltinus Kalns rises near
Saldus, and the Kreivenkalns, the
highest hill (184 metres/602 feet) in
Curonia between Saldus and Liepaja.
Curonia was a favoured area to settle
for the German Balts, making it possible to find a large number of estates
in this region. On the point near Kolka
is an area formerly occupied by the
Soviets, the Slitere Reserve. Kurzeme also has the third largest city in
Latvia, the port of Liepaja.

Aizpute (Hasenpoth)

One of the oldest cities in Latvia can
be found 50 kilometres (31 miles)
northwest of Liepaja on the Tebra
River: Aizpute. The rural Curonia
town with a population of 6,200 has a
coat of arms depicting a fortress
crowned in stars. This city was awarded the rights of a city in 1378 and
was a bustling commercial and administration centre up into the 18th
century – then the harbour silted up.
The attraction of this small town
which is sooner a sleepy little town
today, are atop the small hills lining
the banks of the Tebra. Rising up on
the right riverbank is the *Lutheran
Church* built from 1242 to 1254; on
the left riverbank, the *ruins of the
Teutonic fortress.* Burial sites from
prehistoric times were discovered in
Misinkalns. Sixteen kilometres (10
miles) to the west is **Cirava** with its
picturesque *church,* built from 1780
to 1781 on the site where the old
wooden church once stood. The
newer stone church was commissioned by *Friedrich Baron Behr,* the
owner of the Edole and Cirava estates.
Information
Café: Kafejnica "Kursa," Atmodas iela
13.
Fuel: On the outskirts of town heading toward Jelgava.
Pharmacy: Atmodas iela 24.

Dobele (Dobeln)

The small city of Dobele on the banks
of the *Berze,* is around 28 kilometres
(17½ miles) west of Jelgava, and was
once renowned as the "heart of Semigallia." A sword in the city's coat of
arms is still reminiscent today of the
city's strategic importance as a border stronghold at the edge of the

highlands of Austrumkurzeme and the flatlands of Zemgale.

History

In 1254, the existence of Dobele was first documented. However, the region along the river was inhabited as early as the 10th century by Semigallian tribes. Their small settlement was protected by a wooden fort on the right riverbanks. After the 80 years of resistance against the Teutonic Knights, the Semigallians ultimately burned their town to the ground in 1289 and fled to Lithuania. The symbol of the new rulers was erected on the foundations of the destroyed wooden fort: in 1335, the Teutonic Order built its stone fortress, garrison and religious seat up to 1542. On the left banks of the river, a centre for commerce and handicrafts developed which was mentioned in 1444 as "Hackelwerk Dobeln" in historical documents. Under the rule of King Jakob during the 17th century, the city was to experience a period of economic prosperity: a watermill, a saw mill and wool-combing mill brought work and money to the city. The cultural upsurge in the city came in 1870 when the First Kurzeme Song Festival was celebrated. The establishment of a rail connection on the route Riga – Jelgava – Liepaja bought a new economic boom. A mere 467 people lived in the city in 1867, a figure which increased to 1,721 in 1897. When Dobele was awarded the status of a city in 1917, it was home to more than 2,000 – the population is a multiple of that today. The town's centre with a church and marketplace is bordered by the streets Zala iela (Green Street), Baz-

nicas iela (Large Church Street), Uzvaras iela (Small Church Street), Viestura iela (Post Street), Brivibas iela (Grand Street), and Skolas iela (School Street).

The whitewashed *church* is presumed to have been built in 1495. Its 50 metre (164 foot) steeple towers above all other buildings in the city. It was first in 1908 that the tower was equipped with a clock when the church was remodelled. A small park connects the church with the old marketplace lined with two-storey houses and numerous shops. A simple Kafejnica which serves delicious blintzes at lunchtime can also be found here. Zala iela (Green Street) once led to the estate and the Krimunas Train Station. The post office (No.12) was built in 1884. Set back somewhat from the street and surrounded by modern apartment buildings, number 31 is a small building housing the *Dobeles Novad Petniecibas Muzejes* (Museum of Local History; open Wednesday and Thursday from 11 am to 4 pm, Saturday from noon to 6 pm and Sunday from noon to 4 pm), which was opened six years ago – albeit in its cramped quarters. While the space on the ground floor is used for special exhibitions, the collection displayed in the attic collects dust. Amid the attic beams is a collection worth seeing which is also happily shown to visitors: typewriters, spinning wheels and samovars, wicker baskets, pottery and irons. Tobacco shears reveal that tobacco is grown in private gardens even today. Old musical instruments can be found among the other pieces and of course Lenin – busts, pictures and bronze figurines – albeit quite dusty.

On the opposite (right) banks of the river are the _Pilsdrupas_ (castle ruins) from 1335. An illustration by _J. R. Sturna_ displayed as a postcard in the Museum of Local History shows just how impressive the castle once was around 1600. Its gradual decay began during the 18th century. Also belonging to the fortress were the monastery building from the 14th century and a residential house from the 16th century. Several kilometres outside of town toward Saldus, Dobele II and Dobele III will confront visitors with the more recent history of this area: these are huge military bases of the Red Army in the middle of the forest.

Information

Accommodation: Hotel Viesnica Dobele, Uzvaras iela 2, Tel: 2 12 29.

Culture Centre: Baznicas iela 6.

Fuel: On the outskirts of town heading toward Jelgava, near the factory entrance.

Hospital: Adama iela 2, Tel: 2 12 29.

Post Office: Zala iela 12.

Restaurants: Kafejnica Berze, open 9 am to 8 pm, in the centre of town; Kafejnica Reprize, Baznicas iela 6, open 10 am to 4 pm; bar open 7 to 11 pm.

Dundaga (Dondangen)

The distance to the Baltic Sea as well as the Gulf of Riga is around 30 kilometres (19 miles) from the intersection at Dundaga in the northern extremities of Curonia. With an area of 728 square kilometres (284 square miles), Dundaga was once the largest estate in the Baltic States. In 1245, Bishop Nicholas of Riga gave a tract of 17 square kilometres (6½ square miles) around Dundaga to the papal legate Wilhelm von Modena. In 1434, the cathedral chapter had to be relinquished to the Bishop of Curonia. The last bishop, in turn, sold the church-owned estate to Martin Bersewicz in 1582 – this was the chancellor of King Stefan of Poland. Thus, Dundaga became a region under direct Polish administration, independent from Curonia. Sold to the Margrave von Bülow in 1588, the estate went to the von Osten family (also called Sacken) after his death and remained in their ownership up to the expropriation in 1920. The manorhouse, built as a water castle, has remained almost completely unchanged. Built as a rectangle surrounding a courtyard, the tower gate leads to 52 rooms. A beautiful _estate park_ with oak trees up to 600 years old also belongs to the castle.

Dundaga's _parish church,_ first documented in 1383, was rebuilt as a stone church by Prince Karl von der Osten in 1766 and renovated in 1882. A neo-Gothic wooden steeple was added in 1897.

Around six kilometres (4 miles) to the north, the _Azu stavakmens_ (Goat's Stone) rises from the flat landscape. Inscriptions and symbols embellish the two metre (6½ foot) erratic block.

Kandava (Kandau)

The small city of Kandava to both sides of the Abava River, is situated

Sliteres Reserve – Untouched Nature

Thirty-six kilometres (22½ miles) north of Dundaga is the beginning of the second largest nature reserve in Latvia, the *Sliteres Reserve.* The region southwest of Kolkarags Point and down to Jaunci (still) encompasses a fantastic, untouched coastal landscape. The reason: this area was a Red Army military zone up to the middle of 1990 with a high level of strategic importance. Today, the area where an old lighthouse on the entrance to the Bay of Riga will evoke dreams of the sea was once patrolled for fifty years by the Red Army. Under state control, the typical coastal landscapes were preserved, albeit unintentionally.

Today, strict classification of this area as a reserve has provided a habitat for beavers, black grouse, wood grouse, moose and even a few wolves. Rare orchids can be found among the flora of this region as well as a respectable number of yew trees. It is planned to have a group of experts research the extent of the damaged caused by the presence of the Red Army – German ministries have been commissioned to undertake this investigation. The only "city" in the reserve is **Mazribe**. *Lake Engures* lies in the hinterlands near **Berciems.** In the fishing village of **Roja,** the *Maritime Museum* (Liepu iela 4) is worth visiting.

only a few kilometres to the south on th A 220, halfway between Riga and Ventspils. The old core of the rural city, first documented in 1231, is on the right riverbanks. On the Castle Hill, also called Hill of Ancestors, are the ruins of the Fortress from the 13th century. The best preserved structure is the Gun Powder Tower. The *church* built in 1763, has a 32 metre (105 foot) tower. Inside, the artistically embellished confession booth is the work of *J. Maerten;* the altarpiece from 1855 was created by K. Arnold. The stone bridge from the 14th century is one of the oldest permanent bridges in the entire Baltic region. Sulphur springs were discovered in 1902, three kilometres (2 miles) downriver in the *snake morass* on

the left banks of the river. This area with its rare flora is protected by nature preservation laws.

Four kilometres (2½ miles) outside of town is the old *parish estate of Kandava,* built on the right banks of the river and including a magnificent columned hall.

Kuldiga (Goldingen)

The oldest city in Curonia, Kuldiga, is simultaneously one of the most picturesque places. Those who stroll through the streets of this city with 13,000 residents will feel as if time has stood still; the boundary between past and present become fluid.

The centre of Curonia developed around 1300 where the *Aleksupite* (Alex Stream) flows into the Venta. In

1368, Kuldiga became a member of the Hanseatic League. Its coat of arms depicts St. Catherine. In 1596, under the Duke of Curonia, the city experienced its golden age. This was brought to an abrupt end when the residence was moved to → *Jelgava* in 1617 – the castle was torn down only one hundred years later. The town on the Venta (Windau) became famous for its "waterfall." A rumour spread to such an extent by brochures, the visitor will probably sooner rub his or her eyes in bafflement: a number of rapids and a small cascade over a length of 110 metres (360 feet) do indeed make a beautiful show of nature called *Rumbla* (Rummel), but a real waterfall is sooner the *Aleksupite* (Baznicas iela), where the stream plummets five metres (16½ feet) into the valley below – and with that, it is the highest natural waterfall in Curonia. The nicest view of the Rumbla is from the small wooden pavilion on Pils iela with a small observation platform.

Sights

Important: when approaching from Saldus, access to the city is only possible via the bypass. The old bridge on Rigas iela is blocked off to all vehicles. The walk to the brick bridge is still worthwhile in spite of this: from here, there is a nice view of the city, the river and the waterfall.

In the *old centre of town* around City Hall Square is an almost uninterrupted ensemble of magnificent Renaissance, Gothic and Baroque buildings, both wooden and stone. A number of Latvian films were made here using this backdrop. Even today it leaves the impression of a vital rural city in old Curonia. The *New City Hall* was built in Italian Renaissance architecture in 1860. The *Old City Hall* from the 17th century is on Padomju iela; the municipal prison is in the basement. Not far from here at No. 7 is the *oldest house in Kuldiga:* built in 1670 and rebuilt in 1742. The Catholic *Trinity Church* (Raina iela 10) from 1640 displays Italian Renaissance architecture. The baroque interior from the 17th century has pronounced rococo elements. The statue "Mary with the Christ Child" was completed in the 15th century and the confession booth dates back to 1691. *Czar Alexander I,* donated the altar in 1820. First historically documented in 1252, the Protestant *St. Catherine's Church* (Baznicas iela 33) was built a second time in 1567. After having been destroyed by two fires in the 17th century and then rebuilt twice, it was most recently restored in 1968. Even more beautiful than the interior with a pipe organ from 1712 with 996 pipes and a artistically carved high-altar from 1660 is the breathtaking *view* from the 25 metre (82 foot) church tower.

Passing the Aleksupite waterfall, a path leads through a small park to the site where the Teutonic fortress once stood (Pils iela). Where the Teutonic Knights once built a fortress which was first incorporated into the city during the 14th century is now an extensive *sculpture park* with bronze and stone statues by Latvian artist – the fortress collapsed in 1735. The stones from the fortress were used in part to build the *Palace Guardhouse* (Pils iela 4).

On the edge of the park, the *Museum of Local History* (Pils iela 5; open Tuesday to Sunday from 11 am to 5 pm) is housed in a wooden villa from the turn of the century. Sculptures by local artists stand in the gardens here as well.

Surroundings

Edole (Edwahlen): 22 kilometres (14 miles) to the west is the town of Edole, first mentioned in historical documents as "Edvalia" in 1230. Its well-preserved *water castle* is presumed to have been built at the end of the 13th century and was the residence of the *Barons von Behr* for over 350 years from 1562 up to the expropriation in 1919. The Teutonic fortress, "Gothicized" at the beginning of the 19th century, is intended to serve as a cultural centre upon completion of the renovations. One of the four legends surrounding this water castle tells the story of a ghost, who would haunt the rooms at night. One Lord of the castle once had two sons. When one killed the other during an argument, the blood of the murdered son appeared on the wall above the fireplace the day after. Tormented by the picture of his brother on the wall, the murderous son had an open fireplace built in the wall – since then, the ghost roams the castle... Also interesting is the church from the 17th century – it houses the *first library in Latvia*.

Lake Nabas, 30 kilometres (19 miles) to the northwest on the road to Ventspils, has a very nice rest stop with a grilling area. There is also a camping area on the shores of this secluded lake, surrounded only by isolated fishing huts.

Information

Accommodation: Hotel "Kursa," Pilseta laukums 6, Tel: 2 24 30 and 2 43 42.

Automobile Repair: Edoles iela 36, Tel: 2 25 58 (equipped with a car wash).

Bus Station: Stacijas iela 2, Tel: 2 20 61.

Café/Bistro: Bar Alan, Rigas iela/at the bridge. Snack bar with tables outside; Ekspresbars, Liepaja iela 18; Vaverite, Baznica iela 32; Vejins, Mucenijeku iela 1; Kafejnica Staburadze, Liepajas iela 8.

Cinema: Kurzeme, Gada iela 6, across from the city park.

Fuel: Graudu iela 5, Tel: 2 22 53.

Hospital: Liepajas iela 37, Tel: 2 25 86.

Library: Baznica iela 34, open weekdays from 10 am to 6 pm.

Post Office: Liepajus iela 34, Tel: 2 26 84.

Liepaja (Libau)

With a population of around 114,000, Liepaja is the western harbour city of Latvia and simultaneously the third largest city in the country. The marine and fishing base is increasingly developing into a tourist centre of southwestern Latvia. An interesting, contradictive city with a diverse cultural calendar and relatively clean Baltic water at its doorstep – this mix is becoming more and more popular with Latvians and holiday visitors alike.

History

On the narrow coastal strip between the sea and the lake where the old city is located today was once the site of the fishing and mariners' village of "Liva," which in the language of the Livs and Cours living there meant nothing more than "sand." Equipped with a small natural harbour, the village came under the ownership of the Brothers of the Sword on April 4, 1253 – a document had long since sealed the fate of the settlement. Around 1300, the fishing village became an appendage of the Grobin prefecture. This possession brought the new owners more grief than satisfaction: the village and harbour often filled in with sand. Although the harbour was moved repeatedly, the order could no longer maintain control over this area in the middle of the 16th century – the last Order master *Gottfried Kettler* mortgaged it off to Prussia without hesitation.

On March 18, 1625, Libau was awarded city rights by *Duke Friedrich* in the Grobin Castle. On that same day, the authentication of the city's coat of arms took place. It depicts a red Curonian lion on a silver background supporting a linden tree with its front paws. In 1640, Libau had just 1,500 residents. The decisive turn in the city's development came in 1700 with the construction of a canal which connected the city's lake with the open Baltic Sea. The other Baltic powers quickly recognized the advantages of the new harbour site: in 1701, the Swedish King Karl XII took the city; in 1795, Liepaja became Russian; in 1812 during the Napoleonic Wars, it was occupied by France and Prussia and by Britons in 1854 during the Crimean War. The beginning of the upswing in the 18th century was continued through the construction of the railway from Liepaja to Romnas (1871-1876) which fostered the development of industrial facilities like a cast iron factory, a wharf and an oil mill. In 1860, the harbour basin was dredged deeper and the ice-free harbour was first expanded into a military facility in 1907 with the addition of a fortress. In 1906, ship lines connected the city of Liepaja with New York and Halifax. As early as 1889, Liepaja became the first city in the Russian Empire to be equipped with an electric streetcar. Looking to the west was also characteristic of politics: the Social Democratic Party of Latvia was founded here in 1904; in 1919, this city was the seat of the provisional government of free Latvia; today, the most critical, most provocative people's movements come from this harbour city. Liepaja is renowned among young Latvians for one of the best pop bands in the country: "Livi" – a group which can be heard each year in August at the Rock Festival.

Walking Tours

Access to the inner city via the city bridge from 1883 which spans the harbour canal is only open to pedestrians due to its desolate structural condition – vehicles are diverted to a more modern bridge around 100 yards upriver.

I. Old Liepaja

In the 17th century, Liepaja was sooner a sleepy town than a booming commercial centre. All around the harbour were black, tarred wooden houses belonging to the merchants and craftsmen; adjacent, the warehouses. Those with the most stately interiors were the property of the Duke. The market and St. Anne's Church were in the centre of town, both wooden buildings then. Even the houses of aristocracy were more similar to combined homes and warehouses or farmhouses than stately palaces.

Peter's House (Kungu/Herren iela 24) ranks among the oldest houses in Liepaja. The wooden cabin with its tiled roof rests on a low foundation. It was named after Peter the Great who lived here occasionally.

Old trading houses and warehouses can still be found on Zivju iela (Fish Street). In the inner courtyard of house number 4/6 is the *oldest warehouse in Liepaja* - it was presumably built in 1690. The *historical storehouse* at house number 10/12 originates from the 18th century. On Stendera iela, named after Mayor H. H. Stenders, are *two warehouses from the 18th century:* on Jauna iela and Kaiju iela are *warehouses from the 19th century.*

Also reminiscent of old Liepaja are the *buildings from the 18th century* at Baznicas iela (Church Street) 8 and Avotu iela (Unger Street) 10. As soon as 1699, Mayor Joachim Schröder had his *brick house* on a high foundation built at Barinu iela 32. In the pedestrian zone (Tirgonu iela) is a modern street lighting system which makes an attractive contrast to the numerous old houses, in which a number of craftsmen have their workshops and ateliers. The *Trinity Church* (Liela iela 9) is probably the oldest and most beautiful church in Liepaja. On July 9, 1742, the cornerstone was laid for this Italian Renaissance structure with baroque and rococo elements. It was completed in 1758. The tower, originally lower than today, was built up to its present height of 55.5 metres (182 feet) the spurred by Mayor Sigismund Ulich. The organ, built by *Contius in Riga* was considered the largest in the Russian empire after it was expanded in 1885 by the Stettin organ builder *B. Grünberg.* Up to 1912 – then the monumental mechanism with 7,000 pipes in 131 registers and 21 auxiliary registers was outdone by the organ in the Riga Cathedral. Also worth seeing is the high baroque altar. The *Roza laukums* (Rose square), a popular meeting place even today, has been the centre of Liepaja since the town's earliest development. The "New Market" was located here up to 1901. This was the city's main market with the butcher blocks moved here from the Louis Street. Sooner sterile today, this green square was acclaimed as the "city's ornament" in historical sources of 1805. While it was paved especially attractively then, today the square is covered with barren, grey cement slabs...

The park, established in 1911 by the municipal gardener Oskar Katterfeld was for the most part destroyed in 1941 – and rebuilt as a Socialist monument in honour of Soviet soldiers.

II. The Empire in Liepaja

The construction of the rural road to

Grobina in 1841, the opening of the railway route from Liepaja to Romnas in 1876 and the growing significance of the harbour brought wealth and prosperity to Liepaja.

The run on the Ruble caused a construction boom. Numerous old wooden houses were burned down to make way for the imperial mansions of Czarist Russia.

Witness to the golden age in the Russian Empire is a stately *City Palace* built from 1805 to 1809 and located at Barinu iela 12. This is also the case for the buildings at Pasta iela 20, 22 and at Veidenbauma iela 20.

III. Maksis Pauls Berci (Bertschy) and Modern Architecture

Maksis Pauls Berci gave Liepaja's architecture the aspiration for modern expression like no other. This architect of German descent was the dominant city planner in Liepaja for thirty years. He arrived in the city in 1871 after having studied in Berlin and St. Petersburg. His red brick buildings characterized the appearance of the industrial city around the turn of the century. Berci built clinics, factories, schools but also private company buildings and villas. The long list of his construction projects includes for example the *Linoleum Factory* (Linoleja rupnica eka), the *former building of confectionery Woldemar Bonitz* at Graudu iela 20 and the *Hospital* at J. Kosas iela 31, built from 1886 to 1900. Berci was especially active on K. Valdemara iela, having built the *Nicholas Secondary School* (No. 4) in addition to several residential houses (No. 14, No. 16, No. 20/26). The *City*

Hall (Rozu iela 6) and the *Fire Station* (Jelgava iela 41) were also created by Berci. His most monumental work is, however, the renovation and remodelling of *St. Anne's Church* in 1892 and 1893. The beginnings of this church at Kursa Laukums 5 date back to the 16th century. Berci, who was only to restore the tower at first, directly made plans to remodel the entire church. He left the tower in its configuration of 1872... The altar of St. Anne's, created in the workshop of *N. Steffenz* in 1697 is a masterpiece of baroque wood carving. Across from the church is the *Vecais tirgus* also called "Petertirgus" (Peter's Market), one of the oldest centres of Liepaja. Berci's project, the modernization of the old trading square from 1560, was to falter due to lacking funds. Only the *central market hall,* a brick structure with white shutters, was restored. The large open area is shared by the vegetable merchants and the flea market. Initiated by Berci in 1890, a construction ordinance was passed – the city was subdivided into two zones dependent on the building materials used to better regulate construction. Around the turn of the century, *Art Nouveau* arrived in Liepaja. Beautiful buildings remain preserved at Dzintaru iela (Amber Street) 18, Rigas iela 3, Kursu iela 17 and 21, and Ausekla iela 9. The *Constructive Movement* can be found at Graudu iela (Grain Street) 45, Liepu iela (Linden Street) 23 and Dzintaru iela 9. Romantic colourings of national folklore are reflected in the *wooden villas* at Dzintaru iela 16, in the schoolhouse at Roza iela (Rose Street) 10 and in the corner house at Raina iela 1 as well as the multi-storey *residential buildings* on Liela iela, built by M. Berci Junior.

IV. Gods, Graves and Gurus

Liepaja is a city of churches. The Catholic *St. Joseph's Cathedral* (Rakstvezu iela/Scribe's Street 13) was built in the architectural style of historism from 1894 to 1900 according to the plans of *L. Melvil* in cooperation with *K. E. Strandmann*. In contrast to the opulent interior with filigree wood carvings and lovely windows is the unpretentious altar.

St. Paul's Chapel (Kursu iela 19) is characterized by the strict lines of neo-classicism. The Baptist house of prayer, built from donations of the congregation, has two simply furnished sanctuaries. The *St Nicholas Marine Cathedral* (Sevastoples iela 5/7) was alienated from its purpose by the Soviet Marines for 46 years. It was only in 1991 that the pastors returned to this church built from 1900 to 1903 by *V. Kosjakov, V. Frolov* and *V. Beljalev* - and they paled at the sight: the soldiers has left the ornate interior with its outstanding mosaics in a heavily damaged condition.

Construction on the Protestant *Martin Luther Church* (Jelgava iela 60) lasted 20 years (1914-1934) – and the church was still not finished when the construction was completed: there was no church tower. The designs for the church with national-romantic elements were drawn up by the architect *K. E. Strandmann*. Also originating from him are the plans for the *Valst Liepaja Teatris* (National Thea-

tre). The stylistic melange of historism, neo-classicism and Art Nouveau was built as the "German Theatre" from 1912 to 1916. The "Latvian Theatre," founded in 1907, has performed on this stage since 1917. The small square on Liela iela is dominated by the neo-classicistic monumental *Pedagogical Academy* building (Liela iela 14). The entryway to the Stalinistic school building is embellished with a columned facade with richly ornamented capitals. The *Vestures un maksalas muzeju* (Museum of History and art; Kurmajas prospektas 16, Tel: 2 23 27 and 2 26 04; open Tuesday to Sunday from 11 am to 7 pm) is acclaimed as the "treasury of culture and craftsmanship in the Liepaja region."

The *Jurmalas Parks* offers an appropriate interlude to recover from the sightseeing stress. The 47 hectare (118 acre) beach park extends 3 kilometres (2 miles) along the Baltic coast. The first trees were planted here around 1870 – today there are 112 different types of trees growing in this park. It also has a number of recreational facilities like the amphitheatre "Püt Vejini," the "Dzintars" cinema and the Folk Festival grounds. Sports enthusiasts will be drawn to the tennis courts or the stadium. Between the beach park and the city is the preferred villa district of Liepaja. impressive *wooden and stone villas* from the turn of the century line the broad residential boulevards lined with trees. These include Dzintaru iela, Jurmalas iela and Ulika iela. The municipal beach with its fine sand is around 70 metres (230 feet) wide and gradually falls off to the sea beyond the belt of sand dunes – a mile long dream for sun worshippers and sandpipers. Even swimming is allowed here: unlike many other towns along the Baltic coast, the tides are relatively clean.

Surroundings

Twenty-five kilometres (15½ miles) northeast of Liepaja is **Durbe** on the banks of Lake Durbe. The site of the historical "Battle of Durbe" in 1260, the settlement was awarded the rights of a city in 1893. It leaves the impression of a typical small Latvian city with its building from the 17th to 19th centuries. Also worth seeing are the *fortress ruins* (1293) and *Ligutu Park.*

Ten kilometres (6¼ miles) east of Liepaja is **Grobina** (Grobin). For 630 years from 1290 to 1920, this town was the administrative centre for the surrounding region. In the 16th century, the first school in Curonia opened its doors here. Grobina became known throughout all of Curonia for its hatmakers. Granted the rights of a city in 1695, Grobina at the gates of Liepaja had a population of around 4,600 in 1989. The old *Order Administration,* first historically documented in 1253 and the seat of the district administration up to 1812, stands in ruins today. Only a few walls and stumps remain of the former fortress with its four bastions, naturally protected by the Aland Stream on two sides. The *Lutheran Church* dates back to the 17th century.

Information

Accommodation: Hotel Baltika, Flotes iela 14, Tel: 5 62 41; Liva, Liela iela 11, Tel: 2 53 45 and 2 01 22, single rooms priced at £6.50 ($12), double rooms at £10.75 ($20) – also payable in Rubles. Simple and clean. Zvejnieku nams, Ganibu iela 131/133, Tel: 2 51 50.

Airport: Outside of town toward Grobina, Tel: 7 39 07. Aeroflot office, Radio iela 12/14, Tel: 2 34 50.

Automobile Repair: Cukura iela 1, Tel: 7 41 21; Plavu iela 9, Tel: 2 27 24; Ganibu iela 105, Tel: 2 25 88.

Banks: Latvijas Bankas, Teatra iela 3, Tel: 2 20 71; branch in the old city, Baznicas iela 4/6, Tel: 2 24 03. Savings & Loans: Liela iela 10, Tel: 2 36 31; Peldu iela 16, Tel: 2 35 41; T. Breiksla iela 45, Tel: 2 38 02; Klaipedas iela 64, Tel: 3 36 09; Kungu iela 30/34, Tel: 2 69 22; Silku iela 19, Tel: 2 64 14; Fabriciusa iela 20, Tel: 5 76 31.

Cafés (Kafejnica): Aromats, Tirgonu iela 20, open from 8 am to 1 pm and 2 to 8 pm. Small and old with a touch of Art Nouveau. Kaiia, Liela iela 12, Tel: 2 52 44. Kalva, Ganibu iela 71, Tel: 2 38 51. Liepava, Kurmajas prospektas 71, Tel: 2 67 28. Majigums, Ziviu iela 12.

Pastry Café Teiksa, Liela iela 7.

Casino: Silku iela 26, open until 4 am.

Cinemas: Dzintars, Peldu iela 66, Tel: 2 45 07. Liepaja, Juras iela 13, Tel: 2 67 76. Palass, Graudu iela 27, Tel: 2 49 23.

Ednicas (Cafeterias): Kosmoss, Graudu iela 42, Tel: 2 91 27; Petertirgus, Siena iela 3, Tel: 2 62 76.

Fuel: Brivibas iela 174/176, Tel: 7 34 38; on the road to Klaipeda, Tel: 2 40 92.

Hospitals: Central Hospital, Grizupes iela 100, Tel: 7 48 97 and 7 33 13. Polyclinics: Republikas iela 5, Tel: 2 64 66; Rigas iela 25, Tel: 2 36 49 Zemnieku iela 8, Tel: 5 11 32; Veca Ostmala 54, Tel: 2 60 57.

Marketplace: Petertirgus, Kursu laukums 7, Tel: 2 35 17. Annas Tirgus, Jelgavas iela 54, Tel: 2 51 32.

Pharmacy: Tirgonu iela 15.

Police: Kris Barona iela 8, Tel: 5 09 31 (responsible for traffic); for other issues: Liela iela 3, Tel: 2 02 69; Cenkones iela 55, Tel: 3 14 18; Silku iela 24, Tel: 4 20 03; Fabriciusa iela 49b, Tel: 7 18 02.

Post Office: Pasata iela 4, Tel: 2 70 00.

Restaurants: Jura, Liela iela 5, Tel: 2 47 37; Liedags, Klaipedas iela 64, Tel: 3 33 53; Liepaja, Rigas iela 14, Tel: 2 67 36; Liva, Liela iela 11, Tel: 2 71 73.

Sports and Recreation: "Daugava" Stadium, Piejuras parka, Tel: 2 49 29; "Dinaomo" Stadium, Ühila iela 3, Tel: 2 35 23. Tennis courts can be found at Piejuras parkas, Tel: 2 51 07.

Theatre: Valsts Liepajas teatris, Teatra iela 4, Tel: 2 21 21 and 2 24 06; Teatra Maza zale, Baznicas iela 3/5; Lelju teatris, Baznicas iela 3/5.

Pavilosta (Paulshafen)

Fifty-eight kilometres (36 miles) north of Liepaja is the village of Pavilosta surrounding the mouth of the Saka River on the Baltic coast. This village was founded in 1879. The town was given its present-day name in 1890 during the construction of the harbour with a small wharf – the old fishing village was called Sakasgriva. Gulls, waves and fish depicted on the city's coat of arms are reminiscent of its origins. In 1989, a population of 13,000 lived in Pavilosta in the old centre or on the edge of town in the modern apartment buildings. The city's *amphitheatre* lies in a small park. Extending to the north of Pavilosta is a steep, sandy coastline. Especially beautiful: the secluded sand beach between Jurkalne and Uzmale.

Planica (Planetzen)

From 1905 to 1914, German colonists from Wohlhynia were settled in the northwestern Ukraine, especially in the districts of Kuldiga and Ainazi. They found a new home in Krussat-Drogen, Valtaiki (Neuhausen), Planica (Planetzen), Kurmahlen and Wirgen.

Sabile (Zabeln)

Around 30 kilometres (19 miles) south of Talsi, the small city of Sabile extends along the *Abava* (Abau) slopes. The sooner inconspicuous town found its way into the "Guiness Book of World Records": The *vineyard* on the southern slopes, with an area of around one hectare (2½ acres), is the northernmost vineyard in the world. Only a few sections of the foundation remain of the former Teutonic fortress complex, built during the middle of the 13th century.

In 1597, the construction of a *parish church* in Sabile was commissioned. In 1876, a complete renovation would follow – only the walls built from the stones of the neighbouring castle ruins remained intact. In the tower, the old clock from the castle church from 1450 strikes the time.

Saldus

The nicest view of Saldus, the city between Riga and Liepaja, is from the parking area when approaching from Broceni: above the old settlement along the *Ciecere River* cement tourist barracks line the slopes. In the centre of this town with a park on the intersection of the A 222 and A 218 is also a *covered market.*

Vegetables are sold in the wooden greenish yellow market hall and farmers sell flowers at stands outside. A high wall built from erratic blocks surrounds the whitewashed *church* across the way with its red tile roof. A few kilometres outside the city, on the northern point of the oblong lake is **Broceni** with its cement factory. It is especially loud here at night: an unexpected detour diverts traffic from the main route here to the bypass roads.

Information

Fuel: Kuldiga iela, on the outskirts of town.

Kafejnica: Kuldiga iela 21

Pharmacy: Liela iela 1a.

Restaurant: "Ciecere," in the department store, Revolucias iela 6.

Talsi (Talsen)

The small rural city of Talsi, like Rome, lies on seven hills – and this, directly in the middle of one of the most beautiful regions of Curonia, the so-called "Switzerland of Curonia." Talsi was first mentioned in 1231 in the contract between the papal envoy from Rome *Alnas Balduin,* and the Cours. In 1291, the settlement appeared once more as "Hakelwerk" in historical documents. Talsi, a fortified castle at that time, formed the centre of the Curonian Province of Vanema. After the Teutonic Order conquered the settlement and fortress, the Swedes pillaged the city in 1651. Under the rule of Duke Jakob, the first cast iron factory began operation in the 17th century not far from the city. Up into the 19th century, commerce and craftsmanship were reserved for the resident Germans. It was especially the manufacture of needles which made this town, the provincial capital since 1819, renowned beyond its borders. Before the First World War, most of the Talsi region belonged to the Stenden, Postenden and Nurmhusen estates. During the census in 1989, a population of 13,000 lived in this idyllic rural city.

Sights

Predominantly buildings from the 19th century are characteristic of the old city centre. Atop the Baznickalns (Church Hill) between Castle Hill and Mill Hill is the oldest building in the city: the *church.* The whitewashed church, built in 1567 and remodelled repeatedly, was already mentioned as being in need of repair in the chronicles of 1609 – although "only the roof" was missing at first, the church was without windows by 1655. It was one hundred years later that the restorations on the church resumed: in the 18th century, the church was equipped with a new tower; in 1802, a red roof followed; and in 1873, when the walls were built higher, a gallery was added. The cross-shaped layout of today is a result of the relatively recent construction work in 1888. The pastor *Karl Ferdinand Amenda,* a friend of Ludwig van Beethoven, preached here from 1802 to 1836. His grave can be found a number of kilometres outside the city. The Dzirnakalns (Mill Hill) is long since a sacred site for the Cours. The Teutonic Order built its fortress here during the 13th century. The stone fortress of faith later made way for a windmill... A division of the French army stopped at Dzirnavu iela 1 in 1812, as stated on the commemorative plaque. The 32.5 metre (106 foot) Pilskalns (Castle Hill) was inhabited as early as the 8th century.

During *archaeological excavations,* a number of finds from the 9th to 12th centuries were unearthed. A very pleasant experience is a stroll through the *Skulpturu darzs* (Sculpture Garden; Liela iela 30): 21 stone and bronze sculptures by Latvian artists stand amid the tall grass, surrounded by radiant flower beds and an old apple tree. Traditional crafts like weaving as well as the History of the Church and Art is covered by the *Local Museum* (Rozu iela 7, Tel: 2 27 70; open Tuesday to Sunday from noon to 6 pm). The exhibitions cover two floors; interesting special exhibits are often displayed on the ground floor. One example is the exhibition on *Lake Vilkmuizas.* More than 3,600 archaeological finds from the 11th to 14th centuries were discovered in the depths of the lake. The Cours once buried their dead in the nearby *City Lake* - an old Viking tradition: the deceased were cremated and the ashes were sunk in the lake.

Surroundings

Laidzi (Laidsen): Eight kilometres (5 miles) northeast of Talsi on a lake is the old *manor* of Laidzi. First mentioned in 1288, this was the property of the Lambsdorff family around 1439. From 1833 to 1886, the Barons von Brüggen built the manorhouse on the lake, which can still be seen today. The last lords of this manor were the Barons von Hahn.

Nurmuize (Nurmhusen): Eleven kilometres (7 miles) east of Talsi is the former domestic farm of the Teutonic Order. The large possession went to Christian von Hoerde in 1561 and, five years later, to the von Fircks family. For 358 years, Nurmhusen remained in the possession of the Fircks, then the noble lords were dispossessed. This well preserved castle goes back to a solid house built by the Teutonic Order during the Middle Ages. The chapel, connected with the manorhouse, later served as a library.

Pastende (Postenden): Three kilometres (2 miles) southeast of Talsi is the oldest Curonian fief. On October 10, 1288, Albert von Helmwadeshusen was enfeoffed with a parcel of land in the village of Padestanden from the Order Master. The estate on the Testenden brook was bequeathed to Hinrik Hane from the Order on November 1, 1476; this "for eternity." The estate stayed in the possession of the same family for 444 years – a continuity quite rare for the Baltic region. For thirteen generations, fifteen lords in uninterrupted succession came from the von Hahn family, whose main residence was in Basedow near the Mecklenburg lake basin. The oldest portions of the manorhouse date back to the 17th century. In 1780 and 1800, remodelling work decisively changed the structure of the manorhouse.

Information

Accommodation: Hotel Kareivju iela 16, Tel: 2 26 89 and 2 12 84.

Automobile Repair: Laidze iela , Tel: 1 63 68.

Bus Station: Dundagas iela 15, Tel: 2 21 05.

Cafés: Kafejnica Mara, Liela iela 16; pastry shop, Valdemara iela 2.

Fuel: Dundagas iela 15, Tel: 2 48 31.

Hospital: Rugena iela 7, Tel: 2 27 91.

Marketplace: Ezera iela 7, open Tuesday to Sunday from 7 am to 3 pm; during the summer season, from 8 am to 4 pm.

Pharmacy: Liela iela 24.

Post Office: Liela iela 4/6.

Restaurants: Kurzeme, Brivibas iela 17a; Bufete Saulite, Baznica laukums 2.

Special Events in Summer: Song Festivals at the Sauleskalns Balustrade.

Tukums (Tuckum)

The old Livonian settlement of Tukums, now a vital small city with a train station, is located around 25 kilometres (15½ miles) from Jurmala. Its name originates from the Finnish-ugrish work "tukku mägi" (Hill Range). The *Milzu Kalns* (Hill of the Giant), the highest elevation in the region offers a fantastic view of this city (first mentioned in 1445) and its picturesque surroundings. Today, only a few remnants of the walls remain of the Teutonic Fortress of Tuckum, built in the second half of the 13th century. In 1605, the Swedes destroyed the settlement to such an extent that only 200 years later in 1798 was Tukums awarded city status. The railway brought an economic boom to the city: in 1878, the route from Tukums to Riga and in 1904, the route from Tukums to Ventspils.

The *Tukums Museum of Art and Regional History* has an extensive collection of works by Latvian artists from 1920 to 1930, among which are the works of *Vilhelms Purvins, Voldemars Tone* and *Janis Rozentals.* The collection of modern paintings includes works by *Karlis Neile, Janis Pauluks, Leo Svempa* and *Otto Skulme.* The *Durbes Manorhouse,* built in 1820 by the Swiss architect *Janis Berlics* is worth seeing as is the Lutheran *church* from 1670. On Karatavu Kalns, also called Kapu Kalns, is the municipal cemetery.

Information

Café: Kafejnica-Restorans Valgums, next to the Universal department store.

Police: Brivibas laukums.

Tourist Information: Tourisma Asocian Kurzeme, Pils iela 6, can be reached by telephone by calling the technical secretary's office in the city hall, Tel: 2 27 07.

Ventspils (Windau)

To find Ventspils, simply follow the stench: the largest port city in Latvia with an ice-free harbour, Ventspils suffers drastically from acute ecological problems. Those who visit this industrial city must accept the health risks involved. The air is heavily polluted and the water highly contaminated – in the sea as well as from the faucet.

History

The Wendans once settled on the site where the Venta River flows into the Baltic. The Baltic tribes, first mentioned in historical documents in the 10th century, gave the city and river their names. Later displaced by the Cours, the crusading Knights moved into this region in the 13th century and secured their new territory with a fortress. At the base of the mighty Teutonic fortress, a settlement of merchants and craftsmen developed and was awarded the status of city in 1378. As a member of the Hanseatic League (14th to 16th century), Ventspils experienced its golden age under the rule of Duke Jakob (1642-1681). Duke Jakob established a wharf for trade and military ships here and had his ships set sail for the Curonian colonies of Tobago and Gambia. The Great Northern War abruptly ended this dynamic development and the plague claimed the lives of almost the entire population of the city – only seven families are said to have survived. It was only in 1904 that the establishment of a railway route to Moscow could raise this city from insignificance. In 1961, the Soviets built up

Ventspils – Latvia's "Environmental Catastrophe"

Ventspils is considered the environmental disaster of Latvia. Gas masks were distributed a number of times during the past years to at least protect the children from the heavily polluted air. The frequency of birth defects is also above average. One will notice the conditions in Ventspils even at a distance: the stench of this city extends for miles.

Ventspils as a centre for the petrochemical industry. A pipeline was built to the harbour; a factory for the production of liquid ammonia and potash was established here by the US company "Occidental Petroleum." Since then thousands of tonnes of liquid ammonia and phosphoric acids are transported here every day. Factories for wood processing were also established. The fish canning combine presses the fresh catch from the fishing fleets of "Sarkana baka" into over one million cans per year. Today, Ventspils is on the verge of collapse: the completely contaminated and overbuilt city is also entirely overpopulated. The population has quadrupled since 1950 due to the resettlement of Russian guest workers which drove the population up over 52,000.

Sights

White brick workers' apartments, almost built overnight, dominate the profile of this city. However, those who expect to find a bustling harbour city will be disappointed upon first glance: dragging, contemplative almost unreal is the impression this small city leaves; a city with a number of sights, but sights which could be questioned once in the city. Where is the "picturesque old city," praised so highly in the travel brochure? And where is the Teutonic Fortress? Even local residents don't know the way there... What remains is a stroll down the main street of Kuldigas iela past a few shops and residential buildings, the façades of which are decorated with restored Art Nouveau emblems. On the southern end of the old city is the marketplace surrounded by the post office, administration offices and the *Museum of the History of Ventspils.* a small street leads off to the Lutheran *St. Nicholas Church.* Consecrated in 1834, above the portal is a German inscription "Gott und dem Kaiser" (For God and Emperor). The church was named after the Russian Czar Nicholas I, who made the construction of this church possible through national funding.

The *Maritime and Fishing Museum* (Rinka iela 2; open daily from 10 am to 6 pm) lies somewhat outside the centre of town toward the Baltic coast. With an area of eight hectares (20 acres), old fishing and nautical maps, old Curonian barges and all kinds of equipment from a time long past illustrate the lifestyle of the fishermen who once lived in the Ventspils region.

Those who crave a hardy breath of fresh air after the stench of this city can hike from here through the dunes and to the beach – swimming is, however, not a good idea due to the proximity of the harbour. The *Gargarin Park* is considered the "green lung" of this city. On the outskirts of town are also the *Busnieku* and *Zvejnieku* parks.

Information

Accommodation: Viesnica Dzintarju-ra, Ganibu iela 26, Tel: 2 27 19. Branch: Lielais prospektas 15, Tel: 3 30 99.

Automobile Repair: Kuldigas iela 20, Tel: 2 20 48.

Bank: Kuldigas iela 3 and 23.

Fuel: Rupniecibas iela 14.

Bus Station: Lauku iela.

Hospitals: Pils iela 2, Tel: 2 21 75.

Post Office: Lauku iela.

Restaurant: Kosmoss, Ganibu iela.

Zegmale (Semigallia)

Zemgale, both historically and ethnographically, is the southernmost region in Latvia. It extends to the south of the Daugava in the interior of Latvia to the Lithuanian border. Since this region is predominantly flat, forests were cut down relatively early in the region's history to make space for agriculture – for this reason, most of the farming villages in Zemgale were, unlike in Curonia, not estate villages, but composed of individual farms. Serfdom was also abolished here earlier than in the rest of Latvia, namely in 1817, and rent was introduced between peasantry and feudal tenure. Zemgale was incorporated into the Duchy of Curonia in 1795.

Bauska (Bauske)

The history of the small city of Bauska, located 80 kilometres (50 miles) south of Riga near the Lithuanian border, is closely connected with the Teutonic Order. In 1443, the Knights built their mighty fortress at the confluence of the Musa (Muß) and Memele (Memel) Rivers. First mentioned in 1443, Bauska already had city status in 1511. In 1599, Duke Friedrich had the fortress expanded; however, this was to prove in vain: in 1625, the fortress and the city were pillaged by the Swedes before the Russians conquered and blew up the fortress in 1706 during the Great Northern War. What was left, is now being carefully restored. The oldest structure in the city is the *Church of the Holy Ghost,* built from 1591 to 1594. The church tower from the 19th century was struck by lightning and has not been repaired to date.

Bauska suffers greatly from the through traffic to Lithuania. The M 12 runs directly through the middle of town. The actual city centre around the oblong marketplace looks rather run-down. A thick layer of dust covers the patinas of the old houses. The few trees left hardly have a chance against the exhaust fumes from the traffic.

Surroundings

Ten kilometres (6¼ miles) to the west of Bauska is probably the most famous architectural monument in Latvia, the *Pilsrundale* (Ruhenthal Castle; closed Monday and Tuesday; open from 10 am to 5 pm during the winter and 10 am to 6 pm during the summer with the last tour beginning at 5:15; small information pamphlet available in several languages). This was the summer palace of the Imperial Count Johann von Biron, designed by the Italian architect *Bartolomeo Francesco Rastrelli,* who also built the winter palace in St. Petersburg. Rastrelli came to Rundale on invitation of von Biron in the autumn of 1735. The count had only purchased the land that summer. Plans for the summer residence of this count who had won the favour of Czaress Anna Ivanovna began with the arrival of Rastrelli. May 24, 1736 marked the laying of the cornerstone.

2,000 workers – only 500 of which were locals – completed the construction of the castle of Rundale from the foundation to the attic within only one year. In the construction of the framework, stones from the former medieval castle were used. After four years, the entire castle was almost completed. Clay was transported from the surrounding regions to be used in the construction. The building site was equipped with a dozen brick kilns for this purpose alone.

While the castle was roofed in 1737, the master craftsmen from St. Petersburg began work on the interior. The ceiling murals on canvas were the work of *Bartolomeo Tarsia;* the plasterwork was conducted by *P. Jefremov.* The tile oven, decorated with blue and white Delft tiles, was created by the master craftsman *Uschakov* and his apprentices. In 1737, the life's dream of the glory-hungry baron came to fruition – Biron was declared the Duke of Curonia. At the apex of his influence, Biron began construction on a second castle in the capital of Jelgava. The pace of construction work on the Rundale Castle slowed. The death of the Czaress in 1740 put an abrupt end to Birons career – he was arrested and sent into banishment for 22 years.

For this reason, the construction on Rundale, although almost finished, could only be brought to an end in 1763. During the following four years, the two Italian artists *Francesco Martini* and *Carlo Zucchi* completed the remaining ceiling murals. The sculpted wall and ceiling ornamentations were the work of the Berlin master craftsman *Johann Michael Graff*. Thirty-one years after construction began, the castle was finally finished in 1767. The excitement over the new summer residence was to be short-lived. In 1795, the Grand Duchy of Curonia was annexed by Russia – and *Catherine II* gave Biron's stately palace to her favoured *Count Valerian Subov*. This dwarf aristocrat, in turn, gave the castle to Count Suvalov, who resided in Rundale up to the dispossession in 1920. Having learned from the heavy damage and pillagings during the First World War, the count wisely sold or brought most of the valuable inventory of the castle to safety. In 1916, the castle served as a military hospital for the German Army. In 1972, restoration work began on the 90 hectare (225 acre) castle complex and still continues today. The work on the eastern wing could be completed by 1981 and the castle was once more opened to the public. Of the 138 rooms in the castle, 43 on the upper floor are used for displaying the castle museum's exhibits. Today, the Biron family lives in France. However, crowned heads have returned to the summer residence: in August 1992, Queen Margarethe II of Denmark and King Gustav Adolf of Sweden accompanied by his wife Sylvia were received here by the Latvian government.

Walking Tours

Chestnut trees line the 500 metre (545 yard) footpath from the parking area to the small bridge over the moat. A passageway leads to a small round plaza, surrounded by rust coloured stall buildings. The lion figures at the gateway to the parade grounds replaced the high tower in 1763, which once stood at the castle gate. Seven staircases lead up to the castle, consisting of a main section and two side wings. The central stairway leads into the foyer of the main wing and farther to the galleries. To the right are the rooms of the Duchess and the dining hall; to the right, the living quarters of the Duke and the reception rooms. Both galleries lead to the Rastrelli parade steps, unparalleled in the world. An oak door which was only opened on festive occasions lead to the reception rooms. The golden hall, also called the throne room, offers majesty and grandeur – this was where the Duke's throne stood. The plasterwork was created by Johann Michael Graff. The ceiling paintings by F. Martini and C. Zucchi acclaim Biron's ruling virtues allegorically: powerful and wise, generous, peace-loving and magnificence. The allegories on the mouldings and garlands on the wall show artistic skill and craftsmanship in music, architecture, animal husbandry and the hunt. The 30 metre (98 foot) grand gallery provided the setting for festive dinners. The small gallery has remained in it original form from the 1830's. The white hall, which served as a ball room and concert hall, is light and airy in comparison to the majestic pomp of the throne room. The allegories presented in the plasterwork depict the four elements fire, water, earth and air as well as the four seasons. These are also the work of Johann Michael Graff. As a sign of luck, Graff set a stork in the middle of the ceiling.

At the front end of the hall is the oval porcelain cabinet with a beautiful collection of Japanese and Chinese vases on 45 rocaille consoles. The entire central structure of the castle houses the rooms of the Duke, furnished with valuable brocade tapestries from Moscow and fireplaces made from Delft porcelain. In two parallel flights, Biron had no less than 20 rooms at his private disposal. Toward the courtyard were the wardrobe, dressing room and two work rooms. In the Rose Hall, a small square in the corner of the ceiling reveals in what pitiful condition the castle was before restorations began. Rococo chairs and paintings by Dutch artists decorated the Blue Salon. In the bedroom of this ruler with royal alcoves are portraits of the family. Providing the necessary warmth were two Delft fireplaces. Also restored, but less lavishly, are the rooms of the Duchess and the guest rooms in the western wing. Tacky be-

yond compare: the boudoir of the Duchess. Tree trunks in which two children are perched frame a seashell divan. In the kitchen which heats the White Hall with the warmth it produces, 1,200 eggs and a bull were used every day according to statements of the late Prince Subov.

The castle park to the south, also designed by Rastrelli, is being planted with new lindens. Where now a sooner bleak tract of land stretches, it is planed to resurrect the old park with pavilions, arcades and pergolas. The hunting park on the opposite side of the canal has better maintained its former appearance. It is also planned to rebuild the domestic buildings from the end of the 18th century, situated to the north; this, despite extreme financial problems.

Ten kilometres (6¼ miles) upstream from Bauska is **Mezotne** (Mesothen). To the left before the entrance to the large agricultural settlement was the residence of Prince *Anatol Lieven* in his magnificent *estate palace.* With the dispossession of 1919, his 4,275 hectare (10,688 acre) estate was sectioned off into 83 new farming plots. 286 hectares (715 acres) of farmland went to the Latvian Agricultural Society, which set up an educational institution on the former estate, even equipped with a livestock farm. Lieven was left 101 hectares (253 acres) of land in 1921 as a residual estate to farm himself. Up to his death on April 3 1937, the prince worked the land as a "common" farmer. Lieven's princely manorhouse, built according to the plans of the Berlin architect *Johann Georg Berlitz,* is now classified as a historical monument. Although the estate house was added once again to the list of historic monuments after the Second World War, it still is used for other purposes – as a warehouse, saw mill and poultry stall. The ceiling beams, window frames and hallway floors were overheated during the cold Baltic winters. The securing of the building began in 1957 and the renovation of the façade commenced in 1966. The nearby church from 1822 was used for more secular purposes in the 1960's, namely as a warehouse for artificial fertilizers. To enable the large transport vehicles to drive up to the building, the portal columns were removed and a portion of the windows were walled up. Only two of the former 35 graves of the princely family remain: a sandstone cross from 1830 and the epitaph for the last owner. In the neighbouring cemetery, gravestones and monuments were removed and brought to Bauska to be processed further; the cemetery was then planed. In the small *estate park*, which gradually drops off to the river are numerous old oak and chestnut trees.

Information

Accommodation: Hotel, Slimnicas iela 7, Tel: 2 38 04 and 2 47 05.
Bus Station: Slimnicas iela 11, Tel: 2 24 77.
Fuel: Code iela, Tel: 2 22 65.
Hospital: Slimnicas iela 2, Tel: 2 31 53.
Marketplace: Rupniecibas iela 11; open 8 am to 5 pm, closed during the winter months.

Post Office: Slimnica iela 9, Tel: 2 22 68.
Restaurants: Pilskalns, Brivibas bulvaris 2; Bauska, slimnicas iela 7; Gliemezitis, Kalna iela 7; Musa, Ratslaukums 1.

Ielcava

The small city of Ielcava, halfway between Riga and Bauska on the M 12 is situated on the banks of the Ielcava River. The large agricultural centre borders the city to the north.
Information
Accommodation: A hotel is located around 4 kilometres (2½ miles) before town on the M 12 when coming from Riga (look for the signs).

Jelgava (Mitau)

Sixty-eight kilometres (43 miles) south of Riga on the southern banks of the Lielupe is the old capital of Zemgale, Jelgava. In this former residence city, with a population of 72,000 today, patinas and problems overshadow the former grandeur.
History
Around 1265, the Teutonic Order built its renowned *Mytowe Fortress* here. The settlement surrounding this fortress was first awarded city rights in 1573 despite its strategic location on the river. Jelgava's golden age began in 1596 when Duke *Friedrich Kettler* moved the residence of the Curonian Dukes to this location. In 1658, Jelgava was conquered by the Swedes and in 1730, the Russian Czaress Anna held her court here. Up to 1860, the bustle of a big city

could be found once a year in Jelgava: On June 12, the main pay-day in Curonia, the nobility found their way to the central market to pay and receive payment. An annual fair with jugglers and travelling folk augmented St. John's Mass.

Beginning in 1870, the railway made goods from Jelgava known throughout the country: honey-gingerbread from the traditional bakery J. Sieslacks, "Original American Shoe Forms" from the Carl shoe house, steam-brewed beers from H. Kroitzsch, ink and cloth from Jelgavan manufacturers.

In 1915, Jelgava became the governmental city of Curonia; in 1918 it was elevated in status to provincial capital of Semigallia. The bombs of the Second World War destroyed 90% of the city centre in 1944. Newer apartment buildings line the edge of the city. in the suburb of Ozolnieki, a satellite city rises above the treetops of the forest. In the new districts toward Dobele, large numbers indicating the year in which each building was built reveal that one brick building has been built here every year since 1987.

Sights

The façade of the *Duke's Castle* runs along 150 metres (490 feet) of the southern banks of the Lielupe River. In the former residence of the Curonian Dukes, built in 1738 by the St. Petersburg court architect *Bartolomeo Francesco Rastrelli* is now an Agricultural Institute. Access to the square complex surrounding a small inner courtyard is provided by two gateways, open weekdays from 7 am to 5:30 pm. A broad driveway leads up to the main wing. On the garden side, a majestic double stairway leads to the narrow sand path along the river. Before the students of agriculture moved into the building, the sand and rust-brown building offered an banished king refuge: from 1798 to 1801 as well as from 1804 to 1807, the successor to the French throne Louis XVIII tarried here.

Next to a small sculpture park is the impressive building of the *Gederts-Elias Museum of History and Art* (Akademijas iela; open Tuesday to Friday from noon to 6 pm, Saturday from 10 am to 4 pm). A makeshift wooden fence conceals the nearby, crumbling ruins of the Russian Orthodox *Church* (Raina iela/corner of Akademijas iela). Construction on the *Trinity Church* was begun in 1574. After a construction halt, the work was postponed until 1592. The church was completed in 1625 – albeit sans tower. This was to be added in 1680. The first restorations began as soon as 1843 on this church which makes a pitiful impression today. The altar, consecrated in 1641, was donated by *Duchess Elizabeth Magdalena*.

The *Vecpilseta iela* is reminiscent of old Jelgava. Although the surface of the street littered with potholes and the old wooden houses are in dire need of renovation, the trip here is still worth the while. Also of interest is the *City Hall.* Among other relics, logbooks of Curonian sea officers were collected in the assembly hall in the 17th century.

Surroundings

On the road to Dobele is the "Nakotne" (Future) Kolkhoz founded in 1946 and situated amid the flat, green landscape. Near the black and white cows, leisurely chewing their cud is a strange scene: nine railway wagons and a large passenger plane rusting in the middle of the field.

Information

Accommodation: Hotel Viesnica Jelgava, Liela iela 6, Tel: 2 61 93 and 2 37 83, also housing Kafejnica Riga. This hotel is located to the right directly beyond the bridge on the outskirts of town.

Bank: Akademija iela/corner of Dirskas iela (across from the pharmacy).

Bus Station: Pasta iela.

Pharmacy: Akademija iela/corner of Dirskas iela; Zvaras iela 5.

Post Office: Pasta iela.

Restaurants: Bernu Kafejnica, Liela iela; Madara Kafejnica, on the church square, Liela iela/corner of Jaunatnes iela; Kafejnica Kulinaria, Jaunatnes iela/corner of Dobeles iela; Restaurant Tonuss, Uzvaras iela.

Olaine

In the small city of Olaine on the Misa River, 23 kilometres (14½ miles) south of Riga on the A 219 and the railway route to Jelgava, a chemical and pharmaceutical combine was set up in the 1960's and 1970's, albeit without any type of safety precautions... Since 1966, the plant (which was later expanded) has produced polyvinyl-chloride plastics. With the independence of Latvia, the first scientific studies of this region were published. They confirm that only nine percent of the children living in this area have "normal" health. Among the workers, around 80 percent have been suffer from work-related health problems and only 20 percent are halfway healthy.

Tervete

South of Jelgava near the rural road to the Lithuanian town of Zagare is Tervete. The idyllic region with forests, lakes and rivers was once inhabited by old Semigallian tribes. Their powerful king Viestur ruled the region with his twelve princes from the wooden fortress. His successor Nameys led an attack in 1280 against the Teutonic knights in nearby Riga. The counterattack followed the next year: 14,000 Teutonic knights drove Nameys into Lithuanian exile. The Teutonic knights built their stone fortress on the ruins of his fort. The historical districts lie in the very attractive *Meza ainavu landscape park.* A map provides information on sights at the large parking area before the hilltop on the way into town. A good point of departure for hikes through the idyllic landscape park is the *Anna Brigaderes Memorial Museum,* also called "Spridise" after the heroine of this author. The author of children's books lived in Spridise up to her death in 1922. The intact landscape surrounding it found a place in her stories. The *Tervetes Landscape Park,* transversed by a dense network of hiking trails is composed of several sections: the Saules noskanu parks (Mood of the Sun Park), the

Veco priezu parks with the oldest and tallest pine tree in Latvia, the Pasaku mezs (Fairy Tale Forest) and the Rukisu mezs (Dwarf's Park).

The mythological and fairy tale character of the forest and meadow park is emphasized through wooden figures from the world of fantasy, for example the giant Lutausis, the dwarfs Rukitis and the forest king Meza kenins. Offering a nice view is the *Sapnu pili* (Castle of Dreams).

Latgale (Latgallia)

Latgale, which belonged to Poland up to 1772, is much different from the rest of Latvia – the majority of the population is Catholic: the first division of Poland which brought Latgale under Russian control, incited a sweeping wave of emigration. Even today, the Russian proportion of the population is well above the national average. At almost 13% (1979) the Latvians are a minority in their own land.

Aluksne (Marienburg)

The small city of Aluksne, 20 kilometres (12½ miles) south of the Estonian border in the northern regions of Latgale is on the shores of Lake Aluksne, an almost perfectly circular body of water.

History

The Teutonic Order built its fortress on an island in the lake. During the Great Northern War, the order's former commander's quarters were conquered in 1702 by the Russian general *Scheremetjev*. The town and fortress were destroyed during the course of these events and the residents were deported to Russia and imprisoned. The present-day city of Aluksne developed from 1881 on a tract of land which was once a part of the Marienburg estate.

Sights

The artery of the city is the Pils iela (Castle Street). Directly in the centre of town are not only a bank, a hotel, a department store, numerous small shops and Kafejnicas but also the *church.* This granite church, plastered in yellowish green is presumed to have been built by the Rigan architect *Christoph Haberlandt* in 1788. The majestic altar was created by the sculptor *Karl Kopolka* from Prague. To both sides of the altar, generous boxes were built for the patrons of the church. To the east, the Pils iela bisects the extensive *park* with its man-made ponds, sculptures, fountains, idyllic paths and open meadows which offer a view of the lake. To the right-hand side of the street is a small, beige-brown *Tudor Castle.* This building now houses the "Liesna" cinema and the Maksla ir Amatu-Skola (Art School). The Russian-Orthodox *church* (Komjaunates iela 56) was built from bricks and erratic blocks during the end of the 19th century

Aluksne is situated in the middle of a fantastic, gently rolling moraine landscape. Birch trees line the mostly sand walkways and now and then, oaks line the broad rural roads.

Near **Paulius** on *Lake Aluksne* a small

bay is used by fishermen and campers for grilling and swimming – one of the few places where the rather dense belt of reeds is interrupted.

Information

Accommodation

Camping: Three kilometres (2 miles) north of town on the shores of the lake; located on the left-hand side of the P 37 to Pleskava.

Hotel: Pils iela.

Bank: Pompous classicistic building next to the church in the centre of town.

Bus Station: Pils iela.

Hospital: On the lakeshore on the outskirts of town.

Post Office: O. Vaciesa iela 8.

Restaurants: Ednica Aluksne, side entrance of the Universalveikals (department store), Pils iela; a Kafejnica is also in the Universalveikals, Pils iela.

Balvi

The spread-out small city of Balvi, 80 kilometres (50 miles) north of Rezekne, is set against the backdrop of *Lake Perkonu*. The city is less interesting in a touristic sense. In addition to the least expensive accommodation in the Baltic region, the city has a beautiful *park*, accessible via the narrow path to the right of the hotel. Smaller and larger erratic blocks with the most diverse mineral composition were stacked to create sculptures. Especially beautiful: the reflection of the stone creation in the waters of a man-made moat with a wooded island.

Information

Accommodation: Hotel Balvi, Tautas iela 14, Tel: 2 23 07. Simple, quiet and clean, only cold running water; very inexpensive.

Kafejnica, cozy wooden decor to the left of the foyer.

Currency Exchange: Brivibas iela 57.

Fuel: On the edge of town when heading toward Gulbene.

Restaurant: Kafejnica-Ednica Balvi, Brivibas iela 63.

Train Station: Four kilometres (2½ miles) west of town in Kurna.

Dagda

On the byway, halfway between Kraslava to Rezekne is the small provincial city of Dagda on the *Guscina River*. The city, dominated by the impressive *baroque church* (Alunes iela), opens to *Lake Dagda* with its twelve islands. Ten kilometres (6¼ miles) to the north heading toward Rezekne is the fishing and resort town of **Ezernieki.** This town on the *Ezezers* is also designated as "Bukmuiza" on some maps. A dense belt of reeds lines the shores of the lake with numerous bays. Rarely is direct access to the water possible. The "tourist station" is on a point in the island, once used by Soviet soldiers and now open to the general public. The small *church* built from erratic blocks on a hill directly by the P 48 motorway offers a nice view of the village and lake.

Information

Bus Station: Daugavpils iela.

Fuel: On the edge of town when heading for Kraslava.

Restaurant: Ednica Lasite, on the intersection of the rural roads P 48 and P 56.

Daugavpils (Dünaburg)

240 kilometres (150 miles) southeast of Riga is Daugavpils, the second largest city in Latvia on the upper Daugava River. Daugavpils, called "Dvinsk" by the Russians, has a population of 130,000. This city in the three country region of Latvia, Lithuania and Belorussia is an important traffic hub: this is the intersection of the A 215 (Riga – Moscow) and the A 226 (Kaunas/Vilnius – St. Petersburg) and the junction of the north-south and east west railway routes. Ships also set off for Riga on the Daugava River.

History

First documented in 1278, when the Teutonic Order built a fortress on the river, Daugavpils was called "Dünaburg." In 1577, *Ivan the Terrible* took the fortress and destroyed it to its foundations. On the ruins of the enemy fortress, the Russian ruler built his own fortress – it still towers over the city today. The history of the city can only be recounted in segments. Colourful posters in the local museum reveal that Daugavpils celebrated a Latgallian song festival in 1940. In the spring of 1946, construction on the streetcar system began – and as soon as autumn of that year, the first streetcar rattled through the city.

The old trade settlement was intentionally built into an industrial region by the Russians. In 1949, the chain factory which produced chains for bicycles and other vehicles moved from Charkov to Daugavpils. The "Electoinstruments" company, called "DAUER" since 1991, was founded in 1952 and a factory for the improvement of railway wagons and locomotives would follow shortly thereafter.

The construction of a gigantic hydroelectric plant 3 kilometres (2 miles) from the city was temporarily stopped by massive protests in 1987. Musical messages can be heard by the five musicians in "Elpa" – the folk-pop band from Daugava is also popular well beyond the borders of Latvia.

Sights

Although the Second World War destroyed Daugavpils up to 80%, the intentional destruction of Daugavpils' religious cultural legacy was to follow under the Soviets. The Russian-Orthodox *Nevski Church* in the centre of town was torn down overnight in 1969. The inner city is laid out in a checkerboard patter with all streets running at right angles. The main shopping street Rigas iela is a pedestrian zone from the railway station to Vienibas laukums.

The rectangular plaza is dominated by *Vienibas nams* (Labour Union House). The monumental building, erected within 17 months in 1937, houses the Aeroflot office, a book store, a restaurant, a department store and a theatre with a large auditorium and a small chamber theatre. The Lenin statue, which gave this square its name during the Soviet regime, was removed in 1991. The majestic *city villa,* in which *Janis Rainis* lived with his wife after returning from exile in April of 1920, now houses the

Daugavpils Novadpet niebibas un maksla muzejs (Daugavpils History and Art Museum; Muzeja iela 23, open Tuesday to Saturday from 11 am to 6 pm) which remains open despite remodelling. Across the street in the *Dubrovnis Park* the "eternal flame" burned up to one year ago – Russia capped the gas line during the energy conflict... The monumental memorial complex for seven Red Army officers who fell in 1944 is a place of pilgrimage (of sorts at least): at night, satanists celebrate black mass here. Not far from the museum is the *Teachers' College* (Instituto iela), founded by *Valerija Seil* in 1922. Today, music students practice in this building. A new teachers' college was built in the centre of town in 1952 – in the Stalinistic pseudo-classicistic monumental style of that era.

The Catholic *St. Peter's Church* was built by Italian architects from 1845 to 1848, inspired by St Peter's Cathedral. Diagonally across from the church is the *central tirgus* (central market, Cietoksna iela), open from 7 am until the afternoon.

The "four churches district" is accessible by taking tram 3 to "Lokomotiv." The tram stop is in the longest street in the city. The present-day "Street of November 18th," named after the first day of independence, was called "Street of the Red Army" during the Soviet regime and "Adolf Hitler Street" from 1941 to 1944 during the German occupation. During the Soviet regime, a boxing school was housed in the red, neo-Gothic Lutheran *church* across from the tram sta-

tion. When the roof burned in 1987, the church was given back to the congregation – the government had insufficient funds to undertake the necessary repairs. Today, reconstruction is financed through donations – only the roof of the tower was still missing in the autumn of 1992. The Catholic *St. Mary's Church,* built as a one-naved church with neo-baroque and neo-Gothic elements, is used by the Polish congregation for their church services. Inside, reliefs on the walls depict Christ's stations of the cross. However, the main attraction of this magnificent white-washed church is the rather tacky St. Mary's Grotto below a painting which shows the grotto of Lourdes. Mary is said to have appeared there in 1854. A gilded frame with lightbulbs surrounds the altarpiece. A very colourful basilica with a pink façade and blue and yellow onion towers belongs to the old Orthodox congregation. Their *Nikolski Chram* (Andreja Pumpura iela/corner of Puskina iela) was built in 1928 by religiously persecuted Russians.

The church may only be entered by those who observe the dress requirements and have their heads covered. Women must have their hair under a scarf; men must place a handkerchief on their heads. Especially worth seeing is the impressive icon wall and the three-storey silver candelabra. Services take place only during weekends: Saturday and Sunday in the morning and evening.

Passing the Polish school (Varszava iela 2), a quiet residential street leads to the *Boris Gelb Cathedral* (Tautas iela) across from the sports field. Its rust-brown and white façade stands in sharp contrast to the apartment buildings. The 40 by 20 by 16 metre (131 by 66 by 53 foot) church built from 1904 was consecrated on June 12, 1905. Portraits of Russian saints, archbishops and martyrs embellish the columns and walls. The unusually large amount of pictures is explained by a belief: each worshipper chose his own saint to whom he or she prayed.

Those who have the opportunity should visit a concert by the famous Boris Gelb Cathedral Choir.

Surroundings

One should travel to **Aglona,** around 50 kilometres (31 miles) northeast of Daugavpils on *Ceresu ezers* (Lake Ceresu) on August 15: in celebration of Mary's Ascension, Catholics come to the *basilica* from all over Latvia for the festive mass. Near Aglona are also Lake Rusonu and Lake Ilzes.

Information

Accommodation: Hotel Latvija, Gimnazijos iela 46, Tel: 2 90 03 (on Vienibas laukums). Nine-storey hotel building with a restaurant and café. Hotel Celtnieks, Jelgavas iela 7, Tel: 5 12 09.

Bus Station: Viestura iela/corner of Laplesa iela.

Cafés: Dzintars, Smilsu iela 94a; Kosmoss, Kandavas iela 6.

Gallery: Maksla salonas, Rigas iela 20; changing exhibits.

Hospital: Polyclinic, Viestura iela 11.

Pharmacy: Rigas iela 54a.

Post Office: Suvorova iela 24.

Restaurant: Daugavpils, Vienibas laukums/Rigas iela 22.

Theatre: In the Labour Union Building, Vienibas laukums.

Gulbene

Gulbene is a town on the A 214 in the northern regions of Latgale with apartment buildings, some industry, several railroad tracks and hardly any old wooden houses. The only highlight: the expansive *cemetery park* with a small chapel, a swan fountain and white benches in front of the individual graves for silent dialogue with the deceased.

Information

Fuel: Akiera iela, railroad tracks across from the cemetery.

Jekabpils

Prince Jekab gave this city, located on the banks of the Daugava, its name. The settlement, having once belonged to Curonia was a popular stopping point for ships on the Daugava River heading for Riga and the city of Daugavpils. Although this region was inhabited since the 13th century, the city was officially founded in 1920. This makes Jekabpils, famous for its School of Navigation, the youngest city in the country. The *ruins of the Teutonic Fortress* from the 13th century on the Krustpils are reminiscent of the earlier significance of the settlement.

While the *Krustpils Church* already stood in 1683, the *Jekabpils Church* as well as the *St. Nicholas Monastic Church* date back to 1769.

Village architecture and the rural traditions are preserved by the *Outdoor*

Museum for Regional Studies. The *Janis Rainis Museum* (Tel: 7 72 51; open May 15 to October 15) has been set up in the house where the national poet spent the first five years of his life. "Tadenava," built in 1895 by Janis Rainis' father repeatedly brings the memory and works of this poet to life. Two rooms in the museum are dedicated to Rainis' father and sister.

Surroundings

Around 30 kilometres (19 miles) northeast of Jekabpils south of the M 9 is the *Teici Nature Reserve.* The 18,000 hectare (45,000 acre) highland moor reserve is threatened since the political shift: since raw materials are lacking in Latvia, industrial extraction of peat is planned for this region in the near future. The environmentalists are irate – nowhere in central Europe is there a highland moor of this type in existence.

Kaunata

The small village of Kaunata on the eastern shores of the huge *Lake Reznas* is surrounded by a pastoral landscape of gently rolling hills. The highest elevations in this "land of the blue lake" are the Makonkalns at 248 metres (811 feet) to the west, the M. Liepu Kalns to the south (266 metres/870 feet) and the L. Liepu Kalns east of town reaching the proud height of 289 metres (945 feet).

Kraslava (Kraslau)

The most beautiful view of Kraslava is from the parking area on the edge of town when approaching from **Daugavpils.** The sweeping view spans the meandering *Daugava River* in the valley all the way to the wooden houses of the city. The buildings, most of which originate from the 19th century, clearly show their age. The Maskava iela runs directly through this sleepy and dusty city. The *Museum of Local History* (Grafu Plateru iela, open Wednesday to Sunday from 11 am to 1 pm and 2 to 5 pm) provides information on the history of this small city near the Belorussian border.

Information

Accommodation: Hotel Kraslava, Raina iela 35, Tel: 2 14 49. 248 Rubles for a double room. Four-storey complex in a quiet residential area with a Kafejnica adjacent. Tourist Inn Saulenskalns, 16 kilometres (10 miles) southwest of town in Kombuli.

Automobile Repair: Vasarnieku iela 92, Tel: 2 13 28.

Bus Station: Maskavas iela 129, Tel: 2 34 00.

Cafés: Café Madara, Tirgus iela 1; Café Marite, Brivibas iela 7; Varaviksne Kafejnica, Maskava iela 141; Kafejnica Janupite, Baznicas iela 1.

Fuel: There is a large service station on the edge of town when heading for Daugavpils.

Hospital: Maskavas iela 215, Tel: 2 35 06.

Marketplace: Krasta iela 1, Tuesday to Sunday from 7 am to 3 pm.

Post Office: Sveta Ludviga laukums.

Restaurants: Restaurant Kraslava, in the Universalveikals, Maskava iela 92; Restaurant Smorugova iela 37.

Ludza (Ludsen)

Ludza: a city at the end of the world; the streets are blocked off or torn up, the houses in desolate condition, the people surly. Living in the small city on Lake Ludza, around 45 kilometres (28 miles) from the Belorussian border on the M 9 are predominantly Russians. The Latgales iela leads directly through town to the *city parish church* with its open bell tower. How beautiful Ludza must have once been is revealed by the intact houses along the lakeshores. These display the names of the residents instead of house numbers.

Only some *remnants of walls and towers* remain of the fortress which once protected the lake and city. Those who would like to investigate Ludza in more detail should visit the *Museum for Regional Studies* (Kulneva iela 2, Tel: 2 39 31; open Tuesday to Sunday from 9 am to 4 pm).

Surroundings

35 kilometres (22 miles) farther east is the train station of *Zilupe* only a few kilometres from the Belorussian border. The Catholic *Pasiene Church* three kilometres (2 miles) south of the small city offers a outstanding panorama of the expansive Russian plain.

Information

Accommodation: Hotel Stacijas iela 42, Tel: 2 24 90.
Bus Station: Kris Barona iela 45/14, Tel: 2 26 83.
Café: Kafejnica, Latgales iela.
Fuel: Latgales iela 255, Tel: 2 30 09.
Hospital: Raina iela 43, Tel: 2 21 11.
Post Office: Latgales iela 110/19
Restaurant: Stacijas iela 30.

Rezekne (Rositten)

At the junction of the M 9 and A 116 in the eastern regions of Latvia is Rezekne. This city lost the struggle over capital city of Latgale to the larger city of **Daugavpils.** The *Rezekne River* runs directly through this small city, which was elevated in status to district capital in 1802. While, during the First World War, "only" one hundred buildings were destroyed, the bombs of the Second World War were to claim up to 80% of the city. Rezekne arose from the ashes – as a pompous Stalinistic provincial city with oversized access roads, a palace and park around the last remnants of the old city. The *Fortress Hill* with the ruins of the Teutonic Fortress from 1285 makes up a portion of the extensive city park today. The *Catholic Church* on Latgales iela was built in 1888. A *Museum* provides information on the history and culture of Latgale (Lenina iela 102, Tel: 2 24 64; open Tuesday to Sunday from 10 am to 5 pm).

Information

Accommodation: Hotel Latgale, Brivibas iela 2, Tel: 2 21 80; 1,600 Ruble per night.
Bus Station: Latgales iela 17, Tel: 2 31 82.
Fuel: Varonu iela 6.
Hospital: 18. novembra iela 41, Tel: 2 21 00.
Marketplace: Liepajas iela 16, open from 7:30 am to 5 pm.
Pharmacy: Brivibas iela 3/corner of Latgales iela.
Restaurant: Latgale, in Hotel Latgale, Brivibas iela 2.

Lithuania

Lithuania at a Glance

Country Name: Republic of Lithuania

Capital City: Vilnius (population: 592,000)

Larger Cities: Kaunas (pop: 500,000), Klaipeda (pop: 200,000)

Area: 65,200 square kilometres (25,428 square miles)

Length of Coastline: 99 kilometres

Population: 3,761,000

Ethnic Groups: Lithuanians (79.6%),

Russians (9.4%), Poles (7%), Belorussians (1.7%), Ukrainians (1.2%), Jews (0.3%)

Economic Structure: Industry and construction (42%), commerce and transportation (24%), service industry (21%), agriculture and forestry (13%)

Declaration of Independence: Recognition by the Soviet Union on September 6, 1991.

Vilnius (Wilna)

Vilnius, in German Wilna, in Polish Wilno and in Yiddish Vilne is located in the southeastern regions of Lithuania. Only 35 kilometres (22 miles) separate this capital city from the White Russian border. The centre of modern-day Vilnius extends along the broad Neris valley between the Medininku Hills on the left riverbanks and the Baltijos Hills on the right side of the river. The Neris River runs directly through this city surrounded by seven hills. Once this river meandered through the city, today, it flows through a canalized riverbed.

History

As soon as the *4th century,* the lovely area at the confluence of the Vilnia Stream and Neris River, the second largest river in the country, was inhabited – this is revealed by an almost seven metre (23 foot) depository layer at the base of Gediminas Mountain full of archaeological finds. Around 500 AD, the scattered settlements grew into a smaller city. The chronicles of the capital of Vilnius begins with the *Message of the Gediminas* in 1323. At that time, the Lithuanian Grand Duke called on merchants, architects, masons and painters together: they were to build his "new" capital city – in return he offered tracts of land and subsidies... In 1395, the *Teutonic Knights* attacked the newly founded city. This was to prove futile: naturally protected on three sides by the Neris and Vilnia, surrounded by seven hills, secured through the mighty fortress on Mount Gediminas and a fortification wall around the lower city (the city of merchants and craftsmen) the aggressive soldiers of God were never able to take the city.

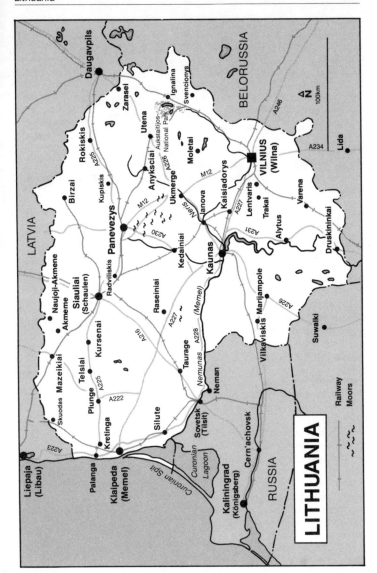

When Lithuania became Catholic in 1387, the "royal city" was awarded the *city rights of Magdeburg*. Cast iron factories and blacksmiths, paper manufacturers and mills made Vilnius renowned beyond the borders of Lithuania.

In 1525, *Franziskus Skorina* founded a printing house and published the oldest Russian books (The Acts of the Apostles). In 1562, postal carriages ran regularly from Vilnius via Krakow to Vienna and Venice. It was especially trade with Russia – Moscow, St. Petersburg and Kiev – which brought prosperity to the city.

In 1597, the Jesuits founded the University of Vilnius. During the 16th century, Vilnius was considered one of the largest cities in Eastern Europe with a population between 25 and 30 thousand. In 1648, it was around 175 hectares (438 acres) within its three kilometres (2 miles) of city walls, secured through nine gates. Today, the city encompasses an area of 263.4 square kilometres (102.7 square miles) – however, only around a third of that is built up.

The golden age of this city ended in the 17th century: *plague epidemics* and several fires brought the population down to around one-half of its former size; during the *Great Northern War*, the Swedes plundered the city. In 1812, *Napoleon's* army attacked the city on their way back from Russia and pillaged, set fires and destroyed. With uprisings, the impoverished populace protested the *oppression in Czarist Russia* - the czar's soldiers brutally shot down the rebels. The German *Wehrmacht* oc-

Legend
1. St. Stanislaus Cathedral
2. St. Anne's Church
3. Church of the Bernardines
4. St. Michael's Church
5. University
6. St. John's Church
7. Observatory
8. University Library
9. Alumnato rumai
10. "Senasis Rusys" Restaurant
11. Memorial Marker
12. Dramos Teatras (Dramatic Theatre)
13. Hotel "Vilnius"
14. Parliament
15. Ausros Gate
16. St. Theresa's Church
17. Basilius Monastery
18. St. Casimir Church
19. Art Museum
20. St. Dvasios Church
21. St. Nicholas Church
22. Reformed Protestant Church
23. Church of St. Peter and St. Paul
24. Opera and Ballet
25. St. Raphael's Church and Monastery

cupied the city from 1915 to 1919 during the *First World War*. In February of 1918, *Antanas Smetona* declared *Lithuania's independence*. During the same year, the Communist Party was founded. During their first party convention in December, they demanded that the conciliatory government under *Vincas Kapsukas* form the Lithuanian-Belorussian Soviet Republic of "Litbel." When the Poles occupied the Vilnius region in 1939, Kaunas became the provisional capital of bourgeois Lithuania. At

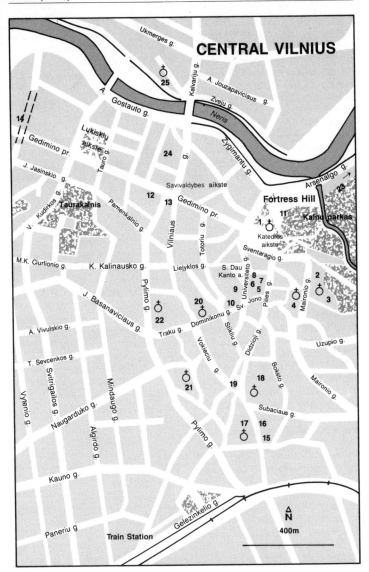

CENTRAL VILNIUS

Ukmerges g.
Kalvariju g.
A. Jouzapaviciaus g.
A. Gostauto g.
Zveju g.
Neris
Zygimantu g.
Arsenalgo g.
Gedimino pr.
J. Jasinskio g.
Lukiskiu aikste
Tauro g.
Savivaldybes aikste
Fortress Hill
Kalnu parkas
Kudirkos g.
Taurakalnis
Pamenkalnio g.
Gedimino pr.
Katedros aikste
V.
M.K. Ciurlionio g.
K. Kalinausko g.
Vilniaus g.
Totoriu g.
Sventaragio g.
S. Dau Kanto a.
Universiteto g.
Pylimo g.
Liejyklos g.
Sv. Jono g.
Pilies g.
Maironio g.
J. Basanaviciaus g.
Traku g.
Dominikonu g.
Sv. Jono
Siklu g.
A. Vivulskio g.
Vokieciu g.
Dizdzioji g.
Uzupio g.
T. Sevcenkos g.
Svitrigailos g.
Mindaugo g.
Pylimo g.
Boksto g.
Maironio g.
Subaciaus g.
Vyenio g.
Naugarduko g.
Algirdo g.
Kauno g.
Paneriu g
Train Station
Gelezinkelio g.
N
400m

14

25

24

12   13

1   11

23

8   7
9   6   5
10

2
4   3

20

22

21

19   18

17   16
15

that time, Vilnius bore the epithet "Lith-uanian Jerusalem." In 1897, the city had a Jewish population of 63,831 (41.5%); in 1923, there were still 55,000 Jews (41%). In 1939, the pro-portion of Jews sank to 28%. The communities around the synagogue were enlightened and politically ac-tive: in 1897, the General Jewish La-bour Party of Vilnius was founded.

When the German troops once again marched into the city in 1941, the hol-ocaust began. Night for night, the Jewish citizens living in the ghettos were deported: in the Paneriai Forest southwest of the city, over 100,000 Jews were systematically murdered in 1941, the corpses dumped into mass graves. In July 1945, the *Red Army* "liberated" the city. The Nazi terror was followed by Stalin's mass deportations. The systematic *Sovieti-zation* of the city is evidenced by massive industrial contamination and monotonous cement apartment houses with the character of bunkers which throttle the inner city. The core of Vilnius is composed of the Sena-miestis (Old City) and the Naujamie-stis (New City) with apartment and administrative buildings from the turn of the century. The district of Turnis-kes, a former residential area of the communist nomenclature, located 15 kilometres (9½ miles) to the north of the city on the Neris River, is now home to the political elite and foreign ambassadors. The old city district of Uzupis on the Neris is called simply "Harlem" by the locals. Newer resi-dential areas were built predominant-ly on the city's periphery. Old wooden houses would be torn down

(in Antakalnis, Zrimunai), open spaces were built up in cement (Lazdy-nai, Karoliniskes, Baltupiai, Seskine). From Gediminas Hill, it is especially interesting to see how green areas separate the suburbs from the actual city. Architects were awarded the prestigious Lenin prize for the Lazdy-nai apartment complex in 1974. "One feels the concern for the people" was to be heard in the laudatio.

The glasnost and perestroika epoch was "responsible" for the develop-ment from 1987 to date in Lithuania as well. On the anniversary of the Hitler-Stalin Pact (August 23), more than 3,000 citizens gathered in Vil-nius for a demonstration. With the establishment of the Lithuania Re-form Movement *Sajudis* goals and expectations were manifested. Their representatives emerged of the first free elections in 1990 as the clear victors. Their chairman *Vytautas Landsbergis* proclaimed the *Independ-ent Republic of Lithuania* on March 11, 1990. However, it was first after the coup against Gorbachev in au-tumn of 1991 was unsuccessful that the Soviet Union recognized this in-dependence on September 8, 1991).
→ *History/Lithuania*

Walking Tours of the City
I. The Old City
The *Katedros aikste* (Cathedral Square), called Gediminas Square from 1951 to 1990, is the pulsing heart of the city. The streets radiate from this square, buzzing with traffic night and day. The lower castle of the

Lithuanian princes once stood here. Under the cement slab on this square are the walls of this old residence. Foundations of the Bishop's Palace as well as those of churches, monasteries and sacred heathen sites reveal that the political and religious power lay adjacent to each other. At the beginning of the 19th century, the marketplace was remodelled under the Russian czar. The last remnants of the castle and the former merchants' and craftsmen's houses were razed. The famous annual market of Vilnius of St. Casimir was held here as well up to 1904. Since flooding often hindered the activity, the city had the market moved to Lukiskiu aikste, once called Lenin Square.

After the high waters of the Neris once more flooded the square in 1941, the Cathedral Square was raised as commissioned by the city in 1941, laid out in a strict square and paved with cement slabs. Buildings from the 19th and 20th centuries line the square, among them numerous administrative buildings and the central telegraph office. In the southeastern portion, a memorial stands in commemoration of the 650th anniversary of Vilnius in 1973. In the centre of the square, the *Sv. Stanislovo Basilica* (St. Stanislaus Cathedral) rises up to the sky. Originally, this was the site of a small stone church: in 1387, Grand Duke *Jogaila* had commissioned a Gothic church, to architecturally document Lithuania's conversion to Catholicism. After a fire in 1419, a Gothic, but larger church with three naves and Gothic arches was commissioned by Prince *Vytautas*. The first reconstruction of the

church commenced one hundred years later, led by an Italian architect. During the course of the subsequent centuries, the church was repeatedly rebuilt after having been destroyed by wars and fires – thus, it was given Renaissance, baroque and classicistic elements. Still, the church threatened to collapse in the middle of the 18th century: wide cracks were in the main façade and western apse. When a tower collapsed in 1769 resulting from an autumn storm, the cathedral was closed immediately due to safety considerations. A young Lithuanian architect won the competition for the reconstruction. *Laurynas Stuoka-Gucevicius,* having just returned from the customary Grand Tour through Europe and to Paris, only retained the floor-plan during his reconstruction work: the Gothic core was given a strict classicistic façade. The reconstruction work began in 1783 and lasted almost 20 years. After the death of Stuoka-Gucevicius, *Michael Schultz* completed the enormous project in 1801. The cathedral was given its present-day form of a Greek temple. This "heathen" style of architecture pointed back to the cathedral's origins – the god of thunder Perkunas was once venerated on the site of the cathedral. Used during the Soviet regime as an art museum, the cathedral became a symbol of the National Awakening and was consecrated anew on February 5, 1989 as the first church of Lithuania.

The front is embellished with an impressive columned hall 20 metres (65 feet) high. Six baroque sculptures by the Italian sculptor *Tomasso Righi* stand in the niches: Abraham, the four evangelists and Moses. The gable relief shows Noah and his family; above the entry portal are scenes from the lives of the apostles. Columns also ornament the symmetrical façades. In the niches on the southern side are sculptures of the Lithuanian dukes; on the northern sides, of the apostles and saints. The interior has remained virtually unchanged for centuries.

Two rectangular rows of columns subdivide the church in three naves of equal size. To the right in the shadows of the cathedral is an architectural jewel: the *St. Casimir Chapel*. The square sanctuary in the southeastern portion of the cathedral was built in honour of the Lithuanian prince *Kazimieras* (Casimir; 1458-1484). While the architect is unknown, the interior was built in cooperation with the Italian architect *Constantino Tencalla*. The chapel was adapted to the baroque architecture of that time in 1692. Decorative elements and ornaments of light plaster were added, domes and walls with allegorical scenes from the life of the pious prince (who was canonized posthumous in 1602) were painted. Two valuable frescoes embellish the side walls: "the opening of the grave of St. Casimir" and "the miracle at the grave of St. Casimir." Also worth seeing are the *Gostautu Chapel* with its grave stones from the 16th century as well as the baroque *Valaviciu Chapel*. The organ, first documented in the 16th century, was rebuilt by the Lithuanian organ builder *Juozapas Radavicius* in 1889 and restored in 1969 by the organ specialists from the Potsdam firm Alexander Schuke.

Slightly askew, the cathedral *clock tower* also called the bell tower, rises up to the heavens. The tower was built on the foundations of a former fortress tower which was once a part of the lower fortress walls. In 1963, during archaeological excavations at a depth of one metre (3¼ feet), an even older foundation from the 13th century was discovered. The rectangular base extends down to a depth of four metres (13 feet). Since the tower has an archway, archaeologists assume that the land here must have been around five metres lower during the Middle Ages than it is today. The upper octagonal portion of the tower with two window openings was built up in two stages in 1522; the uppermost clock portion dates back to the end of the 16th century. After the bell tower had burned to the ground several times during the course of the centuries, the upper portion was covered with an eight metre (26 foot) pyramid crowned by a five metre (16 foot) cross. Thus, the tower reaches its present-day height of 57 metres (187 feet). The tower clock was built during the 17th century. The mechanism of today was created in 1803 by the local clock maker *Jozefas Bergmann*. The 728 kilogramme (1,470 pound) masterpiece is driven by three weights which hang down to the base on cables. Those who try to read the exact time from the four golden faces will find themselves staring up quite baffled: the clock shows only the hour. The small bells, poured in 1758 by the German

G. Mörk signal each quarter hour; the large bell, made in 1673 by the Dutchman *J. Delamar* rings at each full hour. In 1967, 17 additional bells of various sizes were installed. During the following year, the clock tower with a carillon would follow – today, the melody serves as the jingle for Lithuanian radio.

The Pilies gatve, now blocked off to traffic, leads to the old city. This street, which was renamed Gorki Street under Soviet rule, is a reminder of the old name Great Fortress Street: one of the oldest streets of the city, it connected the Vilnius fortified castles with the centre of the city, City Hall Square. To the left, a small archway leads to *Bernadinu gatve* (named Pilies-Skersi-gatvis under the Soviets), a typical alleyway of old Vilnius. On house number 11 is a commemorative plaque of the University of Vilnius in memory of *Adam Mickiewicz*. He, the most famous Polish poet, lived and worked here for a few months during the spring and summer of 1822. At the end of the alleyway is the Maroniu gatve with the *Sv. Onos Church* (St. Anna's Church; No. 8). A quote by Napoleon made this Gothic church famous: he wanted to carry the church to Paris in his hand, is what the Frenchman said enthusiastically. Only speculations as to the appearance of the first St. Anna's Church remain – the original structure burned to the ground. It is unknown whether construction took place from 1520 to 1572 or 1581, but what is certain is that St. Anna's was built by unknown architects during the reign of *King Zymunt August*. For

this reason its value in architectural history is undisputed: the church is considered a climax in the Gothic religious architecture in Lithuania. During construction of the 19 by 8.7 metre (62 by 28 foot) church, sooner a smaller structure, 33 different types of bricks were used in the façade.

Leaving an especially plastic impression is the western façade with its slender turrets of equal length. The plain interior is somewhat of a disappointment after seeing the impressive exterior: the entire interior was damaged by fire. For this reason, the baroque altar from the 17th century and portions of the vaulting do not match the Gothic architecture of this church. The neo-Gothic belfry was also added to the church in 1874 by *Nikolai Tschagin*. In 1469, the Franciscan monks came to Vilnius via Poland. They were given a plot of land near the fortress at the bend in the Vilnia River. When the wooden ensemble comprising a church and monastery burned down at the end of the 15th century, the Bernardines built a new stone church. As soon as 1500, the first cracks appeared in the façade, shortly thereafter, the vaulting collapsed. Only the choir and sacristy remained undamaged. Led by the royal architect *Michael Enkinger* a new church was built on the foundations in 1516. Consecrated in 1520, the *St. Bernard Church* was, according to early travel reports, one of the most beautiful and largest buildings in the city. The church integrated into the fortifications of the city as a fortified church, it makes a dark and stern impression even today. Portly beams support the thick walls, the rectangular towers seem squat, gun slits protrude from under the roof of the northern façade. Four pairs of octagonal columns subdivide the area of the church (42 metres/137 feet in length and 24 metres/78 feet in width) into three naves of equal sizes and a height of 22.5 metres (74 feet).

The 20 metre (65 foot) choir ends in an apse. Narrow, high windows and banisters emphasize the "Gothic aspiration to the heavens." Baroque elements can be found on the gables of the façade and the tips of the ancillary towers. The high altar in the central nave was created by a Lithuanian artists in 1720. The twelve side altars were carved by the Italian craftsman *Daniel Giotto* from 1766 to 1784. The octagonal bell tower, not very tall at a height of only 37 metres (121 feet) makes a lighter and finer impression with its embellishments made from ten different types of bricks in comparison to the church – and the tower was even built at the same time as the church. Adjacent to the church on the northern side is the *monastery*. Originally two storeys equipped with colonnades for processions, an additional storey was added to the medieval building during the 19th century. The monastery was closed in 1864. During the Socialist era, the rooms housed the national art academy.

Across from St. Anna's Church at Volano gatve 13, the *Sv. Mykolo Church* (St. Michael's Church) was built from 1594 in the style of the Lubinian Renaissance. The church was commissioned by *Lew Sapieha*, chancellor of the Grand Duchy of Lithuania, who also had the adjacent Bernardine Convent built to the south side of the church. While the convent began operation in 1604, the church was first completed in 1625 under the direction of the mason *Jonas Kajetka*. Only thirty years after the structure was completed, it burned down. Reconstruction lasted up to 1633. In 1703, new colonnades were added and the bell tower above the entry gate was built in 1715. The wall which shields the church from the street today dates back to 1874. Due to the lengthy period of construction, the interior is from the Renaissance. In the northern nave with a length of 30 metres (98 feet) and a width of 13.5 metres (44 feet) is the sacristy.

To the left of the altar, one can enter the family mausoleum of Lew Sapieha and his two wives. The mausoleum is embellished with multi-coloured marble and a wealth of sculpted ornamentations. The mummified corpses lay one floor lower in the catacombs. The church has served as a museum of architecture since 1972. However, the congregation and religious leaders hope that it will soon fulfil its original purpose once again.

The picturesque alleyway near the church leads back to Pilis gatve. The buildings on the right-hand side of the street are already part of the *University*. One can reach the large *University Courtyard* by going through a gateway at house number 15/17/19. The university, founded in 1579 as "Alma Mater Vilnensis" by the privileged Grand Duke *Steponas Batoras* as the successor of the Jesuit Seminary, began higher education with

500 students. For two hundred years, the university was under the control of the Jesuit order, who determined education in Lithuania.

In the opinion of the fathers, the university should serve the church and combat reformatory ideas. For this reason, the subjects offered were philosophy and theology. Juris prudence was to follow in 1641; medicine, only after the abolition of the Jesuit order in 1773. The duration of study for the office of priest was twelve years. To elevate the prestige of the alma mater, the Jesuits called upon numerous leading minds of that time to teach at their university. After the Order was abolished in 1773, its possessions and schools became property of the state. In 1781, the university was renamed as the "institution of higher education in the Grand Duchy of Lithuania." After annexation of Lithuania by the Russians (1795) the czar confirmed the status of the university. On April 4, 1831 the university was renamed in "Imperial University of Vilnius." The expansion of the subjects offered to include Agriculture, Engineering, Diplomacy and Statistics caused the student body to double in size. After the Polish uprising against the czarist regime, *Czar Nicholas* dissolved the university on May 1, 1832. The provisionally faculties of Medicine and Theology continued to operate and were restructured as academies of Medicine and Surgery and the Theological Academy. In 1842, the medical school was moved to Kiev; in 1844, theology was moved to St. Petersburg. A secondary school moved

into the university building. As the Polish Stephan Bathory University, teaching was continued from 1919 to 1939. After the Red Army marched into Vilnius, the university remained open up to 1943 with a number of interruptions until it was ultimately closed in October and the undesirable professors, deported to concentration camps. One year later, the sciences "returned." During winter semester in 1944/45, over 1,000 students were registered. In 1955, on the 75th birthday of *Vincas Kapsukas,* the old university was given the honorary name of the co-founder of the Lithuanian Communist Party. In its 414th year of existence, the once oldest university in the former Soviet Union was simply called "University of Vilnius." Just as impressive as the list of scientists who worked at the alma mater is the list of its partner universities: Greifswald, Carl's University in Prague, University of Krakow, Technical University of Marburg, University of Brazzaville Congo, and Koshut University in Debrecen, Hungary. The collection of old university buildings comprises an extensive complex with inner courtyards and buildings from the 16th to 20th centuries. The large courtyard from the 17th century, built in honour of the first rector of the University *Petras Skarga* (1536-1612) was called Skarga Court earlier is characterized by Mannerism, the transition from the Renaissance to the Baroque period. The courtyard is surrounded on three sides by yellow three-storey buildings with arcades. The main entrance to the university is located in the two-storey classicistic building with the Latin inscription "Alma Mater Vilnensis." The columned hall on the second floor is used as an assembly and celebration hall. The fourth edge of the courtyard is the site of the magnificent façade and bell tower of the *Sv. Jonas Church*. Construction on this Gothic church began in 1387, which was then given to the Jesuits by Zygmunt August in 1571. With the abolition of the order in 1773, the church became the property of the university. The late-baroque church which stands here today dates back to the restorations after the massive fire of 1737. Under the Soviets, the church was transformed into a museum for scientific thought. Church services have been held once again in this church as of October 1991. Portraits of famous academians and scientists still decorate the walls. The main altar is a composite of ten altars and is very much worth seeing. Originally, 13 side altars from the 18th century, formerly on the supporting beams of the dome, were destroyed during remodelling around 1820.

Around the end of the 19th century, busts and commemorative plaques were exhibited for personalities who proved themselves deserving at the Vilnius University – for example, the poet *Adam Mickiewicz,* the author *Simonas Daukantas* and the composer *Stanislav Moniuszko.*

Through a gateway across from St. John's Church, one will reach the small inner courtyard of the *Observatory.* The former building of the astronomic observatory on the right-hand side of the courtyard is crowned with two cylindrical towers – from their domes, the heavenly bodies were once observed. The façade from the last quarter of the 18th century was designed by the professor of Architecture at the university, *Martin Knackfuß,* and shows a relief of the twelve astrological signs on its broad façade. Returning to the larger courtyard, a passageway to the left of St. John's Church leads to the *Mykolas Sarbievijus Courtyard* and from there, farther to the smaller courtyards of the university. One of the oldest university buildings houses the *Universiteto Biblioteka* (University Library; Universiteto 3, Tel: 61 06 16). The oldest library in the country, it was founded in 1570 by the Jesuit seminary in Vilnius and with 4,500,000 volumes it has the largest collection of old Lithuanian books. Also among its collections: 180,000 manuscripts from the 13th to 16th centuries. The extensive cartographic collection with over 4,000 specimens has 740 old atlases. No wonder that the enormous library in the white hall was considered one of the best libraries in Europe during the 16th century. The entrance to the library is on *S. Daukanto aikste.*

The small triangular plaza is dominated by a two-storey *palace* from the end of the 18th century. This former residence of the Bishop of Vilnius was declared the seat of the Russian Governor General after Lithuania was annexed. At the beginning of the 19th century, extensive remodelling followed according to the plans by the Governor's architect *Karl Schildhaus;* later, the opulent

What may appear strange to visitors is an everyday sight for the Balts: the Hill of Crosses in Siauliai Lithuania

A national monument with special meaning for the Lithuanians: the medieval fortress of Trakai

Historical architecture in Klaipeda: built in 1857, this theatre was recently renovated

building was changed once more according to the plans of the St. Petersburg architect *Wassili Stassov*. In 1975, the interior restorations were concluded. Since then, concerts often take place in five halls in the palace. More impressive than the façade facing the square is the side toward the park. In the courtyard is still the booth for the honorary guard. Also used for concerts now is the *Bonifrater Church* from the 17th and 18th centuries. The "small baroque hall," equipped with a new organ in 1976, can accommodate an audience of up to one hundred for organ and chamber music concerts.

Above the Dominikonu gatve past the *Alumnato rumai,* an aristocratic palace from the 17th and 18th centuries, one will quickly reach Sv. Ignoto gatve where the "Senasis Rusys" (= old wine cellar) Restaurant is an inviting place to stop for a break. Returning to Cathedral Square, one can reach Lielyklos gatve and L. Stukos gatve within only a few minutes.

II. The Polit-Promenade: from the Upper Fortress to the Parliament

The Lithuanian national flag flutters in red, yellow and green atop the Gedinimas tower on Fortress Hill. From Katedros aikste, a gradually ascending sand trail leads up to the 48 metre (157 foot) *Pilies Kalns* (Fortress Hill). At an elevation of 142 metres (464 feet) above sea level, the Upper Fortress once protected the city here. Its ruins from the 14th and 15th centuries are presently being restored. The landmark of Vilnius is the well-preserved western tower, better known as *Gediminas Tower.* Its three octagonal storeys rest on a massive, rectangular foundation. The tower, almost 20 metres (65 feet) high today was originally one storey higher with a pointed tiled roof. A narrow spiral staircase leads by a small *Museum for the History of the Fortress and the City* (→ *Museums)* to the actual attraction, the observation platform at a height of 20 metres (65 feet). Admission for the panorama must be paid in the museum. A compass card provides information on the sights below. A greenbelt was laid out all around the fortress at the end of the 19th century. In commemoration of the 100th birthday of the poet *Alexander Puschkin* this park was named after him in 1899. The memorial unveiled in 1900, destroyed during the First World War, has been replaced with a new statue by the sculptor *Bronius Vysniauskas* since 1955. Crossing the Katedros aikste (→ *Tour I)* continue to *Gediminio prospektas.* This bustling, main axis of the city had several names over the years: from the Russian "Katedralnaja" to the Polish "Mickiewicza" to the Lithuanian "Mickeviciaus"; from the postwar names "Laisves (Freedom) prospektas," to the "Stalino prospektas" and "Lenino prospektas." Today, the street which connects the three large squares Katedros aikste, Savivaldybes aikste and Luiskiu aikste is once again named after the founding father of Vilnius. Those who stroll along the boulevard should not only pay attention to the façades of the businesses and the Art Nouveau houses but also glance at the ground: occasionally one will spot old sewer covers with the German inscription "Magistrat M. Wilna."

Three black robed figures with golden faces signal the *Dramos Teatras* on the left-hand side of the street. This theatre was founded in 1940 and seats 700.

Passing the main post office on the street leads to Savivaldybes aikste on the intersection of Vilniaus gatve. The Chernkakovski Square under the Soviets is flanked to the left by the "Universal," the largest department store in Vilnius; next to this, the time-honoured Hotel "Vilnius" where even the sign complements the cast iron lanterns at the entrance. A boulevard lined with lindens encircles *Lukiskiu aikste,* with an area of four hectares (10 acres), this is the largest square in the centre of the city. Eight footpaths lead to the centre of the square. Up to September 1991, a monumental sculpture of Lenin towered to the sky from the granite base, which had lent this square its name "Lenino aikste" since 1952. On the northern end of the square toward the Neris River are the *St. Jacob and St Phillip's Church* as well as the *Dominican Church* from the 17th century. The nearby clinical hospital no. 1, one of the oldest hospitals in Vilnius has been in operation since 1723.

Beyond Lukiskiu Square, on which weekly markets took place since 1904 is the governmental district with several ministries and the national library. Long after independence, the Lithuanian citizens army guarded the parliament building, and the high tank barriers made of cement slabs and the sand bags inside the building are a reminder of the shots fired in 1991. Directly before independence was achieved, the barbed wire fence which surrounded the parliament was similar to a type of wailing wall: with irate protest, accusatory photographs, written requests and red roses, the citizens supported the struggle for independence in their own way. "Gorbi = Hussein" was written on one poster, and "Freedom for the Baltics" on another. A tree trunk was transformed into a stake for the Communist Party: piles and piles of party pins, old medals and badges of rank were discarded here. A plain cement bridge spans the multi-lane motorway surrounding the city. Beyond it, the silver domes of the Russian Orthodox *Maria Manifestation Church* from 1903.

III. From Trains to the Baroque

From the train station surrounded by a dense group of stands and street merchants selling candy, fruits and all kinds of stuff, it is only a few steps on the Gelhinkelio gatve to the southern edge of town with the *Ausros Gate* also called the "Medininkai Gate" or "Ostra brama" (= pointed gate). The only of nine city gates which is still standing today, the "Gate of Dawn" was built by *Jonas Skydelis* as the southern gateway to the city when approaching from the town of Medininkai. The chapel in the interior of the old gate tower is one place of prayer for the city's Catholic population. The wondrous *Mother of God picture,* painted on oak by an unknown Renaissance master is framed in silver. Since the mother of God is depicted without the Christ child or any other artifacts, art critics assume that this is a secular portrait – probably of the Lithuanian Princess *Barbora Radvilaite* (1520-1551). Carmelite monks consecrated the icons in the 17th century. Since then thousands of Catholics pilgrim to them. The stairway to the chapel is on Ausros vartu gatve behind a wooden door across from house number 19. In the classicistic chapel from the 18th century, church services are held regularly. Continuing down Ausros vartu gatve, an early baroque church stands to the right, this is the *Sv. Theresia* (St. Theresa Church).

This three-naved basilica was built from 1635 to 1650, presumably according to the plans of *Constantino Tencalla* or *Ulrik*. The three-storey bell tower was built next to the presbyterium in 1783. Cloisters, built by *Pietro Rossi* in 1789 connect the church with its small chapel. An archway leads a few steps farther down to a small inner courtyard with the pink *Sv. Dvasios Cerkve* (Church of the Holy Ghost; Ausros Vartu 10).

This, the most significant orthodox church in Lithuania was presumably built in the middle of the 17th century for the Russian-Orthodox population and is now the seat of the archbishop. While exterior changes during the 18th and 19th centuries destroyed the original appearance of the building, the baroque interior is definitely worth seeing. This is the final resting place of the martyrs Antonius, Ivan and Eustachius, who were executed by Prince *Algirdis* in 1937 for their belief. The three saints wear white during the Christmas season, black during the spring and red clothing the rest of the year.

The building to the left of the square housed a monastery in the 16th century, to which a school, hospital and printing house belonged as well. Ornate and interesting façades line the *Ausros vartu gatve* - one example is at "Restoranas Medininkai" (No. 8) a quaint restaurant in the old city with a nice inner courtyard, and house number 4, the former home of the composer *A. Kacanauskas*. On the opposite side of the street is the art gallery "Arka" and the adjacent "Arka Café," where students meet in the courtyard from 11 am to 11 pm for coffee and cognac. Next to this is the gate to the *Basilius Monastery,* built in 1761 by *Johann Gaubitz.* A cobblestone alleyway leads gradually up to the *Svenciausios Trejybes bazinica.* The Unitarian church in the inner courtyard surrounded by university buildings, like for example the electrotechnical department. Returning to Ausros vartu gatve, the street leads past a stately *city palace* from the 17th and 18th centuries, now housing the music school (Didzioji gatve 34), to *Sv. Kazimiero* (St. Casimir Church). The first baroque church in Vilnius, an opulent and lavish structure in pink, is dedicated to the Lithuanian patron saint. During the construction of this church from 1604 to 1615 according to plans by *Jan Prochowicz,* the Jesuits had this built after their main church Il Gesu in Rome. Therefore, a "Roman cross" forms the floor-plan: there, where the side naves cross the long middle nave, a 40 metre (131 foot) high and 17 metre (56 foot) wide dome accentuates the centre of the church – a completely new type of church for Vilnius at that time. The exterior is crowned with a golden dome – a sign of the royal origins of Casimir. The church, which depicts the powerful connection of church and state like no other church in Vilnius, became a popular object of persecution. Converted to the Russian-Orthodox St. Nicholas Church during the reign of the czar, an onion tower replaced the noble crown of the church. During the German occupation in the First World War, it was forced to be converted to Protestantism; from 1924, it was Catholic again and St. Casimir was then converted to a Museum for Atheism and Religious History in 1965. Masses in Lithuanian and Russian have been held here once more since 1988. Across from the church is Hotel "Astorija," a posh hotel. The impressive building housing the *National Philharmonic Orchestra,* built in 1902 as a municipal assembly hall for conferences, concerts and theatre performances experienced the premiere of the first Lithuanian opera "Biruta" by *Mikas Petrauskas* in 1906. On December 15, 1918, the national people's deputies convened here for its first meeting. It was only in 1940 that music would return. The Didzioji gatve leads to a large, elongated square. The southern side of this old marketplace is dominated by the building of the *Lietuvos Dailes Muzeijs* (Art Museum). Several steps lead up to the temple building, its entrance embel-

lished with 6 Dorian columns. The monumental classicistic structure (like the Cathedral) was built by *Laurynas Stuoka Gucevicius* around 1785 as a city hall. From 1845, the city theatre troupe performed here before the graphic arts moved in 1940. A *branch of the art museum* is at Vokieciu gatve 2 (formerly Muziejaus gatve): special exhibitions have been displayed here on 2,000 square metres (19,620 square feet) of floor space, special exhibitions have been shown since 1967 on the first floor. To the left-hand side of the former city hall is the beginning of *Stikliu gatve.* This narrow alleyway in the old city was beautifully renovated as a pilot project. It leads by the handicrafts shops, souvenir shops and simple but attracted city palaces from the 15th to 19th centuries to the Dominikonu gatve. The façade of the bookstore on the corner displays animal ornaments: a buck's head in a wreath of flowers is perched above several lions the heads of which are made of medallions. Those who are hungry should stop at "Restoranas Seasis rusys."

Down to the left, one will come to the Dominikonu gatve leading by the *Sv. Dvasios Church* from the 16th to 18th centuries to Vokieciu gatve, a broad commercial street with a green median. Due to the destruction during the Second World War, it is rather unattractive. House number 24, a typical old Vilnius house with two inner courtyards one behind the other, is the only bright spot on this street. Not far from here, the narrow Sv. Mikalojaus gatve leads to the oldest remaining church in Lithuania. *Sv. Mikalojaus* (St. Nicholas, Sv. Mikalojaus 4) was built in 1320 before the Christianization. Founded by German merchants, the Gothic Church simultaneously served as a warehouse.

Following the Siauliu gatve and the Mesiniu gatve, one will come to Ligonines gatve. Beyond the passageway near house number 9 is a bustling area – the large, elongated inner courtyard is lined with boutiques and shops. The steps at the opposite end lead up to Pylimo gatve. The main traffic artery of the old city leads from the train station to the river. The first Calvinistic church was built here in 1555, the *Evangelistu Reformatu baznycia* (Evangelical Reformed Church; Pylimo 29). The present-day reformed church (1830-1835) is considered one of the most beautiful examples of late classicism.

When the Soviets had the church closed in 1953, it was first used as an exhibition hall and later as a cinema. On January 1, 1990, the church was returned to the evangelical reformed congregation of Vilnius.

The *Sv. Petro ir Povilo* (St Peter and Paul's Church; Antakalnio 1) is best reached by bus from here. Built on the former sacred site for the heathen goddess Milde in the suburb of Antakalnis which was already settled at that time, this is one of Vilnius' main attractions: the church has hardly been changed from the period of high baroque. Located outside the city walls, the church never fell victim to fires or enemy attacks. Grand Duke *Michael Kazimieras Pacas* commissioned this church. The design

was the work of the Krakow architect *Jan Zaora*. After the cornerstone was laid on June 29, 1668, construction progressed quickly. When the Italian architect *Giovanni Baptist Frediani* took over the direction, construction on the main façade had already begun. The domes were completed in 1674 and 1675. The work on the interior followed in 1677, by the Italian sculptors *Pietro Petri* and *Giovanni Maria Galli.*

After the death of the financier Pacas in 1682, construction was halted at the beginning of 1686. Even the interior work from 1691 to 1704 by the sculptors *Andrea Sanctini Capone* and *Giovani Pensa* was to remain a fragment, the main altar, paintings and reliefs unfinished. During the restoration of the church at the beginning of the 19th century, the baroque structure was augmented with two smaller altars. The baroque view of life as a theatre of the world characterizes the opulent interior. Over 2,000 figures depicting people of differing occupations and origin are grouped in mythical or biblical scenes: shepherds and saints, the devil and heir to the throne in plaster; a skeleton shows the end of the path through life: from child to old man. In the wall to the right of the entrance, the inscription "Hic jacet pecator" marks the grave of the famous general Pacas, entombed in the wall. A legend arose in connection with the founding of the church: when originally a wooden church went up in flames during a war with Russia before his very eyes and Pacas only barely escaped death, he swore he would show his thanks for the divine salvation by building the most magnificent church in the city.

IV. Modern Vilnius

From Savivaldybes aikste, the Vilniaus gatve leads to the *Opera and Ballet Theatre* on the Neris riverbanks. The complex was built according to the plans of the Institute for Municipal Planning under the head architect *Nijole Buciute.* Granite, marble and red ceramic plates, copper, wood and glass embellish the reinforced concrete building before the cascades which gush down through a small green area. The house, opened in 1973 can accommodate an audience of up to 1,150 in the auditorium. The *Bridge,* built in 1952 on the site of the "green bridge" which was blown up in 1944, is ornamented with groups of figures created by Lithuanian sculptors. Passing the *St. Raphael Church and Monastery* a stairway leads up to the pedestrian zone. Planned during the 1960's as a cultural and shopping centre according to Soviet criteria, this is also the site of the largest "supply facility" in the city, the "Planetarium" department store. Towering 22 storeys high at the end of this Soviet shopping mile is the former "Intourist" Hotel with 650 beds. The Ukmerges gatve and Zveju gatve lead to the "Zalgris" sports complex. This *sports palace* opened in 1971 and was designed and built in the form of a ship by the architects *Eduardas Chlomauskas, Zigmas Liandzbergis, Jonas Kriukelis* the two engineers *Algimantas Katilius* and *Henrika Karvelis.*

In the highest portion of the "bow" is the grandstand for 2,876 spectators. The large sports hall, whose main arena has the area of three basketball courts (61 by 66 metres/200 by 216 feet) has a capacity of up to 6,000 spectators. In addition to sporting events, this is also used for pop concerts. In 1950, the "Zalgris" Stadium was completed with 20,000 seats. The ice palace was designed by Eduardas Chlomauskas. In 1978, the rowing training station was built on the banks of the Neris River.

V. Lazdynai – Exemplary Socialist City Planning

Above the right banks of the Neris River, around 6 kilometres (4 miles) from the city centre is Lazdynai.

In the middle of the 1960's, the local architects *Vytautas Cekanauskaus* and *Vytautas Bredikis* were commissioned to develop an open area of 174 hectares (435 acres) into a residential area for 40,000 people. The Kosmonautu prospektas divides this suburb in two portions of unequal size. The houses, on the other hand, are grouped in four residential complexes which are connected by the 3.5 kilometre (2¼ mile) ring street Architektu gatve. The shopping and cultural centre is on Erfurto gatve at the focal point of the residential complex. Due to the varying height of the buildings – five, nine, twelve and sixteen storeys – and the construction of fifteen different types of houses, the 10,000 apartments are supposed to make up an attractive, diverse residential district. The architects and construction workers were awarded the Lenin medal for by the Vilnius Construction Combine in 1974 for their exemplary architectural achievements in Lazdynai. The 326.5 metre (1,068 foot) television tower is on the border to the neighbouring district of Karolinskes, developed between 1971 and 1976 for an additional 44,000 people.

The lower portion of the highest television tower in Lithuania is built from reinforced concrete; the upper portion a metal spire. The base of the television tower is surrounded by maintenance buildings, and a maintenance platform in the shape of a bowl hangs at a height of 165 metres (540 feet). On the first level atop the tower is the observation platform and a café-bar; the upper two levels contain the technical equipment. A lift takes visitors to the top of the tower in less than one minute. Here, visitors will not only experience a fantastic view; a note also provides information on the total weight of the tower: 410 tonnes. In the night of January 13, 1991, the tower gained tragic fame: 14 unarmed Lithuanians were killed by OMON riflemen and tanks during the raid on the television tower (→ *History/Lithuania*).

VI. Jewish Vilnius

Up until the Second World War, Vilnius was called "The Jerusalem of the East." *Elijah ben Solomon,* the Gaon (spiritual leader) of Vilnius, had made the city into a centre for Jewish enlightenment (Haskala) – Warsaw did have the largest eastern Jewish population and Lodz, the largest Jewish trade centre, but Vilnius was home to the Jews with the most political ambition. In 1897, the Jewish-Socialistic World Union was founded.

Since 1991, David Smith leads the Jewish community of 5,500 as their new Rabbi. The Jewish population lived since the 1940's – almost five decades – without a religious leader. Smith, presently living in London, travels to Vilnius once a month. He holds services in the last remaining *Synagogue* (Pylimo 39) – in pre-war Vilnius there were 96 Jewish synagogues... The synagogue built in 1894 was spared the Nazi destruction and vandalism because of its beauty and was used as a warehouse for medications during the Soviet regime. Today, it is a place of prayer every day at 6 pm. Not far from the synagogue square, the Shulhoyfs, was once the Strashun Library.

Matityahu Strashun donated his collection of books to the congregation in the 19th century, a collection which ranks among the largest Jewish libraries in the world. In the ghetto, a broad education was highly valued: a Jewish secondary school, a technical school in which lessons were in Yiddish, several Yiddish primary schools and five daily Yiddish newspapers covered the need for information and education. Today, around 4,000 Jews still live in Vilnius.

Museums and Galleries

– *Artukerujos Bastionas,* Boksto 20/18, Tel: 61 21 49, open from 11 am to 7 pm. This bastion from the 17th century displays medieval cannons and armaments.

– *Lietuvos Dailes Muziejus* (Museum of Lithuanian Art): Didzioji 31, Tel: 62 86 79, open daily except Monday from noon to 6 pm.

– *Lietuvos Valstybinis Zydu Muziejus* (State Jewish Museum of Lithuania): Pamenkalnio 12, Pylimo 6, Tel: 61 58 77. Open from 9 am to 5 pm, closed during the weekend. The Jewish composed around 40% of the total population of Vilnius during the early 20th century. 94% were killed during the Second World War; around 40,000 of them in Paneriai.

– *Paneriu Muziejus* (Museum of the Jewish Genocide): Agrastu 15, Tel: 64 18 47; open Monday and Wednesday to Friday from 11 am to 6 pm.

– *Lietuvos Valstybes Muziejus* (Lithuanian National Museum): Studentu 8, Tel: 35 51 70; open from 11 am to 7 pm. This museum is housed in the former Revolutionary Museum and it brings the struggle for independence alive with barricades, fortification and other documentation. The heroes who died in this struggle are honoured in the "Hall of Fame." Also documented here are the mass-deportations which took place under Stalin.

– *Adam Mieckiewicz Memorial:* Bernadinu 11; open Fridays from 2 to 6 pm and Saturdays from 10 am to 20 pm. "Pan Tadeusz," the emphatic anthem praising Lithuania, which begins with "Oh my fatherland" has made Adam Mieckiesicz to the most widely known Polish-Lithuanian poet. The exhibition in this house, which was the residence of Mieckiewicz in 1822, is a tribute to his work and artistic development.

– *Taikomosios Dailes Muziejus* (Museum of Applied Art): Arsenalo 2, Tel: 22 18 13 and 62 80 80; open from 11 am to 7 pm, closed Mondays and Tuesdays. The spacious hall on the ground floor is reserved for German and French works: one can view porcelain and furnishings from the 14th to 19th century. Contemporary Lithuanian ceramics and tapestries are on the uppermost floor. In the cellar are excavations of the foundations of the first settlement in Vilnius.

– *Museum of Architecture:* Volano 1, Tel: 61 64 09 and 61 04 56; in St. Michael's Church. Open daily except Tuesdays from 11 am to 7 pm. The exhibition informs visitors about the development of architecture in Lithuania from 1918 to present.

– *Lietuvos Istorijos ir Etnografijos Muziejus* (Museum for History and Ethnography): Arsenalo 1, Tel: 62 77 74 and 62 94 21; open daily except Saturdays from 11 am to 7 pm. This museum was founded in 1855 and later closed by the Czar's troops. It has once more exhibited 270,000 archaeological specimens since 1967, shedding light on the ethnography and history of Lithuania.

– *Rysiu Muziejus* (Communications Museum): Pilies 23, Tel: 61 37 58; open Wednesday and Friday from 3 to 7 pm and Saturdays from 11 am to 2 pm.

– *Vilniaus Universiteto Mokslo Muziejus* (Museum of Science): Sv. Jono 12, Tel: 61 17 95. Open from 10 am to 6 pm except Mondays and Tuesdays. Murals of famous scientists in the Sv. Jono Church.

– *Puschkin Memorial:* Subaciaus 124, Tel: 69 00 80, open 11 am to 6 pm except Mondays and Tuesdays. Located somewhat outside of the city and built in 1867, this was formerly the residence of Puschkin's son Alexander. The building with its dark furnishings from the 19th century radiates peace and solitude. This poet's sitting room is just as impressive: nothing has been changed since the poets death. Puschkin planned the unsuccessful uprising against the czar in 1863 with his confidants, in the adjacent park with an area of 47 hectares (118 acres).

– *Radvilu Rumai:* Vilniaus 22, Tel: 22 01 66; open Wednesday to Sunday from noon to 8 pm. The museum is housed in the former City Palace of the Radziwill Families and sooner leaves the impression of a museum of ancestry: in one room alone, 165 members of this influential family look down from the walls onto the visitors below. The portraits, commissioned by Nicholas Kasimir Radziwill in the 18th century, all originate from one and the same painter. In addition to these, there are also etchings of Vilnius from the 18th century and on the upper floor are works by the Lithuanian exile artist Vytautas Kasuba.

– *Verkiai Palace Exhibition:* Turistu 49, Tel: 77 61 56; open Wednesday, Saturday and Sunday from 11 am to 6 pm. Neo-classicistic pomp and stately extravagance dictate the ambiance in this old bishop's palace. It's picturesque location atop a hill overlooking the Neris River adds to the attraction. Although the main building was destroyed, a visit to the remaining collection is still worth the trip (10 km/6¼ miles).

– *Vilnius Pilies Muziejus* (Castle Museum): Castle Hill, Tel: 61 74 35; open from 11 am to 6 pm, except Tuesdays. Seventy-four steps lead up into the tower from the 13th century. The collection exhibited here covers the history of this tower. At the top of the tower, an observatory platform offers visitors a panorama of the city.

– *Vilniaus planetariumas* (Planetarium): Ukmerges gatve 12a.

A Stop in the Park

– *Trijiu Kryziu Kalnas* (Three Crosses Hill): According to the legend, seven Franciscan monks were murdered at this site. Three were crucified and the other four, were tied to crosses and cast into the river. The first crosses in memory of these martyrs were erected in the 17th century. Under Stalin's rule, they were dismantled and on June 14, 1989, the memorial could be rebuilt according to the old plans. In addition to the function as a memorial, these crosses symbolize the hope of the populace.

– *Kalnu Park:* Located at the foot of the Hill of Crosses, adjacent to the Sereikiskiu Parkas. This hilly park with old trees is transversed by the Dainu valley in which dance festivals and rock concerts take place.

– *Sereikiskiu Park:* Formerly the Jaunimo (Youth) Park. Bordered by the old city and the Altarijos Hill, this is Vilnius' oldest park. In the 15th century, it belonged to the Benedictine monks from the nearby monastery who tended fruit and vegetable gardens here. From the end of the 18th century to the middle of the 19th cen-

The Cemeteries of Vilnius – Definitely Worth a Visit

The last resting places of Vilnius are definitely worth seeing – especially for the impressive old gravestones, the memorials and the pictures of the deceased or the white benches used for silent dialogue with the deceased. The cemeteries are open from April 1 to September 30 from 8 am to 8 pm; from October 1 to March 30, from 9 am to 10 pm.

– *Rasu Cemetery (Rossa):* The pantheon of Lithuanian personalities was laid out as a cemetery in 1801.

Atop a rise surrounded by oaks, birches and pines are also the graves of Polish politicians and prominent artists. Buried within the 10 hectare (25 acre) complex are the poets *Vladyslav Syrokomla* and *Ludvik Kondratowicz* as well as the graves of the painter *Franciszek* and the historian *Joachim Lelewel*. In a separate military cemetery under a black granite slab is the gravesite of the Polish national hero Marshall *Josef Pilsudski* (1867-1935).

Patriotic Lithuanians are also attracted to other graves, like to that of the composer *Mikalojus Konstantinas Ciurlionis* and that of the author and journalist *Jonas Basanavicius*. The capacity of this cemetery is meanwhile exhausted. No one has been buried here since 1967. A small pamphlet provides information on the history and location of the more than 200 graves.

– *Saules Cemetery* (Saules 1) is famous for its beautiful view of Vilnius.

– *Antakalnis Cemetery:* Kariu Kapu 11, Tel: 74 05 87. The cemetery is also called "Soldiers' Cemetery" by the local residents. The first soldiers to be buried here were those who fell during the First World War. Later, German, Russian, Polish and Lithuanian soldiers who also lost their lives in war would follow. The area for Soviet soldiers in the heart of the cemetery is still used by the Red Army. Death united all opponents: honoured Communists like Anatas Sniekus lies here united with the victims of the January Uprisings and the seven Lithuanian border guards who were shot by Red Army riflemen on July 31, 1991.

– *Bernadinu Cemetery:* Zvirgzdyno 3, Tel: 22 06 79. The cemetery of the Bernardine monks was laid out at an idyllic location along the river in 1810. Even after the secularization of the monastery in 1864, the cemetery retained its old name – despite its conversion into a public park. Especially worth seeing here is the "Columbinarium" the only remaining grave site memorial from the early 19th century.

tury, this was the site of the University's botanical gardens. In 1864, the park was placed under municipal administration which opened access to the public. Today, this park is very popular with the residents of Vilnius. It is also equipped with a playground and tennis courts.

– *Burbiskiu Park:* Burbiskiu 5, Tel: 26 48 75. In this park, located near the Paneriai Forest, wooden carvings line the walking and jogging paths.

– *Pasaku Park:* This fairy-tale park in the Karolioniskes district is especially popular with children. Large wooden statues portray Lithuanian legends and fairy tales.

– *Vingis Park:* The pine forest measuring 395 hectares (988 acres), makes up the largest woodland park in the city. Located in the western portion of Vilnius, it extends along the meandering Neris River which borders this park on three sides. The park was first mentioned in historical documents as early as the 16th century. As reported in anecdotes, Czar Alexander is said to have heard of the invasion of Napoleon at a ball which took place in this park in 1812. The main entrance to the park lies on the Ciurlionio gatve. In 1947, the first National Song Festival was held here. A large "Estrada" was built after the prototype in Tallinn for the 20,000 singers, dancers and musicians who gather here every five years. A miniature pioneer railroad will draw the attention of the younger visitors; adults will be attracted by the botanical gardens that the University of Vilnius planted here in 1920. The summer restaurant Lakstinagala (Tel: 63 14

87, open from 11 am to 11 pm) is a nice place to stop for a break.

Sports and Recreation

Culture and Recreation Centre: Operated by the Ministry of the Interior.
Hot-Air Ballooning: Laisves Balionu Klubas, Conelaicio 20-3, Tel: 63 75 42, Fax: 62 48 72. Robertas Kozma offers tours in his red, white and blue striped hot-air balloon.
Swimming: outdoor pool, Atviras plaukiomo baseinas, Rinktines 3/19, Tel: 35 10 13; indoor pool, Vandens sporto rumai, Erfurtas 13, Tel: 26 90 41 and 26 90 30.
Tennis: Tennis-Club "Zalgiris," Barbors Radvilaites 6, Tel: 61 25 34; open daily from 7 am to 10 pm, ten cinder and one artificial grass court.
Cultural and Sports Hall of the Ministry of the Interior: Sporto 21, Tel: 75 10 30; open during the summer from 10 am to 10 pm. Four cinder courts.

Shopping

Amber: Amber, Austros vartu 9.
Antiques: Antikvariantiniu Daiktu Komisas, Dominikonu 14, Tel: 62 40 71; Antikvarine Komiso, Mesiniu 5, Tel: 62 49 70; Knygynas Antikvariatas, Pylimo 13. Second hand books; Kolekcionierius, Mesiniu 9, Tel: 61 51 31. Postage stamps, medallions, coins, medals; Solda, Dominikonu 9, enter from Stikliu, Tel: 62 35 68.
"Art" Galleries: Whether kitch or art – that is a matter of taste. During the past few months an increasing number of souvenir merchants have trad-

ed their street stands for shops; artists have also found "real" galleries to finally exhibit and sell their works. The motto is look around. Since then the customs officials have abolished the absolute ban on exporting works of art, the limit is now a total of ten works of art – handicrafts, antiques or paintings – independent on what the value of the objects is. For each additional work of art, a tax of 100% is levied.

Andromeda, Ukmerges 12a, Tel: 73 11 73. Paintings on the ground floor, ceramics on the upper floor. Arka, Ausros vartu 7, Tel: 22 13 19, open Tuesday to Friday from 11 am to 7 pm, Saturdays from noon to 7 pm. Lithuanian Avant-Garde in addition to shockingly beautiful paintings. Dailes Centrinis Salonas, Vokieciu 2, Tel: 61 95 16; Tuesday to Saturday from 11 am to 2 pm and 3 to 7 pm. Hundreds of paintings by Lithuanian artists are exhibited by this state-run art centre, also pottery and leather. Dizaino Salonas '89, Mesiniu 4, Tel: 22 01 79, open Monday to Friday from 11 am to 2 pm and 3 to 7 pm. Leather, amber, costume jewellery of clothing – a colourful melange of kitsch and craftsmanship. Galerija '91, Latako 2, open Tuesday to Saturday from noon to 2 pm and 3 to 6 pm. Interesting works by students at the Art Academy. Kuparas, Sv. Jono 3, Tel: 62 37 38 and 22 27 87, Lithuanian folk art is exhibited on the first floor on weekdays from 11 am to 7 pm. Langas Asmenos 8, Tel: 22 15 05, open Monday to Friday from 11 am to 7 pm, Saturday from noon to 4 pm. Medaliu Galerija, Sv.

Jono 11, open Monday to Thursday from 10 am to 6 pm, Friday from 10 am to 5 pm. Statues and medallions displayed in a beautiful hall. Paroda-Pardavimas Sauluva, Pilies 22, Tel: 22 16 96, open weekdays from 10 am to 7 pm. Especially on Palm Sunday, this out-of-the-way shop in an inner courtyard draws a large crowd. This is the only shop in the city which specializes in traditional "verba" crafts – dried flower and wheat stalk arrangements. Some arrangements are only sold for hard currencies. Siauras Atenai, Pylimo 8, Tel: 22 47 09, open Monday to Friday from 11 am to 2 pm and 3 to 7 pm. Permanent exhibition of works by professional goldsmiths. Vartai, Vilniaus 39, Tel: 22 29 49, open Monday to Friday from noon to 7 pm, Saturday from noon to 5 pm. This small hallway gallery on the second floor of the teacher's college displays modern paintings by Lithuanian and Russian artists. Vilnius ir daile, Barboros Radvilaites 6, Tel: 22 66 11, open Tuesday to Saturday from 11 am to 7 pm. Landscapes and scenes of the city have been brought to canvas by professional Lithuanian artists, offered for sale by this the first private gallery in Lithuania.

Books: Ausra, Gedimino 2, Tel: 61 18 23. Large selection of Polish literature; Penki continenti (Five Continents): Vilniaus 39, Tel: 62 66 40. Foreign books, prices in hard currencies; Littera, Sv. Jono 12, Tel: 61 34 60. University Bookstore; Vilnius, Gedimino 13, Tel: 61 60 84.

Commission Stores (Komiso parduotove): Hundreds of private "commis-

In Search of the Heart of Europe

The heart of Europe lies kilometres (15½ miles) north of Vilnius near the rural road to Moletai. The geographical centre of Europe between the Atlantic Ocean and the Ural Mountains is situated in the middle of nothing. Even local residents do not know the way to the black granite slab which is exactly at 25 degrees 19 minutes eastern longitude and 54 degrees 54 minutes northern lattitude. Those who would still like to begin the search should first drive to Purnuskes, turn left and cross over a small bridge and park at the parking area after around 400 yards. Take the unmarked trail over the hill and cross a small wooden bridge to reach the centre of Europe.

sion shops" offer everything which is otherwise "officially" hard to come by: American cigarettes, Italian spaghetti, German coffee filters, perlon stockings – and sometimes antiques at bargain prices. A commission is added onto the price of all the goods meaning that this is the percentage the shop takes for selling the goods from third parties.

Department Stores: Vilniaus Centrine Universaline Parduotuve (VCUP): Ukmerges 16, Tel: 73 05 59; Vilniaus Universaline Parduotuve (VUP): Gedimino 18, Tel: 62 16 27.

Groceries: Bitinelis, Sopeno 12/26, Tel: 63 05 70, open Monday to Friday from 9:30 am to 1 pm and 2 to 6 pm, Saturday from 9 am to 2 pm. The Bee-keepers Association of Vilnius runs this small shop selling only honey – hand spun and heavenly...

Handicrafts ("Daile" Shops): Arka, Ausros vartu 3, Tel: 22 13 19; Dailes Centrinis Salonas, Vokieciu 2, Tel: 61 95 16; Dizaino Salonas '89, Mesiniu 4, Tel: 22 01 79; Galerija 91, Pilies 44; Langas, Asmenos 8, Tel: 22 15 05; Paroda-Pardavimas Salu-

va, Pilies 22, Tel: 22 16 96; Vartai, Vilniaus 39, Tel: 22 29 49.

Marketplaces (Turgavietes): Mazoji kolukine turgaviete (flower market), Basanaviciaus 42; Sendaikciu turgaviete, Gariunai, Tel: 64 94 15, open every morning except Mondays... There is a large bazaar near the motorway exit Vilnius – Kaunas: from machine guns to toothbrushes – everything can be found here... Centrine turgaviete (central market), Pylimo gatve 62; Hale, Pylimo gatve 58/1, Tel: 62 55 36. Meat, milk, fruit and flowers; Kolukine turgaviete, Kalvariju gatve 71, closed Monday. Private farmers' market with a flea market section. Prices run around a third higher than the state run shops, but the quality and selection are equally as good. Caution: pickpockets.

Music: Melodija, Tilto 13/15, Tel: 62 01 68; Muzikas Prekes, Gedimino prospekt 33/17, Tel: 61 31 02. The Beatles as a cheap Soviet product – who would have thought it possible? Valstybines Munitines parduotuve (state customs shop): everything that has been confiscated on the new national borders is sold here at inexpensive prices...; Gedimino prospekt 25.

Theatres and Concert Halls

– *Operos ir Baleto Teatras,* A. Vienuolio 1, Tel: 62 06 36, Fax: 62 35 03. Opera and Ballet Theatre, built in 1974, seats 1,300.

– *Akademinis Dramos Teatras,* Gedimino prospektas 4, Tel: 62 97 71.

– *Lietuviu Tautinis Teatras,* Basanaviciaus 13, Tel: 65 20 30.

– *Teatras Lele* (Puppet Theatre), Arkliu 5, Tel: 62 86 78.

– *Rusu Dramos Teatras* (Russian Theatre), Basanaviciaus 5, Tel: 62 05 52.

– *Jaunimo Teatras* (Youth Theatre), Arkliu 5, Tel: 62 67 32 and 61 61 26.

– *Kiemo Teatras* (University Theatre), Universiteto 3, Tel: 61 40 96.

– *Nacionaline Filharmonija* (National Philharmonic Symphony): Didzioji 45, Tel: 62 71 65.

– *Mazoji baroko sale,* S. Daukanto aikste 1.

– *Lietuvos Muzikos Akademija,* Gedimino prospekt 42, Tel: 61 26 91.

Cinemas

There are over 25 cinemas in Vilnius. Most of the films shown are dubbed in Russian with Lithuanian subtitles. Aidas, Dzuku 1; Adrija, Didzioji 18/2; Draugyste, Pergales 1; Helios, Didzioji 28, Tel: 62 48 50; Lazdynai, Erfurto 1; Lietuva, Pylimo 17a, Tel: 62 34 84; Neris, Antakalno 37; Pergale, Pamenkalnio 7/8, Tel: 22 71 48; Planeta, A. Gostauto 2, Tel: 61 05 05; Taika, Seskines 20; Tevyne, Kalvariju 85, Tel: 75 25 33; Vilnius, Gedimino prospekt 3a, Tel: 60 09 94; Vingis, Savanoriu 7, Tel: 63 76 16.

Beer Halls (Alaus Baras)

Alaus Baras, next to the Lietuva Hotel, Tel: 35 61 32; Aukstaiciu, Zirmunu 27, Tel: 76 68 06, upper floor; Rudininkai, Rudininku 14, Tel: 62 46 68; Stikliai, Stikliu 7, Tel: 22 21 09; Tauro Ragas, Janskio 2, Tel: 62 89 25; Zemaiciu Aline, Vokeiciu 24, Tel: 61 65 73, beer bar in the cellar.

Cafés (Kavine)

Alumnatas, Universiteto 4, Tel: 61 20 43. Popular with university students: wooden tables in two rooms, heavy brown drapes, popular music; Ansamblis Svetaine, Universiteto 6, entrance from the inner courtyard; Arka Kavine, Austros Vartu 3, next to the Arka Gallery, therefore it is very popular with young artists, students and intellectuals, tables in the courtyard, open from 11 am to 11 pm; Arkadina, Sv. Jono 3; Gluosnis, Totoriu 3, Tel: 22 01 53; Kavine, Upes 5; Kretinga, Zemaitijos 8/11, Tel: 61 11 36; Pasazas, Didzioji 45, Tel: 22 13 83; Savas Kampas, Sauletekio al. 19, Tel: 77 98 11; Viktoria, Pamenkalnio 7.

Restaurants (Restoranas)

– Airport Restaurant, Tel: 66 74 76; open 10 am to 8 am; the only thing out of the ordinary that this restaurant has to offer is the fact that night owls can enjoy a hot meal well into the early morning hours.

– Akimirka, Gedimino prospekt 31, Tel: 61 64 40; centrally located near the cathedral, the menu is in English.

– Amantininku Uzeiga, Didzioji 19/2, Tel: 62 65 06, after 8 pm it remains in question whether guests will be served.

– Astorija, Didzioji 35, Tel: 22 40 43, closed for renovations at present, but otherwise an elegant address.

– Bociu, Sv. Ignoto 4/3, Tel: 62 37 72; housed in the former Jesuit refectory, one is surrounded by magnificent frescoes; however, the food is less colourful. The menu is in English, French and German.

– Dainava, Vienuolio 4, Tel: 61 74 81; large dining hall in the Soviet style; shows during the evening.

– Draugyste, Ciulionio 84, Tel: 66 16 51. Live music every evening, English menu, the food is average and the atmosphere is pseudomodern.

– Gintaras, Sodu 14, Tel: 63 53 70; interesting clientele, extremely slow service.

– Laura, Zirmunu 147, Tel: 77 96 11; located on the northern outskirts of town; the food is far better than the location.

– Literatu Svetaine, Gedimino prospekt 1; Tel: 61 29 39; located next to the cathedral. Good restaurant, quick service and delicious food; English menu.

– Lokys, Stidliu 8, Tel: 62 90 46; wild boar and moose are the specialities of this brick Gothic cellar.

– Medininkai, Ausros Vartu 4, Tel: 61 40 19; medieval cellar with a nice atmosphere and delicious blintzes (Blynai).

– Palanga, Vilniaus 10/16, Tel: 62 01 86; the restaurant is up for sale; better for dancing than for dining.

– Panorama, Lietuva Hotel, Tel: 35 61 38; on the 22nd floor of the hotel, nice view of the city but the food is nothing special. A 30-minute variety show takes place at 10 pm with dancing afterwards (admission is charged).

– Pauksciu Takas, Television Tower, Tel: 45 88 77, entry fee, open 10 am to 11 pm, reservations are required; average food.

– Seklycia, Lietuva Hotel, Tel: 35 60 69; in the Lietuva Hotel, ground floor, serving Lithuanian cuisine; charging admission when bands perform.

– Senansis Rusys, Sv. Ignoto 16, Tel: 61 11 37.

– Stikliai, Gaono 7, Tel: 62 79 71; one of the best restaurants in Lithuania; excellent, very expensive cuisine which has been enjoyed by François Mitterrand, Princess Caroline of Monaco and the Finnish President Mauno Kolvisto.

– Vilnius, Gedimino prospect 20, Tel: 61 61 97; in the hotel. Gloomy – both the atmosphere and the food.

– Viola, Kalvariju 3; Russian restaurant – very good!

– Vizitas, Zveju 18, near the sports stadium somewhat difficult to find; only a few tables.

– Zaliasis, "Green," Jankiskiu 43a, Tel: 65 32 33; located outside of town toward Kaunas – worth the trip.

Night Life

After midnight, Vilnius has little to offer night-owls other than the tourist hotels and private parties. Before midnight, disco dancing is offered in the restaurants Dainava, Palanga and Panorama.

– Ritmas, Ugniagesiu 5, Tel: 63 22 68; open noon to 6 pm and 7 pm to midnight, Mondays from noon to 3 pm; serves pizza and soft drinks during the day and has disco dancing beginning at 7 pm. Video shows during the weekend at 8:30 pm.

– VRM Kulturos ir Sporto Rumai (Palace of Sports and Culture): Sporto 21, Tel: 73 35 78. Teenagers and the younger crowd from 16 to 23 dance here Mondays, Tuesdays, Thursdays and Sundays. Wednesday is "Retro Day": the Lithuanian pop band "Sodzius" performs oldies; Friday night is somewhat softer with the "Blues Makers." "Unforgotten Melodies" draw the seniors to the dance floor on Saturdays.

Accommodation
Hotels

– Astorija, Didzioji 35/2, Tel: 62 99 14; 37 rooms priced from £22 to £54 ($40 to $100), Norwegian management in a stately house from 1901.

– Draugyste, M. K. Ciurlionio 84, Tel: 66 27 11, Fax: 26 31 01. 185 rooms priced at £19 ($36) for a single room, £22 ($40) for a double room; the residence of numerous diplomats near Vingis Park.

– Gintaras, Sodu 14, Tel: 63 44 96; 308 rooms, located near the train station.

– Germa, Vilniaus 2/30, Gedimeno prospekt, Tel: 61 54 60.

– Kolukietis, Rinktines 42.

– Lietuva, Ukmerges 20, Tel: 35 60 16 and 35 60 90; 747 rooms on 23 storeys, former "Inturist Hotel" in the typical Soviet "tourist ghetto" style on the opposite banks of the Neris River; this hotel does, however, offer a beautiful view of Vilnius. Single room, £40 ($75); double room £47 ($90).

– Marbre, Maironio 13, Tel: 61 41 62; the best and most expensive hotel in Vilnius offers guests four luxury suites – priced at £47 ($90) per night including breakfast.

– Narutis, Pilies 24, Tel: 62 28 82; central location in the old city near the university on the Pilies gatve, formerly closed off to traffic. Men's and Women's showers are on the ground floor, the rooms are simple.

– Neringa, Gedimino prospekt 23, Tel: 61 05 16. 21 rooms on the main shopping street, most facing the street making them somewhat loud. Single room £35 ($65); double room, £43 ($80) without breakfast; often completely booked. The rooms are quite spacious and are equipped with a large refrigerator.

– Sarunas, Raitininku 4, Tel: 35 38 88; reservations: Tel: 35 48 88. 26 rooms priced at £34 ($64) for a single and £43 ($81) for a double. The Lithuanian basketball star Sarunas Mardiulionis opened this hotel and the "Rooney" Bar (accepting only hard currencies) in 1992. Saunas, with a height of 6'6" still plays for the Golden State Warriors.

– Skrydis, Rodunios Kelias 8, Tel: 66 94 67 and 66 94 62; near the airport. 89 rooms, singles £13.50 ($25); doubles from £13 to £20 ($24 to $38).

– Sportas, Bistrycios 13, Tel: 74 89 53 and 74 89 46.

– Trinapolis, Verkiu 66, Tel: 77 87 35 and 77 89 13. 60 rooms priced at £13.50 ($25) for a single and £11 ($20) for a double room. Bungalow complex on the northern outskirts of town, not all rooms have western standards; the clientele are mostly Polish and Russian tour groups.

– Turistas, Ukmerges 14, Tel: 73 30 02; 115 rooms, single £27 ($50), double £34 ($64).

– Vilnius, Gedimino prospekt 20, Tel: 62 14 57; 200 beds, single rooms £27 ($50), double rooms £20 ($37). A stately building in the pedestrian zone with Patina in the bathroom and room...

– Zalgris, Seimyniskiu 21a, Tel: 35 34 28, reservations: Tel: 35 20 78. 12 rooms, singles from £21.50 to £28 ($40 to $52) and doubles from £42 to £67 ($80 to $126); quiet and clean, spacious rooms.

– Zaliasis Tiltas, Vilniaus 2/30, Tel: 61 54 60. Gedimino prospekt 12, reservations: Tel: 22 17 16. 100 rooms, singles £19 ($36), doubles £29 ($54).

– Zebis, Sibiro 6, Tel: 69 08 90 and 69 07 07; Three rooms, one luxury apartment; opened in October of 1991 southeast of the old city in the Markucia district, this hotel is somewhat difficult to find.

Guest Houses

– Ekspresas Kooperatinis, Tel: 26 17 17, on the outskirts of Vilnius, no breakfast included.

– Litinterp, Vokieciu 10/15, Tel: 61 20 40; £11 ($20) per night, located in the old city.

– Viesnage, Kooperatinis, Rodunios kelias 8, Tel: 63 45 41.

Camping

– Trinapolis, Verkiu 66, Tel: 77 87 35 and 77 89 13.

– Turistine Base Trakuose → *Trakai*.

Surroundings

– *Valakampiai:* The popular excursion destination on the Neris River can be reached from Prieplauka (= Quay) by boat. There is no set schedule for departures – the boats depart as soon as they are full. Information: T. Kosciuskos 4, Tel: 61 29 72.

– *Keturiasdesimt Totoriu* (40 Tartars): 16 kilometres (10 miles) to the southwest. In 1397, 40 Tartars were settled here by Grand Duke Vytautas, who had brought them here as prisoners of war from the Crimea. Their settlement still extends around the 183 metre (599 foot) hill, on which the cemetery is located. The centre of town is the wooden mosque with onion towers.

– *Naujoji:* Eight kilometres (5 miles) east of Vilnius. The construction of the railway route from Warsaw to St. Petersburg brought industry to the one small village in 1860; later the town became known through a tragic historical event: this was the last stop on the way to Siberia for trains transporting those deported under Stalin.

– *Forest of Paneriai:* Eight kilometres (5 miles) southwest of Vilnius. A foreboding atmosphere dominates the pine forest on the southern edge of the city. During the Nazi occupation of Lithuania, over 100,00 people, mostly Jews, were murdered here from 1941 to 1944. A small museum

stands as a reminder of this period.
– _Rykantai:_ Fifteen kilometres (9¼ miles) west of Vilnius. The Catholic church dates back to the year 1585 – however, at that time it was a Protestant church since the Reformation had caught hold especially early in Rykantai. Leo Tolstoy reported in "War and Peace" that Napoleon has stopped here in 1812 on his march eastward. The town was to see the Grande Armee once more in the same year during its retreat.
– _Silos Ezeras_ (Lake Silos): 12 kilometres (7½ miles) north of Vilnius on the Nemencimes Motorway is a popular swimming area, where young pioneer tent camps were often set up.
– _Zalieji Ezerai_ (Green Lakes): 12 kilometres (7½ miles) north of Vilnius on the motorway to Moletai. Several hills surround the 7,320 hectare (18,300 acre) woodland park with its lakes up to 40 metres (130 feet) deep. Those who prefer not to hike through the Verkiu and Jeruzales Forests can rent a boat at the lakes, swim or simply enjoy the magnificent landscape.

Transport

Automobile

Automobile Repair: Autoservisas, Kirtimu 41a, Tel: 64 17 60; breakdown service Tel: 64 08 54. Garage Eva, Jocioniu 14, Tel: 64 34 19, Fax: 64 34 19, payment accepted only in hard currencies. Service Station, Eisiskiu pl. 34, Tel: 63 23 79.

Car Rental: Eva, Jacioniu 14, Tel: 64 94 28; payment required in cash and in hard currency. Litinterp, Culture Centre, Sporto 21, Tel: 75 61 72 and 35 70 14, Fax: 62 34 15; Rent a Car Baltiv Optima, Tel: 46 09 98.

Fuel (Degaline): Bariunai (Kauno pl.), Tel: 64 07 81; Karoliniskiu 6, Tel: 45 70 47; Lentvario 1, Tel: 66 05 78; Moletu motorway, Tel: 58 73 08; Polocko, Tel: 69 60 20; Pramones 12, Tel: 67 27 87; Savanoriu prospekt 119, Tel: 63 10 11; Sv. Stepono 41, Tel: 63 02 12; Ukmerges 156a, Tel: 75 34 42; Vakampiu 3, Tel: 76 85 22.

Train

"Stotis," Gelenzkelio 16, Tel: 63 00 88. Tickets for domestic travel. Foreign visitors must pay higher prices for all routes outside of Lithuania, and this in hard currencies. Reservations can be made by contacting the reservations office, Sopeno 3 (near the train station), Tel: 62 30 44. Tickets are also available through the travel agency in the Lietvu Hotel, Ukmerges 20, Tel: 35 62 25.

The Suvalki – Sestokai railway route was out of service for 47 years, but was reopened in 1992. A White Russian visa is required for travel on the route to Poland via Grodno.

Bus (Autobusu Stotis): Sodu 22 (next to the train station), Tel: 26 24 82; advance reservations, Tel: 26 29 77; reservations on the same day, Tel: 26 22 93. Latvia Minibuses to Kaunas are 10 min. quicker, departing from the central bus terminal.

Air Travel

Airport (Aerouostos): Information for domestic flights: Tel: 63 02 01 and 63 55 60; international flights Tel: 66 94 81.

Airline Offices: Lietuvos Availinijos: Ukmerges 12, Tel: 75 25 88 and 75 32 12; Austrian Airlines/SAS/

Swissair: Airport, upper floor, Tel: 66 20 00 and 66 02 02, Fax: 66 01 39; LOT (Polish Airline): in Hotel Skrydis, room 104, Tel: 63 01 95; Lufthansa: Airport, upper floor, Tel: 63 60 49 and 63 76 99; Hamburg Airlines: Ukmerges 12, Tel: 75 25 50, Fax: 35 48 52; Airport, upper floor, Tel: 63 01 16 and 63 78 17; Malev (Hungarian): in Hotel Skrydis, room 103, Tel: 63 08 10.

Travel Agencies

Asmara, Justenisku 48-24, Tel: 41 06 65; Baltic Travel Service, Subajaus 2, Tel: 62 07 5; Balticorp, Gedimino 26, room 217, Tel: 22 03 03; Datour, Konarskio 18-52, Tel: 65 05 97; Ilies, Naugarbuno 91, room 205, Tel: 26 37 18; Irtavik, Taikosta 195-11, Tel: 46 611 679; Kernave P.O. Box 25 90, Tel: 63 83 24; Senansis Vilnius, Basancaviciaus 15, second floor, Tel: 65 622 638; Trinapolis, Verkju 66, Tel: 76 57 76; Vosso, Gedimino 26, third floor, Tel: 61 99 28.

Municipal Transport
Trolleybus

2 Stotis	– Katedros aikste – Antakalnis
3 Karoliniskes	– Zverynas Katedros aikste – Antakalnis
4 Antakalnis	– Katedros aikste – Pylimo gatve – Savanoriu prospekt – Zemieji Panerai
5 Stotis	– City Centre – Kalvariju gatve – Zirmunai
6 Zemieji Paneriai	– Savanoriu prospekt – Lukiskiu aikste – Kalvariju gatve – Verkiu gatve
7 Stotis	– Zverynas – Laisves prospekt – Justiniskes
8 Justiniskes	– Laisves prospekt – Zverynas – Seimyniskiu gatve – T. Kosciuskos gatve – Katedros aikste – Paupys
9 Karoliniskes	– Zverynas – Seimyniskiu gatve – Zirmunai
10 Antakalnis	– Kalvariju gatve – Lukiskiu aikste – Svitriailos gatve – Naujininkai
11 Antakalnis	– Kalvariju gatve – Lukiskiu aikste – Savanoriu prospekt – Lazdynai – Karoliniskes – Virsuliskes – Pasilaiciai
12 Zemieji Paneriai	– Savanoriu prospekt – J. Vasanaviciaus gatve – Pylimo gatve – City Centre – Katedros aikste – Zirmunai
13 Zirmunai	– T. Kosciuskos gatve – Lukiskiu aikste – Svitrigailos gatve – Naugarduko gatve

14 Antakalnis	– Valakampiai
15 Stotis	– Kauno gatve – Zemaitis gatve – Savanoriu prospekt – Zemiehi paneriai
16 Stotis	– Kauno gatve – Zemaitis gatve – Savanoriu prospekt – Ladzynai – Karoliniskes – Virsuliskes – Pasilaiciai
17 Zirmuni	– T. Kosciuskos gatve – Lukisku aikste – Svitrigailos gatve – Naujininkai
18 Zemieji Paneriai	– Savanoriu prospekt – Karoliniskes – Virsuliskes – Justiniskes

Bus Lines

1 Train Station	– Airport – Kirtimai
2 Airport	– Svitfigailos gatve – Lukiskiu aikste – Kalvariju gatve – Ukmerges gatve – Seskine
4 Tito gatve	– Katedros aikste – Maironio gatve – Zarasu gatve – Naujoji Vilna
5 Antakalnis	– Zirmunai – Kalvariju gatve – Zalgirio gatve – Ukmerges gatve – Seskine
8 Train Station	– Savanoriu prospekt – Aukstieji Paneriai
9 Vilkpede	– Svitrigailos gatve – Lukiskiu aikste – Ukmerges gatve – Seskine – Justiniskes
10 Markucia	– Maironio gatve – Katedras aikste – Kalvariju gatve – Baltupiai – Fabijoniskes
11 Virsuliskes	– Zverynas – Lukiskiu aikste – Uzupis
13 Stotis	– Kauno gatve – Dzuku gatve – Liepkalnis gatve
21 Lazdynai	– Savanoriu prospekt – Pamenkalnio gatve – Pylimo gatve
22 Lazdynai	– Savanoriu prospekt – Lukiskiu aikste
23 Zirmunai	– Olandu gatve – Stotis – Savanoriu prospekt – Lazdynai
31 Stotis	– Pavilnis – Naujoji Vilna

33 Zalgirio gatve	– Pasilaiciai
34 Stotis	– Olandu gatve – Kalvaiju gatve – Baltupiai – Jeruzale – Santariskes – Visoriai
35 Zalgirio gatve	– Kalvariju gatve – Baltupiai – Jeruzale – Verkiai – Naujieiji Verkiai
36 Zalgirio gatve	– Kalvariju gatve – Baltupiai – Jeruzale – Verkiai – Zalieji ezerai
40 Lukiskiu aikste	– Ukmerges gatve – Fabinoniskes
43 Lukiskiu aikste	– Ukmerges gatve – Justiniskes – Pasilaicial
46 Pasilaiciai	– Ukmerges gatve – City Centre
48 Sekinie	– Pasilaiciai – Santariskes
52 Stotis	– Savanoriu prospekt – Auksteji Paneriai – Trakai

Taxi
Tel: 77 29 29 and 77 48 88.

Information
Banks: Lietuvos Bankas, Gedimeno prospekt 6, Tel: 22 40 15; Bansanaviciaus 17. Litimpeks Bankas, Verkiu 37, Tel: 35 40 48, Fax: 35 56 15. Vilnius Bankas, Gedimino prospekt 12, Tel: 62 65 57.
Boat Trips: on the Neris River, departing from dock 1/3, Tel: 76 68 15.
Hospitals: Antakalnio Hospital, Antakalnio 124, Tel: 76 40 41; Emergency Hospital, Siltnamiu 29, Tel: 26 90 96; Red Cross Clinic, Zygimantu 3/1, Tel: 61 35 06; Santariskiu Hospital, Santariskiu 2, Tel: 77 99 12; Vilnius Clinic No. 6, Antakalnio 57, Tel: 74 45 19.
Lost and Found Office: Rastu Daiktu Fiuras, Mindaugo 14, Tel: 62 46 06. Monday to Friday from 9 am to 1 pm and 2 to 6 pm.

Pharmacy (Vaistines): Gedimeno Vaistine, Gedimeno prospekt 27, Tel: 61 01 35; Gulbe, Didzioji 39, Tel: 62 97 17; Pharma-Tech, Seimyniskiu 21, Tel: 75 00 36 – a German-Lithuanian joint venture, only accepts hard currencies; Senamiesci, Vilniaus 22, Tel: 61 83 87; Vaistine, Vokieciu 11, Tel: 61 10 52.
Post Office: Main Post Office, Gedimeno prospekt 7, Tel: 61 66 14, Post Office, Vilniaus 33; express letters, Post Office 24, Vokiecu 7, Tel: 62 56 70; Telephone Centre, Vilniaus 33/2, Tel: 61 99 50; Telegraph Office: Vilniaus 33/2, Tel: 61 96 14.

Literature Tip
Antanas Papsys, Vilnius. Moscow: Progress, 1989.
Justinas Marcinkevicius, Hubert Metzger, Vilnius (Photography), Rostock: Hinstorff-Verlag, 1992.

Aukstaitija

The region of Aukstaitija lies in the eastern portions of Lithuania, bordering on Belorussia. Including Vilnius and Kaunas, this is the largest Lithuanian region encompassing the two most important cities in the country. It also includes the lake basin around Ignalina, the most beautiful national park in Lithuania, Aukstaitija National Park.

Anyksciai

Anyksciai with a population of 1,500 and located on the Sventoji on the railway route from Utena to Panavezys is considered the "Weimar" of Lithuania. This town was made especially famous by the poet *Antanas Baranauskas* (1835-1902) through his poem "The Grove of Anyksciai." The town, on the trade route from Vilnius to Riga, was first mentioned in 1516. In 1557, the Crusaders came, pillaged and set fires. Nine years later, the recently rebuilt city burned down once again.

Up to 1858, the city disappeared into the darkness of history, having hardly any historical structures. Then Antanas Baranauskas came here, moved into a straw-roofed storehouse, the so-called "Klete," and wrote his most famous poem. The theme: the threat to nature through mankind. The protagonist: a greedy wood merchant. The setting: the *Grove of Anyksciai*, today a 150 hectare (375 acre) tract of land under protection to the south of the city. In the middle in a clearing is the 256 tonnes erratic block "Puntuskas." Since 1943, a portrait of the Lithuanian Atlantic pilots *Darius* and *Gireno* can be seen on the stone, almost seven metres (23 feet) tall. A protective glass pavilion now stands above the *Klete of Baranauskas*. It belongs to a *museum,* which commemorates the life and work of this poet.

Standing in the centre of town since 1899 is the neo-Gothic *Church of the Apostle Matthew* across from the culture centre built in 1977.

Surroundings

Eight kilometres (5 miles) to the north on the banks of the Sventoji is the small town of **Niuronys.** In the *Horse Museum,* housed in the former Community College and the neighbouring barn not only displays around 600 pieces of old equipment having to do with horses and horsemen but also offer carriage rides. During the summer, the horseman festival games draw a number of visitors and participants. The *birth house of the Literary Classicist Jonas Billunas* (1879 - 1907) was converted into a small memorial museum in 1932. Thirty-four kilometres (21¼ miles) to the west is **Raguvele.** This well-preserved estate from the 18th to 20th century once belonged to the Komar family. The *wooden church* with its stone bell tower was built at the end of the 18th century. The *Brewery Building* in the neo-Gothic architectural style dates back to the end of the 19th century.

Information

Accommodation: Hotel "Puntukas," Baranausko gatve 8, Tel: 5 13 45.
Restaurants: Silelis, Vilniaus gatve 80; Ziburys, Baranausko gatve 12.

Aukstaitija National Park

A nature reserve as a symbol of revolt? Aukstaitija could be considered just that. When Moscow planned to build an nuclear power plant with six reactor blocks in the middle of the expansive lake landscape on the border to Belorussia and Latvia, Lithuania answered by declaring the area a national park. It was feared especially that the water from the cooling system would warm Lake Druskiai and the lakes connected to it. Moscow ignored the protest. As early as 1975, the construction on the nuclear power plant with the reactor type RMBK (Chernobyl type) began. In 1983, the first reactor was put into operation with 1,500 megawatts; a second reactor went on-line despite the protest of environmentalists.

The 30,000 hectare (75,000 acre) national park to the west of the main town of *Ignalina* lies in the provinces of Ignalina, Utena and Svencionys. The region of Aukstaitija (Mountain-land) encompasses the plateau to the west, the Neris-Zeimena depression at the centre and the plateau of Svencionys to the east. In addition to this, the park is subdivided into three zones: economic, protective and recreational zones. The protective zones may only be entered with permission from the park administration. In the recreational zones are recreational and holiday facilities like camping areas, holiday complexes, cycling trails, canoeing routes and rest areas with grills. A group of four villages are also under governmental protection: Vaisnoriske, Suminai, Strazdai and Salos II.

Information

Nacionalino parko direkcija (National Park Administration), Paluses pastas 23 47 59, Tel: 5 31 35 and 5 59 16. The office in Meironis can provide a detailed map of the national park. Unfortunately, all of the remarks on the maps are still only in Lithuanian and Russian. A better option: stop by Viktorija Luneckiene in the Turizmo biuras (tourist office), Ligonines gatve 1, Ignalina, Tel: 5 38 05 and 53 39 64.

Lake Baluosas

On the northern shores of this 427 hectare (1,068 acre) lake with its seven islands is the *Azvinciai Forest*. On the lakeshores are also the villages of Strazdai, Simunai and Trainiskis *(→ individual entries)*.

Lake Dringis

With an area of 721 hectares (1,803 acres) and five islands, Lake Dringis is not only the largest lake in the national park, but in all of Lithuania. In the northern shores is the former raft village of *Vaisniunai*.

Gaveikenai

Eight kilometres (5 miles) west of Ignalina is the small town of Gaveikenai not far from Lake Dringis. Worth seeing here is the old *water mill* – now a pleasant country restaurant.

Ginuciai

Around ten kilometres (6¼ miles) northeast of Paluse on the shores of Lake Almajas is the small town of Ginuciai. Its old *watermill* was converted into a rustic tourist inn. From there it is not far to the 155 metre (507 foot) *Ledakalnis* (ice mountain), two kilometres (1¼ miles) away. The hilltop offers the most beautiful view of the six lakes and forests of Aukstaitija.

Ignalina

The Chernobyl-type nuclear power plant brought national recognition to the district capital of Ignalina in the northeastern regions of Lithuania near the Belorussian border. The rather plain city in which around 10,000 people live today came into existence at the end of the 19th century on the railway route from St. Petersburg to Warsaw. Before that, there was only one farm here – the administration centre was in the nearby town of Paluse at that time. First mentioned in 1810, Ignalina was first awarded the status of city in 1950. An scattered industrial area extends along the edge of town.

Information

Accommodation

Camping: Five kilometres (3 miles) outside of town.

Hotel: Gavaitis, Aukraicius 37, Tel: 5 23 45. 120 to 220 Rubles per night.

Bank: Ateities gatve 9.

Bus and Train Station: Gelenzinkelio gatve.

Fuel: Two kilometres (1½ miles) outside of town when heading toward Vilnius, on the right hand side above a small lake.

Pharmacy: Laisves gatve 60.

Police: Vasario gatve 7.

Post Office: Laisves aikste 2.

Restaurant: Dringis, Laisves aikste, next to the department store, open from noon to midnight.

Kaltanenai

The railway station of Kaltanenai on the southern edge of the national park is around 16 kilometres (10 miles) from Ignalina. It is situated at the source of the Zeimena River on the shores of Lake Zeimena. This village with its beautiful wooden houses and villas is dominated by its *brick church.* The *marketplace* is classified as a historical monument.

Meironys

On the northern shores of the 391 hectare (978 acre) Lake Lusiai is the small village of Meironys, the seat of the national park administration (→ *Ankstaitija National Park*). The path along the shores are lined with a number of *wooden sculptures,* which were created in 1977.

Mincia

Mincia is located to the north of the national park. The old *mill* has been converted into an inn.

Paluse (Beim Luchs)

Four kilometres (2½ miles) west of Ignalina on the shores of Lake Lusiai (almost 400 hectares/1,000 acres in area) is the idyllic collection of wooden houses called Paluse. It has an unparalleled *church ensemble built from natural wood.* A church from 1750 rises behind the wooden fence to the left of the street on a small hill overlooking the lake. Under the wood shingle roof are no less than three rococo altars as well as paintings from the 17th and 18th centuries. As with the church, the separate *bell tower* is also completely wooden. The octagonal tower and the church were both built without a single nail.

Information

Accommodation: Turistine Baze/Holiday Village: Paluses pastas, Tel: 5 28 91 and 5 74 77.

Sakarva

A hiking trail leads from Paluse to Sakarva, an old village on the shores of Lake Lusiai, the smaller arm of which is also called *Lake Sakarvai.* This lake arm with an area of 75 hectares (188 acres) is around 2.5 kilometres (1½ miles) long, ½ kilometre (¼ mile) wide and has a depth of around 40 metres (131 feet).

Stripeikiai

Ten kilometres (6¼ miles) southeast of Tauragnai, a narrow trail leads by and old *watermill* to the *Senovines Bitinikystes Muziejus* (Beekeeping Museum), which is housed in several wooden cabins. Displayed is everything having to do with beekeeping. One interesting aspect: at the focal

---

Seimatis – and he turned to stone

Hard to believe: the three metre (10 foot) tall and three metre (10 foot) long *erratic block "mokas"* is said to have once been a man. The legend: since people seem to have forgotten how to think for themselves despite all the good advice, this wise man grieved to such an extent that he truned to stone... Today, "he" lies in Seimatis.

---

point of the complex is a *wooden statue* of the heathen god of bees and beekeeping: Babila.

Suminai

A trail through the forest leads to the village of Suminai, situated idyllically on a point in Lake Baluosas. The wooden hoses with thatched roofs were built during the 19th and 20th centuries. The entire village has been place under governmental protection.

Tauragnai

Tauragnai is located on the western shores of the 208 hectare (520 acre) *Lake Tauragnai,* the deepest lake in Lithuania reaching a depth of 60.5 metres (198 feet).

Trainiskes

The entire village of Trainiskes south of Ginuciai on Lake Baluosas is under governmental protection as an *ethnographic ensemble.* A natural wonder can be seen on the lakeshore: an *oak* with a trunk circumference of more than six metres (19 feet).

Lake Utenos

This lake in the northern regions of the national park has an area of 200 hectares (500 acres) and a depth of up to 21 metres (65 feet).

Vaisniunai

The old raft village of Vaisniunai from the 16th century is located on the northern shores of Lake Dringis.

Vaisnoriske

Linden blossom honey made this village famous, located on the fork of the Buka Stream. The *Azvinciu Mincios Forest* begins in the northeastern area of town. The 10,000 hectare (25,000 acre) nature reserve in which even bears can be found may only be entered with special permission from the reserve administration.

Lake Zeimenu
(also: Lake Zeimenys)

Lake Zeimenu is 445 hectares (1,113 acres) in area nd reaches a depth of up to 23.5 metres (77 feet) and is situated in the southern regions of the national park. To both ends of the 12 kilometre (7½ mile) lake is a *camping area.* The name of this lake comes from the Zeimenu River which begins at this lake and then flows into the Neris River after about 60 kilometres (37½ miles).

Birstonas

On the right banks of the Neman River is the popular beach and spa resort of Birstonas, located 40 kilometres (25 miles) southeast of Kaunas. The very generously laid out (13 hectares/33 acres) almost park-like city is still accented by *villas from the turn of the century,* with magnificent carvings on the gables, windows and verandas.

History

The town was first mentioned in history in 1382 as the seat of the "Bierstein" fortress on a nearby hill, the hunting castle of Prince Vytautas during the autumn. As soon as 1518, the town was referred to as a city. During the 17th century, Birstonas declined – only 30 families were still registered here in 1826. The beginning of mineral water extraction during the 19th century revitalized the city. The water, used for medicinal purposes, made Birstonas into a spa town in 1846. Before the First World War, more than 2,000 guests flocked here every year – today, the number is ten times that. The population grew just as rapidly. In 1923, only 268 residents were registered here; in 1970, the population had grown to 2,228. Two years later in 1972, Birstonas became the Olympic training centre for rowing.

Sights

With the exception of a neo-Gothic *church* from the 19th century (Birutes 10) and the beautifully restored wooden villas, the town has no special sights worth seeing. However, what is always surprising is just how modern and experimental the new architecture in Lithuania actually is – the new residential area on the edge of town with its futuristic brick buildings on a green pasture is a good example of this.

One nice walk is along the *dike promenade* along the Nemuna which leads to a forest park outside the city. Also worthwhile is a visit to the *Museum of History* (Vytauto 9; Tel: 5 63 94), a branch of the historical museum in Kaunas.

Surroundings

12 kilometres (7½ miles) to the south on the Nemunas River is the town of **Punia.** Both the town and the surrounding regions have been placed under governmental protection. A wooden defence fortress was built here in 1382 on a hill overlooking the river. From this outpost, the Teutonic Order began their missions with the Bible and the sword.

Information

Accommodation

Camping: Zveryno sile, on the Nemunas River.

Hotels: Nemuna, Algirdo gatve 5. A beautiful wooden villa from the late 19th century, situated directly next to the Nemuna dike promenade.

Turist, Turistu 1, Tel: 5 63 31.

Bank: Tel: 5 66 39.

Bus Station: Vaizganto 20, Tel: 5 63 33.

Cafés: Baras Nida, Algirdo 1, Tel: 5 69 96; Henda, Nemuno gatve; Birute, M. Melnikaites gatve 32, Tel: 5 63 57; Seklytele, Prienu gatve 17, Tel: 5 62 11.

Cinemas: Knygynas, M. Melnikaites gatve 4, Tel: 5 63 58.

Hospital: Jaunimo gatve 87, Tel: 5 67 81.

Pharmacy: Jaunimo gatve 8, Tel: 5 62 52.

Restaurant: Druskupis, Algirdo gatve1 17, Tel: 5 67 81.

Birzai

The district capital of Birzai in the northeastern regions of Lithuania, around 25 kilometres (15½ miles) south of the Latvian border on *Lake Sirvenos* is the terminal station of a side route of the train from Panevezys. A single family determined the fate of this city for three hundred years beginning in 1575: the aristocratic Radvila (Radziwills) family. *Perkunas Radvila* had a fortress built on his extensive tracts of land in the centre of town from 1575 to 1589. The fortress was already conquered by the Swedish king *Gustav Adolf* in 1625 and was consequently rebuilt in the Renaissance style in 1662. In 1704, the Radvilan castle was destroyed once more by the Swedes – and rebuilt yet another time. After extensive restoration work (1978-1985) it how houses the *Museum of Local History*. Displayed here are historical documents pertaining to the Radvila family and the city. One interesting collection shows Lithuanian musical instruments.

The *old city* has suffered considerably under the frequent wars. What have remained preserved despite this are a medieval *pharmacy* (Bielinio 1) as well as the reformed *parish church* from 1874.

At the northern end of Lake Sirvena is the *Palace of Prince Tiszkiewicz*, now used for exhibitions and concerts.

Kaunas
(Kauen; Russian: Kovno)

Kaunas is located where the Neris River flows into the Neman and, with a population of around 500,000, it is the second largest city in Lithuania. The economic heartbeat of Lithuania can be found in Kaunas: in the factories in and around the 121 square kilometre (47 square mile) city is a district in which the industrial production of the country is determined.

History

Even as early as 10,000 BC, this fertile area between the two rivers was inhabited. During the 4th and 5th centuries, a small settlement developed here. Kaunas was first mentioned in historical documents in 1361: *Martin von Wiegand* reported of the destruction of the Lithuanian fortress by the Teutonic Knights. After the defeat of the Teutonic Knights

in the *Battle of Tannenberg* in 1410, the *golden age* of Kaunas began. Two years prior, Kaunas was awarded the city rights of Magdeburg; the Hanseatic League carried out their east-west trade here; and, in 1441, merchants from Elbing, Danzig and Thorn set up offices here. In 1540, a city construction plan set the streets at right angles, as can be seen in the old city today.

Central functions insured the city's influence: in 1566, Kaunas became an administrative seat; in 1648, the Jesuits opened the first school; from 1665 on, the Grand Dukes had their currencies printed here.

Pillaging by the Swedish troops in 1701 and the great city fire of 1732 ended the almost 300 years of prosperity. Napoleon's men ravaged through the city twice: on their glorious march to Russia – and on their way back after having been defeated.

The designation of the city as the *Governeurial Centre of the Russian Empire* in 1843, brought a new upsurge to the city. Incorporation into the main railway routes and the expansion of domestic shipping on the Nemunas fostered the economic development. Kaunas, a border city to Prussia at that time, was built up to one of the most mighty fortifications from 1882 to 1887 as commissioned by the czar. The *Polish occupation* of Vilnius made Kaunas the *provisional capital of Lithuania* for twenty years beginning in 1920. Culture especially profited from this favoured status. The Opera and Ballet Theatre was founded in 1920; in 1922, the first

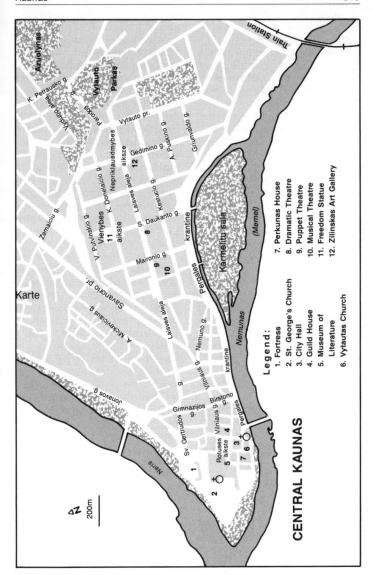

CENTRAL KAUNAS

Legend:

1. Fortress
2. St. George's Church
3. City Hall
4. Guild House
5. Museum of Literature
6. Vytautas Church
7. Perkunas House
8. Dramatic Theatre
9. Puppet Theatre
10. Musical Theatre
11. Freedom Statue
12. Zilinskas Art Gallery

university – with classes held in the Lithuanian language.

While the bourgeois were delighted in this boom, slums called "Brazilkas" developed on the outskirts of the city. On June 24, 1941, the *German Wehrmacht* marched into the city. The czar's fortresses were converted into concentration camps. In the ninth fort, played down as "operation 1005-B," over 80,000 were tortured to death. A memorial stands in memory of these atrocities. The Jewish ghetto was – clearly separated from the actual city – in Viljampole, on the opposite banks of the Neris River. After the war, when most of the public offices and administration returned to Vilnius, the development of Kaunas stagnated. However, this was not the case with the revolts among the populace against the Soviet occupation. 1972 marked the first mass demonstration after the student *Roman Kalantas* set fire to himself.

Walking Tours of the City
I. The Old City

The earliest origins of the city lie at the confluence of the Neris and Nemunas Rivers. The first stone fortress was built on the foundations of the old wooden fort at this strategic location. Destroyed in 1362 by the Teutonic Order after a long period of occupation, the Lithuanians built a new *fortress with four corner towers* at the beginning of the 15th century. The fort itself had walls three metres (10 feet) thick and was surrounded by a broad trench. In order to keep

pace with the spread of firearms, the fortress was fortified during the middle of the 16th century. Powerful cannon bastions were built in front of the southwestern tower, underground corridors ensured the safe connection between the tower and the outpost. In the middle of the 19th century, the fortress lost all function after having been used as a prison periodically. The fortress decayed. It was only in 1954 that the structure was first secured. Today, only portions of the walls and two towers remain standing – one has housed a small museum since the middle of the 1960's.

Next to the fortress is the *St. George's Church.* This Gothic church, built from 1471 to 1504, was remodelled and rebuilt a number of times during the 16th and 17th centuries. Once a portion of the *Cistercian monastery,* this naved church without a tower has unusually high Gothic windows.

The *Rotuses aikste* (City Hall Square) forms the centre of old Kaunas. In the middle of the square lined with chestnut tress is the "White Swan of Kaunas." The slender, light coloured tower is part of the *City Hall.* The administrative building, built by *B. Choinauskas* first in the Gothic style without a tower from 1542 to 1562, was heavily damaged in 1655. During reconstruction lasting from 1771 to 1780, according to the plans drawn up by *J. Mateker,* baroque elements were added. The tower built during the 16th century was built up to a height of 53 metres (174 feet). In the 19th century, the city hall served the czar as a residence during his travels; later, the Russian governor general lived here. Since 1973, the city hall functions as a "wedding palace," as the justice of the peace was called in the former Soviet Union. A *ceramics museum* has occupied the cellar since 1973. Typical Gothic merchants' houses line the City Hall Square to the east, The façades of which are tastefully decorated with traditional motifs. One of these is the *Guild House* (Rotuses aikste 2). The former trade office is now used by the restaurant "Gildija" with a beer cellar. In an old pharmacy on the northern side is the *Museum for Medical and Pharmaceutical History (→ Museums).* The former *residential house of Maironis,* in which the poet lived from 1910 to 1932, now houses a *literary museum* (Rotusas aikste 13). To the southern side of the square are the *Jesuit Church and Monastery* (Rotusas aikste 8). The monks founded a school of higher education here in 1648. Today, it proudly bears the name *Adam Mickiewicz.* The Polish poet taught here from 1819 to 1823. The Gothic *Vytautas Church* built around 1400 is one of the oldest churches in Lithuania. The only nave church in the country with side chapels was built for the Christians who had emigrated to Kaunas. Next to the church on the southeastern side at Karaliaus dvaro gatve 1a is the house of a heathen lord.

The *Perkunas House* bears the name of the Lithuanian god of thunder. The two-story Gothic house was presumably built as a warehouse for Hanseatic merchants – the reason that this is assumed is the absence of a kitchen, an important indication. During the 18th century, the adjacent warehouse was added. The most unusual aspect of this residential warehouse with a cellar and reception rooms in the upper storey is the façade: over 16 different kinds of bricks were used during its construction. A small exhibition in the Perkunas House (restored from 1965 to 1968) provides information about the old city and its restoration. Vilniaus gatve leads from City Hall Square to Laisves aleja in the modern districts of Kaunas. The Vilniaus gatve is a pedestrian zone over its entire length. Gothic, baroque and historism are harmonically united in the *Arkikatedra basilica* (St. Peter and Paul's Church; Vilniaus gatve 26). Construction on the cathedral began in 1413, which was first built as a one-naved Gothic church. Later, the two-storey sacristy to the north would follow, a structure which has the largest console vaulting in Europe – with a span of almost eight metres (26 feet). During the middle of the 17th century, the largest Gothic structure in Lithuania – 80 metres (262 feet) long and 30 metres (98 feet) high at the centre nave – was rebuilt as a basilica. After having been destroyed by wars and fires, the church was extensively restored during the 18th century in the late baroque architectural style. From 1893 to 1897, a neo-Gothic chapel was added to the choir. Nine altars, all facing the main central altar accent the late baroque interior in which only the ribbed and console vaulting is reminiscent of its Gothic origins. The grave of the poet *Maironos* is in the southern exterior wall. The Zemaite bishop *Valancius,* a famous author and historian in Lithuania, is also buried here.

Among the restored façades on Vilniaus gatve, a *corner house* (No. 20) is especially striking, which was built in two stages – as revealed by the façade. A black rhombus pattern of clinker bricks embellishes the brick building on the ground floor – a typical Gothic ornamentation. The upper storey incorporates early elements of the three-stepped gables, an early masterpiece of the Renaissance.

The colourful Savanoriu prospektas separates the old from the new city which was developed from 1847 to 1871 according to the general construction plans to both sides of the axial street Laisves aleja (Freedom Boulevard).

II. The New City

Beyond the underpass, the 1.7 kilometre (1 mile) long Laisves aleja (Freedom Boulevard) continues. *Neo-classicistic buildings,* among them the bank (1929), the main post office (1932), the M. K. Ciurlionis Art Museum (1936) and the clinic (1931) line the majestic boulevard, which was converted to the first pedestrian zone in the Baltic States in 1982. Café "Tulpe" (No. 49) was a popular meeting place for literaries, artists and politicians when Kaunas was the provisional capital of the country during the period between the two world wars. Several *theatres* also line the boulevard: the Dramatic Theatre (No. 71), the Puppet Theatre (No. 87a)

and, somewhat concealed in the trees, the Musical Theatre (No. 91). The Lithuanian parliament was established in 1920 in the theatre building erected from 1890 to 1892 and remodelled by the architect *V. Zelmkanis* in 1932. Daukanto gatve to the left of the "Mercurijus" department store leads to Vienybes aikste (Unity Square), on which the obligatory Lenin statue stood up to autumn of 1991 – today the *freedom statue* stands here. In 1960, the "Palace for Political Education," was built here. Today, this is the seat of the Vytautas University.

Continuing back along the Laisves aleja, it is only a few yards to the Nepriklausomybes aikste. The majestic exterior of the neo-Byzantine *church* (built in 1895 as a church of the czar's municipal garrison) stands in crass contrast with the shabby interior in dire need of repairs. To the right, a stairway leads up to the postmodern, ostentatious entryway of the *Zilinskas Art Gallery.*

To the east of Vytauto prospektas are the "green lungs" of the city. Following the small *Vytautas Parkas* is the 60 hectare (150 acre) *Oak Forrest of Azuloynas.* Those who stroll through the extensive grove heading east passing trees over 100 years old will ultimately come to the only zoo in Lithuania. The *Zoological Gardens of Kaunas* lie in the Adam Mickiewicz Valley – the famous Polish poet is said to have enjoyed taking long walks in this area.

Museums and Galleries

– *Balys Sruogos memorialinis mu-*

A picturesque wooden house in Nidden on the Curonian Spit: "Curonian blue" is the term for this expressive colour

Impressions of the Curonian Spit: a holiday paradise for everyone — even Wilhelm von Humboldt and Thomas Mann were enthused about this region

zuejus (Sruogos Memorial Museum): This museum is a memorial to the poet and dramatist B. Sruogos; B. Sruogos gatve 21, Tel: 73 80 01.

– *Cvirka memorialinis muziejus* (Cvirka Memorial Museum): Donelaicio gatve 13, Tel: 20 64 88, open Wednesday to Monday from 11 am to 7 pm.

– *Dailes A. Zmuidzinaviciaus kuriniu u rinkiu muziejus* (Devil's Museum): V. Putvinskio gatve 64, Tel: 20 35 14 open noon to 6 pm; a collection compiled by the Lithuanian landscape artist Antanas Muidzinaviciaus, who collected statues of the devil as a hobby.

– *Fotomeno galerija* (Photo Gallery): Rotuses aikste 1, Tel: 20 26 74, open daily from 11 am to 7 pm.

– *Gruodis memoralinis muziejus* (Gruodis Memorial Museum): Gruodis was a composer and the museum in his honour is located at Salado 18, Tel: 73 24 98.

– *Kipras Petrausko memoralinis muziejus* (Petrauskas Memorial Museum): Petrausko was the composer of the first Lithuanian operetta and opera; K Petrausko gatve 31, Tel: 73 33 71, open Wednesday to Sunday from noon to 6 pm.

– *Keramikos muziejus:* Rotuses aikste 15, Tel: 20 35 72, open Tuesday to Sunday from noon to 6 pm; in the basement of the city hall.

– *Maironio Liutuvio literaturos muziejus* (Museum of Literature): Rotuses aikste 13, Tel: 20 12 84, open Wednesday to Sunday from 11 am to 7 pm, Sunday from 11 am to 5 pm.

– *M. K. Ciurlionis Dailes Muziejus* (Art Museum): V. Putvinskio gatve 55,

Tel: 20 52 05; open Tuesday to Sunday from noon to 6 pm. This museum displays works by the famous Lithuanian painter Ciurlionis in addition to other Lithuanian and Asian works of art.

– *Museum in the Ninth Fort:* Zemaiciu plentas 73, Tel: 26 05 74, open Tuesday to Sunday from noon to 6 pm. Eighty thousand people were killed by the Nazis in the Ninth Fort, an addition 35,000 died in the Sixth Fort. In a forest near Alytus, around 95,000 lost their lives and did 100,000 in the Forest of Paneriai near Vilnius – the memorial exhibition can only provide a short glimpse of the horrendous deeds performed in the name of the Führer.

– *Museum of Musical Instruments:* Zamengoso gatve 12/corner of Kurpiu gatve, Tel: 20 68 20, open Wednesday to Sunday from 11 am to 7 pm.

– *Mykolo Zilinsko dailes galerija* (Art Gallery): Nepriklausomybes aikste 12, Tel: 22 75 13 and 22 28 53; open Tuesday to Sunday from noon to 6 pm. A post modern monumental building out of marble, steel and glass exhibiting works of art on three floors.

– *Medicinos ir farmacijos istorijos muziejus* (Museum of Pharmaceutical and Medical History): Rotuses aikste 28, Tel: 20 74 01.

– *Paveikslu galerija:* K. Donelaicio gatve 16, Tel: 20 02 31, open daily from noon to 6 pm.

– *Pedagoginis Muziejus:* Zemaiciu gatve 85, Tel: 22 81 94.

– *Salomeja Neries memorialinis muziejus* (Neris Memorial Museum; Mrs.

Meris is known as the "literary nightingale"): Palemonas, S. Neris gatve 7, Tel: 73 73 34, open Monday to Wednesday from 11 am to 7 pm.
– _T. Ivanausko zoologijos muziejus_ (Zoological Museum): Laisves aleja 106, Tel: 20 02 92. On the lower level are protective slippers to be worn by visitors, the tour begins on the upper floor.
– _Vytauto Didziojo karo muziejus_ (Military Museum): K. Donelaicio gatve 64, Tel: 22 27 56, open Wednesday to Monday from 10 am to 6 pm.

Theatres
– Valstybinis leliu teatras, Laisves aleja 87a, Tel: 2 21 69.
– Valstybinis akademis dramos teatras (Dramatic Theatre): Laisves aleja 71, Tel: 22 40 64 (administration), 22 31 85 (reservations). Performances of plays by Lithuanian dramatists – unfortunately only in the Lithuanian language.
– Valstybinis muzikinis teatras (operas, operettas and musicals), Laisves aleja 91, Tel: 22 87 84 (administration), 22 09 33 (reservations).
– Puppet Theatre: Laisves aleja 7a, Tel: 20 89 93 (administration), 22 16 91 (reservations).
– Pantomime Theatre: Sapeigos 5, Tel: 22 84 78.

Concert Halls
Philharmonic Society, Tolstojaus 5, Tel: 22 25 58 (Administration), 22 04 78 (reservations). Classical and traditional music are performed in the large hall; changing art exhibitions are displayed in the foyer.

Cinemas
Planeta, Vytauto pr. 6, Tel: 22 85 49; 100 yards from the train station, showing current films.
Azuolynas, Radvilenu plentas 74, Tel: 73 40 50.
Daina, Savanoriu prospekt 74, Tel: 73 01 19.
Dainava, Chemijos prospekt 11, Tel: 75 38 82.
Eiguliai, P. Luksio gatve 66, Tel: 72 86 93.
Kankles, Laisves aleja 36, Tel: 20 58 90.
Kaunas, Savanoriu prospekt 350, Tel: 77 24 09.
Laisve, Laisves aleja 54, Tel: 20 52 03.
Pasaka, Savanoriu prospekt 124, Tel: 20 88 16.
Taika, A. Juozapaviciaus prospekt 67, Tel: 74 00 14.
Vilnius, Sajungos aikste 3a, Tel: 26 14 98.
Kankles, Laisves aleja 36, Tel: 20 58 90.
Romuva, Laisves aleja 54, Tel: 20 55 82.
A cinema for intellectuals is up for sale: Rotuses aikste 23. The name is Programm and demanding films are presented to an equally demanding audience.

Bars
Antis, Vilnius gatve 22, Tel: 20 66 92; Aukso kiausinis, Vilnius gatve 11; Desertinis, Laisves aleja 61; Grill, K. Donelaicio gatve 27, Tel: 20 52 07; Kepsniai, Laisves aleja 70; Kosmosas, Savanoriu prospekt 105; Pas Pranciska, Jonavos gatve 62a, Tel: 72 25 14. Pieno Baras, Vilniaus gatve

13; Rambynas, Vasario16/Osios gatve 1, Tel: 20 89 73; Sokoladine, Vilniaus gatve 20; Ugne, Rotuses aikste 23, Tel: 20 82 80.

Cafés

Architektu, K. Donelaicio gatve 62, Tel: 20 52 53; Astra, Laisves aleja 76; Berneliu uzeiga, M. Valanciaus gatve 9, Tel: 20 63 62; Curkraine, Vytauto prospekt 69; Dviese, Vilnius gatve 8, Tel: 20 36 38; Ledaine, S. Daukanto gatve 14, Tel: 20 65 88, Liepaite, K. Donelaicio gatve 56; Muza, Kumeliu gatve 16, Tel: 20 35 65. Pasaka, Laisves Aleja 27, Tel: 20 72 12; Pegasas, Rotuses aikste 13, Tel: 20 76 75; Pyragas, Sv. Gertrudos gatve 38; Tartu, K. Petrausko gatve 79; Tulpe, Laisves aleja 47/49, Tel: 22 17 36; Velnele, Vytauto prospekt 51, Tel: 20 89 47.

Restaurants

Baltija, Vytauto prospekt 71, Tel: 29 32 44.

Bialystokas, Vytauto prospekt 56, Tel: 20 58 68.

Gelezinkelio st., M. K. Ciurlionio gatve 16, Tel: 29 24 39.

Gildija, Rotuses aikste 2, Tel: 20 08 04; in a house built in 1602 and renovated in 1978.

Kaukas, S. Simkauzs aleja 2, Tel: 73 01 90.

Mediziotoju uzeiga, Rotuses aikste 10, Tel: 20 83 74.

Metropolis, Laoisves aleja 61, 20 44 27.

Neris, K. Conelaicio gatve 27, Tel: 20 62 07

Vakaras, Vasario16/Osios gatve 1, Tel: 22 76 66.

Zalias Kalnas, Savanoriu prospekt 111, Tel: 22 33 75.

Night Life

Kolegos: Juro 63, Tel: 75 47 00 and 75 64 67, weekend disco showing video clips, open 8 to 11 pm.

Kulturos Namai (Culture Centre): Vytauto prospekt 79. This address draws a clientele from kids to grandpas – with separate dance halls for the resepective age groups. Open Wednesday and Friday to Sunday from 8 to 11:15 pm; showing videos from 8 to 9 pm.

Lzua: Noreikiskiu gatve, Tel: 22 82 55 and 29 65 94; open Thrusday to Sunday from 8 pm to midnight. This disco belongs to the Lithuanian Agricultural University and is referred to as "the aquarium" by insiders.

Ramove: Mickeviaus gatve 19, open Saturday and Sunday from 8 pm to midnight. Gays only.

Veterinariojs Disco: Adomausko 18, Tel: 26 03 83 and 26 74 30. A meeting place for the veterinarians and dance-crazed students, open during the weekend at irregular hours.

Tresta: Mickeviciaus 8a, open Wednesday, Saturday and Sunday. A large proportion of Russian clientele, more ruffian than refined; not exactly a good tip for singles or women.

Sports Hall: Perkuno aleja 5, Tel: 20 22 78 and 20 14 70, open only Thursdays from 7 to 10 pm. Rap and Techno.

Accommodation

Joldija (formerly Baltija), Vytauto prospekt 71, Tel: 22 36 39. 330 beds at quite reasonable prices, hotel parking area.

Neris, K. Donelaicio gatve 27, Tel: 20 42 24. 319 beds. Expensive and gloomy – and popular with thieves. Hotel parking area to the rear; foreign currency shops inside.

Sportis, Auros 42a, Tel: 79 69 32. 217 beds; predominantly rooms with three and four beds, often without separate facilities – but the sauna and swimming pool do provide refreshment. No café or restaurant in the hotel.

Lietuva, S. Daukanto gatve 21, Tel: 20 59 92. 180 beds, elevated standards, TV, telephone and refrigerator in the rooms, hotel parking area. Branch hotel at Laisves aleja 35, Tel: 22 17 91, somewhat less expensive, located in the pedestrian zone.

Nemunas, Laisves aleja 88, Tel: 22 31 02. Three and four bed rooms without bath, but with TV and telephone.

Vairas, Dariuaus ir Gireno 102, Tel: 20 54 05, the least expensive alternative in Kaunas; a tip for sound sleepers.

Parks and Gardens

Botanikos soda (Botanical Gardens): Botanikos gatve 4, Tel: 29 86 58.

Zoologijos soda (Zoo): Radvilenu plentas 21, Tel: 73 06 30. The only zoo in Lithuania is within the Azuolynas Park in the Adam Mickiewicz valley.

Surroundings

Kaunas marios (Kaunian Lake): This reservoir, 83 kilometres (52 miles) in length to the east of the city is a popular recreation area – especially during the summer. The lake, up to 20 meters (66 feet) deep and 3.3 kilometres (2 miles) wide was laid out in 1959 during the construction of a hydraulic power plant. Four turbo turbines which began operation in 1959 and 1960 each have a capacity of 25,200 kilowatts and produce over 100 megawatts.

On the southwestern shores is the *Pazaislis Monastery* one of the most famous baroque ensembles in Lithuania. The construction of the monastery and church for the Kamaldulensian Order was financed by the Lithuania chancellor *Krystof Zigmant Pacas* - he had met these monks during his youth in Italy. The Kamaldulensians are the only order that still live in closed monk cells – the monks have themselves walled up in hermitage huts for a period of strict prayer. The construction of the church commenced in 1667 under the direction of the Italian architect *Carlo Putini* and was later continued by Brother Pietro, lasting up to 1712. Western European and Lithuanian architecture are united in this church. Sculptures originate from the German sculptor *M. Wollscheid;* the bells, from the Frenchman *de la Mars;* the frescoes and murals, from the workshop of *M. Arcangelo Poloni* and *Fernando della Croce.* Heavily damaged during the Napoleonic Wars, the church and monastery were handed over to the orthodox church under the czar. After repeated alteration, Pazaislis became the seat of the congregation of St. Casimir from 1920 to 1940. Under the Soviets, an asylum moved into the monastery before the first modifications began in 1964. Since 1980, the monastery is open to visitors as a museum. The gallery exhibits western European and Polish paintings from the 17th and 18th centuries.

Twenty-six kilometres (16¼ miles) east on the northern lakeshore is the *Rumsiskes Ethnological Outdoor Museum.* Displayed on the 175 hectare (438 acre) complex opened in 1974 are traditional farmhouses, workshops and residential houses from the four Lithuanian regions Aukstaitija, Zemaitija, Suvalkija and Dzukija. Over fifteen farms and homesteads form an interesting microcosm of the country. During the summer, the village comes alive: folk dance groups and singing ensembles perform during the weekends, craftsmen sell traditional ceramics, iron or textile work, and special exhibitions are on display occasionally.

Information

Banks: Lithuanian Bank, Maironio 25, Tel: 20 04 80; Ukio Bankas, Gruodzio 9, Tel: 2 00 36 51; it is also possible to exchange currency at the VERTA service office, Kestucio 38, Tel: 20 59 97.

Hospitals: Raudonias Kryzius (Red Cross Clinic), Laisves aleja 17, Tel: 22 61 54; Polyclinic, Januskeviciaus 2, Tel: 73 33 77.

Pharmacies:

Post Office: Laisves aleja 102, Tel: 22 62 20.

Tourist Information: Service office for foreign tourists, Tel: 20 42 89; excursions office, Roruses aikste 11, Tel: 22 05 32.

Transport

Automobile: Trans-Lithuania Motorway from Vilnius to Klaipede.

Automobile Repair: NECA, Donelaicio 26, Tel: 20 19 28 (specialising in western automobiles; repairs are payable only in DM or $); Autoservisas, Taikos prospekt 151, Tel: 71 23 78.

Car Rental: NECA, Donelaicio 26, Tel: 20 19 28.

Fuel (Degalines): Asigalio gatve, Tel: 72 45 31; Chemijos pr. Tel: 7 55 45 67; Draugytes pr. Tel: 74 73 10; Kestucio gatve 63, Tel: 22 40 75; Raudondvario pl. 82, Tel: 26 10 91.

Towing Service: Tel: 71 89 22.

Traffic Police: Tel: 22 81 12.

Train: Gelezinkelio stotis, M. K. Ciurlionio gatve 16, train information, Tel: 22 10 93.

Bus: Autobusu stotis, Vytauto pr. 24, bus information, Tel: 22 79 42.

Funiculaires (cableway): Zaliakalns, Ausros 6, Tel: 20 58 82; Aleksotas. Skriandzus 8, Tel: 22 31 28.

Airport: Aerouostos Karmelavoje, Tel: 54 14 00. Several kilometres outside of town near Karmelava; there are evening flights to Riga and Tallinn several times during the week; during the summer, there are also flights to the Baltic seaside resorts near Palanga.

Ship Travel: Nemuno laivininkyste, Prieplauka – Raudondvario pr. 107, Tel: 26 13 48, Kauno mariu prieplauka, Tel: 75 82 66. The ship Nemuna travels between Klaipeda and Nida. The "Raketa" hydrofoils depart daily early in the morning and arrive at the towns along the Baltic coast around noon. It is questionable whether the ship routes on the Kanos Marios to Rumsiskes and Birstonas will continue to be operated – schedules for 1993 were not yet available at the end of 1992.

Taxi: Tel: 23 44 44, 23 55 55, 23 66 66 and 77 77 77.

Kernave

The small city of Kernave on the Neris River, around 40 kilometres (25 miles) northwest of Vilnius, is considered the first capital city of Lithuania. In 1279, the village of 250 in the Sirvintos regions was first mentioned in history. During *archaeological excavations,* the remains of the former fortress and other remnants from a medieval settlement from the 12th century were found behind the *neo-Gothic brick church* from 1920. The fortress of Kernave – together with the Fortresses of Trakai and Medininkai – formed the eastern Lithuanian lines of defence against attacks by the Teutonic Order. The view from this ridge is simply breathtaking.

Medininkai

Thirty-two kilometres (20 miles) southwest of Vilnius on the M 12 toward Minsk is the village of Medininkai with a population of 600. This village on the Belorussian border was founded by monks and gained a tragic fame during the uprisings for independence – the massacre of seven young Lithuanian border guards on July 31 1991 remains unforgotten today.

The *fortress ruins* from 1311 was once one of the largest castles in Lithuania with an area of 7½ hectares (19 acres). Of the former four towers, only the *watchtower* to the northeast has remained preserved to date. In front of the up to 14 metre (46 foot) walls, an earthen wall and a trench protected the complex against attacks by the Teutonic Order. During the Second World War, the German Wehrmacht set up an supplies storehouse.

Restorations on the fortress began in 1916 which now houses a small museum covering the history of this structure. South of Medininkai is the highest elevation in Lithuania, the 292 metre (955 foot) *Juozapines Kalnis.*

Moletai

A key, the wings of a bird and a number of waves are depicted on Moletai's coat of arms, located around 50 kilometres (31 miles) southwest of Ignalina on the rural road from Vilnius to Itena. Several lakes surround the city. The baroque church in the centre of town was built during the 16th century. Around 13 kilometres (8 miles) outside of town toward Utena is the *Observatory of Moletai* on the 193 metre (631 foot) Kaldiniu-Kalnis. A small museum provides information on the history of astronomy in Lithuania.

Information

Accommodation: A hotel is located

on the Inturkes gatve. It is a red, dilapidated building across from a pond.
Restaurant: Moletai, Vilniaus gatve 41, Tel: 5 13 69.

Panevezys (Ponewiesch)

Panevezys, the fifth largest city in Lithuania with a population of 150,000 has a less typical structure for industrial cities: Ninety-two percent of the residents of this city on the Nevezis River are Lithuanian. The economic significance of this central Lithuanian city stands in contrast to the touristic importance of Panevezys: drive right through it – unless overcome a nostalgic hankering to search for Soviet traces.

History

Panevezys, a rather young city, was the result of the consolidation of three towns. Construction on the Mikolajavas as a planned city on the right banks of the Nevezis began in 1780. The settlement, awarded city rights in 1796, is now called Smelyne. In 1857, 5,900 residents lived there. At the end of the 19th century, the two villages, old and new Panevezys were combined with Mikolajavas to form one city. The construction of the railroad brought industry and workers to this city. In 1927, Panevezys became the seat of the bishop. Almost completely burned to the ground during the first world war, the city was occupied during the Second World War on June 26, 1941 by the German *Wehrmacht* and then almost completely destroyed three years later when they retreated from the Red Army. Today Panevezys is a modern residential and industrial city

without any out of the ordinary sights.

Sights

The "old city" (Senamiestis) extends between the Nevezis River and the railway route from Siauliai to Daugavpils; the new city (Naujamiestis), on the left banks of the Nevezis. Serving the spiritual needs of the residents are the *cathedral* (Katedros aikste 12), the *St. Peter and St. Paul's Church* (Smelynes 10), and the *Holy Trinity Church* (Sodu 2). The classicistic *Piarist Church* was built in 1803. One of the oldest buildings in the city is the War Court from 1614.

During the 1960's, modern critical performances at the *theatre* (Liaves aleja) under the direction of *Juozas Miltinis* were renowned beyond the borders of the former Soviet Union. Scheduled performances included innovative productions of Arthur Miller, Wolfgang Borchert and Friedrich Dürrenmatt – a courageous undertaking at that time. Three museums can also be visited: the *art gallery* (Respublikos 3, Tel: 6 36 75; open Thursday to Sunday from noon to 8 pm), the *Regional Museum* (Vasario 16, Tel: 6 27 77; open Tuesday to Sunday from Noon to 8 pm) and the *Folk Museum* (Respublikos 56).

Around 15 kilometres (9¼ miles) south of Panevezys is the *Flax Museum* (presently being restored) near the town of **Upyte** housed in a mill.

Information

Accommodation

Hotel: Nevezis, Laisves aleja 26, Tel: 3 51 17. Located in the centre of town, with a bar and restaurant. Rambynas, Republikos 34, Tel:

6 10 07. Upyte, Republikos 38, Tel: 6 67 47. The latter accommodation is in need of renovation – and not the quietest.

Airport: Tel: 3 32 98.

Automobile Repair: "Autoservisas," Velzio kelias 48, Tel: 3 31 13.

Banks: Respublikos 56, Tel. 6 10 35.

Bus Station: Savanoriu aikste 5, Tel: 6 41 85.

Fuel: Klaipedos gatve, Tel: 3 39 48. Velzio kelias, Tel: 3 33 13. Smelynes gatve, Tel: 3 74 29.

Marketplace: Ukmerges 26, Tel: 3 39 65.

Post Office: Republikos 60, Tel: 6 44 45.

Restaurants: Agounele, Laisves aikste 15, Tel: 3 38 09; Biciulis, Marijonu 27, Tel: 6 88 65; Grillbaras, Laisves aikste 1, Tel: 3 57 54; Stumbras, Aukstaitju 4, Tel: 3 54 84; Zaraus, Dariaus ir Gireno 4, Tel: 2 62 10.

Theatre: Dramos teatris, Laisves aleja, Tel: 6 28 37.

Train Station: Stotis gatve, Tel: 6 30 51 and 6 36 15.

Rokiskis

The district capital of Rokiskis in the northeastern regions of Lithuania is located 16 kilometres (10 miles) from the Latvian border and is home to a population of 25,000.

Sights

During the 18th century, the aristocratic family von Tiessenhausen commissioned the architect *Stuoka-Gucevicius* with the construction of a new residence in the classicistic style. This *castle,* from 1801 (remodelled during the 20th century) has housed the *Museum of Local History* (Tysenhauso aleja) for over fifty years. The scientific library is also in a stately building. The archives of the old estate and parish also belong to this library.

The neo-Gothic *St. Matthew's Church,* built by *Gustav von Schacht* and *G. Werner* from 1866 to 1883 ranks among the most important architectural monuments in the history of Lithuania. The 60 metre (196 foot) bell tower to the north of the three-naved church is connected to the main building by a short, roofed walkway. The interior is a successful union of western European and Lithuanian art: Belgian master craftsmen from Leuven worked together with local wood carvers on the oak pulpit. The gilded alter is from Paris; the glass windows were made by Viennese artists.

Some *old merchants' houses* from the 19th century have remained preserved on Vytauto gatve.

Information

Accommodation: Hotel Rokiskes, Nepriklausombyes aikste, Tel: 5 23 45.

Restaurant: Nemunelis, Nepriklausombyes aikste 20, Tel: 5 23 68.

Siauliai (Schaulen)

The fourth largest city of Lithuania with a population of 160,000 was closed off to foreign visitors up until 1987 because of its military facilities. The 70 square kilometre (27 square mile) area of the city is an important traffic and transport hub: this is the junction of the motorways A 225 (Palanga – Panevezys) and the A 216 (Riga – Kaliningrad/Königsberg); the railway route from the Latvian capital of Riga meets up with the route from Klaipeda to Daugavpils. Among the most important industries of the city is the "Gubernija" Brewery in which beer and other beverages have been produced since 1789. "Nuklonas" has a total of 3,200 employees. This electro-technical factory was founded in 1968 and exports to 19 countries. Bicycles have been produced by "Vairas" since 1948; "Elnias" delivers leather shoes to Italy.

History

A battle made this city famous: in 1236, the Lithuanians defeated the Livonian Order's army near the city of Saule. In the middle of the 15th century, a small settlement developed which was awarded the city rights of Magdeburg during the 16th century. During the 17th and 18th centuries, the centrally located town was pillaged and occupied a number of times: the Swedes and Russians are only two examples. In 1812, Napoleon's troops marched through, setting fire to the city. In 1875, a large fire almost destroyed the entire city which was mostly composed of wooden buildings. The construction of the rural road from Königsberg to St. Petersburg in 1839 and the railway route to Liepaja in 1871 made Siauliai into a commercial and industrial centre. Completely destroyed during the First and Second World Wars, Siauliai was rebuilt as a modern Soviet city. Siauliai has a pedestrian zone since

1975: the Vytauto gatve leads from Draugyste prospektas to the railway station built in 1871.

Sights

Surrounded by modern apartment buildings, the highest church tower in Lithuania has risen up where the old centre of Siauliai once was since the end of the 19th century. The six-storey tower is 70 metres (229 feet) in height and belongs to the *St. Peter and Paul's Church.* The church built in the Renaissance style from 1617 to 1634 in the form of a Roman cross has been restored a number of times. The interior has a noteworthy gallery which leads around the entire church nave to the choir at a height of 9 metres (30 feet).

In the *park on Lake Talsos,* a huge *sundial* commemorates the 750th anniversary of the city. Serving as the pointer is a long pole on which a gilded archer is perched at a height of 22 metres (72 feet).

The *Zubova Palace,* built at the end of the 18th century, is now used as an educational institution.

Museums and Galleries

– *Ausra Museum for History and Ethnography:* Building 1: Ausros aleja 47, Tel: 3 87 22, open Wednesday to Sunday form 11 am to 6 pm; Building 2: Vytauto gatve 89, Tel: 3 38 37. Over 70 000 pieces are displayed in this museum which opened in 1923; the collection of paintings is also worth seeing.

– *J. Kriksciunas Jovaras Museum:* Vytauto gatve 116, Tel: 3 73 25, open Tuesday to Friday from 10 am to 5 pm. This former residence of the Lith-

uanian poet (1880-1967) now houses a memorial.
- *Museum of Photography:* Vytauto gatve 140, 2nd floor, Tel: 3 72 03, open Thursday to Monday from noon to 7 pm.
- *Bicycle Museum:* Vilniaus gatve 189, Tel: 3 37 88, open Wednesday to Sunday from 11 am to 7 pm.
- *Cat Museum:* Zuvininku 18, Tel: 3 89 14, Wednesday to Sunday from 11 am to 5 pm.
- *Radio and Television Museum:* Vilniaus gatve 174.

Surroundings

Eighteen kilometres (11¼ miles) northwest toward Meskuiciai is the *Kryziu Kalns* (Hill of Crosses). Thousands upon thousands of crosses made from wood, metal or plastic and covered with relicts, pictures of saints and even more crosses cover the 16 metre (52 foot) hill. The tradition of setting up crosses began during the czarist uprisings of 1831 and 1863. It later became a symbol of resistance against the Soviet dominance. The hill on the Kulpe River accentuates the suffering of the Lithuanian people like no other place in the country. The Soviets were well aware of the significance of the Kryziu Kalns – in 1961 and 1973, they destroyed the crosses. The national monument is now a popular place for newlyweds to have their picture taken. After the wedding ceremonies, the couple first lays roses at the foot of the statue of Mary, cross themselves before the Christ child and end the pilgrimage with a picture against this pious backdrop.

On the northeastern edge of Siauliai is the road to Pasvalys in **Ginkunai,** the *manorhouse* of the Russian Count's family Zubov, surrounded by the school grounds and a cemetery. *Alexander Zubov* became famous as a favoured subject of Czaress Catherine the Second.

Information

Accommodation

Hotels: Siauliai, Draugyste pr. 25, Tel: 3 73 33. Branch hotel: Vytauto gatve 74, Tel: 3 29 33; Salduve, Donelaicio 70, Tel: 56 16 79.
Airport: Meskuicial, Tel: 3 26 61 and 7 77 18. The former military airport is now opened to civilian air traffic.
Automobile Repair: Vilniaus gatve 8, Tel: 3 64 65.
Bus Station: Tilzes gatve 109 (when heading out of town to the west, before the railway bridge), Tel: 3 38 64.
Cafés: Kavine, Tilzes gatve 147. Kavine Kastonas, Ausros aleja 52.
Cinema: Tiesa, Ausros aleja 62.
Fuel: Kosmonautu gatve, Tel: 5 31 91, Kursenu pervaza, Tel: 3 62 71; Bielskio 47, Tel: 4 03 70; Tilzes gatve 223, Tel: 3 73 54; Vilnius gatve 12, Tel: 3 65 75; Zemaites gatve, 5 54 09.
Handicrafts: Daile, Vytauto gatve 136, Tel: 3 46 81; fabrics, ceramics, leather, paintings.
Hospital: Kurdikos gatve 99; bus 4 and 18.
Lost and Found Office: Tel: 9 73 27.
Marketplace: Turgaus gatve, Tel: 3 08 72.
Pharmacy: Ausros aleja 66.
Police: Ausros aleja 29.

Post Office: Ausros aleja 42, Tel: 3 06 20.

Restaurants: Blaiva, Vytauto gatve 145; Siauliai, in the Blaiva hotel, Draugyste pr. 25, Tel: 3 66 73.

Taxi: Tel: 4 22 01, Information Tel: 4 00 04.

Theatre: Ledaine Pie Teatro/Siauliai Dramos Teatros, Tilzes gatve 55/57, Tickets, Tel: 3 29 40 (open 11 am to 2 pm and 4 to 7 pm). Mazasis Teatro, Vilniaus 147, Tel: 3 67 00.

Tourist Information: Tel: 3 36 51.

Train Station: Dubijos 44, information, Tel: 3 06 52.

Ukmerges

Several kilometres to the north of the city at the edge of the plain and plateau of Austaitija is Ukmerges, an important traffic hub in Lithuania: this is the junction of the M 12 (Riga – Vilnius) and the A 226 (Kaunas – Daugavpils).

The Kauno gatve runs directly through the centre of this rather faceless city. The cultural centre, a pub and a department store are all on Kauno gatve. The economic backbone of this city is the furniture factory with around 900 employees. Founded in 1941, the factory exports desks and furniture for children and youths to Great Britain, Austria and Belgium.

Information

Bus Station: On the outskirts of town toward Utena.

Fuel: On the outskirts of town toward Kaunas.

Utena

A beer ... mous ... "Uten ... since ... ear th... tazas" knitt... 1967. A large amoun... is underway in this industrial ... kilometres (87½ miles) north of Kaunas on the A 226 and around 60 kilometres (37½ miles) from the Latvian border – countless houses and apartment complexes are being built on the outskirts of the city. Leading through the centre of town is the Basanaviciaus gatve. The city park is adjacent to the central bus terminal.

Information

Accommodation: Hotel Ledva, Autros gatve 45, Tel: 5 13 45; priced from £12 to £17 ($22 to $32). Located next to the Cultural Centre (Kulturas Nams).

Bus Station: Basanaviciaus gatve.

Fuel: On the outskirts of town toward Ukmerges on the left-hand side.

Pharmacy: Ausros gatve 24.

Post Office: Basanaviciaus gatve 59.

Visaginas

In the three-country region of Latvia, Belorussia and Lithuania is the "Russian island" of Visaginas near Lake Druksiai – 85% of the population are workers from other nations in the former Soviet Union. They were sent here in 1975 when a labour force was needed for the nearby Ignalina power plant. Originally named after the Communist official *Antanas Sniek-*

32,000 was first given
...ay name in 1991.

...ai

...small city of Zarasai, 4 kilome-
...s (2½ miles) south of the Latvian
...order in the northeastern regions of
Lithuania, is on the shores of Lake
Zarasu. The A 226 runs directly
through town. Zarasai is not only a
centre for administration and shopping for the Zarasai district, but is
also the central point of the small *lake
basin* with around 300 larger and
smaller bodies of water, making it a
popular holiday and recreation area –
although not necessarily the most
beautiful: wooden houses and apartment buildings stand directly next to
each other.

The baroque *St. Marijos* (St Mary's
Church) dominates the city with its
two whitewashed towers. The *Zarasai Krasto Muziejus* (Museum of
Local History; D. Bukanto gatve 20,
open Tuesday to Sunday from 10 am
to 6 pm) is reminiscent of the rural
and agricultural origins of the city.
Especially worth seeing: the silhouette collection.

Surroundings

One of the oldest and largest *oak
trees* in Europe stands in **Stelmuze**,
a village near Zarasai. The giant tree
measures 13.5 metres (44 feet) in
diameter and is estimated at being
1,500 years old. It is very difficult to
determine the exact age of the tree –
the annual rings have meanwhile begun to decay. The *wooden church*
from 1650 and remodelled in the 18th
century has a magnificent pulpit from

the end of the 18th century, embellished with sculptures and reliefs.
One beautiful example of Lithuanian
folk are is the free-standing bell
tower.

Touring Tip: A visit to the wood
carver *Robertas Matulionis* in **Anta-
zave,** Dembu pasode, Tel: 4 14 98.
Matulionis, whose works can be seen
in a number of museums, mostly
carves religious motifs. The folkloric figures are then painted.

Information

Accommodation: Hotel at D. Bukanto
gatve 7, Tel: 5 13 45.

Fuel: A 226, on the outskirts of town
toward Utena.

Pharmacy: Siauliai gatve 1.

Post Office : Seliu aikste.

Restaurants: Ednica in the Universal
department store, D Bukanto gatve
(next to the hotel).

Dzukija

In the southeastern regions of the
country is the province of Dzukija, a
landscape characterised by a highland plateau. The region has a large
pine forest with a number of very old
trees. The main town is Druskininkai,
the premiere beach and spa resort.

Alytus

Around 90 kilometres (56 miles)
southwest of Vilnius is the 34 square
kilometre (13 square mile) district city
of Alytus. 75,000 people live in this,
the southern centre of Lithuania.
Lethargically and heavily polluted,
the Nemunas River flows directly

through the centre of town. The old city centre is in the valley to both sides of the river; on the southern banks, concrete buildings and ugly grey apartment buildings line the river on the slope.

History

In 1377, the Lithuanians built a wooden fortress on the right banks of the river. A settlement was first mentioned in 1387. In 1501, the settlement was awarded the city rights of Magdeburg and then sank into insignificance during the 17th century until it was expanded into a Russian border fortification. The Second World War hit Alytus hard: 60% of the buildings were destroyed. In 1941 and 1942, 35,000 people died in the Alytus Nazi prisoner of war camp. A memorial also stands in the nearby forest – a reminder of the 60,000 Soviet citizens who were also killed here.

Under Soviet rule, Alytus was developed into an economic centre. Since 1929, the "Astra" factory with 1,450 employees has produced washing machines, ironing machines and electrical household appliances. 3,200 employees have produced refrigerators at the "Snaige" factory since 1964, which are exported to Spain, Hungary and Greece. Paints and lacquers have been produced in the chemical plant since 1936. A construction firm has provided work for around 4,000 employees since 1979, producing pre-fabricated homes. The main employer in this city is the cotton mill, where almost 6,000 employees produce thread, yarn and fabrics for export. The soft drink and champagne factory provides refreshments. Their wines, apple juice and champagnes are also exported to Germany. The economic significance of Alytus stands in sharp contrast to its touristic importance. The museum alone is worth visiting: the *Anthropological Museum* with its collection of early archaeological finds.

The city park, also called "sculpture park" because of the statues set up recently, confronts visitors with modern arts where the adults sooner stand baffled while the children have long since recognized their function – they climb, balance and play on the sculptures to their heart's content.

Information

Accommodation

Hotel: Dzukija Hotel, Pulko gatve/ corner of Jotvingu gatve, Tel: 5 13 45. Signalas, Santaikos gatve 31; built in 1984, on the outskirts of town toward Marijampole, across from the service station; guests are predominantly soldiers.

Bus Station: Jotvingu gatve 5/7.

Fuel: On the outskirts of town toward Marijampole.

Marketplace: Jotvingu gatve 10.

Police: Jotvingu gatve 8.

Post Office: Pulko gatve/corner of Jotvingu gatve.

Druskininkai

One hundred kilometres (62½ miles) south of Trakai is the city of Druskininkai near the Belorussian border. Around 2,200 residents enjoy every day what holiday visitors have valued since 1938: the mineral water springs, mud-baths and beaches on the Nemunas and the extensive pine forests surrounding the town.

Sights

Druskininkai is a "yellow" city, especially during the autumn: the colours of the linden leaves and the yellow brick buildings lend this city a golden radiance. This year, the few remaining residential streets with their *wooden houses* were especially beautiful – for example Cvirkos gatve. The *M. K. Ciurlionis Memorial Museum* (Ciurlionio 41, Tel: 5 27 55; open Tuesday to Sunday from noon to 6 pm) keeps the memory of the painter and composer *Mikalojus Konstantinus Ciurlionis* alive. He lived in Druskininkai during his youth. The museum is in the house of a close relative.

In commemoration of the 100th birthday of this national artist, a *memorial* was erected in the Nemunas Park in 1975. During the same year, the *Ciurlionis trail* was built, leading from Druskininkai to Varena and lined with wooden folk sculptures by local artists.

Surroundings

South of the road to Frodno is the picturesque *Reigardas Valley,* before the gates of the city. Especially during the autumn, the residents of Druskininkai take off to the nature reserve baskets in hand – countless mushrooms grow in the extensive forests.

Large pine forests in the eastern portions of the city make up the *Dzukijos National Park,* bisected by a straight road, one kilometre (½ mile) in length. Clearings offer views of the extensive forests of the highland plateau –

tree after tree as far as the eye can see. Offering a little more diversity is our tour tip. The gravel road to Marcinkonys leads through one of the most secluded areas in the country to towns and villages where time seems to have stood still. Old wooden houses, weathered dark by the wind and elements, crouch behind the impressive, richly decorated cross at the entrance to town; colourful gardens open to the streets. German shepherds bark, announcing each stranger in town and sheep and cows graze along the roadside. Dreams of old Lithuania – for example in **Purciai** (on the lake), and **Kasetos.** The roadside village of **Zervynos** has been preserved from the 18th century in its entirety. The beautiful wooden house village of **Marcinkonys** is dominated by a sunshine-yellow wooden church on a small hill. In the staunch wall of erratic blocks, devotional chapels recount the stations of the cross. A glaring contrast to this is nearby **Varena:** black billows of smoke rise from the middle of the forest; the military and a huge freight train station seem alien in this landscape. In **Mautizos** is a huge cement factory in the middle of the forest; gravel is quarried nearby.

Four kilometres (2½ miles) south of the Marcinkonys train station is the beginning of the *Cepkeliai Nature Reserve.* The 8,500 hectare (21,250 acre) area near the Belorussian border has the oldest swamp forests and the second largest moor area in the country, the 6,000 hectare (15,000 acre) "Cepkeliu raistas." This unparalleled habitat is still quite se-

The "Wonder-Water" of Druskininkai

Up to the middle of the 19th century, Druskininkai was a small village. The name is derived from the Lithuanian word "druska" meaning salt. The "wonder water of Druskininkai," praised highly in old legends, was first analyzed as commissioned by the Polish king and the Grand Duke of Lithuania *Stanislav August* by his personal physicians. The report, having disappeared for centuries, was rediscovered in 1835 by *Ignacy Fonberg*. Three years later, the first spa facilities were opened. The construction of the railway which runs past the town at a distance of 16 kilometres (10 miles) fostered the development as a health resort. Postal carriages ran regularly between the train station of Porecje (now in Russia) and Druskininkai, until a sideroad was built to the resort. Before the First World War, during which the mineral springs were polluted, 50,000 spa guests came to Druskininkai annually. Occupied by Poland from 1920 to 1939, Druskininkai became a part of the Belorussian SSR from October 1939 to August 1940.

After the Second World War, Druskininkai went back to Lithuania without any ado. The quiet return of this town is a point of controversy today: immediately after the announcement of independence, Minsk raised territorial claims on Druskininkai. This remains unresolved to date.

Despite this pending situation, Druskininkai is beginning with the restructuring and privatization of the formerly state-owned resort.

Nine sanatoria with over 5,000 beds were available to spa patients before the independence. Today, a number of buildings have been closed because of unresolved ownership.

Meanwhile, the eight mineral springs bubble up from the ground as ever. The "Grozis" is especially popular for drinking water therapy – the Grozis is the "spring of beauty." The *spa and therapy centre* of Druskininkai is at Dineikos 6. Mudbaths, inhalations, massages and gymnastics provide therapy for digestive and cardio-vascular ailments as well as treating rheumatism and arthritis.

cluded and hardly visited, offering numerous rare species of animal and plant life a refuge. Over 150 endangered species of birds, among them cranes, eagles, wood grouse and black grouse have found sanctuary here. Pine martens, lizards and am-

phibians can still find their natural habitats here. Over 43 species of plants which are otherwise listed as endangered grow here – arnica and hellebore, for instance. However, Cepkeliai is most famous for its cranberries. Around 900 kilograms per hectare

(727 pounds per acre) are harvested each year.

Information

Accommodation

Camping: Nemuno 26, Tel: 5 25 77.

Hotel: Druskininkai, Kurdikos 41, Tel: 5 25 66.

Airport: Tel: 5 10 25.

Automobile Repair: Baravyku 5a, Tel: 5 27 98.

Bank: Kurdikos 31, Tel: 5 34 54.

Bus Station: Gardino 1, information Tel: 5 13 33.

Cinema: Tel: 5 15 17.

Fuel: Gardino 53, Tel: 5 23 05.

Hospital: Ligonines gatve.

Polyclinic: Ciurlioni gatve/corner of Vytauto gatve.

Marketplace: Ciurlionio gatve 133a, Tel: 5 20 38.

Pharmacy: Ciurlionio gatve 105.

Post Office: Kurdikos 41, Tel: 5 21 11.

Restaurants: Astra, Vilniaus aleja 10, Tel: 5 33 35; Bebenciukas, Ciurlionio gatve 103, Tel: 5 35 14.

Taxi: Tel: 5 26 02.

Train Station: Gardino 3, information, Tel: 5 34 43.

✓ Trakai (Troki)

Twenty-eight (17½ miles) west of Vilnius on a narrow peninsula between three lakes is the island city of Trakai. East of the city is _Lake Luka,_ to the west is _Lake Totoriskiai._ In the middle of _Lake Galve_ the largest of the twenty islands rises up dark red and majestic, crowned by the famous _Water Fortress of Trakai._

History

The history of this city begins in the 12th century. Even then, Trakai was a fortified settlement. It is said that _Prince Gediminas_ moved the capital of Lithuania to this site in 1321. _Grand Duke Vytautas_ chose Trakai as his preferred residence from 1392 to 1430. He settled the Tartars and the Kara-Kalpak people (also spelled Qaraqalpaq) here, financed a church and monastery and brought monks from Tyniec in Poland. In 1409, Trakai was one of the first cities to be granted the city rights of Magdeburg. The old city castle, once belonging to the Grand Duke of Kestudies was replaced at the beginning of the 15th century by Vytautas with a magnificent fortified castle on an island in Lake Galve: the water castle. It remains the main attraction of the small city with a population of 8,000. Every summer the international elite of the rowing sport come to Trakai for the "Amber Rowing Competition."

Sights

The entire inner city is blocked off to traffic. Vytauto gatve, the main street through the island city in the lake, is lined with wooden houses and stone buildings from the 19th century. The _old fortress,_ of which only a few remnants of the two to three metre thick walls built from erratic blocks and ruins of the small tower remain standing, was presumably built from 1362 to 1382 by _Grand Duke Kestutis._ The Knights of the Order repeatedly occupied the fortress. And were successful at that – according to several sources, while the Lithuanian city chronicle reports that the Knights of the Holy Sword retreated. Passing the _Vytautas Church_ from the

16th to 18th century, one will come to the hotel and restaurant "Trakai." The way to the water castle leads along the Karaimu gatve to the *residential district of the Kara-Kalpak people*. At the end of the 14th/ beginning of the 15th century, these Turkic-speaking people were brought here from the Crimea Peninsula as prisoners of war and were given land by Grand Duke Vytautas or served in his royal guard. Their one-story, gabled wooden houses in yellow, green and brown characterize this portion of the city. The Kara-Kalpak still hold their Jewish religious services in the yellow *Kinessa* built in 1812 to replace the original building from the 15th century. The *Kara-Kalpak Ethnographic Museum* (Karaimu gatve 22) displays objects from daily life and introduces visitors to the art and handicrafts of the Kara-Kalpak – unfortunately, only in Lithuanian and Russian.

A long wooden bridge leads over to the fortress island with the impressive *water castle* (open Tuesday to Sunday from 10 am to 6 pm). Increasing attacks by the Crusading Knights prompted Grand Duke Vytautas to move his residence to the largest island in Lake Galve. Built around 1406 as a Gothic water fortress, an narrow strait around 500 yards wide now separates the old fortress from the new fortress. One can enter the masterpiece of Lithuania fortress architecture through the gate tower. Beyond this is the outer fortress. The large, trapezoidal inner courtyard is surrounded by walls of up to seven metres (23 feet) and

round corner towers. On the western side of the walls are two-storey, on the eastern side, three-storey casemates used to store weapons, ammunition and supplies as well as serving as a post for the fortress guards. A deep moat separates the fortress from the Duke's palace. A drawbridge leads to a gate, simultaneously a watchtower and living quarters, in the inner courtyard. The first and second floors of the inner fortress are connected by wooden galleries. The reception hall with an area of ten by twenty metres (98 by 65 feet) is the largest room in the palace and is located in the right wing. A spiral stairway leads to the uppermost floor in the 33 metre (108) foot tall residential tower. The *Museum of City and Fortress History* is on two floors of the palace. In the outer fortress, the *Historical Museum* is worth visiting with an occasional rarity or anecdotal object. In the hunting room, all of the tables and chairs were made from antlers and pelts. One seat rests on deer's feet – and on the table, a deer foot serves as a chalice. The pipe collection includes valuable cigar and cigarette holders made of Meerschaum or Meißen porcelain. A set table with blue and white china from the 19th century accents the dining room. In the bedroom, a statue of Amour shoots his arrow of love from the foot of the bed... Also worth seeing is the collection of enamel painting, enamelwork and enamel miniatures from the early 18th to 20th centuries. Works of Art Nouveau in pewter and glass, ivory and tortoiseshell from the 18th to

20th century are also on display. The art of glass-making came from Krakow to Kaunas in the 17th century, where the first glazer's workshop came into being. A visit to a hall with beaded embroidery is displayed as well as the porcelain room with works from Vienna, St. Petersburg and France concludes the tour.

After the fortress lost its importance in defence, its continual decay set in. It was only at the end of the 19th century that new interest in the fortress germinated in the scope of the National Awakening. The securing of the building began in the early 20th century. Extensive renovations were to follow from 1929 to 1940, an endeavour that was recognized with a governmental prize in 1967 – and rightfully so.

Surroundings

Lake Galve, with an area of 317 hectares (793 acres), was developed within the scope of an extensive recreational project in 1970. Today it is the heart of tourism in the Trakai region. During the summer, tour steamboats depart for the eastern banks to **Uztrakis.** The former *Palace of Duke Tyszkiewicz,* a neo-classicistic building from the 19th century, now accommodates tourists. The castle is within a 40 hectare (100 acre) park which was designed at the end of the 19th century by the then famous French landscape architect *Eduoard André.*

Information

Accommodation

Camping: Turistine Base Tarkuose, 4 kilometres (2½ miles) outside of town on the road to Vievis, Tel: 5 17 45; on the northern shores of Lake Galve near Slenis. On the western shores of Lake Totoriskiai is a well equipped camping area where rental boats are also available.

Hotel: Karaimu gatve 41, Tel: 5 13 45; brown wooden building; plain and dirty... very inexpensive and located directly on the lakeshore.

Boat Rental: on the lakeshore.

Restaurant: Nendre, Karaimu gatve, Tel: 5 20 08 at the north parking area.

Suvalkija

Suvalkija is the smallest province in Lithuania. It lies in the southwestern regions of the country and borders on Poland. The rather hilly region which suffered greatly under the war, has hardy any significant towns and is predominantly characterized by agriculture.

Kybartai (Kybarten)

The small city of Kybartai on the border to the Russian enclave of Kaliningrad is a legendary railway hub. Up to 1910, the beginning of the regauging technology, travellers had to debark with their luggage, pass through customs and passport control and board the wide-gauge Russian trains on the opposite side of the platform. The reason for this inconvenient procedure: the German trains ran on the normal gauge and the Russian trains, on the wide gauge. Unique in railway technology near Mockava: normal and wide gauge tracks run parallel here – in one set of tracks.

Lazdijiai

The small city of Lazdijiai is situated in an idyllic landscape of hills, 140 kilometres (87½ miles) west of Vilnius. Traffic jams miles in length make this otherwise inconspicuous city quite infamous: the travellers must calculate a wait of up to twenty hours on the Polish-Lithuanian border into their travel itinerary. Those who are completely distraught spend the night in the simple *hotel* in the centre of town and try their luck the following morning.

Marijampole

On the intersection of the A 119 and A 226 motorways, around 30 kilometres (19 miles) from the Polish border is the small city of Marijampole. The city of almost 20 square kilometres (8 square miles) on the Sesupe River was called *Vincas Kapsukas* up to the independence of Lithuania. The city, with a population of 29,000 originates from the establishment of a monastery here. A small city with the name "Marijampole" was first mentioned in 1756, and awarded the city rights of Magdeburg in 1792. 1828 brought the Incorporation into the railway network on the route from Warsaw to St. Petersburg. In 1866, a secondary school opened its doors and in 1919, a teachers college was founded in this predominantly Jewish city. The unusual population structure caused Marijampole to particularly suffer during the Second World War: the old city was almost entirely destroyed by bombs and fire. When the city was renamed in "Kapsukas" in 1955, the Christian origins of this now Soviet state were intended to be eradicated. It was only in 1991, that Marijampole was able to distance itself from its "artificial" name – Vincas Kapsukas, the leader of the Lithuanian Communist Party, as well as the name were pensioned-off.

Surroundings

Twenty-three kilometres (14½ miles) west of Marijampole on the A 229 is **Vilkaviskis.** A *castle* was built here during the 18th century by a German by the name of Knackfuß. Only recently restored, the building houses a small painting gallery.

Information

Accommodation: Hotel Sudeva, in the centre of town directly next to the town hall, Tel: 5 39 70 and 5 46 41.

Prienai

The administrative city of Prienai, 35 kilometres (22 miles) south of Kaunas, is situated on the western banks of the Nemunas. At the bridgehead above the meandering river is the *Memorial of the Grand Duke Kestutis* which has stood here since 1990. It had been stormed and torn down by the Red Army in 1954.

This small city typical for rural Lithuania has one of the nicest inns in the region: Hotel "Revuona" is housed in an old mill.

Information

Bus Station: Vytauto gatve shortly before the bridge over the Nemuna River.

Fuel: On the outskirts of town toward Birstonas.

Pharmacy: Basanaviciaus gatve/corner of Vytauto gatve.
Police: Basanaviciaus gatve.
Post Office: Basanaviciaus gatve.

Zuvintas

Southeast of Marijampole is the Zuvintas Nature Reserve with an area of 5,400 hectares (13,500 acres). The reserve comprises the nearly silted up *Zuvintas Lake* around 11 square kilometres (4¼ square miles) in area, 30 square kilometres (12 square miles) of *marshlands* and 12 square kilometres (4½ square miles) of *forests* as well as the largest *moor area* in the country.

Zemaitija (Schemaiten)

In the region of Zemaitija, the 15 to 20 kilometre (9½ to 12½ mile) wide coastline rises from the Baltic Sea to the Hills of Zemaicin, portions of which are under governmental protection. The highest elevation here is the 234 metre (765 foot) Medvegalis. With Klaipeda, the only harbour city is located in Zemaitija and with Palanga, the most famous beach resort.

Klaipeda (Memel)

Klaipeda, the old city of Memel, is not only the third largest city in Lithuania with a population of 203,000, but also has the only harbour in the country. The city extends along both sides of the Dane (Dange) River: on the left banks is the old city (Senamiestis) and on the right banks, the new city (Naujamiestis).

The Bird Paradise of Zuvintas

In addition to 258 species of birds – among them ospreys, white-tailed eagles and various types of falcons and hawks – there are over 600 different types of plants in the Zuvintas Nature Reserve. The special attraction of Zuvintas are, however, the "mute swans," which have brooded here since 1937.

History

Klaipeda was first founded as "Memele" (Memelburg) in 1252 by the Brothers of the Sword. At the base of the fortress, a settlement quickly developed which was awarded the city rights of Lübeck as early as 1258. As the only city between Riga and Königsberg, it was also the object of embittered battles as a "bridge" between the influential Teutonic Order and the Brothers of the Sword. The united Lithuania troops stormed the city under the leadership of *Grand Duke Gediminas*. When the city was allocated to the Teutonic Order in the *Treaty of Melne* in 1422, the Grand Duke attacked it anew – however, this time he would be forced to accept his defeat.

In 1525, Klaipeda came under Prussian rule. the *golden age* of this harbour and commercial centre commenced: in 1593, the first ships were built; in 1597, Klaipeda was awarded trade privileges. After a short Swedish interlude from 1629 to 1635, Klaipeda returned to the King of

Prussia in 1701. From 1709 to 1711, over 3,000 citizens died of the *plague.* The gap left behind was quickly filled by German colonists who resettled in Klaipeda. Klaipeda recovered from the wars and crises of the past decades. Leather processors began production from 1725 to 1731. In 1770, according to the chronicles, 500 ships were docked in the harbour of Klaipeda.

From 1863 to 1873, the construction of the *Klaipeda Canal* connected the Nemuna and Minija, offering better access to the Baltic for domestic shipping. The wood processing plant founded here in 1899 remains in operation today. This traditional factory employs 1,200.

Up to 1918, Klaipeda belonged to the German Empire. Resulting from the Treaty of Versailles the city and Memelland came under the *supervision of the League of Nations* before it was placed under the fiduciary administration of France on January 15, 1920. Occupied by Lithuanian volunteer corps in 1923, the region came under Lithuanian administration in 1924 before *Hitler's ultimatum* brought the city and Memelland back into the German Empire on March 22, 1939. The Red Army marched into Klaipeda on January 28, 1945. Almost the entire population fled west to Germany. The battle over Klaipeda, lasting months, destroyed two-thirds of the city. The planned resettlement changed the old structure of the population radically – today, around one-third of the residents are non-Lithuanian citizens.

Sights

The old centre with its streets laid out at right angles has been classified in its entirety as a historical monument since 1959; other sources say since 1969. The first restorations began in 1971 and continue even today. What has been completed, however, are almost all of the thirty individual buildings. One street that turned out especially nice is the Austoji gatve (High Street). The once extremely dilapidated craftsmen's houses from the 18th and 19th centuries have been reawakened and now house handicrafts shops, offices and bistros. Right in the middle is the oldest half-timbered building in the city, a renovated *warehouse from 1819.* Today, it is used for exhibitions. The *oldest house* in Klaipeda is a few metres farther: the brick building with

Annie of Tharau

Donations to the "Annie of Tharau Society" made it possible that a statue of the Klaipeda's most famous resident stands in memory since December 1989. The *statue* of a girl by *Arnold Haacke* has a medallion by *Simon Dach* (1605-1659) on its pedestal. With some notes from the famous folk song "Annie of Tharau" – sculpted onto the base – the memory of the poet born in Klaipeda is kept alive. The original Annie Statue was lost – in 1939, it first made way for a bust of Hitler and was then set up on Libauer Square where it suddenly disappeared.

the magnificent mansards dates back to 1775. In the *old post office* (No.13) letters are cancelled with a special stamp. The heart of the old city pulsates on *Teatro aikste* (Theatre Square). The former "new market," remodelled during the 19th century is dominated by the *Dramatic Theatre/Municipal Theatre.* The theatrical tradition of this square goes back a number of centuries: as soon as 1775, travelling theatre troupes would perform their plays on stage wagons. The comedy playhouse was built in 1819. A fire broke out in the rigging loft in 1854. Construction on a new building began as soon as 1857. The facade of the former German Theatre has shone in its former grandeur since May of 1990 after restoration totalling over six million Rubles. The balcony of this theatre played a role in world politics when *Adolf Hitler* held his "Anschluss speech" from there.

The *Green Pharmacy* on Tiltu gatve (Bridge Street) has also been lovingly restored. Built in 1677 by *Jakob Grund,* a small exhibition informs visitors about the pharmaceutical history of the city. In the late spring months when the chestnuts bloom, a walk along *Neris gatve* is a special experience. Art Nouveau buildings line the street: for instance the former Swedish Consulate (No. 8) and the former girls' secondary school (No. 4) now used as a conservatory.

The *ruins of the old Memelburg Fortress* (Zveju gatve 12) have meanwhile been secured in part.

Whether a reconstruction of the fortress from 1252 will be undertaken remains questionable: opponents are for the construction of university buildings on the historical foundations.

Walking Tours

I. The New City

The "new city" begins on the northern, right banks of the Dane River. A linden-lined boulevard was laid out in 1769 and 1770 leading off from the "geese market." The old Linden Street, renamed in 1802 to Alexander Street in honour of Czar Alexander I, is meanwhile called "Liepu iela" (Linden Street) once more. Surrounded by impressive merchants' houses, the *main post office* is a neo-Gothic brick building from 1890. Its carillon plays the melody "Annie of Tharau"... A few metres farther, a visit to the *Clock Museum* (No. 12) is worthwhile.

On the corner of Kristijonas Donelaicio Street, the former Auguste Viktoria School survived the bombs of the war. The Donelaicio aikste, formerly the sports field, is now complemented by a *memorial* for the classic Lithuanian author *Kristijonas Donelaicio* (1714-1780).

To the east of Liepu iela toward the train station is the *Mazvydas Park.* This park on the grounds of the old municipal cemetery was designed as a *sculpture park.* 106 sculptures are set up on the 10 hectare (25 acre) park grounds.

II. Post-War Klaipeda

The Taikos prospektas (Peace Street) runs directly through Klaipeda. Retail stores line the broad boulevard. To the south, the main artery leads to the residential district of Aksnyne; to the north, to residential districts in the forest. To the left-hand side of the main street is the Soviet *Military Cemetery*. 527 fallen soldiers are buried under the cement slab at this 1,000 square metre (10,690 square foot) plaza. The names of the fallen are listed on a marble plate at the head of the square. A huge sword rests on its point next to the eternal flame.

Museums and Galleries

– *Aquatic Museum* (Juru muziejus ir akvariumas): Smiltynes 3, Tel: 3 57 32; open 11 am to 6 pm. Take the ferry to the Curonian Spit to Smiltyne. The museum is in the old Neringa woods.

– *Laikroduziu muziejus* (Clock Museum): Liepu gatve 12, Tel: 1 36 94; open 11 am to 6 pm.

– *Laudies meno muziejus* (Ethnographic Museum): Pakalnes gatve 2, Tel: 1 56 51; open 11 am to 7 pm.

– *Mazosios Lietuvos muziejus* (Museum of Regional History): Didzioji Vandens gatve 6, Tel: 1 46 35; open 11 am to 7 pm. Presenting the history of small Lithuania as well as the city of Klaipeda; also a collection of coins and maps.

– *Dailes Parodu Rumai* (Painting Gallery): Aukstoji gatve 1; open 11 am to 7 pm. Exhibiting modern works of art.

– *Galeria Bohema:* Aukstoji gatve 3, entrance beyond the gateway to the left in the silo; open 11 am to 2 pm and 3 to 6 pm.

Sports and Recreation

Baltija Stadium, Dubysos gatve; Zalgiris Stadium, Sportininku gatve 46,

Voilà – the Lithuanian National Dish

Prusija, S. Simkaus gatve 6, Tel: 1 85 91. A Kavine-Bar-restaurant with an adjacent hotel. Restaurant: six nicely set tables in a small, cozy dining room predominantly frequented by locals. The service is prompt and friendly, the food is good and the coffee is excellent – all at moderate prices. This restaurant also has the Lithuanian national dish on its menu: "Cepelinai" – long dumplings made from raw potatoes and filled with minced meat, served in a light bacon sauce.

Tel: 9 77 90; Cycling Race Track, Divizijos gatve 16, Tel: 9 77 28; Gymnasium, Taikos prospektas 50, Tel: 9 41 10; tennis courts, M. Mazvydo parkas, Tel: 1 33 13.

Restaurants

Klaipeda, Naujo sodo 1, Tel: 5 70 17.

Meridianas, Danes krantine, Tel: 1 68 51. Restaurant aboard a three-mast ship.

Regata, Danes krantine, Tel: 1 25 06; a modern ship restaurant on the Dane River.

Neptunas, Tiltu 18, Tel: 1 41 68.

Neringa, Spalio pr. 40a, Tel: 4 03 32.

Vetrunge, Taikos pr. 28, Tel: 5 48 18.

Zuvedra, Kepeju 10, Tel: 1 52 34.

Viktorija, M. Melnikaites 12, Tel: 6 28 38.

Accommodation

Camping: Seven kilometres (4½ miles) to the north in Firuliai; simple and dirty but a nice location.

Hotels

Baltija, J. Janonio 4, Tel: 1 49 67.

Juragis, Debreceno, Tel: 3 89 50.

Klaipeda, M. Melnikaites 12, Tel: 1 99 60; diagonally across from, the old Queen Louise School. 400 beds on seven floors, ten-storey tower with a panorama bar and café on the ninth floor. Predominantly German tour groups chose this, the most expensive accommodation in town. This red brick building tends toward western standards and can sooner be recommended for the service facilities on the ground floor.

Pamarys, Sauliu (formerly Tarybines Armijos) 28, Tel: 1 99 39.

Smiltyne, Smiltynes 17, Tel: 9 11 49. On the Curonian Spit.

Vetrunge, Taikos pr. 28, Tel: 5 48 01.

Viktoria, S. Simkaus 12, Tel: 1 36 70; simple, inexpensive and quiet, located only a stone's throw from Hotel Klaipeda. Once a category III hotel. Rooms with cold running water, extra charge for warm showers.

Surroundings

Curonian Spit: → *individual entry*

Giruliai (Forestry Office): Seven kilometres (4½ miles) north of Klaipeda and readily accessible by train is the famous Baltic Sea resort of Giruliai. In 1863, the summer residence of wealthy Klaipedan merchants even became a spa town. Under the Soviets, Giruliai became known as the "Artek of Lithuania." As in Artek, a huge pioneer camp on the Black Sea,

eight central pioneer camps for children were set up here from June to August as well. A beautiful walk leads between the Baltic coast and the pine forests along the promenade to **Mellneraggen.**

Information

Airport: Aereouosto, Tel: 3 04 09.

Bus Station: Tarpmiestine autobusu stotis, Butku Juzes 9, Tel: 1 14 32, information: Tel: 1 48 63.

Cafés: Baras Bohema, Aukstoji gatve 3, with an inner courtyard; open 11 am to 4 pm and 5 to 11 pm.

Cinemas: Baltijos, Zviju 3, Tel: 1 67 28; Jurate ir Kastytis, Taikos pr. 105, Tel: 3 04 01; Svyturys, H. Manto gatve 27, Tel: 1 28 70; Vaidila, Paryziaus komunos 4, Tel: 5 29 87; Vaiva, H. Manto gatve 11, Tel: 1 73 54; Zemaitija, H. Manto gatve 31, Tel: 1 55 13.

Ferry to the Curonian Spit: Ferries from Klaipeda to the Curonian Spit depart from two locations: the ferry for pedestrians and automobiles departs from the old harbour to Smiltyne; the last ship leaves Klaipeda at 9 pm, the trip lasts around ten minutes. Prices (one way): buses 600 Rubles, cars 90 Rubles, pedestrians 9 Rubles. There is also a new ferry in the district of Smeltne, but using this ferry does unfortunately require a longer wait; the trip itself also takes around ten minutes.

Fuel (Degalines): Kretingos pientas, Tel: 9 72 44; Spalio prospektas, Tel: 2 22 88; Paryziaus Komunos, Tel: 1 28 16; Zyejybos uostas, Tel: 7 27 01.

Post Office: Main Post Office, Liepu gatve 12, Tel: 1 37 30; main Telegraph Office, Liepu gatve 16; telegram service around the clock, Tel: 06. Telephone office, Liepu gatve 30, also open around the clock.
Theatre: Dramos teatros, Danges 19, Tel: 1 30 12; Muzikinis teatras, Danges 19, Tel: 1 25 89.
Train Station: Gelezinkelio stotis, Priestoties 1, Tel: 1 44 38, information: Tel: 1 46 14.

Curonian Lagoon/Curonian Spit

Louis Passarge wrote "The most strange thing is the absence of any scale of comparison," during a ride through the dunes of the Curonian Spit in 1878. *Wilhelm von Humboldt* came to the enthusiastic conclusion in 1809 that "The Curonian Spit is so peculiar that one should have seen this area just as much as Spain or Italy if a wonderful impression is not

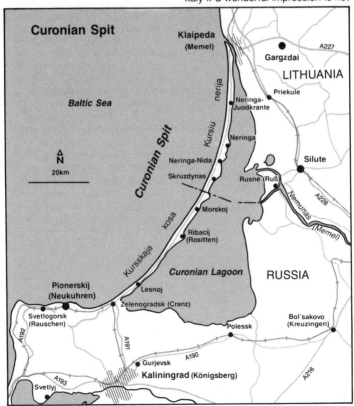

to be missing from one's mind's eye." The strange, breathtaking beauty of the Curonian Spit attracted painters – *Max Pechstein, Karl Schmidt-Rotluff, Ernst Mollenhauer, Lovis Corinth* – and even a Nobel prize winner for literature: the summer residence of *Thomas Mann* in Nida is now a heavily frequented museum. Of the former 79 kilometres (49 miles) of dunescapes, only 35 kilometres (22 miles) remain. The largest of the in total four regions of wandering dunes is on Russian territory. In Lithuania, the dunescapes extend from the Negeln Hook to Perwalka on the Palwe River and the highest dune is south of Nida.

In 1961, the five towns Nida, Preila, Pervalka, Juodkrante and Smiltyne were consolidated into an artificial city called "Neringa." The consequences remain evident: paved banks, large parking areas, cement highrises in the heart of the city. When the Spit threatened to suffocate in an avalanche of dust and stone, cement and sheet-metal, the officials' surprising change in policy followed at the last second: the Curonian Spit was declared a national park. A botanists' conference in Juodkrante confirmed the "natural wonder of the Curonian Spit" in June of 1976 and called for strict protective regulations.

One of these regulations is financed from the pockets of visitors: a police outpost before Juodkrante charges admission for a visit to paradise. The "spa tax" serves the preservation and protection of the Curonian Spit: pedestrians 39 Rubles, motorcycles 49 Rubles, day-pass for a car and one

The Everyday of the Curonian Fishermen

The *Ethnographical Museum* tells of the daily routine of the Curonian fishermen. Displayed here are straw-roofed fishing cottages from the turn of the century, a Curonian barge with a Curonian flag from Purwin as well as a "caterpillar wagon" from the early years of sea rescue. In an old villa, the *House of Animals* provides information on flora and fauna as well as the geological evolution of the Curonian Spit. The old Neringa Forest has been the site of the main attraction of this area since 1979: the unparalleled *Maritime Museum* with an adjacent aquarium. Over 11,000 shells and coral are on display here. In the aquarium it is more lively with not only endemic fish but tropical species as well. The three dolphin pools are filled with water from the Atlantic. Up to 1,000 spectators can experience a trained seal show daily at 12:30 and 5:30 pm.

person 243 Rubles, buses 340 Rubles. The main road to Nida runs along the old postal route from Königsberg via Memel (Klaipeda) to St. Petersburg. Rest areas and parking areas, some of which are equipped with picnic tables line the paved road today. The route is 98 kilometres (61 miles) long, leading to the Russian beach resort Cranz. Around 60 kilometres (38 miles) on the Lithuanian side lead up to the Russian border crossing point beyond Nida.

Smiltyne (Sandhof)

The lively beach resort and excursion destination near the ferry to Klaipeda was named after a historic tavern in the sand. First mentioned in 1616, this inn on the 15 metre (49 foot) dune was destroyed in 1945. On the west side of the Curonian Spit, a broad sandy beach begins toward the Baltic Sea which extends along the entire length of the peninsula. A cement promenade leads to a "linguistic peculiarity with a view." The northern end of the Curonian Spit is called the "Süder Spitze" (southern point). It was so named because opposite it was the southern mole of the city of Klaipeda – therefore, the Curonian Spit lay to the south of the city from that perspective. This point offers a very nice view of the harbour of Klaipeda.

Information

Accommodation: Hotel Smiltyne, Smiltynes 17, Tel: 9 11 49; the former main spa building has been transformed into a hotel.

Transport: Bus connections to Juodkrante, Pervalka, Preil and Nida departing from the ferry docks. On the lagoon side of the peninsula the main road along the eastern shore runs by a construction zone for the new yacht harbour ant to the junction with the road leading to the second ferry to Klaipeda (2.5 km/1½ miles). Three carved resort pennants on the lefthand side greet visitors. The road continues through a series of curves through a pine forest gently ascend-

ing up to *Hageno kalva* (Hagen's Hill) at an elevation of 38 metres (124 feet), then back down to *Bear Canyon*. Passing the Budnischen Haken, one will pass close to the *Liebestal* (Valley of Love) before toll is charged in Alksnyne (Almins Bay) at a police outpost with a tollgate.

Juodkrante (Schwarzort)

Twenty kilometres (12½ miles) from the ferry docks and 30 kilometres (19 miles) before Nida is the first larger fishing and holiday town of Juodkrante, extending along the bay on the Curonian Spit. During the middle of the 17th century, the present-day site of Villa Hubertus was where the tavern "Black Town" (German: Schwarzort) was founded. A small settlement developed surrounding the tavern which simultaneously served as a postal station. After permission for the construction of fishing cottages was granted in 1680, the first six already stood in 1697. A village school provided education for the youth beginning in 1743. Raised in status in 1795 to a parish, the parsonage was built in 1831. The church, first built of wood with a stray roof fell victim to a fire in 1878. The new neo-Gothic structure served other purposes under the Soviets, namely as a museum. On July 4, 1922, the "collapse of the Schwarzort Dune" shook the city: one beautiful sunny day, portions of the dune broke off and plummeted into the valley. At the northern entrance to town is the Amber Bay, where the "Baltic gold" was industrially extracted from

The Curonian Lagoon – A never-ending battle against the sandy destruction

The name Neringa is derived from the Lithuania word "neria" which describes a strip of land protruding from the water, created by the action of the waves.

Up to the Seven Years' War, the old Neringa Forest covered the dunes – then this natural protection against erosion was used to build ships and for firewood, which almost completely destroyed the forest. The consequences: seven villages were buried in sand dunes over the course of the centuries – Kunzen, Neustadt, Predin, Negeln, Karwaiten, Pillkoppen and Lattenwalde.

In 1882, a postmaster from Nida undertook the battle against the sandy destruction by planned planting and afforestation programmes. A gravestone in the Nida Lake Cemetery commemorates the pioneering achievements of *Georg David Kuwert.*

However, the constant shifting of the Spit continues even today. In 1980, a severe storm broke the Curonian Spit in two at the narrowest point near Sarkanu near the Russian town of Cranz – the peninsula temporarily became an island. Before the crevice could become a trench, it was closed up, thanks to the enormous efforts of the workers.

The maximum height of the wandering dunes is 70 metres (230 feet) – the strong winds do not allow the accumulation of sand above this point. The typical ripple marks on the dunes were explained during the past century by *Hermann von Helmholz:* "Ripples always form where two bodies moving at different speeds come into contact."

The "Helmholz ripples" are formed on the meeting point of air and sand – similar to those on the ocean floor.

The "Kupsten" (dead dunes) are evidence of earlier sand dunes. These knolls, similar to stork nests, are what remains of the humus soil after the dune is eroded away. The bizarre world of forms evolving from the play of wind, sand and moisture holds every beauty and every danger. Dark areas before hollows indicate the danger of quicksand – avoid these areas at all costs and give them a generous berth. If moisture is too low, dunes break off into pieces which fall down the dune similar to an avalanche. During extremely dry periods, entire dunes can collapse.

A Fairytale Hike on the Blocksberg...

The *hiking trail* built from 1979 to 1981 on the 53 metre (173 foot) *Blocksberg* in *Juodkrante*, which begins next to the large parking area is lined with around 40 artistically carved tree-trunks by Lithuanian artists. The carved wooden *sculptures* take up motifs from the fantasy world. Some depict, quite humorously, Curonian traditions. One example is the larger-than-life sculpture of King Naglis with his wooden club, the devil and a witch gamble, or Siegfried battles a dragon. Also interesting is the statue of a woman, hugging a tree on which a number of birds are perched...

1862 to 1899. In 1883 alone, 75,546 kilograms (around 70 tonnes) were extracted in this area. Today, the bay is calm. With a bit of luck, some moose can be observed drinking here at dusk. Large holiday complexes like "Pilkope," "Gintaras," "Juras" and "Nerijas" dominate the modern centre of town today, in which construction is still underway. Only one *wooden villa* at Kalno gatve 4 is reminiscent of the period of promoterism.

More traditional is the district of Karwaiten. Surrounding the old *Aalfang Square* where the fishing baskets still lay out to dry in the wind, are fishing cottages from the 20th century in brown and blue. To the right-hand side of the main road is the *Raganu Kalnu Muziejus* (Wood Sculpting Museum; admission free of charge).

Surroundings

The *Heron Hills* rise 44 metres (144 feet), the name of which goes back to the former heron colony on the Curonian Spit. Worth seeing here is the panorama from this vantage point which makes the climb worthwhile. If tired of walking and driving is preferred, there is a parking area at the top.

Information

Accommodation: Gintaras, Kalno gatve 12, Tel: 5 22 15 (only with reservations).
Transport: Bus connections to Smiltyne, Perwalka, Preila and Nida.

Beyond the Heron Hills, the main road leads to a parking area from which it is only a short was up the 40 metre (131 foot) *Avikalnis* (Sheep Hill) with a beautiful view. A serpentine trail leads back down. Halfway to Perfalka, several parking areas line the road. To the left-hand side on the horizon one can recognize the old sand hills of the *Great Dunes*. The landscape is also called the "dead dune" due to its age. The most beautiful view is from the 53 metre (173 foot) *Neegelsche Mountain* which is around 2 kilometres (1¼ miles) north of Pervalka. The dunescape, a fantastic hiking area, is transversed by narrow, unmarked trails. During the autumn, a large number of people gather mushrooms in this area. Through the grey dunes, grown with heather and grass and passing the scattered dwarf pines and birch trees, the way leads to the sand dune belt which falls off steeply into the lagoon.

A wooden pillar stands atop the 53 metre (173 foot) Skirpstas (Kirbste Mountain) on the side-street to Pervalka to the left-hand side. This is a *memorial pillar* for the *Theology Professor Ludwig Reza* (1776-1840) from the sunken village of Karwaiten quotes a few lines from his poem "The Sunken Village," published in 1797 in "Prutena."

Pervalka (Perwelk)

Pervalka is the smallest village on the Curonian Spit after Sandkrug. It is home to a population of 175. The former fishing village now lives from tourism: the new holiday complex along the lagoon side is unusually moderate in its dimensions, green and inviting. The name of this village "Pervalka" (= "dragged here"; per = here, wilk = drag) is reminiscent on the fate of the first residents – the inhabitants of the villages that were buried in sand dragged what was left of their possessions here. A *hiking trail* leads from the parking area on the northern edge of the city along the coast to a picnic area on a small bay. The red "lagoon light" rises out of the water: it warns fishermen and navigators of the "Horseshoe" shoal. To the south of the village is the spacious "Baltininkas" holiday complex; beyond it, a basketball court and a parking area.

Information

Kavine/Baras Venta: in the centre of town.

Paddle Boat Rental: Holiday Hostel "Baltija."

Post Office: Pervalka gatve 12.

Preila

Preila, once an inside tip for those on holiday on the Curonian Spit is now more metropolitan than Pervalka – and that with only 220 residents... This town was founded by refugees from the villages buried in sand. Preila was first discovered as a resort by the painters *Max Beckmann* and Erich Heckel. Only a few, isolated but lovingly restored *fishermen's cottages* are reminiscent of old Preila. The centre of town, marked by a *sculpture* of four gulls on posts, is composed of modern buildings which have successfully incorporated elements from the fishermen's houses. Less nice, in fact, is the cement *promenade* along the lagoon. On the southern outskirts of town is the small harbour of Preila. The nearby *Wetzekurgsberg* is considered the highest "mountain" on the Curonian Spit region. Some sources state its elevation at 63 metres (206 feet), others at 66 metres (216 feet). As a wandering sand dune, it is however subject to differing altitudes. The Wetzekurgsberg is in constant competition for "highest dune" with the high dune south of Nida and the Pillkoppener Dune in the Russian portion. All three of these "mountains" are over 60 metres (196 feet) high. The *Palwe* is the smallest of the remaining wandering sand dunes in this area.

The *Moose Forest* begins south of Preila. At the *Bulwikkschen Hook* the Curonian Spit reaches its widest point, measuring four kilometres (2½ miles). The narrowest area is near Sarkau near the Russian town of Cranz.

The secluded cement slope on the lagoon serves in summer as a runway for the air traffic from the Polangen airport, otherwise it is used as a parking area.

Nida (Nidden)

The largest and probably most well known city on the Curonian Spit, Nida, came into being as a result of the consolidation of the three villages of Purwin, Nida and Skrusdin. From three parking areas (the way is marked) on the motorway with bus stops, a network of trails leads past the holiday and residential complexes in the pine forests over the dunes and into town which is blocked off to traffic.

Walking Tours of the City
I. "On the Hook" – Old Nidden

All of the old *Nida wooden houses* are without exception classified as historical monuments. On especially beautiful example is the *Peleikis House.* In front of the yellow building in the centre of town in a small garden is the *sculpture of the "sitting lady."* The *Villa Charlotte* (Pamarios gatve 4), built in 1909 now houses the Music School; the reading halls are now in the former Froese department store. The neo-Gothic *brick church* of Nida, consecrated on October 10, 1888, was used for exhibitions and concerts beginning in 1959. Since Christmas 1988, church services are held here once more. The old *Forest Cemetery* was captured on canvas by *Lovis Corinth.* The strange graveyard with its old gravestones, now classified as historical monuments, is presently being restored.

To the south id the *Muziehas Etnografinis Skyrins* (Ethnographic Museum; Nagliu gatve 4, open Wednesday to Sunday from 11 am to 7 pm). The rooms in the blue fisherman's house from 1935 have been kept in their original condition. In the garden is a black tarred Curonian barge – one of the 70 barges that docked in Nida. Next door is a fish restaurant. The other houses on the *Nagliu gatve,* most of which were built from 1910 to 1930, are reminiscent of the days of yore in Nida.

II. Nida – The New Centre

The entire city centre of Nida was newly developed. Men fish from the pier, painters attempt to capture the atmosphere of the city with oils on canvas. Before the harbour pier is the three-storey *city hall.* The brick building with its four-fracture roof picks up on the gable forms of the old Nidan fishing cottages. Sooner grey and gloomy is the service complex with

Encounters with Thomas Mann

The brown estate with the light blue window frames on "Mother-In-Law's Mound" formerly stood at the disposal of Hermann Göring as the "Elchwald hunting cottage" – however, he never made use of it. Thus, the Mann family came here. In 1929, Thomas Mann wrote "so taken with the indescribable character and beauty of nature, the fantastic world of wandering dunes, the pine and birch forests populated with moose between the lagoon and the Baltic Sea, the wild wonder of the beach, we decided to make a permanent residence of this secluded area." Shortly prior to this, Thomas Mann had been awarded the Nobel Prize for Literature.

On July 16, 1930, Thomas Mann moved into his cottage in the dunes and returned every summer with his family – until the Manns were forced to leave Germany in 1933. The summer house was converted into a museum in 1967 – on the ground floor, exhibits provide information on the work of this author; on the upper floor are the study rooms. Only the view from the upper floor is a disappointment: the much quoted "Italian view" is now almost completely blocked by bushes and shrubs.

the "agila" recreation centre, the "Gilija" shopping market and a simple café. The hideousness of the residential area along Pillkoppener Way in the middle of the dune forest was corrected during recent years by extensive architectural alterations. Stalin's monotonous architecture was "beautified" with new roofs, balconies and facades; trees and green areas were also planted.

III. Nida-Skrusdin –
the Artist Colony

Around the turn of the century, artists discovered the attraction of Nida. In 1888, a genre-painting by *Bishop Culm* made this town known within literary and painting circles. *Lovis Corinth* sketched the well at the old village inn and captured the "Cem-

etery of Nidden" on canvas in gloomy robust brushstrokes. *Hans Kallmayer* is considered the "moose painter" of Nida. *Ernst Mollenhauer,* who last resided in the artists' colony in 1945 remained true to Nida in his later years as well. In 1953, for example, he painted the "Rescue Station of Nidden." Those who did not stay at Hotel "Hermann Bode" directly at the beginning of a small steep coastline on the lagoon at least visited here: today, only a metal plaque on the exterior of the building stands as a reminder of the former artists' lounge. The film industry also discovered Nida. A few scenes for the film "Journey to Tilsit" were filmed here on the lagoon beach. The poet *Agnes Miegel* ultimately dedicated her poem to the "women of Nidden." Passing Gulbis Court, the horseshoe complex owned by the Gulbis siblings and the painter *Knauf's* house, a paved street leads to the most famous artist's domicile in Nida, the *Tomas Mano Manelis* (Thomas Mann's House; Skruzdynes 19; open Tuesday to Sunday from 11 am to 5 pm).

IV. Nida Naturally

A chain of hills separates the town on the lagoon and the beach on the Baltic Sea. The *Angiu Kalns* (Snake Hill) is 50.5 metres (165 feet) in elevation. The new cemetery of Nida extends around the modern cemetery chapel. Recently, the tradition of the old wooden crosses is being continued. Since times long past, the *lighthouse of Nida* stands atop the 51 metre (167 foot) *Urbo Kalns.* The old stone tower was replaced in 1874 by a red and white striped metal beacon.

The *Parniddener Mountain* to the south of Nida is a 51 metre (167 foot) sand dune. Those who prefer not to hike to the top along the stairway lined with benches, can drive to the top on the paved side-street from Pillkoppener to the parking area. Hiking trails lead from the Parnidden Mountain to the *Valley of Silence* and to the *High Dune* – a hike that is definitely worth the while.

Information

Accommodation: Jurate, Pamario gatve 3, Tel: 5 26 18 and 5 26 19; a spacious holiday complex laid out around a central fountain and the old fishermen's house "Villa Udine."

The Grove of Hope – A Lovely Tradition

Another something worth seeing in Junknaiciai is the *Grove of Hope:* With every birth, a small tree is planted – a linden for each girl and a oak for each boy.

Beach: Lagoon side: a narrow sand beach on the outskirts of town when heading toward the dunes. Baltic side (at the sand dune); is not accessible. A nudist beach for women is in the beach area directly near the border.

Boat Rental: Lotsmikio 1.

Bus Station: Tarybu gatve, near the town hall.

Pharmacy: Taikos gatve 7 (in the polyclinic).

Polyclinic: Taikos gatve 7.

Restaurants: Seafood Restaurant Eserine, Nagliu gatve 2 (next to the Ethnographic Museum); Nida, Pamario 1, open 11 am to 5 pm, a simple but good cafeteria with a bar located in the park.

Special Events: Sailboat regatta during the summer.

Transport: Blue and white sightseeing train departing from the pier daily from 10 am to 6 pm. The tour lasts around ten minutes and costs 10 Rubles.

Travel Agency: Modum, Taikos gatve 4.

Lagoon Villages and the Nemunas Delta

(in the former Memelland)

Junknaiciai (Jugnaten)

Fifteen kilometres (9¼ miles) south-east of Silute is the agricultural centre which was once developed as a model kolkhoz. Today, around 2,000 people live in Junknaiciai. The town's name first appeared in historical documents in 1540. In 1761, the establishment of a village school was reported; in 1872 came the incorporation into the railway route from Tilsit to Klaipeda. The model kolkhoz, nestled in a well-tended park has a _Health and Culture Centre_ with a swimming pool, sauna and underwater massage – a rarity in Lithuania and especially in rural regions like this.

Near the "Grove of Hope" is the highest elevation in the Silute district. The _Alge Kalnis_ rises to a height of 34 metres (111 feet). According to the legend, a castle is buried within the hill.

Kintai (Kinten)

The old village of Kintai, located along the birch-lined avenue became the centre of a gigantic kolkhoz under the Soviet regime. The large high-rise apartment blocks dominate the district of Sakucia especially with their monotonous grey and flat roofs. The village is favourably situated at the wooden bridge spanning the Minjia River. In the main town of Kintai,

however are a few old farmhouses and craftsmen's houses.

In the centre of the village is the old Protestant _church_ (Ciulados gatve 27) from 1704. The church, hardly damaged in the war, was confiscated in 1950 and used as a concert hall. Meanwhile church services take place here once more. The former _Hallische Villa_ now houses a bank (Ciulados gatve 33). The stately building rests on a foundation of erratic blocks. Brick niches and ornaments decorated the light plastered building.

The _swimming beach_ on the lagoon is also beautiful; it falls off gradually into the water.

Information

Pharmacy: Ciulados gatve 9.
Post Office: Ciulados gatve 7.

Minija (Minge)

The fishing village of Minija on the river with the same name has the epitaph "Little Venice" – a little exaggerated for the few fishing cottages which line the right and left banks of the river. The town itself which is often cut off from the outside world during the spring due to flooding and is only accessible by boat then, has been discovered by artists in recent years. Painters, authors and craftsmen have converted some of the old houses to studios and ateliers.

Priekule (Prökuls)

Municipal stone buildings, hardly any wooden houses, point to the small city of Priekule's German cultural legacy, a city located on the A 228 between Klaipeda and Silute. Before the gates to this rather ordinary city is a small *amber warehouse*.

Information

Bank: Klaipedos gatve 6.
Fuel: One kilometre (½ mile) out of town on the rural road to Klaipeda.
Pharmacy: Klaipedos gatve 2.
Post Office: Turgaus gatve.

Saugos (Saugen)

Earlier, Saugos was one of the most affluent villages in the Memelland. Surrounded by excellent soil, even the train from Königsberg stopped here to obtain the farmer's deliveries. A sawmill brought affluence to the city. Today, there is little left of the former rural village. To ensure that the village's history is not lost forever, the former schoolhouse is presently being converted into a museum.

Silute (Heydekrug)

Forty-four kilometres (27½ miles) south of Klaipeda is the district city of Silute, situated on the A 228. Only 11 kilometres (7 miles) to the south is the Nemunas River, the border River to the Kaliningrad region. The pop vocalist *Alexandra* who was in the charts during the 1960's, comes from this region. An automobile accident abruptly ended her life.

History

Resulting from the consolidation of the villages Shilokarcema (Heydekrug), Czibai (Szibben), Verdaine (Werden) and Cintijonischkai (Cintio-

nischken) was the city of Silute. The name of this town can be traced back to a grant from 1511, allowing the operation of a tavern (Krug) in the heath (Heide). The first church in this young city was built in the district of Verdaine in 1541 on the present site of the textile mill. The city grew; a postal station, pharmacy and library would follow. In 1842, the first dairy in the Memelland began producing butter and "Tilsit cheese" in 1842. After the Second World War, it was expanded to a state cheese factory where 3,460 tonnes of cheese, milk, cream, kefir, and other dairy products in 1990. Where once oxen and cattle once changed hands at the central livestock market of the regional is now the "Baldaiu" furniture factory. That which began as a small furniture workshop has produced kitchen furnishings, stools and tables since 1958. In 1991, the Silute furniture factory exhibited 13 lines at a special exhibition in the Paris Furniture Museum. The pump factory founded during the early post-war years, manufactures hydraulic apparatuses for Germany, China and India. In the textile mill over 1.5 million yards of fabric in twelve colours and patterns and almost 700 tonnes of yarns are manufactured annually. The distillery has produced around five million litres of liquor since 1936.

In autumn of 1941, Silute was awarded city status. The administrative and economic centre of Memelland with around 22,000 residents is the seat of an Agricultural Technical Academy. Diverse cultural life also characterizes the small city: the dancing group "Fezginele," folklore groups, folk song ensembles and a mixed choir have been renowned well beyond this region for 46 years. The city newspaper "Pamarys" appears on weekdays and provides information on local events with a circulation of 15,000; a radio programme is broadcast three times weekly from Silute. In 1991, Silute celebrated its 480th anniversary.

Sights

A ring of modern buildings surrounds the old city. The 50 metre (164 foot) neo-Gothic tower belonging to the Protestant *church* towers above all other buildings in the city. This church, built in 1926, seems a bit odd at this location – the whitewashed building is strikingly similar to a rural southern German church.

The Catholic *Holy Cross Church* was built of red brick in 1854. The small *Silutes Muzeigus* (Museum of Local History; Lietuvininku gatve 16, open Tuesday to Friday from noon to 6 pm, Saturday and Sunday from 11 am to 4 pm) is very much worth visiting. On display here are rustic furniture from the 18th century from the collection of the former estate owner Dr.h.c. *Hugo Scheu.* The highlights of the exhibit by this publisher and collector of lesser Lithuanian cultural relics are the wardrobe with rural paintings from 1795 and a table from 1783. An old Memelland room with a bed, trunk and a floor clock has been preserved. A second room shows the regional wildlife. The Museum of Local History, at present quite cramped, is planned to be moved to the old estate on the banks of the Sysa

when renovations are completed. The stately *Fire Department* was built in 1911.

One pleasant walk leads on the *promenade along the Sysa* through the "Crane Forest" to Verdaine.

Surroundings

Four kilometres (2½ miles) east of Silute is **Macikai** (Matzicken). The author *Hermann Sudermann* was born on September 30, 1857 in the old estate village, now dilapidated and over built with monotone apartment buildings. The house where he was born, a yellow plastered house to the left of the entrance to town keeps the memory of Hermano Udermano (Hermann Sudermann) alive. The *memorial museum* on the ground floor is open from 11 am to 6 pm and can also be visited at times other than the official hours – the museum curator lives on the upper floor. The famous dramatist of the turn of the century wrote socially critical dramas like "Honour" and "Sodom's End," but also narratives and novels like "Lithuanian Stories" (1917) and "Journey to Tilsit" (1917).

Traksedziai (Trakseden) is the economic centre of the over 3,000 hectare (7,500 acre) *Aagstumal Moor.* Peat has been extracted here since 1882. The current industrial extraction of peat ensures a raw material basis for the state-operated peat processing plant, which exports 150 to 160 tonnes of peat to Denmark, Belgium and Austria.

Eight kilometres (5 miles) west of Silute is *Kroku Lunka.* The large inland lake at the delta of the Nemunas and Minija Rivers not far from Ruguldi belongs to the Nemunas River Delta National Reserve, which has protected this unique alluvial land area since 1975.

Information

Accommodation: Hotel Nemuna (formerly Deim's Hotel), Lietuvininku gatve 70, Tel: 5 23 45; with a Kavine.

Airport: Six kilometres (4 miles) to the east.

Culture Centre: Lietuvininku gatve 6.

Fuel: On the outskirts of town toward Klaipeda.

Hospital: Rusnes gatve 1.

Police: Lietuvininku gatve 29.

Restaurant: Rambynas, Lietuvininku gatve 68.

Tourist Information: Tourist Association, Lietuvininku gatve 36 (on the first floor of the museum), Tel: 5 12 47.

Rusne (Ruß)

Eight kilometres (5 miles) southwest of Silute is Rusne, an old "raft city." For the crossing over the Curonian Lagoon and farther to Klaipeda, the rafts coming from Lithuania were maintained and repaired here. Due to the location on the three rivers Athmath, Skirwieth and Pokallna – all tributaries of the Rusne River – the town is often flooded during the winter thaw. Access via the bridge is then closed off – Rusne can only be reached by amphibian vehicle, boat or helicopter. The water that floods the meadows is heavily polluted. The sewage from the nearby paper factory in **Sovjetsk** (Tilsit) ultimately lead to an absolute ban on swimming in the rivers. The murky water fits in well with the gloomy city. Despite a few rather attractive new buildings in the centre of town, the city (whose coat of arms depicts a boat with fishing nets) makes a rather dilapidated impression. The former fishing harbour is now used by the coast guard. The *church,* in existence at the time of the Teutonic Order, was rebuilt after a fire in 1809. The small *museum of Rusne* can be visited by appointment: contact Mr. Banys, Tel: 5 81 69.

A cobblestone street, partially unpaved, leads in a ring over the alluvial island in the Nemunas Delta. Lined with scattered pollard willows and drained areas of land, a narrow pathway leads to **Pamarys** with its large goose farm at the entrance to town. Grey herons nest beyond the village: birds as far as the eye can see. Crouched behind the dike is the village of **Syskrante** with its dark wooden houses and fishing cottages along the gravel road. A cobblestone alleyway leads to the fishing village of **Skirytele** on the Pokallna.

Vente (Windenberg)

On the point in the Curonian Lagoon is the small fishing village of Vente, 10 kilometres (6¼ miles) southwest of Kintai. A small fishing harbour at the entrance to town, four scattered residential houses and a small sand beach on the lagoon hardly reflect Vente's former importance and power.

Up to the 16th century, the mighty Lithuanian fortress stood here, defending the land against attacks by the Teutonic Order. In the side of the old fortress is now the *lighthouse*. The beacon is now combined with the living quarters of the lighthouse caretaker. The lighthouse is classified as a technical monument.

The main attraction of Vente is the birds which nest here. The migratory species have been captured and tagged by ornithologists since 1929. The small *Ornithological Museum* (open 10 am to 6 pm) provides information in two large display cases on the ornithological world of the Curonian Lagoon.

On the upper floor, a balcony enclosed in glass serves as an observatory. The nets used to catch the birds are quite impressive, a huge rigging amid the underbrush.

Vente is especially beautiful during the evening: the gulls perch on the stone pier. The evening sun floods the calm waters of the lagoon in deep gold before the smouldering red orb sinks beyond the dunes of the Curonian Spit.

Mainland Coastline north of Klaipeda / Hinterlands

Kretinga

Twenty kilometres (12½ miles) north of Klaipeda on the A 225 is the railway junction of Kretinga in the upper Dane Valley. This city with a population of 22,000 in the coastal hinterlands is popular with visitors from the nearby city of Palanga who seek diversion from the beaches.

A fortress called Kretinga first appeared in the old annals in 1253 – the Zemaites conquered the fortress of the Brothers of the Sword at that time. During the numerous battles against these warriors from Klaipeda, the Zemaites were repeatedly successful in defending their fortress during the subsequent centuries.

In the 16th century, the *Duke Zubov* and *Duke Tyskiewicz* built their magnificent *aristocratic palaces*. The vocational school is now housed in these stately mansions.

Beer has been brewed in Kretinga since 1838. The main square built in the 17th century with the *church* and the adjacent *Franciscan Monastery* forms the centre of this small city. Built from 1610 to 1617 by the master builder Akron, originally as a one-naved church with a tower, it was expanded and remodelled into a three-naved baroque basilica. The high, pointed Gothic windows point to the church's origins; paintings on the ribbed vaulting originate from the Renaissance. Especially worth seeing are the artistically ornamented Renaissance doors to the sacristy and the anterior hall. The silver statues on the pulpit disappeared during the Great Northern War. In the monastery, the large library, the refectory and the old dining hall make a visit worthwhile.

Also beautiful is the nearby *Orangery* from the 19th century with over 100 exotic plants and flowers.

A small *Museum of Local History* (Vilniaus gatve 2) offers information on the history of Kretinga. In the district of Bajorai in the southern portions of the city near the railway, a gatepost separated the German enclave of Memelland from the Russian empire up to the First World War.

Mazeikiai

The industrial town of Mazeikiai in northern Lithuania on the A 222 lies 12 kilometres (7½ miles) south of the Latvian border. The economic backbone of the city has been an oil refinery since 1980. Almost 3,000 employees produce various fuels, bitumen and other petroleum products. As soon as 1965, a compressor factory settled into Mazeikiai; 3,200 employees manufacture electric motors in another plant. The workers live in gigantic apartment complexes south of the railway tracks.

The "old" centre of town north of the railway tracks is mostly just one street, the Laisves aleja, with a hotel, department store and administrative buildings. During the evening there is not a soul on the streets – city life is confined to the newer areas of town.

Information

Accommodation: Hotel Tulpes, Laisves aleja, not far from the train station.

Restaurant: Putinas, Tel: 5 33 35; in the new section of town to the south.

Mosedis

The small city of Mosedis, with a population of 1,300 in the northwestern Zemaitija province probably has the most peculiar collection in the country: the physician *Vaclovas Intas* founded his *Rock Museum* here in 1979. The medical doctor collected over 5,000 rocks from the fields in this region. He didn't even stop at heavy boulders – even rocks weighing ten tonnes are exhibited in the small park.

Even more absurdities can be seen in **Gargzdele** at the *Orydai Absurdas Museum:* mosaics, sculptures and mysterious looking runic inscriptions on stones.

Palanga (Polangen)

The largest resort town in Lithuania, Palanga, is around 25 kilometres (15½ miles) north of Klaipeda and is closed off to through traffic. Those who travel here by car must pay a "spa tax" at a police outpost. Beyond the gate is one of the most beautiful beach resorts in the Baltic States: 22 kilometres (14 miles) of fine, sandy beach, swamplands and mineral springs make Palanga a travel destination during the entire year. Around a half of a million people visit this city each year – a city with a permanent population of almost 22,000. Resulting from an administrative reform by which the neighbouring towns of Vanagupe, Kunigiskiai, Monciske, Nemirseta and Sventoji were incorporated into the city, Palanga now extends over 24 kilometres (15 miles) from Nemerseta (Nimmersatt) all the way to the Latvian border.

History

The history of this town goes back a long time: the now extinct Cour tribe had already settled here as evidenced by archaeological finds –

among them, tools used to process amber.

Palanga was first mentioned in 1161. In 1167, the Danes conquered the small fortress before the Brothers of the Sword destroyed the fishing village in the 14th century. After repeated attacks by the Teutonic Knights, Palanga ultimately remained under Lithuanian rule from 1422; the expansion of the city as a commercial harbour began. The only Baltic Sea harbour in the country, all shipments to Holland, England and Sweden were handled in Palanga. In 1639, Palanga was awarded privileges of free trade. Sweden and England set up their own offices here. The Great Northern War ended the golden age of Palanga abruptly: in 1701, Swedish troops destroyed the harbour. In 1779, Palanga came under the control of the *Bishop of Vilnius;* in 1793, under Russian rule.

As the beach resort grew in popularity at the beginning of the 19th century, *Count Tyskiewicz* recognized its potential. In 1824, the aristocrat bought the entire town, had a sea bridge built and erected a majestic castle which now houses the Amber Museum.

Sights

Gintaro Muziejus (Amber Museum; Vatauto gatve 17, Tel: 5 35 01, open Tuesday to Sunday from 11 am to 6 pm). The castle of the Tyskiewicz family from 1897 houses the main attraction of the city. The Amber Museum has provided information on the evolution of amber, its extraction and processing of the Baltic gold into jewellery since 1963 with 25,000 dis-

plays. Magnifying glasses help in examining the 5,000 specimens more closely.

The *Castle Park* is the work of the French landscape architect *Eduoard André.*

Less renowned but still worth seeing is the *Museum of Local History* (Vytauto gatve 23a, open daily from noon to 5 pm, Tel: 5 45 59).

Growing in the 70 hectare (175 acre) *Botanical Gardens* on Birute Kalns are over 200 different types of tress and shrubs. The rose gardens alone exhibit over 80 different types of roses. Passing a *Grotto with a picture of the Mother of God,* a trail leads to the top of the 22 metres (72 foot) dune with a neo-Gothic brick chapel from 1869. Even the less religious should climb the hill – the vow of the town and the nearby Baltic Sea from the *Birute Kalns* is magnificent. The neo-Gothic *Ascension Church,* built from 1897 to 1907, was designed by the German-Balt Strandmann. Also worth seeing are the *old pharmacy* from 1827 and the half-timbered complex on J. Basanaviciaus gatve. The main traffic artery through town, the straight Vytauto vardu, was converted to a pedestrian zone in the city centre.

Information

Accommodation: Hotel Broliai, Daukanto gatve; Pajuris Hotel, Basanaviciaus gatve 9/corner of Daukanto gatve, Tel: 5 33 45, simple hotel, almost exclusively Russian clientele.

Airport: information, Tel: 5 30 31; reservations: Tel: 5 34 31, located north of the city. Flights to Kaunas, Vilnius, Moscow and St. Petersburg as well as to the Curonian Spit.

Lithuania's Youngest National Park – Zemaitija

After a 5 kilometre (3 mile) drive on the Plunge gravel road strewn with potholes, one will arrive in **Plateliai.** This village on the shores of the large Lake Zemaitija forms the centre of *Zemaitija National Park.* The relatively young national park places the hill country of Zemaitija under governmental protection. *Lake Plateliai* with an area of 12 square kilometres (3 square miles) and its seven islands is a popular area for boat tours and sailing.

Information
Accommodation: Hotel Vilnius, Nemuno gatve 3.

Automobile Repair: Vytauto gatve 106, Tel: 5 24 91.
Bank: Jurates gatve 17, Tel: 5 34 54.
Bus Station: Jasinskio gatve 1.
Cinemas: Jaunyste, Basanavicius gatve 16, Tel: 5 28 31; Naglis, Vytauto gatve 82, Tel: 5 18 94.
Concert Hall: Vytauto gatve 43, Tel: 5 22 10; summer concerts.
Fuel: Kretingos gatve 9.
Marketplace: Berzu gatve 12, Tel: 5 32 13.
Post Office: Tel: 5 34 44.
Restaurants: Ausringe, Vytauto gatve 98, Tel: 5 20 69; in the same complex as Baltija and Meta. Banga Basanaviciaus gatve 2, Tel: 5 13 70. Birute, Vytauto gatve 64, Tel: 5 15 26. Gabija, Vytauto gatve 40, Tel: 5 19 11. Café Klumpe, Neries gatve 9, Tel: 5 39 00. Pajuris, Basanavicius gatve 9, Tel: 5 35 39. Vakaris, Vytauto gatve 64, Tel: 5 37 15 – dining under a ceiling of stars. Virbaliske, Klaipedos pr. 62a, Tel: 5 61 29.

Sports and Recreation
Swimming: In the resort complex, Vytauto gatve 155, Tel: 5 84 78; Neries 44, Tel: 5 26 96.
Sports Fields: Dariaus ir Gireno gatve.
Sports Arena: Pozelos gatve 18.
Sports Stadium: Sporto gatve 9.
Tennis Courts: Geliu aikste.

Plunge

Fifty-six kilometres (35 miles) east of Palanga is the district capital of Plunge which is home to a population of 28,000. Around 10,000 of them work in the factory for synthetic leather products. The plant, founded in 1971, which once lived from export to the Comecon-nations (Council for Mutual Economic Assistance), is now plagued by enormous sales problems. High unemployment determines the mood of the city. In Plunge, which was awarded the rights of a city in 1792, the neo-classicistic *manorhouse* of the Oginskis family is situated in the middle of an extensive park. The palace was designed by the German architect *Karl Lorenz* and built in the style of historism: the main building has elements of classicism and the Renaissance, the side buildings exhibits English Tudor Gothic, the gardener's house was built as a tiny Florentine palace.

The famous Lithuanian painter and composer *Ciurlionis* also came to Plunge. He visited the music school which was in a wing of the castle from 1873 to 1902. Ultimately, Ciurlionis moved here in 1909 with his wife-to-be.

The Vytauto gatve is the main traffic artery of the street. In from of a department store is the *carved wooden figure of S. George*. The *brick church* at the end of the street is from 1933.

Silale

The spread-out, modern small city of Silale on the edge of the hills and the Nemuna valley plateau lies five kilometres (3¼ miles) to the south on the A 227. The Lokysta River flows directly through the centre of town. During the autumn of 1992, power shovels dredged through the swampy stream bed – a new park is being built along the banks. The main street Basanaviciaus gatve lined with retail shops leads to a small square. Surrounding the green area are the bus terminal, a department store and a cinema. A rather impressive neo-Gothic *church* rises up not far from the centre of town on the opposite side of the river.

Information

Accommodation: Hotel Asutis, Basanavicius gatve 4, Tel: 5 13 45.
Cinemas: Ausra, S. Gaudesiaus gatve 4, beyond the park in the centre of town; an impressive cinema with columns at the entrance and wooden gables; the façade is kept in brown and white tones.

Culture Centre: Basanaviciaus gatve 1.
Restaurant: Medvegalis, Basanaviciaus gatve 3.

Taurage (Tauroggen)

The small city of Taurage on the Jura River lies on the A 216 around 30 kilometres (19 miles) from the Russian border near **Sowjetsk** (Tilsit). This is the focus of the Protestant Church in Lithuania. This rather faceless city became much more renowned through an episode in world history, which took place before the gates of the city in the village of **Pozerunai** on December 30, 1812: it was then that the field Marshall *Count Yorck von Wartenburg* and *Czar Alexander* signed the "Tauroggen Convention" through which York revoked the alliance with Napoleon. A *memorial* commemorating this historical event has stood in the small village since 1976.

Telsiai

The small city of Telsiai on Lake Mastis is around 80 kilometres (50 miles) east of Palanga on the northern edge of the hills of Zemaitija. It ranks among the oldest cities in Lithuania. As soon as 1398, the town on the Durbinis Stream was mentioned in historical documents. In the middle of the 18th century, Telsiai was made a district capital together with three other Lithuania cities. The greater influence is also reflected in the buildings of this city. In 1765, the *Cathedral of St. Anthony of Pauda* was consecrated. Built on an elevation in the middle of the city centre, the opulent baroque building makes a majestic impression. The interior of the cathedral was already characterized by the transition from the baroque to classicism. The *Bishop's Palace* was built during the beginning of the 20th century – Telsiai has only been the seat of the Bishop of ZEmaitija since 1926. The *Bernardine Monastery* from the 17th century is on Spaudos gatve as is the an old *schoolhouse* from the 18th century, both very much worth seeing.

The *Krastotyros Muziejus* (Museum of Culture; Muziejus gatve 25) is not only worth visiting for its large collection covering regional history. Also on display is a collection of Flemish, French and Italian paintings, among them "Homage of the Kings" by *Lucas Cranach*. Just as interesting is the branch of the museum in the city park: Zemaitic *farmhouses* including *windmills* - outdoors and beautiful.

Varniai

Located in the middle of the Zemaitija Hills surrounding a number of lakes it the city of Varniai with a population of 1,000. A rather inconspicuous town today, Varniai (granted the rights of a city in 1735) experienced a *golden age* for more than 400 years as the seat of the Bishop of Zemaitija from 1417 to 1864.

Reminiscent of this importance of yore is the *St. Peter's and St. Paul's Church* (M. Kalanciaus gatve) built in 1691. The main and ancillary naves have a lavish baroque interior. The painting of Mary with the Christ child

is a continuation of the icon tradition – gold and silver plates cover and augment the oil painting. The paintings on the walls all around the church depict the stations of the cross. In the crypt is a macabre sight: the last remains of two bishops who died in 1838 and 1844 lay under glass plates in open coffins. Plain but beautiful is the *Sv. Aleksandro Church* (Vytauto gatve/corner of Birute gatve). The yellow wooden church is presently being restored.

Surroundings

A swampy meadow landscape extends to the south of the city. To the north is a landscape of gently rolling hills. *Lake Lukstas* lies three and a half kilometres (2 miles) south of Varniai. Fifteen kilometres (9¼ miles) to the south near the motorway from Kaunas to Klaipeda is **Laukuva** with its *village church* built out of erratic stones and plastered white. On the square in front of the church, a *war memorial* stands in memory of the soldiers who died between 1918 and 1928; a *cemetery with a small chapel* lies on the highest point in town. Medical care in this typically rural Lithuanian town is provided by an out-patient clinic and a pharmacy on the road to silale. Sixteen kilometres (10 miles) to the west, accessible by a broad sand road is **Tvereai** with its *wooden church* with two towers. It lies beyond an unusually high wall of erratic stones. Small devotional chapels are recessed into the wall.

Information

Bus Station: Vytauto gatve 3.
Fuel: On the outskirts of town toward Uzvenys.

Zemauciu Kalvarija

The town of pilgrimage Zemauciu Kalvarija with its population of 6,000 lies 25 kilometres (15½ miles) north-east of Plunge. At the beginning of June, Catholic pilgrims flock to this town and walk in prayer along the seven kilometre (4½ mile) *cloisters with 19 chapels,* the stations of the cross, before attending the services in the *Chapel of Mary's Trial,* consecrated in 1896. Before the bishop of Zemaitija had the pilgrim's path laid out from 1637 to 1639, "Kalvarienberg" was only a small village with the name "Gardai." Under the Soviets, it was renamed in Varduva.

Index